CURRENT READINGS IN LIFESPAN DEVELOPMENT

CURRENT READINGS IN LIFESPAN DEVELOPMENT

DENISE R. BOYD

HOUSTON COMMUNITY COLLEGE

GENEVIEVE D. STEVENS

HOUSTON COMMUNITY COLLEGE

Allyn and Bacon

Boston   London   Toronto   Sydney   Tokyo   Singapore

Series Editor: Tom Pauken
Marketing Manager: Caroline Croley
Editorial-Production Service: Omegatype Typography, Inc.
Composition and Prepress Buyer: Linda Cox
Manufacturing Manager: Joanne Sweeney
Cover Administrator: Kristina Mose-Libon
Electronic Composition: Omegatype Typography, Inc.

Copyright © 2002 by Allyn & Bacon
A Pearson Education Company
75 Arlington Street
Boston, MA 02116

Internet: www.ablongman.com

Between the time Website information is gathered and then published, it is not unusual for some sites to have closed. Also, the transcription of URLs can result in unintended typographical errors. The publisher would appreciate notification where these occur so that they may be corrected in subsequent editions. Thank you.

Library of Congress Cataloging-in-Publication Data

Current readings in lifespan development / [edited by] Denise Boyd, Genevieve Stevens.
    p. cm.
   ISBN 0-205-32219-0 (alk. paper)
    1. Developmental psychology. I. Boyd, Denise. II. Stevens, Genevieve.

  BF713 .C87 2002
  155–dc21

                                2001022113

Printed in the United States of America

10 9 8 7 6 5 4 3   06 05

CONTENTS

LATE ADULTHOOD

**EARLY, MIDDLE,
AND LATE ADULTHOOD**

DEATH

PREFACE

TO THE INSTRUCTOR

We have been teaching developmental psychology to undergraduates, the intended audience of this book of readings, for more than a decade. Readings are arranged by chronological age periods to correspond with most lifespan development textbooks. We hope that they will be helpful to instructors who wish to provide their students with a deeper understanding of developmental psychology and to familiarize them with contemporary research in the field.

In addition to considering student interest and relevance to the topics covered in most lifespan development textbooks, we adopted two objectives in article selection. First, we selected articles that we believe will be useful in teaching students about the process of development and will familiarize them with both long-standing and contemporary questions about human development. Second, we chose readings that will familiarize students with the ways in which cultural variables shape the process. There are readings that address both objectives for each major chronological period.

To help prevent readers from becoming distracted and confused by methodological and statistical details, the "To the Student" section outlines a general strategy for reading research articles. Furthermore, the introductions we have written for the articles include brief explanations of the methodology employed by each researcher. To further aid reader comprehension, we have also included definitions for terms and concepts with which students may not be familiar. Finally, multiple-choice and essay questions follow each article.

TO THE STUDENT

There are many types of reading materials: newspaper articles, novels, textbooks, and so on. Each type calls for a different approach to comprehension. This book of readings contains articles selected from scientific journals, a kind of reading material you may never have encountered before. It will be very helpful to you to take a few minutes to learn how to go about understanding them before you undertake the task of reading them.

Before reading each article, be sure to read the introductory material. We have provided you with brief explanations of the research methods and statistical analyses reported in each. We have also included definitions for various terms and concepts you will need to know to understand the article. It may also help to turn to the end of the article and preview the self-study questions you will find listed there.

Many of the articles report one or more research studies. Such articles are organized into the following blocks of information: *introduction, method, results,* and *discussion*. Different journals may use different labels for these sections. For example, some use the term *method,* while others refer to the same information as *procedure.* Others do not use such labels at all. However, the order of presentation of information is typically the same no matter which journal is involved or what terms are used. It will be very helpful to you to make notes on the articles that are organized in the same way.

Each block of information communicates something different from the others. The *introduction* outlines prior research that is relevant to the study being reported along with questions the study attempted to answer or the hypotheses it tested. Understanding the ideas in this section is critical to comprehending the rest of the article. Rather than focusing on the details of the studies the author cites, try to understand the general concepts he or she has derived from them. You may have to read some parts of the introduction more than once, and you should ask your instructor about any parts you don't understand after rereading. You may also understand the article's introduction better if you read relevant sections of your textbook prior to reading the article.

The purpose of the *method* section is to enable readers who want to repeat the study to do so. As a result, it contains many specific details. The section usually describes research participants, any tests that were used, and the conditions under which the study was conducted. One characteristic of the participants that is very important to your comprehension is age. Demographic characteristics—race, socioeconomic status, and the like—are also important. Understanding of every detail of methodology and statistical analysis is not critical to understanding these articles. The introductory material provided for each article includes a section on methodology that should give you some help understanding the specific methods used in each study.

The *results* section is geared toward readers who have an interest in and an understanding of statistics. This section explains the outcomes of the study's statistical analyses. Figures have been provided to assist in understanding this section at a conceptual level. Readers who do not have a thorough knowledge of statistics should not let the technical information distract them from focusing on understanding the main ideas of the article.

In the *discussion* section, the study's author or authors interpret the results. They do so by relating them to the questions and/or hypotheses put forward in the *introduction.* They also typically explain the study's limitations and may include practical implications for parents, teachers, or others. In most cases, authors also outline directions for future research. Like the *introduction,* you may have to read the *discussion* more than once to fully comprehend it.

Once you're fairly certain that you understand the article, try to answer the multiple-choice questions at the end. If you can't, go back through the article and try to find the relevant information. After answering the multiple-choice questions, try to respond to the essay questions. Reviewing and summarizing your notes can be useful at this point in the process as well.

Keep in mind that repetition helps enormously in learning to use a new learning strategy. The first selection you read will be the most difficult, but the process should become easier with each ensuing article. Moreover, following the procedures we have outlined should result in your acquiring a new reading comprehension strategy that will be useful to you in future courses.

ACKNOWLEDGMENTS

We wish to thank the publishers and authors who allowed us to use their work. In addition, interactions with our colleagues at Houston Community College have been helpful to us in deciding both which articles to include and how to present each most effectively to students. Finally, we would like to acknowledge the important role our students have played in teaching us how to teach.

CURRENT READINGS IN
LIFESPAN DEVELOPMENT

INFANCY

"Infants' Perception of Dynamic Affective Expressions: Do Infants Distinguish Specific Expressions?"

OVERVIEW

Developmentalists have known for a long time that infants can tell the difference between positive and negative categories of emotional expressions. For example, they respond differently to smiling and frowning faces. This article describes a study in which researchers sought to determine whether babies can tell the difference between specific emotions, such as anger and sadness or interest and happiness, within the general categories.

METHODOLOGY

Infant research is very challenging because researchers can't communicate with babies verbally. To solve this problem, infant researchers have invented some remarkable techniques. This study used one such method called *preferential looking*. The baby's attention was drawn to the center of a blank monitor screen with a dot or light and then two pictures were presented at the same time on both sides of this fixation point. Researchers then recorded how the baby divided his or her attention to the two pictures. If most or all of the infants looked at one particular kind of picture more than another, researchers assumed that the characteristics of that picture were more interesting to or better understood by them. In some conditions, facial expressions were combined with *concordant* vocal expressions, while in others facial and vocal stimuli were *discordant*. For example, a person who is smiling while humming an upbeat tune is exhibiting concordant visual and auditory expressions of emotion. Conversely, one who is yelling at someone in a hostile way while smiling is demonstrating discordant visual and auditory expressions.

GLOSSARY TERMS

- **Affect, affective** emotion, emotional
- **Dynamic expressions** constantly changing facial expressions (as we experience them in everyday life)
- **Static expressions** expressions of emotion that are fixed, rather than changing, such as those in still photographs
- **Multimodal information** information presented to more than one sense at a time such as stimuli that pair sights with sounds

- **Temporal synchrony** at the same time
- **Intermodal matching** correctly coordinating information from different senses, such as associating the smell of an orange with a picture of an orange
- **Condition** the particular situation in which a participant is exposed to a stimulus
- **Child-centered speech** baby talk
- **Interrater reliability** the degree to which independent observers agree about what was observed

Infants' Perception of Dynamic Affective Expressions: Do Infants Distinguish Specific Expressions?

Seven-month-old infants' perception of positive (happy, interested) and negative (angry, sad) affective expressions was investigated using a preferential looking procedure (n = 20 in each of 6 conditions). The infants saw two videotaped facial expressions and heard a single vocal expression concordant with one of the facial expressions. The voice on the soundtrack was played 5 s out of synchrony with the ongoing affective visual display. Infants participated in one of six conditions (all possible pairs of the four expressive events). Infants' visual fixations to the affectively concordant and affectively discordant displays were recorded. Infants looked longer at the affectively concordant displays than at the affectively discordant displays in all conditions except the happy/sad and interested/sad conditions. For these two comparisons, facial discrimination was demonstrated by the infants' preferential looking at happy and interested expressions compared to the sad expression. Thus, 7-month-old infants discriminate among happy, interested, angry, and sad expressions, demonstrating differentiation among specific, dynamic expressions. The results are discussed in terms of the information specifying facial and vocal affect and the possible role of familiarity in learning to differentiate among affective expressions during infancy.

INTRODUCTION

Theories of emotion have emphasized the role of facial expression in providing, information for people making judgments about another person's affect (Ekman, 1984; Izard, 1971, 1977; Plutchik, 1980). A common hypothesis is that there are specific, universally recognized facial expressions. Thus, specific facial expressions can provide affective information and facilitate social communication and interchange. For example, an angry expression might warn of an impending attack and a happy expression might promote social bonding and a sense of good feeling (Malatesta & Wilson, 1988). Adults and young children from different cultures are able to distinguish between specific facial expressions (See Ekman, 1982; Ekman et al., 1987; Izard, 1971). This investigation examines whether the boundaries that distinguish specific, dynamic facial expressions (e.g., happy, interested, sad, and angry) are the same for adults as for infants. Specifically, do infants distinguish between dynamic facial expressions that share

Reprinted from *Child Development*, 1999, 70, 1275–1282. Copyright Society for Research on Child Development. Reprinted with permission.

the same emotional tone (positive or negative) but specify different expressions? For example, can infants distinguish happy from interested or do they treat such expressions as qualitatively the same?

Infants can discriminate among some expressions depicted in photographs. For example, 7-month-old infants can tell happy from surprised, angry, sad, and fearful expressions, and can discriminate among angry, sad, and fearful expressions (Kestenbaum & Nelson, 1990; Ludemann & Nelson, 1988; Oster & Ewy, 1980; Schwartz, Izard, & Ansul, 1985; for reviews of facial expression research with photographs, see Nelson, 1987, and Oster, Daily, & Goldenthal, 1991). It is an empirical question, however, whether discriminability of static, perfectly posed representations of expressions generalizes to perceiving dynamic expressions of affect characteristic of normal social interactions between infants and caregivers or other people. A few studies have explored the role of motion information in the perception of facial expressions and have found that specific movement patterns of the face (Soken & Pick, 1992) and motion providing multiple views of the face (Nelson & Horowitz, 1983) may facilitate perception. The present study focuses on infants' ability to differentiate dynamic facial expressions.

From the studies in which dynamic displays of facial expressions have been used, it is clear that infants distinguish happy from angry and sad expressions (Haviland & Lelwica, 1987; Kreutzer & Charlesworth, 1973; Walker, 1982). There is limited evidence, however, that infants distinguish between negative expressions (e.g., angry and sad), and one study that included a positive expression other than happy (i.e., surprise) did not yield evidence that infants distinguish between happy, surprised, and woeful expressions (Kreutzer & Charlesworth, 1973). It is a question, then, whether infants distinguish between dynamically presented positive and negative expressions but treat expressions within the positive or negative affect dimension as qualitatively the same. In order to answer this question, it is necessary to present infants with more than one positive and more than one negative facial expression. In the present study, we presented infants with happy, interested, angry, and sad expressions.

In normal expressive interactions, infants are presented with multimodal information, e.g., visual, auditory, olfactory, and tactile. Infants see the face and gestures, hear the person's voice, smell the person, are often touched by the person, in an interactive context. The live presentations of facial expressions used in some studies (Haviland & Lelwica, 1987; Kreutzer & Charlesworth, 1973; Termine & Izard, 1988) have the advantage of preserving much of the multimodal information characteristic of social interactions. However, this procedure presents two problems. First, the basis of infants' discrimination is not clear (e.g., visual, vocal, tactile, or gestural information). Second, the equivalence of facial, vocal, and gestural presentations from infant to infant cannot be assured.

Videotaped presentations of affect retain some of the dynamic quality of normal social interaction and also ensure equivalence of the affect displays to each infant. There is evidence that infants, as well as adults, are sensitive to motion information specifying some affective expressions in video displays (Bassili, 1978, 1979; Soken & Pick, 1992).

Walker (1982) conducted a series of studies of infants' perception of dynamic facial expressions that were both seen and heard. In these studies a preferential looking procedure was used in which two filmed facial expressions were shown side by side while a single vocal expression specific to one of the facial expressions was played from a centrally-located speaker. Walker observed when the infants looked preferentially at the affective display corresponding to the vocal display they were hearing. Infants discriminated the expressions happy and neutral (7-month-olds), happy and sad (5- and 7-month-olds), and happy and angry (7-month-olds) when presented with synchronous visual and vocal displays. Walker-Andrews (1986) also found discrimination between happy and angry expressions by 7-month-olds even when the mouth region was occluded. Thus, simple lip matching or featural information (e.g., "toothiness" of happy) was not the basis for the infants' intermodal perception.

Walker (1982) also explored whether temporal synchrony is necessary for intermodal matching of happy and neutral expressions. In a preferential looking procedure, the soundtrack of each film was played 5 s out of synchrony with the film of the appropriate facial expression. Seven-month-olds still preferred to look at the facial expression corresponding to the soundtrack. Apparently, the infants were sensitive to rhythm information of the face and voice that specify facial expressions. In the present study, we also presented infants with visual and vocal affective displays 5 s out of synchrony in order to exclude synchrony as a basis for intermodal matching.

In summary, research with dynamic visual and vocal affective displays has shown that, at least by 7 months of age, infants distinguish the positive affect happy from some negative affective expressions. In the present study, the question investigated is whether, by means of intermodal matching, infants distinguish between specific positive affective expressions (e.g., happy and interested) and specific negative affective expressions (e.g., angry and sad), as well as between positive and negative expressions (e.g., happy and angry, interested and sad).

METHOD

Displays

Prior to videorecording, an actress was provided with information about facial characteristics associated with the affective expressions happy, interested, sad, and angry (Izard, 1971, 1977). She was shown static pictures of the expressions portrayed at their apex as well as descriptions of the position of particular facial features. Also, she was instructed to think of events or situations, portrayable in approximately 2 min, that would elicit each affect. This method of eliciting particular emotions has been used in previous studies with facial expressions (Ekman, 1973; Haviland & Lelwica, 1987). The actress was cautioned not to rehearse dialogues to the extent that they might become overly practiced and contrived.

The actress was videorecorded from the shoulders upward under normal lighting while portraying each of the expressions facially and vocally four times for 2 min each. Initially, the actress was videorecorded for a period of time and shown the displays to allow her to see how her facial and vocal behavior appeared. After the first attempt at portraying an expression, the actress was shown the display and the experimenter and actress reviewed the display in terms of the emotional quality of the facial and vocal content. The facial expressiveness and vocal content were adult-centered and did not have the qualities of exaggerated facial and vocal expressiveness of child-centered speech or motherese (Fernald, 1985; Fernald & Kuhl, 1987).

Four adults rated each of the video displays for overall expressiveness and emotional quality. The highest-rated happy, interested, sad, and angry displays were selected. These affective expressive events were edited so as to produce video displays in which the voice was 5 s out of synchrony with the ongoing, appropriate facial expression. The final versions of the affective displays were presented to 15 naive adult observers who all correctly labeled the displays as happy, interested or "mildly happy," sad, or angry.

Procedure

All possible pairs of happy, interested, sad, and angry expressions were used in this study. This yielded six combinations, each of which served as one condition of the study. Infants participated in only one of the six conditions.

Infants sat on their parent's lap approximately 60 cm from two 48 cm color monitors. The monitors were separated by 25 cm with a speaker located centrally between them. A grey partition occluded the equipment (except for the monitors), experimenter, and observers from the infant's view. The infants' eye movements were observed through a 1 cm × 1 cm hole located 31 cm below the monitors and 76 cm from the infant.

The infants were presented with six 1-min trials of the same two affective visual displays shown side by side (one on each monitor) while one of the corresponding soundtracks was played from a centrally-located speaker. Prior to each trial, the infant's gaze was attracted to the center of the screen with a penlight from an aperture located between the two monitors. When the observer judged the infant's fixation to be between the monitors, the trial began. The entire experimental session lasted approximately 10 min.

The six experimental trials for an infant within a condition consisted of three affectively concordant displays of each of the two expressions (e.g., three happy and three angry affectively concordant displays). The two visual expressions were presented to the left and right and were counterbalanced across the infants within a condition. Thus, across the 20 infants in a condition (e.g., happy and angry), the number of affectively happy and angry expressions

presented to left and right were equal. Lateral position of expressions and sound-specification of the expressions were counterbalanced for each condition in this way.

One of three observers was used in each experimental session. The observers were naive to the lateral positions of the various displays. The observer had two buttons connected to a computer with which she could record a fixation to the left monitor or to the right monitor (or a fixation to neither monitor if no button was depressed). Interrater reliability was established by each pair of observers carrying out the procedure with individual babies. A second peephole and pair of buttons were used in these cases, and the computer recorded and compared the two observers' simultaneous inputs. To achieve an appropriate level of reliability, each pair of observers carried out the procedure with three to five (pilot) babies. The mean reliability achieved by the three observer pairs was (Cohen's κ) $r = .91$ and (Pearson) $r = .97$.

Data

The amount of looking time to each of the two affective displays for the six trials of a condition was recorded for each infant. The mean looking times and their standard deviations for concordant and discordant displays for each condition are displayed in Table 1.

The looking times to the pairs of affective expressions were analyzed in the same manner as in earlier studies of Walker-Andrews (Walker, 1982; Walker-Andrews, 1986, 1988, p. 194) and Soken and Pick (1992). The amount of looking to each expression of the pair was converted to the proportion of the *total* looking time to the two expressions. For each expression, the proportion of the infants' total looking time to that expression with the affectively concordant and discordant soundtracks was compared using matched sample t tests. Thus, for the happy/angry condition, the proportion of looking time to the happy expressions with the happy soundtracks (i.e., happy affectively concordant) and with the angry soundtracks (i.e., happy affectively discordant) was compared. Likewise, the proportion of looking time to the angry expressions with the angry soundtrack (i.e., angry affectively concordant) and with the happy soundtrack (i.e., angry affectively discordant) was compared. The computation of the tests for pairs of expressions is identical since the values for one expression are one minus the values for the other expression. Thus, if the difference between the proportions for one expression is statistically significant, the difference between the proportions for the other expression has to be also. Hence, only one t test is reported for each set of comparisons. Additional t tests

TABLE 1	Looking Times in Seconds to the Visual Displays in Each Condition with Concordant and Discordant Vocal Expressions		
CONDITION	AFFECTIVE DISPLAY TYPE	M	SD
Happy/interested	Happy affectively concordant	69.25	21.44
	Happy affectively discordant	60.32	15.00
	Interested affectively concordant	77.66	21.32
	Interested affectively discordant	68.92	22.07
	Overall	276	
Happy/sad	Happy affectively concordant	87.01	19.30
	Happy affectively discordant	79.87	20.81
	Sad affectively concordant	48.65	10.76
	Sad affectively discordant	47.06	12.28
	Overall	263	
Happy/angry	Happy affectively concordant	83.15	17.25
	Happy affectively discordant	69.10	15.93
	Angry affectively concordant	61.08	13.26
	Angry affectively discordant	56.59	11.12
	Overall	270	
Interested/sad	Interested affectively concordant	82.11	24.58
	Interested affectively discordant	73.87	20.47
	Sad affectively concordant	50.19	13.93
	Sad affectively discordant	46.06	16.80
	Overall	252	
Interested/angry	Interested affectively concordant	75.89	16.13
	Interested affectively discordant	68.34	20.06
	Angry affectively concordant	66.38	15.50
	Angry affectively discordant	56.13	17.32
	Overall	267	
Sad/angry	Sad affectively concordant	60.78	15.14
	Sad affectively discordant	47.96	14.26
	Angry affectively concordant	78.87	17.31
	Angry affectively discordant	68.70	18.08
	Overall	256	

were conducted to explore whether there were affect or side preferences. In all cases, the significance levels reported are two-tailed ($\alpha = .05$).

RESULTS

Condition 1: Happy and Interested Expressions

Twenty 7-month-old infants (M = 213 days, SD = 3 days), 12 males and 8 females, participated. The data for two additional infants were excluded due to fussiness. Infants for this and the other five conditions were recruited through birth announcements in a newspaper, and were all healthy, normal-term infants.

The infants looked longer at the affectively concordant displays than at the affectively discordant displays. The infants' proportion of looking time to the affectively concordant happy displays (M = .50) was greater than that to the affectively discordant happy displays (M = .44), $t(19)$ = 2.32, p < .05. Likewise, their proportion of looking time to the affec-

tively concordant interested displays (M = .56) was greater than that to the affectively discordant interested displays (M = .50). Thus, the infants in this condition discriminated between happy and interested. They detected invariant information from the auditory and visual displays for happy and interested affective expressions. There was no statistically significant preference for either expression but there was a right side preference, $t(19)$ = 3.20, $p < .005$.

Condition 2: Happy and Sad Expressions

Twenty 7-month-old infants (M = 213 days, SD = 4 days), 11 males and 9 females, participated in this condition. Data for four additional infants were excluded: three because of fussiness, and one because of equipment failure.

The infants' proportions of looking times to the affectively concordant displays (happy M = .65, sad M = .38) did not differ from those to the affectively discordant displays (happy M = .62, sad M = .35), $t(19)$ = 1.69, p = .11. The infants looked proportionately longer at the happy expression (M = .66) than at the sad expression (M = .33), $t(19)$ = 9.22, p < .001. There was also a right side preference, $t(19)$ = 2.24, p < .05. Infants in this condition failed to look longer at the affectively concordant displays, but their visual discrimination between the happy and sad displays was apparent from their significant preference for looking at the happy display regardless of which soundtrack they heard.

Condition 3: Happy and Angry Expressions

Twenty 7-month-old infants (M = 214 days, SD = 3 days), 10 males and 10 females, participated in this condition. Data from nine additional infants were excluded: three due to crying and fussing, and six due to experimenter error or equipment failure.

Infants looked longer at the affectively concordant displays than at the affectively discordant displays. The infants' proportion of looking times to the affectively concordant happy displays (M = .60) was greater than that to the affectively discordant happy displays (M = .53), $t(19)$ = 3.16, p < .005. Likewise, the infants' proportion of looking times to the affectively concordant angry displays (M = .47) was greater than that to the affectively discordant angry displays (M = .40). The infants showed a significant preference for looking at the happy expression, $t(19)$ = 3.44, p < .005. In addition, infants looked longer to the right side, $t(19)$ = 2.97, p < .01.

Overall, these infants looked longer at the affectively concordant displays and preferred to look at the happy display. Infants in this condition detected invariant information from the auditory and visual displays for happy and angry affective expressions. In addition, their visual discrimination between expressions is reflected in their preferential looking toward the happy expression. These results replicate those of two previous studies using a similar procedure (Soken & Pick, 1992; Walker-Andrews, 1982).

Condition 4: Interested and Sad Expressions

Twenty 7-month-old infants (M = 214 days, SD = 3 days), 10 males and 10 females, participated in this condition. The data from five additional infants were excluded: two because of fussiness, and three because of equipment failure or experimenter error.

The infants' proportion of looking times to the affectively concordant displays (interested M = .63, sad M = .40) was not significantly different from those for the affectively discordant displays (interested M = .60, sad M = .37), $t(19)$ = 1.29, p = .21. The infants looked proportionately longer at the inter-

ested expression (M = .64) than at the sad expression (M = .36), $t(19)$ = 7.59, p < .001.

The infants in this condition failed to look longer at the affectively concordant displays. However, the infants' visual discrimination between interested and sad expressions was indicated by their preferential looking at the interested expression.

Condition 5: Interested and Angry Expressions

Twenty 7-month-old infants (M = 214 days, SD = 3 days), 8 males and 12 females, participated. The infants looked longer at the affectively concordant displays than at the affectively discordant displays. The proportion of the infants' looking times to the affectively concordant interested displays (M = .57) was greater than that to the affectively discordant interested displays (M = .51), $t(19)$ = 2.46, p < .05. Likewise, the infants' proportion of looking times to the affectively concordant angry displays (M = .49) was greater than that to the affectively discordant angry displays (M = .43). In addition, the infants showed a significant preference for the interested display, $t(19)$ = 2.10, p < .05, as well as a significant right side preference, $t(19)$ = 2.91, p < .01.

The infants in this condition detected invariant information from the auditory and visual displays for the interested and the angry affective expressions. In addition, their visual discrimination between expressions is reflected in their preferential looking to the interested expression.

Condition 6: Sad and Angry Expressions

Twenty 7-month-old infants (M = 214 days, SD = 4 days), 10 males and 10 females, participated in this condition. The data for four additional infants were excluded: two because of fussing, and two because of equipment failure or experimenter error.

The infants in this condition looked longer at the affectively concordant displays than at the affectively discordant displays. The infants' proportion of looking times to the affectively concordant sad displays (M = .47) was greater than that to the affectively discordant sad displays (M = .38), $t(19)$ = 4.35, p < .001. Likewise, the infants' proportion of looking times to the affectively concordant angry displays (M = .62) was greater than that to the affectively discordant angry displays (M = .53). In addition, the infants looked longer at the angry expressions than at the sad expressions, $t(19)$ = 5.15, p < .001, and they also showed a right side preference, $t(19)$ = 2.25, p < .05.

The infants in this condition discriminated between the angry and sad expressions as evidenced by their proportionately longer looking at the angry and sad displays when they were accompanied by their affect-appropriate soundtrack. Additional evidence of the infants' visual discrimination between expressions was their preferential looking at the angry expression compared to the sad expression.

DISCUSSION

The question asked in this study was whether infants discriminate discrete dynamic affective expressions conveyed facially and vocally, or whether they distinguish between positive and negative expressions but not among expressions that share the same emotional tone. The answer is that 7-month-old infants do discriminate between discrete dynamic expressions, both positive and negative.

The six conditions of this study included all paired combinations of the affective expressions happy, interested, sad, and angry. The infants looked proportionately longer at the affectively concordant displays than at the affectively discordant displays in the happy/interested, happy/angry, sad/angry, and interested/angry conditions. Thus, the infants differentiated the affective expressions conveyed facially and vocally. The infants in the other two conditions, happy/sad and interested/sad, looked proportionately longer to happy and interested, respectively, demonstrating discrimination among the specific facial expressions. In fact, these infants looked longer at the positive facial expressions in these conditions than they did in any other context, suggesting the possibility that their preferential looking to positive facial expressions masked evidence that they also detected the facial-vocal correspondences of the affective expressions.

A right side preference was observed in five of the six conditions. There were no apparent reasons for this preference (e.g., mother or equipment visible on the right, etc.) and there is no obvious explanation for it, but counterbalancing of trials prevented confounding of affectively concordant looking and lateral position. In any case, side preference is a nuisance variable that increases variability and therefore reduces the likelihood of observing reliable results for the variables of interest. (For a more detailed discussion of how side preferences affect the interpretation of results with paired comparison paradigms, see Soken and Pick, 1992.)

What is the developmental progression for discriminating dynamic affective expressions? Some investigators have speculated that seeing and hearing affective expressions may promote infants' learning to discriminate among them (Caron, Caron, & MacLean, 1988; Kuchuck, Vibbert, & Bornstein, 1986; Ludemann & Nelson, 1988; Malatesta, Grigoryev, Lamb, Albin, & Culver, 1986; Malatesta & Haviland, 1982). Malatesta and colleagues (Malatesta et al.,

1986; Malatesta & Haviland, 1982) observed parents and their infants interacting and found that by 7 months, for the four expressions used in the present study, infants have seen and heard the positive expressions of happy and interested most frequently, expressions of anger next most frequently, and expressions of sad least frequently. The overall looking times to these expressions by the infants in the present study corresponds to the relative frequency of their occurrence observed by the earlier investigators (M overall looking times: happy = 448 s, interested = 447 s, angry = 388 s, sad = 301 s).

In a test of the familiarity hypothesis, Ludemann and Nelson (1988) conducted an habituation study using photographs of the expressions happy, surprised, and fearful. They hypothesized that less familiar expressions would be more difficult to habituate to, and thus discrimination would not be apparent when a less familiar expression was the habituating stimulus. Seven-month-old infants were presented with either surprised/happy or surprised/fearful expression pairs. From the observations of Malatesta and colleagues (Malatesta et al., 1986; Malatesta & Haviland, 1982), it was assumed that expressions of surprise would be of intermediate familiarity in comparison to expressions of happy and the relatively unfamiliar expressions of fearful. As predicted, discrimination between the expression pairs surprised/fearful and surprised/happy was obtained only when the more familiar expression was presented during habituation and the less familiar expression during the subsequent test phase (e.g., happy followed by surprised, and surprised followed by fearful). These results were consistent with previous studies (Ludemann & Nelson, 1988; Nelson & Dolgin, 1985; Nelson, Morse, & Leavitt, 1979) in which similar order effects were observed, and they support the hypothesis that less familiar expressions are more difficult to habituate to, at least when the affective expressions are represented as photographs.

Is there support for the familiarity hypothesis with dynamic facial expressions? Some evidence from the present study is consistent with the hypothesis that familiarity promotes infants' learning to discriminate between dynamic facial expressions. Infants in the two conditions in which the most familiar expressions were paired with the least familiar expression, happy/sad and interested/sad, did not look proportionately longer at the affectively concordant displays. Instead, the infants looked longer at the presumably more familiar happy and interested expression displays than at the presumably unfamiliar sad displays. There also were significant preferences for the more familiar expression in five conditions (e.g., happy over sad, happy over angry, interested over sad, interested over angry, angry over sad). The sixth condition, happy/interested, in which both expressions are familiar, yielded no preferential looking.

In the present study we have established that 7-month-old infants discriminate between specific positive and negative affective expressions. A next step is to investigate the development of recognition of meanings or affordances of specific expressions. There are at least two ways of conceptualizing such recognition of the affordances of specific expressions. First, if infants' own emotional expressions, bodily movements, and vocalizations are related to the discrete expressions portrayed by another individual, then recognition may be demonstrated. Second, recognition of the meaning of facial expressions is demonstrated if infants are shown to use the facial affective information of another individual to guide their behavior in an ambiguous situation. For example, investigators of the development of social referencing have found that infants are able to recognize the broad positive or negative signal value of facial expressions, but that they are not necessarily sensitive to the signal value of specific facial expressions (Klinnert, 1984; Sorce, Emde, Campos, & Klinnert, 1985; Zabatany & Lamb, 1985).

In the future, we plan to explore the development of the recognition of the affordances of affective expressions longitudinally. A social referencing task can be devised that uses an early emerging infant behavior—specifically reaching and grasping—with a range of facial affective expressions presented by mothers with and without vocal accompaniment. This will allow us to see whether and when infants' behavior is differentially affected by their mothers' discrete expressions. For example, we can observe what effect a mother's facial expression has on a child about to grasp an attractive object. This is an important component of the study of recognition of expressions because in order to make claims about naturalistic social situations and the perception of affective meaning, context is necessary. An advantage of using an early-emerging infant behavior such as grasping is that we can investigate the development of recognition of expressions earlier in development than previous social referencing studies, which have depended on the infants' ability to locomote independently (e.g., Sorce et al., 1985).

ACKNOWLEDGMENTS

This article is based on a doctoral dissertation submitted by the first author to the University of Minnesota. The research was supported in part by the Center for Research in Learning, Perception, and Cognition; and the National Institute of Child Health and Human Development (HD-07151). Portions of the research were presented at the International Conference on Infant Studies, Miami, FL, May 1992. The authors would like to thank Maureen Bigbee and Patricia Melendez for their assistance with data collection and other aspects of carrying out the research.

REFERENCES

Bassili, J. N. (1978). Facial motion in the perception of faces and emotional expression. *Journal of Experimental Psychology: Human Perception and Performance, 4,* 373–379.

Bassili, J. N. (1979). Emotion recognition: The role of facial movement and the relative importance of upper and lower areas of the face. *Journal of Personality and Social Psychology, 37,* 2059–2070.

Caron, A. J., Caron, R. F., & MacLean, D. J. (1988). Infant discrimination of naturalistic emotional expressions: The role of face and voice. *Child Development, 59,* 604–616.

Ekman, P. (1973). Cross-cultural studies of facial expression. In P. Ekman (Ed.), *Darwin and facial expression: A century of research in review* (pp. 169–222). New York: Academic Press.

Ekman, P. (1982). *Emotion in the human face* (2nd ed.). New York: Cambridge University Press.

Ekman, P. (1984). Expression and the nature of emotion. In K. Scherer & P. Ekman (Eds.), *Approaches to emotion* (pp. 329–343). Hillsdale, NJ: Erlbaum.

Ekman, P., Friesen, W. V., O'Sullivan, M., Diacoyanni-Tarlatzis, I., Krause, R., Pitcairn, T., Scherer, K., Chan, A., Heider, K., LeCompte, W. A., Ricci-Bitti, P. E., Tomita, J., & Tzavaras, A. (1987). Universals and cultural differences in the judgments of facial expressions of emotion. *Journal of Personality and Social Psychology, 53,* 712–717.

Fernald, A. (1985). Four-month-old infants prefer to listen to motherese. *Infant Behavior and Development, 8,* 181–195.

Fernald, A., & Kuhl, P. K. (1987). Acoustic determinants of infant preference for motherese speech. *Infant Behavior and Development, 10,* 279–293.

Haviland, J. M., & Lelwica, M. (1987). The induced affect response: 10-week-old infants' responses to three emotion expressions. *Developmental Psychology, 23,* 97–104.

Izard, C. E. (1971). *The face of emotions.* New York: Appleton-Century-Crofts.

Izard, C. E. (1977). *Human emotions.* New York: Plenum Press.

Kestenbaum, R., & Nelson, C. (1990). The recognition and categorization of upright and inverted emotional expressions by 7-month-old infants. *Infant Behavior and Development, 13,* 497–511.

Klinnert, M. D. (1984). The regulation of infant behavior by maternal facial expression. *Infant Behavior and Development, 7,* 447–465.

Kreutzer, M. A., & Charlesworth, W. R. (1973, March). *Infants' reactions to different expressions of emotion.* Paper presented at the biennial meeting of the Society for Research in Child Development, Philadelphia.

Kuchuck, A., Vibbert, M., & Bornstein, M. H. (1986). The perception of smiling and its experiential correlates in three-month-old infants. *Child Development, 57,* 1054–1061.

Ludemann, P. M., & Nelson, C. A. (1988). Categorical representation of facial expressions by 7-month-old infants. *Developmental Psychology, 24*, 492–501.

Malatesta, C. Z., Grigoryev, P., Lamb, C., Albin, M., & Culver, C. (1986). Emotion socialization and expressive development in preterm and full-term infants. *Child Development, 57*, 316–330.

Malatesta, C. Z., & Haviland, J. M. (1982). Learning display rules: The socialization of emotion expressions in infancy. *Child Development, 53*, 991–1003.

Malatesta, C. Z., & Wilson, A. (1988). Emotion/cognition interaction in personality development: A discrete emotions, functionalist analysis. *British Journal of Social Psychology, 27*, 91–112.

Nelson, C. A. (1987). The recognition of facial expressions in the first two years of life: Mechanisms of development. *Child Development, 58*, 889–909.

Nelson, C. A., & Dolgin, K. (1985). The generalized discrimination of facial expressions by 7-month-old infants. *Child Development, 56*, 58–61.

Nelson, C. A., & Horowitz, F. D. (1983). The perception of facial expressions and stimulus motion by 2- and 5-month-old infants using holographic stimuli. *Child Development, 54*, 868–877.

Nelson, C. A., Morse, P. A., & Leavitt, L. A. (1979). Recognition of facial expressions by seven-month-old infants. *Child Development, 50*, 1239–1242.

Oster, H., Daily, L., & Goldenthal, P. (1991). Processing facial affect. In A. Young & H. Ellis (Eds.), *Handbook of research on face processing*. Amsterdam: North Holland Press.

Oster, H., & Ewy, R. (1980). *Discrimination of sad vs. happy faces by 4-month-olds: When is a smile seen as a smile?* Unpublished manuscript, University of Pennsylvania, Philadelphia.

Plutchik, R. (1980). *Emotion: A psychoevolutionary synthesis.* New York: Random House.

Schwartz, G. M., Izard, C. E., & Ansul, S. E. (1985). The 5-month-old's ability to discriminate facial expressions of emotion. *Infant Behavior and Development, 8*, 65–77.

Soken, N. H., & Pick, A. D. (1992). Intermodal perception of happy and angry expressive behaviors by 7-month-old infants. *Child Development, 63*, 787–795.

Sorce, J. F., Emde, R. N., Campos, J. J., & Klinnert, M. D. (1985). Maternal emotional signaling: Its effects on the visual cliff behavior of 1-year-olds. *Developmental Psychology, 21*, 195–200.

Termine, N. T., & Izard, C. E. (1988). Infants' responses to their mothers' expressions of joy and sadness. *Developmental Psychology, 24*, 223–229.

Walker, A. S. (1982). Intermodal perception of expressive behaviors by human infants. *Journal of Experimental Child Psychology, 33*, 514–535.

Walker-Andrews, A. S. (1986). Intermodal perception of expressive behaviors: Relation of eye and voice? *Developmental Psychology, 22*, 373–377.

Walker-Andrews, A. S. (1988). Infants' perception of the affordances of expressive behaviors. In C. K. Rovee-Collier & L. Lipsitt (Eds.), *Advances in infancy research* (Vol. 5, pp. 173–221). Norwood, NJ: Ablex.

Zabatany, L., & Lamb, M. E. (1985). Social referencing as a function of information source: Mothers vs. strangers. *Infant Behavior and Development, 8*, 25–33.

SELF-STUDY QUESTIONS

Multiple Choice

1. Prior research has shown that infants
   a. respond to all kinds of facial expressions in the same ways as adults
   b. do not respond facial expressions at all
   c. discriminate between positive and negative categories of facial expressions
   d. respond to facial but not vocal expressions of emotion

2. Based on this study, which of the following generalizations is most accurate?
   a. Infants prefer to look at negative expressions.
   b. Infants prefer to look at positive expressions.
   c. Infants have no preference for one kind of expression over another.
   d. Infants do not seem to process vocal expressions of emotion.

Essay

1. What is the *familiarity hypothesis*, and how do the authors use it to explain the results of their study?

2. How do the authors explain infants' tendency to look to the right?

INFANCY

"Cultural Differences in Maternal Beliefs and Behaviors: A Study of Middle-Class Anglo and Puerto Rican Mother–Infant Pairs in Four Everyday Situations"

OVERVIEW

People often say they believe one thing or another, but psychologists have found that beliefs are not always expressed behaviorally. Thus, one of the enduring questions in developmental psychology concerns the degree to which parents in a particular culture manifest cultural beliefs about child-rearing in their parenting behavior. In this study, researchers examined differences between Anglo and Puerto Rican mothers in both beliefs and practices. They were particularly interested in how varying ideas about the relative importance of individual and societal needs influenced participants' ideas and behaviors.

METHODOLOGY

The methods used to gather data in this study are typical of those employed by researchers who want to learn how real people behave in everyday situations: structured interviews and naturalistic observation. The statistical analyses allowed the researchers to identify interactions among variables. An interaction occurs when two variables are related under one condition, or in one situation, but not another. For example, one interaction question these researchers examined was whether cultural beliefs were expressed in maternal behavior across both play and teaching situations.

GLOSSARY TERMS

- **Interpretive approach** a way of studying culture in which the researcher explains as well as describes cultural beliefs and practices
- **Individualism** a culture's tendency to emphasize individual needs over societal needs
- **Collectivism** a culture's tendency to emphasize societal needs over individual needs; also known as *sociocentrism* and *interdependency*
- **Instantiation** a cue or set of cues that lead to particular behaviors; for example, being in a res-

taurant *instantiates* your knowledge of how to behave in a restaurant
- **Construct** an abstract psychological trait that cannot be directly measured; for example, height is not a construct because it can be directly measured with a ruler or tape measure; intelligence is a construct because we measure it with vocabulary and reasoning tests, from which we must make an inference about a person's intelligence

Robin L. Harwood, Axel Schoelmerich,
Pamela A. Schulze, and Zenaida Gonzalez

Cultural Differences in Maternal Beliefs and Behaviors: A Study of Middle-Class Anglo and Puerto Rican Mother-Infant Pairs in Four Everyday Situations

This study examines cultural patterning in situational variability in mother-infant interactions among middle-class Anglo and Puerto Rican mothers and their 12 to 15-month-old firstborn children. Forty mothers were interviewed regarding their long-term socialization goals and childrearing strategies, and videotaped interacting with their infants in four everyday settings: feeding, social play, teaching, and free play. Results suggest that: (1) Anglo mothers place greater emphasis on socialization goals and childrearing strategies consonant with a more individualistic orientation, whereas Puerto Rican mothers place greater focus on goals and strategies consistent with a more sociocentric orientation; (2) coherence was found between mothers' childrearing beliefs and practices, with Puerto Rican mothers more likely to directly structure their infants' behaviors; and (3) situational variability arose in mother-infant interactions, but this variability showed a cultural patterning consistent with mothers' long-term socialization goals and childrearing beliefs.

INTRODUCTION

The past decade has brought increased interest among researchers in understanding the cultural context of childhood. Along with this concern has come a heightened consideration of appropriate theoretical frameworks for the study of culture and child development. In particular, interpretive approaches have been articulated among several researchers (Cole, 1996; Harkness & Super, 1996; Shweder, 1996). Despite their diversity, interpretive approaches generally share the assumption that human beings construct meaning through their cultural symbol systems, with language being one of culture's most powerful symbol systems. Many of these approaches go on to assert that this construction occurs within a matrix of social interaction, in which the child as participant actively produces and reproduces culturally meaningful patterns of beliefs and behaviors (e.g., Corsaro & Miller, 1992; Goodnow, Miller, & Kessel, 1995; Rogoff, Mistry, Goncu, & Mosier, 1993; Schieffelin & Ochs, 1986).

Reprinted from *Child Development*, 1999, *70*, 1005–1016. Copyright Society for Research in Child Development. Reprinted with permission.

As interpretive approaches become more widely used and recognized, certain themes appear to recur and to demand continued refinement. One salient question involves the use of terms like "individualistic/independent" or "collectivistic/interdependent" as heuristic devices to characterize broad-level cultural belief systems and practices (cf. Greenfield & Cocking, 1994; Markus & Kitayama,1991; Shweder & Bourne, 1984; Triandis, Bontempo, Villareal, Asai, & Lucca, 1988). Briefly, American culture is often described as "individualistic" in that it conceives of the individual as an "independent, self-contained, autonomous entity who (a) comprises a unique configuration of internal attributes…and (b) behaves primarily as a consequence of those internal attributes" (Markus & Kitayama, 1991, p. 224; see also Kessen, 1979; Sampson, 1989; Shweder & Bourne, 1984; Spence, 1985). This construal of the self is described as a key component of the beliefs and practices which organize perceptions of and interactions with children in America, thus constituting a primary aspect of the cultural context of childhood in this country (Harkness & Super, 1996; Harwood, Miller, & Lucca Irizarry, 1995; Rogoff et al., 1993; Schieffelin & Ochs, 1986).

In contrast, many other cultures are described as sociocentric" or "interdependent" in that they emphasize the fundamental connectedness of human beings to one another: "Experiencing interdependence entails seeing oneself as part of an encompassing social relationship and recognizing that one's behavior is determined, contingent on, and, to a large extent organized by what the actor perceives to be the thoughts, feelings, and actions of *others* in the relationship" (Markus & Kitayama, 1991, p. 227). Again, this emphasis on interdependence is depicted by many researchers as a key component of the beliefs and practices that organize perceptions of and interactions with children in a variety of non-Western cultures, thus constituting a primary aspect of the cultural context of childhood in these countries (cf. Greenfield & Cocking, 1994; Kurtz, 1992; Tobin, Wu, & Davidson, 1989; Triandis, Marin, Lisansky, & Betancourt, 1984).

Critics of this approach have maintained that such global characterizations are unidimensional and do not tap "the multitude of social orientations that constitute the social life of individuals in most cultures" (Wainryb, 1995, p. 390). The use of phrases like "the individualism of American culture" or "the interdependence of Japanese culture" has drawn critical rejoinders highlighting instances where American mothers emphasize cooperation, and Japanese or Indian parents provide their children with choice (Derne, 1995; Mines, 1994; Nucci, 1994).

The reality, of course, is that no substantive researcher (to our knowledge) claims that cultures are monolithic, homogeneous entities devoid of internal variation, or that "individualistic" cultures lack a concept of relatedness, and "sociocentric" cultures lack a concept of personal choice. As Miller, Fung, and Mintz (1996) note, however, one of the major challenges in cultural psychology today consists of "finding effective ways to represent the intricate patterning of similarities and differences among cultures—without subduing the complexity of particular meaning in each" (p. 239). More specifically, if childhood's cultural context is indeed patterned at a broad level, then how do we understand and represent internal variations in parental beliefs and practices?

Culture and Situational Variability

Situational effects have long been recognized as a source of internal variation in the beliefs and behaviors of individuals, and indeed it could be argued that parental beliefs and practices show considerable variability across situations, thus belying any attempt at broad-level group characterizations such as "individualistic" or "interdependent." Alternatively, it is possible that situational variability in mother-infant interactions will be culturally patterned, thus suggesting that within-group variation exists, but

needs to be examined within the larger context of broad-level group differences.

In this study, we sought to investigate the cultural patterning of situational variability in mother-infant interactions by examining middle-class mother-infant pairs in northeastern Connecticut and in San Juan, Puerto Rico. Briefly, there were three hypotheses:

1. Consistent with previous research (cf. Harwood et al., 1995) indicating that Anglo-American culture can generally be described as more "individualistic," whereas Puerto Rican culture can generally be described as more "sociocentric," it was expected that the two groups would differ in the extent to which they emphasize socialization goals and childrearing strategies consonant with these broad constructs.

2. Although previous studies have suggested that long-term socialization goals represent salient cultural constructs (Harwood, 1992; Harwood et al., 1995), research has not directly examined these goals in relation to mothers' interactions with their infants. Consistent with the idea that culture consists of meaningful patterns of beliefs and behaviors (Corsaro & Miller, 1992; Rogoff et al., 1993; Schieffelin & Ochs, 1986), we thus hypothesized that coherence would exist between mothers' beliefs regarding socialization goals and the ways in which they organize interactions with their infants. In particular, it was predicted that Anglo mothers would structure interactions with their infants in such a way as to encourage independence and self-confidence, whereas Puerto Rican mothers would structure their interactions in such a way as to encourage respectfulness and attentiveness to others.

3. It was anticipated that situational variability would arise in mother-infant interactions, but that this variability would show a cultural patterning consistent with mothers' long-term socialization goals.

Selection of Study Participants

The reasons for choosing middle-class Anglo[1] and Puerto Rican mothers include: (1) Middle-class An-

---

[1]We have chosen the term "Anglo" to describe the white American women of nonHispanic European ancestry who participated in these studies. Although "white Americans of nonHispanic European ancestry" is the most accurate name for this group, it is far too cumbersome for repeated use. In addition, alternative labels like "Euro-American," or "U.S." ignore the fact that many Puerto Ricans are not only also of (Hispanic) European ancestry, but are also all United States citizens. In addition, "Anglo" has a long history of use as a cultural term contrasting the English-speaking Americas with the Spanish-speaking Americas.

glo mothers were expected to provide an index of the mainstream culture that has shaped the articulation of theories of child development within the United States (Kessen, 1979), thus providing an appropriate comparison point for the study of other groups; and (2) Middle-class Puerto Rican mothers in San Juan represent an educated, professional group in a society that, due to its commonwealth status, shares the technology, industry, and urbanization of the United States. Nonetheless, it was anticipated that Puerto Rican mothers would demonstrate beliefs concordant with a cultural meaning system different from that of the middle-class Anglo mothers. In particular, Puerto Rican culture is generally considered to emphasize a more sociocentric, and Anglo culture a more individualistic, view of the person and of interpersonal relationships (Diaz Royo, 1974; Harwood et al., 1995; Lauria, 1982). Significantly, Puerto Rico's status as a U.S. commonwealth has made socioeconomic status more comparable across the two cultures than is normally the case, thus facilitating a comparison of these two middle-class groups.

METHOD

Participants

Forty middle-class mothers (Anglo = 22, Puerto Rican = 18) participated as paid volunteers. All mothers were at least 20 years of age, and had one firstborn infant between the ages of 12 and 15 months. There were no group differences in the age of each mother's child ($M = 13.5$ months), and gender distribution (Anglo = 11 female, 11 male; Puerto Rican = 10 female, 8 male) was similar across the two groups. The Anglo mothers were drawn from urban areas within eastern Connecticut, were White American mothers of nonHispanic European ancestry who had been born, reared, and educated in the United States, spoke English as their first language, and had male partners who met these same ethnic criteria. The Puerto Rican mothers were drawn from the San Juan metropolitan area (Puerto Rico's largest city, situated in the north-eastern quadrant of the island), had been born, reared, and educated in Puerto Rico, spoke Spanish as their first language, and had male partners who met these same ethnic criteria. In both settings, mothers were recruited primarily by an invitational letter from the principal investigator that was distributed through the offices of pediatricians who agreed to identify for us mothers who met the sampling criteria; in both settings, a few mothers also were solicited by this same method through day care centers and in mother-infant activity groups.

Socioeconomic Status and Demographic Characteristics. Hollingshead's (1975) Four Factor Index was used to determine socioeconomic status (SES). This scale computes a weighted average score based on both parents' occupations and educational levels when both are employed outside the home, and on the income-receiving parent only in other cases. In this study, "middle-class" mothers were defined as women living in a home where the household occupational prestige score fell within Levels I and II (major and minor professional) of Hollingshead's scale.

Analyses were performed on 10 demographic variables (child's age, mother's age, mother's education in years, maternal employment status, hours worked outside the home, total number people in household, father's education in years, father's age, household Hollingshead score, and mother's marital status). As can be seen in Table 1, results indicated that the groups were demographically similar, differing significantly on just one variable: Anglo mothers were older than were Puerto Rican mothers, *mean* = 31.5 and 27.9 years, respectively, $p < .05$. The two groups were thus comparable, both comprised of highly educated, financially stable mothers.

Procedure

Interviews were conducted in two sessions in mothers' homes by ethnically matched, trained interviewers. The first session included videotaped observations of each mother interacting with her infant in four everyday settings. The second session included an interview with each mother regarding her long-term socialization goals and childrearing beliefs. The videotaped observations were done prior to the interviews in order to avoid biasing mothers' interactions with their infants during the observations. The interview sessions were

TABLE 1   Demographic Characteristics of Participants

CHARACTERISTIC	ANGLO		PUERTO RICAN	
	M	SD	M	SD
Child's age (months)	13.7	1.1	13.3	1.3
Mother's age	31.5	5.0	27.9	4.6*
Mother's education (years)	16.5	1.9	15.9	1.5
Percent mothers employed	78.0		78.0	
No. hours worked/week	32.1	12.2	37.3	6.3
No. people in household	3.0	0.0	3.2	0.4
Father's education (years)	16.2	2.4	15.6	2.2
Father's age	32.8	6.0	30.3	5.8
Hollingshead score	53.3	9.1	50.9	8.9
Percent mothers married	95.0		78.0	

*$p < .05$.

tape-recorded and transcribed verbatim for further analysis. Each of the two sessions took about 1½ hours to complete, and were conducted approximately 1 week apart. The Spanish version of the interview protocol was obtained through a committee of three bilingual, bicultural master's level research assistants at the Behavioral Sciences Research Institute, University of Puerto Rico Medical School. Spanish interviews were transcribed and translated into English in the first author's laboratory by bilingual, bicultural (Puerto Rican) graduate students.

Maternal Beliefs

Long-Term Socialization Goals.

To provide an index of long-term socialization goals, mothers were administered an abbreviated version of the Socialization Goals Interview (SGI), a semistructured, individually administered interview consisting of four open-ended questions in which parents are asked to describe the qualities they (1) would and (2) would not like their children to possess as adults, and to describe toddlers they know who possess at least the beginnings of those (3) positive and (4) negative qualities (Harwood, 1992). Because previous research (Harwood et al., 1995; Harwood, Schoelmerich, Ventura-Cook, Schulze, & Wilson, 1996) has indicated that the first two questions, which probe for adult socialization goals, may provide a better index of broad cultural belief systems than the two questions regarding desirable and undesirable child behavior, mothers in this study were asked only the first two questions.

Childrearing Strategies.

To investigate the specific childrearing strategies that mothers espouse for accomplishing their expressed socialization goals, each mother also was asked to describe what parents could do to help a child come to possess the desirable qualities, or to not come to possess the undesirable qualities, that she mentioned. An open-ended format rather than a standardized questionnaire was used for this task in order to obtain, as much as possible, mothers' indigenous beliefs on this topic.

Coding of Interviews

Socialization goals. As in previous research using the SGI (Harwood et al., 1995, 1996), mothers' responses to the questions regarding long-term socialization goals were coded at the level of individual word and phrase descriptors into one of six mutually exclusive categories identified through previous work as culturally relevant to Anglo and Puerto Rican mothers (Harwood, 1992; Harwood et al., 1995):

(1) Self-Maximization, (2) Self-Control, (3) Lovingness, (4) Decency, (5) Proper Demeanor, and (6) Miscellaneous. Fewer than 5% of mothers' responses across both groups were coded as Miscellaneous, attesting to the broadly encompassing character of the five content categories.

Reliability in coding mothers' responses to the SGI was calculated between two independent judges blind to the study hypotheses as well as to each mother's sociocultural group on 50% of the sample. Overall agreement reached a level of .78 (*range* = .72–.84, Cohen's κ).

Childrearing strategies. Mothers' responses to the question regarding what parents could do to encourage or discourage the development of specific qualities in their children were coded into seven categories derived from the most common types of responses generated by mothers in both groups. These included: (1) Model the desirable behavior, (2) Provide Opportunities for child to develop the quality on his or her own, (3) Provide an Emotional Environment that will allow the quality to flourish, (4) Praise the child for desirable behavior, (5) the child learns through the parent's Direct Instruction, (6) the characteristic is innate or Inborn, and thus the parents' influence is negligible, (7) Other: the parent gives an ambiguous or otherwise uncodeable response, such as, "I'll worry about that later." Fewer than 5% of mothers' responses across both groups were coded as Other.

Reliability in coding mothers' responses to the question regarding childrearing strategies was calculated between the third author and one independent judge blind to the study hypotheses as well as to each mother's sociocultural group on 50% of the sample. Overall agreement reached a level of .92 (*range* = .90–.95, Cohen's κ).

Mother-Infant Interactions

In order to investigate coherence between maternal beliefs and practices, as well as to examine cross-situational variability in maternal practices, mothers were videotaped interacting with their infants in four everyday situations:

1. *Feeding.* Mothers were instructed to, "Feed your child as you normally would," and videotaped for the first 10 min of the feeding session. Few feeding sessions lasted beyond the allotted 10-min time period.
2. *Social Play.* Mothers were instructed to, "Play with your child without using toys," and videotaped for 5 min.

3. *Teaching.* Mothers were supplied with materials and instructed to spend 3 min on each of the following three tasks:

"Teach your child to draw a line on the pad of paper with a crayon";

"Teach your child to stack one block on top of another";

"Teach your child to push one toy with another along the floor."

Total time spent videotaping mothers in the teaching situation was 9 min.

4. *Free Play.* Mothers were supplied with a variety of developmentally appropriate toys and instructed to, "Play with your child as you normally would using toys." Videotaping lasted for 8 min.

Coding of Mother-Infant Interactions.   The videotaped mother-infant interactions were coded in real time using Interact (Dumas, 1993), a software program that computes frequencies of different types of behaviors, and durations of different types of settings. In our mother-infant interactions, we chose to code two types of data: (1) frequency of behaviors (maternal nonverbal, maternal verbal, and infant) common across the situations; and (2) frequency of behaviors and duration of settings specific to each situation.

Maternal nonverbal behaviors.   In order to investigate situational variability in mothers' nonverbal strategies for organizing interactions with their infants across four everyday situations, the frequency of five specific types of maternal nonverbal behaviors was examined in each situation as follows. The mother: (1) attempts to signal infant's attention by tapping or pointing, (2) praises infant by clapping and cheering, (3) positions infant, (4) restrains infant when infant attempts to pull away or wander off, and (5) offers affection by hugging/kissing infant.

Maternal verbal behaviors.   In order to investigate situational variability in mothers' verbal strategies for organizing interactions with their infants across four everyday situations, the frequency of five specific types of maternal verbal behaviors was examined in each situation as follows. The mother: (1) signals infant's attention by calling infant's name, (2) praises infant, (3) offers infant affection by using term of endearment, (4) directly structures infant's behavior by commanding infant to perform or not perform a given action, and (5) indirectly structures infant's behavior by suggesting that infant perform or not perform a given action.

Infant behaviors.   Although we were primarily interested in mothers' behaviors in this study, in order to control for the possibility that group differences in maternal behavior reflect differences in infant behavior, we also examined three behaviors thought to index the infant's overall activity level and cooperation with the mother: (1) resists maternal intervention, displaying negative affect; (2) disengages from direct physical contact with the mother without signs of negative affect; and (3) wanders away by retreating out of arm's length of mother.

Situation-specific behaviors and settings.   In addition to behaviors examined across the situations, a few behaviors and settings specific to each situation also were coded:

1. *Feeding.* Mother feeds the infant by directly placing spoon in infant's mouth; mother encourages autonomy in feeding (e.g., places spoon in infant's hand); and infant feeds self.
2. *Social Play.* Duration of time each mother spent in one of four types of dyadic social games: clapping/singing games; bouncing games (e.g., swinging child up and down in parents' arms); hiding-chasing games; and touching/turn-taking games (e.g., tickling, or games involving some kind of back-and-forth interaction between the mother and infant, such as tugging a diaper back and forth).
3. *Teaching.* Duration of total time infants spent on-task for each of the three tasks: crayon, block, and pushtoy; and duration of total time mothers spent attempting to teach the tasks.
4. *Free Play.* Duration of time each dyad spent in the following states of coordinated activity: mother and infant play together; infant plays alone while mother watches; mother attempts to shift infant's attention to a new toy while infant is still playing with another toy; mother attempts to gain infant's attention with a new toy while infant is not involved in any play activity; and no play activity.

The videotapes were coded in the first author's laboratory in Connecticut by three trained graduate students. In particular, a native English-speaking student was the primary coder for the Anglo videotapes, and a bilingual Puerto Rican student was the primary coder for the Puerto Rican videotapes. Reliability was established: (1) between the two primary coders by having the bilingual student code 9% of the Anglo videotapes in addition to all the Puerto Rican tapes, and (2) between the two primary coders and a third independent judge, by having an additional bilingual Puerto Rican student code 27% of the Anglo videotapes, and 33% of the Puerto Rican videotapes.

Because the coders were viewing videotapes of mother-infant interactions among two linguistically different groups, it was not possible to blind them to each mother's sociocultural group membership; however, all three students remained blind to the hypotheses of the study. Overall agreement reached a level of .70 *(range = .54–.85, Cohen's κ)*.

RESULTS

In order to control for possible gender effects, preliminary analyses were performed with child's sex entered as a factor. There was only one significant gender effect among all analyses: mothers of girls were more likely to give verbal signals during free play than mothers of boys. Due to the general lack of significant gender effects, this variable will not be discussed further.

Maternal Beliefs

Socialization goals. An analysis of variance (ANOVA) indicated no group differences in total number of descriptors generated by Anglo and Puerto Rican mothers in response to the open-ended questions regarding long-term socialization goals (M = 18.59 and 17.84, respectively). Because of the relatively small number of responses generated, however, categories were combined for the purposes of analysis, according to previous research (Harwood et al., 1995, 1996), which has indicated that the categories of Self-Maximization and Self-Control tend to be more characteristic of the responses of Anglo mothers, whereas the categories of Decency and Proper Demeanor tend to be more characteristic of the responses of Puerto Rican mothers. Thus, the categories used in this analysis were: Self-Maximization/Self-Control; Decency/Proper Demeanor; and Lovingness.

In order to investigate cultural differences in mothers' long-term socialization goals, a 2 × 3 (Group × Category-Type) multivariate analysis of variance (MANOVA) was performed on the number of mothers' descriptors falling into the three experimenter-derived categories. This analysis yielded a significant Group × Category-Type interaction, $F(3, 36) = 6.5, p < .01$. Follow-up one-way ANOVAs revealed significant cultural differences in the number of descriptors generated for two of the three categories. Consistent with previous research, the Anglo mothers, compared to the Puerto Rican mothers, were more likely to generate descriptors falling into the combined Self-Maximization/Self-Control category (M = 9.95 and 5.89, respectively, $p < .05$), and less likely to generate descriptors falling into the combined Decency/Proper Demeanor category (M = 3.82 and

9.17, respectively, $p < .01$). There were no group differences in the use of the category Lovingness (M = 4.82 and 2.78, respectively).

Childrearing strategies. An ANOVA was performed on the total number of answers generated by mothers in response to the question regarding what parents can do to encourage or discourage the development of desirable and undesirable qualities in their children. This analysis indicated that Anglo mothers gave a larger number of answers to this portion of the interview than did Puerto Rican mothers (M = 59.2 and 34.6, respectively, $p < .05$). Therefore, data were transformed to represent percentages of the total number of answers for each subject, and the resulting scores were treated as compositional data by log-transforming the scores to remedy the problems of nonindependence of variation associated with data of this type (Aitchison, 1986; see Bersoff & Miller, 1993). Analyses were then performed on the transformed data. Two of the seven categories (Inborn and Other) together represented less than 6% of mothers' responses, and thus were dropped from the final analysis.

Specifically, to compare mothers' open-ended responses regarding parenting strategies, a 2 × 5 (Group × Category-Type) MANOVA was performed. This analysis yielded a significant Group × Category-Type interaction, $F(5, 34) = 9.05, p < .01$. Follow-up one-way ANOVAs indicated that the Anglo mothers, compared to the Puerto Rican mothers, were (1) more likely to generate childrearing strategies falling into the categories of Modelling, $p < .05$, and Provide Opportunities, $p < .01$; and (2) less likely to generate childrearing strategies falling into the category of Direct Instruction, $p < .001$. The categories of Provide Optimal Emotional Environment and Praise did not yield significant group differences.

Mother-Infant Interactions Common across the Settings

Infant behaviors. Preliminary analyses revealed that infant behaviors between the two groups differed on just two variables across the four situations. In particular, compared to Anglo infants, Puerto Rican infants were less likely to retreat out of arm's length during teaching (M = 2.86 and 0.33, respectively, $p < .01$), and more likely to engage in resistive behaviors during feeding (M = .50 and 5.28, respectively, $p < .01$). This low incidence suggests that group differences in mothers' behavior were not a result of group differences in infant behavior. Because of this low incidence, and because our primary interest was in maternal behavior, the analyses described below will focus on maternal variables.

Maternal nonverbal behaviors. Preliminary analyses indicated that the use of highchairs rendered the maternal nonverbal behaviors of interest uncommon among both Anglo and Puerto Rican mothers; feeding therefore was omitted as a situation from this analysis. To investigate cultural differences in mothers' nonverbal strategies for organizing interactions with their infants, a MANOVA with group (2) as a between factor, and situation (3) and behavior (5) as repeated factors was performed on the frequency of different types of maternal nonverbal behaviors occurring in each of the situations except feeding. This MANOVA yielded significant main effects for group, $F(1, 37) = 11.58$, $p < .01$, situation, $F(2, 74) = 3.27$, $p < .05$, and behavior, $F(4, 148) = 43.79$, $p < .001$, as well as a significant Situation × Behavior interaction, $F(8, 296) = 15.45$, $p < .001$.

Follow-up one-way ANOVAs (see Table 2) indicated that, compared to Anglo mothers, Puerto Rican mothers: (1) exhibited a higher overall frequency of nonverbal behaviors during social play, $p < .01$, and teaching, $p < .05$, but not during free play; and (2) were more likely to restrain their infants during social play, $p < .001$, and to position their infants during teaching, $p < .05$. No group differences arose in mothers' use of nonverbal behaviors toward their infants during free play.

Maternal verbal behaviors. To investigate cultural differences in mothers' verbal strategies for organizing interactions with their infants, a MANOVA with group (2) as a between factor, and situation (4) and behavior (5) as repeated factors was performed on the frequency of different types of maternal verbal behaviors occurring in each of the four situations. This MANOVA yielded significant main effects for group, $F(1, 37) = 7.64$, $p < .01$, situation, $F(3, 111) = 95.95$, $p < .001$, and behavior, $F(4, 148) = 58.34$, $p < .001$, as well as significant Group × Behavior, $F(4,148) = 32.61$, $p < .001$, Situation × Behavior, $F(12, 444) = 17.32$, $p < .001$, and Group × Situation × Behavior, $F(12,444) = 13.36$, $p < .001$, interactions.

Follow-up one-way ANOVAs (see Table 3) indicated that, compared to the Anglo mothers, Puerto Rican mothers were more likely to: (1) signal their infants' attention in all four situations, (2) offer affection during teaching, (3) issue directives in the form of commands in all situations except social play, and (4) emit a greater overall number of verbal behaviors towards their infants during free play. Conversely, compared to the Puerto Rican mothers, Anglo mothers were more likely to: (1) praise their infants' efforts in all situations except social play, and (2) issue directives in the form of suggestions in all situations except free play.

Situation-Specific Maternal Behaviors

Behaviors specific to feeding. To investigate group differences in the organization of feeding, a 2 × 3 (Group × Behavior) MANOVA was performed. The three feeding behaviors examined were: mother feeds infant, mother encourages autonomy in feeding, and infant feeds self. This analysis yielded a significant Group × Behavior interaction, $F(3, 34) = 38.7$, $p < .001$. As can be seen in Table 4, follow-up one-way ANOVAs indicated that Anglo mothers, compared to Puerto Rican mothers, were more likely to encourage autonomy in feeding ($M = 7.64$ and 1.39, respectively, $p < .01$), and less likely to directly feed their infants ($M = 8.36$ and 41.94, respectively, $p < .001$). Concomitantly, Anglo infants were more likely than Puerto Rican infants to self-feed ($M = 23.82$ and 2.78, respectively, $p < .001$).

Behaviors specific to social play. An ANOVA indicated no significant group difference in total amount of time that the Anglo and Puerto Rican mothers spent playing dyadic social games (clapping/singing; bouncing; hiding/chasing; touching/turntaking) with their infants ($M = 93.1$ s and 112.1 s,

| | | | PUERTO | | |
| | ANGLO | | RICAN | | |
BEHAVIOR	M	SD	M	SD	p
TABLE 2 Mean Frequency of Maternal Nonverbal Behaviors by Situation					
Social Play					
Nonverbal signal attention	1.3	3.3	2.7	4.4	
Position infant	2.4	1.8	3.7	2.6	
Restrain infant's movements	1.6	1.4	5.1	4.6	***
Nonverbal praise	.1	.5	.2	.6	
Nonverbal affection	1.8	2.0	2.6	3.8	
Overall nonverbal	7.2	4.7	14.3	9.4	**
Teaching					
Nonverbal signal attention	6.4	4.9	9.1	6.7	
Position infant	.9	1.2	2.4	2.3	*
Restrain infant's movements	1.8	2.2	2.6	2.5	
Nonverbal praise	.4	.9	.7	1.4	
Nonverbal affection	.3	.8	.6	1.0	
Overall nonverbal	9.8	6.6	15.4	6.7	*
Free Play					
Nonverbal signal attention	5.7	5.7	5.5	4.8	
Position infant	.9	1.2	1.0	1.5	
Restrain infant's movements	.6	.7	1.3	2.4	
Nonverbal praise	.2	.4	.7	1.5	
Nonverbal affection	.6	1.2	.7	1.2	
Overall nonverbal	8.0	7.0	9.1	6.6	

*$p < .05$; **$p < .01$; ***$p < .001$.

TABLE 3 Mean Frequency of Maternal Verbal Behaviors by Situation

BEHAVIOR	ANGLO		PUERTO RICAN		
	M	SD	M	SD	p
Feeding					
Verbal signal attention	1.7	2.2	9.7	13.4	**
Verbal praise	3.6	5.7	.6	1.5	*
Verbal affection	.6	.8	.9	1.6	
Command	4.0	3.9	18.1	16.2	***
Suggest	7.2	4.4	10.7	8.9	
Overall verbal	17.1	9.4	40.0	24.3	***
Social Play					
Verbal signal attention	1.2	1.5	6.3	6.2	***
Verbal praise	1.6	2.1	.6	.9	
Verbal affection	1.2	2.2	1.5	2.2	
Command	6.8	5.3	10.3	8.8	
Suggest	5.7	4.5	2.8	2.9	
Overall verbal	16.3	8.5	21.4	12.3	
Teaching					
Verbal signal attention	14.8	8.0	37.1	15.9	***
Verbal praise	9.3	5.6	4.8	4.8	*
Verbal affection	.9	1.9	3.2	4.3	*
Command	21.7	15.4	34.3	17.9	*
Suggest	28.4	9.6	6.9	6.9	***
Overall verbal	75.1	25.0	86.4	30.9	
Free Play					
Verbal signal attention	7.5	4.2	16.0	9.5	***
Verbal praise	4.8	3.1	1.3	2.0	***
Verbal affection	1.3	2.1	3.0	3.4	
Command	9.8	9.4	26.2	16.2	***
Suggest	19.6	8.8	3.6	2.9	***
Overall verbal	43.0	19.4	50.1	23.0	

$*p < .05$; $**p < .01$; $***p < .001$.

respectively). Types of social games played were thus analyzed according to number of seconds mothers spent engaged or attempting to engage their infants in each type of game.

To investigate group differences in types of social games played, a 2 × 4 (Group × Game-Type) MANOVA was performed. This analysis yielded a significant group × game-type interaction, $F(4, 32) = 3.3$, $p < .05$. Follow-up one-way ANOVAs (see Table 4) indicated that, compared to the Anglo mothers, Puerto Rican mothers were significantly more likely to engage in touching/turntaking games with their infants, $p < .05$. Group differences for clapping/singing, hiding/chasing, and bouncing games did not reach significance.

Behaviors specific to teaching. A *t* test of total time spent on-task in the teaching situation yielded a sig-

nificant group difference, with Anglo mother-infant pairs spending on average 330.2 s on-task, compared with an average of 194.1 s on-task among the Puerto Rican mother-infant pairs. A by-task breakdown of on-task time indicated that in both groups, infants spent approximately 87% of their time on-task during the crayon portion of the teaching situation, but that on-task time dropped to an average of 67% among the Anglo infants, and 35% among the Puerto Rican infants for the block and pushtoy portions. Moreover, a *t* test of total time spent on the teaching situation (see Table 4) indicated that Anglo mothers persisted with this situation longer than did Puerto Rican mothers ($M = 459.4$ s and 371.2 s, respectively, $p < .05$).

Behaviors specific to free play. To investigate group differences in the coordination of mother-infant activity during free play, a 2 × 5 (Group × Activity) MANOVA was performed. The five activities examined were: (1) mother and infant play together with object, (2) infant plays alone while mother watches, (3) mother attempts to shift infant's attention to a new toy while infant is still playing with another toy, (4) mother attempts to gain infant attention while infant is unoccupied, and (5) no play activity. This analysis yielded a significant Group × Activity interaction, $F(4, 152) = 5.25$, $p < .01$. Follow-up one-way ANOVAs (see Table 4) indicated that, compared to the Anglo mothers, Puerto Rican mothers spent (1) more time attempting to shift or gain their infants' attention, $p < .05$, and (2) less time watching while their infants played alone, $p < .01$.

DISCUSSION

Consistent with a broad characterization of Anglo cultural belief systems as more individualistic, and Puerto Rican cultural belief systems as more sociocentric, the Anglo mothers in this study were more likely to generate long-term socialization goals falling into the combined categories of Self-Maximization and Self-Control, whereas the Puerto Rican mothers were more likely to generate long-term socialization goals falling into the combined categories of Proper Demeanor and Decency. Moreover, when asked what parents could do to encourage or discourage these qualities in their children, mothers were likely to generate childrearing strategies that corresponded to these broad cultural constructs. In particular, Anglo mothers were more likely to say that they would model positive behaviors and provide their children with opportunities that allow them to learn for themselves, whereas Puerto Rican mothers were more likely to say that they would teach their

TABLE 4   Mean Frequency of Behaviors, and Duration of Settings Specific to Each Situation

BEHAVIOR/SETTING	ANGLO		PUERTO RICAN		
	M	SD	M	SD	p
Feeding					
Mother spoon-feed infant	8.4	8.7	41.9	11.5	***
Mother encourage autonomy	7.6	8.3	1.4	2.9	**
Infant feed self	23.8	12.6	2.8	4.3	***
Social Play					
Hiding/chasing games	35.1	40.4	15.4	31.8	
Clapping/singing games	15.6	28.6	31.3	32.5	
Bouncing games	22.2	25.6	15.6	21.8	
Touching/turntaking games	20.2	21.5	49.8	46.7	*
Teaching					
Time on-task crayon	135.8	38.5	107.8	38.1	*
Time on-task blocks	98.4	49.8	47.2	37.8	**
Time on-task pushtoy	96.1	51.8	39.1	33.0	***
Total time on-task	335.5	77.9	204.7	80.9	***
Total time in situation	459.4	128.9	371.2	82.3	*
Free Play					
Play together	190.6	85.8	181.9	73.7	
Infant play, mother watch	207.7	92.9	125.3	57.9	**
Attempt to shift attention	7.6	15.9	25.4	29.7	*
Attempt to gain attention	2.3	10.7	12.0	18.4	*
No play activity	37.5	37.6	61.9	50.7	

*$p < .05$; **$p < .01$; ***$p < .001$.

children through the direct exercise of parental authority. These results suggest a greater emphasis among the Anglo mothers on childrearing strategies that indirectly structure the child's learning experiences, thus optimizing the child's own sense of autonomy and personal choice; and a greater focus among the Puerto Rican mothers on childrearing strategies that directly guide the child's learning experiences, thus highlighting the child's sense of interpersonal obligation.

Of course, it should be noted that statements falling into the categories of Proper Demeanor and Direct Instruction were not absent among the Anglo mothers, any more than statements falling into the categories of Self-Maximization and Provide Opportunities were absent among the Puerto Rican mothers. What is significant is not the presence or absence of each of these response categories, but their relative patterning across the two groups. Long-term socialization goals and childrearing strategies that emphasize the individual's own agency were foregrounded for the Anglo mothers, whereas goals and strategies that focus on the individual's obligations

and connectedness to others were foregrounded for the Puerto Rican mothers.

Group commonalities in socialization goals and strategies also emerged. In particular, there were no group differences in the use of adjectives falling into the category of Lovingness when describing long-term goals, and no significant differences in the use of Provide Optimal Emotional Environment and Praise as childrearing strategies. These findings suggest that the capacity for emotional intimacy, and the desire to provide the child with an emotionally supportive environment, is equally valued among mothers in both groups. Where the two groups differ is in the relative emphasis placed on dimensions consonant with the broad cultural constructs of individualism and interdependence.

Greater differential emphases on individualism and interdependence also were evident when examining mother-infant interactions across the four every-day situations, providing evidence of coherence between mothers' childrearing beliefs, and the ways in which they chose to structure interactions with their infants in four everyday situations. In particular, Puerto Rican mothers were more likely than Anglo mothers to structure their infants' behavior directly. This was evident in all four situations and expressed in a variety of verbal and nonverbal maternal behaviors, including greater tendencies to physically position and restrain the infant, to signal the infant's attention and issue direct commands, and to spoon-feed the infant. Conversely, consistent with a greater emphasis on individualism, Anglo mothers were more likely than Puerto Rican mothers to praise the infant verbally, to attempt to structure the infant's behavior indirectly through the use of suggestions, and to encourage autonomy in feeding.

It could be argued that Puerto Rican and Anglo mothers' behavioral differences reflect temperamental differences in the infants. In particular, Puerto Rican mothers might be more directive because their infants are either more or less active than Anglo infants. There were few group differences in infant behavior, however, and those that arose did not form a coherent pattern. These findings do not suggest a pattern whereby either group of infants appears to be more or less active than the other group. It thus seems unlikely that differences in maternal behavior are explicable as responses to preexisting group differences in the temperament or activity level of Puerto Rican versus Anglo infants.

It also should be noted that group commonalities in mother-infant interactions also occurred. Consistent with the finding of no group differences in emphasis on Lovingness as a socialization goal, or in Providing an Optimal Emotional Environment as a childrearing strategy, there were generally no group differences in mothers' physical or verbal affection to their infants. There was one exception: Puerto Rican mothers were more likely than Anglo mothers to show verbal affection to their infants during teaching.

The finding of Puerto Rican mothers' greater verbal affection during teaching is interesting in light of the lesser tendency of Puerto Rican infants to be on-task during this situation, and to spend less time overall on the teaching tasks. Group differences in on-task time during teaching can be interpreted in at least two possible ways: (1) The nondirective methods used by the Anglo mothers are more effective at sustaining infant attention in these tasks than the more directive methods used by the Puerto Rican mothers, or (2) the teaching tasks were less salient and meaningful for the Puerto Rican dyads than they were for the Anglo dyads. The latter interpretation is supported by the fact that the proportion of infant on-task times for the two groups was roughly equivalent at around 86% during the crayon task (which most infants this age find inherently interesting), but

dropped dramatically for the two remaining tasks to around 67% for the Anglo infants, and to around 35% for the Puerto Rican infants. In other words, both groups of infants found the crayon task to be relatively more interesting than the other two tasks, but this was especially true for the Puerto Rican infants, and this may be related to the relative lack of persistence on these tasks among the Puerto Rican dyads. It is conceivable that the teaching tasks were perceived as less age-appropriate and less interesting by the Puerto Rican mother-infant pairs than they were by the Anglo dyads; the Puerto Rican mothers' greater use of verbal affection during this situation may indicate that they viewed themselves as trying to coax their infants to do something that was difficult or uninteresting. This possibility highlights the importance of employing culturally meaningful tasks, as well as the importance of looking at mother-infant interactions across a variety of situations when attempting to understand cultural differences.

As suggested by the example above, situational variability did occur in mother-infant interaction, manifesting itself in at least three different ways: (1) Overall frequencies of maternal nonverbal and verbal behaviors differed according to the situation, (2) some behaviors showed significant group differences in one situation but not in another, and (3) certain behaviors and activities were unique to each situation (such as types of social games played, or spoon-feeding versus self-feeding).

In terms of overall activity levels, both groups of mothers were more verbally active during teaching and free play than they were during feeding and social play. Although some of these differences reflect differential lengths of observation, observation time alone cannot account for these differences. For instance, even if all social play maternal frequencies are doubled, they still do not reach the levels exhibited by mothers during the teaching tasks. Mothers in both groups thus appear to be differentially responsive to the demands of each situation. Significantly, however, when group differences arose in maternal behavioral frequencies, they were in the direction of the Puerto Rican mothers being more active, particularly with regard to nonverbal behaviors.

Variability also arose in terms of mothers' differential selection of strategies for organizing each situation. This was particularly true for nonverbal behaviors. For instance, Puerto Rican mothers were more likely to restrain their infant's free movements about the room during social play, but not during teaching or free play; similarly, they were more likely to physically position their infants during teaching, but not during social play or free play.

Moreover, free play was unique among the four situations in that it did not yield any group differences in maternal nonverbal behavior. Group differences in mothers' verbal behaviors, however, showed considerable cross-situational consistency. In particular, compared to Anglo mothers, Puerto Rican mothers were more likely to signal the infant's attention and to use commands, and less likely to praise the infant or to use suggestions.

These findings point to maternal responsiveness to differential situational demands among both groups of mothers. It is noteworthy, however, that the significant differences that occurred were in the expected direction. In other words, the differences were consistent in all four situations with a greater degree of direct structuring of the infant's behavior among the Puerto Rican mothers, and a greater offering of personal choice to the infant among the Anglo mothers. What differed by situation was the specific strategy that mothers chose to communicate either greater directiveness or greater choice.

Together, these findings suggest that situational variability occurs in the instantiation of broad cultural constructs. This variability remained coherent in this study with larger cultural goals, however, appearing to consist primarily of different manifestations of the same concern, or of situationally specific interactional opportunities. Although mothers did not behave identically across all four situations, they did behave in ways that were consistent with cultural goals and expectations. These findings add to our understanding of culture's role in child development by: (1) demonstrating coherence among long-term socialization goals, maternal beliefs regarding strategies for realizing those goals, and the structuring of mother-infant interactions in four everyday situations; (2) providing evidence for the usefulness of 'individualism' and 'sociocentrism' as general heuristic devices for understanding broad cultural differences in the context of child development; and (3) suggesting that more localized, intragroup variations in childrearing beliefs and practices need to be understood within the context of broader cultural belief systems, goals, and values. As Wiley, Rose, Burger, and Miller (1998) note, an appreciation of the "subtle patterns of similarities and differences within and across cultural groups…is essential if we are to move beyond dichotomous comparisons of sociocultural groups" (p. 844).

These findings, though suggestive, are limited by a small sample size of just 40 mothers, and concomitantly lowered reliability coefficients for maternal behaviors, two of which fell below .60. Because reliability coefficients, along with group differences, become more robust with sample size, the findings presented here bear further study and replication with a larger number of mothers. In addition, future research in this domain would benefit from a closer examination of patterns of within-group variability, and the ways in which local variations can be understood as situated within broader cultural goals and values. Finally, as Super and Harkness (1986) have noted, parents' cultural beliefs work in concert with other important dimensions of everyday life to shape childhood's context. Further research in this domain needs to continue to examine the multiple paths through which parents create settings in which children come to construct and reconstruct their own cultural understandings of self and others. These include not only parental beliefs, but also other aspects of the child's setting, such as number and type of social contacts, and amount of time spent engaged in a variety of activities throughout the day (Leyendecker, Lamb, Schölmerich, & Fracasso, 1995).

Rogoff et al. (1993, p. 1) stated that "development occurs through active participation in cultural systems of practice in which children, together with their caregivers and other companions, learn and extend the skills, values, and knowledge of their community." Consistent with this, our findings suggest that children engage repeatedly in situationally specific instantiations of larger cultural values in a variety of everyday settings. Situationally appropriate behavior may itself be culturally patterned, further illustrating the ways in which homogeneity and heterogeneity can coexist coherently within a larger cultural belief system.

ACKNOWLEDGMENTS

This research was made possible through a grant to the first author from the National Institute of Child Health and Human Development (HD32800). We also are grateful to Glorisa Canino of the University of Puerto Rico School of Medicine for making available the resources of her laboratory for the collection of the Puerto Rican data. We would like to express appreciation to Eugenio Avala, Delia Collazo, Helena Mendez, and Stephanie Wilson, for their assistance with interviewing, translation, and data coding. We also would like to thank Penn Handwerker for many lively discussions concerning the conceptualization of culture. Portions of this paper were presented at the biennial meetings of the Society for Research in Child Development in Washington, DC, April, 1997, and of the International Society for Infant Studies in Providence, RI, April, 1996.

REFERENCES

Aitchison, J. (1986). *The statistical analysis of compositional data.* London: Chapman & Hall.

Bersoff, D. M., & Miller, J. G. (1993). Culture, context, and the development of moral accountability judgments. *Developmental Psychology, 29,* 664–676.

Cole, M. (1996). *Cultural psychology: A once and future discipline.* Cambridge, MA: Harvard University Press.

Corsaro, W. A., & Miller, P. J. (Eds.). (1992). *Interpretive approaches to children's socialization. New Directions for Child Development, 58.* San Francisco: Jossey-Bass.

Derne, S. (1995). *Culture in action: Family life, emotion, and male dominance in Banaras, India.* Albany: State University of New York Press.

Diaz Royo, A. (1974). The enculturation process of Puerto Rican highland children. *Dissertation Abstracts International, 35-12A,* 7646. (University Microfilms No. 75-12506, 324).

Dumas, J. *(1993). Interact Software System, v. 2.0.* Lafayette, IN: Purdue University.

Goodnow, J. J., Miller, P. J., & Kessel, F. (Eds.). (1995). *Cultural practices as contexts for development. New Directions for Child Development, 67.* San Francisco: Jossey-Bass.

Greenfield, P. M., & Cocking, R. R. (Eds.). (1994). *Cross-cultural roots of minority child development.* Hillsdale, NJ: Erlbaum.

Harkness, S., & Super, C. M. (Eds.). (1996). *Parents' cultural beliefs sytems: Their origins, expressions, and consequences.* New York: Guilford.

Harwood, R. L. (1992). The influence of culturally derived values on Anglo and Puerto Rican mothers' perceptions of attachment behavior. *Child Development, 63,* 822–839.

Harwood, R. L., Miller, J. G., & Lucca Irizarry, N. (1995). *Culture and attachment: Perceptions of the child in context.* New York: Guilford.

Harwood, R. L., Schoelmerich, A., Ventura-Cook, E., Schulze, P. A., & Wilson, S. P. (1996). Culture and class influences on Anglo and Puerto Rican mothers' beliefs regarding long-term socialization goals and child behavior. *Child Development, 67,* 2446–2461.

Hollingshead, A. B. (1975). *Four Factor Index of Social Status.* Unpublished manuscript, Yale University, New Haven, CT.

Kessen, W. (1979). The American child and other cultural inventions. *American Psychologist, 34,* 815–820.

Kurtz, S. N. (1992). *All the mothers are one: Hindu India and the cultural reshaping of psychoanalysis.* New York: Columbia University Press.

Lauria, A. (1982). *Respeto, relajo,* and interpersonal relations in Puerto Rico. In F. Cordasco & E. Bucchioni (Eds.), *The Puerto Rican community and its children on the mainland* (2nd ed., pp. 58–71). Metuchen, NJ: Scarecrow Press.

Leyendecker, B., Lamb, M. E., Schölmerich, A., & Fracasso, M. P. (1995). The social worlds of 8- and 12-month-old infants: Early experiences in two subcultural contexts. *Social Development, 4,* 194–208.

Markus, H. R., & Kitayama, S. (1991). Culture and the self: Implications for cognition, emotion, and motivation. *Psychological Review, 98,* 224–253.

Miller, P. J., Fung, H., & Mintz, J. (1996). Self-construction through narrative practices: A Chinese and American comparison of early socialization. *Ethos, 24,* 237–280.

Mines, M. (1994). *Public faces, private voices: Community and individuality in South India.* Berkeley: University of California Press.

Nucci, L. (1994). Mothers' beliefs regarding the personal domain of children. In J. G. Smetana (Ed.), *Beliefs about parenting: Origins and developmental implications, New Directions for Child Development, 66* (pp. 81–97). San Francisco, CA: Jossey-Bass.

Rogoff, B., Mistry, J., Goncu, A., & Mosier, C. (1993). Guided participation in cultural activity by toddlers and caregivers. *Monographs of the Society for Research in Child Development, 58*(Serial No. 236).

Sampson, E. E. (1989). The challenge of social change for psychology: Globalization and psychology's theory of the person. *American Psychologist, 44,* 914–921.

Schieffelin, B. B., & Ochs, E. (Eds.). (1986). *Language socialization across cultures.* Cambridge, UK: Cambridge University Press.

Shweder, R. A. (1996). True ethnography: The lore, the law, and the lure. In R. Jessor, A. Colby, & R. A. Shweder (Eds.), *Ethnography and human development: Context and meaning in social inquiry.* Chicago: University of Chicago Press.

Shweder, R. A., & Bourne, E. J. (1984). Does the concept of the person vary cross-culturally? In R. A. Shweder, & R. A. LeVine (Eds.), *Culture theory: Essays in mind, self, and emotion* (pp. 158–199). Cambridge, UK: Cambridge University Press.

Spence, J. T. (1985). Achievement American style: The rewards and costs of individualism. *American Psychologist, 40,* 1285–1295.

Super, C. M., & Harkness, S. (1986). The developmental niche: A conceptualization at the interface of child and culture. *International Journal of Behavioral Development, 9,* 545–569.

Tobin, J. J., Wu, D. Y. H., & Davidson, D. H. (1989). *Preschool in three cultures: Japan, China, and the United States.* New Haven, CT: Yale University Press.

Triandis, H. C., Bontempo, R., Villareal, M. J., Asai, M., & Lucca, N. (1988). Individualism and collectivism: Cross-cultural perspectives on self-ingroup relationships. *Journal of Personality and Social Psychology, 54,* 323–338.

Triandis, H. C., Marin, G., Lisansky, J., & Betancourt, H. (1984). *Simpatia* as a cultural script of Hispanics. *Journal of Personality and Social Psychology, 47,* 1363–1375.

Wainryb, C. (1995). Reasoning about social conflicts in different cultures: Druze and Jewish children in Israel. *Child Development, 66,* 390–401.

Wiley, A. R., Rose, A. J., Burger, L. K., & Miller, P. J. (1998). Constructing autonomous selves through narrative practices: A comparative study of working-class and middle-class families. *Child Development, 69,* 833–847.

SELF-STUDY QUESTIONS

Multiple Choice

1. Which of the following statements best expresses what cultural psychologists mean when they say that Anglo-American child-rearing is "individualistic"?
   a. Anglo-Americans socialize children to be concerned only about themselves and not about others.
   b. Anglo-Americans socialize children to value individual rights and needs more than social obligations when the two are in conflict.
   c. Anglo-Americans teach their children that society should support individuals who are in need.
   d. Anglo-American parents are more likely to treat siblings differently than are those in other cultures.

2. Which of the following statements about the parenting goals of Anglo and Puerto Rican mothers who participated in this study is true?
   a. Their goals were very similar.
   b. Puerto Rican mothers were more concerned about independence than Anglo mothers.
   c. Anglo mothers were more concerned about independence than Puerto Rican mothers.
   d. Both groups were more concerned about socialization than independence.

3. The researchers found that
   a. Puerto Rican mothers were more likely than Anglo-American mothers to expend effort to maintain their infants' attention
   b. Anglo-American mothers were more engaged with their infants in teaching situations than in play situations
   c. Anglo-American mothers allowed the infants to do more things, such as feeding themselves, on their own
   d. all of the above

Essay

1. The researchers did not examine how maternal behavior affected infants' development. Some cross-cultural researchers have found that cultural differences in parental behavior do not lead to differences in children's development, but others have found just the opposite. How do you think the parental differences found by these researchers is likely to affect their children's behavior when they are older? For example, do you think cross-cultural differences in maternal attention-maintaining behavior will lead to differences in attentional behavior when these infants enter school? What about other differences such as those in self-care skills and verbal behavior? How would you test your predictions?

2. Write an essay outlining your own parenting goals that includes justifications for them. For example, if you believe teaching children to be independent at an early age is important, explain why.

EARLY CHILDHOOD

"Universal, Developmental, and Variable Aspects of Young Children's Play: A Cross-Cultural Comparison of Pretending at Home"

OVERVIEW

In this study, researchers examined how a universal behavior of preschool-aged children, pretending, is influenced by culture. Using primarily naturalistic observation, they compared Irish American and Chinese preschoolers' tendency to play with objects, to pretend with other children, to engage their parents in pretend play, and to employ specific play themes (e.g., superheroes). Their observations resulted in an interesting mix of both consistencies and differences across the two cultures.

METHODOLOGY

The statistical analyses employed by these researchers allowed them to identify interactions among variables. An interaction occurs when two variables are related under one condition, or in one situation, but not another. For example, one interaction question these researchers examined was to what degree cultural differences in play behavior held true for both younger and older preschoolers.

GLOSSARY TERMS

- **Confucian thought** a system of philosophy based on the writings of Confucius; generally, Confucian thought emphasizes working hard to do one's best in order to bring honor to one's family and nation
- **Ethnographic fieldwork** a research method in which an in-depth description of a culture is based on observations of behavior in everyday situations; ethnographies also often include descriptions of a culture's physical environment, symbols, rituals, and so on

Wendy L. Haight, Xiao-lei Wang, Heidi Han-tih Fung,
Kimberley Williams, and Judith Mintz

Universal, Developmental, and Variable Aspects of Young Children's Play: A Cross-Cultural Comparison of Pretending at Home

Using longitudinal data from five Irish American families in the United States and nine Chinese families in Taiwan, in conjunction with an emerging body of evidence in the cultural psychology literature, we propose universal, culturally variable, and developmental dimensions of young children's pretend play. Possible universal dimensions include the use of objects, and the predominantly social nature of pretend play. Developmental dimensions include increases in the proportion of social pretend play initiated by the child, the proportion of partner initiations elaborated upon by the child, and caregivers' use of pretend play initiations to serve other, nonplay social functions. Culturally variable dimensions include the centrality of objects, the participation of specific play partners, the extent of child initiations of social pretend play with caregivers, the various functions of social pretend play in interaction, and specific themes. These findings raise the theoretical issue of how universal and variable dimensions of pretend play interact in specific communities to create distinctive development pathways.

INTRODUCTION

Pretend play has been documented in a wide variety of cultural groups. Recently, researchers have begun to explore the cultural dimensions of children's play (e.g., Farver, 1999; Farver & Shin, 1997; Gaskins, 1996; Goncu, Tuermer, Jain, & Johnson, 1999; Haight & Miller, 1992, 1993; Roopnarine, Johnson, & Hooper, 1994; Schwartzman, 1978). This research both reflects and contributes to the attempts of cultural psychologists, activity/practice theorists, and others to articulate a culture-sensitive theory of development, one that seeks to understand how child and culture are co-created (e.g., Corsaro & Miller, 1992; Jessor, Colby, & Shweder, 1996; Rogoff, Mistry, Goncu, & Mosier, 1993). Although play often is assumed to be universal in its characteristics, these perspectives challenge us to understand play as a culturally mediated activity that may take different forms in different groups (Miller, Gaskins, Goncu, & Haight, 1999).

The goal of this paper is to use data from preschool-aged children's pretend play in Irish American families in the United States and Chinese families in Taiwan, in conjunction with the emerging body of evidence in the cultural psychology literature, to propose universal, developmental, and culturally variable dimensions of young children's pretend play. As discussed below, the addition of Chinese and Irish American cases to the existing literature will be useful in illuminating the following dimensions of pretend play: 1) physical ecology (e.g., available objects), 2) interpersonal context (e.g., available people), 3) social interaction (e.g., patterns of adult–child interactions), 4) social functions (e.g., the use of pretend play in teaching), and 5) content (e.g., daily living and fantasy).

Universal Dimensions of Pretend Play from 2.5 to 4 Years

Physical ecology. Scholars with diverse theoretical perspectives agree that objects support and shape young children's pretend play (e.g., see Garvey, 1990; Newson & Newson, 1979; Rubin, Fein, & Vandenberg, 1983; Vygotsky, 1978). Empirical evidence

Reprinted from *Child Development*, 1999, 70, 1477–1488. Copyright Society for Research in Child Development. Reprinted with permission.

indicates that the spontaneous pretend play of European American, middle-class children typically occurs in relation to objects, particularly toy miniatures such as dolls, cars, dishes, and phones (e.g., Haight & Miller, 1993; Pulaski, 1973). In cultural groups where toy miniatures are scarce (Heath, 1983) or nonexistent (Gaskins, 1990), children enjoy active play lives (Schwartzman, 1986), constructing props from the materials at hand (Roopnarine, Hossain, Gill, & Brophy, 1994). In this study, we expected to observe the use of objects in both middle-class Irish American and middle-class Chinese families. We argue that the use of objects in early pretend play is a potential universal.

Interpersonal context. Debate continues concerning the extent to which pretend play emerges in interaction with others and the significance of such interactions (e.g., Bornstein & Tamis-LeMonda, 1995; Fein & Fryer, 1995). Recent empirical evidence from naturalistic home observations indicates that within European American (e.g., Beizer & Howes, 1992; Haight & Miller, 1992, 1993; Haight, Parke, & Black, 1997), English (e.g., Dunn & Dale, 1984; Dunn & Wooding, 1977), Turkish (Goncu & Mosier, 1991), and Mexican (Farver, 1993) families, pretend play occurs primarily in interaction with others in the first years of life; and caregivers, siblings, and friends are important participants. For example, the interactive pretend play of young, middle-class European American children is more sustained (Dunn & Wooding, 1977; Haight & Miller, 1993; Slade, 1987), more complex (Fiese, 1987; Haight & Miller, 1992, 1993; Slade, 1987), and more diverse (O'Connell & Bretherton, 1984) than is their solo pretending; and young children incorporate their caregivers' pretend talk into their own pretending (Haight & Miller, 1993). In contexts in which pretend play is not sanctioned, toddlers' initial pretend gestures may remain unelaborated, older children may incorporate younger children into their games, or older children may pretend among themselves outside of the context of adults (e.g., Gaskins, 1996; Lancy, 1996; Rogoff et al., 1993). We expected to observe that the pretend play of young Chinese and Irish American children is predominantly social. We argue that young children's pretend play is fundamentally a social activity.

Developmental Dimensions of Pretend Play from 2.5 to 4 Years

Social interaction. Naturalistic observations within European American families indicate that as children develop social and communicative competency, they become increasingly active in initiating episodes of pretend play (Haight & Miller, 1992) and increasingly successful in elaborating upon their partners' initiations (Haight et al., 1997). We expected that Chinese and Irish American children would become increasingly active in initiating and elaborating upon caregiver–child pretend play. We argue that the way in which caregiver–child pretend play is socially conducted varies with development.

Social functions. As with other social activities, pretend play may serve multiple social functions as participants capitalize upon the others' interest in pretend play to achieve a variety of outcomes. Relatively few researchers, however, have described the various social functions of pretending. Within European American middle-class families, Haight, Masiello, Dickson, Huckeby, and Black (1994) described the emergence of caregiver–child pretend play from mundane contexts such as household chores which both shaped and were shaped by pretending. Although the initiations of children and mothers were primarily playful, mothers increasingly initiated pretend play to guide their children toward more socially desirable behaviors, for example, diverting a toddler's attention from a tantrum or gaining a young child's cooperation in picking up toys.

Some researchers have argued that the functions of social pretend play change with development, for example, supporting communication in toddlers versus intimacy among school-aged friends (see Howes, 1992). We expect that, initially, caregiver participation may function predominantly to socialize toddlers into pretend play. Once children become fluent pretenders, however, caregivers may capitalize on these interests and skills to socialize preschoolers into other, culturally appropriate social interactions. In this study, we expected to observe both Irish American and Chinese caregivers using pretend play to encourage socially appropriate interactions. We also expected to observe an increase in such usages. We argue that nonplay functions of caregiver initiations vary with development.

Variable Dimensions of Pretend Play from 2.5 to 4 Years

Physical ecology. Relatively little attention has been paid to the significance of variation in the availability of particular types of objects, particularly toy miniatures, for the development of pretending. The scarcity or absence of toy miniatures may require that children and caregivers make relatively greater use of other types of available objects, or other types of support (e.g., language), in constructing a nonliteral world. Given the limited space for personal possessions in the compact apartments typical of Taipei, as well as relatively less emphasis on personal ownership (Fung, 1994), we expected to observe greater use of objects such as toy miniatures in Irish American families. We argue that the centrality of objects, particularly toy miniatures, in pretend play varies across cultures.

Interpersonal context.   It is important to consider children's pretend partners because different partners may contribute in different ways to children's pretending (Dunn & Dale, 1984; Farver, 1993). Whether other people are available as potential play partners, and who is available (mothers, fathers, siblings, extended family, and friends), depend on routine arrangements of time and space, with their concomitant distributions of persons (see Whiting and Edwards, 1988). The availability of various partners also depends upon adult beliefs regarding pretend play. For example, in middle-class European American families, caregivers generally view pretend play as facilitative of children's development; they view their own participation as both appropriate and desirable and participate actively in children's pretending (Haight et al., 1997). In contexts in which pretend play is not viewed as having a special role in children's development, or adult participation is not viewed as appropriate (e.g., Gaskins, 1996; Lancy, 1996; Rogoff et al., 1993), adult participation is atypical and children pretend among themselves.

We expected that caregivers would be important participants in Irish American families and—given Fung's (personal communication) evidence that middle-class Chinese mothers generally view pretend play as facilitative of development and endorse maternal participation—in Chinese families as well. We also expected that when other children were present in the home, they would pretend with target children. We argue that young children's pretend play partners vary.

Interaction.   Western researchers (e.g., Haight & Miller, 1992, 1993) have argued that caregivers may facilitate their children's pretending through mutual, responsive engagement, neither participating minimally, nor dominating with pretending that is too complex or of little interest to the child. Indeed, naturalistic observations of pretend play within European American and English families indicate that caregivers and children mutually initiate episodes of pretend play (Dunn & Wooding, 1977), and respond to one another's initiations (Haight & Miller, 1992). Current theories of pretend play, however, have not addressed variation in the ways in which caregivers in culturally diverse communities participate in chil-

dren's pretend play-particularly in communities where adult–child interactions generally are more hierarchically organized. In many communities, young children are not expected to interact with adults as peers, initiating interactions and participating as equals in conversation (e.g., Heath, 1983; Ochs & Schieffelin, 1984; Rogoff et al., 1993; Ward, 1971). For example, Chinese caregivers initiate a relatively greater proportion of episodes of interaction with their young children than do European American caregivers (Fung, 1994; Wang, Goldin-Meadow, & Mylander, 1995), and relatively fewer Chinese caregiver–child interactions are characterized by mutuality (Miller, Fung, & Mintz, 1996). In this study, we expected that relatively more episodes of caregiver–child pretend play would be initiated by Irish American than by Chinese children. We argue that the way in which caregiver–child pretend play is socially conducted varies across cultures.

Social functions.   Little evidence exists concerning the diverse social functions served by caregiver–child pretend play in non-Western communities. Although children's and caregivers' initiations of pretend play may be primarily playful, variation in caregivers' initiations may relate to diverse socialization goals. Overall, in interactions with their young children, Chinese mothers have been described as heavily didactic relative to European American mothers. They extensively expose their children to explicit models of proper conduct, often focusing on the acquisition of those values and behaviors necessary for group acceptance and participation (Fung, 1994; Wang et al., 1995). This same didactic orientation and emphasis on rules and children's rule violations have been documented with respect to personal story telling (Miller et al., 1996). Pretend play may be another vehicle through which Chinese caregivers teach proper conduct to young children. Indeed, Confucian thought has emphasized "playing rites" in which children enact roles to learn social rules and adult customs (Pan, 1994). In this study, we expected that Chinese caregivers would focus more on teaching proper conduct than would Irish American caregivers. We argue that the functions of caregiver initiations of pretend play vary across cultures.

Content.   Pretend play has been viewed as a supportive context for the transmission and creation of meanings (e.g., Farver, 1993; Haight & Miller, 1992, 1993; Slade & Wolfe, 1994). Available cross-cultural research suggests that children enact cultural-specific themes reflecting activities and values important within specific communities. For example, children in the Marquesas Islands pretend to paddle canoes, hunt, and fish (Martini, 1994). Children in India enact traditional celebrations and folk tales (Roopnarine, Hossain, et al., 1994). Korean American children focus on family role themes, while European American children focus on fantasy themes such as superhero adventures (Farver & Shin, 1997).

The themes of caregiver–child pretend play also may reflect variation in socialization values and goals. For example, European American caregivers generally emphasize individuality, independence, and self-expression (e.g., Chow, 1994; Fung, 1994; Greenfield, 1994), while Chinese caregivers generally emphasize harmonious social interaction obtained through obeying, respecting, and submitting to elders, adherence to rules, and cooperation (see Chow, 1994; Fung, 1994; Ho, 1994; Pan, 1994). Consistent with these socialization goals, narratives within European American families often highlight children's positive and unique characteristics, while narratives within Chinese families focus on moral and social standards (Miller et al., 1996; Miller, Wiley, Fung, & Liang, 1997). We expected that in the content of caregiver–child pretend play would vary between Chinese and Irish American families, particularly with respect to themes involving social standards and routines. We argue that the centrality of particular themes varies across cultures.

METHOD

The data for this project were collected as part of a larger comparative project undertaken from 1988 to 1991 by Peggy J. Miller and her students. The purpose of that project was to investigate the role that personal storytelling played in the socialization of young children within the family context (see Miller, 1996; Miller et al., 1996; Miller, Mintz, Hoogstra, Fung & Potts, 1992; Miller et al., 1997). Key features of the design of Miller's project, however, allow for the comparative study of other important dimensions of social development, including pretend play. Miller et al. refer to the Irish American community as "Long wood."

Participants

In keeping with standard ethnographic practices, the families were selected through networks of personal contacts. Fourteen middle-class, two-parent families were recruited, primarily through referrals from preschool teachers, local church leaders, and other community residents. Families had from one to three children, and the target children were 2.5 years of age. All of the fathers and most of the mothers had college educations. All families owned their own homes and were economically secure. In many respects, families were not typical Chinese or European American families. They were relatively privileged, and they created a particular cultural idiom at a particular moment in history (see Miller et al., 1996). Our objective is to provide an in-depth, highly contextualized description of particular, localized groups. The resulting information is essential to understanding socialization cross-culturally, and is not readily obtained through other methods (see Miller et al., 1998).

The United States subsample consisted of five Irish American families (three with girls and two with boys) living in Chicago. The Chinese subsample consisted of nine Mandarin-speaking families (five with girls and four with boys) living in Taipei. We chose to sample more Chinese than European American families because of the relative paucity of research describing pretend play within this cultural community.

Procedures

The first phase of the study involved ethnographic fieldwork. Researchers were assigned to cultures with which they were familiar: a Chinese researcher, a native of Taipei, worked with the Chinese families, and a European American researcher worked with the Irish American families. Researchers familiarized themselves with their communities through informal observation and collection of documentary material. Fieldnotes included descriptions of homes and play areas (see Miller et al., 1996.)

The second phase of the study involved naturalistic observations. Children were videorecorded at home at 2.5, 3, 3.5, and 4 years of age. This project is based on videorecordings at 2.5, 3, and 4 years of age. At each of these ages, children were observed on two occasions lasting 2 hr each. Multiple, sustained observations are important because previous naturalistic research conducted in the home indicates that the most sustained and complex episodes of pretend play occur subsequent to the first hour of observation (Haight & Miller, 1992).

Prior to the first observation session, researchers made repeated visits to the families' homes so that they and the families could become comfortable with one another. Observations occurred at a time that was convenient for the primary caregiver, usually a weekday morning or afternoon. The primary caregiver was always present, and siblings were often present. Fathers were usually at their places of employment.

Caregivers were told that we wanted to learn more about how young children learn to communicate as part of ordinary family life, including how they learn to tell stories, to play, and to express emotions. Each researcher participated as a family friend who had stopped by for a casual visit. At the same time, they were careful not to structure the sessions, but to allow them to unfold naturally (see Miller et al., 1996, 1997).

In the final phase of the study, researchers conducted formal interviews with primary caregivers to obtain basic information about the child and family, including the child's everyday routines and caregivers' socialization beliefs and practices.

Transcription and coding of videotapes.

All episodes of pretend play, both verbal and nonverbal, were identified and transcribed verbatim from the videorecordings and then coded. Chinese data were transcribed and coded by a Chinese, native Mandarin speaker. Irish American data were coded by a European American, native English speaker. Transcripts also described the participants, any objects used, and nonverbal behaviors. Codes were developed collaboratively by Chinese (Wang and Fung) and American (Haight, Mintz, and Williams) members of the research team.

Following Garvey (1990), pretend play was defined as a subcategory of play in which actions, objects, persons, places, or other dimensions of the here-and-now are transformed or treated nonliterally. An episode of pretend play began with the first action of pretend play produced by or directed at the child, and continued as long as the chain of transformational actions and supporting responses on a given topic or theme continued.

We coded the proportion of pretend play time involving toy miniatures. A toy miniature is a realistic toy which the child uses conventionally during play, pretending, for example, to feed a doll, drive a toy truck, or eat from toy dishes. We also coded the proportion of pretend play time spent using no objects at all, for example, pretending to address a guest or to be Qiye or Baye (figures in Chinese folk history) strutting in a parade.

Social pretend play occurred when the child directed pretend play to another person or attended to the pretend play directed to him or her by another person. Pretending could be directed at the other verbally, for example, by addressing the other by name; or nonverbally, by directing an action toward the other. Caregiver–child pretend play occurred when the caregiver served as a social pretend-play partner. The initiator of social pretend play was the first person to direct pretending toward the other person, either verbally or nonverbally. An elaborative response to a partner's initiation offered new material thematically related to the initiation. For example, a child is pretending to drive a car and her mother queries, "Where are you going?"

Several social functions of pretend initiations were inferred on the basis of the preceding and ongoing social interaction. Negotiating problematic interaction was coded if, at the time of the initiation, one or both partners were expressing negative affect, or routinely expressed negative affect in this situation. For example, an Irish American caregiver suggests that she and her bored and tantruming toddler "have a parade." Practice proper conduct was coded when pretending was initiated in the context of demonstrating or teaching particular social skills, manners, or conventions. For example, a Chinese caregiver initiates pretend play which involves bowing to the "teacher."

The content of each episode of caregiver–child play was inferred on the basis of pretend actions, gestures, and talk. Fantasy involved the enactment of literary or media portrayals involving magic or fantasy. Caretaking was coded if the episode involved caring for the self or other (e.g., cooking, feeding, or dressing), or the home (e.g., cleaning, shopping, or yard work). Episodes were coded as social routines involving nonkin adults if they focused upon routine social interactions involving the child and teachers, public officials, merchants, or other nonkin adults.

Intercoder reliability.

Reliabilities were obtained for all behavioral codes following extensive training using videotapes and transcripts. Reliabilities were obtained between the first author and the European American and Chinese coders. First, reliabilities were obtained for the identification of pretend play based on 26 min of randomly chosen videotape segments at each of the three age levels for each of nine European American children from a larger data set (Haight & Miller, 1992). The proportion of agreement across pairs of raters for identifying episodes of pretend play and episode boundaries (i.e., the opening and final actions or utterances) ranged from .86 to .92. Reliabilities also were calculated for all the other codes based on approximately 10% of the total number of transcribed episodes. Kappas between pairs of coders ranged from .70 to 1.0. (Details are available upon request.)

RESULTS

Fourteen hours of pretend play (5 in Taiwan and 9 in Chicago) were produced from 168 hours of home observations (108 in Taiwan and 60 in Chicago). All of the 14 children engaged in spontaneous pretend play at all three ages. An age (30, 36, and 48 months) × community (Taipei, Chicago) repeated measures ANOVA on the rate of pretending revealed no significant main effects or interactions. To avoid violating the assumptions of ANOVAs, arc sine-transformed variables were used in this and all subsequent analyses involving proportions.

The Physical Ecology of Pretend Play

Ethnographic description. Our ethnographic descriptions draw heavily upon the data of Fung (1994), Mintz (1998), and Miller et al. (1996).

All of the Irish American families resided in spacious, single-family homes. The parents provided child-scaled objects and furniture, and abundant toys. Indeed, most of these homes contained playrooms or family rooms that were filled with children's toys. All Irish American children possessed extensive and elaborate collections of toy miniatures, including multiple dolls and accessories, stuffed animals, action figures, costumes, cars, trains, dishes, pretend food, kitchen sets, and pedal cars. These toy collections typically included toys commercially marketed in association with children's movies (e.g., stuffed animal characters from *The Lion King*) or TV programs (e.g., *Power Rangers* action figures).

The Chinese children lived within single-family, compact apartments. Although their parents generally spoke of them as spoiled with respect to material possessions, Chinese children had a modest number of possessions relative to the Irish American children. Their collections of toy miniatures typically included a stuffed animal and a few toy cars or a doll.

Observations of pretend play. All but one child (from Taipei) incorporated toy miniatures into their play, but this practice was more typical of Irish American than Chinese children. As indicated in Table 1, an Age × Community repeated measures ANOVA on the proportion of pretend play time involving toy miniatures revealed a main effect of community, $F(1, 12) = 8.7$, $p < .05$, but not of age, and no Age × Community interaction. Collapsing across ages, the mean (and standard error of the mean) proportion of pretend play time involving toy miniatures was .28 ± .07 for Chinese children and .57 ± .06 for Irish American children.

All children also engaged in some pretending that involved no objects at all, but this practice was more typical of Chinese children. As indicated in Table 1, an Age × Community repeated measures ANOVA on the proportion of pretend play time involving no objects revealed a main effect of community, $F(1, 12) = 16.3$, $p < .01$, but not of age, and no Age × Community interaction. The mean (and standard error of the mean) proportion of pretend play time involving no objects at all was .36 ± .04 for Chinese children and .10 ± .03 for Irish American children.

The Interpersonal Context of Pretend Play

Ethnographic description. There was considerable variability in the social ecologies of the communities and families. Taipei is not organized into neighborhoods, and there is little residential segre-

TABLE 1 Potential Universal, Variable and Developmental Dimensions of Children's Pretend Play from 2 to 4 years

	UNIVERSAL	DEVELOPMENTAL	VARIABLE
Physical ecology	Use of objects		Play with toy miniatures (A > C, $p < .01$) Play without objects (C > A, $p < .01$)
Interpersonal context	Social activity		Proportion of pretend play that is social (C > A, $p < .001$) Specific partners, especially caregivers (C > A, $p < .01$) and other children (A > C, $p < .01$)
Interaction		Child initiations increase ($p < .01$) Child elaborations increase ($p < .05$)	Extent of child initiations (A > C, $p < .01$)
Social functions		Caregiver nonplay uses increase ($p < .05$)	Proportion of caregiver initiations functioning as play (A > C, $p < .01$) Practice proper conduct (C > A, $p < .01$)
Content			Fantasy (A > C, $p < .03$) Caretaking (A > C, $p < .02$) Social routines with nonkin adults (C > A, $p < .001$)

Note: Direction of effect is denoted for Irish American (A) and Chinese (C) families.

gation by class and ethnicity. Middle-class families in Taipei tend not to have strong ties to particular locales. Perhaps as a consequence, the Chinese families typically did not have extensive contact or friendships with their neighbors despite their close physical proximity (see Miller et al., 1997). In addition, Chinese families were small. Five of the Chinese target children had one older sibling, and the other four children had one younger sibling. During the first year of life, children were in the full-time care of their mothers or another close female relative at home. Chinese children had more extensive social contact with other children outside of the home when they attended formal preschool programs.

In contrast, the Irish American children had extensive contact with other children and adults within their homes and neighborhood. Irish American families lived within an ethnically and economically distinct neighborhood in Chicago that has been home to Irish Americans for nearly a quarter of a century. All parents came from large families of six or more children, and these large, extended families lived in the area and frequently visited one another. Two of the target children had one older sibling, two had both an older and a younger sibling, and one had a younger sibling. All of these children were cared for at home full-time by their mothers until they reached school age. During the day, children participated in informal playgroups consisting not only of siblings and cousins, but of neighbors. Preplanned playdates, birthday parties, and holiday parties also were regular events. In addition, children had regular contact with neighborhood children and adults through their active participation in a local Catholic church.

Observations of pretend play.   All 14 children displayed social pretend play and, with one exception, more than 50% of pretend play time at each age was social. On average, however, social play was more typical of Chinese children's pretending. As indicated in Table 1, an Age × Community repeated measures ANOVA on the proportion of pretend play that was social revealed a main effect of community, $F(1, 12) = 22.6$, $p < .001$, but not of age and no Age × Community interaction. The mean (and standard error of the mean) proportion of pretend play time that was social was .98 ± .01 for Chinese children and .89 ± .04 for Irish American children.

All 14 children pretended with their caregivers at each age. On average, however, caregiver–child play was more typical of Chinese children's social pretending. As indicated in Table 1, an Age × Community repeated measures ANOVA on the proportion of social pretend play time involving caregivers revealed a main effect of community, $F(1, 12) = 9.2$, $p = .01$, but

not of age, and no age by community interaction. The mean (and standard error of the mean) proportion of social pretend play time involving caregivers was .90 ± .06 for Chinese children and .64 ± .13 for Irish American children.

All five Irish American children pretended with other children, while only three of nine Chinese children pretended with other children. As indicated by Table 1, an Age × Community repeated measures ANOVA on the proportion of social pretend play time involving other children revealed a main effect of community, $F(1, 12) = 10.8$, $p < .01$, but not of age, and no Age × Community interaction. The mean (and standard error of the mean) proportion of pretend play time involving other children was .13 ± .09 for Chinese children and .64 ± .13 for Irish American children.

Interactions within Caregiver–Child Pretend Play

Ethnographic description.   When interacting with their children across a variety of contexts, Chinese caregivers generally were highly didactic, directive, and demanding of mature behavior relative to Irish American caregivers. They generally expected children to listen attentively to their elders, understand what was said, and behave accordingly (see Fung, 1994; Miller et al., 1996). Overall, Irish American caregivers were relatively more focused on meeting their children's perceived individual needs, and supporting their individual interests. They often allowed their children to initiate and lead interactions around topics of the children's own choosing.

Observations of pretend play.   All 14 children initiated episodes of caregiver–child pretend play, and 13 did so increasingly with age, but initiations were more typical of Irish American children. As indicated in Table 1, an Age × Community repeated measures ANOVA on the proportion of caregiver–child pretend play episodes initiated by the child revealed a main effect of age, $F(2, 24) = 8.9$, $p < .01$, and community, $F(1, 12) = 14$, $p < .01$, but no Age × Community interaction. The mean (and standard error of the mean) proportion of caregiver–child pretend play episodes initiated by the children ranged from .09 ± .04 at 30 months to .34 ± .06 at 48 months for the Chinese children, and .70 ± .14 at 30 months to .94 ± .07 at 48 months for the Irish American children.

Both Chinese and Irish American children and their caregivers generally were responsive to one another's initiations of pretend play, with children becoming increasingly responsive over time. As indicated in Table 1, an Age × Community repeated measures ANOVA on the proportion of children's responses to caregivers' initiations that were elaborative, revealed a main effect of age, $F(2, 22) = 3.7$, $p < .05$, but no main effect of community, and no Age × Community interaction.[1] The mean (and standard error of the mean) proportions of these responses that were elaborative ranged from .56 ± .07 at 30 months to .82 ± .07 at 48 months.

The Social Functions of Caregiver–Child Pretend Play

Ethnographic description. Although both Irish American and Chinese caregivers viewed adult–child pretend play as appropriate, neither group prioritized it as a primary socialization goal. Irish American caregivers prioritized the development of self-esteem through focused attention from the parent (Mintz, 1998). Pretend play was one context in which such focused attention could occur. Chinese caregivers prioritized moral development (Fung, 1994) and viewed adult–child play as an engaging context for teaching culturally sanctioned forms of social interactions. They discussed the concept of *ji-hui jiaoya*, or "opportunity education," that is, utilizing everyday activities and ongoing interactions of interest to children (presumably including pretend play) as a context for instruction (Fung, 1994).

Observations of pretend play. The mean proportion of children's initiations of pretend play that functioned only as play was .99 ± .10. The functions of caregiver-initiated play showed more variation. Indeed, 13 caregivers initiated pretend play to serve some other nonplay purpose. As indicated in Table 1, an Age × Community repeated measures ANOVA on the proportion of caregivers' initiations functioning as play revealed a significant main effect of community $F(1, 11) = 12.1$, $p < .01$, and age, $F(2, 22) = 4.1$, $p < .05$, but no Age × Community interaction (see Footnote 1). The mean (and standard error of the mean) proportion of caregivers' pretend play initiations that functioned only as play ranged from .51 ± .09 at 30 months to .30 ± .09 at 48 months for Chinese caregivers, and .97 ± .04 at 30 months to .71 ± .04 at 48 months for Irish American caregivers.

An Age × Community repeated measures ANOVA on the proportion of caregivers' initiations that served to manage problematic interactions revealed no significant main effects or interactions.

The mean (and standard error of the mean) proportion of these initiations was .10 ± .02.

In contrast to Irish American caregivers, Chinese caregivers routinely initiated caregiver–child pretend play to practice proper conduct (see Table 1). An Age × Community repeated measures ANOVA on the proportion of caregivers' initiations functioning as a way to practice proper conduct revealed a main effect of community, $F(1, 11) = 11.6$, $p < .01$, but not of age, and no Age × Community interaction. The mean (and standard error of the mean) proportion of caregivers' pretend play initiations that functioned as a means to practice proper conduct was .38 ± .06 for Chinese caregivers and .00 ± .00 for Irish American caregivers.

The Content of Caregiver–Child Pretend Play

The pretend play of Irish American caregivers and their children included relatively more fantasy than that of Chinese caregivers and children. As indicated in Table 1, an Age × Community repeated measures ANOVA on the proportion of caregiver–child episodes of pretend play that involved fantasy themes revealed a main effect of community, $F(1, 12) = 6.7$, $< .03$, but not of age, and no Age × Community interaction. The mean (and standard error of the mean) proportion of pretend play episodes that depicted fantasy themes was .05 ± .02 for Chinese caregivers and children and .21 ± .07 for Irish American caregivers and children.

Irish American caregiver–child pretend play focused relatively more on caretaking. An Age × Community repeated measures ANOVA on the proportion of caregiver–child episodes of pretend play that involved caretaking revealed a main effect of community, $F(1, 12) = 7.7$, $p < .02$, but not of age, and no Age × Community interaction. The mean (and standard error of the mean) proportion of pretend play episodes depicting caretaking was .07 ± .04 for Chinese caregivers and children, and .29 ± .08 for Irish American caregivers and children.

Chinese caregiver–child pretend play focused relatively more on routine social interactions with non-kin adults. As indicated in Table 1, an Age × Community repeated measures ANOVA on the proportion of caregiver–child episodes of pretend play that involved such social interactions revealed a main effect of community, $F(1, 12) = 21$, $p < .001$, a main effect of age, $F(2, 24) = 5.1$, $p < .02$, and an Age × Community interaction, $F(2, 24) = 38$, $p < .04$. The mean (and standard error of the mean) percentages of pretend play episodes depicting such social interactions for Chinese caregivers and children at 30, 36, and 48 months were .50 ± .10, .74 ± .12, and .86 ± .06,

---

[1]Because several children did not initiate caregiver–child pretend play at every age level, caregivers were not included in a formal analysis of partner response to initiations, and children were not included in a formal analysis of initiation functions.

respectively, for Irish American caregivers and children, .02 ± .03, .20 ± .16, and .02 ± .03, respectively.

DISCUSSION

This project is part of an emerging body of research describing the cultural dimensions of children's play. These data suggest universal, developmental, and culturally variable dimensions of young children's pretend play. They also suggest that enriching existing theories of pretend play to understand pretend play as a culturally mediated activity will require attention to the interaction of a complex set of ecological and ideological factors.

Universal Dimensions of Pretend Play

We argued that there are a variety of potential universals in children's pretend play. Consistent with research in a variety of other cultural communities (e.g., Roopnarine, Hossain, et al., 1994), Chinese and Irish American children incorporated objects into their pretend play. These findings may reflect the general utility of objects for supporting children's participation in pretend play. For example, Vygotsky (1978) argued that for toddlers, objects may facilitate the transition from the literal to the nonliteral world: "in order to imagine a horse, he (the child) needs to define his action by means of using 'the horse-in-the-stick' as the pivot" (pp. 97–98). In preschool-aged children, objects may continue to serve as important reference points. For example, Newson and Newson (1979) suggest that, "...because the human imagination is so extensive and complex...children seem to look for solid tangible reference points, as it were, from which to range more freely. Just as language makes subtle and complicated thought possible, perhaps toys do the same for play" (p. 12).

We also argued that young children's pretend play is fundamentally a social activity. Consistent with research in other cultural communities, pretend play in Irish American and Chinese families was primarily a social activity embedded within interactions with family members and friends (e.g., Beizer & Howes, 1992; Dunn & Dale, 1984; Dunn & Wooding, 1977; Farver, 1993; Goncu & Mosier, 1991; Haight & Miller, 1992, 1993; Haight et al., 1997). These findings point to the importance of developing theories and methods which consider pretend play as a social activity. For example, paralleling Vygotsky's (1978) view that language develops from the social to the private, El'Konin (1966) argued that pretend play develops from the interpersonal to the intrapersonal.

Developmental Dimensions of Pretend Play

We also argued that there are a variety of developmental dimensions of young children's pretend play from 2.5 to 4 years of age. Consistent with previous work in European American communities (Haight & Miller, 1992; Haight et al., 1997), Chinese and Irish American children became increasingly active in their initiations of caregiver–child pretend play, and they increasingly elaborated upon their caregivers' initiations. These findings may reflect children's emerging ability to participate in a variety of cultural activities.

Over time, we also observed that caregivers became less playful in their initiations of pretending. This finding may reflect developmental changes in the social functions of caregivers' participation in children's pretending. Initially, caregiver participation may function predominantly to socialize toddlers into pretend play. Once children become fluent pretenders, however, caregivers may capitalize on these interests and skills to lead preschoolers into other, culturally appropriate social interactions. This interpretation is consistent with other observations that the functions of social pretend play change with children's development (see Howes, 1992).

Variable Dimensions of Pretend Play

We also argue that there is considerable cross-cultural variation in children's pretend play. First, the interpersonal context of pretend play varies. Children's pretend partners depend in part on the availability of various partners, as well as on adult beliefs concerning the appropriateness of their own participation in pretend play (Gaskins, 1996; Lancy, 1996; Rogoff et al., 1993). In our study, Chinese children pretended more with their caregivers while Irish American children pretended more with other children. Given that Chinese and Irish American caregivers viewed their own participation in children's pretend play as appropriate and desirable, these findings may reflect Irish American children's greater access to siblings and neighbors.

Second, the extent to which pretend play is social varies across cultures. Relative to the Irish American children, a greater proportion of Chinese children's pretend play was social. This finding may reflect variation in play partners. For example, generally speaking, adult caregivers may be more consistently responsive to, and supportive of, a young child's participation in social exchanges such as pretend play than are slightly older siblings. This finding also may reflect variation in the structure of play groups. In contrast to the Chinese children, Irish

American children frequently engaged in multiparty pretending in groups of three or more players, often including slightly older children. The pattern of Irish American children's participation in these multiage small groups consisted of periods of intense engagement in social pretending alternating with periods of solo pretending alongside the ongoing social pretending of older individuals. Multiparty pretend play at home may be one context in which Irish American children watch the pretending of more competent children, and practice entering into and negotiating pretend play with other children. Indeed, Rogoff et al. (1993) describe multiparty interactions as important contexts for learning through observation. The Chinese children may have similar learning opportunities in the context of their preschools.

Third, the way in which caregiver–child pretend play is socially conducted varies across cultures. Caregiver–child pretend play in Irish American families was more typically initiated by children. These observations are consistent with previous observations that Chinese caregivers initiate a relatively greater proportion of episodes of interaction with their young children than do European American caregivers (Fung, 1994; Wang et al., 1995).

Fourth, the nonplay functions of caregiver initiations vary across cultures. Chinese caregivers' initiations more often functioned as a way to practice proper conduct. This didactic orientation and emphasis on conduct is consistent with observations of Chinese caregivers in other contexts (Fung, 1994; Wang et al., 1995) including narrative (Miller et al., 1996).

Fifth, the centrality of particular themes varies across cultures. Many of the toy miniatures around which the pretend play of Irish American children revolved were commercially marketed in relation to children's movies. The role of these toys in suggesting play themes may account in part for the relatively greater emphasis on fantasy themes in the Irish American families. The emphasis on caretaking themes may be related to the relatively larger immediate and extended families within Irish Catholic communities. The apparently greater overall concern of Chinese caregivers with proper conduct may account for the relatively greater proportion of social pretend play episodes depicting social routines with nonkin adults.

Finally, the centrality of objects, particularly toy miniatures, varies. Researchers and theorists have emphasized the importance of objects as pivots from a literal into a nonliteral context. Consistent with previous reports about European American communities (e.g., Haight & Miller, 1993), Irish American caregivers purchased many objects for children's pretending, and the majority of children's pretend play time re-

volved around toy miniatures. These young European American children appeared to beneficially utilize the shared scripts suggested by their toy miniatures to propel their social play. Other researchers have pointed out that when caregivers do not provide children with abundant toys, children will construct props for pretend play from the materials at hand (Gaskins, 1990; Heath, 1983; Roopnarine, Hossain, et al., 1994; Schwartzman, 1986). Our data suggest a third possibility, namely, that there are a variety of nonpalpable pivots that support the pretend play of young children from diverse communities. In the Chinese families, where space was limited and children had relatively few personal possessions, children typically did not construct props from other available materials. Indeed, a sizable proportion of their pretend play involved no objects at all throughout the age range. They appeared to rely upon nonpalpable supports such as shared knowledge of social routines to propel their joint play. Similarly, Sperry and Sperry (1996) found that in a rural African American community where caregivers routinely evoked imaginary characters to control children's behavior, young children made extensive use of the characters in these familiar stories, not of objects, in constructing their own fantasy.

Understanding Pretend Play as a Culturally Mediated Activity

Existing theories of pretend play do not account for variation in children's pretend play, nor do they consider how such variation relates to the development of pretend play (Gaskins & Goncu, 1988). Accounting for cross-cultural variation will require attention to a complex set of ecological and ideological factors. Whether particular objects and persons are available for children's pretend play clearly depends upon a complex set of ecological factors such as economic resources, parents' work load, and so forth. Ecological factors, however, cannot adequately account for variations in caregivers' support of children's pretend play. For example, in another study involving European American caregivers in and around Chicago (Haight & Miller, 1993), where families lived in small apartments similar in physical and social ecology to the Chinese families in the current study, caregivers supported their children in ways similar to those of the Irish American caregivers and distinct from those of the Chinese caregivers in this study. For example, despite their similar physical constraints, European American caregivers purchased large quantities of toy miniatures for their children.

Variation in dimensions of children's pretend play also may be attributable to caregivers' broader socialization goals and practices. European American families generally have been described as child centered in their approaches to socialization (e.g., Chow, 1994; Fung, 1994; Greenfield, 1994). Such child centered approaches are reflected in practices such as the use of personal storytelling to highlight children's positive and unique characteristics (Miller et al., 1997). They also may be reflected in the extent to which children are provided with toys and allowed to initiate and lead pretend play, and the extent to which play functions primarily as play and focuses on children's fantasy themes. Confucian principles have been described as guiding socialization practices in modern Taiwan (see Chow, 1994; Fung, 1994; Ho, 1994; Pan, 1994); note for example, the didactic use of personal storytelling to convey moral and social standards (Miller et al., 1997). They also may be reflected in the extent to which caregivers initiate and lead pretend play, employ pretend play for didactic functions, and focus on proper conduct with nonkin adults.

In conclusion, we have made an analytic distinction between universal, developmental, and variable dimensions of pretend play. This heuristic is useful in illuminating the complex, multifaceted phenomenon of children's pretend play. The next step in understanding pretend play as a culturally mediated activity, however, is to articulate how universal and variable dimensions of pretend play come together in specific, localized communities to create distinctive developmental pathways for play.

ACKNOWLEDGMENTS

This research was supported by a Spencer Foundation grant to the first author. We would also like to thank Peggy J. Miller for her helpful comments on earlier drafts. The order of the fourth and fifth authors was determined by the flip of a coin.

REFERENCES

Beizer, L., & Howes, C. (1992). Mothers and toddlers: Partners in early symbolic play: Illustrative study #1. In C. Howes (Ed.), *The collaborative construction of pretend: Social pretend play functions* (pp. 25–44). Albany: State University of New York Press.

Bornstein, M., & Tamis-LeMonda, C. (1995). Parent-child symbolic play: Three theories in search of an effect. *Developmental Review, 15,* 382–400.

Chow, R. (1994). Beyond parental control and authoritarian parenting style: Understanding Chinese parenting through the cultural notion of training. *Child Development, 65,* 1111–1119.

Corsaro, W. A., & Miller, P. J. (Eds.), W. Damon (Series Ed.). (1992). Interpretive approaches to children's socialization. *New Directions for Child Development: Vol. 58.* San Francisco: Jossey-Bass.

Dunn, J., & Dale, N. (1984). I a daddy: 2-year-olds' collaboration in joint pretend with a sibling and with mother. In I. Bretherton (Ed.), *Symbolic play: The development of social understanding* (pp. 131–158). New York: Academic Press.

Dunn, J., & Wooding, C. (1977). Play in the home and its implications for learning. In B. Tizard & D. Harvey (Eds.), *Biology of play* (pp. 45–58). London: Heinemann.

El'Konin, D. (1966). Symbolics and its function in the play of children. *Soviet Education, 8,* 35–41.

Farver, J. (1993). Cultural differences in scaffolding pretend play: A comparison of American and Mexican American mother-child and sibling-child pairs. In K. MacDonald (Ed.), *Parent-child play: Descriptions and implications* (pp. 349–366). Albany: State University of New York Press.

Farver, J. (1999). Activity setting analysis: A model for examining the role of culture in development. In A. Goncu (Ed.), *Children's engagement in the world: A sociocultural perspective* (pp. 113–148). Cambridge, UK: Cambridge University Press.

Farver, J., & Shin, Y. (1997). Social pretend play in Korean- and Anglo-American preschoolers. *Child Development, 68,* 544–556.

Fein, G., & Fryer, M. (1995). Maternal contributions to early symbolic play competence. *Developmental Review, 15,* 367–381.

Fiese, B. (1987, April). Mother-infant interaction any symbolic play in the second year of life: A contextual analysis. Paper presented at the biannual meeting of the Society for Research in Child Development, Baltimore, MD.

Fung, H. H. (1994). *The socialization of shame in young Chinese children.* Unpublished doctoral dissertation, University of Chicago.

Garvey, C. (1990). *Play.* Cambridge, MA: Harvard University Press.

Gaskins, S. (1990). *Exploration and development in Mayan infants.* Unpublished doctoral dissertation, University of Chicago.

Gaskins, S. (1996). How Mayan parental theories come into play. In S. Harkness & C. Super (Eds.), *Parents' cultural belief systems* (pp. 345–363). New York: Guilford Press.

Gaskins, S., & Goncu, A. (1988). Children's play as representation and imagination: The case of Piaget and Vygotsky. *The Quarterly Newsletter of the Laboratory of Human Cognition, 10,* 104–107.

Goncu, A., & Mosier, C. (1991, April). *Cultural variations in the play of toddlers.* Paper presented at the meeting of the Society for Research in Child Development, Seattle, WA.

Goncu, A., Tuermer, U., Jain, J., & Johnson, D. (1999). Children's play as cultural activity. In A. Goncu (Ed.), *Children's engagement in the world: A sociocultural perspective* (pp. 173–202). Cambridge, UK: Cambridge University Press.

Greenfield, P. M. (1994). Preface. In P. M. Greenfield & R. R. Cocking (Eds.), *Cross-cultural roots of minority child development*. Hillsdale, NJ: Erlbaum.

Haight, W., Parke, R., & Black, J. (1997). Mothers' and fathers' beliefs about and spontaneous participation in their toddlers pretend play. *Merrill-Palmer Quarterly, 42*, 271–290.

Haight, W., Masiello, T., Dickson, L., Huckeby, E., & Black, J. (1994). The everyday contexts and social functions of spontaneous mother-child pretend play in the home. *Merrill-Palmer Quarterly, 40*, 509–522.

Haight, W., & Miller, P. (1992). The development of everyday pretend play: A longitudinal study of mothers' participation. *Merrill-Palmer Quarterly, 38*, 331–349.

Haight, W., & Miller, P. (1993). *Pretending at home: Development in sociocultural context*. Albany: State University of New York Press.

Heath, S. B. (1983). *Ways with words: Language, life and work in communities and classrooms*. Cambridge, UK: Cambridge University Press.

Ho, D. Y. F. (1994). Cognitive socialization in Confucian heritage cultures. In P. M. Greenfield & R. R. Cocking (Eds.), *Cross-cultural roots of minority child development* (pp. 285–314). Hillsdale, NJ: Erlbaum.

Howes, C. (Ed.). (1992). *The collaborative construction of pretend: Social pretend play functions*. Albany: State University of New York Press.

Jessor, R., Colby, A., & Shweder, R. (Eds.). (1996). *Ethnography and human development: Context and meaning in social inquiry*. Chicago: University of Chicago Press.

Lancy, D. F. (1996). *Playing on the mother-ground: Cultural routines for children's development*. New York: Guilford Press.

Martini, M. (1994). Peer interactions in Polynesia: A view from the Marquesas. In J. Roopnarine, J. Johnson, & F. Hooper (Eds.), Children's play in diverse cultures. Albany: State University of New York Press.

Miller, P., Fung, H., & Mintz, J. (1996). Self construction through narrative practices: A Chinese and American comparison. *Ethos, 24*, 1–44.

Miller, P., Gaskins, S., Goncu, A., & Haight, W. (1999). The sacred, the profane, and the prosaic: Insight and issues in the cultural study of children's play. Manuscript submitted for publication.

Miller, P., Mintz, J., Hoogstra, L., Fung, H., & Potts, R. (1992). The narrated self: Young children's construction of self in relation to others in conversational stories of personal experience. *Merrill-Palmer Quarterly, 38*, 45–67.

Miller, P., Wiley, A., Fung, H., & Liang, C. (1997). Personal storytelling as a medium of socialization in Chinese and American families. *Child Development, 68*, 557–568.

Mintz, J. (1998). *The socialization of self in middle-class, Irish American families*. Unpublished doctoral dissertation, University of Chicago.

Newson, J., & Newson, E. (1979). *Toys and playthings*. New York: Pantheon Books.

Ochs, E., & Schieffelin, B. (1984). Language acquisition and socialization: Three developmental stories and their implications. In R. Schweder & D. Levine (Eds.), *Culture theory: Essays on mind, self and emotion*. Cambridge, MA: Cambridge University Press.

O'Connell, B., & Bretherton, I. (1984). Toddlers' play alone and with mother: The role of maternal guidance. In I. Bretherton (Ed.), *Symbolic play: The development of social understanding* (pp. 337–368). Orlando, FL: Academic Press.

Pan, H. W. (1994). Children's play in Taiwan. In J. L. Roopnarine, J. E. Johnson, & F. H. Hooper (Eds.), *Children's play in diverse cultures* (pp. 31–50). Albany: State University of New York Press.

Pulaski, M. (1973). Toys and imaginative play. In J. L. Singer (Ed.), *The child's world of make-believe* (pp. 74–103). New York: Academic Press.

Rogoff, B., Mistry, J., Goncu, A., & Mosier, C. (1993). Guided participation in cultural activity by toddlers and caregivers. *Monographs of the Society for Research in Child Development, 58*(1, Serial No. 183).

Roopnarine, J., Hossain, Z., Gill P., & Brophy, H. (1994). Play in the East Indian Context. In J. Roopnarine, J. Johnson, & F. Hooper (Eds.), *Children's play in diverse cultures*. Albany: State University of New York Press.

Roopnarine, J., Johnson, J., & Hooper, F. (Eds.). (1994). *Children's play in diverse cultures*. Albany: State University of New York Press.

Rubin, K., Fein, G., & Vandenberg, B. (1983). Play. In E. M. Hetherington (Ed.), P. H. Mussen (Series Ed.), *Handbook of child psychology: Vol. 4. Socialization, personality, and social development* (4th ed., pp. 693–774). New York: Wiley.

Schwartzman, H. (1978). *Transformations: The anthropology of children's play*. New York: Plenum Press.

Schwartzman, H. B. (1986). A cross-cultural perspective on child-structured play activities and materials. In A. W. Gottfried & C. C. Brown (Eds.), *Play interactions: The contribution of play materials and parental involvement to children's development* (pp. 13–29). Lexington, MA: Lexington Books.

Slade, A. (1987). A longitudinal study of maternal involvement in symbolic play during the toddler period. *Child Development, 58*, 367–375.

Slade, A., & Wolfe, D. (1994). Preface. In A. Slade & D. Wolfe (Eds.), *Children at play: Clinical and developmental approaches to meaning and representation*. Oxford, UK: Oxford University Press.

Sperry, L., & Sperry, D. (1996). Early development of narrative skills. *Cognitive Development, 11*, 443–465.

Vygotsky, L. W. (1978). *Mind in society: The development of higher mental processes*. Cambridge, MA: Harvard University Press.

Wang, X., Goldin-Meadow, S., & Mylander, C. (1995, March). *A comparative study of Chinese and American mothers interacting with their deaf and hearing children*. Paper presented at the meeting of the Society for Research in Child Development, Indianapolis, IN.

Ward, M. (1971). *Them Children: A study in language learning*. Prospect Heights, IL: Wavelength Press.

Whiting, B. B., & Edwards, C. P. (1988). *Children of different worlds: The formation of social behavior*. Cambridge, MA: Harvard University Press.

SELF-STUDY QUESTIONS

Multiple Choice

1. The authors state that prior research suggests which of the following?
   a. Children play with objects only in cultures where children possess their own toys.
   b. Object use is a universal feature of children's play.
   c. European American children play with objects, but Chinese children do not.
   d. Object use slows down the development of pretend play behavior.

2. Which of the following best describes differences between European American and Chinese parents' beliefs about pretend play?
   a. Both groups believe pretend play is important to children's development.
   b. European American parents believe pretending is important, but Chinese parents do not.
   c. Chinese parents believe pretending is important, but European American parents do not.
   d. Both groups believe pretend play does not play an important role in preschoolers' development.

3. Which of the following was found by these researchers?
   a. Irish American children possessed fewer toys than Chinese children.
   b. Chinese parents used pretend play situations to teach their children moral rules.
   c. Chinese children spent more time playing with other children than Irish American children.
   d. Irish American parents were less concerned about children's self-esteem than Chinese parents.

Essay

1. The authors stated that "European American families generally have been described as child centered in their approaches to socialization" (p. 35). Explain what they mean by this statement. Do you agree? Why or why not?

2. How do the authors explain Chinese children's less frequent use of objects in pretend play?

EARLY CHILDHOOD

"Effects of Repeated Exposures to a Single Episode of the Television Program *Blue's Clues* on the Viewing Behaviors and Comprehension of Preschool Children"

OVERVIEW

Have you ever wondered why preschoolers prefer to hear the same stories read to them over and over again, or to watch the same videos day after day? This study provides some interesting and important insights into this peculiar developmental characteristic.

The researchers examined how various aspects of 3- to 5-year-olds' behavioral responses to a *Blue's Clues* video changed each time they watched it. They also measured how much and what kind of information the young viewers had learned after each viewing.

METHODOLOGY

This study is a *multifactorial experiment.* This means that the researchers examined how several variables, or *factors,* interacted. The factors were one-time versus repeated viewing, type of content, gender, and age. This kind of design allows researchers to deter-mine whether the effects of one-time and repeated viewing are the same for different kinds of content (educational versus entertainment), for 3-, 4-, and 5-year-olds, and for boys and girls in each age group.

GLOSSARY TERMS

- **Curriculum-based** a stimulus designed to teach a specific skill
- **Inverted U-shaped function** a particular kind of curvilinear relationship between two variables. For example, conformity and age are related in this way. When we are very young (low in num-ber of years), we exhibit very little conformity to social expectations. As we get older, we conform more and more, so age and conformity are both increasing. When we reach middle and late adulthood, though, we conform somewhat less. In other words, as age increases, conformity de-creases. When you make a graph with age on the X-axis and conformity on the Y-axis, the line looks like an upside-down U, so it is called an *inverted U-shaped function.* Some psychologists think that children's attention to repeated presentations of a video increases until they are very familiar with it, at which time their attention begins to decrease. Thus, if you graph repeated viewing against at-tention, you get an inverted U-shaped line.
- **Polynomial trend analysis** a type of statistical analysis that allows researchers to determine whether a relationships between two variables is curvilinear in nature

Alisha M. Crawley, Daniel R. Anderson, Alice Wilder, Marsha Williams, and Angela Santomero

Effects of Repeated Exposures to a Single Episode of the Television Program *Blue's Clues* on the Viewing Behaviors and Comprehension of Preschool Children

A single episode of the preschool educational television program Blue's Clues *was shown once or repeated on 5 consecutive days for 3- to 5-year-old viewers. A comparison group watched a different preschool program one time. Viewer behavior was videotaped, and comprehension and learning of* Blue's Clues *content was tested. With repetition, looking at the television screen remained at a high level. Only 5-year-old boys' looking decreased. Verbal and nonverbal interactions with the program (such as answering questions and pointing at the screen) increased, especially during educational content. Comprehension improved with repetition. Episode repetition is an effective strategy for enhancing learning and program involvement for a preschool audience.*

Preschool children often ask for repetition of storybooks and videos. Mares (1998) surveyed parents of children aged 2 to 17 years about frequency of repeated videotape viewing. Sixty-nine percent of parents of children aged 2 to 4 reported that their children "almost always" watched videos repeatedly. The parents of less than 10% of the children in this age group reported that their children "very rarely" or "never" watched videos repeatedly. The percentage of children who "almost always" watched repeatedly substantially decreased with age beyond the preschool years.

Almost any theory of comprehension would predict that children's comprehension of a television program improves with repetition. In the small amount of research concerning television that has examined this issue, the prediction has been supported. Peracchio (1992) studied the effects of repetition on the acquisition of the event knowledge of a product-exchange story presented aurally or audiovisually. Five- and 7-year-old children were shown either once or three consecutive times a televised version of a child returning a birthday present to a store. Repetition benefited comprehension in both versions, but the benefit for the audiovisual version was primarily for younger children.

Mares (1997) had 4- and 9-year-old children watch a televised story that had been misunderstood in previous research. Experimental versions of the story concerned an old woman who was pretty and mean or ugly and kind; viewers watched either once or four times, a week apart. Mares found that comprehension of the younger children was worse than comprehension of the older children for the group that saw the story only once, but there was no age difference for comprehension following repetition. The younger children who watched the story four times reached the ceiling comprehension score that the older children achieved with one viewing. Children who saw the story only once rated their enjoyment as slightly more than those who saw it four times.

Mares (1997) conducted a second study in which 6- to 9-year-olds watched an edited version of a children's feature film and compared children who were watching the film for the first time with those who had seen it before. She measured comprehension by asking the children to name characters, make inferences about the movie, and state the moral. She found that children who had seen the film previously did better on character identification and inferences.

Sell, Ray, and Lovelace (1995) had 4-year-olds watch an edited version of a *Sesame Street* tape depicting a muppet game show ("Alphabet Treasure

Hunt") three times over a 3-week period. After each viewing, the children were asked, "How do you play 'Alphabet Treasure Hunt'?" With repetition, children increased their knowledge of the game show script, focusing more on relevant details. This study confounded repeated questioning with repeated viewing, so some of the increase may have come from alerting the children to the relevant features of the program.

In addition to the work on repetition of television programs, there has been a small amount of research on repeated reading of stories to young children, which appears to occur quite commonly. With repeated readings, young children asked more questions and made more comments; they also shifted the focus of their questions from relatively superficial aspects of the books to the meaning of the text. The more the children understood the books that were repeatedly read, the more they appreciated them (Beaver, 1982; Martinez, 1983; Martinez & Roser, 1985; Morrow, 1988; Snow, 1983; Snow & Goldfield, 1983; Sulzby, 1985; also see Samuels, 1979).

Despite the apparent benefits of repetition to learning, curriculum-based television programs are not systematically repeated. We assume that broadcasters avoid repetition because they believe that attention to the program would habituate and that audiences would thereby be diminished. If so, this assumption flies in the face of observations that children repeatedly watch videotapes. The primary question addressed in this article is whether preschool viewer attention and behaviors indicating program involvement necessarily diminish with moderate amounts of program repetition.

Theories of attention to television provide conflicting perspectives. Singer (1980) argued that young children's attention to television is primarily attracted and held by movement, scene changes, and other formal features that elicit orienting reactions. From its simplicity, this theory provides the most straightforward prediction for the present study. Because orienting reactions readily habituate with stimulus repetition, attention should decrease as the viewer habituates. This should happen equivalently for each age group.

Anderson and Lorch (1983) proposed that young children's attention to television is primarily driven by their comprehension of the content of television. Because television programs are frequently difficult for preschoolers to understand, this theory emphasizes comprehensibility of the content. Anderson and Lorch argued that to the degree to which the television program is optimally comprehensible, it holds attention. If a program is unfamiliar but somewhat understandable, attention should

increase with repetition until the program becomes optimally comprehensible. Beyond that point, when the content becomes overly familiar and predictable, attention should decrease. Huston and Wright (1983, 1989) provided a more comprehensive theory along similar lines, explicitly arguing that attention may follow an inverted U-shaped function related to, among other things, familiarity with the content.

Based on unpublished formative research done by the producers, the episode of *Blue's Clues* used in the present study was designed to be optimally comprehensible but intellectually challenging to 4-year-olds. From this consideration, our predictions, based on the Anderson and Lorch (1983) and the Huston and Wright (1983, 1989) theories, are that 4-year-olds' attention should either be sustained or increase with repetition. Because repetition should make the program more comprehensible to 3-year-olds, their attention should increase. Five-year-olds, on the other hand, would be the most likely to show some decrease in attention because the program may begin to become overly predictable.

There is another theory that is relevant to the present work. Salomon (1983) argued that children invest more or less mental effort in processing media. The amount of mental effort that is invested depends on the degree to which the medium is perceived as demanding such effort. For example, elementary school children who are told that they will be tested on the contents of a television program invest more effort than children who do not receive such instructions (Salomon & Leigh, 1984; van der Molen & van der Voort, 1997). Field and Anderson (1985) replicated this result for younger children and found that visual attention was correlated with the children's reports of invested mental effort.

Blue's Clues differs from other curriculum-based television programs insofar as the audience is frequently asked to "help" solve various problems presented during the program. After delays designed to allow the audience time to overtly or covertly provide answers, feedback on solution strategies as well as correct answers are provided by the program. In designing *Blue's Clues*, the creators hoped that the opportunity to "participate" would increase the mental effort the viewers invest in the program. This, combined with the sense of mastery instilled by solving the problems or otherwise knowing the answers, would help children sustain interest in and enjoyment of the program. Salomon's (1983) theory does not directly predict the effects of episode repetition, but it is reasonable to suppose that as children become familiar with the *Blue's Clues* format, they increase the effort they invest in solving the problems and helping provide answers. On this basis, it might be predicted that visual attention should be maintained and that overt interactions with the program should increase.

Only two prior studies examined visual attention to television in relationship to repetition. These studies found no changes in visual attention to several repetitions of very brief television segments (Anderson & Levin, 1976; Wright, Kotler, Hughes, and Donley, 1997). Otherwise, there has been no prior research on viewing behavior during repeated presentations of a television program. Given the likelihood that repeated experience with a television program extends and deepens comprehension by young children, the relative lack of research is surprising. Especially for curriculum-based television and videotapes, repetition provides a potentially inexpensive means of increasing learning.

METHOD

Design

One group of children (3-, 4-, and 5-year-olds) viewed the *Blue Clues* episode once, with comprehension testing immediately following. A second group viewed the same *Blue's Clues* episode on 5 consecutive days, with comprehension testing occurring immediately following the fifth exposure. A comparison group watched an episode of a different preschool television program one time. The comparison group was included in order to provide an indication of baseline knowledge of the curriculum items included in the *Blue's Clues* episode. The design of the analyses for comprehension was Condition (3) × Age (3) × Gender (2), with all factors between subjects. The design of the analyses for viewer behavior focused on the repeated exposure group and is a mixed design of Age (3) × Gender (2) × Repetition (5) × Content Type (2), with Repetition and Content Type within-subjects factors. Content Type refers to content that is primarily either educational or entertaining in intent.

Participants

Participants were recruited from three day-care centers in New York and Connecticut. The 108 participants included 36 three-year-olds (range was 2 years 11 months to 3 years 11 months; mean age was 3 years 7 months; 13 girls), 38 four-year-olds (range was 4 years 0 months to 4 years 11 months; mean age was 4 years 6 months; 18 girls), and 34 five-year-olds, (range was 5 years 0 months to 5 years 10 months; mean age was 5 years 3 months; 16 girls). The broad ethnicities of the participants were 41% African

American, 36% White, 21% Hispanic, and 2% Asian American.

The participants were assigned to one of the three experimental groups based on their age, gender, and ethnicity. For example, 3 children of the same age, gender, and ethnicity were put in three different groups. Unfortunately, there were not enough participants to match perfectly by these criteria, so 6 of the children were assigned randomly, consequently producing unequal numbers of participants in the Conditions × Age × Gender design. In the comparison group, there were 12 three-year-olds (4 girls), 12 four-year-olds (6 girls), and 12 five-year-olds (6 girls). In the one-exposure group, there were 12 three-year-olds (5 girls), 14 four-year-olds (8 girls), and 10 five-year-olds (4 girls). In the repeated-exposure group, there were 11 three-year-olds (3 girls), 13 four-year-olds (6 girls), and 12 five-year-olds (6 girls).

Of the 52 participants who watched on the 1st day, there were 36 who watched all 5 days and were tested. Fourteen were dropped because of absence, and 2 were not tested although they did watch from the 1st to the 4th day and were present on the 5th. In addition, there were 13 children who were in the comparison or one-exposure group who completed the session but were not used in the final sample for reasons of equipment failure or other violation of the experimental procedure.

Setting

Participants were observed at their day-care centers. One, in Stamford, Connecticut, provided 60 participants (19 in the repeated-exposure group, 21 in the one-exposure group, and 20 in the comparison group). Another, in Queens, New York City, provided 20 participants (7 in the repeated-exposure group, 6 in the one-exposure group, and 7 in the comparison group). The third, from Harlem, New York City, provided 28 participants (10 in the repeated-exposure group, 9 in the one-exposure group, and 9 in the comparison group). The research was conducted in rooms that were quiet and away from most distractions. The television was set up near an electrical outlet, and the video camera was on a tripod next to the television. The experimenter sat behind or next to the camera, in order to move it if the child moved out of camera range.

Stimulus Programs

The experimental tape was *Blue's Clues*, episode 101, "Snack-time," (Santomero, 1996) with a running time of 23.8 min, excluding closing credits. The series is designed to teach preschool children cognitive skills and to exercise new and already acquired cognitive skills and knowledge. A human host, Steve, guides the child viewers through his animated world, solving problems left by his puppy Blue. In this episode, Blue gives Steve and the viewers three clues to try to figure out what Blue wants with her snack. On the way, Steve and Blue invite viewers to help elephants paint their family (using color identification), help characters put food of different shapes away (using shape recognition), and help chicks find their friends with matching hats (using matching skills). The series is designed to elicit overt verbal and behavioral reactions from the preschool audience watching. This is accomplished by having Steve or other characters ask questions of the audience that can be answered verbally or through nonverbal behaviors such as pointing. The series had not yet been telecast at the time of the study and was therefore new to the participants in this study.

The comparison program was episode 41 of *The Busy World of Richard Scarry,* (LaPierre, 1996) with a running time of 22.8 min without closing credits. This episode features the animated residents of Busytown. This series was chosen as a comparison because it is popular with preschool children but represents a more traditional approach insofar as it presents stories without attempts to elicit overt behaviors from the audience. This episode, too, had not been telecast at the time of the study.

Procedure

Children were brought to the viewing room individually. The child was seated on the floor in front of the television, with paper, crayons, and blocks as distractors within reaching distance. The experimenter talked to the child for a few minutes and then played the videotape. Children were not told that they would subsequently be tested on their knowledge of the program. During the program, interaction with the child was kept to a minimum. If the child asked a question or directed a comment to the experimenter, she would indicate that she was doing work and that the child should go back to playing or watching television. On the 5th day, the children in the repeated-exposure group were tested after viewing. The children of the comparison and one-exposure groups were tested after their first and only viewing session.

The two comprehension tests for *Blue's Clues* and *Busy World* viewers were almost identical. During the test, the participant was shown pictures and asked questions about them. The test consisted of five types of items. Educational items contained questions about the educational content, primarily

the games in which the audience was invited to provide the answers (e.g., using the clues *cup, straw,* and *cow* to infer what Blue wanted with her snack). Entertainment items contained questions about the entertainment content, including names of characters and questions such as what happened when the telephone rang (Steve fell down). The third type we called *far transfer.* In these items, the concepts of the thinking games (color identification, shape recognition, and matching) were tested using stimuli different from those shown in the episode. The fourth type examined a strategy that was modeled in the program for solving the matching problems (placing the standard next to the comparison stimuli). How often the child used this strategy was assessed for the items using the same stimuli shown in the episode, as well as for far transfer problems using different stimuli. For example, in the matching part of the comprehension test, children matched chicks with matching hats, as shown in the show. In the far transfer matching game, children matched kangaroos with matching shoes.

These same items were given to the comparison group to establish baseline knowledge. There were also questions regarding the specific content of the episodes. These questions were different depending on which show the child watched. All children were also asked to answer the question "What did you just see?"

Immediately after the video, the experimenter moved to the floor near the participant. After a brief warm-up, the experimenter administered the comprehension tests without feedback. The repeated-exposure children watched with the same experimenter for the first 4 days, but on the 5th day, they watched with and were interviewed by one of the other two experimenters, randomly chosen. This latter procedure was designed to reduce the possible effect of a familiar researcher eliciting more answers from the repeated-exposure children.

Videotape Coding

The videotapes that were used to record the children included standard vertical interval and serial time code, allowing for frame accurate computer-assisted coding. Looking at the television screen was coded on a continuous basis. A coder advanced the tape to the exact frame where she judged the child to be visually oriented to the television screen. The coder then pressed a button on the computer and held it until she judged the look ended. The computer recorded the video frame numbers concurrent with the button push and release. Because of the clarity of these tapes, there was little difficulty in deciding where the child was looking. However, there were some parts of the session when the coder was uncertain about where the child was looking, as when the child moved out of camera view. Here, the coder pressed a button on the computer at the exact frame where the uncertainty began, and released it at the exact frame where uncertainty ended.

Program-related verbal and nonverbal behaviors other than looking were also coded. The verbal behaviors were answers directed to the television host or other characters, verbalizations about the television that were not answers, and other (including laughing and singing). The coded nonverbal behaviors were nonverbal direct responses to a query by a television character (such as nodding and pointing), imitation, and other. There were two uncertainty codes, one for verbal uncertainty and one for nonverbal uncertainty. An example of an answer directed to the television is "Steve, the clue is on the cow!" A verbalization about the television that is not an answer would be "I have a puppy, too." Behaviors not related to the program, such as talking in general and playing, were not coded.

Interobserver reliability for looking at the television screen was assessed by having each of the five coders code a tape in common. Phi correlations (based on judgments of looking vs. not looking) between pairs of coders ranged from .97 to .99, consistent with corresponding reliabilities in previous research (e.g., Anderson & Levin, 1976).

Interobserver reliability for interactions with the television was also assessed by having each of the coders code a tape in common. Phi correlations were based on judgments of whether or not an interaction occurred during each second of the show. They ranged from .76 to .92.

RESULTS

Viewing Behavior

Combining the single session and first exposure session of the repeated-exposure *Blue's Clues* groups, we compared percentage looking, verbal interactions per minute, and nonverbal interactions per minute with the same for *The Busy World of Richard Scarry*. The Groups (2) × Age (3) × Gender (2) analyses of variance (ANOVAs) revealed greater looking at *Blue's Clues*, $F(1, 96) = 10.09$, $p < .01$ (77.4% looking vs. 62.2%), and more nonverbal interactions, $F(1, 96) = 7.85$, $p < .01$ (.17 per minute vs. .06). The difference in verbal interactions (.41 per minute for *Blue's Clues* vs. .30) was not significant.

Blue's Clues is designed to elicit active audience participation in problem solving and other educa-

tional activities. The program, nevertheless, is designed to entertain as well as educate. Although the entertainment portions of the program invite audience participation, these require less intense cognitive involvement than do the educational portions of the program. Accordingly, we parsed the show into constituent content units on the basis of whether the units were strongly educational in nature or whether the intent was primarily entertainment (consensus decisions by two of the investigators). More of the episode involved educational content (14.5 minutes or 61%) than entertainment content (9.3 minutes or 39%). An example of educational content is a pattern matching game, and an example of entertainment occurs when Blue, hiding from Steve, is sitting on top of his head.

The primary analyses of the viewer behaviors were Age (3) × Gender (2) × Content Type (2) × Repetition (5) multivariate analyses of variance (MANOVAs) with polynomial trend analysis (up to the quadratic component) of the repetition factor. In these analyses, scores were estimated for 1 participant whose session was missing due to a lost videotape. This session was from the fourth exposure of a 3-year-old boy. The missing data point was estimated using a formula advocated by Myers and Well (1991, p. 258). All analyses were repeated deleting this participant; there were no differences in significance of effects.

Looking. The mean percentage of coder uncertainty for looking was 0.57%, with a range from 0% to 15.17%. An Age (3) × Gender (2) × Exposure Number (5) mixed-design ANOVA revealed no significant effects of uncertainty, indicating that it was approximately evenly distributed across conditions. Periods of uncertainty were not included in the looking data. If, for example, a child had a cumulative total of 1 min of uncertainty during a given type of content, the denominator for calculating percentage looking was reduced by that amount.

Percentage looking was measured as the number of frames spent looking at the screen divided by the total number of frames in the program times 100. An Age (3) × Gender (2) × Content Type (2) × Repetition Number (5) mixed-design MANOVA trend analysis yielded a significant Content Type × Repetitions (linear trend) interaction, $F(1, 30) = 11.77$, $p < .01$, which is illustrated in Figure 1. There was a significant Age × Repetition (linear trend) interaction, $F(2, 30) = 6.03$, $p < .01$, which was qualified by an Age × Gender × Repetition (linear trend) interaction, $F(2, 30) = 4.33$, $p < .05$. That is, the linear trend over repetitions differed by age and gender.

The interaction of repetition with age and gender was analyzed by performing Gender × Exposure

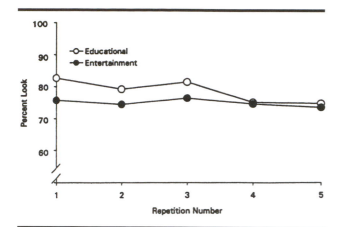

FIGURE 1 Mean percentage looking as a function of repetition number and content type.

trend analyses for each age group, collapsing across content type. There were no significant effects for the 3- or 4-year-olds; the linear function of repetition was $L = 72.16\% + 1.55R$ for the 3-year-olds, and $L = 84.59\% - 2.06R$ for the 4-year-olds, where L is percentage looking and R is repetition number. The analysis for the 5-year-olds revealed the source of the omnibus interactions involving age and gender. There was a significant main effect of repetitions, $F(1, 10) = 20.44$, $p < .001$, and a marginally significant interaction with gender, $F(1, 10) = 4.93$, $p = .051$. The 5-year-old boys' linear function of repetition was $L = 88.91\% - 4.88R$, whereas the 5-year-old girls' function was $L = 75.89 - 1.67R$. Looking declined with repetition among 5-year-olds, but more so for boys (a loss of nearly five points per repetition) than girls (a loss of less than two). It should be noted, however, that boys initially looked more at the program than did girls.

Interactions directed at the television. The interactions were coded as verbal or nonverbal in nature. Verbal interactions were further coded as answers, imitations, comments about the program, and other. Nonverbal interactions were coded as answers (usually pointing), imitations, and other. As with looking, there were occasional points at which a coder was uncertain about the behavior or utterance. When the child was not visible, nonverbal interactions were not coded. Verbal interactions were coded in these cases because the child could still be heard. Nonverbal uncertainties were coded if the child made a nonverbal motion that was ambiguous. There was a mean of 0. 15 episodes of nonverbal uncertainties, with a range from 0 to 2. Verbal uncertainties were coded if the child made a verbalization and the coder could not understand what was said. There was a mean of 1.22 episodes of verbal uncertainties, with a range from 0 to 10. Verbal and nonverbal uncertainties are ignored for the rest of the analyses.

The analysis for total interactions (see Table 1) revealed a significant linear trend of repetitions, $F(1, 30) = 4.46$, $p < .05$, which varied as a function of content type, $F(1, 30) = 8.60$, $p < .01$, as illustrated in Figure 2. Separate analyses for each content type showed a significant linear trend for the educational content, $F(1, 30) = 5.96$, $p < .05$, $I = .38 + .17R$, where I is interactions per minute. The trend for entertainment content was not significant, $I = .47 + .08R$. We further analyzed the interactions according to whether they were verbal or nonverbal.

	TABLE 1	Total Interactions per Minute as a Function of Age, Content Type, and Repetition Number				
		REPETITION NUMBER				
AGE		1	2	3	4	5
			Educational content			
3		0.63 (1.00)	0.60 (0.92)	0.79 (0.83)	0.78 (0.86)	0.79 (0.91)
4		0.51 (1.02)	0.77 (1.33)	1.18 (1.93)	1.61 (2.11)	1.44 (2.47)
5		0.40 (0.80)	0.70 (0.95)	1.13 (1.33)	0.71 (0.83)	1.29 (2.09)
	Total	0.51 (0.92)	0.69 (1.07)	1.04 (1.43)	1.05 (1.46)	1.19 (1.94)
			Entertainment content			
3		0.96 (1.19)	0.65 (0.66)	0.58 (0.52)	0.70 (0.50)	0.74 (0.61)
4		0.57 (0.51)	0.73 (0.83)	0.88 (0.84)	1.14 (1.09)	0.99 (1.36)
5		0.33 (0.55)	0.29 (0.42)	0.59 (0.66)	0.50 (0.60)	0.91 (1.35)
	Total	0.61 (0.81)	0.56 (0.67)	0.69 (0.69)	0.79 (0.81)	0.89 (1.15)

Note. The values represent the mean interactions per minute with the standard deviations in parentheses. There were significant linear trends for both educational and entertainment content but no effects of age.

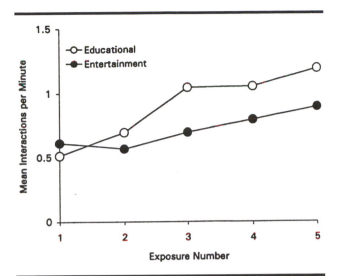

FIGURE 2 Mean interactions per minute as a function of repetition number and content type.

For verbal interactions per minute, there was a significant linear trend for repetitions, $F(1, 30) = 4.52$, $p < .05$, which varied as a function of content type, $F(1, 30) = 7.75$, $p < .01$. Separate analyses for each content type revealed a significant linear trend for the educational units, $F(1, 30) = 5.85$, $p < .05$, $I = .24 + .14R$, but not for the entertainment units, $I = .31 + .07R$.

Verbal interactions were coded as answers, imitations, and talking about the program. Because some cells contained very few responses, the data for each type of verbal interaction were analyzed collapsed across gender of participant. The analyses were thus Age (3) × Content Type (2) × Repetitions (5) MANOVAs with trend analysis. Analyses indicated that talking about the program did not increase with repetition whereas imitations did, $F(1, 33) = 6.81$, $p < .05$, $I = -.02 + .06R$. Of more educational importance with respect to the educational goals of the program were verbal answers. There was a significant interaction (linear trend) of repetitions with content type, $F(1, 33) = 5.75$, $p < .05$. Verbal answers increased with repetition, $F(1, 33) = 7.95$, $p < .01$, but more so for educational, $F(1, 33) = 7.16$, $p < .05$, $I = .13 + .07R$, than for entertainment content, $F(1, 33) = 5.98$, $p < .05$, $I = .02 + .014R$.

Verbalizations about the television program varied only by type of content, $F(1, 33) = 10.33$, $p < .01$. The means and standard deviations were .11 (.27) for the educational content and .22 (.31) for the entertainment content.

For total nonverbal interactions per minute, a linear trend of repetitions varied significantly by content type, $F(1, 30) = 4.87$, $p < .05$, which was further complicated by an interaction of linear trend of repe-

titions with gender and content type, $F(1, 30) = 6.57$, $p < .05$. This interaction was due to a linear increase in girls' nonverbal interactions with educational content, $I = .10 + .04R$, whereas there was no such increase for entertainment content, $I = .15 - .003R$. Boys showed no significant increase in nonverbal interactions for either type of content, $I = .16 + .02R$, for both educational and entertainment content.

Nonverbal interactions were coded as answers, imitations, and other (such as dancing to the music). Because there was substantially less nonverbal interaction than verbal interaction and because the overall analysis of nonverbal interactions indicated that the interactions varied by gender of viewer, we concluded that there were too few data for meaningful analysis.

Comprehension

The comprehension test yielded five separate scores. Summing the scores on the five types of items produced a total score. The highest possible total score was 49 (22 points were possible for educational, 10 for entertainment, 11 for far transfer, and 3 points each for strategy use in the two matching games). Free recall to the question "What did you just see?" was also coded for how many units of information were provided by the child. This was scored only for the *Blue's Clues* viewers and was analyzed separately.

Mean percentages of the total possible scores (with standard deviations) for each of the five question types may be seen in Table 2. An Age (3) × Gender (2) × Conditions (3) × Question Type (5) MANOVA, with question type as a repeated measure, was used to analyze percentage of correct answers. There was a main effect of age, $F(2, 90) = 21.56$, $p < .001$, due to better comprehension with age. A main effect of condition, $F(2, 90) = 16.16$, $p < .001$, was due to better performance following five repetitions of *Blue's Clues* than after one repetition, which in turn was better than performance by the group that saw a different program. There was a main effect of question type, $F(4, 360) = 168.53$, $p < .001$, with far transfer strategy use being the most difficult and far transfer items being easiest (see Table 2). There was also an Age × Item Type interaction, $F(8, 360) = 4.14$, $p < .001$, and a Conditions × Item Type interaction, $F(8, 360) = 3.48$, $p < .01$. To determine the source of these interactions, we ran separate between-subject ANOVAs, Age (3) × Gender (2) × Conditions (3), on each comprehension category.

For educational items, there were main effects of age, $F(2, 90) = 26.10$, $p < .001$, and condition, $F(2, 90) = 27.66$, $p < .001$, and for entertainment items, main effects of age, $F(2, 90) = 22.73$, $p < .001$, and condition,

TABLE 2   Percentage Comprehension by Question Type, Age, and Condition

AGE & QUESTION TYPE	GROUP			
	C	1X	5X	TOTAL
3-year-olds				
Far transfer matching	2.78 (9.62)	0.00 (0.00)	15.15 (22.92)	5.88 (15.29)
Original matching	11.11 (29.59)	15.15 (22.92)	15.15 (31.14)	13.73 (27.36)
Entertainment	10.83 (12.40)	20.91 (16.40)	37.27 (21.02)	22.65 (19.74)
Educational	31.82 (15.14)	41.74 (17.58)	57.44 (13.68)	43.32 (18.50)
Far transfer	46.97 (30.73)	36.36 (22.64)	56.20 (24.33)	46.52 (26.74)
Total comprehension	27.89 (12.98)	32.10 (13.78)	47.87 (13.08)	35.71 (15.54)
4-year-olds				
Far transfer matching	11.11 (21.71)	9.52 (20.37)	25.64 (38.86)	15.38 (28.46)
Original matching	0.00 (0.00)	11.90 (30.96)	35.90 (44.02)	16.24 (34.09)
Entertainment	31.67 (14.67)	45.00 (22.10)	54.62 (16.13)	44.10 (19.96)
Educational	46.21 (9.85)	63.96 (18.48)	70.98 (15.80)	60.84 (18.17)
Far transfer	71.97 (23.72)	77.27 (18.78)	76.92 (18.78)	75.52 (20.02)
Total comprehension	44.05 (8.98)	56.56 (15.67)	64.05 (11.41)	55.21 (14.67)
5-year-olds				
Far transfer matching	8.33 (20.72)	0.00 (0.00)	22.22 (35.77)	10.48 (25.27)
Original matching	5.56 (12.97)	9.09 (30.15)	30.56 (38.82)	15.23 (30.62)
Entertainment	28.33 (12.67)	55.45 (18.09)	67.50 (15.45)	50.29 (22.56)
Educational	48.86 (12.58)	75.21 (10.63)	79.55 (8.99)	67.66 (17.42)
Far transfer	81.06 (16.65)	84.30 (17.76)	81.82 (13.98)	82.34 (15.74)
Total comprehension	46.77 (9.31)	64.56 (8.07)	71.09 (5.49)	60.70 (12.98)
All participants				
Far transfer matching	7.41 (18.01)	3.70 (13.28)	21.30 (33.00)	10.80 (24.04)
Original matching	5.56 (18.69)	12.04 (27.78)	27.78 (38.63)	15.12 (30.70)
Entertainment	23.61 (15.88)	40.83 (23.47)	53.61 (21.00)	39.35 (23.65)
Educational	42.30 (14.49)	60.61 (20.76)	69.70 (15.67)	57.53 (20.52)
Far transfer	66.67 (27.83)	66.92 (28.26)	72.22 (21.73)	68.60 (25.99)
Total comprehension	39.57 (13.30)	51.53 (18.61)	61.45 (13.98)	50.85 (17.77)

Note. The values represent the mean percentage correct with the standard deviations in parentheses. C = *Busy World of Richard Scarry* comparison group; 1x = *Blue's Clues* one-exposure group; 5x = *Blue's Clues* repeated-exposure group.

$F(2, 90) = 25.53$, $p < .001$. These effects were due to better performance with age, as well as better performance following five repetitions than one repetition, and both were superior to the group that saw a different program.

The analysis for far transfer (same tasks but different problems than in the episode) yielded only a main effect of age, $F(2, 90) = 25.96$, $p < .001$, due to better performance with age. There were main effects of condition for strategy use (due to greater use of the demonstrated strategy by the repeated *Blue's Clues* viewers) in both the original matching game, $F(2, 90) = 4.11$, $p < .05$, and the far transfer matching game, $F(2, 90) = 4.11$, $p < .05$. There was low performance in some of the cells used for the analysis of strategy use, leading to the problem of artificially constrained variability. Therefore, the Kruskal-Wallis one-way ANOVA, a nonparametric test, was also used to test the effects of condition on strategy use.

Again, there was a significant effect of condition on both the original matching game, $\chi^2(2, N = 108) = 9.7$, $p < .01$, and for the far transfer matching game, $\chi^2(2, N = 108) = 10.2$, $p < .01$.

An Age (3) × Gender (2) × Condition (2) ANOVA on free recall by the two *Blue's Clues* groups revealed only a significant age effect, $F(2, 60) = 11.71$, $p < .001$. The means and standard deviations of the number of recalled units were .59 (.73), 1.85 (2.13), and 3.17 (2.33) for the 3-, 4-, and 5-year-olds.

DISCUSSION

Although preschooler demand for repetition of books and videos is widely known among parents and other caretakers of young children (Mares, 1998), the phenomenon has been the subject of remarkably little formal research. We examined the effects on 3- to 5-year-old viewers of repeating an educational television program, *Blue's Clues*, for 5 consecutive days.

Blue's Clues is designed to provide cognitive challenges and teach cognitive skills to preschool viewers while entertaining them. More than any prior television program, *Blue's Clues* encourages audience participation. Based on ideas that learning would improve and the audience would feel empowered by meeting the program's cognitive challenges, the Nickelodeon network adopted a novel broadcast strategy of showing an identical episode on 5 consecutive days each week. This strategy seems well founded. We found that, with repetition, visual attention remained constant, with the exception of some decline among 5-year-old boys. Verbal and nonverbal interactions, especially answers and imitations, greatly increased with episode repetition. Comprehension improved, and children increased their application of a demonstrated problem-solving strategy to problems both shown and not shown by the program.

With respect to theories of television viewing, the results are least consistent with Singer's (1980) orienting response theory that predicted attention should decline with repetition at all ages. The Anderson and Lorch (1983) and Huston and Wright (1983, 1989) theories, which emphasize the importance of the viewers' engagement with the content, provided predictions that are consistent with observed results, although not in detail. The results are also broadly consistent with Salomon's (1983) theory of invested mental effort. Because *Blue's Clues* overtly invites viewer participation and active problem solving, we hypothesized that invested mental effort would increase as the children became familiar with the program's formats and demands. Consequences of this increased mental effort would be increased overt viewer participation, maintained visual attention, and improved comprehension, all of which were found.

Practically speaking, repetition has not hurt and may have helped audience ratings for *Blue's Clues*. Since the beginning of the second season (October 1997), *Blue's Clues has* attracted more preschool viewers than any other preschool show on television (Nielsen Media Research, based on K2–5 weekly cume AA [000]). In both educational and audience terms, therefore, the repetition strategy appears to be a success.

There are several important empirical questions that are left unanswered by the present research. Because *Blue's Clues* is unusual both in its cognitive challenge and in its ability to elicit audience participation, we do not know what the effects of episode repetition might be for more traditional television programs. Based on Salomon's (1983) theory of invested mental effort, furthermore, traditional educational television programs that do not invite active participation may not be perceived by young viewers as requiring sustained mental effort. These programs may not bear repeating to the same extent that *Blue's Clues* does.

We also do not know if the beneficial effects of repetition are limited to the ages examined in the present study. Repeated viewing of videos at home declines among school-age children (Mares, 1998), and repetition of an educational television program for older children may not have the desired effects.

Theories of child development and cognitive theories of learning have remarkably little to say about the effects of repetition other than that comprehension and memory should benefit. We suggest that any such theory must incorporate notions of optimal comprehensibility, active participation, and a need for cognitive mastery. Regardless of the form such a theory may take, the present research indicates that repetition can be a useful tool to increase enjoyment and learning from media for young children.

REFERENCES

Anderson, D. R., & Levin, S. R. (1976). Young children's attention to "Sesame Street." *Child Development, 47*, 806–811.

Anderson, D. R., & Lorch, E. P. (1983). Looking at television: Action or reaction? In J. Bryant & D. R. Anderson (Eds.), *Children's understanding of television: Research on attention and comprehension* (pp. 1–33). New York: Academic Press.

Beaver, J. M. (1982). Say it! Over and over. *Language Arts, 59*, 143–148.

Field, D. E., & Anderson, D. R. (1985). Instruction and modality effects on children's television attention and comprehension. *Journal of Educational Psychology, 77*, 91–100.

Huston, A. C., & Wright, J. C. (1983). Children's processing of television: The informative functions of formal features. In J. Bryant & D. R. Anderson (Eds.), *Children's understanding of television: Research on attention and comprehension* (pp. 35–68). New York: Academic Press.

Huston, A. C., & Wright, J. C. (1989). The forms of television and the child viewer. In G. Comstock (Ed.), *Public communication and behavior* (pp. 103–158). Orlando, FL: Academic Press.

LaPierre, T. (1996). A trip back in time (M. Da Silva, Director). In M. Charest (producer), *The busy world of Richard Scarry*. New York: Nickelodeon.

Mares, M. L. (1997, May). *Re-examining children's comprehension of television: The potential effects of the VCR.* Paper presented at the annual conference of the International Communication Association, Montreal, Quebec, Canada.

Mares, M. L. (1998). Children's use of VCRs. *Annals of the American Academy of Political and Social Science, 557,* 120–131.

Martinez, M. (1983). Exploring young children's comprehension through storytime talk. *Language Arts, 60,* 202–209.

Martinez, M., & Roser, N. (1985). Read it again: The value of repeated readings during storytime. *Reading Teacher 38,* 780–786.

Morrow, L. M. (1988). Young children's responses to one-to-one story readings in school settings. *Reading Research Quarterly, 23,* 89–107.

Myers, J. L., & Well, A. D. (1991). *Research design and statistical analysis.* New York: HarperCollins.

Peracchio, L. A. (1992). How do young children learn to be consumers? A script processing approach. *Journal of Consumer Research, 18,* 425–440.

Salomon, G. (1983). Television watching and mental effort: A social psychological view. In J. Bryant & D. R. Anderson (Eds.), *Children's understanding of television: Research on attention and comprehension* (pp. 181–198). New York: Academic Press.

Salomon, G., & Leigh, T. (1984). Predispositions about learning from print and television. *Journal of Communication, 34,* 119–135.

Samuels, S. J. (1979). The method of repeated readings. *Reading Teacher, 32,* 403–408.

Santomero, A. C. (1996). Blue's snacktime (T. Kessler, Director). In T. Kessler (Producer), *Blue's Clues.* New York: Nickelodeon.

Sell, M. A., Ray, G. E., & Lovelace, L. (1995). Preschool children's comprehension of a Sesame Street video tape: The effects of repeated viewing and previewing instructions. *Educational Technology Research and Development, 43*(3), 49–60.

Singer, J. L. (1980). The power and limitations of television: A cognitive-affective analysis. In P. H. Tannenbaum (Ed.), *The entertainment functions of television* (pp. 31–65). Hillsdale, NJ: Erlbaum.

Snow, C. E. (1983). Literacy and language: Relationships during the preschool years. *Harvard Educational Review, 53,* 165–189.

Snow, C. E., & Goldfield, B. A. (1983). Turn the page please: Situation-specific language acquisition. *Journal of Child Language, 10,* 551–569.

Sulzby, E. (1985). Children's emergent reading of favorite story-books: A developmental study. *Reading Research Quarterly, 20,* 458–481.

van der Molen, J. H., & van der Voort, T. H. (1997). Children's recall of television and print news: A media comparison study. *Journal of Educational Psychology, 89,* 82–91.

Wright, J. C., Kotler, J. A., Hughes, K. P., & Donley, S. M. (1997, April). *Brief educational segments on PBS' Ready-to-Learn series: Effects of program relevance and repetition.* Poster session presented at the biennial meeting of the Society for Research in Child Development, Washington, DC.

SELF-STUDY QUESTIONS

Multiple Choice

1. Research on repeated presentations of stories to young children suggests
   a. children learn more each time
   b. children learn all they're going to learn the first time they hear a story
   c. repetition benefits older but not younger children
   d. children enjoy a story more each time they hear it

2. Which of the following conclusions about children's responses to repeated viewing of *Blue's Clues* episodes is best supported by this study?
   a. Children learn little from repeated viewing because they are easily bored.
   b. The entertainment portions of the program are more interesting to children than those that are educational.
   c. Children only interact with the characters the first time they see an episode.
   d. Repeated viewing seems to help children learn the program's educational content.

Essay

1. According to this article, how do theorists explain children's attention to television?

2. What advice would you give to a parent who told you that she never plays an educational video for her preschool-aged child more than once because she doesn't want the child to be bored? Use information from the article to justify your recommendations.

MIDDLE CHILDHOOD

"Myths and Realities about Words and Literacy"

OVERVIEW

This article, written by two leading reading researchers, presents ideas about the reading process in a myths-and-realities format that cites several common beliefs about reading that research suggests are false. It includes discussions of both beginning reading and the kinds of knowledge older children need to become expert readers.

METHODOLOGY

This article is a brief summary of reading research that is relevant to the points made by the authors. Therefore, there are no references to specific research procedures or statistical analyses.

GLOSSARY TERMS

- **Phoneme**   a single unit of sound in a particular language; for example, the sound [b] at the beginning of the word *bat*
- **Morpheme**   a single unit of meaning; for example, the word *bat* has one morpheme that, when used as a noun, refers to a type of rodent or a piece of baseball equipment. However, the word *bats* has two morphemes, *bat-*, with the same meaning as the single morpheme *bat*, and *-s*, meaning that the word describes more than one such animal or object.
- **Etymology**   the history and derivation of a particular word
- **Nexus**   a bond or connection between two entities

Marilyn Jager Adams and Marcia K. Henry

Myths and Realities about Words and Literacy

Six myths about beginning and developing reading instruction are examined and debunked. The importance of teaching phonological awareness and decoding in beginning reading and of teaching syllable patterns and morpheme patterns from Anglo-Saxon, Greek, and Latin roots and affixes in developing reading is discussed.

Reading is the first of the three Rs. And well that it should be, for being educated depends integrally on reading. It depends on being literate.

Webster's *Ninth Collegiate Dictionary* (1989) indicates that the word *literate* is derived from the Latin word for *letters*. Thus, the word *literate* literally means "marked with letters" or able to read and write. In usage, however, its meaning more broadly extends to being "educated, cultured," being "versed in literature," being "lucid, polished," and even to "having knowledge or competence" in general (as in "computer-literate"). Similarly, beyond something produced in writing, *literature* means "writings having excellence of form or expression and expressing ideas of permanent or universal interest"; *literary* means "having the characteristics of humane learning"; and the *literati* are not merely those who can read and write, but the "educated class," the "intelligentsia." Conversely, the word *illiterate* is used as a synonym for ignorance in any field, regardless of whether the impugned can read or write.

No wonder that being literate and being educated are so thoroughly intertwined in our cultural minds. Historically, print has been where our culture has stored its knowledge—ready for usage and between users. (Note that *prehistoric* is defined as antedating writing). Further, although other media that are at least as capable of storing information are rapidly being invented, there is at least some indication from research that print remains unrivaled in terms of the information that people can retrieve. For example, work by Cunningham and Stanovich (1991) suggests that, even if we watch television with inter-

est and understanding, we tend not to retain or learn from it as we do from print.

For the time being, in any case, an inability to read stands as an enormous barrier to one's potential knowledge and social participation. What is in balance is not merely the information in instructions, newspapers, memos, and manuals but, further, the major archives of human invention, philosophy, literature, study, and experience. Literacy affords access to people, events, places, times, language, perspectives, thoughts, and modes of thought that extend broadly and deeply beyond what any person could ever encounter in her or his day-to-day existence.

Perhaps it is because of its fundamental educational importance that there are so many disparate beliefs about the underlying nature of the reading process. Ironically, in view of the etymology of the word, many of these vying beliefs center on the relation and even the relevance of letters and words to literacy. In turn, these beliefs have strongly influenced approaches to teaching people how to read. Given the tight interdependence of education and literacy, the validity of these beliefs warrants examination. After all, and especially considering the social and connotative baggage of the term *illiterate,* how could any literate person label any other person "illiterate" if it were the illiteracy of our educational practices that had caused them to be so. The goal of this article is to debunk a few of the more broadly held and enduring myths about learning to read and to highlight the instructional implications of their alternatives.

THE MYTHS AND THE REALITIES

Myth 1 and The Reality

Myth 1. Good readers exploit the semantic and syntactic predictability of text so that they do not have to plod through text in a word by word manner.

Reprinted from *School Psychology Review*, 1997, 26, 425–436. Copyright 1997 by the National Association of School Psychologists. Reprinted by permission of the publisher.

Reality. True, good readers are far more sensitive to the semantic and syntactic nuances and constraints of text than are poor readers. Also true, a defining characteristic of good readers is the speed and fluency with which they course through text—upward of 5 words per second or 300 words per minute. However, it is *not* true that good readers gain this speed and fluency by using context to skip, guess, or otherwise shortcut the words of the text. To the contrary, it is the efficiency with which good readers are able to take in the words of a text to which both their speed and their interpretive advantages are owed.

Think about your own efforts at writing. Think about how hard you work to craft your text with clarity and precision. Why would you do that if the words didn't matter? The words and wordings of a text are authors' only means of conveying their intended meaning and message. If comprehension were mostly a matter of readers using their prior knowledge and expectations to guess the author's meaning, then it would render text incapable of communicating anything new to readers in information or affect. Why, then, would we read?

During the past 25 years, research using computer-mediated eye-monitoring technology has affirmed that, when reading meaningful text, good readers normally pause their eyes on very nearly every word of text. Where text is easier or more predictable, the durations of their visual fixations tend to be briefer, but the pattern is otherwise unchanged. How do practiced speed readers attain speeds upward of 600 words per minute? They do so by skipping large blocks of text—and commensurately forfeiting their meaning. When reading for understanding, readers proceed through text through what is essentially a left to right, line by line, word by word process, and this is so whether or not they feel like that is what they are doing. (For reviews, see Just & Carpenter, 1987; Patterson & Coltheart, 1987; Rayner & Pollatsek, 1989.)

Myth 2 and The Reality

Myth 2. Beginning readers should be taught to use context and pictures to guess the meanings of difficult words.

Reality. Human attention is limited. People can actively attend to only one dimension of thought at a time. Furthermore, what people notice, learn, or remember from any experience depends exactly and only upon that to which they have attended.

If the principle goal of beginning reading instruction is to teach children to read with understanding, then there follows a dilemma. Specifically, young readers unavoidably encounter previously unseen words in the texts they are asked to read. Yet, if they take extra time and effort to work these words out, then—because of the dynamics of attention—they are liable to lose track of the text's larger meaning.

Herein lies the motivation for predictable text. Predictable text is text that has been especially designed to ensure that wherever a new word arises, its identity—or at least its gist—will be obvious from the surrounding language, plot, or illustration. In many first-grade classrooms predictable text has all but displaced the conventional primer. The ostensible advantage of predictable text is that it offers a means by which children can get past troublesome words without diverting their attention from the meaningful plane of the story.

But is this really an advantage? Whether predictable or unpredictable, authentic or "basalese," the primary purpose of all of the texts that we give to beginners is to help them learn to read. Encouraging children to rely on the picture to avoid decoding a visually new word may boost their sense of success with the story at hand, but it can do nothing to bolster their success with that word in the next story they read. Encouraging them to rely on context is of similarly limited value. After all, until a child can actually read some of the words, there is effectively no context upon which he or she can lean. Further, the difficult, to-be-guessed words of today's text will soon enough become the easy, context-setting words in some other text down the line. In lending primacy to the meaningfulness of the immediate reading experience, predictable texts shortshrift the larger endeavor.

Again what people notice, learn, or remember from any experience depends exactly and only upon that to which they attend. Except as they attend to a new word, children can learn nothing about it that will make it less troublesome on the next occasion. Although there are costs associated with decoding a new word, they are greatly outweighed by the benefits, both direct and indirect. For normally developing readers, research shows that pausing once to decode a word significantly eases its recognition on next encounter. By the third or fourth encounter and quite enduringly thereafter, the word is typically recognized with no noticeable pause at all (Reitsma, 1989). Further, because the spelling of no word is unique, every word studied indirectly eases the recognition of a number of others. Thus learning to read *mat* eases the reading of *cat, map,* and *met;* learning to read *light* eases the reading of *bright, sight,* and *delighted;* and so on. (e.g., Adams, 1990).

If too many words of a text are unfamiliar, then the reading experience becomes tedious and frustrating. In these cases, children should be given help or, better yet, an easier text. On the other hand, as readers gain control of more and more words, fewer and fewer will require the kind of effort that disrupts comprehension. In the meantime, the best way to help them reach that point is by encouraging them to lend new words the attention they require.

Myth 3 and The Reality

Myth 3.   Phonics is, at best, a transitional skill

Reality.   It has sometimes been said that the reason for learning phonics is so that phonics will not be needed any more. The belief behind this statement is that good readers recognize familiar words directly, holistically, and without analysis of their component letters or sounds. However, this is not so.

If researchers were surprised to learn that reading is generally a left to right, word by word process, they were astounded to learn that skillful readers visually process virtually every individual letter of every word they read while automatically, irrepressibly translating the print to speech as they proceed. It is not that good readers must explicitly and methodically sound out each letter to identify a word. Rather, these translations are nearly reflexive; the associations from letters and spelling patterns to speech sounds have become deeply and intricately imprinted in the readers' memories as the cumulative result of their lifetime of reading.

Research has now taught us that people's knowledge of phonology—of the pronunciations of word—is the nexus of the reading system. On one hand, people's knowledge of the phonological structure of words serves as the glue that holds together the identities and order their letters in memory. On the other, this knowledge serves as the portal from text to language, allowing not only for the child's language to receive and guide his or her reading, but for the reading to impact and alter that child's language beyond the book. In keeping with this, difficulty in reading aloud well-spelled nonsense words is found to be a singularly powerful indicator of specific reading disability (Rack, Snowling, & Olson, 1992).

Myth 4 and The Reality

Myth 4.   The value of teaching children phonics depends on their perceptual strengths and learning styles.

Reality.   This is one of the most enduring and broadly held myths in the field of reading instruc-

tion: Phonics, it is argued, may be fine for children who are auditorily attuned and analytically natured; however, for those who are not so predisposed, reading may better be developed without phonics by emphasizing the global, visual, or meaningful dimensions of the challenge. Because of the widespread popularity of this belief, scores of studies have been conducted to demonstrate its validity—but they have been to no avail (for reviews, see Arter & Jenkins, 1979; Stahl, 1988). Despite the many, many efforts to demonstrate otherwise, however, research has not produced any solid, positive evidence for this sort of interaction between program effectiveness and preferred modalities.

It is true that some children experience far more difficulty in learning phonics than others. However, those children need more support with phonics, not less. Children with reading disabilities are commonly and repeatedly found to benefit most when given a reading program that directly emphasizes decoding and word recognition skills rather than more general reading strategies (Lovett, Ransby, & Barron, 1988; Lovett, Ransby, Hardwick, Johns, & Donaldson, 1989).

Myth 5 and The Reality

Myth 5.   The most difficult and critical phonics lesson is that of teaching children to blend.

Reality.   Most children can successfully learn to recognize and name the letters of the alphabet without too much difficulty. Further, for children who know their letter names, learning the sounds of the letters does not seem to be a major obstacle. Rather, reading difficulty most often asserts itself when "even when able to sound printed letters and letter groups, they cannot blend these to form whole words," (Vernon, 1971, p. 128). No wonder then that the question of how best to help children learn to blend has by long tradition been central to beginning and remedial reading instruction.

We now realize that the inability to blend is not the root cause of reading difficulty. Instead it is a symptom of a more fundamental problem: poorly developed phonemic awareness. Very simply, phonemic awareness is the insight that every spoken word can be conceived as a string of elementary speech gestures, the phonemes.

In every human language, phonemes are basic building blocks of speech. In an alphabetic language, however, they also are the linchpins of the writing system. It is to phonemes that the basic printed symbols—letters—are intended to refer. It is the separable existence of the phonemes that anchors the very logic of the writing system.

To be sure, children's sensitivity to the phonemic structure of words and syllables grows substantially in breadth and depth as their reading and writing skills mature. Yet, at its most fundamental level, the basic awareness of the nature and existence of phonemes seems to qualify as a genuine insight. It is, moreover, an insight that has been shown to escape roughly 25% of American first-graders, and if the samples were restricted to children from print-poor preschool environments, then that percentage would be substantially larger (Adams, 1990).

There are wholly understandable reasons for the elusiveness of this insight. First, in the course of normal language production or comprehension, the perception and production of individual speech sounds occurs nearly effortlessly and subattentionally, rather like the recognition of individual printed letters by skillful readers. Indeed, it is only because children have so thoroughly automated their processing of speech sounds that they have attention and capacity for the higher-order meaning and nuances of spoken language, and by the age of three or four, children really are remarkably proficient with spoken language. Second, because the phonemes tend to be seamlessly blended together and, in any case, quite variable in normal running speech, it is difficult for children to understand what to listen for even when trying (Liberman & Liberman, 1990).

Faced with an alphabetic script, the child's level of phonemic awareness upon entering school is widely held to be the strongest single predictor of the success she or he will experience in learning to read and of the likelihood that she or he will fail (e.g., Adams, Treiman, & Pressley, 1997). It does little good for a child to memorize that the letter *b* says /b/ unless that /b/ is recognized as the sound that is heard in such words as *bubble, ball*, and *banana*. Without that recognition, the sounds of letters are arbitrary: they yield no access to the speech system, and the speech returns no guidance as to how they might be "blended" together. Without phonemic awareness, the only recourse for learning how to recognize or spell words is rote memorization. Yet, rote memorization is tedious and fallible at best, and there are far too many words to be learned.

Developing phonemic awareness does not eliminate the need for phonics instruction. Children must still be taught the patterns and conventions of their language's spelling system and also to attend to those patterns and conventions in their own reading and writing. Even so, children who approach

phonics with an awareness of the phonemic structure of language and a solid familiarity with the letters are found to learn letter-sound correspondences easily and to begin to use them independently to read and write. Similarly, for children who understand the essential logic of the alphabetic system, spelling and decoding instruction is more effective as well. Thus, programs of games and activities designed to develop phonemic awareness are repeatedly shown to result in significant acceleration of children's subsequent reading and writing achievement (e.g., Ball & Blachman, 1991; Bradley & Bryant, 1983; Byrne & Fielding-Barnsley, 1989, 1991; Lundberg, Frost, & Peterson, 1988).

Myth 6 and The Reality

Myth 6. Phonics instruction is a sufficient basis for children to learn to read and spell words well.

Reality. Teachers often observe students in upper elementary grades, middle school, and high school who actually know phonics, and may have even been trained in phonological awareness, but who are reading at a primary level. Their phonological knowledge helps them decode only phonetically regular words of one syllable. Readers require other word attack strategies for the longer words found in upper grade literature and textbooks. Therefore, we must think of the decoding/spelling curriculum extending beyond the primary grades and incorporating strategies for learning longer words.

The continuum extends the teaching of decoding and spelling to two additional elements of English word structure. Understanding frequently used syllable patterns as well as morpheme patterns (the meaning units in words consisting of compound forms, prefixes, suffixes, and roots) provide additional strategies for decoding unfamiliar multisyllabic words. When teachers instruct children across such a continuum, all students benefit including those learning English as a second language and those with specific learning disabilities (Henry, Calfee, & LaSalle, 1989).

Syllable Patterns

Syllables refer to units of spoken language consisting of a single uninterrupted sound formed by a vowel or vowel digraph alone or combined with one or more consonants. Johnson and Baumann (1984) reviewed research on syllabication and concluded that results remain mixed concerning the effectiveness of syllabication instruction. However, when placed in the context of the decoding/spelling continuum, syllabication does offer an alternative strategy for decoding longer, unfamiliar words, especially those words that do not contain affixes and roots.

Moats (1995) noted that children with spelling difficulties benefit from learning the basic syllable types. She concluded that benefits occur because

> redundant patterns in longer words can be much more quickly discerned; another is that the rules for adding endings to words and the way in which syllables are combined into longer words depend on the type of syllable(s) in the word; and finally, spellings become more predictable when the type of syllable is taken into account. (p. 101)

Hanna, Hodges, and Hanna (1971) suggested syllabication be taught as an inductive approach rather than by rote memorization of rules. By examining lists of words, students can form their own rules (e.g., *tennis, grammar, napkin,* = 2 consonants preceded by a short vowel: divide between the consonants).

Activities for encouraging syllable division include counting the number of syllables in words of 2 to 5 syllables, discussing possible syllable division points, dividing multisyllabic words while reading them, and spelling words, being sure to count syllables before writing and saying each syllable while writing.

The most common syllable patterns are shown in Table 1. Students in grade two should be introduced to the VC/CV pattern; third graders need to understand V/CV, VC/V, and /consonant -le patterns. Only older students need to learn the V/VC patterns.

Knowing these six common patterns for dividing words into syllables makes words easier to read and to spell. When spelling, students should sound out syllable-by-syllable. In this way words like *artichoke, remember,* and *populate* can readily be spelled. When the schwa sound in an unaccented syllable causes problems (e.g., *invitation, excellent*), students should

try to figure out the base word (i.e., *invite* and *excel*) to better hear the appropriate vowel sound. Obviously, in the words invitation and excellent, students will also benefit by knowing the suffixes *-tion* and *-ent*.

Morpheme Patterns

Possibly the most important strategy for decoding and spelling is often overlooked in instructional programs. Morpheme patterns, the meaning units within words, make up hundreds of thousands of words in English. Morphemes are the constituent words in compound words, and also the prefixes, suffixes, and root words. Students need to know that depending on the language origin of a word, base and root words either compound or affix. The majority of English words have either Anglo-Saxon, Latin, or Greek origins.

Several researchers have studied students' acquisition of morphological knowledge as well as the ability to use this knowledge in spelling (Bruck & Waters, 1990; Carlisle, 1987; Scott, 1992). All found that good readers and good spellers exhibit better morphological knowledge than poor readers and spellers. They suggest that by being able to read more, better readers acquire knowledge of morphological patterns and word families. Bruck and Waters (1990), studying the nature of the relationship between reading and spelling skills, suggested that reading experiences may provide a foundation for those spelling tasks that involve "higher levels of linguistic knowledge, especially those involving use and knowledge of morphological information" (p. 201). The findings also suggest that explicit teaching of morphological patterns may be useful, especially to students with reading disabilities.

Adams (1990) found it useful to both spell and understand meaning of words by looking at morphological clues (e.g., the common *fid* in *confidence, fidelity, fiduciary,* and *bona fide*). She acknowledged, however, that "it is also my impression that such insights are never automatic. The only way I seem to discover such relations is by consciously looking for them" (p. 155).

Henry (1988, 1989) found that teaching the common morpheme patterns within the context of language origins brought marked gains not only in morphological knowledge, but also in decoding and spelling ability. (See Henry [1993] for a review of research on morphological instruction.)

Torneus (1990) in Sweden and Elbro (1990) and Elbro and Ambak (1996) in Denmark studied young children's morphological awareness, most extensively in using inflected endings. Both noted that to

TABLE 1	Common Syllable Patterns	
LABEL	PATTERN	EXAMPLES
Closed (short vowel)	VC/CV	rabbit, interruption
Open (long vowel)	V/CV	hobo, vacation
Closed	VC/V	solid, limit
Consonant -le	/Consonant -le	tumble, bugle
Unstable digraph	V/VC	theater, hierarchy
Non-digraph	V/VC	triumph, diary

use morphemes as decoding units, the student must have developed awareness of morphemes. Torneus hypothesized that while metaphonological skills are related to the very first phases of reading development, "when the child has developed metaphonological skills and masters the basic decoding rules, the relationship between reading and morphological awareness is expected to become more pronounced" (p. 157). She concluded that in grade 3, reading skill is for the first time related to metamorphological ability and that later phases of reading development seem to be dependent upon abilities other than metaphonological ability.

Elbro (1990) studied disabled readers and hypothesized that readers have "a third possibility in decoding a word—apart from whole-word recognition and letter-level recoding—namely, an analysis and synthesis in morphemes" (p. 122). He noted that the morphemic principle acts to preserve the spelling of morphemes independently of context and phonemic alternations.

Anglo-Saxon morphemes. Anglo-Saxon based words can be characterized by being the short, everyday words found commonly in both elementary and secondary text. One can see that Anglo-Saxon words both regularly compound and affix. The compound words combine short Anglo-Saxon words to create new words (e.g., flashlight, railroad). Words also can be expanded by affixing beginnings and endings to the common Anglo-Saxon base word (e.g., unlikely, forgetful).

Anglo-Saxon base words often compound to form words such as flashlight, lamppost, and pigtails. In addition, these base words often affix by adding common prefixes and suffixes (e.g., *like, unlike, unlikely*). Common affixes can be introduced as early as mid-second grade.

Un-, in-, dis-, mis-, re-, be-, and *de-* are among the first prefixes to be learned. These units can be taught with their corresponding meaning. (For a sequence for introducing morphemes, see Henry, 1990, and Henry & Redding, 1996.)

Suffixes may hold specific meaning, but they are often grammatical markers. Early suffixes to learn include *-ing, -er, -ed, -less, -ful,* and *-ly*. While the meanings of the adjective endings *-less* and *-full* are clear, the meanings of -ed and -ly are not (i.e., -ed marks a past tense verb and -ly an adverb).

Students begin reading and spelling of those words for which the spelling is straightforward. Words like *heating, speller, milked,* and *blameless* require no special rules. However, adding suffixes to many base words requires knowing three basic suf-fix-addition rules: (a) the one-syllable doubling rule, (b) the silent e rule, and (c) the final y rule. Words of one syllable, ending in one consonant preceded by one vowel, must double the final consonant when adding a suffix beginning with a vowel. For example, *hot–hotter, step–stepping*. Base words ending in a silent *e* drop the final *e* when adding suffixes beginning with a vowel (e.g., *blame, blaming,* but *blameless*). The final *y* rule requires the speller to change the *y* to *i* when the *y* is preceded by a consonant, and the suffix begins with any letter except *i* (e.g., *try, tried,* but *trying*).

Latin morphemes. Brown (1947) noted that 80% of the English words borrowed from other languages come to us from Latin and Greek and make up approximately 60% of our language. He analyzed Latin and Greek word roots and concluded that 12 Latin and 2 Greek roots in combination with 20 of the most frequently used prefixes would generate an estimated 100,000 words. He designed an instructional program for building vocabulary for college content area reading based on these roots and prefixes.

Romance words, comprised primarily of words of Latin and French origin, usually affix to bound roots (meaningless when they stand alone, as the *rupt* in *disruption)*. The reader will notice that neither the root nor the affix stands alone (e.g., *interrupted, transmitting, prevention)*. The root generally receives the primary accent. Bound roots remain constant as prefixes and suffixes are added (e.g., the *vis* in *vision, visible, invisible, visionary, visual, television, revise*). Henderson (1990) noted that this constancy clarifies the spelling of many unaccented syllable (or schwa) patterns such as *divide-division, serene-serenity, confide-confidential, local-locality,* and *compete-competition*. Beyond the schwa, letter-sound correspondences are quite regular. Indeed, the troublesome vowel digraphs found in words of Anglo-Saxon origin are rare in Latin-based words. That is one reason students learn roots relatively easily when they know basic consonant and vowel sounds.

Because each root holds specific meaning, learning the Latin roots and corresponding prefixes and suffixes enhances not only decoding and spelling but vocabulary as well. Learning Latin roots such as *form, port, rupt, spect, struct, tract, scrib/script, dic/dict,* and *vers/vert* are extremely useful for students studying for the PSAT and SAT.

Greek morphemes. Words of Greek origin compound two roots, or combine forms, rather than affix (e.g., example *tele + graph, phon + ology,* and *anthro +*

pod). Greene (1967) noted that the Greek root *pseudo* forms the beginning of more than 800 words in an unabridged dictionary! Greek-based words are often found in words appearing largely in scientific texts (e.g., microscope, hemisphere, physiology). Letter-sound correspondences are similar to those used in Anglo-Saxon and Latin based words, but words of Greek origin frequently use the sounds of ph, ch, and y found in *chlorophyll*.

With approximately 25 prefixes, 40 suffixes, 50 Latin roots, and 50 Greek roots creating many thousands of words, teaching these forms to all children makes excellent sense. Before teaching these word parts, however, the school psychologist or teacher should assess children's morphological knowledge. Although we know of no standardized instruments, test administrators can readily evaluate this knowledge by giving students lists of words containing various word parts. For example, students can be asked to circle the prefixes (e.g., in *misplace, return, belong, midlife*), the suffixes, the Latin word roots, and the Greek word roots in corresponding lists of words. Words that do not include the targeted word part should be included in each list.

Lesson Procedures

We suggest that in teaching letter-sound correspondences, syllable patterns, and morpheme patterns teachers use a discussion model. One such model has been described by Calfee and Henry (1985) and Calfee and Patrick (1996). Each lesson contains an opening, middle activities, closing, and follow-up activities. In the opening, teachers state the purpose and goals for the lesson and introduce a new concept, pattern, and/or generalization. During the middle segment of the lesson, students discuss word features as they read words fitting a specific pattern, generate new words, and spell numerous words fitting frequently used patterns. They often contrast this pattern to other similar patterns and become aware of how word structure influences spelling. To close the lesson, teacher and students summarize and reflect upon the lesson content, structural patterns, and procedures. Follow-up exercises promote reinforcement of the concepts. For example, students might look for Greek words based on their under-

standing of the features inherent in these words in their science texts, or look for affixes in the evening newspaper.

Appendix A provides an example of a lesson introducing students to several new Greek combining forms. This lesson would be taught after students become familiar with Anglo-Saxon and Latin morphemes. The lesson should be adapted for students' ability levels. That is, when teaching new roots to students with reading disabilities, present only 2 to 4 specific roots at a time.

A final unit could provide practice with strategies for analyzing long words for both decoding and spelling. Here students synthesize the information from previous units of instruction as they decode and spell long, unfamiliar words. Students follow the sequence used by most fluent readers. They first check for affixation and roots; if further analysis is necessary, then students look for syllable segments. Only if these two strategies fail, do students use letter-sound correspondences. As students spell dictated words, they repeat the word, listen for syllables, and try to identify common affixes and roots. Students are encouraged to use letter-sound correspondences only after they attempted the morpheme and syllable strategies.

CONCLUSION

Research proves that children must learn to recognize words quickly and accurately to read with fluency and comprehension. Because of this, instruction on decoding and spelling is very important for primary-grade students. Moreover, such instruction should be built on phonemic awareness, and it should be complemented and reinforced through use in reading and writing activities. Older children need to learn word recognition and spelling strategies that extend beyond phonics. These strategies include the ability to recognize syllable junctures, and to understand the form and meaning of common prefixes, suffixes, and roots. By developing students' word recognition and spelling abilities along this continuum, we can arm them with efficient, effective strategies for learning to read, spell, and understand most words in English.

REFERENCES

Adams, M. J. (1990). *Beginning to read: Thinking and learning about print*. Cambridge, MA: The MIT Press.

Adams, M. J., Treiman, R., & Pressley, M. (in press). Reading, writing, and literacy. In I. Sigel and A. Renninger (Eds.), *Mussen's handbook of child psychology,*

Volume 4: Child psychology in practice. New York: Wiley.

Arter, J. A., & Jenkins, J. R. (1979). Differential diagnosis—prescriptive teaching: A critical appraisal. *Review of Educational Research, 49*, 517–555.

Ball, E. W., & Blachman, B. A. (1991). Does phoneme awareness training in kindergarten make a difference in early word recognition and developmental spelling? *Reading Research Quarterly, 26,* 49–66.

Bradley, L., & Bryant, P. E. (1983). Categorizing sounds and learning to read—a causal connection. *Nature, 301,* 419–421.

Brown, J. L. (1947). Reading and vocabulary: 14 master words. In M. J. Herzberg, (Ed.), *Word study* (pp. 1–4). Springfield, MA: Merriam.

Bruck, M., & Waters, G. S. (1990). An analysis of the component spelling and reading skills of good readers-good spellers, good readers-poor spellers, and poor readers-poor spellers. In T. H. Carr & B. A. Levy (Eds.), *Reading and its development* (pp. 161–206). San Diego: Academic Press.

Byrne, B., & Fielding-Barnsley, R. (1989). Phonemic awareness and letter knowledge in the child's acquisition of the alphabetic principle. *Journal of Educational Psychology, 81,* 313–321.

Byrne, B., & Fielding-Barnsley, R. (1991). Evaluation of a program to teach phonemic awareness to young children. *Journal of Educational Psychology, 83,* 451–455.

Calfee, R. C., & Henry, M. K. (1986). Project READ: An inservice model for training classroom teachers in effective reading instruction. In J. V. Hoffman (Ed.), *The effective teaching of reading: Research into practice* (pp. 199–229). Newark, DE: International Reading Association.

Calfee, R. C., & Patrick, C. L. (1995). *Teach our children well.* Stanford, CA: Stanford University Alumni Association.

Carlisle, J. F. (1987). The use of morphological knowledge in spelling derived forms by learning-disabled and normal students. *Annals of Dyslexia, 37,* 90–108.

Cunningham, A. E., & Stanovich, K. E. (1991). Tracking the unique effects of print exposure in children: Associations with vocabulary, general knowledge, and spelling. *Journal of Educational Psychology, 83,* 264–274.

Elbro, C. (1990). *Differences in dyslexia.* Copenhagen: Munksgaard International.

Elbro, C., & Arnbak, E. (1996). The role of morpheme recognition and morphological awareness in dyslexia. *Annals of Dyslexia, 46,* 209–240.

Greene, A. (1967). *Word clues.* Evanston, IL: Harper & Row.

Hanna, P. R., Hodges, R. E., & Hanna, J. S. (1971). *Spelling: Structure and strategies.* Boston: Houghton-Mifflin.

Henderson, E. H. (1990). *Teaching spelling* (2nd ed.). Boston: Houghton-Mifflin.

Henry, M. K. (1988). Understanding English orthography: Assessment and instruction for decoding and spelling. *Dissertation Abstracts International, 48,* 2841A. (University Microfilms No. 88-00-951)

Henry, M. K. (1989). Children's word structure knowledge: Implications for decoding and spelling instruction. *Reading and Writing, 2,* 135–152.

Henry, M. K. (1990). *WORDS: Integrated decoding and spelling instruction based on word origin and word structure.* Austin, TX: Pro-Ed.

Henry, M. K. (1993). Morphological structure: Latin and Greek roots and affixes as upper grade code strategies. *Reading and Writing, 5*(2), 227–241.

Henry, M. K., Calfee, R. C., & LaSalle, R. A. (1989). A structural approach to decoding and spelling. In S. McCormick & J. Zutell (Eds.), *Thirty-eighth yearbook of the National Reading Conference* (pp. 155–163). Chicago: National Reading Conference.

Henry, M. K., & Redding, N. C. (1996). *Patterns for success in reading and spelling.* Austin, TX: Pro-Ed.

Johnson, D. D., & Baumann, J. F. (1984). Word identification. In P. D. Pearson (Ed.), *Handbook of reading research* (pp. 583–608). New York: Longman.

Just, M. A., & Carpenter, P. A. (1987). *The psychology of reading and language comprehension.* Boston: Allyn & Bacon.

Liberman, I. Y., & Liberman, A. M. (1990). Whole language vs. code emphasis: Underlying assumptions and their implications for reading instruction. *Annals of Dyslexia, 40,* 51–76.

Lovett, M., Ransby, M. J., & Barron, R. W. (1988). Treatment subtype and word type effects in dyslexic children's response to remediation. *Brain and Language, 34,* 328–349.

Lovett, M. W., Ransby, M. J., Hardwick, N., Johns, M. S., & Donaldson, S. A. (1989). Can dyslexia be treated? Treatment specific and generalized treatment effects in dyslexic children's response to remediation. *Brain and Language, 37,* 90–121.

Lundberg, I., Frost, J., & Petersen, O. P. (1988). Effects of an extensive program for stimulating phonological awareness in preschool children. *Reading Research Quarterly, 23,* 263–284.

Moats, L. C. (1995). *Spelling: Development, disability and instruction.* Baltimore: York Press.

Patterson, K. E., & Coltheart, V. (1987). Phonological processes in reading: A tutorial review. In M. Coltheart (Ed.), *Attention and performance XII: The psychology of reading* (pp. 421–447). London: Erlbaum.

Rack, J. P., Snowling, M. J., & Olson, R. K. (1992). The nonword reading deficit in developmental dyslexia: A review. *Reading Research Quarterly, 27,* 28–53.

Rayner, K., and Pollatsek, A. (1989). *The psychology of reading.* Hillsdale, NJ: Erlbaum.

Reitsma, P. (1989). Orthographic memory and learning to read. In P. G. Aaron & R. M. Joshi (Eds.), *Reading and writing disorders in different orthographic systems* (pp. 51–73). The Netherlands: Kluwer.

Scott, R. (1992, April). *Spelling and reading strategies of seventh grade good readers/good spellers, good readers/poor spellers, and poor readers/poor spellers.* Paper presented at the annual meeting of the American Educational Research Association, San Francisco.

Stahl, S. W. (1988). Is there evidence to support matching reading styles and initial reading methods? A reply to Carbo. *Phi Delta Kappan, 70,* 317–322.

Torneus, M. (1990).The importance of metaphonological and metamorphological abilities for different phases of reading development. In G. T. Pavlidis (Ed.), *Perspectives on Dyslexia* (Vol. 2). New York: Wiley.

Vernon, M. D. (1971). *Reading and its difficulties.* Cambridge: Cambridge University Press.

Webster's ninth new collegiate dictionary. (1989). Springfield, MA: Merriam-Webster.

APPENDIX A

Opening: Discuss reasons for learning Greek word roots (combining forms) and relevance to reading, spelling, and writing.

Middle Activities: As you introduce the combining forms, have students write each form in a notebook with its meaning. Introduce

micro (small)	bio (life)
meter (measure)	scope (watch, see)
therm (heat)	hydro (water)

Students generate words containing phon, photo, ology, graph-gram, tele (all taught in a previous lesson), therm, bio, meter, micro, and hydro

Students read words such as

microscope	microgram	microphone
micrometer	speedometer	pedometer
barometer	audiometer	thermometer
thermal	thermostat	thermodynamics
biology	biography	autobiography
hydroscope	telescope	autobiographical
hydrogen	hydrophone	hydrostat

Students read the following sentences. (Note both Latin and Greek word parts.)

The biography contained unusual dialogue.

The automobile's speedometer and thermostat needed repair.

Oxygen and carbon dioxide are necessary for respiration.

Students spell the following sentences:

The biologist wrote his autobiography.

The instructor used a microphone to transmit his message.

The telescopic lens suggested temperature changes in space.

Set the thermometer to a comfortable temperature.

Closing: Discuss relevance of Greek roots to science and math text reading and scientific writing.

Follow-up: Find Greek roots in this week's assignment in students' science textbook.

(Adapted from Henry & Redding, 1996)

SELF-STUDY QUESTIONS

Multiple Choice

1. According to the authors, which of the following is NOT true?
   a. Once children have learned to read, they no longer need instruction in word structure.
   b. Even highly skilled readers mentally process individual words when they read.
   c. Some children have difficulty learning phonics skills.
   d. Learning phonics skills depends on phonemic awareness.
2. Which of the following recommendations could be derived from this article?
   a. Beginning readers should be encouraged to use context clues to guess what an unfamiliar word is.
   b. Older children can benefit from learning about the morphemic structure of words.
   c. When children have problems learning to read, teachers should not use phonics methods to try to help them.
   d. If left to their own devices, children will figure out word structures on their own.

Essay

1. Summarize what this article suggests about the role of a reader's ability to decode and understand individual words in the reading comprehension process.
2. How does the article suggest teachers can best facilitate students' comprehension of individual written words?

MIDDLE CHILDHOOD

"Social Risks and Psychological Adjustment: A Comparison of African American and South African Children"

OVERVIEW

This article illustrates the difference between race and culture. To distinguish between the two, it is necessary to hold race constant across two or more cultures. The authors accomplished this by comparing black South African to African American school-aged children. They compared the two both in terms of developmental outcomes and with respect to family structure variables such as the presence of an adult male in the home. Their findings suggest that black-white differences within the United States are more likely to represent cultural variations than biological race.

METHODOLOGY

A variety of strategies were used to measure family variables such as structure, poverty, and social class. Children's problem behavior (e.g., inappropriate use of aggression) was rated by parents using an instrument that had been used in previous studies. After compiling the data, the researchers used a statistical technique called *multiple analysis of variance (MANOVA)* to identify relationships among the variables. This kind of analysis also allowed the researchers to identify interactions among variables. An interaction occurs when two variables are related under one condition, or in one situation, but not another. For example, one interaction question these researchers examined was whether the effects of poverty were the same in both cultures.

GLOSSARY TERM

- **Hollingshead system**   a technique for categorizing socioeconomic status that takes into account several variables (e.g., education, type of job) as well as income

Oscar A. Barbarin

Social Risks and Psychological Adjustment: A Comparison of African American and South African Children

In the United States, race is highly associated with social risk factors such as poverty and family structure that may account by themselves for developmental outcomes often attributed to race alone. This cross-national study assesses the effects of social risks on adjustment of racially similar groups of 306 African American and 625 South African 6-year-olds. Poverty and gender were confirmed as risk factors but single female headship was not. Moreover, poverty and gender posed less risk for South African than for African American children. Poverty placed children at risk for immaturity, hyperactivity, and difficulty in peer relations. Boys were more likely to have behavior problems than were girls. African Americans exhibited higher rates of emotional symptoms but lower rates of bullying, destructiveness, and social rejection than did South Africans. African Americans, particularly the males, scored higher on the opposition and hyperactivity scales than did South Africans. Distinctive social contexts and cultural resources may account for differences in adjustment.

INTRODUCTION

Considerable evidence links social risk factors such as poverty, gender, and family structure to a range of adverse psychological outcomes in children (Brooks-Gunn & Duncan, 1997; Costello, 1989). For example, emotional distress, behavioral disorders, and cognitive deficits have all been associated with poverty (Capaldi & Patterson, 1994; Werner & Smith, 1989). The magnitude of the impact of poverty, however, appears to differ considerably by psychological domain. The largest effects are observed for cognitive development and academic achievement (McLoyd, 1998). In the same vein, Brooks-Gunn, & Duncan (1997) report data in which effect sizes of poverty are greatest for cognitive functioning, followed by behavioral functioning, and then emotional functioning. Moreover, even though poor children are more likely than non-poor children to present with symptoms of emotional distress and behavioral problems, poverty is inconsistently associated with higher-than-expected rates of diagnosable mental disorders as defined by the DSM IV criteria (Gore, Aseltine, & Coldon, 1993; Hammen & Rudolph, 1996; Whitaker et al., 1990). Recent studies also show that the effects of poverty are more per-vasive and detrimental when poverty is chronic or when it occurs early in the life of the child than when it is acute, temporary, or first appears after the child has reached adolescence (McLoyd, 1998).

Gender is another widely recognized risk factor for psychological problems. Compared to girls, boys are more likely to exhibit deficits in regulation of behavior and attention (Offord, Alder, & Boyle, 1986). They are more often conduct-disordered and under-controlled and are more aggressive than girls. Alternatively, girls are more likely than boys to encounter problems of emotion regulation such as irritability, depression, anxiety, and mood swings. The social risks identified in broadly representative samples of American children appear to operate in similar ways within specific populations such as African Americans. For example, Barbarin & Soler (1993) observed, in a nationally representative sample of African American children, that young boys under 12 years of age were more likely than young girls to act impulsively, exhibit anger, break things, be withdrawn, feel worthless, have problems concentrating, be disobedient, and have problems getting along with adults. At the same time, children from single adult households tend to have more symptoms of anxiety-depression, oppositional behavior, immaturity, and difficulties with peers than children living in two-adult and multi-generational households (Barbarin & Soler, 1993).

Race, too, has come to be viewed as a social risk factor for problems of achievement and psychological adjustment. A growing body of comparative research reveals what has been identified as the "race gap" in educational achievement (Frederick D. Patterson Research Institute, 1997). In addition, African Americans fare more poorly than do other racial groups on a host of psychological indicators. In spite of methodological limitations and conceptual problems associated with the use of race as an independent variable in the social sciences, the empirical basis of our understanding of the psychological and developmental status of African American children rests largely on a foundation of Black–White comparative research. For example, alarm about emotional and behavioral functioning arises from the comparatively higher rates of anxiety, depressive symptoms, and conduct problems found for African American children than for White children (Garrison, Jackson, Marsteller, McKeown, & Addy, 1990; Neal, Lilly, & Zakis, 1993; Ollendick, 1983). Comparative data on academic status of African American children paints a similar portrait of suboptimal functioning (Lyons, 1996; Stevenson, Chen, & Uttal, 1990). Although African American and White children do not differ in reading competence in the first grade, by third grade they have significantly lower reading scores than do White children (Wood, Felton, Flowers, & Naylor, 1991). The gap widens so quickly that by fourth grade only 31% of African American children score at or above the proficient level in reading, as compared to 71% of White students (Frederick D. Patterson Research Institute, 1997).

A variety of explanations have arisen in the public discourse about race to account for the comparatively poor outcomes of African American children. Some explanations such as genetic inferiority, inadequate moral guidance, and self-marginalizing underclass values (e.g., Herrnstein & Murray, 1994) have been widely discredited. The validity of these accounts specifically and the interpretability of conclusions from Black–White comparative designs more generally have been questioned on both conceptual and methodological grounds (Foster & Martinez, 1995; Kincheloe, Steinberg, & Gresson, 1996; Suzuki & Valencia, 1997). Conceptually, comparative studies rarely specify whether race refers to biological, cultural, or social categories. Claims for a biological explanation seem indefensible on several grounds. Methodologically, assignment to a racial group is frequently unreliable. Few studies employ an explicit verifiable procedure and rely instead on interviewer assignment based most often on observations of skin color and hair texture or on self-designations by research participants. Although self-designation is ac-

ceptable for studies which treat race as a social construct, this method provides an inadequate basis from which to draw conclusions that involve biological and genetic interpretations of race.

Because within-group genetic variability is as great as, if not greater than, between-group variation, genetic explanations do not offer a credible account of racial differences in development, particularly in light of more compelling alternatives (Kincheloe et al., 1996). Plausible explanations of the findings from racially comparative studies include poverty, stress, and stigma resulting from encounters with racist attitudes and behaviors, and the many adverse sequelae in family and community life associated with economic disadvantage (Halpern-Felsher et al., 1997). Brooks-Gunn and Duncan (1997) point out that poverty defined only in terms of low family income does not entirely explain the differences observed in child functioning. Instead, they argue, the relationship between poverty and children's outcomes may be mediated by additional factors in the community and in the family such as female headship and mother's age and educational attainment. Thus, differences between Black and White children in academic achievement and mental health may arise, for example, from family processes, from social denigration and marginalization of Blacks, or from high concentrations of poverty in Black communities that result in unequal access to resources and opportunities (Nielsen, 1997). To complicate matters even more, among African Americans, race is treated not simply as a biological/genetic category but also as a sociocultural category that implies a distinctive set of ethnic group values or world views (e.g., see Jagers & Mock, 1993). Effects of these putative cultural dispositions overlap with and are difficult to distinguish from the effects on children's socialization attributed to differences in economic status and social class. Thus, for African Americans, socially denigrated racial categorizations, racial identities infused with cultural meanings, and economic and political inequalities are inextricably bound. Consequently, interpretations of Black–White comparative research often do not distribute effects accurately among plausible sources that include: 1) race as a biological/genetic category, 2) race as a sociocultural category, 3) inequality of resources due to social denigration and racism, and 4) social risks related to economic status or family structure. Research intended to illuminate the effects of one of these factors without controlling for the effects of the others will be mired in ambiguity. Consequently, the use of White children as a solo comparison group in studies of African American children is a conceptually ambiguous and flawed strategy. This is an especially relevant issue in the case of phenomena that are likely to be influenced by income and social inequality, or in which questions of cultural processes are the focus of scholarly inquiry. Developmental researchers are unlikely to resist the appeal of comparative designs. Nevertheless, it seems wise to select and devise comparisons which strengthen explanatory power by minimizing or avoiding these problematic confounds.

Designs comparing one ethnic minority group with another is one approach to this problem that has been used with increasing frequency, because it offers controls for economic disadvantage and a history of social denigration. An equally attractive option involves a cross-national comparative design which draws economically diverse samples from identical racial groups residing in two or more nations. Accordingly, selection of South African Blacks as a comparison group to explore the effects of social risk factors on psychological and academic development of African American children is fortuitous, first because this design controls for race as a biological category, and second because such a comparison controls for the experience of discrimination and social stigma. Even a cursory examination of the social and historical conditions endured by urban South Africans reveals striking parallels to the situation of African Americans. For example, in South Africa 40% of Black families live below the poverty level in contrast to 1% of Whites. In the United States, approximately 46% of Black children live in poverty compared to only 14% of White children. The relative economic disadvantage endured by South Africans and African Americans can be traced to a history of racial oppression that is fueled by educational inequality and sustained by extraordinarily high rates of unemployment. As a consequence, both groups suffer inordinately from hunger, nutritional deficiencies, inadequate housing, cycles of rural-urban migration, degradation of physical environment, exposure to pollution and toxins, and unequal access to health care (Barbarin & Khomo, 1997). The social challenges and community problems confronting South Africans resonate within African American communities: rising numbers of children born to unmarried women living in poverty, concerns about crime and violence, child abuse and neglect, and spiraling rates of substance abuse which tear apart the fabric of family life (Richter, 1994).

Depending on the sampling design, cross-national comparisons which hold constant the variable of racial categorization can facilitate testing of the impact of cultural resources or social risk factors on children's adjustment. For example, the effects on development of risks associated with material inadequacy or parental marital status can be distinguished from effects of membership in a stigmatized group by comparing children from groups that have similar histories of racial discrimination. By minimizing the confound of racial group identity and economic status, this approach offers a more stringent test of the effects of poverty or of being raised in a single adult household headed by an unmarried mother. In this way, cross-national comparison of African American and South African children is an attractive option.

Although the similarities are substantial, significant differences are also noted between African Americans and South African-Blacks with respect to family life, history, culture, geography, language, minority status, and experience of colonization. A subtle but important difference is that, unlike African Americans, South African Blacks constitute an overwhelming majority in their own country where they make up approximately 79% of the South African population of 37.5 million. Majority status may afford Black South Africans a psychological advantage not enjoyed by African Americans. In addition, Black South Africans organize themselves into ethnic, clan, and family groupings which forge a common identity through shared languages, traditions, and ideologies. These ethnic group identifications bring with them culturally defined views, for example, of childhood and gender roles that are reflected in socialization goals, discipline, and expectations of unquestioning compliance with parental, familial, and male authority (Richters, 1993). The ability to control for racial categorization and discrimination in comparisons between South Africans and African Americans opens the possibility of testing the independent effects of social risks and resources on children's psychological development.

RESEARCH QUESTIONS

The extent to which factors identified as social risks in the United States have similar effects in other national contexts is unclear. For example, growing up as a black, poor, and female child of an unmarried mother may involve a different experience and have different significance in South Africa than in the United States. These differences, in turn, may augment or attenuate the hazards associated with gender, poverty, and family structure. With respect to racial group identity, being among the majority may convey to Black South Africans a psychological advantage in the form of self-efficacy and hope not enjoyed by African Americans. Perhaps majority status confers protection against the effects of racially based social and economic inequality on emotional and behavioral problems. In light of the majority status and cultural differences, will the consequences of economic status, family structure, and gender for behavioral, emotional, and academic functioning be the same for South African Blacks as it is for African American children growing up in the United States? The cross-national comparisons undertaken here offer the advantage of controlling for socioeconomic status and racial subordination, thus making possible a clearer test of the relation of psychological adjustment to other social risks and cultural resources.

METHOD

Participants include a sample of 625 Black children representative of the Birth-to-Ten longitudinal study cohort from the Black townships within the metropolitan area of Johannesburg, South Africa, and 306 African American children selected as part of a nationally representative sample of American children. All children were between 5 and 6 years old at the time of interview.

Sample 1: African American Sample and Data Collection Procedure

Data from the African American sample reported in this paper were collected as part of the 1988 National Health Interview Survey, the Child Health Supplement (NHIS-CHS), under the auspices of the United States Department of Health and Human Services, the National Center for Health Statistics (National Center for Health Statistics, 1988). The National Health Interview Survey (NHIS) provided a summary of the child's physical and social development and targeted, specifically, symptoms of physical illness, emotional difficulties, and behavioral disorders. The purpose of the NHIS was to gather information about physical developmental and psychological conditions of children. Trained project staff visited children's homes to conduct face-to-face interviews with parents or parental surrogates. They posed structured questions on health status, school adjustment, problems of learning, and psychological functioning. The information was used to identify service needs of children and their families. Additional information was gathered on household composition; demographic status of the biological mother, father, and primary care taker; and data related to pregnancy, birth, and child care. The universe of the sample was a civilian noninstitutionalized population of the 50 states and the District of Columbia. The sampling methodology involved a multistage probability sample from 1,924 geographically defined primary sampling units. When more than one child resided in a selected household, a single target child was randomly selected from each household. The resulting

sample is therefore a representative sample of the population of the United States, with a large national probability sample of African American children aged 0 to 17 years.

Sample 2: South African Sample and Data Collection Procedure

The South African data were collected as part of the Birth-to-Ten study (BTT), a longitudinal study of the effects of urbanization on physical growth and psychological development (Richter, Yach, Cameron, Griesel, & deWet, 1995). The group of children whose data are reported here represent a subgroup of children primarily from Black townships. The entire sample was a prospective birth cohort of all children born in the seven-week period from March 23 to May 7, 1990 in the Johannesburg-Soweto metropolitan area. The sampling procedure and its outcome are described in greater detail elsewhere (Barbarin & Khomo, 1997). Mothers or primary caregivers of the children were recruited into the study at several different points until the cohort reached the age of 1 year. Extensive data on physical growth, psychological development, and family life were collected in data waves in 1992, 1994, and 1995. The data reported here were collected between January and April 1996 by trained interviewers fluent in a variety of languages spoken by Black South Africans in the Guateng Province: Zulu, South Sothto, Tswana, Xhosa, English, and Afrikaans. Interviews were conducted by five trained multilingual community residents who had experience in collecting similar data from prior BTT panels.

MEASURES
Poverty Index

To assess the effects of material hardship on children's behavioral and emotional adjustment, indices of poverty were assessed for each family. In both the United States and South Africa, standards have been developed by the national government which are sensitive to a local context for assessing material hardship and poverty (U.S. Bureau of the Census, 1993; Bureau of Market Research, 1995). For the sample in the United States, the United States government poverty standard was utilized; children falling at or below the poverty line were designated as poor, and those falling above it were designated as not poor. Generally these guidelines are based on the amount of funds needed to provide a minimally adequate food supply plus a small allowance for housing and other costs. The most recent poverty line for a family of four—two adults and two children—is approximately $14,000. In the African American sample, 44% of the children live below the poverty line. For the most part, the social and economic conditions in South Africa—characterized by high unemployment (estimated by the World Bank at 40%), low wage rates, and nonmonetary methods of consumption—were emphasized in poverty designations. Therefore, consumption rather than income was used to estimate economic status and assign South African families to poverty groups (Barbarin & Khomo, 1997). Consumption was measured in terms of expenditures for housing, utilities, appliances, and transportation. In our South Africa sample, 57% of the children lived in households which were at or below the median consumption level for our urban sample. For the purposes of this study these children were designated as *the poor.*

Family structure index. Previous research suggests that several key family structures may account for significant differences related to levels of behavioral and emotional adjustment; one of the key factors is whether the parent is the single adult in the household or has a partner to aid in parenting. This variable is used to test the effects of family structure. Single parents are those who live with dependent children with no other adults in the household. For both the South African and African American samples, the majority of single adults were women; only 5% were men, mostly fathers and a few grandfathers. The female solo parents consisted of mothers, grandmothers, and aunts. While most of the multiple-adult households consisted of biological mothers and fathers, household constellations also included grandparents or aunts and their spouses, or mothers and their mothers or sisters.

Behavior problem index. The Behavior Problem Index (BPI; Zill, 1985) was developed for the NHIS and used as an index of significant behavioral problems with clinical cutoff scores (total raw score of 14, or 90th percentile) that effectively differentiated between children referred and those not referred for mental health services (Bussing, Halfon, Benjamin, & Wells, 1995). Items were selected by a group of developmental consultants from extant screening tools assessing behavior and emotional adjustment of children aged 4 years and older (Achenbach, Howell, Quay, & Conners, 1991). The evidence supporting the construct validity and reliability of the BPI scales is substantial (Peterson & Zill, 1986; Zill, 1985). Subscales for the BPI were developed using a principle components analysis of items. The factor analysis yielded five scales made up of the sum of

constituent items scored 0 or 1. Estimates of internal consistency average about .85 for young children (Bussing et al., 1995). The scales are as follows

> *Anxiety/depression* includes symptoms normally categorized under the rubric of internalizing disorders. They refer generally to emotional agitation and disturbances of mood or affect. This scale contains five items: mood changes, feeling unloved, fearfulness, worthlessness, and sadness.
>
> *Immaturity* is a four-item scale that refers to excessive dependence on others, particularly adults. It is suggestive of a lack of self-assurance. High scores in this item suggest a lack of autonomy and overly dependent behavior.
>
> *Oppositional behavior* assesses treated disposition, best characterized as difficult to control and influence. Scores indicate the extent to which the child is noncompliant. This scale contains six items: stubbornness, strong temper, disobedience at home, disobedience at school, arguing, and being high strung.
>
> *Hyperactivity* assesses the constellation of behavioral symptoms—such as difficulty in concentration and maintaining cognitive focus—so often associated with attention deficit disorder. It also includes heightened activity and inability to inhibit or control movement that is synonymous with hyperactivity. The scale contains five items pertaining to inability to concentrate, being easily confused, impulsivity, and restlessness.
>
> *Social problems* measures social withdrawal and problems in social functioning. The five items making up this scale assess shyness, social withdrawal, peer acceptance, and the extent to which the child is able to get along with other children.

The substantial cultural and linguistic differences between the United States and South Africa undoubtedly complicate issues of measurement and interpretation of findings. Consultation with a group of parents was undertaken to assess the clarity, sensitivity, and relevance of measures to parenting as construed by South Africans. Adaptations were made in language and content to address concerns identified in pilot studies prior to using these measures. For example, "to make a face" was substituted for "to pout" because the latter expression is not in common use among South African Blacks. (Questions used in the study are available from the author.) Typically, the BPI was completed by the mother or primary guardian. For each of the 25 BPI items included in this study, the respondent indicated whether it was often true, sometimes true, or not true of the target child. This study adopted a stringent scoring approach, summing up only those items for which the respondent indicated that it was often true, because by inference these represented the most serious manifestations of the symptom.

RESULTS

Demographic profiles. A comparison of the South African and African American samples suggests that they are relatively similar along a number of important dimensions. Statistical tests reveal no significant differences between the two groups with respect to gender composition, maternal education, and maternal employment. In both samples there is a relatively even distribution of males and females. With respect to parents, only one of five mothers in each sample had education beyond the high school level, and two of every three mothers described themselves as employed or seeking employment. However, South African mothers are significantly younger ($M = 25.1$, $SD = 6.4$) than the mothers of the African American sample ($M = 27.1$, $SD = 9.5$), $F(1, 928) = 13.3$, $p = .001$.

Hollingshead Social Class Factor scores were computed for households in both nations (Hollingshead, 1957). No differences were observed in the proportion of South African and African American households at the lowest end of the SES spectrum. Moreover, with the exception of Class I, the two samples have roughly the same proportion of households in each of the Hollingshead social class groupings. Over one third of both groups were assigned to the lowest Hollingshead social class. However, very few in the South African household sample are in the top social class (1), and about 1 in 10 African American families could be categorized as Class 1. Likewise, African American children were less likely than South African children to live in households that fell below the poverty lines of their respective countries. This may be due to the extraordinarily high rate of Black unemployment, large household size, and absence of a social welfare system for Blacks in South Africa.

With respect to family structure and household composition, there is again rough parity between the South African and African American samples. The two groups are equivalent with respect to the proportion of mothers who were married, and close in the proportion of households headed by single mothers. A much larger proportion of the South African mothers have never been married but live with partners. Although mothers in the South African sample are younger, the size of South African households is larger ($M = 7.2$, $SD = 3.4$) than the African American

families ($M = 4.1$, $SD = 1.7$), $F(1, 928) = 229.3$, $p = .001$. Significant differences between African American and South African samples occur with respect to nonmaternal figures residing in the household with mother and children. Grandmothers resided with mother and child in one of three South African families but in only one of five African American families. The significantly larger household size for South Africans is due not only to the larger number of dependent children but also to the greater likelihood of multiple generations living in the same home. Newly formed families find it increasingly difficult to obtain housing. By policy, the former apartheid government in South Africa constrained the supply of new housing in urban areas. Thus the high rate of multigenerational households resulted from a combination of poverty, acute housing shortages for urban Blacks, and historical cultural patterns of living arrangements such as family compounds in which extended family members live in close proximity. In spite of the comparatively lower marital rate for South African mothers, South African children were more likely than their African American counterparts to reside with a father figure. This may in fact represent both an acceptance of informal marriages and cohabitation among those who intend to marry but who cannot afford *Labola*[1] offerings to the woman's family, and the greater likelihood for multiple generations to reside in the same household. (See Table 1 for the demographic data for each sample.)

Hierarchical log linear analysis of symptom frequencies. Table 2 presents the results of the hierarchical log linear analysis which examined the relation of national origin and gender to the prevalence of behavioral and emotional symptoms among children in the study. In addition, the analysis tested the significance of the nation × gender interaction on the occurrence of symptoms. Children who do not have serious difficulties will occasionally exhibit many of these symptoms. Consequently, a conservative approach to scoring the items considers the symptom as contributing to a pattern of difficulty only when the parent indicates that it occurs often. Accordingly, the log linear analysis is applied to the responses, recoded so that "never occurs" and "sometimes occurs" become 0, and "often occurs" becomes 1.

Across both samples, high proportions of children were characterized as restless, squirming, and

---

[1]*Labola* are obligatory payments somewhat like dowries paid to the family of the bride. Traditionally these were in the form of cattle but in urban areas they took the form of cash payments or material goods.

TABLE 1	Demographic Profile of the African American and South African Samples		
	AFRICAN AMERICANS ($n = 306$)	SOUTH AFRICANS ($n = 625$)	χ^2
% Male	52.3%	49.6%	ns
Mother's education, less than high school	83.0%***	83.0%	
Mother in labor force	63.7%	65.9%	
Marital status			
Never married	40.4%	59.7%	
Widowed/divorced	23.9%	5.2%	$\chi^2 (2) = 73.6$**
Married	35.7%	35.1%	
Father figure in home	49.7%	60.3%	$\chi^2 (2) = 9.49$*
Grandmother in home	19.0%	32.8%	$\chi^2 (2) = 19.4$**
Single adult, female-headed household	39.2%	33.4%	
Hollingshead two-factor social class rating			
Class I (highest)	10.5%	.3%	
Class II	8.2%	13.0%	
Class III	18.3%	17.8%	
Class IV	26.1%	31.6%	
Class V (lowest)	36.9%	37.3%	
Percent living in poverty	44.1%	57.1%	$\chi^2 (2) = 13.8$**

*$p < .05$; **$p < .01$; **$p < .001$.

frequently demanding attention. The results of the partial χ^2 for the effects of national origin reveal significant differences on 17 of the 25 symptoms. African American children had higher prevalence rates than did the South Africans on 12 of the 17 items for which significant national origin effects were found, (viz., anxiety, nervousness, sadness, disobedience at home and school, temper tantrums, concentration problems, being confused, complaining about love, dependence, clinging to an adult, and crying without reason). South Africans, however, had higher prevalence rates for symptoms related to social and behavioral adjustment, such as breaking the rules, destroying others' possessions, bullying, not being liked by others, and demanding attention.

With respect to gender, boys more often than girls were rated as evidencing symptoms of disruptive behavior such as disobeying, breaking rules, acting impulsively, destroying others' possessions, and bullying or acting with cruelty. A significant interaction between national origin and gender was observed for problems of concentration. In this case, African American boys were much higher than any other group. Moreover, the differences in concentration between boys and girls in the South African sample were negligible, but African American boys were significantly more likely than African American girls to evidence concentration problems. A similar pattern obtains with respect to bullying behavior: African American boys scored significantly higher than did girls; South African boys and

girls were not different, and as a group their scores were higher than those of African Americans. A different pattern occurs with respect to feelings of worthlessness. African American girls and South African boys are more frequently rated as often feeling worthless. The exact opposite patterns occur for demanding attention, where the South African girls and African American boys are higher than their gender counterparts.

Multiple analysis of variance (MANOVA). The individual symptom items from the BPI combine linearly to comprise five distinct scales: anxiety/depression, immaturity, oppositional behavior, hyperactivity, and social problems. These five scales were entered as dependent variables into a MANOVA. The independent variables for this analysis included national origin, poverty status, and gender. When we tested the main effects and interactions, several factors emerged as significant on the test for overall multivariate effect. First, the overall multivariate F value for national origin was significant, $F(5, 918) = 14.02$, $p \leq .001$. Also significant were the main effects for poverty, multivariate $F(5, 918) = 3.98$, $p \leq .001$, and gender, multivariate $F(5, 918) = 2.47$, $p \leq .03$. Two interactions approached significance: nation × poverty status, multivariate $F(5, 918) = 2.15$, $p \leq .05$, and nation × gender, multivariate $F(5, 918) = 2.16$, $p \leq .05$. The two-way interaction between poverty status and gender, and the three-way interaction between nation, poverty status, and gender, were not significant.

TABLE 2 Hierarchical Log Linear Analysis: Cell Percentages and Partial χ^2 Testing Significance of the Associations between National Origin, Gender, and Interaction with BPI Symptoms

| | AFRICAN AMERICANS | | SOUTH AFRICANS | | | PARTIAL χ^2 | | |
	BOYS ($n = 160$)	GIRLS ($n = 146$)	BOYS ($n = 310$)	GIRLS ($n = 315$)	TOTAL	NATION	GENDER	NATION × GENDER
Anxious	35.6	35.6	8.7	7.9	17.2	100.61***		
Argues	42.5	38.4	43.2	43.8	42.5			
Disobedient at school	27.5	11.6	8.4	5.1	11.1	33.47***	13.86***	
Breaks rules	18.1	17.1	29.4	21.6	22.9	7.61***	4.09*	
Impulsive	37.5	30.8	40.3	33.7	35.5		4.50*	
Withdrawn	8.1	5.5	7.1	5.4	6.4			
Destroys others' possessions	14.4	4.8	41.6	26.7	26.1	74.10***	22.69***	
Mood changes	46.3	41.1	38.1	36.5	39.4			
Worthless	2.5	6.2	4.5	2.9	3.9			3.72*
Complains about love	18.1	19.9	9.0	10.8	12.9	11.05***		
Sad	10.0	8.9	4.5	1.6	5.2	15.84***		
Nervous	3.0	2.9	1.8	1.3	2.0	66.66***		
Dependent	36.9	33.6	25.2	29.4	29.9	6.40**		
Disobedient at home	36.3	29.5	10.6	8.9	17.4	72.30***		
Stubborn	43.1	38.4	47.7	34.6	41.1		10.44***	
Temper tantrums	30.0	23.3	19.7	18.1	21.5	7.28**		
Unable to concentrate	43.8	28.8	18.7	18.4	24.5	43.38***		4.02*
Confused	16.9	12.3	2.3	3.2	6.7	43.86***		
Bullies, cruel, mean	17.5	12.3	43.9	32.4	30.5	57.35***	10.34***	4.56*
Unable to get mind off certain things	19.4	12.3	16.8	16.2	16.3			
Squirms, restless	50.0	45.9	50.3	53.7	50.7			
Clings to adults	23.8	15.8	13.9	12.7	15.5	6.40**		
Cries without reason	28.8	21.2	10.6	12.4	16.0	26.84***		
Demands attention	48.1	41.1	56.1	61.9	54.4	16.73***		3.50*
Not liked by other children	6.9	3.4	8.4	9.5	7.7	14.29*		

* $p < .05$; ** $p < .01$; *** $p < .001$.

Table 3 presents the means and standard deviations for the behavior problem inventory subscales by national origin, poverty status, and gender. In examining the significance of the univariate F for the main effects and interactions on which multivariate Fs were significant, we noted several distinct patterns. The univariate F values for the main effect of national origin were significant for anxiety/depression, $F(1, 928) = 57.09$, $p \leq .001$, immaturity, $F(1, 928) = 3.83$, $p \leq .05$, oppositional behavior, $F(1, 928) = 29.56$, $p \leq .001$, and social problems, $F(1, 928) = 4.73$, $p \leq .03$. In each case, the African American children scored significantly higher on these problems than did the South African children. When we examine the univariate F values for poverty status, we observe a significant F value for immaturity, $F(1, 929) = 5.03$, $p \leq .03$, hyperactivity, $F(1, 929) = 13.4$, $p \leq .001$, and social problems, $F(1, 929) = 9.86$, $p \leq .002$. In each case, poor children score significantly higher on problem scales than do children from more advantaged backgrounds.

Significant univariate Fs are found for gender on oppositional behavior, $F(1, 928) = 6.65$, $p \leq .01$, and hyperactivity, $F(1, 928) = 9.39$, $p \leq .002$. Inspection of the means shows that boys score significantly higher than girls on opposition and hyperactivity.

In interactions between national origin and poverty status, we find significant univariate Fs for anxiety/depression, $F(1, 926) = 4.00$, $p \leq .05$, and for hyperactivity, $F(1, 926) = 5.89$, $p \leq .015$. Inspection of the means for the four groups suggests that the difference on anxiety between the nonpoor and poor for African Americans is greater than the difference between nonpoor and poor South Africans. A similar pattern obtains for hyperactivity.

Significant univariate Fs for the nation x gender interaction were found for immaturity, $F(1, 926) = 5.12$, $p \leq .02$ and for hyperactivity, $F(1, 926) = 3.87$, $p \leq .05$. Again, inspection of the means related suggest that gender differences are much greater for African Americans than they are for South Africans.

TABLE 3 Means and Standard Deviations for BPI Subscale by National Origin, Poverty Status, and Gender

| | | AFRICAN AMERICANS | | | | | | | SOUTH AFRICANS | | | | | | | |
| | | POOR | | | NONPOOR | | | | POOR | | | NONPOOR | | | | |
	n	BOYS (67)	GIRLS (68)	BOTH (135)	BOYS (93)	GIRLS (78)	BOTH (171)	TOTAL (306)	BOYS (129)	GIRLS (139)	BOTH (268)	BOYS (180)	GIRLS (176)	BOTH (356)	TOTAL (624)	GRAND TOTAL (930)
Anxiety/ depression	*M*	1.34	1.13	1.24	.97	1.10	1.03	1.12	.69	.63	.66	.62	.57	.60	.62	.79
	SD	(1.3)	(1.3)	(1.3)	(1.1)	(1.3)	(1.2)	(1.2)	(.8)	(.8)	(.8)	(.9)	(.8)	(.8)	(.8)	
Immaturity	*M*	1.48	1.31	1.39	1.30	.95	1.14	1.25	1.06	1.07	1.07	1.06	1.23	1.15	1.11	1.16
	SD	(1.5)	(1.4)	(1.4)	(1.4)	(1.1)	(1.3)	(1.4)	(1.1)	(1.0)	(1.0)	(.9)	(1.0)	(1.0)	(1.0)	(1.1)
Opposition	*M*	2.03	1.47	1.75	1.54	1.55	1.54	1.63	1.21	1.01	1.10	1.31	1.15	1.23	1.18	1.33
	SD	(1.7)	(1.6)	(1.7)	(1.6)	(1.5)	(1.5)	(1.6)	(1.1)	(.9)	(1.0)	(1.1)	(1.0)	(1.1)	(1.1)	(1.3)
Hyperactivity	*M*	1.82	1.31	1.56	1.23	.95	1.10	1.30	1.28	1.22	1.34	1.31	1.19	1.25	1.28	1.29
	SD	(1.5)	(1.5)	(1.5)	(1.3)	(1.1)	(1.2)	(1.4)	(1.0)	(1.2)	(1.2)	(1.1)	(1.0)	(1.1)	(1.0)	(1.1)
Social problems	*M*	.34	.24	.29	.19	0	.15	.21	.12	.14	.13	.18	.16	.17	.15	.17
	SD	(.7)	(.6)	(.6)	(.5)	(.29)	(.4)	(.5)	(.3)	(.4)	(.4)	(.4)	(.4)	(.4)	(.4)	(.4)

To test the effects of family structure—specifically single parenthood—a four-way MANOVA was computed in which national origin, poverty status, gender, and single parenthood were the independent factors. The main effect for family structure was not significant nor was there a significant interaction between parenthood and any of the other variables, whether two-way, three-way, or four-way. Thus, single parenthood does not explain the variance on behavior problems beyond what can be accounted for by poverty status.

DISCUSSION

This research analyzes differences between South African Blacks and African American children in psychological adjustment, and evaluates the cross-cultural robustness of several social risk factors. Taken together, the results of the log linear analysis and the MANOVA analyses suggest interesting differences for behavioral and emotional problems among young African American and South African children. Overall, African American children evidenced greater prevalence for most, though not all, symptoms and scored higher than South African children with respect to the clinical scales. For example, the symptom-level data show that African American children scored much higher on the emotional symptoms such as anxiety, nervousness, sadness, complaining about love, and dependence, than did the South African children. In addition, African American children scored significantly higher than South Africans on the scale scores for anxiety/depression, immaturity, opposition, and hyperactivity. These data lead to the conclusion that African Americans are, in

general, more troubled and more susceptible to risk of psychological dysfunction than are South Africans. African American boys, in particular, evidenced a pattern of heightened vulnerability for behavioral and emotional difficulties. For example, of all groups in the study, African American boys have the greatest difficulty with concentration problems. It is not immediately evident why African American boys should have more difficulty in this area than African American girls. Plausible explanations include gender-differentiated socialization, and biological vulnerability early in life which compound the effects of other risks such as malnutrition and early exposure to toxins and metals that severely compromise neurological development necessary for acquisition of self-regulation (Politt & Gorman, 1994).

Although African American children evidence behavioral and emotional difficulties to a significantly greater extent than South African children, South Africans evidence greater vulnerability within a subset of symptoms related to antisocial and disruptive behavior. Specifically, South Africans were rated much higher on symptoms such as bullying, breaking rules, destroying others' property, not being liked by others, and demanding attention. These data suggest a differential pattern of dysfunction—namely, African American children tend to have greater vulnerability with respect to internalizing symptoms, suggestive of over-regulation among African Americans, and South African children have greater vulnerability to socially disruptive behavior, suggestive of suboptimal regulation (Hammen & Rudolph, 1996). The differences may be related to high levels of disruption in family and community life associated with political turmoil in South Africa and the wave of violent criminal activity that has risen in its place (Barbarin, Richter, deWet, & Wachtel, 1998). In addition, the excesses of physical punishment at home and at school, ethnic conflict, and a steadily increasing wave of criminal violence may create in children the unmistakable impression that violence and coercion are socially acceptable and sanctioned strategies for resolving interpersonal difficulties (McKendrick & Senoamadi, 1996; Swarts, 1997). Moreover, during the protracted period of the liberation struggle against apartheid, defiance of authority became an accepted norm, particularly among youth. This sentiment may still be commonplace in the post-apartheid transformation period.

Poverty, family structure, and gender have broad empirical support as risk factors for behavioral and emotional difficulties (Barbarin & Soler, 1993). The evidence from this study is consistent, for the most part, with the existing research on these issues. The gender differences expected on the basis of this earlier work were found for behavior and conduct problems. Predictably, boys were more often rated as having conduct problems than were girls. However, our data do not provide support for differences between girls and boys on emotional symptoms. Poverty was also confirmed as a risk factor. Poor children scored significantly higher on immaturity, hyperactivity, and social problems than nonpoor children. However, family structure, as indexed by single parenthood, was unrelated to children's behavioral and emotional adjustment when poverty status was controlled. This finding is important because so much of the data confirming a relation between single-adult households and poor development fail to control for the confound of economic status. If economic status is the active ingredient, then policy efforts focused exclusively on marital and family life are misguided at best.

Although poverty and gender are confirmed as risk factors for African American children, this is not the case for South African children. Why are South African children protected relative to African Americans? Possible explanations include the psychological protections afforded by majority status and the stress-buffering resources of support from extended family networks.

Even though South African children grow up under conditions that are as adverse as, if not more adverse than, those for African Americans, the social and cultural context may afford them some protections not available to African American children. A different consciousness of self, founded in the perception of self as part of a majority group, may be an important resource for South African children and their families. This notion could be tested by comparisons

of African Americans and Africans to the mixed race groups in South Africa classified under the apartheid system as Coloured—a mixed race group formed from a combination of Whites, Africans, and Malay Indians. If the supposition about the effect of majority status is accurate, African children would show better outcomes than both Coloured and African American. Many Coloureds, by language, culture, and politics, tend to identify more with Afrikaans-speaking Whites than with Black Africans. In the shifting landscape of South Africa's racial group politics, Coloured children, situated uncomfortably between Whites and Africans, occupy an uncertain position in the Black-majority ruled democracy. Absent the psychological protections afforded Blacks by their majority status, the position of Coloureds is analogous to that occupied by Blacks in the United States. For this reason, it could be argued that comparisons of Coloureds to African Americans would reveal less striking differences in psychological adjustment.

Another explanation is that a more adequate foundation of social and material support is available to South African parents who are living in multigenerational households (which tend to be more of a standard). The forces of apartheid, by limiting the supply of housing, may inadvertently have contributed to a level of family interdependence which makes some form of adult nurturing and guidance more consistently available to children than is the case among African Americans. Moreover, ideological resources may be available to South African families from the resistance struggle to seek liberation from apartheid. Participation in the liberation movement may help form explanatory schemas that permit families to transcend the demoralizing effects of adversity by reinterpreting it as an externally imposed condition. Moreover, retention of traditional family practices in a modified form (ritualization; family, clan, or ethnic group identification) also affords protection to the developing child.

In the absence of confirming empirical data, these ideas amount to little more than plausible speculations. Additional research might examine other cultural resources and identify the ways in which they impact on child development.

It is hoped that the data on South African–African American differences presented here will stimulate more focused investigations of the social and cultural contexts of psychological adjustment and development (e.g., Robertson & Kottler, 1993). Advancement of knowledge about these issues may result from several lines of research. At the heart of suggestions for future research are efforts to understand how differing conceptions of childhood, socialization goals, parental roles, and family relations combine to create culturally distinctive social environments for children. Future research might examine differences in how adults understand the inner lives and emotional experiences of children. It could document how parents set standards for children's emotional regulation, behavioral compliance, and social competencies. It could explore whether different outcomes result from the tendency of adults to encourage some responses to developmental challenges children face and to sanction others. It would be important to know how much attributes thought to be valued in the United States are related to positive outcome in the developing world. These attributes include parents' investment in their children's lives, promotion of psychological autonomy, and functional independence. Differences in these domains are suggested by notable differences in the ratings made by South African parents of their children's behaviors, emotions, and social functioning. South African parents are less likely than African Americans to ascribe aversive cognitive or emotional states to their children. Typically these experiences of anxiety or sadness are not readily observable, and inferences are guided by a conception of childhood that includes differentiated affect. The views of African American parents about the emotional experiences of their children are not clear. Thus the connection between differential views of childhood and ratings of emotional function is speculation that must be subjected to empirical tests. Differences between African Americans and South Africans are most pronounced on symptoms that involve observable and potentially disruptive or disturbing behavior. South African parents make markedly higher ratings than do African American parents on these items. This difference does not occur with symptoms that are cognitive, emotional, or social in nature and which are not easily observable.

South Africans, however, are no more ready to characterize their children as disobedient than are African American parents. Differences in the behavioral ratings of South Africans and African Americans may reflect a stricter standard held by South African parents for compliance on the part of their children. Some support for this higher expectation is available in the comparatively high frequency with which South African parents report that their children break rules, are impulsive, and destroy things. This interpretation is consistent with the commonly held belief that African parents value compliance and demand immediate and complete obedience (Liddell, Kvalsvig, Shabalala, & Qotyana, 1994). If this belief is true, it appears that African children, for the most part, meet this expectation.

The results of this cross-national comparative study provide support for claims of an independent effect of social risk factors of gender and poverty. At the same time they cast doubt on a role of female headship that is independent of economic status. In light of the controls for racial categorization, the differences observed between African American and South African children provide an opening for explanations of child outcomes that are based on culture and sociopolitical context. This study demonstrates that there are identifiable similarities between urban dwellers in the United States and those in South Africa with respect to socioeconomic situations, and that there are putative differences with respect to cultural mores and world views. The differences reported here justify additional research on how, on the one hand cultures mediate development of behavioral and emotional problems, and on the other they serve as a basis for resilience and coping. Future research programs on ethnicity, culture, and child adjustment could specifically explore possible health-promoting factors such as spirituality, racial identity, and sociocultural resources that seem to safeguard South African children from deleterious effects of adverse social conditions.

REFERENCES

Achenbach, T. M., Howell, C. T., Quay, H. C., & Conners, C. K. (1991). National survey of problems and competencies among four- to sixteen-year-olds: Parents' reports for normative and clinical samples. *Monographs of the Society for Research in Child Development, 56*(3, Serial No. 225).

Barbarin, O. A., & Khomo, N. (1997). Indicators of economic status and social capital in South African townships: What do they reveal about the material and social conditions in families of poor children? *Childhood: A Global Journal of Child Research, 4*, 193–222.

Barbarin, O., Richter, L., deWet, T., & Wachtel, A. (1998). Ironic trends in the transition to peace: Criminal violence supplants political violence in terrorizing South African Blacks. *Peace and Conflict: Journal of Peace Psychology, 4*, 283–305.

Barbarin, O., & Soler, R. (1993). Behavioral, emotional and academic adjustment in a national probability sample of African American children: Effects of age, gender and family structure. *Journal of Black Psychology, 19*, 423–446.

Brooks-Gunn, J., & Duncan, G. (1997). The effects of poverty on children. *The Future of Children: Children and Poverty, 7*, 55–71.

Bureau of Market Research (1995). *The October Household Survey*. Pretoria, S.A.: University of Pretoria.

Bussing, R., Halfon, N., Benjamin, B., & Wells, K. (1995). Prevalence of behavior problems in U.S. children with asthma. *Archives of Pediatrics and Adolescent Medicine, 149,* 565–572.

Capaldi, D. M., & Patterson, G. R. (1994). Interrelated influences of contextual factors on antisocial behavior in childhood and adolescence for males. In D. C. Fowles, P. Sutker, & S. H. Goodman (Eds.), *Progress in experimental personality and psychopathology research* (pp. 165–198). New York: Springer.

Costello, E. J. (1989). Child psychiatric disorders and their correlates: A primary care pediatric sample. *Journal of the American Academy of Child and Adolescent Psychiatry, 28,* 851–855.

Duncan, G. J., & Brooks-Gunn, J. (1997). *Consequences of growing up poor.* New York: Russell Sage Foundation.

Foster, S. L., & Martinez, C. R., Jr. (1995). Ethnicity: Conceptual and methodological issues in child clinical research. *Journal of Clinical Child Psychology, 24,* 214–226.

Frederick D. Patterson Research Institute. (1997). *The African American education data book* (Vol. 2). Alexandria, VA: United Negro College Fund.

Garrison, C. Z., Jackson, K. L., Marsteller, F., McKeown, R., & Addy, C. (1990). A longitudinal study of depressive symptomatology in young adolescents. *Journal of the American Academy of Child and Adolescent Psychiatry, 29,* 581–585.

Gore, S., Aseltine, R. H., & Colton, M. E. (1993). Gender, social-relational involvement, and depression. *Journal of Research on Adolescence, 3,* 101–125.

Halpern-Felsher, B., Connell, J. P., Spencer, M., Aber, J., Duncan, G., Clifford, E., Crichlow, W., Usinger, P., Cole, S., Allen, L., & Seidman, E. (1997). Neighborhood and family factors predicting educational risk and attainment in African American and White children and adolescents. In J. Brooks-Gunn, G. Duncan, & J. Aber (Eds.), Neighborhood poverty: Context and consequences for children (Vol. 2, pp. 146–173). New York: Russell Sage Foundation.

Hammen, C., & Rudolph, K. D. (1996). Childhood depression. In E. J. Mash & R. A. Barkley (Eds.), *Child psychopathology* (pp. 153–195). New York: Guilford Press.

Herrnstein, R. J., & Murray, C. (1994). *The bell curve: Intelligence and class structure in American life.* New York: Free Press.

Hollingshead, A. B. (1957). Two factor index of social position. New Haven, CT: Yale University, Department of Sociology.

Jagers, R., & Mock, L. (1993). Culture and outcomes among inner-city African American children: An Afrographic exploration. *Journal of Black Psychology, 19,* 391–405.

Kincheloe, J., Steinberg, S. R., & Gresson, A. (1996). *Measured lies: The bell curve examined.* New York: Saint Martin's Press.

Liddell, C., Kvalsvig, J., Shabalala, A., & Qotyana, P. (1994). Defining the cultural context of children's everyday experiences in the year before school. In A. Dawes & D. Donald (Eds.), Childhood and adversity: Psychological perspectives from South African research (pp. 51–65). Cape Town, SA: David Phillip.

Lyons, R. K. (1996). Attachment relationships among children with aggressive behavior problems: The role of disorganized early attachment patterns. *Journal of Consulting and Clinical Psychology, 64,* 64–73.

McKendrick, G., & Senoamadi, W. (1996). Some effects of violence on squatter camp families and their children. In L. E. Glanz & A. D. Spiegel (Eds.), *Violence and family life in contemporary South Africa: Research and policy issues* (pp. 15–28). Pretoria, SA: Human Sciences Research Council Publishers.

McLoyd, V. C. (1998). Socioeconomic disadvantage and child development. *American Psychologist, 53,*185–204.

National Center for Health Statistics. (1988). *Child Health Supplement National Health Interview Survey.* Hyattsville, MD: Public Health Service.

Neal, A. M., Lilly, R. S., & Zakis, S. (1993). What are African American children afraid of? A preliminary study. *Journal of Anxiety Disorders, 7,* 129–139.

Nielsen, F. (1997). Inequality by design: Cracking the Bell Curve myth. *Social Forces, 76,* 701–704.

Offord, D. R., Alder, R. J., & Boyle, M. H. (1986). Prevalence and sociodemographic correlates of conduct disorder. *American Journal of Social Psychiatry, 4,* 272–278.

Ollendick, T H. (1983). Fear in children and adolescents: Normative data. *Behavior Research and Therapy, 23,* 465–467.

Peterson, J., & Zill, N. (1986). Marital disruption, parent-child relationships, and behavior problems in children. *Journal of Marriage and the Family, 48,* 295–307.

Pollitt, E., & Gorman, K. (1994). Nutritional deficiencies as developmental risk factors. In C. A. Nelson (Ed.), *The Minnesota Symposium on Child Psychology: Vol. 27. Threats to optimal development: Integrating biological, psychological, and social risk factors* (pp. 1–31). Hillsdale, NJ: Erlbaum.

Richter, L. M. (1994). Economic stress and its influence on the family and caretaking patterns. In A. Dawes & D. Donald (Eds.), Childhood and adversity: Psychological perspectives from South African research (pp. 28–50). Cape Town, SA: David Phillip.

Richter, L. M., Yach, D., Cameron, N., Griesel, R. D., & de Wet, T. (1995). Enrollment into Birth to Ten (BTT): Population and sample characteristics. *Pediatrics and Perinatal Epidemiology, 9,* 109–120.

Richters, J. E. (1993). Community violence and children's development: Toward a research agenda for the 1990s. *Psychiatry, 53,* 3–6.

Robertson, B. A., & Kottler, A. (1993). Cultural issues in the psychiatric assessment of Xhosa children and adolescents. *South African Medical Journal, 83,* 207–208.

Stevenson, H. W., Chen, C., & Uttal, D. H. (1990). Beliefs and achievement: A study of Black, White, and Hispanic children. *Child Development, 61,* 508–523.

Suzuki, L. A., & Valencia, R. R. (1997). Race-ethnicity and measured intelligence: Educational implications. *American Psychologist, 52,* 1103–1114.

Swarts, M. (1997). The family: Cradle of violence in South Africa. *Human Sciences Research Council: In Focus Forum, 4*(5), 40–44.

U.S. Bureau of the Census. (1993). *Poverty in the United States: 1992* (Current Population Reports, Series P-60, No. 185). Washington, DC: U.S. Government Printing Office.

Werner, E., & Smith, R. (1989). *Vulnerable but invincible: A longitudinal study of resilient children and youth.* New York: Adams, Bannister, and Cox.

Whitaker, A., Johnson, J., Shaffer, D., Rapoport, J. L., Kalikow, K., Walsh, B. T., Davies, M., Braiman, S., & Dolinsky, A. (1990). Uncommon troubles in young people: Prevalence estimates of selected psychiatric disorders in a non-referred adolescent population. *Archives of General Psychiatry, 47,* 487–496.

Wood, F. B., Felton, R. H., Flowers, L., & Naylor, C. (1991). Neurobehavioral definition of dyslexia. In D. D. Duane & D. B. Gray (Eds.), *The reading brain: The biological basis of dyslexia* (pp. 1–26). Parkton, MD: York Press.

Zill, N. (1985). Behavior Problem Scales developed from the 1981 Child Health Supplement to the National Health Interview Survey. Washington, DC: Child Trends.

SELF-STUDY QUESTIONS

Multiple Choice

1. The authors compared black South African and African American children in order to
   a. hold constant the effects of biological race
   b. hold constant the effects of culture
   c. hold constant the effects of family structure
   d. none of the above

2. Which of the following was found by the authors?
   a. Black South African children exhibited more behavior problems than their African American counterparts.
   b. Black South African children were more likely to live in a household in which an adult male also resided.
   c. African American children were less aggressive than peers in South Africa.
   d. The effects of family structure were very different in the two cultures.

Essay

1. Outline the difference between race as a biological/genetic category and a sociocultural category as explained by the authors of this study.

2. How do the authors explain their finding that poor and nonpoor African American children differed more than their counterparts in South Africa? Do you agree? Why or why not?

MIDDLE CHILDHOOD

"Moral Theme Comprehension in Children"

OVERVIEW

You may remember the story of *The Little Red Hen*, about a hen who works hard to raise wheat, grind it into flour, and bake bread. While she is working, the other farm animals refuse to help. However, when the bread is baked, they all expect a share. The hen explains that only those who helped with the work involved are entitled to a share of the final product.

As adults, we have little trouble identifying the moral theme in this story, and as parents or teachers, we use such stories to teach children about morality. But what do children get out of these tales? Can they identify the moral without help from adults? These were the questions examined by the study reported in this article.

METHODOLOGY

The researchers employed two common statistical techniques: *ANOVA* and *ANCOVA*. ANOVA stands for *analysis of variance*, a technique that allows researchers to test for differences between groups. ANCOVA signifies *analysis of covariance*, a strategy that enables researchers to statistically control a variable they think may influence the study's results. In this case, the researchers thought vocabulary and reading achievement might influence the outcome because their procedure required participants to read moral stories and to generate verbal responses to questions. Consequently, they used a standardized achievement test to determine participants' general reading and vocabulary skills. Participants' test scores were then added to the analysis of the study's other variables. This procedure allowed the researchers to know exactly how much of participants' moral theme comprehension was due to their overall reading ability. It also enabled them to determine the contribution of developmental variables, as measured by school grade level, to moral theme comprehension over and above the contribution of verbal ability and reading achievement.

GLOSSARY TERM

■ **Story schema**   the general concept that stories have settings and characters, and that they contain a plot that progresses from a beginning, through a middle, to an end. The story schema allows us to distinguish between a collection of random sentences and a real story.

Darcia Narvaez, Tracy Gleason, Christyan Mitchell,
and Jennifer Bentley

Moral Theme Comprehension in Children

Although some claim that reading moral stories to children will improve their moral literacy (see, e.g., Bennett, 1993), little research has been done that bears on this question. The purposes of this study were to (a) test the idea that children can extract the theme from a moral story and (b) test for developmental differences in moral theme comprehension. Participants from 3rd and 5th grades and a university were tested on whether they understood the lessons (i.e., the moral themes) from several moral stories. They were asked to identify both the theme from a list of message choices and which of 4 alternative vignettes had the same theme. Participants also rated the set of message and vignette choices for closeness of match to the original story. Reading comprehension was used as a covariate. Developmental differences in moral theme understanding were significant even after accounting for reading comprehension.

Although some claim that reading moral stories to children will improve their moral literacy (see, e.g., Bennett, 1993), little research has been done that focuses on this question. Bennett and others (e.g., Kilpatrick, 1992; Lickona, 1991; Wynne & Ryan, 1993) have stated that children need to hear moral stories to develop moral literacy and moral character. Regardless of the paucity of research examining such assumptions or the educational effects of reading moral stories on the reader (Leming, 1997), these assertions raise questions: What do children extract from a moral text? What do they understand as the theme or message? The purposes of this study were to test character educators' implicit claim that children can extract the theme from a moral story and to test for developmental differences in moral theme comprehension. The questions we sought to answer include the following: Do readers understand a moral text in the manner intended by the author? Can any listener extract the theme or message from a moral text? Is reading ability the sole determinant of moral theme comprehension? In this study, we integrated theory from both moral development and text comprehension to examine development in moral theme comprehension.

Reprinted from *Educational Psychology*, 1999, *91*, 477–487. Copyright © 1999 by the American Psychological Association. Reprinted with permission.

TEXT COMPREHENSION

Generally, when a reader reads a text, she or he tries to create a coherent mental representation of the text both by integrating text elements and by elaborating on the text with prior knowledge about the world (van den Broek, 1994). For example, consider this text: "Missy was looking for her car keys. She looked on the dining room table. Then she looked on the kitchen counter. She found them." When reading the last sentence, the reader must integrate current and prior text elements by recalling car keys from memory of earlier text events to understand the referent *them*. Without an integration of the earlier text, the reader cannot know what the referent means. The text continues, "Missy took her car keys and went out the door. She pulled out of the driveway." To understand this section of the text, the reader must infer from background knowledge that Missy got into a car, put the keys in the ignition, started the engine, and so forth. Otherwise, the reader might wonder what Missy was pulling out of the driveway. Through the process of integrating prior and current text elements and making inferences from prior knowledge to bridge text elements, the reader builds a mental model of what the text is about (McNamara, Miller, & Bransford, 1991; van Dijk & Kintsch, 1983). However, even when reading an identical text, different readers do not build the same mental model.

Two factors are cited in explaining why all readers do not understand a text the same way: prior knowledge and individual differences in reading skill (see Gernsbacher, 1994, for examples). Prior knowledge can occur in the form of general knowledge structures such as schemas (see, e.g., Anderson & Pearson, 1984; Bartlett, 1932; Bobrow & Norman, 1975; Rumelhart, 1980; Rumelhart & Ortony, 1977). The reader's schemas affect how the text is understood. For example, a reader raised in the United States is likely very familiar with a birthday party schema. The birthday party schema is an activated set of birthday-related concepts such as a birthday cake, birthday presents, the person celebrating the birthday, and party guests. When the reader reads, "They celebrated Jesse's birthday. He ate a lot," the related set of concepts about birthday parties is activated. If a reader later recalls "Jesse ate a lot of cake" (an inference that was not part of the original text), such added information would be evidence for a birthday party schema in operation. Schema effects have been documented where readers had different levels of familiarity with text material (see, e.g., Chiesi, Spilich, & Voss, 1979; Spilich, Vesonder, Chiesi, & Voss, 1979) and with culture-specific texts (Bartlett, 1932; Harris, Lee, Hensley, & Schoen, 1988; Pritchard, 1990; Reynolds, Taylor, Steffensen, Shirey, & Anderson, 1982). For example, Reynolds et al. (1982) had participants recall two stories about weddings. One wedding was traditional in the United States, the other was traditional in India. Participants recalled better the wedding that matched their cultural background, tending to distort recall of the unfamiliar wedding practices from the other text. However, although prior knowledge has a measurable effect on the comprehension of a text, differences in reading skill also play a part.

Reading skill differences help explain some of the developmental differences in understanding a text. Comprehension is affected by reading skill tasks such as decoding words and sentences, word recognition, vocabulary, and the ability to integrate the individual meanings of words and sentences into a general understanding of the text or theme (Oakhill, 1994). For example, research in narrative comprehension has demonstrated that children do not understand narratives in the same way adults do: Children remember less of the story overall and have difficulty making inferences to connect goal-action-outcome chains of events (see, e.g., Collins, 1983; Perfetti, 1985; van den Broek, Lorch, & Thurlow, 1997). When Wilder (1980) asked children to recall a moral story by recreating it with puppets, he found differences between older and younger children in terms of type and amount of story elements recalled.

Stein and Trabasso (1982) used moral texts to test the mental models children built of texts. By varying information about motives, goal-relatedness of motives, and severity of consequences within stories, the authors manipulated aspects of a character's intentions. A key component in interpretive ability is the ability to generate causal inferences (by which events in the text are mentally connected to other events in the text, as shown in the car key example), an ability that increases with age and cognitive development. Accordingly, with our example, children would have a more difficult time making the string of inferences about Missy and her car keys.

Children's interpretive (inferential) abilities, skills relevant to theme comprehension, have been tested by various means. An example from moral text comprehension can be found in the work of D. F. Johnson and Goldman (1987) in which children were presented with Bible stories that illustrated "rules of conduct" (e.g., helping, obeying, or not being afraid). Children were tested on their ability both to recognize the rules in the stories and to group stories according to the rules. Young children tended to group stories according to actions and concrete items rather than by rule similarity.

Several researchers have suggested that young children have difficulty extracting themes from stories. Taylor (1986) reported that summarizing the point of a narrative was difficult for fourth and fifth graders. N. S. Johnson (1984) found that summarization was more difficult than recall for elementary school children. When Goldman, Reyes, and Varnhagen (1984) asked kindergarten through sixth-grade children to extract lessons from fables, children were generally unable to extract a lesson until fourth grade (age 10); younger children were able to extract only concrete, story-specific lessons. Lehr (1988) tested theme comprehension in kindergartners and second and fourth graders with realistic stories and folktales. Both age and previous experience with literature were related to theme identification. Overall, children were better at extracting themes from realistic fiction than from fantasy fiction.

Adults also have difficulties extracting themes from texts (Afflerbach, 1990; Reder & Anderson, 1980; Williams, 1993). Afflerbach found that experts automatically constructed the main idea of topic-familiar texts significantly more than they did for texts about unfamiliar topics. Afflerbach concluded that main idea construction generally is neither automatic nor fundamental unless the topic is familiar. Not only does prior knowledge influence the comprehension structures built from reading texts, it can also affect the mental representations important in moral development.

MORAL DEVELOPMENT

Research in moral development has often focused on moral judgment (i.e., reasoning used to advocate a certain action choice in a moral dilemma; Colby & Kohlberg, 1987; Rest, 1986). In this tradition, researchers have recognized that people conceptualize moral problems differently on the basis of age and education (see, e.g., Kohlberg, 1984).[1] As individuals develop in moral judgment, transformations occur in how they construe their obligations to others. These transformations can be viewed as moral schemas about how it is possible to organize cooperation (Rest, Narvaez, Bebeau, & Thoma, 1999). As moral judgment matures, an individual's concerns expand, and he or she is able to consider the welfare of more and more others when conceptualizing ideal forms of cooperation (e.g., at the lowest schema, one is primarily concerned for self, whereas in the most developed schema, one includes concern for strangers).

Several methods have been used to measure changes in moral judgment, including moral comprehension. Moral comprehension studies present participants with someone else's reasons for a moral action. Participants are asked to respond by paraphrasing, recalling, or selecting the identical reasoning from a list of paraphrased reasons. For example, Rest (1973; Rest, Turiel, & Kohlberg, 1969) presented moral arguments based on different Kohlbergian stages in separate paragraphs to participants who were asked to restate them. The schemas that a participant could paraphrase were credited as being understood. The comprehension of moral stage arguments is cumulative. That is, as understanding expands to include higher, more complex stages, the individual retains comprehension of the simpler stages. By providing an inventory of a participant's moral schema capacity across stages, moral comprehension studies support the developmental nature of moral schemas.

Another type of moral comprehension is moral text comprehension. Narvaez (1998) studied the effects of moral judgment development on the comprehension of narratives. After reading narratives about moral dilemmas in which various stages of Kohlbergian moral reasoning were embedded, participants were asked to recall the narratives. Differences in recall corresponded to differences in moral judgment development as measured by the Defining Issues Test (DIT). Persons with higher scores in moral judgment on the DIT not only had better recall of the texts and the high-stage moral arguments within them but also distorted their recall differently. Although all readers tended to distort the text in their recall, high-stage moral reasoners were significantly more likely to add new high-stage reasons to their recall of the narratives in comparison with lower stage reasoners. This research also supports the view that developmental differences in moral judgment influence the comprehension of moral texts.

The current study brings together moral comprehension with text and theme comprehension by focusing on whether children are able to extract the theme from a moral story. This research differs from previous studies in the following ways:

1. Unlike previous moral comprehension researchers who asked participants to restate moral reasoning advocating a particular course of action, we asked participants to extrapolate and identify the moral message from a story. We examined whether children understood the themes of moral stories as the author intended or whether they distorted the themes.

2. Unlike those who have discussed moral stories elsewhere (e.g., Bennett, 1993), our definition of *moral* involves cooperating or getting along with others (Piaget, 1932/1965; Rest et al., 1999). For us, a *moral story* has a theme about a specific aspect of getting along with others. Therefore, in the selection of texts for this study, we did not choose texts such as Aesop's fables, because they focus mostly on types of prudence (e.g., don't be vain, plan wisely, don't be fooled, etc.).

3. We focused on correct versus incorrect choice of the moral theme from among distractors. Thus, the focus of responses is on veridical choice rather than on theme generation or personal interpretation of a story theme.

4. To control the clarity and complexity of the moral stories and moral themes, we developed our own stories. We had conducted an earlier study using texts from children's books (Narvaez, Bentley, Gleason, & Samuels, 1998) but were unable to find complex moral stories with a variety of moral themes (within our strict definition) that were suitable for this research. For this study, we created well-constructed (i.e., with a beginning, middle, and end), nonreligious, literary stories.

5. In each story, we adopted the complex notion of moral behavior as theorized by Rest's four component model (Rest, 1983). In this model, moral action

---

[1]Kohlberg's (1984) moral stage theory has engendered a great deal of research and supportive findings. The Defining Issues Test (DIT; Rest, 1979) is an offspring of his theoretical approach. The DIT, systematically validated through a series of studies (see Rest, Thoma, & Edwards, 1997, for a review), indicates that moral judgment based on justice changes with age and education from a preference for preconventional thinking to a preference for conventional thinking to one for postconventional thinking.

requires moral sensitivity (being aware of cause–consequence chains of actions and reactions), moral judgment (selecting the most moral action), moral motivation (applying one's values and prioritizing a moral action), and moral character (implementing and following through on the moral action). All four components were included in each story.

6. We selected themes that were understandable to younger children (e.g., persevere for the good of others, be honest with strangers, do not lie for friends, be responsible and trustworthy by completing your duties to others), not more adult themes on topics such as the complexities of constitutional democracies.

METHOD

Participants

There were 132 participants: 50 third graders (average age, 8 years, 6 months; 28 girls, 22 boys) and 54 fifth graders (average age, 10 years, 9 months; 34 girls, 20 boys) from a city elementary school. We pilot tested tasks and stories with children from 6 to 12 years old. Our pilot testing confirmed earlier findings that children younger than those in fourth grade have difficulty extracting the themes (Goldman et al., 1984). Thus, we selected third- and fifth-grade students for three reasons: (a) On the basis of the results of an earlier study (Narvaez et al., 1998), fifth graders were found to be quite competent at identifying moral themes in relatively simple stories in which distractors were clearly wrong (e.g., "Never trust a monkey or a rabbit"); (b) third graders performed the tasks competently in the aforementioned study (although they were more likely to be incorrect in their answers); and (c) most students had the skills to be able to move beyond the concrete and to generalize a theme by fourth grade (Goldman et al., 1984). To confirm the authors' criterion of veridical themes, 28 adults were recruited (average age, 27 years, 9 months; 15 women, 7 men, 6 who did not indicate gender) from educational psychology classes at a public university. Each adult received course credit for participating.

Materials

Stories. Four stories about moral dilemmas were written. Each story has a complex moral message and contains a dilemma that the protagonist must resolve. In each story, the protagonist resolves the dilemma by affirming the values of the theme. Of the four stories, two are about helping strangers ("Kim" and "California"). "Kim" concerns a girl whose family is moving across the country and stops at a gas station where Kim receives too much change from the cashier. The moral messages concern being honest with everyone, even strangers, and using self-control to be honest. (See Appendix A for the full text of "Kim.") "California" is a version of Hans Christian Andersen's "The Boy and the Dike." Set in the Western United States at the turn of the century, the story is about a girl who saves cattle in which the community has invested by holding the gate of a corral closed during a storm throughout the night. The moral messages are self-sacrifice and perseverance to help others. The other two stories are about helping friends or family ("Jed" and "Malcolm"). "Jed" is about a boy who is tempted away from his home responsibilities. The moral messages concern doing one's duty and being trustworthy. "Malcolm" is about a boy whose friend is an arson suspect and expects Malcolm to lie to keep the friend out of trouble while getting an innocent stranger into trouble. The moral messages are about telling the truth about strangers even at great cost.

To measure moral theme comprehension, we used two types of stimuli after a story was read: vignettes (paragraph-long stories with same or different themes) and messages (brief sentence-long themes). Participants responded to each type of stimulus with two types of tasks: (a) rating the closeness of the original story theme to the theme in each vignette or message and (b) selecting the vignette or message with the same theme. Two of these tasks (the selection tasks) had been used successfully in a previous study (Narvaez et al., 1998), and two (the rating tasks) were pilot tested successfully with children for this study.

Themes and distractors. The list of themes and distractors for the multiple-choice message and theme selection task was generated from two pilot groups: a group of adults (enrolled in an education class) who were asked to generate as many themes as possible for each story and a group of children (faculty and staff offspring) who were interviewed individually about what they thought the themes of the stories were. The themes were further corroborated with another group of adults (graduate students).

Keeping in mind the distortions that had occurred in previous research on moral comprehension and moral narrative recall, we attended to the distortions of moral themes that emerged in our pilot studies. These types of distortions were used as the basis for constructing distractor items for the multiple-choice message task. Distortions in the pilot studies often were based on three low-stage Kohlbergian moral reasoning stages, so we included distractor variables based on these stages (Stages 1–3), categorized according to Rest's version of Kohlberg's moral judgment stage typology (see Rest, 1979). We had five different categories of distractors (each scored as *incorrect*) and two theme choices (both scored as *correct*) for each story. The five distractor types were as follows: Stage 1 theme distortion (a focus on reprisal), Stage 2 theme distortion (a focus on prudence, i.e., personal gain or loss), Stage 3 theme distortion (a focus on losing or gaining the approval of others), an item using multisyllabic, "grown-up" words (an item that made sense but was not the theme), and an item focusing on the priority of the "in-group" (an item emphasizing collectivism). See Table 1 for the list of messages for "Kim." The in-group item was included because we thought it might provide information about cultural differences by attracting some cultural groups more than others. Although our hunch was correct, that analysis is not provided in this article.

There were three distractors for the multiple-choice vignette selection task. All used the same gender of protagonist as the target story did. The distractors varied systematically on superficial characteristics: One vignette type used the same actions (i.e., the same plot characteristics) but had different actors and a different theme, a second vignette type used the same actors but involved different actions and themes, and the third type of vignette had only the same setting. The target (correct) vignette had different actions and actors but the same theme. See Appendix B for examples.

Tasks.   After reading a story, the participants completed several tasks to measure comprehension. First, we measured reading comprehension by asking participants to answer 10 true–false questions about the story. Then came four tasks that measured moral theme comprehension:

TABLE 1 Message Choices and Categories from "Kim"	
ITEM	CATEGORY
Good children don't embarrass their parents.	Stage 3
If you give up what isn't yours now, your parents will reward you later.	Stage 2
If you think of others first instead of your family, your family may suffer.	In-group
Monetary interchanges need to be monitored scrupulously.	Complex
Treat all people with honesty no matter what tempts you.	Theme
You might get caught if you keep money that isn't yours.	Stage I
You shouldn't keep what isn't yours even from strangers.	Theme

1. Vignette rating: Participants rated four vignettes for how closely each one's theme matched the original story's theme. A 5-point Likert-type scale was used. Unlike the message choice task described below, the vignette rating task measured a more implicit understanding of the theme because the theme was not specified.

2. Vignette choice: Participants selected the vignette that best matched the theme of the original story. This task also measured a more implicit understanding of the story by not requiring a word-based understanding of the themes.

3. Message rating: Participants rated each of seven or eight messages for how well they matched the theme of the original story (using a 5-point Likert-type scale). This task measured a type of theme recognition.

4. Message choices: From the list of choices just rated, participants selected the two message choices that best matched the theme of the original story. This task measured their preference for presented themes.

Scoring.   To minimize the effect of response sets (individuals consistently rating widely or narrowly), we standardized (adjusted) rating scores in the following manner: For each task and participant, the sum of the ratings for the theme items in a story was subtracted from the rating for each choice in a story. Analyses refer to the adjusted scores whereas unadjusted scores are reported in the tables as noted.

Each of the four tasks was examined separately for each story in the following manner: (a) For the vignette rating task, the difference between the average ratings for the distractor (incorrect) items was subtracted from the rating for the correct vignette choice; (b) for the vignette selection task, the correct vignette choice was credited as 1 point; (c) for the message rating task, the difference between the average ratings for the distractor (incorrect) items was subtracted from the average rating for the correct theme choices; and (d) for the message selection task, the total correct theme choices were summed. Each score type was combined across stories. The scores for each of these four combination variables were added together for a composite score indicating moral theme comprehension. The reliability of the composite score (across four stories and four tasks) using Cronbach's alpha was .89. The combination of rating and ranking tasks has been a powerful tool in other studies of moral thinking, such as the N2 score for the DIT (Rest, Thoma, Narvaez, & Bebeau, 1997).

Responses to the ratings of distractor items were also analyzed. Ratings for each category of distractor were added together across stories and then compared by age group.

Reading comprehension. Ten true–false questions about the story were used to measure reading comprehension (general, not specifically moral) and served as a covariate in the analyses. These questions measured factual recall and inferences about the story.

True (mentioned) facts are facts explicitly stated in the story. *False (unmentioned) facts* are factual statements that are not in the story. *True inferences* are inferences a good reader would make while reading the story. *False inferences* are inferences a good reader would not make while reading the story. In other words, true inferences are those that have causal supporting evidence in the story whereas false inferences do not. Over all four stories, there were 12 true facts, 11 false facts, 7 true inferences, and 10 false inferences. The questions for each story were randomly ordered. See Table 2 for the questions used for "Kim." The reading comprehension score was composed of the correct answers to the set of 10 true-false questions for each story added together (*n* = 40). Cronbach's alpha reliability for these 40 questions was .81. As a secondary control for general reading ability, the children's standardized test scores (Metropolitan Achievement Test 7, hereafter MAT7) for reading comprehension and vocabulary were also collected.

Procedure

The children were tested in three groups by grade in two 50-min sessions 1 week apart. To minimize reading comprehension differences that were not the focus of study, we put the stories and tasks on audio tape as well as on paper for the children. Adults received only the written version and completed the tasks at home.[2]

Participants were guided through a practice story first. In each of two sessions, the children read along as two stories and questions about them were played on tape. After hearing and reading a story, participants were asked to think about the message of the story ("What do you think the author would like you to learn about getting along with others? Think about what would be the *best lesson* from this story about getting along with others.") After thinking about the message, participants completed several tasks:

1. Reading comprehension: Participants answered 10 true-false questions about the story. ("Here are some True-False questions about the story [story name]. Circle 'True' if the statement is true about the story or circle 'False' if the statement is false about the story. Answer these questions without looking back at the story.")

2. Vignette rating: Participants read four vignettes (paragraph-length) and then rated each one according to how well its message matched what they thought was the target story message. A 5-point Likert-type scale was used. ("Please read the following four stories. As you read each one, decide how well its message matches the *best* message from [story name].")

3. Vignette selection: Participants were next asked to select the vignette with the message that best matched the message in the original story. ("Now mark which of the four stories above has a message that most closely matches the *best* message of [story name]. You may look back at the four stories and what you thought about their messages.")

4. Message rating: The participants read and rated seven or eight possible messages or themes according to what they thought was the message of the target story. A 5-point Likert-type scale was used. ("Below are several possible messages for [story name]. Mark how good a match each message is with what you think is the *best* message of [story name].")

5. Message selection: Participants then identified which two messages had themes closest to that of the original story. ("Below, we list the possible messages again. Please circle the numbers of the two messages that you think most closely match the *best* message from [story name]. Circle two.")

There were three story orders. Each order presented two stories in each session for two sessions.

TABLE 2	True–False Comprehension Questions for "Kim"
QUESTIONS	TYPE
Kim didn't want to pay for the gas.	False fact
Kim wanted to buy snacks.	True fact
Kim's father stopped the car at a grocery store.	False fact
The family planned to go out for lunch.	False inference
Kim's parents were from Minnesota. Kim's father wanted the children to stay in the car.	False fact
Kim played the alphabet game with her father.	False fact
Kim's father was upset that she didn't keep the extra money.	False inference
Some boxes fell in the store.	True fact
The clerk was worried about her son.	True inference

---

[2]In the several pilot studies on the university campus, adults found the tasks to be extremely easy, so we decided there would be no threat to internal validity by allowing the adult participants to take the protocols home.

Each session included one story about a boy and one about a girl.

RESULTS

Several hypotheses were tested using analyses of variance (ANOVAs). In our primary analyses, we formed variables on the basis of (a) two kinds of ranking tasks: vignette choice and message choice; (b) two kinds of rating tasks: vignette rating and message rating; and (c) the composite score, which added the rankings and ratings across the four types of variables across stories (i.e., 16 units). Each analysis was conducted with alpha set at .05 and all t tests were two-tailed. There were no gender differences so analyses were combined for gender. When a participant failed to complete every instance of a response type, we eliminated that participant from the analysis of that type of response. Hence, the number of participants across the analyses varied.

Moral Theme Comprehension: Selection Variables

Two of the four tasks used to measure moral theme comprehension involved selecting the theme-based items. We first describe the results for each story and then the summary variables across stories. On the story level, the percentage of each group selecting the correct vignette was the following: For "Kim," third graders selected correctly 14% of the time; fifth graders, 59% of the time; and adults, 100% of the time. For "Jed," third graders were correct 18% of the time; fifth graders, 40% of the time; and adults, 75% of the time. For "Malcolm," the percentages were 10, 48, and 93, respectively; for "California," the percentages were 2, 35, and 96, respectively. Therefore, although all participants heard the same moral stories, there were significant differences in comprehending the moral themes.

Summarizing across stories, the third graders selected the correct vignette (one out of four possible choices) about 11% of the time ($M = 0.44$, $SD = 0.64$), and fifth graders selected correctly 45% of the time ($M = 1.81$, $SD = 1.67$), whereas adults selected correctly 91% of the time ($M = 3.64$, $SD = 0.56$). We used ANOVAs to compare the difference among the age groups and found it to be significant, $F(2, 129) = 118.74$, $p < .0001$. There was an increasing linear probability with age for selecting the correct vignette and, at the same time, a decreasing linear probability for selecting the third graders' favorite type of vignette, the distractor with the same actions as the target story. The third graders were consistent in selecting this distractor more than the others, suggest-

ing that they were competent in the task, although incorrect. If the third graders had been overwhelmed by the task, their responses would have been distributed equally across choices. Instead, their responses indicate a systematic pattern of response (an attraction to the vignette with the same actions) that the fifth graders reflected less and the adults still less.

For the list of messages, we used ANOVAs to compare group scores for selecting the two correct theme choices for each story (message choice). Table 3 has the percentages of each grade that selected the theme items from the message choices. Although among the stories there were different findings, there was a consistent linear age trend for each story (third grade: $M = 2.72$, $SD = 1.51$; fifth grade: $M = 4.67$, $SD = 1.26$; adult: $M = 6.00$, $SD = 0.86$): $F(2, 129) = 63.28$, $p < .0001$.

Moral Theme Comprehension: Rating Variables

Participants rated each choice they were given. Table 4 lists the average unadjusted ratings by grade for correct vignettes (vignette rating). Summarizing across stories, the results of ANOVA testing for differences in the ratings of the vignettes (using adjusted scores) were significant (third grade: $M = -2.57$, $SD = 3.17$; fifth grade: $M = 3.76$, $SD = 3.75$; adult: $M = 9.22$, $SD = 2.86$): $F(2, 129) = 116.52$, $p < .0001$.

Table 5 lists the average unadjusted ratings by grade for theme messages (message rating). Using ANOVAs on adjusted scores, we found a significant developmental trend for some theme rating variables. Overall, there were strong developmental differences for theme messages combined across stories (third grade: $M = 2.74$, $SD = 2.95$; fifth grade: $M = 5.74$, $SD = 2.40$; adult: $M = 8.32$, $SD = 2.01$): $F(2, 129) = 45.73$, $p < .0001$. In other words, the higher the age, the higher the rating of correct theme choices and the greater the differentiation between correct and incorrect choices.

ANOVAs were conducted for each set of rating variables. The findings for the incorrect vignettes were as follows for same-action vignettes (third grade $M = 3.72$, $SD = 0.56$; fifth grade $M = 3.53$, $SD = 0.73$; adult $M = 2.36$, $SD = 0.60$): $F(2, 129) = 43.82$, $p < .001$; for same-character vignettes, $F(2, 129) = 23.37$, $p < .001$; and for same-setting vignettes, $F(2, 129) = 13.30$, $p < .001$. For the ratings of the message distractors, all tests were significant: for Stage 1, $F(2, 29) = 22.58$, $p < .0001$; for Stage 2, $F(2, 29) = 4.00$, $p < .02$; for Stage 3, $F(2, 29) = 12.82$, $p < .0001$; for complex word, $F(2, 29) = 14.77$, $p < .0001$; and for in-group, $F(2, 29) = 13.28$, $p < .0001$.

TABLE 3   Percentage of Third Graders, Fifth Graders, and Adults Who Selected the Theme from the List of Message Choices

STORY AND SELECTION	THIRD GRADE	FIFTH GRADE	ADULTS
"Kim"			
Selected both themes	22	59	93
Selected only one theme	52	39	7
Selected neither theme	26	2	0
"Jed"			
Selected both themes	14	47	93
Selected only one theme	52	41	7
Selected neither theme	34	13	0
"Malcolm"			
Selected both themes	10	28	64
Selected only one theme	44	52	32
Selected neither theme	46	21	4
"California"			
Selected both themes	26	61	54
Selected only one theme	48	35	43
Selected neither theme	26	4	4

TABLE 4   Average Unadjusted Ratings (1–5) for Theme Vignettes for Each Story by Grade

TARGET VIGNETTE	THIRD GRADE		FIFTH GRADE		ADULTS		$F(2, 129)$
	M	SD	M	SD	M	SD	
"Kim"	2.34	1.36	3.93	1.18	4.50	0.58	38.83**
"Jed"	2.46	1.36	3.74	1.08	4.54	0.74	33.25**
"Malcolm"	1.58	0.84	2.80	1.14	3.46	1.04	35.71**
"California"	2.22	1.15	2.87	1.29	4.29	0.76	29.44**

**$p < .001$.

TABLE 5   Average Unadjusted Ratings (1–5) for Theme Messages for Each Story by Grade

STORY AND THEME	THIRD GRADE		FIFTH GRADE		ADULTS		$F(2, 129)$
	M	SD	M	SD	M	SD	
"Kim"							
Theme 1	3.65	1.35	4.65	0.68	4.57	0.69	14.88**
Theme 2	3.02	1.61	4.17	1.16	4.46	0.74	15.12**
"Jed"							
Theme 1	3.00	1.41	4.33	0.86	4.75	0.44	31.68**
Theme 2	4.04	1.12	4.44	0.82	4.43	0.69	2.90
"Malcolm"							
Theme 1	3.88	1.32	4.02	0.98	3.93	0.86	0.21
Theme 2	3.98	1.29	4.00	1.15	4.68	0.55	4.24*
"California"							
Theme 1	3.90	1.16	4.13	0.89	4.25	0.93	0.29
Theme 2	3.72	1.21	4.00	1.15	4.14	1.04	0.25

*$p < .02$. **$p < .001$.

Moral Theme Comprehension: Composite Variables

As mentioned previously, combining rating and ranking tasks can be more powerful than either task alone (Rest, Thoma, Narvaez, & Bebeau, 1997). Analyses of covariance (ANCOVAs) were conducted for each of the four dependent variables added across stories (i.e., target vignette choice, target vignette rating, target message choice, target message rating) and for all four added together. In the first set of analyses, scores on the reading comprehension items answered after each story were used as a covariate to control for general reading skill. See Table 6 for summary scores and significance. Analyses were significant for each dependent variable and their combination. There was a main effect for grade on the composite theme comprehension score, $F(2, 129) = 135.62$, $p < .0001$; even with reading comprehension as a covariate, $F(2, 129) = 74.65$, $p < .0001$.

A second set of ANCOVAs was performed for the children only; as a secondary control for general reading ability, two standardized subtest scores (MAT7 scores for reading comprehension and for vocabulary) along with the true–false reading comprehension measure were used. Again, the dependent variable was the composite theme comprehension score (all four dependent variables added together across stories). Covarying out both sources of reading comprehension scores (standardized test scores and study-specific true–false item scores) still produced a main effect for grade between the two groups, $F(1, 92) = 61.61$, $p < .0001$. When each source of reading comprehension (true–false items, MAT7 vocabulary, MAT7 reading comprehension) was tested independently for its prediction to composite scores, the effect was strongest for the true–false reading comprehension measure: for the true–false measure, $F(1, 91) = 5.67$, $p < .02$; for the MAT7 vocabulary,

$F(1, 91) = 3.92$, $p < .051$; and for the MAT7 reading comprehension, $F(1, 91) = 1.37$, $p < .24$.

Order Effects

There were order effects. As it turned out, there were more third graders in one group, and so this group's overall means were significantly lower for the main variables. However, an ANOVA conducted for Order × Age showed no significant differences, $F(2, 129) = .561$, $p < .572$, indicating that the order differences were accounted for by the disproportionate number of third graders in the one group.

DISCUSSION

The age groups performed differently on the tasks designed to measure moral theme comprehension. There were developmental differences on the message ratings and choices and on the vignette ratings and choices. These differences remained significant even after controlling for reading comprehension. With increasing age, correct performance improved. A separate analysis of the children's scores involved using as a covariate their standardized test scores (MAT7) along with the study-specific reading comprehension scores (true–false items). Differences between third and fifth graders were still large and significant. Reading comprehension could not explain all the variance in moral theme comprehension. We come to three specific conclusions as follows.

First, reading moral stories to children does not guarantee that they will understand the moral message or theme as intended by the author. Although we do not argue that children should not listen to moral stories that they understand differently from adults, we do advise that adults who educate for character should be aware of children's differential

TABLE 6	Means, Standard Deviations, and *F*s with Covariate for Combination Variables (Adjusted Scores)							
	THIRD GRADE (*n* = 50)		FIFTH GRADE (*n* = 54)		ADULTS (*n* = 28)			*F*(2, 129)
VARIABLE	*M*	*SD*	*M*	*SD*	*M*	*SD*	*F*(2, 129)	WITH COVARIATE
Vignette choice	0.44	0.64	1.81	1.67	3.64	0.56	118.74***	57.18***
Vignette rating	−2.57	3.17	3.76	3.75	9.22	2.86	116.52***	65.99***
Message choice	2.72	1.51	4.67	1.26	6.00	0.86	63.28***	25.43***
Message rating	2.74	2.95	5.74	2.40	8.32	2.01	45.73***	86.82***
Composite of four	3.31	6.04	15.99	7.00	27.19	4.98	135.62***	74.65***

Note. Vignette rating: possible range = −15–15; vignette choice: range = 0–4; message rating: possible range = −35–35; message choice: range = 0–8. Composite score combines the four other scores into one score.

***$p < .0001$.

interpretations of stories that seem perfectly clear to adults. Even among grade school children, the stories were understood differently—children only 2 years apart (third and fifth grade) varied significantly in their performance. This finding has serious implications for curriculum development and implementation. For example, character education curricula should be thoroughly pilot tested to gauge what is understood by the target audience. A curriculum that works with one age may not work for another.

Second, there are developmental differences in moral theme comprehension, as has been found in other moral comprehension research (e.g., Narvaez, 1998; Rest, 1973; Rest et al., 1969). Despite the fact that the correct themes were provided as choices to the respondents, the younger child was less likely to choose the correct message or vignette or to rate them highly. For all ages, the most attractive distractor type for the vignettes was the one with the same actions as the target story (a surface similarity). This attraction decreased with age as the attraction to the target vignette increased. Perhaps part of children's difficulty in grasping moral themes is that they tend to be distracted by superficial details.

Third, moral theme comprehension requires something beyond general reading comprehension. The age trends were not due simply to reading comprehension, as measured by standardized test scores and our reading test scores. Even when standardized reading comprehension and vocabulary scores were used as covariates along with our reading comprehension items, there were still significant differences between the third- and fifth-grade students on moral theme comprehension tasks. Because of the greater attraction to lower moral judgment stage distortions for themes in younger participants, we believe that moral judgment development is a factor in moral theme comprehension. The reader seems to impose a level of moral sophistication on the initial interpretation of the moral story.

We speculate that there are several tasks that must be completed to successfully complete the theme comprehension tasks generally: one must "pick up" the message by integrating intention–action–outcome chains of events, remember the message, put it into words, make a generalization, and apply it. It is not clear where the younger students go wrong. Do they choose the superficially similar distractor because they did not pick up the message to begin with, or because they did not remember it, or because they could not put it into words, or because they could not generalize, or because they could not apply the generalization they had formulated? Further research must determine where children have difficulty.

Researchers should also explore questions like the following:

1. What are the elements of moral theme comprehension? What is the difference between moral and nonmoral theme comprehension? Researchers have found that extracting embedded information from a narrative is difficult, and readers rely on factors such as their concerns at the time and their perspective on the topic (Britton, 1984; Rosenblatt, 1991). General theme extraction is especially difficult for children, although it becomes better established by fifth grade (Goldman et al., 1984). It has been established that stories contain story grammar categories such as initiating events, actions, goals, and outcomes that are differentially recalled by children in contrast with adults (see, e.g., Collins, 1983, van den Broek et al., 1997). Does moral theme comprehension require something over and above these simpler elements, such as more sophisticated social knowledge?

2. What kinds of story structure and affective focus (Brewer & Lichtenstein, 1982) facilitate moral theme comprehension? How does the causal connection strength (Trabasso & van den Broek, 1985) of a moral theme relate to its comprehension (i.e., is a theme with more causal connections to events in the story better comprehended)?

3. What determines whether a reader conjures a moral or a nonmoral theme for a story? For example, *The Little Engine That Could* (Piper, 1930) has both a nonmoral theme (keep trying and you will be successful) and a moral theme (persevere to help others). Does the generation of a moral theme (instead of a nonmoral theme) become a more automatic rather than a consciously controlled process with age?

4. What is the relation between moral theme comprehension and scores on moral judgment measures? Does moral theme comprehension require sophisticated moral judgment? In other studies, moral reasoning comprehension was strongly related to moral judgment, for example, $r = .67$ (Rest, Thoma, & Edwards, 1997). Does a reader have to share a particular set of moral schemas to extract a theme based on such schemas?

5. Are some moral themes understood sooner developmentally than other moral themes, or are some themes just easier to comprehend than others?

6. What kinds of instruction facilitate moral theme comprehension? Williams, Brown, Silverstein, and de Cani (1994) have demonstrated that middle-level students can understand the theme of a narrative only with deliberate, structured guidance. Answers to some of these questions will facilitate work on interventions for moral theme comprehension and ultimately allow the improvement of character education curricula.

REFERENCES

Afflerbach, P. P. (1990). The influence of prior knowledge on expert readers' main idea construction strategies. *Reading Research Quarterly, 25,* 31–46.

Anderson, R. C., & Pearson, P. D. (1984). A schema-theoretic view of basic processes in reading comprehension. In P. D. Pearson (Ed.), *Handbook of reading research* (pp. 225–291). New York: Longman.

Bartlett, F. C. (1932). *Remembering.* Cambridge, England: Cambridge University Press.

Bennett, W. (1993). *The book of virtues.* New York: Simon & Schuster.

Bobrow, D., & Norman, D. (1975). Some principles of memory schemata. In D. Bobrow & A. Collins (Eds.), *Representation and understanding: Studies in cognitive science* (pp. 131–149). New York: Academic Press.

Brewer, W. F., & Lichtenstein, E. H. (1982). Stories are to entertain: A structural-affect theory of stories. *Journal of Pragmatics, 6,* 473–486.

Britton, J. N. (1984). Viewpoints: The distinction between participant and spectator role in language research and practice. *Research in the Teaching of English, 18,* 320–331.

Chiesi, H. L., Spilich, G. J., & Voss, J. F. (1979). Acquisition of domain-related information in relations to high and low domain knowledge. *Journal of Verbal Learning and Verbal Behavior 18,* 257–274.

Colby, A., & Kohlberg, L. (1987). *The measurement of moral judgment* (Vols. 1 & 2). New York: Cambridge University Press.

Collins, W. A. (1983). Interpretation and inference in children's television viewing. In J. Bryant & D. R. Anderson (Eds.), *Children's understanding of television.* New York: Academic Press.

Gernsbacher, M. A. (Ed.). (1994). *Handbook of psycholinguistics.* New York: Academic Press.

Goldman, S. R., Reyes, M., & Varnhagen, D. (1984). Understanding fables in first and second languages. *NABE Journal, 8,* 35–66.

Harris, R. J., Lee, D. J., Hensley, D. L., & Schoen, L. M. (1988). The effect of cultural script knowledge on memory for stories overtime. *Discourse Processes, 11,* 413–431.

Johnson, D. F., & Goldman, S. R. (1987). Children's recognition and use of rules of moral conduct in stories. *American Journal of Psychology, 100,* 205–224.

Johnson, N. S. (1984). What do you do if you can't tell the whole story? The development of summarization skills. In K. E. Nelson (Ed.), *Children's language* (Vol. 4). New York: Gardner Press.

Kilpatrick, W. (1992). My *Johnny can't tell right from wrong.* New York: Simon & Schuster.

Kohlberg, L. (1984). *The psychology of moral development: The nature and validity of moral stages.* New York: Harper & Row.

Lehr, S. (1988). The child's developing sense of theme as a response to literature. *Reading Research Quarterly, 23,* 337–357.

Leming, J. (1997). Research and practice in character education: A historical perspective. In A. Molnar & K. J. Rehage (Eds.), The *construction of children's character* (pp. 31–44). Chicago: University of Chicago Press.

Lickona, T. (1991). *Educating for character* New York: Bantam Books.

McNamara, T. P., Miller, D. L., & Bransford, J. D. (1991). Mental models and reading comprehension. In R. Barr, M. L. Kamil, P. B. Mosenthal, & P. D. Pearson (Eds.). *Handbook of reading research* (Vol. 2, pp. 490–511). New York: Longman.

Narvaez, D. (1998). The influence of moral schemas on the reconstruction of moral narratives in eighth grade and college students. *Journal of Educational Psychology, 90,* 13–24.

Narvaez, D., Bentley, J., Gleason, T., & Samuels, J. (1998). Moral theme comprehension in third graders, fifth graders, and adults. *Reading Psychology, 19,* 217–241.

Oakhill, J. (1994). Individual differences in children's text comprehension. In M. A. Gernsbacher (Ed.), *Handbook of psycholinguistics* (pp. 821–848). New York: Academic Press.

Perfetti, C. (1985). *Reading ability.* New York: Oxford University Press.

Piaget, J. (1965). *The moral judgment of the child* (M. Gabain, Trans.). New York: Free Press. (Original work published 1932).

Piper, W. (1930). *The little engine that could.* New York: Platt & Munk.

Pritchard, R. (1990). The effects of cultural schemata on reading processing strategies. *Reading Research Quarterly, 25,* 273–295.

Reder, L. M., & Anderson, J. R. (1980). A comparison of texts and their summaries: Memorial consequences. *Journal of Verbal Learning and Verbal Behavior, 19,* 121–134.

Rest, J. R. (1973). The hierarchical nature of moral judgment. *Journal of Personality, 41,* 86–109.

Rest, J. R. (1979). *Development in judging moral issues.* Minneapolis: University of Minnesota Press.

Rest, J. R. (1983). Morality. In P. Mussen (Gen. Ed.) *Manual of Child Psychology,* J. Flavell & E. Markham (Eds.) *Vol 3: Cognitive development* (pp. 556–629). New York: Wiley.

Rest, J. R. (1986). *Moral development: Advances in research and theory.* New York: Praeger.

Rest, J. R., Narvaez, D., Bebeau, M., & Thoma, S. (1999). *Postconventional thinking: A neo-Kohlbergian approach.* Mahwah, NJ: Erlbaum.

Rest, J. R., Thoma, S. J., & Edwards, L. (1997). Devising and validating a measure of moral judgment: Stage preference and stage consistency approaches. *Journal of Educational Psychology, 89,* 5–28.

Rest, J. R., Thoma, S. J., Narvaez, D., & Bebeau, M. J. (1997). Alchemy and beyond: Indexing the Defining Issues Test. *Journal of Educational Psychology, 89,* 498–507.

Rest, J. R., Turiel, E., & Kohlberg, L. (1969). Level of moral development as a determinant of preference and comprehension of moral judgments made by others. *Journal of Personality, 37,* 225–252.

Reynolds, R., Taylor, M., Steffensen, M. L., Shirey, L., & Anderson, R. (1982). Cultural schemata and reading comprehension. *Reading Research Quarterly, 17,* 353–366.

Rosenblatt, L. M. (1991). The reading transaction: What for? In B. M. Power & R. Hubbard (Eds.), *Literacy in process* (pp. 114–127). Portsmouth, NH: Heinemann.

Rumelhart, D. E. (1980). Schemata: The building blocks of cognition. In R. J. Spiro, B. C. Bruce, & W. F. Brewer (Eds.), *Theoretical issues in reading comprehension* (pp. 33–58). Hillsdale, NJ: Erlbaum.

Rumelhart, D. E., & Ortony, A. (1977). The representation of knowledge in memory. In R. C. Anderson, R. J. Spiro, & W. E. Matague (Eds.), *Schooling and the acquisition of knowledge* (pp. 99–135). Hillsdale, NJ: Erlbaum.

Spilich, G., Vesonder, G., Chiesi, H., & Voss, J. (1979). Text processing of domain related information for individuals with high and low domain knowledge. *Journal of Verbal Learning and Verbal Behavior 18*, 275–290.

Stein, N. L., & Trabasso, T. (1982). Children's understanding of stories: A basis for moral judgment and dilemma resolution. In C. J. Brainerd & M. Pressley (Eds.), *Verbal processes in children: Progress in cognitive development research* (pp. 161–188). New York: Springer-Verlag.

Taylor, K. (1986). Summary writing by young children. *Reading Research Quarterly, 21*, 193–207.

Trabasso, T., & van den Broek, P. (1985). Causal thinking and the representation of causal relations in stories. *Discourse Processes, 12*, 1–12.

van den Broek, P. (1994). Comprehension and memory of narrative texts: Inferences and coherence. In M. A. Gernsbacher (Ed.), *Handbook of psycholinguistics* (pp. 539–588). New York: Academic Press.

van den Broek, P., Lorch, E., & Thurlow, R. (1997). Children's and adults' memory for television stories: The role of causal factors, story-grammar categories, and hierarchical level. *Child Development, 67*, 3010–3028.

van Dijk, T. A., & Kintsch, W. (1983). *Strategies of discourse comprehension.* New York: Academic Press.

Wilder, P. G. (1980). The moral of a story: Preschoolers' gradual comprehension of a narrative on Sesame Street. *Moral Education Forum 5,* 2–14.

Williams, J. P. (1993). Comprehension of students with and without learning disabilities: Identification of narrative themes and idiosyncratic text representations. *Journal of Educational Psychology, 85*, 631–641.

Williams, J. P., Brown, L. G., Silverstein, A. K., & de Cani, J. (1994). An instructional program in comprehension of narrative themes for adolescents with learning disabilities. *Learning Disability Quarterly, 17*, 205–221.

Wynne, E., & Ryan, K. (1993). *Reclaiming our schools.* New York: Merrill.

APPENDIX A

Kim

Kim pushed against the heavy boxes as they leaned towards her on the sharp curve. Her dad noticed that the boxes were sliding so he slowed down on the freeway ramp. Her dad had lost his job. They were moving to another city where jobs grew on trees. So people said. They were headed for Minneapolis.

The car was packed with everything they owned. The dinner table and chairs were on top of the car and on top of two mattresses. They gave away the old sofa and stuffed chair before they left Detroit. But they still had the room-sized rug. It drooped off the roof over the back window. Every couple of hours they stopped to tighten the ropes and push the rug and mattresses back from crawling off the car.

Kim had her own box. It had her clothes, her favorite (and only) doll, the dancing ballerina jewelry box she got for her birthday, and the fancy gold vanity set she inherited from her rich godmother when she died. The comb had lost some of its teeth, but the brush and mirror still looked new.

She felt a punch on her arm.

"Stop it, Martin!"

Her little brother squirmed next to her, having gotten bored with rereading the one comic book he owned. He looked like his father, a Puerto Rican mix of many races—curly hair, blue eyes, olive skin. Kim looked like her mother, a Filipino-Chinese. She had almond eyes, straight dark hair and olive skin. Their parents had given them "good American names" so that they would not be teased in school.

"That looks like a good place," Mrs. Perez said softly as they found a small gas station with a grassy lot behind.

Mr. Perez pulled into the gas station. "Everybody out for a stretch!" He didn't have to convince anyone. They all jumped right out.

As her dad filled the gas tank, Kim leaned against the car. Martin was off running and bouncing an old tennis ball in the grassy lot. She watched him for a moment, thinking about whether or not to join him. She decided not to. She was tired of his company after sitting next to him in the car all day long.

"You should get some exercise, girl! Here take this $20 and go pay for the gas. You should get back $1.15."

Her dad was very careful with money. They didn't have much of it. They barely had enough for gas to Minneapolis. The only thing they were eating was baloney sandwiches made from day-old bread and thin slices of baloney. Not even any ketchup! They would buy a carton of milk and a carton of juice and pass them around while they ate the sandwiches. Martin always spilled. Mom said it was because he had a small mouth.

Once inside the gas station store, she eyed the potato chips at the counter but then looked away as her mouth watered. She handed the clerk the $20 bill. As the clerk opened the cash drawer there was a loud crash in the corner of the store. They heard a loud cry.

The clerk became alarmed. "It's my 3-year-old son." She had the 15 cents in her hand. She quickly reached for a bill, pushed it into Kim's hand and went running to help her son. Kim watched. The boy was all right. He had pulled down a stack of cereal boxes but didn't look hurt.

Kim went outside. Her father was playing catch with Martin and her mother was still in line for the bathroom. She looked at the change in her hand. Then she looked again. Instead of $1.15 she had $5.15. The clerk had given her a five-dollar bill instead of a one-dollar bill.

She thought of the candy that she could buy with the extra money. She could go in the store and pretend she had forgotten to buy fruit rollups, potato chips, and pop. The whole family could have a treat, something they rarely had money for. Or she could go ask for change, give her dad the $1.15 and then save the $4 for herself. She wanted to buy a Teacher Barbie doll because she wanted to be a teacher when she grew up.

She couldn't decide, candy and treats now or save for the doll. Then she heard her mother's voice in her head, "You are a Kwong. Kwongs know that the path to success is self-control. Don't do what your feelings tell you to do without thinking about it first. Stop and think. Plan for the future. What you do today affects all your tomorrows." Kim decided not to buy the treats.

She thought about the money. Then she heard her father's voice inside her head from a time when his boss had given him too much money in his paycheck: "If you want to be a good person, you should always try to be honest. And you must always be honest because you are a Perez. We Perez are all honest, good people. Everybody knows that."

Was she being dishonest by keeping money put in her hand by someone she didn't even know? She would never see this clerk again. The clerk didn't know the Kwongs or the Perez family, and they didn't know her. Did it really matter to be honest with people that you didn't know and didn't know you? She entered the store and went to the counter and held out the money to the clerk.

Later, when everyone was back in the car, Kim handed the money to her father. "Here's the change, Papa. She gave me too much, but I gave it back."

"Good for you, sweetheart, good for you." Mr. Perez started up the car and they drove out of the lot.

Martin said, "Let's play alphabet—there's an 'A'!"

"Okay, amorcito—I see a 'B'!" Kim responded. She smiled and felt grown-up.

APPENDIX B

Example of Vignette Choices from "Kim": Same Setting, Same Characters, Same Actions, Same Theme

VIGNETTE WITH SAME SETTING

For summer vacation, Dawn was going to visit her Aunt Sandy. It would take 3 days to get there. Dawn prepared for her trip very carefully, making sure she had enough money for gas. She planned ahead for each stop she would need to make. On the second day of driving Dawn noticed a gas station ahead. It wasn't where she expected it. She had planned to stop at the gas station 20 miles from there. Dawn looked at her gas gauge. She knew she had enough gas to make it the 20 miles but not much farther. She decided that she should get gas at this station just to be safe. She pulled over and filled the gas tank.

While she was paying for the gas, the cashier told her that the gas station 20 miles away was closed. Dawn was glad she had stopped there.

VIGNETTE WITH SAME CHARACTERS

When Kim's family arrived in Minneapolis, they went to stay with Kim's uncle. Martin and Kim were happy to finally get out of the car. Kim took her box of things inside. Martin took his ball and comic book to show his cousins. The uncle and his family thought that Kim's family might be hungry, so they made them a big dinner. Kim and her family ate until they were full and forgot all about baloney sandwiches. After dinner, Kim and Martin played games with their cousins.

VIGNETTE WITH SAME ACTIONS

The Nicholson family was driving to Detroit. Theresa was not looking forward to moving. She didn't want to have to meet new friends, but she thought meeting new people would be better than hanging out with Chet, her brother. Chet was starting to bother her big time—especially after being in the car with him for so long.

Mr. Nicholson finally pulled off the highway so that they could eat dinner in a small town. They had an enjoyable meal at the town cafe. After receiving the bill for their food, Mr. Nicholson gave Theresa some money. "Sweetheart, will you please go pay the bill for our food? You should receive $4.50 back. Be sure to count your change." Theresa loved having adult responsibilities. She happily took the money from her father and went to pay the bill.

VIGNETTE WITH SAME THEME

Rhonda helped her mother unload the bags of groceries from their car. They had spent the day picking up groceries for the poor. Now, at dinner time, they were delivering them to poor families. This family was the last one. After they took the groceries inside, her mother sent Rhonda back to the car while she finished inside. Rhonda reached to shut the trunk. Then she noticed a tiny bag in the corner that they had missed. She looked inside. It contained several chocolate bars. Her stomach growled. The candy would fit into the pockets of her big winter coat. The family wasn't expecting the candy, so they would never know if she kept it. But it had been given for the family and therefore belonged to them. She ran quickly inside to deliver the bag.

SELF-STUDY QUESTIONS

Multiple Choice

1. According to the authors, research suggests that
   a. adults seldom have difficulty understanding text themes
   b. children often do not understand moral themes in stories
   c. children can make inferences about stories as well as adults
   d. reading moral stories to children is a waste of time
2. Which of the following best describes the outcome of this study?
   a. Third-graders were completely unable to understand moral themes.
   b. Third- and fifth-graders were very similar in moral theme comprehension.
   c. Moral theme comprehension was found to result mostly from general reading ability.
   d. There were important differences in comprehension across the two age groups.

Essay

1. Write a paragraph or two explaining the implications of this study for the use of moral stories in encouraging children's moral development.
2. Conduct your own study of moral theme comprehension. Make up a simple story such as those used by the authors of this article or use a literary story that is unfamiliar to the children you test. It must be unfamiliar because it is likely that adults have told children what the moral themes are of familiar stories such as *The Three Little Pigs*. Read the story to children of different ages (perhaps a 6-year-old, 8-year-old, and 10-year-old) and ask them questions like those used by the researchers. For comparison, use the same procedure with an adult. Write up a description of your findings.

ADOLESCENCE

"Why Abstinent Adolescents Report They Have Not Had Sex: Understanding Sexually Resilient Youth"

OVERVIEW

Typically, research on socially discouraged behaviors among adolescents focuses on teens who choose to engage in the discouraged behavior. Consequently, there is a great deal of research that identifies the variables that predict teen sexual behavior, smoking, drug use, and the like. This article is unusual because it seeks to identify the factors involved in a teen's decision to remain sexually abstinent.

METHODOLOGY

Like many social science researchers, the author of this article designed an instrument, the Reasons for Abstinence Scale (RAS), to measure the specific variable in which she was interested. The instrument was embedded in a 137-item survey that included questions about participants' family backgrounds and sexual experience. A statistical analysis called *factor analysis* was used to group the 18 RAS questions into three sets of items. Participants received a total score for each of the three sets that the researcher labeled: (1) fear-based postponement; (2) confusion and emotionality; and (3) conservative values. Once scores were tallied, the researcher determined whether a variety of variables (e.g., gender, alcohol use) predicted participants' reasons for remaining abstinent.

GLOSSARY TERMS

- **Risk factors**   variables correlated with risky behavior such as unprotected sex, alcohol use, and the like
- **Protective factors**   variables correlated with refraining from risky behavior

- **Psychometric properties**   characteristics of a psychological test or research instrument such as reliability and validity

Lynn Blinn-Pike

Why Abstinent Adolescents Report They Have Not Had Sex: Understanding Sexually Resilient Youth

The sample in this study consisted of 697 students from 20 schools in Missouri who indicated on a survey of sexual attitudes and behaviors that they had not had sex. The subjects completed the 18-item Reasons for Abstinence Scale and identified those items that were reasons why they had not had sex. The most frequent reasons for not having sex were related to fears of pregnancy and disease (including HIV/AIDS). The least frequent reasons were related to problems concerning the cost and availability of birth control and protection. Principal components factor analysis revealed three factors that were labeled "fear-based postponement," "emotionality and confusion," and "conservative values." Factor scores differed by gender, grades, alcohol consumption, family structure, father's education, and urbanicity. The discussion centers on the need to design different prevention strategies to build protective factors that result in "sexual resilience" in target groups of adolescents.

The debate over what messages to give adolescents about the prevention of sexually transmitted diseases (including HIV/AIDS) and pregnancy has proven to be confusing to youth and has proven conflictual and polarizing in many communities. The diverse messages that U.S. adolescents receive can be summarized as: (a) remain abstinent until marriage; (b) remain abstinent until emotionally and developmentally ready to become sexually active; (c) remain abstinent but, if not able to, have accurate information about birth control and protection; and (d) have accurate and factual information on how to use birth control and protection effectively because abstinence is not a realistic expectation. While many adults feel strongly about promoting one of the above positions with youth, it is not well understood how adolescents understand and incorporate these disparate admonitions into personal behavior patterns.

In the battle over the most appropriate approaches to reduce adolescent high risk sexual behaviors in the United States, more emphasis has been placed on understanding adolescents who report they have had sex than on understanding adolescents who report they have remained abstinent. For example, the Centers for Disease Control administered the Youth Risk Behavior Survey (YRBS) to a national sample of more than 16,000 high school students in 1997 and reported that 48% of the students had engaged in sexual intercourse. This figure was a significant decline from 54% in 1991 (MMWR, 1998) and generated great interest on the part of politicians, researchers, and practitioners. However, there were little empirical data on which to explain this decline. Both supporters of conservative abstinence-only and more liberal comprehensive sex education programs claimed responsibility. No research was found that asked the adolescents who have not had sex why they have remained abstinent. Therefore, the present study used a protective factor model of resiliency to address why diverse groups of adolescents report they have not had sex and to examine how to support youth who make the decision to remain abstinent to become "sexually resilient."

LITERATURE REVIEW

While much research and discussion has occurred in the last decade about fostering both sexually abstinent youth and resilient youth, few researchers have attempted to merge the two areas to provide direction for adolescent HIV, sexually transmitted disease, and pregnancy prevention. Although none of them specifically examined abstinence. Brooks-Gunn and Paikoff (1993), Small and Luster (1994), and Perkins, Luster, and Villarruel (1998) were unique in applying the concept of resilience, originally developed in the

Reprinted from *Family Relations,* 1999, *48,* 295–301. Copyrighted 1999 by the National Council on Family Relations, 3989 Central Ave. NE, Suite 550, Minneapolis, MN 55421. Reprinted with permission.

field of developmental psychopathology, to understanding adolescent sexual well-being. Brooks-Gunn and Paikoff (1993) explored the roles of cultural (moral standards, gender, culture, and media), individual (biology and social cognition), and environmental (peers, family, and school) factors in understanding how to promote sexual well-being among adolescents. They stated that most of the interventions to promote healthy adolescent sexuality, while promoting principles of positive behavioral change, have not been explicitly linked to the developmental literature on risk and protective factors. Small and Luster (1994) and Perkins et al. (1998) used an ecological risk-factor model to examine adolescents' sexual activity in relation to ethnicity, history of physical abuse, neighborhood monitoring, and attachment to schools.

Abstinence

Significant numbers of adolescents in the U.S. are putting themselves at risk for HIV, sexually transmitted diseases, and pregnancy at younger ages (MMWR, 1996, 1998). However, not all individuals become sexually active before adulthood and little attention has been paid to the group of adolescents who can be labeled as sexually resilient in the face of peer and media messages that make early sexual behaviors appear attractive and normal. Abstinence was catapulted into the public sphere when, on August 22, 1996, Congress appropriated $50M in the controversial Personal Responsibility and Welfare Reform legislation (Public Law 104-93) for the promotion of abstinence education each year from 1998-2002. The portion of this funding allocated to each state was determined by the proportion of the number of low income children in that state compared to the number of low income children nationally. In this legislation, the term "abstinence education" was defined as encompassing eight tenets: (a) There are social, psychological, and health gains from abstaining from sexual activity; (b) abstinence from sexual activity before marriage is the expected standard for all school age children; (c) abstinence from sexual activity is the only certain way to prevent out-of-wedlock pregnancy, sexually transmitted diseases, and other associated health problems; (d) a mutually faithful and monogamous relationship in the context of marriage is the expected standard of human sexual activity; (e) sexual activity outside of marriage is likely to have harmful psychological and physical effects; (f) bearing children out-of-wedlock is likely to have harmful consequences for the child, the parents, and society; (g) young people need to learn how to reject sexual advances and how alcohol and drug use increases vulnerability to sexual advances; and (h) young people need to attain self-sufficiency before engaging in sexual activity.

Organizations such as the National Abstinence Clearinghouse, Project Reality, and the National Coalition for Abstinence Education heralded this as much needed legislation. On the other hand, organizations such as the Sexuality Information and Education Council of the United States, the National Coalition to Support Sexuality Education, Advocates for Youth, the Alan Guttmacher Institute, and the National Commission on Adolescent Sexual Health disagreed and supported the provision of funding for "abstinence-based" rather than "abstinence-only" programs. The former include information on contraception and the latter do not. It has yet to be determined what impact this abstinence-only legislation will have on adolescent sexual decision making in the future.

Resilience

According to Masten, Best, and Garmezy (1990), resiliency refers to "the process of, capacity for, or the outcome of successful adaptation despite challenging or threatening circumstances" (p. 425). Remaining abstinent or making responsible sexual decisions during the adolescent years may be one of the most significant challenges facing youth today. The number of sexual messages that adolescents receive via the print and mass media each day makes it a challenging circumstance to be sexually resilient. According to Perry, Kelder, and Komro (1993), during the 1960s the adolescent issues dealt with on television were rather innocuous and included dates, blemishes, after-school jobs, and cars. During the 1990s, adolescent issues portrayed on television included suicide, pregnancy, HIV/AIDS, sexual harassment, and sexual abuse. Lowry and Towles (1989a) found that in heterosexual relationships in daytime dramas, the ratio of unmarried to married partners was 24 to 1, reinforcing the message that sexual behavior is more likely to occur outside of marriage. They also reported that adolescents watch 11 sexual behaviors per hour during prime time television (Lowry & Towles, 1989b). Brown, Childers, and Waszak (1990) reported that the average teenager watches almost 2,000 hours of sexual references on television each year and that references to birth control or to sexually transmitted diseases are almost nonexistent. Add the impact of films, music, videos, the world wide web, and magazines to that of television and it becomes evident that adolescents in the United States today learn about sexuality through almost unlimited exposure to sexual scenes where protection and responsibility are absent (Perry, Kelder, & Komro, 1993).

Bogenschneider, Small, and Riley (1992) described how the study of resiliency has moved from an epidemiological risk-focused approach in the 1960s and 1970s to the present protective factor etiological perspective. The later perspective asks not only what is wrong with children, but what is right with children. What protects them? How can we enhance the child's ability to resist stressful life events and promote positive adaptation and competence? In addition, Bogenschneider (1996) moved the field a step further ahead by proposing an ecological risk/protective model of resilience based on Bronfenbrenner's (1976, 1986) ecological theory of human development and Lerner's (1995) developmental contextualism. Bogenschneider's model contends that human development is shaped by multiple processes that must be identified in multiple levels of human ecology, and that these processes are shaped by the dynamic and reciprocal nature of development.

Risk factors are defined as individual or environmental hazards that increase an individual's vulnerability to negative developmental outcomes. Risk factors do not necessarily guarantee negative consequences, but may increase the likelihood that problem behaviors will occur (Werner & Smith, 1990). As the number of risk factors increases, the probability of problem behaviors increases. The following are examples of risk factors for youth that can develop into persistent behavioral patterns: involvement in alcohol or other drugs, sexuality, depression/suicide, anti-social behaviors, poor academic standing, and eating disorders (Rutter, 1979).

Protective factors are defined as individual or environmental safeguards that enhance an individual's ability to resist stressful life events while adapting to the situation and developing competency in dealing with it (Garmezy, 1983; Werner & Smith, 1990). In the protective model of resilience, protective factors, such as positive adult role models, good schools, and community involvement, are thought to buffer the impact of risk factors by improving coping, adaptation, and competence building. In the protective model, it is considered important to focus on those factors that foster health-promoting behaviors and competence in children. Protective factors are considered to work in interaction with risk factors to promote resiliency by moderating the effects of social or environmental risks so that more positive adaptation can take place than if they were not present.

Benson, Blyth, Deville, and Wachs (1997) contributed to the protective factor literature when they identified 40 developmental assets of resilient youth and divided them into those that were internal and external assets. The internal assets fall into three categories: commitment to learning, positive values, and social competencies. The external assets fall into four categories: support, empowerment, boundaries and expectations, and constructive use of time.

There have been several longitudinal studies of resiliency that have provided valuable insight into how individuals fare after long term exposure to poverty, dysfunction, mental illness, and physical disability and these have consistently pointed to specific positive traits of resilient children (see Garmezy, Masten, & Tellegen, 1984; Rutter, 1979; Werner & Smith, 1992). The positive traits that have emerged from these studies can be grouped into three categories. The first category involves their ability to seek out and cultivate positive relationships because they: (a) are attractive and popular with other people, (b) have more positive social relationships with friends and teachers, and (c) have a well-developed sense of humor. The second category involves their better cognitive and intellectual abilities that result in: (a) being perceived by themselves and others as being competent in at least some areas, (b) having positive school experiences, and (c) having better verbal skills.

The third category involves their positive world view an outlook on life, exhibited as having: (a) better impulse control, (b) higher self-esteem and internal locus of control, (c) the ability to delay gratification, and (d) the ability to maintain a positive future orientation. The characteristics listed above act as protective shields that assist children in avoiding regulating, or coping with aversive environmental or developmental conditions. In turn, they are better able to modify the negative impact of stressors and experience less damaging consequences.

However, the growing body of research on resilience has not been adequately applied to understanding adolescent abstinence, sexual decision making and risk taking behaviors. The following are unanswered questions concerning external protective factors and adolescent sexuality: Are the same external factors that have been identified as fostering resilience in areas such as drug prevention and delinquent behavior applicable in the prevention of early sexual activity (see Block, Block, & Keyes, 1988)? What community and family characteristics predict positive resistance to sexual pressure? What cultural and environmental assets help youth become proactive about securing and using birth control and protection? And what support system factors assist in overcoming feelings of embarrassment when attempting to communicate with adults and peers about sexual feelings and behaviors? The following are unanswered questions concerning internal protective factors. Are resilient youth: (a) more creative in refusing unwanted sexual advances, (b) more adept at building relationships with caring adults who can serve as confidants concerning sexual relationships, (c) more competent in negotiating the use of condoms, (d) more skilled in manipulating social situations so that they do not find themselves in high risk environments, and/or (e) better able to synthesize conflicting messages into a coherent set of personal standards?

RESEARCH QUESTIONS

The research questions addressed in this study were as follows. First, what reasons do abstinent adolescents give for not becoming sexually active? Second, what are the underlying dimensions of adolescents' reasons for not being sexually active? And third, how do adolescents differ in their reasons for being abstinent based on individual (alcohol use, school grades, age), cultural (race, gender), and environmental (family structure, father's education, and urbanicity) factors related to resiliency?

METHOD

Sample

The sample in this study consisted of 697 early adolescents (8th through 10th grade) attending 20 schools across the state of Missouri. Out of a larger sample of 1,112 subjects, the 697 students made up the 65% of the sample who responded that they had not had sex. Table 1 shows that the sample was approximately equally divided on gender (59% female). The highest percentages of subjects were from nonurban areas (67%), in ninth grade (43%), White (74%), had fathers with high school educations or less (42%), and lived with both parents (73%). The students who were classified as urban lived in two designated metropolitan statistical areas (MSA): Kansas City and St. Louis. A MSA is a large population nucleus, together with adjacent communities that have a high degree of economic and social integration with that nucleus. Each metropolitan area must contain either a place with a minimum population of 50,000 or a Census Bureau defined urbanized area and a total metropolitan population of at least 100,000 (U.S. Census Bureau, 1993). The students not living in these two official metropolitan areas were classified as nonurban.

Instrumentation

The results reported here are based on the 18-item Reasons For Abstinence Scale (RAS) that was devel-

TABLE 1   Demographic Data on Subjects (N = 697)

Age ($\bar{x}/SD$)	14.56/.88
Gender	
Male	288 (41%)
Female	414 (59%)
Urbanicity	
Urban	227 (32%)
Nonurban	468 (67%)
Father's Education	
High School or less	278 (42%)
Some college	114 (17%)
4 or more years of college	120 (18%)
Not sure	147 (22%)
Race	
African-American	145 (21%)
White	516 (74%)
Other	52 (5%)
Live With	
Two parents	512 (73%)
Mother or stepmother	127 (18%)
Father or stepfather	12 (2%)
Other	44 (6%)
Grades (self-reported)	
A-B	373 (57%)
B-C	228 (35%)
C-D	55 (8%)

oped for this study and part of a larger instrument (137 questions) administered to 1,112 students in the fall of 1998. The RAS was administered by trained classroom teachers in intact classrooms. The RAS questions were derived from an extensive review of the literature on adolescent sexual activity and field tested with 45 seventh through ninth grade students in one urban and two rural schools. Care was taken to insure that data collection was consistent across the 20 sites. Prior to the administration of the survey, the involved teachers attended a one-day workshop in which instructions were given for securing parental consent and gathering data in a systematic and ethical manner.

In addition, it was considered important that the students understand the vocabulary used in the survey. Prior to administration of the survey, the teachers wrote the following definition on the board and read it to the students: "Having sex means having intercourse or going all the way." The instructions for the RAS read: "Below are 18 reasons for not having sex. If you have never had sex, read each statement and mark 'yes' if it is one of the reasons why you have not had sex. Mark 'no' if it is not one of the reasons why you have not had sex. If you have had sex, leave the questions blank." Examples of the 18 questions included: "I have never had sex because I would be too embarrassed," "I have never had sex because I am not ready," and "I have never had sex because I do not want to get AIDS." As a reliability check, the student was asked if he or she had had sex at five points in the 137-item survey. All of the 697 students responded five times that they had never had sex.

Analyses

The first step in the analyses was to determine the frequencies of the reasons for not having sex. The second step was to determine the underlying nature of the adolescents' perceptions of why they had not had sex using principal components factor analysis. The number of factors retained for rotation was determined by several criteria: (a) examination of the eigenvalue magnitudes using Kaiser's (1974) normalization, (b) application of Cattell's (1952) screen test, and (c) examination of the variance explained. Factors were rotated using varimax procedures (Kaiser, 1958). Factors were interpreted by examining questions with both positive and negative loadings above .40.

In the third analysis, unweighted summed scales were calculated based on the factor results. Univariate analysis of variance (ANOVA) was used as a test for significant main and interaction effects by subjects' family structure (two-parent family or other situation), grades in school (A-B, B-C, C-D), alcohol usage (never drink, less than one drink per month, more than one drink per month), ages (13,14,15,16), gender, fathers' education (high school or less, some college, four or more years of college), urbanicity (urban and nonurban), and race (African-American and White). When adolescents with missing data were eliminated, the sample size for the ANOVA procedures was 596.

RESULTS

The items with means below 1.20 or the most frequent reasons for not having sex were (1 = *yes*, 2 = *no*): fear of AIDS ($\bar{x} = 1.18/SD = .39$), fear of becoming pregnant or getting someone pregnant (1.18/.39), and fear of getting a disease (1.19/.39). The moderately frequent reasons were: believing it is wrong to have sex before marriage (1.50/.50) and waiting until marriage (1.50/.50). The least frequent reasons were: not knowing where to get birth control or protection (1.90/.29), being embarrassed to use birth control or protection (1.90/.28), and not having enough money to buy birth control or protection (1.93/.24).

In the second analysis, the nature of the adolescents' reasons for remaining abstinent were explored. The results of principal components factor analysis on the 18 questions revealed three factors that explained 48% of the variance (25%, 13%, and 10%, respectively). All of the items, but one, loaded on one of three factors using the .40 criteria. The loading for the item "I do not have a partner at this time" was .32 and was dropped from further analysis. Reliability of the factor solution was assessed using theta. According to Carmines and Zeller (1979) the advantage of theta is that it provides a single coefficient for estimating reliability. Theta for the 17 items was .84.

The three factors were labeled: (a) fear-based postponement (6 items), (b) emotionality and confusion (8 items), and (c) conservative values (3 items). Table 2 shows a summary of the items and factor results. The label "fear-based postponement" was used to describe an adolescent who had considered the consequences and did not feel ready for sex because

TABLE 2	Summary of Means and Factor Loadings for the Reasons For Abstinence Scale (N = 697)		
FACTOR	MEAN/*SD*	LOADING	QUESTIONS
Fear-Based Postponement	1.27/.42	.61	not ready for sex
		.55	waiting for the right person
		.66	waiting until I am older
		.77	fear of pregnancy or getting someone pregnant
		.84	fear of AIDS
		.43	parents would be upset
Emotionality and Confusion	1.85/.26	.47	friends think it wrong before marriage
		.57	too embarrassed
		.50	partner does not want to have sex
		.67	do not know where to get birth control or protection
		.56	afraid it might hurt
		.78	embarrassed to use birth control or protection
		.65	not enough money to buy birth control/protection
		.73	embarrassed to buy condoms
Conservative Values	1.53/.44	.87	wrong to have sex before marriage
		.81	religion says it is wrong to have sex before marriage
		.84	waiting until I get married

he or she believed it would be unwise due to the risk of pregnancy or disease and reprisal from parents.

The label "emotionality and confusion" was given to the items in the second factor because of fears surrounding pain, embarrassment, lack of money for birth control or protection, and peer or partner disapproval. This person appeared to allow a mixed set of environmental or contextual factors to determine his or her level of sexual activity, as opposed to making a personal decision.

The label "conservative values" was given to the items that dealt with religion and waiting until marriage to have sex. The KR-20 reliability for each scale was "fear-based postponement" (.81), "emotionality and confusion" (.78), and "conservative values" (.84).

In the third analysis, the factors identified above were compared based on the age, grades, family structure, race, fathers' education, urbanicity, and gender. There were insufficient numbers of observations in some cells to test for interaction effects.

Scores on factor 1 (*fear-based postponement*) were significantly different by gender and alcohol use. Females had lower (more affirmative) scores on this factor than males ($\bar{x}$ = 1.19/SD = .24 versus 1.37/ .33); $F(1,595)$ = 53.10, p < .001). Scheffe follow-up procedures showed that adolescents who did not drink were significantly more likely than adolescents who drank less than once a month or more than once a month to give factor 1 as a reason for not having sex ($\bar{x}$ = 1.22/SD = .27, 1.28/.31, and 1.36/.32, respectively) ($F(2,592)$ = 11.55, p < .001.)

Scores on factor 2 (*emotionality and confusion*) showed that there were significant differences due to alcohol usage. Scheffe follow-up procedures showed that adolescents who did not drink at all ($\bar{x}$ = 1.83/ SD = .20) were significantly more likely than the adolescents who drank less than once a month ($\bar{x}$ = 1.90/SD = .16) or the adolescents who drank more than once a month (1.89/.16) to affirm that factor 2 was a reason for remaining, abstinent ($F(2,592)$ = 6.94, p < .001.)

Factor 3 (*conservative values*) revealed differences based on alcohol use, father's education, urbanicity, grades, and family structure. Table 3 shows the means and significance levels for these groups. Adolescents who did not use alcohol, had better educated fathers, were from nonurban areas, had higher grades, and lived with both parents were more likely to agree that factor three (*conservative values*) represented a reason for not having sex.

Scheffe follow-up procedures on factor 3 revealed that: (a) All three pairwise comparisons were significant for alcohol use, (b) adolescents who had fathers with high school educations or less were significantly different from either the students who had fathers

TABLE 3	Significant Variables Related to Factor 3-Conservative Values (N = 596)	
	GROUP ($\bar{x}$/SD)	F
Alcohol use		44.08*
no drinking	1.41/.41	
less than once a month	1.64/.40	
more than once a month	1.78/.35	
Father's education		8.63*
four or more years of college	1.45/.44	
some college	1.47/.44	
high school or less	1.59/.41	
Urbanicity		7.18*
nonurban	1.51/.43	
urban	1.61/.40	
Grades		8.68*
A-B	1.34/.44	
B-C	1.63/.40	
C-D	1.67/.33	
Family structure		4.59*
two parents	1.51/.43	
other	1.62/.40	

*p < .01.

with some college or four or more years of college, and (c) adolescents who reported their grades were As and Bs were significantly different from the students who had either Bs and Cs or Cs and Ds.

DISCUSSION

The present study was unique in that it asked abstinent adolescents why they had not had sex. Abstinent adolescents can be labeled as "sexually resilient" because they face the same opportunities and pressures to have sex as their sexually active peers. The results showed that the lack of an available partner did not appear to be a strong reason for remaining abstinent. Five hundred and four (71.5%) of the subjects stated that lack of a partner was not a personal reason for remaining abstinent. The adolescents in this study were young ($\bar{x}$ = 14 years) and, as can be expected, many of them had not yet initiated sexual activity. Nationally, only 7% of adolescents report having sexual intercourse before 13 years of age (MMWR, 1998). However, it is noteworthy that only approximately one-third reported making a conscious decision to delay sexual activity. This is evident in the following results: did not feel ready for sex (32% or 229), waiting for the right person (25% or 178), or waiting until they are older (35% or 251). Fears of pregnancy and AIDS were the most frequent reasons for not having sex. Issues related to the use of birth control and protection, such as cost, embarrassment, and lack of availability, did not surface as important reasons for abstinence.

The adolescents showed that they had absorbed multiple and diverse messages about sex and synthesized them into three distinct abstinence-related factors, each of which was explained by either gender, alcohol use, family structure, grades, father's education, and/or urbanicity. Age may not have been a significant independent variable because of the limited age range of the sample.

The present research did not provide evidence of differences between Whites and African-Americans on the three identified factors. On one hand, it might be hypothesized that there would be racial differences on the first factor because previous research has shown that Black adolescents feel more vulnerable to health risks such as cancer, pregnancy, and AIDS than do White adolescents (Eisen, Zellman, & McAllister, 1985; Price, Desmond, Wallace, Smith, & Stewart, 1988). On the other hand, it might be hypothesized that there would be racial differences on the third factor due to differences in religiosity (Billy, Brewster, & Grady, 1994; Day, 1992). Perkins et al. (1998) conducted an ecological risk factor examination of individual, extrafamilial, and familial risks related to sexual experience in over 15,000 Black, White, and Latino adolescents. They reported little support for the hypothesis that risk factors for sexual activity differed significantly among ethnic groups. Low religiosity was the only risk factor that varied by ethnicity. Low religiosity was a significant predictor of sexual activity for White and Latino males and White and African American females. It remains to be seen if racial differences are revealed on these factors in future research. Future research in this area may need to include a specific measure of religiosity.

As the results revealed, drinking alcohol was a significant independent variable across all three factors. This is consistent with previous research that has pointed to alcohol consumption as a strong predictor of early sexual activity (Flick, 1986; Perkins et al., 1998; Small & Luster, 1994).

Factor 1

The first factor had the lowest of the three means indicating it contained items that were some of the most frequent reasons for not having sex. It was called fear-based postponement because the author imagined an adolescent saying, "Having sex is stupid and I am going to wait because you can get pregnant or die, and besides my parents would kill me." Females were more likely to make such a statement. Of the three that were identified here, this subscale

appears to be the most cognitively-based. Factor 1 represents primarily females who have weighed the consequences and decided not to have sex yet. The fact that females were more likely to express this position is consistent with the resiliency literature that has pointed to gender differences in relation to cognitive ability and adjustment. Werner (1993) found that internal protective factors (e.g., temperament and cognitive skills) tended to have a greater impact on the adult adaptation of high risk females than of high risk males. The opposite was true for males who benefitted more from external support from family and community.

Much research exists about gender differences in risk factors, but very little exists about gender differences in protective factors (Clark, 1995). According to the Centers For Disease Control (MMWR, 1998), the decline in adolescent sexual activity in the U.S. from 1991 to 1997 was significant for males but not females. There is little research on the characteristics of effective gender-based messages to help adolescents become sexually resilient.

Factor 2

The second factor had the highest mean indicating that of the three, it contained items that were the least likely to be selected as reasons for not having sex. It represented emotionality and confusion because adolescents who were low on this factor would be more likely to say, "I haven't had sex because it might hurt and it is embarrassing and hard to get the stuff you need to protect yourself." This was especially true for adolescents who did not drink alcohol. The items in this scale point to an individual who has not clearly delineated why he or she has not had sex and is operating with a mix of loosely related contextual factors. This individual may be at high risk for early initiation of sexual behavior because of a lack of a specific reasoning process that can act as a protective factor.

Factor 3

The third factor revealed a more *conservative value* stance on the part of adolescents who lived in nonurban areas, lived with their parents, did not drink, had better grades, and had better educated fathers. Previous research has identified these variables as significant in the prevention of risky sexual activity (e.g., Costa, Jessor, Donovan, & Fortenberry, 1995; Flick, 1986; Small & Luster, 1994). However, no research was found that examined the relationship between adolescents' reasons for being abstinent and protective factors such as: refraining from alcohol use, having better educated parents, having a higher grade point average, and living in a two-parent household. An adolescent whose views were represented by this factor might say, "I am waiting until marriage to have sex because my religion says that is what I am supposed to do."

In terms of urbanicity, it was not surprising that the nonurban adolescents held more conservative values. Previous research has shown that, compared to their urban counterparts, rural residents consider religion and the role of the church to be very important in community life, hold more traditional moral values, expect greater conformity to community norms, and are less tolerant of diversity (Rounds, 1988). However, such values may not impact behavior because few differences have been found between urban and rural adolescents in their ages of initiation of sexual activity, extent of contraceptive use, or rates of adolescent pregnancy (Skatrund, Bennett, & Loda, 1998; McManus & Newacheck, 1985; Yawn & Yawn, 1987, 1993).

IMPLICATIONS FOR PREVENTION

While the resilience literature contains various related terms such as protective factors, risk factors, assets, and positive traits, it coalesces around an ecological model that stresses the roles of the individual, culture, and environment in protecting youth from engaging in high risk behaviors and experiencing negative consequences from exposure to environmental stressors. The results reported here point to the significant roles that specific individual (alcohol consumption, fear of pregnancy, and disease), culture (gender), and environmental (father's education, urbanicity, family structure) factors play in the adolescent's decision about when to begin having sex.

The "sexually resilient" youth has received little attention in the prevention literature. Based on the results reported above, two messages need to be given to early adolescents to build resiliency and to support behaviors that delay the initiation of sexual activity. The first message is that abstinence is the only 100% effective way of preventing unwanted pregnancy and disease. Some educators may choose to combine this with information on birth control and condoms, depending on local and cultural values. This first message is recommended because early adolescents have been shown to (a) be sporadic users of contraception (Ford, Zelnick, & Kantner, 1981; Herz & Reis, 1987), and (b) misunderstand facts about pregnancy, contraceptive techniques, and the consequences of unintended pregnancy and parenthood (Herz & Reis, 1987). It appears that such

a concrete message will be particularly effective with early adolescent females who fear pregnancy and disease.

While educational programs and media that attempt to reduce barriers to birth control and condoms (accessibility, cost, embarrassment) are important, they may not get the attention of early adolescents because the barriers are not perceived as salient. They may not have had experiences where they attempted to acquire or use birth control or protection and are not sensitized to the issues involved.

And second, given that alcohol consumption is a risk factor that is strongly related to early sexual activity, anti-drinking messages need to target adolescents in the age group studied here, below 15 years of age. Magazines and television shows that are popular with young females could emphasize the security and freedom from fear that comes with abstinence. While media outlets that are popular with both genders could place more emphasis in the anti-alcohol message.

Finally, communities need to work together to foster the messages stated above, as well as to support the kinds of programs and services that are conducive to healthy adolescent development. These could include mentoring, academic tutoring, faith-based recreational activities, and broad-based family support. Parents, family life educators, and teachers can use the RAS as an informal needs assessment tool and then target messages to build resiliency around the feelings of particular groups of adolescents.

CONCLUSION

Although the RAS needs research and documentation concerning its psychometric properties with different groups of adolescents, the results reported here point to three broad reasons why adolescents perceive they have not had sex: fear, confusion, and religion. Sexually abstinent adolescents have not received the same amount of attention as their sexually active peers. Increasing our understanding of why some adolescents choose not to have sex is in keeping with the trend toward identifying protective, rather than risk factors, that contribute to resiliency. The pertinent question is: What have nonsexually active adolescents done right rather than what have their sexually active peers done wrong? Practitioners and researchers need to recognize that the diverse messages that have been given to American adolescents concerning sexuality have resulted in multiple reasons for some of them remaining abstinent. Some sexual resiliency in adolescents may be attributable to individual, cultural, and/or environmental characteristics. No one message, no one philosophical base or value stance, and no one approach to resilience is going to be equally effective with all adolescents.

Perkins et al. (1998, p. 663) stated, "There are different pathways to sexual activity…the risk factors that are important may differ from individual to individual." In light of the results presented here, the statement could be rewritten as, "There are many different pathways to sexual abstinence…the protective factors that are important may differ from individual to individual and from group to group."

REFERENCES

Benson, P. L., Blyth. D. A., Deville, C., & Wachs, J. (1997). *Developmental assets among Seattle youth.* Minneapolis: Search Institute.

Billy, J. O. G., Brewster, K. L., & Grady, W. R. (1994). Contextual effects of sexual behavior of adolescent women. *Journal of Marriage and the Family, 56,* 387–404.

Bogenschneider, K. (1996). An ecological risk/protective theory for building prevention programs, policies, and community capacity to support youth. *Family Relations, 45,* 127–138.

Bogenschneider, K., Small, S., & Riley, D. (1992). *An ecological. risk-focused approach for addressing youth-at-risk issues.* Chevy Chase, MD: National 4-H Center.

Block, J., Block, J. H., & Keyes, S. (1988). Longitudinally foretelling drug usage in adolescence: Early childhood personality and environmental precursors. *Child Development, 59,* 336–355.

Bronfenbrenner, U. (1976). *The ecology of human development: Experiments by nature and design.* Cambridge. MA: Harvard University Press.

Bronfenbrenner, U. (1986). Ecology of the family as a context for human development: Research perspectives. *Developmental Psychology, 22,* 723–742.

Brooks-Gunn, J., & Paikoff, R. L. (1993). "Sex is a gamble, kissing is a game": Adolescent sexuality and health promotion. In S. G. Millstein, A. C. Petersen, & E. O. Nightingale (Eds.), *Promoting the health of adolescents: New directions for the twenty-first century* (pp. 180–209). New York: Oxford.

Brown, J. D., Childers, K. W., & Waszak, C. S. (1990). Television and adolescent sexuality. *Journal of Adolescent Health Care, 11,* 62–71.

Carmines, E., & Zeller, R. (1979). *Reliability and validity assessment.* Beverly Hills, CA: Sage.

Cattell, R. B. (1952). *Factor analysis.* New York: Harper & Row.

Clark, P. (1995). Risk and resiliency in adolescence: The current status of research on gender differences. *Equity Issues, 1,* 1–13.

Costa, F. M., Jessor, R., Donovan, J. E., & Fortenberry, J. D. (1995). Early initiation of sexual intercourse: The influence of psychosocial unconventionality. *Journal of Research on Adolescence, 5,* 93–121.

Day, R. D. (1992). The transition to first intercourse among racially and culturally diverse youth. *Journal of Marriage and the Family, 54,* 749–762.

Eisen, M., Zellman, G. L., & McAllister, A. L. (1985). A health belief model approach to adolescent fertility control: Some pilot program findings. *Health Education Quarterly, 12,* 185–210.

Flick, L. H. (1986). Paths to adolescent parenthood: Implications for prevention. *Public Health Reports, 101,* 132–147.

Ford, K., Zelnick, M., & Kantner, J. (1981). Sexual behavior and contraceptive use among socioeconomic groups of young women in the United States. *Journal of Biosocial Science, 13,* 31–45.

Garmezy, N. (1983). Stressors of childhood. In N. Garmezy & M. Rutter (Eds.), *Stress, coping and development in children* (pp. 43–84). New York: McGraw-Hill.

Garmezy, N., Masten, A., & Tellegen, A. (1984). The study of stress and competence in children: A building block for developmental psychopathology. *Child Development, 55,* 97–111.

Herz, E. J., & Reis, J. S. (1987). Family life education for young inner-city teens: Identifying needs. *Journal of Youth and Adolescence, 16,* 361–377.

Kaiser, H. F. (1958). The varimax criterion for analytic rotation in factor analysis. *Psychometrika, 23,* 187–200.

Kaiser, H. F. (1974). An index to factorial simplicity. *Psychometrika, 89,* 31–36.

Lerner, R. M. (1995). *America's youth in crisis: Challenges and choices for programs and policies.* Thousand Oaks. CA: Sage.

Lowry, D. T., & Towles, D. E. (1989a). Soap opera portrayals of sex, contraception, and sexually transmitted diseases. *Journal of Communication, 39,* 76–83.

Lowry, D. T., & Towles, D. E. (1989b). Prime time TV portrayals of sex, contraception and venereal diseases. *Journalism Quarterly, 66,* 347–352.

Masten, A. S., Best, K. M., & Garmezy, N. (1990). Resiliency and development: Contributions from the study of children who overcome adversity. *Development and Psychopathology, 2,* 425–444.

McManus, M. A., & Newacheck, P. W. (1985). Rural maternal, child, and adolescent health. *Health Services Research, 23,* 807–848.

MMWR. (1996). *Youth Risk Behavior Surveillance, 45* (SS-4), Atlanta: Centers for Disease Control, 1–86.

MMWR. (1998). *Youth Risk Behavior Surveillance, 47* (SS-3), Atlanta: Centers for Disease Control, 1–86.

Perkins, D. E., Luster, T., & Villarruel, F. A. (1998). An ecological, risk-factor examination of adolescents' sexual activity in three ethnic groups. *Journal of Marriage and the Family, 60,* 600–673.

Perry, C. L., Kelder, S. H., & Komro, K. A. (1993). The social world of adolescents: Family, peers, schools and the community. In S. Millstein, A. Petersen, & E. Nightingale (Eds.), *Promoting the health of adolescents: New directions for the twenty-first century* (pp. 73–97). New York: Oxford.

Price, R. H., Desmond, S. M., Wallace, M., Smith, D., & Stewart, P. M. (1988). Differences in Black and White adolescents' perceptions about cancer. *Journal of School Health, 58,* 66–70.

Rounds, K. A. (1988). AIDS in rural areas: Challenges to providing care. *Social Work, 33,* 257–261.

Rutter, M. (1979). Protective factors in children's responses to stress and disadvantage. In M. W. Kent & J. E. Rolf (Eds.), *Primary prevention in psychopathology, Vol. 3: Social competence in children* (pp. 49–74). Hanover, NH: University Press.

Skatrud, J. D., Bennett, T. A., & Loda, F. A. (1998). An overview of adolescent pregnancy in rural areas. *Journal of Rural Health, 14,* 17–26.

Small, S. A., & Luster, T. (1994). Adolescent sexual activity: An ecological, risk-factor approach. *Journal of Marriage and the Family, 56,* 181–192.

U.S. Census Bureau. (1993). Census of Population and Housing: Summary Tape File 4 Technical Documentation, Washington, DC.

Werner, E. E. (1993). Risk, resilience, and recovery: Perspectives from the Kauai Longitudinal Study. *Development and Psychopathology, 5,* 503–515.

Werner, E. E., & Smith. R. S. (1990). Protective factors and individual resilience. In S. J. Meisels & J. P. Shonkoff (Eds.), *Handbook of early childhood intervention* (pp. 97–116). Cambridge, England: Cambridge University Press.

Werner, E. E., & Smith, R. S. (1992). *Vulnerable but invincible: A study of resilient children.* New York: McGraw-Hill.

Yawn, B. P., & Yawn, R. A. (1987). Teenage sexual activity in rural Minnesota. *Minnesota Medicine, 70,* 38–39.

Yawn, B. P., & Yawn, R. A. (1993). Adolescent pregnancies in rural America: A review of the literature and strategies for primary prevention. *Family and Community Health 16*(1), 36–45.

SELF-STUDY QUESTIONS

Multiple Choice

1. Which of the following best describes the author's view of the relationship between research on youth resilience and adolescent sexual behavior?
   a. Resilience researchers have examined adolescent sexuality issues extensively.
   b. Resilience research has little relevance to questions about teen sexual behavior.
   c. The factors that predict general resilience and sexual resilience are different.
   d. Application of findings about general resilience may be useful in understanding adolescent sexual decision-making.

2. Adolescents with high scores on the *conservative values* factor were more likely than participants with lower scores to

   a. live in urban areas
   c. have lower grades
   b. live in single-parent homes
   d. abstain from alcohol

Essay

1. Critics of studies of risky behavior among adolescents claim that such research often leads to negative stereotypes of teens. Explain how the article's Literature Review section supports or does not support this assertion.

2. Suppose you were asked to design an educational program for 13- to 15-year-olds to encourage them to delay becoming sexually active until adulthood. How could you use the findings and recommendations in this article in developing such a program?

ADOLESCENCE

"Perceived Competence and Self-Worth during Adolescence: A Longitudinal Behavioral Genetic Study"

OVERVIEW

You are probably familiar with the *nature-nurture debate*, the ongoing discussion about the relative contributions of genes and environment to human development. For the most part, these discussions have centered on intelligence and personality traits. Variables such as self-esteem are believed to be primarily the result of learning, and, as such, have not been examined by behavior geneticists. However, these authors used longitudinal data derived from twins and siblings to address nature-nurture questions about such variables.

METHODOLOGY

Twin studies are arguably the most important kind of research in the study of behavior genetics. Identical twins, whose genetic inheritance is exactly the same, are typically compared to fraternal twins, who are no more genetically similar than non-twin siblings. Many studies, including this one, also compare identical twins to non-twin sibling pairs and adopted sibling pairs. Researchers correlate the scores of the different kinds of siblings on measures of the variables of interest, in this case competence and self-worth. If the scores of identical twins are more highly correlated than other types of sibling pairs, researchers can conclude that heredity is involved to some degree.

GLOSSARY TERMS

- **Nonshared environmental influences** environmental influences that vary across siblings; for example, one child gets an allowance but another does not because she is thought by parents to be irresponsible
- **Shared environmental influences** environmental influences that do not vary across siblings; for example, a parent uses rewards to encourage desirable behavior in all the children in a family
- **Attrition effects** the effects of some participants dropping out of a longitudinal study
- **Genotype versus phenotype** a person's genetic inheritance is his genotype, while his actual observable traits are his phenotype. For example, an individual may get a gene for type A blood from his mother and one for type O blood from his father, making his genotype AO. His phenotype, though, will be type A because the gene for this type is dominant over the gene for type O blood.

Shirley McGuire, Beth Manke, Kimberly J. Saudino,
David Reiss, E. Mavis Hetherington, and Robert Plomin

Perceived Competence and Self-Worth during Adolescence: A Longitudinal Behavioral Genetic Study

This investigation is the first longitudinal behavioral genetic study of self-concept during adolescence. It is a follow-up of a previous study examining genetic and environmental contributions to children's perceived self-competence and self-worth using a twin/sibling design. The study investigated adolescents' reports 3 years later and stability across two time points. Participants included 248 pairs of same-sex twins, full siblings, and stepsiblings between 10 and 18 years old. The results showed that six of the seven subscales were heritable at the second time point. None of the scales showed significant shared environmental effects. Longitudinal analyses revealed genetic contributions to stability for perceived scholastic competence, athletic competence, physical appearance, and general self-worth. Social competence, on the other hand, showed nonshared environmental mediation across time. These findings highlight the importance of genetically influenced characteristics and unique experiences as correlates of individual differences in self-concept during adolescence.

INTRODUCTION

The literature on children's self-concept is vast (e.g., Bracken, 1997; Cicchetti & Beeghly, 1990; Harter, 1983; Wylie, 1979). Given the central role of the self in the development of social relationships and adjustment, it is crucial that researchers understand the correlates of adolescents' perceived competence and of stability and change in these perceptions over time (see e.g., Cicchetti & Beeghly, 1990). The prevailing view is that individual differences in adolescents' self-concept are due to differences in their social experiences. The family environment, in particular, has been highlighted as a central source of children's perceived competence (Grotevant & Cooper, 1986; Isberg et al., 1989; Lamborn, Mounts, Steinberg, & Dornbusch, 1991; Noller, 1995; Whitbeck et al., 1991). Most studies, however, have examined the role of the family from a "shared environment" angle. That is, links between the family environment and adolescents' self-perceptions have been investigated for only one child per family. This approach is unable to determine whether children in the same family are similar or different in

levels of self-concept. The *assumption* is that children that share certain family characteristics (e.g., a warm family climate) will have similar levels of self-worth and perceived competence.

Recently, a twin/sibling study of adolescents found that siblings living in the same home differed considerably in their perceived self-worth and competence (McGuire, Neiderhiser, Reiss, Hetherington, & Plomin, 1994). The results suggest that experiences that are unique to siblings, rather than shared environmental experiences, are important correlates of self-concept. The study also found genetic contributions to individual differences in four of the seven areas assessed: perceptions of scholastic competence, athletic competence, social competence (i.e., popularity with peers), and physical appearance (i.e., attractiveness). In addition, children's reports of scholastic and social competence were still heritable after controlling for genetic contributions to vocabulary and temperament. Surprisingly, no significant shared environmental influences were found for any of the areas of self-concept. The only other twin study of perceived competence found that adults' perceived interpersonal, work-related, intellectual, domestic, and athletic abilities were significantly heritable. There were no shared environmental influences; instead, the remaining variance appeared to be due to nonshared experiences and measurement error (McGue, Hirsch, & Lykken, 1993). In fact, the sibling similarity pattern in both studies was comparable to a pattern found for some personality traits. Specifically, behavioral genetic studies of personality sometimes show a nonadditive genetic pattern with fraternal twin and sibling correlations that are "too low" (Buss & Plomin, 1984; Goldsmith, 1983; Loehlin, 1992; Lykken, McGue, Tellegen, & Bouchard, 1992; Matheny & Dolan, 1980; Plomin, Chipuer, & Loehlin, 1990; Saudino, McGuire, Reiss, Hetherington, & Plomin, 1995).

Thus, it appears that unique social experiences and genetically influenced characteristics, not shared family experiences, are the main contributors to individual differences in perceived competence. To our knowledge, this study is the first longitudinal behavioral genetic study of self-concept during adolescence. It is the longitudinal follow-up to a study published in this journal (McGuire et al., 1994). The goals were to examine genetic and environmental contributions (1) to perceived self-worth and competence 3 years after the initial study, and (2) to stability and change in self-concept across time.

A 3-year longitudinal follow-up of the sample provided an opportunity to address two developmental questions about self-concept from a behavioral genetic perspective: (1) Does the magnitude of genetic and environmental influences on self-concept change over time?; and (2) what are the contributions of genetic and environmental influences to stability and change during adolescence? One could argue that genetic influences exert most of their effects early in life and diminish across development as environmental forces accumulate over time (Plomin, DeFries, McClearn, & Rutter, 1997). Indeed, shared or nonshared environmental effects on perceived competence and self-worth may increase as children get older. Individual differences in intelligence, however, tend to show higher heritability and lower shared environment effects across the lifespan (Fulker, DeFries, & Plomin, 1988; Pedersen, Plomin, Nesselroade, & McClearn, 1992; Plomin, 1986). The heritability of some aspects of self-concept may increase across adolescence because genetic effects present early in life help create larger phenotypic differences across time, or because the nature of the construct itself has changed (Plomin et al., 1997). On the other hand, the heritability of personality characteristics seems to remain stable, at least across adulthood (Goldsmith, 1983; Loehlin, 1992; McCartney, Harris, & Bernieri, 1990; Plomin & Nesselroade, 1990). In fact, a cross-sectional study of adult twins found that the heritability of perceived competence was consistent across adulthood (McGue et al., 1993). Individual differences in adolescents' per-

ceived self-competence and self-worth might show the same consistent pattern across time.

Although no study has examined genetic and environmental contributions to stability in self-concept, there have been longitudinal behavioral genetic studies of related constructs in the personality area (e.g., Loehlin, 1992; Matheny, 1989; Matheny & Dolan, 1975; McGue, Bacon, & Lykken, 1993; Saudino, DeFries, & Plomin, 1996). These studies typically found significant genetic contributions to stability, whereas change appeared to be due to nonshared environmental effects. A few studies, however, have found evidence of genetic contributions to change in personality characteristics during early childhood and adolescence (Eaves, Eysenck, & Martin, 1989; Goldsmith & Gottesman, 1981).

In summary, the present study had two goals: (1) To examine genetic and environmental influences on adolescents' perceived self-worth and competence at two time points during adolescence; and (2) to investigate genetic and environmental contributions to stability and change across time. It was expected that adolescents' reports of self-concept at Time 2 would replicate the results found at Time 1. That is, perceived scholastic competence, social competence, athletic competence, and physical appearance would be significantly heritable and all of the subscales would suggest significant nonshared environmental influences. It was also expected that stability in self-concept would be linked to genetic factors and change would be due to unique environmental influences and measurement error.

METHOD

Participants

Participants were 248 same-gender sibling pairs taking part in two measurement sessions of the Nonshared Environment and Adolescent Development (NEAD) Project, a regionally representative sample of two-parent families with a pair of same-sex adolescent siblings no more than 4 years apart in age. Nondivorced families were obtained through random-digit dialing of 10,000 telephone numbers throughout the United States; most twin families and stepfamilies, however, were recruited throughout a national market panel of 675,000 households. The families were primarily middle class and of European ancestry. The average years of education were 13.6 for mothers and 14.0 for fathers. The nondivorced and stepfamilies did not differ with respect to demographic characteristics, such as the ages of the two children, family size, income level, ethnicity, and religion. The father's education level, mother's age, and number of years married were higher in nondivorced families, but none of these variables were significantly correlated with the measures used in this report (see Reiss et al., 1994, for a more detailed description of sample characteristics and recruitment procedures).

Of the original 720 pairs, 315 pairs participated at Time 1 and not at Time 2 because the families were out of the scope of the project (*n* = 288) or refused to participate (*n* = 27). Families were considered in the scope of the project if the family was still together and both children lived in the parental household at least part of the time. For the purposes of the present paper, another 145 pairs had to be excluded from the analysis because one of the siblings did not complete all of the scales, or completed them incorrectly at either Time 1 or Time 2. Twelve pairs of twins were also excluded because their zygosity could not be classified with certainty. Thus, the present study focused on 248 sibling pairs who had full data for all self-concept subscales at both time points.

The sample included children with an average age of 13.6 years (*SD* = 2.0) at Time 1 and 16.2 years (*SD* = 2.1) at Time 2; their siblings averaged 12.1 years (*SD* = 1.9) at Time 1 and 14.7 (*SD* = 1.8) at Time 2. The design included six sibling categories: 45 monozygotic twin pairs (19 boys, 26 girls) and 51 dizygotic twin pairs (28 boys, 23 girls); 39 full sibling pairs (19 boys, 20 girls) in nondivorced families; and 57 full sibling pairs (26 boys, 31 girls), 29 half sibling pairs (16 boys, 13 girls), and 27 unrelated sibling pairs (14 boys, 13 girls) in stepfamilies.

Zygosity (MZ or DZ) of the twins was determined by tester, self-reports, and parent reports of physical similarity (e.g., eye and hair color) using a modified questionnaire designed for adolescents. Twins were classified as dizygotic (DZ) if any of the respondents reported differences in physical characteristics. In addition, the questionnaire asked if the twins were "as alike as two peas in a pod," if people ever mixed them up, or if people used special marks to tell them apart. Twins were classified as DZ if respondents reported never being confused about each twin's identity. The measure has yielded over 90% accuracy when compared to tests of single-gene markers in the blood (Nichols & Bilbro, 1966).

Procedure

At both Time 1 and Time 2, the families were interviewed and videotaped twice in their homes approximately 2 weeks apart. The Time 1 and Time 2 data collections were, on average, 2.6 years apart. The present analyses used only data collected during the interview sessions. Each home visit was conducted by two testers and lasted approximately 3 hours.

Measure. Perceived competence and self-worth were assessed using Harter's (1988) Self-Perception Profile for Adolescents. The measure is based on a multifaceted view of self-concept with general self-worth assessed as a separate dimension rather than the average of the other areas of competence (Harter, 1983). The measure contains nine 5-item subscales including scholastic, social, and athletic competence, physical appearance, morality, friendship, romantic appeal, and job competence, as well as global self-worth. The adolescent version was used for the entire sample, with two exceptions for children below the seventh grade: (1) The word "teenager" was replaced with "kid" for each item, and (2) the job competence and romantic appeal subscales were not included. Children completed the questionnaire on their own, although interviewers were on hand to answer any questions concerning the scale. The present study used the seven subscales completed by the entire sample. The internal consistency reliabilities ranged from .70 to .83 at Time 1 and from .74 to .90 at Time 2; however, the reliability of the morality subscale was lower, .55 at Time 1 and .63 at Time 2, which warrants caution in interpretations involving this subscale. The intercorrelations across the subscales ranged from .15 to .86, with the majority below .49. Correlations between general self-worth and the perceived competence subscales ranged from .37 to .68.

Design and model-fitting. The present study employs a combined twin and stepsibling design to disentangle similarity that can be attributed to shared environment from that attributed to shared genetic heritage. Behavioral genetic models use quantitative genetic theory and quasi-experimental methods to decompose phenotypic (measured) variance into genetic and environmental components of variance (Plomin et al., 1997). According to this theory, if shared environment is important the siblings will be correlated across all sibling types. In the present design, the correlation between biologically unrelated siblings is the most direct index of shared environment because these siblings share only environmental influences. If genetic influences are important, the correlations will show the following pattern: MZ twins > DZ twins = full siblings > half siblings > unrelated siblings. The theory can be applied to examine both patterns of sibling correlations and those of cross-sibling correlations. A cross-sibling correlation is the correlation between the child's score on one measure and the sibling's score for a second variable. Common genetic influence between two measures is implied if the cross-sibling correlations show the pattern mentioned above.

A model-fitting approach provides a more powerful analysis of sibling resemblance than examining patterns of correlations. Model fitting analyzes the data for different sibling types simultaneously, tests for the fit of the model, makes assumptions explicit, and permits tests of alternative models (Eaves, Last, Young, & Martin, 1978; Jinks & Fulker, 1970; Loehlin, 1987). In this study, maximum-likelihood model-fitting analyses were performed using LISREL VIII (Jöreskog & Sörbom, 1993). These modeling techniques have been explained in more detail elsewhere (see Boomsma, Martin, & Neale, 1989; Boomsma & Molenaar, 1986; Fulker, Baker, & Block, 1983; Neale & Cardon, 1992). Variance/covariance matrices were used for these analyses because correlation matrices may modify the model and produce incorrect χ^2 values and standard errors. In addition, information about variability is especially important when comparing multiple groups and using equality constraints (Cudeck, 1989; Neale & Cardon, 1992). Two models were used in this study: univariate and bivariate. The univariate model was used to decompose the variance of the individual scales at each time point. This model is depicted as a path diagram in Figure 1. Sibling covariances were used to decompose the variance of a measure into genetic and environmental components. Four parameters were derived: additive genetic variance (G_a), nonadditive

genetic variance (G_d), shared environmental variance (E_s), and nonshared environmental variance (E_n), which includes error variance. This path diagram also indicates the assumptions of the model: no assortative mating, no selective placement of step-siblings, nonadditive genetic variance due to dominance and not epistasis, genotype–environment correlation and interaction are negligible, and shared environment is equal across sibling group. The design of the current model allowed us to test the last assumption using two submodels. The first submodel estimated separate shared environment parameter for twins versus nontwins and the second model for nondivorced versus stepfamilies.

The bivariate models were used to examine the sources of stability and change across the two time points. These models use cross-sibling covariances to decompose the covariance between two measures into common and unique genetic and environmental components. Figure 2 represents a bivariate model with eight latent variables (see Neale & Cardon, 1992). Four latent variables (G_a, G_d, E_s, E_n) reflect genetic and environmental influences *common* to both measures across the two time points. That is, the phenotypic association between two measures may be due to common genetic or environmental sources. The covariance between the two measures was decomposed into these sources. If the association is the

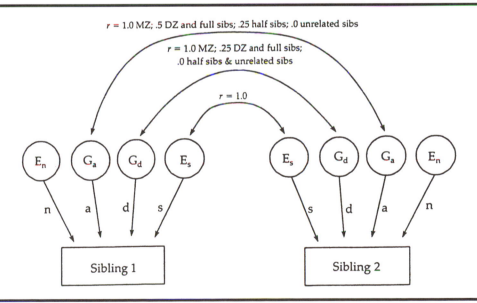

FIGURE 1   A univariate behavioral genetic model. Sibling 1 and Sibling 2 are measured variables for the two siblings, G_a and G_d are latent variables representing, respectively, additive and nonadditive (dominance) genetic variance. E_s is a latent variable representing shared environmental influence common to the sibling pair. E_n represents residual variance that does not result in sibling covariance; this includes nonshared environment and measurement error. The curved, two-headed arrows indicate correlations between the variables they connect; the one-headed arrows represent paths, standardized partial regressions of the measured variable on the latent variable.

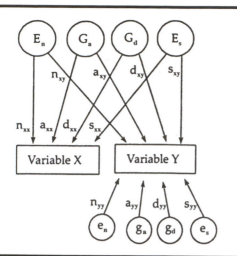

FIGURE 2 A bivariate behavioral genetic model. G_a and G_d are latent variables representing, respectively, additive and nonadditive (dominance) genetic variance common to variables X and Y. E_s and E_n are latent variables representing shared and nonshared environmental influences common to the two measures. The four remaining latent variables represent genetic (g_a and g_d) and environmental (e_s and e_n) influences specific to variable Y.

result of shared environmental influences, then the cross-sibling correlations will not differ across the six groups. The four additional latent variables (g_a, g_d, e_s, and e_n) reflect genetic and environmental influences *unique to* the measure at Time 2.

RESULTS

First, attrition effects were tested by comparing perceived competence scores of the longitudinal sample to those who participated only at Time 1. Next, mean differences were examined for age and gender effects, and variance differences were tested across the six sibling groups. Then, sibling intraclass correlations were calculated for the measures at Time 1 and Time 2, and heritability and environmentality indices were estimated. Finally, genetic and environmental contributions to stability and change were explored.

Attrition

Attrition effects were assessed for pairs in which both children participated in Time 1 and Time 2 data collections (i.e., the longitudinal sample) versus pairs who only participated at Time 1. Analyses were conducted separately for Child 1 (older siblings and first twin entered) and Child 2 (younger siblings and second twin entered) data sets resulting in 14 t tests. The longitudinal samples included the 248 pairs and the

Time 1 only sample included 350 pairs. Four out of the 14 comparisons (29%) showed significant mean differences between the longitudinal and nonlongitudinal sample. The longitudinal sample was significantly higher in scholastic competence in both Child 1, $t = 2.62$, $p < .01$, and Child 2, $t = 2.52$, $p < .01$, data sets. The longitudinal sample was also significantly higher in morality, $t = 2.75$, $p < .01$, and general self-worth, $t = 2.00$, $p < .05$, in the Child 1 data set; these differences, however, were not replicated in the Child 2 data set. The longitudinal sample appears to be a slightly better-functioning group compared to those who did not participate in the Time 2 data collection; however, the attrition effects do not appear to be large or pervasive.

Mean and Variance Differences

Age and gender effects can inflate sibling correlations because siblings are close in age (twins are identical in age) and the study included only same-sex sibling pairs. To prevent inflation of the sibling correlations, older and younger siblings' scores at Time 1 and Time 2 were corrected for age, gender, and gender × age interaction effects (see McGue & Bouchard, 1984). Gender and age effects explained more than 9% of the variance for only 2 of the 28 analyses. These variables explained 13% of the variance in older siblings' athletic competence at Time 2 and younger siblings' physical appearance at Time 2. In addition, homogeneity of variances across the six sibling groups were tested using a likelihood ratio test (Morrison, 1976). Only one scale, social competence at Time 2, showed a significant difference, $\chi^2(5, N = 496) = 12.30$, $p < .03$. Table 1 shows the means and variances for the seven subscales by sibling group while collapsing over birth order.

Genetic and Environmental Contributions

The magnitude of genetic and environmental contributions to the self-concept scales were examined. Table 2 presents sibling intraclass correlations for the perceived competence and self-worth scales at both Time 1 and Time 2. The Time 1 data for the longitudinal sample was analyzed to test whether results would be similar to those found for the original sample (see McGuire et al., 1994). In general, the pattern of correlations across sibling groups at both time points indicated some genetic contribution, but little shared environmental influence. For most scales, MZ twin correlations were double or more than double the DZ and full sibling correlations, and the half and unrelated correlations were low or not significant. It should be noted, however, that the sample

TABLE 1   Means and Standard Deviations for Perceived Self-Competence and Self-Worth by Sibling Group ($N = 496$)

	MZ ($n = 90$)	DZ ($n = 102$)	FN ($n = 78$)	FS ($n = 114$)	HS ($n = 58$)	US ($n = 54$)
Scholastic competence						
Time 1	16.5 (2.8)	15.9 (3.2)	15.0 (3.1)	15.7 (3.0)	14.4 (3.5)	15.1 (3.4)
Time 2	16.2 (3.2)	15.8 (3.2)	15.0 (3.5)	14.8 (3.7)	14.0 (4.1)	14.6 (3.2)
Athletic competence						
Time 1	14.8 (3.3)	14.0 (4.0)	13.6 (4.0)	13.7 (4.1)	13.9 (3.1)	14.4 (3.6)
Time 2	14.1 (4.1)	13.5 (4.4)	13.0 (4.0)	12.8 (4.0)	12.8 (4.3)	14.2 (4.0)
Social competence						
Time 1	16.4 (2.7)	15.5 (3.0)	15.4 (3.3)	16.1 (2.8)	15.6 (3.3)	16.1 (2.9)
Time 2	16.0 (3.2)	15.9 (2.7)	15.5 (3.5)	16.1 (2.8)	16.1 (3.4)	17.0 (2.7)
Physical appearance						
Time 1	14.7 (3.2)	13.5 (3.6)	13.0 (4.1)	13.6 (3.4)	13.9 (4.2)	13.7 (3.4)
Time 2	14.2 (3.7)	13.4 (3.8)	12.3 (4.1)	12.9 (3.8)	13.5 (3.9)	12.9 (3.3)
General self-worth						
Time 1	16.8 (2.7)	15.7 (2.8)	15.0 (3.4)	15.3 (3.2)	16.2 (3.3)	15.6 (3.2)
Time 2	16.4 (2.9)	15.8 (3.1)	14.9 (3.9)	15.3 (3.3)	15.2 (3.5)	15.5 (3.3)
Morality						
Time 1	15.5 (2.2)	14.8 (2.5)	14.6 (2.6)	14.3 (2.6)	14.1 (2.5)	13.8 (2.7)
Time 2	15.4 (2.4)	14.8 (2.3)	13.8 (2.5)	13.7 (2.7)	13.3 (3.1)	13.6 (2.6)
Friendship						
Time 1	16.6 (3.0)	16.1 (2.8)	16.3 (3.0)	16.2 (3.0)	16.3 (2.9)	16.2 (2.7)
Time 2	16.5 (3.1)	16.8 (2.6)	16.8 (3.0)	16.5 (3.1)	16.5 (3.3)	16.5 (3.1)

Note: MZ = identical twins in nondivorced families; DZ = fraternal twins in nondivorced families; FN = full siblings in nondivorced families; FS = full siblings in stepfamilies; HS = half siblings in stepfamilies; US = unrelated siblings in stepfamilies. Standard deviations are in parentheses.

TABLE 2   Sibling Intraclass Correlations for Perceived Self-Competence and Self-Worth at Time 1 and Time 2 by Sibling Group

	TIME 1						TIME 2					
	MZ ($n = 45$)	DZ ($n = 51$)	FN ($n = 39$)	FS ($n = 57$)	HS ($n = 29$)	US ($n = 27$)	MZ ($n = 45$)	DZ ($n = 51$)	FN ($n = 39$)	FS ($n = 57$)	HS ($n = 29$)	US ($n = 27$)
Scholastic competence	.63*	.25*	.18	−.01	−.10	.09	.61*	.08	−.03	.45*	.11	.38*
Athletic competence	.49*	.36*	.14	−.04	.15	−.14	.55*	.01	.14	.21	.32*	.21
Social competence	.43*	.19	.05	.06	−.23	.08	.70*	.08	.28	.30*	.22	.08
Physical appearance	.41*	.34*	−.13	.01	.06	.29	.51*	.27*	.10	.19	.15	.13
General self-worth	.17	.05	.01	−.07	−.02	.27	.55*	.31*	−.09	.21*	−.02	.32*
Morality	.11	.38*	.34*	.18	.03	.04	.29*	.26*	−.07	.07	.10	.18
Friendship	.27*	.06	.28*	−.27*	−.05	.11	.55*	−.09	.08	.19	.30*	.23

Note: MZ = identical twins in nondivorced families; DZ = fraternal twins in nondivorced families; FN = full siblings in nondivorced families; FS = full siblings in stepfamilies; HS = half siblings in stepfamilies; US = unrelated siblings in stepfamilies.

*p < .05.

sizes for both the half and unrelated sibling groups were too small to detect low levels of shared environment. The genetic pattern was not evident for all subscales. General self-worth and friendship at Time 1, and morality at both Time 1 and Time 2, showed correlations for MZ twins that were no greater than correlations for other sibling pairs.

Univariate maximum-likelihood model-fitting confirmed the impressions gleaned from the patterns of sibling correlations. Table 3 contains the components of variance and χ^2 values for the univariate model fitting results. The χ^2 values were significant for 3 of the 14 models. The Goodness-of-Fit index (GFI) for each analysis indicated good to excellent fit to the data. The GFI's ranged from .92 to .99 at Time 1, and from .79 to 1.00 at Time 2.

To test the importance of a parameter for the model, that parameter would be set to zero and the change in $\chi^2(1)$ would be calculated. In every case, the additive genetic (G_a) and shared environment (E_s) parameters could be dropped from the model without a significant degradation in fit. The nonadditive genetic parameter (G_d) was significant for four of the seven self-concept subscales at both Time 1 and Time 2. In addition, two self-concept scales, general self-worth and friendship, show genetic influences at Time 2, but not at Time 1. Only the children's reports of morality showed no evidence of genetic influence at either time point. For all of the subscales, the nongenetic variance was accounted for solely by the nonshared environmental parameter, which includes error of measurement. It should be noted that the lack of shared environmental and genetic influences for the morality scale may be due to the low reliability.

Two other alternative models were tested: separate twins versus nontwin shared environments, and separate nondivorced versus stepfamily shared environments. The shared and nonshared environmental

parameters for the two groups were freed and the change in the χ^2 value was calculated (i.e., new model compared to the original model). This was done for each subscale at both Time 1 and Time 2. Five of the 14 models fit significantly better with separate twin and nontwin environments, and two of the 14 models fit significantly better with separate nondivorced and stepfamily environments. Four cases showed significantly higher shared environment for twins compared to nontwins: physical appearance at Time 1 (.31 versus .01), $\Delta\chi^2(2) = 8.71$; general self-worth at Time 1 (.04 versus .005), $\Delta\chi^2(2) = 7.38$, and at Time 2 (.26 versus .00), $\Delta\chi^2(2) = 10.27$; and morality at Time 2 (.28 versus .07), $\Delta\chi^2(2) = 7.86$. Social competence at Time 2 showed a significantly higher shared environment for nontwins compared to twins (.15 versus .00), $\Delta\chi^2(2) = 7.82$. Scholastic competence at Time 2, $\Delta\chi^2(2) = 7.12$, and morality at Time 2, $\Delta\chi^2(2) = 7.68$, showed significantly higher shared environments for siblings in stepfamilies compared to those in nondivorced families (.00 versus .24, and .06 versus .09, respectively). There is some evidence of a shared twins environment for a few measures. For the most part, the differences were not consistent across time (except for general self-worth) and none of the shared environment estimates were large.

Genetic and Environmental Contributions to Stability

The next question was whether there are genetic and environmental contributions to stability and change across time. These analyses were conducted for the scales that showed stability coefficients above .35. Two of the scales, morality, $r(496) = .34$, and friendship, $r(496) = .29$, did not meet this criteria. Stability coefficients for the other five scales are shown in Table 4 and range from .61 to .39. These results are con-

---

TABLE 3	Variance Components and χ^2 Values from the Univariate Model-Fitting Results at Time 1 and Time 2							
	TIME 1				TIME 2			
	h^2	e_s^2	e_n^2	$\chi^2(8)$	h^2	e_s^2	e_n^2	$\chi^2(8)$
Scholastic competence	.71*	.01	.28*	7.47	.53*	.12	.35*	14.52
Social competence	.49*	.00	.51*	6.70	.51*	.09	.40*	19.57*
Athletic competence	.61*	.00	.40*	13.17	.61*	.09	.30*	6.56
Physical appearance	.46*	.02	.52*	18.20*	.43*	.10	.47*	3.09
General self-worth	.16	.01	.83*	10.92	.60*	.00	.40*	18.31*
Morality	.18	.12	.70*	9.19	.25	.07	.68*	13.42
Friendship	.22	.00	.77*	9.30	.40*	.10	.51*	12.06

Note: h^2 = genetic variance; e_s^2 = shared environmental variance; e_n^2 = nonshared environmental variance.

*$p < .05$, and significant change in χ^2 for reduced models when additive effects of genes (G_a) and nonadditive effects of genes (G_d) are set to zero or when shared environment (E_s) is set to zero.

TABLE 4   Stability Coefficients and Cross-Sibling Correlations for Perceived Scholastic Competence, Social Competence, Athletic Competence, and Physical Appearance by Sibling Relationship Group

	STABILITY[a] (N = 496)	CROSS-SIBLING CORRELATIONS[b]					
		MZ (n = 45)	DZ (n = 51)	FN (n = 39)	FS (n = 57)	HS (n = 29)	US (n = 27)
Scholastic competence	.50*	.53*	.05	.08	.18	.14	.27
Social competence	.43*	.39*	−.01	.11	.04	.24	.21
Athletic competence	.61*	.61*	.19	.19	.14	.06	.04
Physical appearance	.50*	.48*	.27*	−.11	.11	−.05	.27
General self-worth	.39*	.41*	.16	−.14	.10	−.08	.16

Note: MZ = identical twins in nondivorced families; DZ = fraternal twins in nondivorced families; FN = full siblings in nondivorced families; FS = full siblings in stepfamilies; HS = half siblings in stepfamilies; US = unrelated siblings in stepfamilies.

[a]Stability coefficients from Time 1 to Time 2 for the entire sample, collapsing over siblings.

[b]A cross-sibling correlation is the correlation between the child's score on one measure and the sibling's score on the second measure.

*p < .05.

sistent with other studies of the stability of adolescent self-concept (e.g., Eccles et al., 1989).

Table 4 also shows the sibling cross-correlations for the scales across sibling types. The patterns indicate possible nonadditive genetic mediation between the measures across the two time points. As with the univariate analyses, the MZ correlations are significant and more than half the DZ and sibling correlations. The other sibling correlations are low or nonsignificant.

Bivariate maximum-likelihood model fitting using the cross-sibling intraclass covariances confirmed the impressions gathered from examining the correlation patterns. The model fit the data well for the five subscales: scholastic competence, $\chi^2(36) = 41.05$, GFI = .91; athletic competence, $\chi^2(36) = 33.51$, GFI = .97, social competence, $\chi^2(36) = 34.85$, GFI = .90; physical appearance, $\chi^2(36) = 36.43$, GFI = .91; and general self-worth, $\chi^2(36) = 36.74$, GFI = .94. In every case the additive genetic effects (common and unique) could be dropped from the model, as expected from the pattern of cross-sibling correlations presented. Figure 3 shows the parameter estimates for the adolescents' perceptions of their scholastic competence. Only the path coefficients for nonadditive genetic mediation were significant, as indicated by the two significant paths (−.79 and −.46) from the latent variable G_d to the measure at Time 1 and Time 2. This means phenotypic stability is largely accounted for by nonadditive genetic stability. Three other scales also showed this pattern of nonadditive genetic mediation: athletic competence, physical appearance, and general self-worth. Social competence, on the other hand, showed significant nonshared environmental stability. Results also showed significant nonadditive genetic contributions to

change for the scholastic competence and social competence subscales. The results of those analyses are summarized in Figure 4.

Figure 4 shows the genetic and environmental components of stability and change that were calculated using the results of the model-fitting analyses (see also Plomin et al., 1994). For example, the components of phenotypic stability for scholastic competence are estimated by multiplying the common paths in Figure 3: .21 × .35 = .07 for shared environmental stability, −.79 × −.46 = .36 for genetic stability, −.58 × −.11 = .06 for nonshared environmental stability. The sum of these components (.07 + .36 + .06)

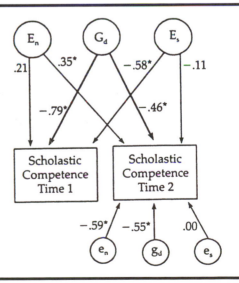

FIGURE 3 Bivariate model-fitting results for the stability in scholastic competence across time. Asterisks denote that the parameters are significant at *p* < .05.

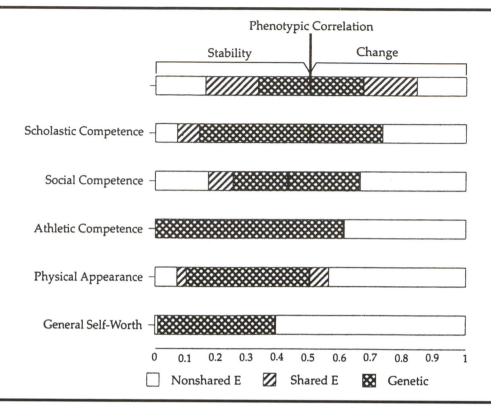

FIGURE 4 Summary of the genetic and environmental components of continuity and change. As shown at the top of the figure, the dark vertical bar indicates the phenotypic correlation. To the left of the bar are the genetic, shared environmental, and nonshared environmental components of the phenotypic correlation; to the right of the bar are the components of change. The key to each component is located at the bottom of the figure. These results were derived from model-fitting parameter estimates, as described in the text.

comes within rounding error of the stability coefficient (.50) for Time 1 to Time 2. Figure 4 shows the ratio of each component to the phenotypic correlation. For example, 73% of the stability in scholastic competence is due to nonadditive genetic stability (.36 ÷ .50 = .73). Similarly, the genetic and environmental components of change were calculated as the ratio of the variance of each change path (e.g., g_d, g_s, e_s, e_n) and the total variance for change. For example, as shown in Figure 3 for scholastic competence, the change path for unique nonadditive genetic latent variable (g_d) is −.55; squaring this path ($-.55^2 = .30$) and dividing by the sum of all the squared change paths ($-.55^2 + .00^2 + .00^2 + -.59^2 = .65$) indicates that almost half the change variance is due to genetic variance (.30 ÷ .65 = .46). The results of the bivariate analyses for all five scales are summarized in Figure 4. In general, nonadditive genetic variance explains a large portion of the phenotypic stability in perceived competence, whereas nonshared environmental factors were the main contributors to phenotypic change.

DISCUSSION

The results of this twin/sibling study point to the importance of nonshared environmental and genetic contributions to individual differences in self-concept during adolescence. As predicted, four of the scales that showed significant genetic influences at Time 1 were also significantly heritable at Time 2. Two additional scales, friendship and general self-worth, showed significant heritability 3 years later. None of the scales showed shared environmental influences at either time point. The longitudinal analyses revealed genetic contributions to stability for four of the subscales; change in self-concept over time appeared to be due to nonshared factors and unreliability of measurement.

Genetic Contributions

Scholastic competence, athletic competence, social competence, and physical appearance were heritable at both time points. There were low to moderate associations across the scales suggesting that the dimensions may have different etiologies. That some areas of self-concept showed significant heritability while others did not, supports the idea of a multidimensional self-concept. It is also likely that genetic contributions to individual differences in some areas of perceived competence are due to links with other genetically linked characteristics. In fact, in our previous study, we found overlap in genetic contributions to scholastic competence and vocabulary and social competence and sociability (McGuire et al., 1994).

It is very interesting that children's self-perceptions of friendship and general self-worth showed significant heritability at Time 2, but not at Time 1. In the previous paper, we argued that friendship and general self-worth would not show significant heritability because of the nature of these self-perceptions in children's lives (McGuire et al., 1994). These interpretations may have been incorrect; the nature of children's self-concept appears to change across development. Our explanations may still apply to children's self-perceptions during middle childhood, but not to the later adolescent years. For example, low general self-worth may become more stable and predictive of adult neuroticism across adolescence. Neuroticism in adulthood has been found to be significantly heritable (Floderus-Myrhed, Pedersen, & Rasmusson, 1980; Heath, Jardine, Eaves, & Martin, 1989; Viken, Rose, Kaprio, & Koskenvuo, 1994; Young, Eaves, & Eysenck, 1980) and adolescent reports of self-worth may begin to tap into this construct and its biological roots. In addition, more areas of self-concept may show genetic influences as children begin to niche pick based on their personality traits and skills (McCartney et al., 1990; Plomin, DeFries, & Loehlin, 1977; Scarr & McCartney, 1983). The emerging developmental behavioral genetic literature points to the conclusion that heritability increases across age for most traits because identical twins stay very similar across time, while all other family members become more different across time (McCartney et al., 1990; Plomin, 1986).

Stability for scholastic competence, athletic competence, physical appearance, and general self-worth were mediated genetically. In addition, significantly heritable scales showed the highest phenotypic stability across time. Genetic contributions to stability in self-concept could occur because the same genetic contributions are present at both time points, or because differences linked to genetic effects early in life are still stable (Plomin et al., 1997). Stability in genetic contributions could also be due to environmental factors. People may be reacting to children's genetically influenced traits in a consistent manner. Children could also be in environments that are based on their genetic differences, and these environments are keeping the children's behavior stable. For example, there is a large literature on ability grouping in school systems (Slavin, 1987; Sorensen, 1986). Children may be placed in different classroom situations initially because of genetically influenced skills; however, the classroom environments would be the stabilizing factor over time. Psychological processes may also play a role in stabilizing genetic contributions to some areas of perceived competence. Children may be rewarded by their culture for excelling in school or being athletic, and this encourages them to continue to achieve in such areas.

Nonshared Environment

Another important finding is that siblings raised in the same family are not similar in self-concept. Indeed, even when one takes into account measurement error, the lack of sibling similarity is striking. The results of this paper and others highlight the need to investigate the nature of children's environmental experiences in a more complex manner (Dunn & Plomin 1990; Hetherington, Reiss, & Plomin, 1994). Studies that examine nonshared environment are part of a general movement away from focusing on only the mother and a single child, toward understanding the implication of the entire family context for children's development. In fact, several studies have linked parental differential treatment by siblings and children's adjustment (e.g., Conger & Conger, 1994; Dunn, Stocker, & Plomin, 1990; McGuire, Dunn, & Plomin, 1995; McHale, Crouter, McGuire, & Updegraff, 1995; McHale & Pawletko, 1992; Mekos, Hetherington, & Reiss, 1996; Pike, McGuire, Hetherington, Reiss, & Plomin, 1996). A previous paper from this project using Time 1 data, found links between nonshared family experiences and the children's reports of self-concept (Anderson, Hetherington, Reiss, & Howe, 1994). Nonetheless, many lasting socialization experiences may not occur in families, but instead may occur in other social contexts such as the peer group (Harris, 1995, 1998). It is likely that the most important nonshared environmental contributions to self-concept lie outside the family with friends, peers, teachers, and other significant adults (Manke, McGuire, Reiss, Hetherington, & Plomin, 1995; McGuire & Fink, 1996; Rowe & Plomin, 1981). In the effort to understand the correlates of individual differences in developmental outcomes, researchers should begin moving the concept of nonshared environment outside the family.

It was also interesting that the stability of social competence was mediated by nonshared environment factors. This result is also somewhat perplexing, given that social competence was significantly heritable at Time 1 and 2, and there was significant genetic mediation between social competence and self-reported temperament at Time 1 (McGuire et al., 1994). In fact, genetic mediation was there, just not statistically significant. The present findings do suggest that only experiences unique to each sibling contribute to stability across time. The most likely candidates are siblings' different peer networks and social activities. Each sibling may enter different types of peer groups during the school-aged years, and these differential experiences contribute to the stability in sibling differences in perceived social competence across time (see Harris, 1998).

Limitations and Future Directions

Due to the design of the study, the model tested contained several assumptions. These assumptions were made because the data needed to test them are simply not available. The first assumption of the model was that assortative mating was negligible. That is, the parents of the children were no more alike in self-concept, and the genetic links to self-concept, than random individuals. Significant assortative mating would have inflated the correlations between all the sibling pairs except the MZ twins. The opposite pattern was found in our data, suggesting that assortative mating is not significant. The second assumption of the model stated that there was no selective placement of stepsiblings. It means that stepchildren are with stepparents that resemble their biological parents genetically. It is a version of the first assumption that only affects the children in stepfamilies. Significant selective placement would inflate the stepsibling correlations and this pattern was not found in our data either. Both of these assumptions, however, can be tested directly by collecting self-concept data on the parents. Studies examining parental similarity for related variables such as personality and well-being suggest that assortative mating is low (e.g., Feng & Baker, 1994).

The third assumption of the model was that nonadditive genetic variance was due to dominance and not to epistasis or environmental factors. The genetic influences found were due to a pattern showing high correlations for MZ twins coupled with low or nonsignificant correlations for the other sibling pairs. As several researchers have pointed out, MZ assimilation effects and sibling contrast effects could produce similar results (Carey, 1986; Plomin et al., 1990). Only a study of twins reared apart could distinguish between these alternative explanations. Some researchers have argued that some personality traits are influenced by genes that do not run in families, that

only identical twins share (Lykken et al., 1992). After reviewing the literature, Loehlin (1992) concluded that adult personality traits are influenced more by additive than nonadditive genetic factors. More data is needed to determine if the genetic architecture of self-concept follows the same pattern.

The fourth assumption of the model stated that genotype–environment correlation and interaction are negligible. Genotype–environment correlation means that people encounter and/or enter different environments because of genetically linked characteristics. Genotype–environment interaction means that genetically influenced behaviors express themselves differently in different environments (see Loehlin, 1992; Plomin, 1986). Our design was able to disentangle family resemblance due to shared family characteristics from shared genetic heritage (i.e., passive genotype–environment correlation). It was not able to address other types of genotype–environment correlations (i.e., evocative or active) or genotype–environment interactions. A few studies have used the adoption design to explore if people react to children based on their biologically based characteristics (i.e., evocative) or if children pick contexts that are correlated with their genetically influenced characteristics (i.e., active; Baker, 1989; O'Connor, Deater-Deckard, Fulker, Rutter, & Plomin, 1998). Other studies have attempted to test for genotype–environment interactions using several designs (e.g., Bergeman, Plomin, McClearn, & Pedersen, 1988; Hood & Cairns, 1989; Plomin & DeFries, 1985). While more empirical work is definitely needed, there has been considerable conceptual work in both of these areas (e.g., Hershberger, 1994; McGue, 1997; Molenaar & Boomsma, 1987; Plomin et al., 1977; Scarr & McCartney, 1983; Wachs, 1992; Wachs & Plomin, 1991).

Another limitation is that stability is not the only way to examine change and continuity over time. Some studies of personality have examined genetic and environmental influences on change scores (Plomin & Nesselroade, 1990). Studies conducted on adolescent and adult twins suggest that such change is due to nonshared environmental effects and error of measurement (e.g., Loehlin, Horn, & Willerman, 1990; McGue et al., 1993; Pogue-Geile & Rose, 1985; Saudino et al., 1996). One study, however, did find genetic influences on changes in personality during the transition from adolescence to adulthood (Dworkin, Burke, Maher, & Gottesman, 1976). In the present study, change scores were calculated by subtracting the Time 2 scores from the Time 1 scores. Cross-sibling intraclass correlations were calculated using the change scores. The pattern showed nonsignificant, near-zero correlations for every sibling group, including the MZ twins. Thus, changes in self-concept during middle childhood and adolescence appear to be due to nonshared environment and/or measurement error. These analyses, however, were not included in the results section because two points of measurement may not be enough information to examine mean level or intraindividual level changes in a construct (Rogosa, Brandt, & Zimkowski, 1982). It is difficult to disentangle meaningful change from methodological problems such as regression to the mean when there are only two time points. Still, investigating genetic and environmental contributions to individual differences in profiles of change across time would be a worthwhile pursuit (Plomin & Nesselroade, 1990).

In conclusion, it was encouraging that this study replicated previous work. Of course, this does not mean that there is little left to learn from behavioral genetic studies of perceived competence and self-worth across development. There are still many unanswered questions: What are the sources of genetic influences on self-concept? Why do siblings differ in perceived competence and self-worth? More multivariate and longitudinal work is needed to illuminate *how and when* genetic and unique environmental factors contribute to the changing structure of the self across development.

REFERENCES

Anderson, E. R., Hetherington, E. M., Reiss, D., & Howe, G. (1994). Parents' nonshared treatment of siblings and the development of social competence during adolescence. *Journal of Family Psychology, 8*, 303–320.

Baker, L. A. (1989). Genotype–environment covariance for multiple phenotypes: A multivariate test using adopted and nonadopted children. *Multivariate Behavioral Research, 24*, 415–430.

Bergeman, C. S., Plomin, R., McClearn, G. E., & Pedersen, N. L. (1988). Genotype–environment interaction in personality development: Identical twins reared apart. *Psychology and Aging, 3*, 399–406.

Boomsma, D. I., Martin, N. G., & Neale, M. C. (1989). Twin methodology using LISREL [Special Issue]. *Behavior Genetics, 19*.

Boomsma, D. I., & Molenaar, P. C. M. (1986). Using LISREL to analyze genetic and environmental covariance structures. *Behavior Genetics, 16*, 237–250.

Bracken, B. A. (1997). *Handbook of self-concept: Developmental, social, and clinical considerations*. New York: John Wiley & Sons.

Buss, A., & Plomin, R. (1984). *Temperament: Early developing personality traits*. Hillsdale, NJ: Erlbaum.

Carey, G. (1986). Sibling imitation and contrast effects. *Behavior Genetics, 16*, 319–341.

Cicchetti, D., & Beeghly, M. (1990). *The self in transition*. Chicago: University of Chicago Press.

Conger, K. J., & Conger, R. D. (1994). Differential parenting and change in sibling differences in delinquency. *Journal of Family Psychology, 8*, 287–302.

Cudeck, R. (1989). Analysis of correlation matrices using co-variance structure models. *Psychological Bulletin, 105*, 317–217.

Dunn, J., & Plomin, R. (1990). *Separate lives: Why siblings are so different*. New York: Basic Books.

Dunn, J., Stocker, C., & Plomin, R. (1990). Nonshared experiences within the family: Correlates of behavior problems in middle childhood. *Development and Psychopathology, 2*, 113–126.

Dworkin, R. H., Burke, B. W., Maher, B. A., & Gottesman, I. I. (1976). A longitudinal study of the genetics of personality. *Journal of Personality and Social Psychology, 34*, 510–518.

Eaves, L. J., Eysenck, H. J., & Martin, N. G. (1989). *Genes, culture and personality: An empirical approach*. London: Academic Press.

Eaves, L. J., Last, K. A., Young, P. A., & Martin, N. G. (1978). Model fitting approaches to the analysis of human behavior. *Heredity, 41*, 249–320.

Eccles, J. S., Wigfield, A., Flanagan, C. A., Miller, C., Reuman, D., & Yee, D. K. (1989). Self-concepts, domain values, and self-esteem: Relations and changes at early adolescence. *Journal of Personality, 57*, 283–310.

Feng, D., & Baker, L. (1994). Spouse similarity in attitudes, personality, and psychological well-being. *Behavior Genetics, 24*, 357–364.

Floderus-Myrhed, B., Pedersen, N., & Rasmusson, I. (1980). Assessment of heritability for personality, based on a short form of Eysenck Personality Inventory: A study of 12,898 twin pairs. *Behavior Genetics, 10*, 153–162.

Fulker, D. W., Baker, L. A., & Block, R. D. (1983). Estimating components of covariance using LISREL. *Data Analyst Communications in Computer Data Analysis, 1*, 5–8.

Fulker, D. W., DeFries, J. C., & Plomin, R. (1988). Genetic influence on general mental ability increases between infancy and middle childhood. *Nature, 336*, 767–769.

Goldsmith, H. H. (1983). Genetic influences on personality from infancy to adolescence. *Child Development, 54*, 331–355.

Goldsmith, H. H., & Gottesman, I. I. (1981). Origins of variation in behavioral style: A longitudinal study of temperament in young twins. *Child Development, 52*, 91–103.

Grotevant, H. D., & Cooper, C. R. (1986). Individuation in family relationships: A perspective on individual differences in the development of identity and role-taking skills in adolescence. *Human Development, 29*, 82–100.

Harris, J. R. (1995). Where is the child's environment? A group socialization theory of development. *Psychological Review, 102*, 458–489.

Harris, J. R. (1998). *The nurture assumption: Why children turn out they way they do*. New York: Free Press.

Harter, S. (1983). Developmental perspectives on the self-system. In E. M. Hetherington (Ed.), P. H. Mussen (Series Ed.), *Handbook of child psychology: Vol. 4. Socialization, personality, and social development* (pp. 275–385). New York: Wiley.

Harter, S. (1988). *The self-perception profile for adolescents.* Unpublished manuscript, University of Denver, Denver, CO.

Heath, A. C., Jardine, R., Eaves, L. J., & Martin, N. G. (1989). The genetic structure of personality: II. Genetic analyses of the EPQ. *Personality and Individual Differences, 10,* 615–624.

Hershberger, S. L. (1994). Genotype–environment interaction and correlation. In J. C. DeFries, R. Plomin, & D. W Fulker (Eds.), *Nature and nurture during middle childhood* (pp. 281–294). Cambridge, MA: Blackwell Publishers.

Hetherington, E. M., Reiss, D., & Plomin, R. (1994). *Separate social worlds of siblings: The importance of nonshared environment on development.* Hillsdale, NJ: Erlbaum.

Hood, K. E., & Cairns, R. B. (1989). A developmental-genetic analysis of aggressive behavior in mice: IV. Genotype–environment interaction. *Aggressive Behavior, 15,* 361–380.

Isberg, R. S., Hauser, S. T., Jacobson, A. M., Powers, S. I., Noam, G., Weiss-Perry, B., & Follansbee, D. (1989). Parental contexts of adolescent self-esteem: A developmental perspective. *Journal of Youth and Adolescence, 18,* 1–23.

Jinks, J. L., & Fulker, D. W. (1970). Comparison of the biometrical, MAVA, and classical approaches to the analysis of human behavior. *Psychological Bulletin, 75,* 311–349.

Jöreskog, K. J., & Sörbom, D. (1993). *LISREL 8 user's reference manual.* Chicago: Scientific Software International.

Lamborn, S. D., Mounts, N. S., Steinberg, L., & Dornbusch, S. M. (1991). Patterns of competence and adjustment among adolescents from authoritative, authoritarian, indulgent and neglectful families. *Child Development, 62,* 1049–1065.

Loehlin, J. (1987). *Latent variable models: An introduction to factor, path, and structural analysis.* Hillsdale, NJ: Erlbaum.

Loehlin, J. (1992). *Genes and environment in personality development.* Newbury Park, CA: Sage.

Loehlin, J. C., Horn, J. M., & Willerman, L. (1990). Heredity, environment, and personality change: Evidence from the Texas Adoption Project. *Journal of Personality, 57,* 221–261.

Lykken, D. T., McGue, M., Tellegen, A., & Bouchard, T. J. (1992). Emergenesis: Genetic traits that may not run in families. *American Psychologist, 47,* 1565–1577.

Manke, B., McGuire, S., Reiss, D., Hetherington, E. M., & Plomin, R. (1995). Genetic contributions to adolescents' extrafamilial interactions: Teachers, best friends, and peers. *Social Development, 4,* 238–256.

Matheny, A. P. (1989). Children's behavioral inhibition over age and across situations: Genetic similarity for a trait during change. *Journal of Personality, 57,* 215–235.

Matheny, A. P., & Dolan, A. B. (1975). Persons, situations, and time: A genetic view of behavioral change in children. *Journal of Personality and Social Psychology, 35,* 1106–1110.

Matheny, A. P., & Dolan, A. B. (1980). A twin study of personality and temperament during middle childhood. *Journal of Research in Personality, 14,* 224–234.

McCartney, K., Harris, M. J., & Bernieri, F. (1990). Growing up and growing apart: A developmental meta-analysis of twin studies. *Psychological Bulletin, 107,* 226–237.

McGue, M. (1997). A behavioral-genetic perspective on children of alcoholics. *Alcohol Health & Research World, 21,* 210–217.

McGue, M., Bacon, S., & Lykken, D. T. (1993). Personality stability and change in early adulthood: A behavioral genetic analysis. *Developmental Psychology, 29,* 96–109.

McGue, M., & Bouchard, T. J. (1984). Adjustment of twin data for the effects of age and sex. *Behavioral Genetics, 14,* 325–343.

McGue, M., Hirsch, B., & Lykken, D. T. (1993). Age and self-perception of ability: A twin study analysis. *Psychology and Aging, 8,* 72–80.

McGuire, S., Dunn, J., & Plomin, R. (1995). Maternal differential treatment of siblings and children's behavioral problems: A longitudinal study. *Development and Psychopathology, 7,* 515–528.

McGuire, S., & Fink, J. (1996). *Moving the concept of nonshared environment outside the family: Sibling differences in educational experiences.* Poster presented at the biennial meeting of the Society for Research in Adolescence, Boston, MA.

McGuire, S., Neiderhiser, J. M., Reiss, D., Hetherington, E. M., & Plomin, R. (1994). Genetic and environmental influences on perceptions of self-worth and competence in adolescence: A study of twins, full siblings, and stepsiblings. *Child Development, 65,* 785–799.

McHale, S. M., Crouter, A. C., McGuire, S., & Updegraff, K. A. (1995). Congruence between mothers' and fathers' differential treatment of siblings: Links with family relations and children's well-being. *Child Development, 66,* 116–128.

McHale, S. M., & Pawletko, T. M. (1992). Differential treatment in two family contexts. *Child Development, 63,* 68–81.

Mekos, D., Hetherington, E. M., & Reiss, D. (1996). Sibling differences in problem behavior and parental treatment in nondivorced and remarried families. *Child Development, 67,* 2148–2165.

Molenaar, P. C., & Boomsma, D. I. (1987). Application of nonlinear factor analysis to genotype–environment interaction. *Behavior Genetics, 1,* 71–80.

Morrison, D. F. (1976). *Multivariate statistical methods.* New York: McGraw-Hill.

Neale, M. C., & Cardon, L. R. (1992). *Methodology for genetic studies of twins and families.* Boston: Kluwer.

Nichols, R. C., & Bilbro, W. C. (1966). The diagnosis of twin zygosity. *Acta Genetica, 16,* 265–275.

Noller, P. (1995). Parent-adolescent relationships. In M. A. Fitzpatrick & A. L. Vangelisti (Eds.), *Explaining family interactions* (pp. 77–111). Thousand Oaks, CA: Sage.

O'Connor, T. G., Deater-Deckard, K., Fulker, D., Rutter, M., & Plomin, R. (1998). Genotype–environment correlations in late childhood and early adolescence: Antisocial behavioral problems and coercive parenting. *Developmental Psychology, 34,* 970–981.

Pedersen, N. L., Plomin, R., Nesselroade, J. R., & Mc-Clearn, G. E. (1992). A quantitative genetic analysis of cognitive abilities during the second half of the life span. *Psychological Science, 3,* 346–353.

Pike, A., McGuire, S., Hetherington, E. M., Reiss, D., & Plomin, R. (1996). Family environment and adolescent depressive symptoms and antisocial behavior: A multivariate genetic analysis. *Developmental Psychology, 32,* 590–603.

Plomin, R. (1986). *Development, genetics, and psychology.* Hillsdale, NJ: Erlbaum.

Plomin, R., Chipuer, H. M., & Loehlin, J. C. (1990). Behavior genetics and personality. In L. A. Pervin (Ed.), *Handbook of personality theory and research* (pp. 225–243). New York: Guilford Press.

Plomin, R., & DeFries, J. C. (1985). *Origins of individual differences in infancy: The Colorado Adoption Project.* Orlando, FL: Academic Press.

Plomin, R., DeFries, J. C., & Loehlin, J. C. (1977). Genotype–environment interaction and correlation in the analysis of human behavior. *Psychological Bulletin, 84,* 309–322.

Plomin, R., DeFries, J. C., McClearn, G. E., & Rutter, M. (1997). *Behavior genetics: A primer* (3rd ed.). New York: W. H. Freeman.

Plomin, R., Emde, R. N., Braungart, J. M., Campos, J., Corley, R., Fulker, D. W., Kagan, J., Reznick, J. S., Robinson, J., Zahn-Waxler, C., & DeFries, J. C. (1994). Genetic change and continuity from fourteen to twenty months: The MacArthur Longitudinal Twin Study. *Child Development, 64,* 1354–1376.

Plomin, R., & Nesselroade, J. R. (1990). Behavioral genetics and personality change. *Journal of Personality, 57,* 191–220.

Pogue-Geile, M. F., & Rose, R. J. (1985). Developmental genetic studies of personality. *Developmental Psychology, 21,* 547–557.

Reiss, D., Plomin, R., Hetherington, E. M., Howe, G., Rovine, M., Tyron, A., & Stanley, M. (1994). The separate worlds of teenage siblings: An introduction to the study of nonshared environment and adolescent development. In E. M. Hetherington, D. Reiss, & R. Plomin (Eds.), *Separate social worlds of siblings: The importance of nonshared environment on development.* Hillsdale, NJ: Erlbaum.

Rogosa, D., Brandt, D., & Zimkowski, M. (1982). A growth curve approach to the measurement of change. *Psychological Bulletin, 92,* 726–748.

Rowe, D. C., & Plomin, R. (1981). The importance of nonshared (E_1) environmental influences in behavioral development. *Developmental Psychology, 17,* 517–531.

Saudino, K. J., DeFries, J. C., & Plomin, R. (1996). Tester-rated temperament at 14, 20, and 24 months: Environmental change and genetic continuity. *British Journal of Developmental Psychology, 14,* 129–144.

Saudino, K. J., McGuire, S., Reiss, D., Hetherington, E. M., & Plomin, R. (1995). Parent ratings of EAS temperament in twins, full siblings, half siblings, and stepsiblings. *Journal of Personality and Social Psychology, 68,* 723–733,

Scarr, S., & McCartney, K. (1983). How people make their own environments: A theory of genotype→environmental effects. *Child Development, 54,* 424–435.

Slavin, R. E. (1987). Ability grouping and student achievement in elementary schools: A best-evidence synthesis. *Review of Educational Research, 57,* 293–336.

Sorensen, A. B. H. (1986). Effects of ability grouping on growth in academic achievement. *American Education Research Journal, 23,* 519–542.

Viken, R. J., Rose, R. J., Kaprio, J., & Koskenvuo, M. (1994). A developmental genetic analysis of adult personality: Extraversion and neuroticism from 18 to 59 years of age. *Journal of Personality and Social Psychology, 66,* 722–730.

Wachs, T. D. (1992). *The nature of nurture.* Newbury Park, CA: Sage.

Wachs, T. D., & Plomin, R. (1991). *Conceptualization and measurement of organism–environment interaction.* Washington, DC: American Psychological Association.

Whitbeck, L. B., Simons, R. L., Conger, R. D., Lorenz, F. O., Huck, S., & Elder, G. H., Jr. (1991). Family economic hardship, parental support and adolescent self-esteem. *Social Psychology Quarterly, 54,* 353–363.

Wylie, R. (1979). *The self-concept: Theory and research on selected topics* (Vol. 2, Rev. ed.). Lincoln: University of Nebraska Press.

Young, P. A., Eaves, L. J., & Eysenck, H. J. (1980). Intergenerational stability and change in the cause of variation in adult and juvenile personality. *Journal of Personality and Individual Differences, 1,* 35–55.

SELF-STUDY QUESTIONS

Multiple Choice

1. According to research cited by these authors, which of the following statements about the influence of families on perceived competence and self-worth is true?

   a. Children who grow up in the same family are very similar.

   b. Family environment seems to have little influence on these variables.

   c. Correlations between family environment and self-esteem exist only in intact families.

   d. none of the above

2. With respect to stability, the researchers found that

   a. participants' self-esteem scores varied considerably from Time 1 to Time 2

   b. identical twins' self-esteem scores were stable, but those of other sibling pairs were unstable

c. Time 1 and Time 2 scores were correlated across all types of sibling pairs

d. self-esteem scores were far less stable in identical twins than in other types of sibling pairs

Essay

1. What does this study suggest about the assumption that parenting practices and family climate determine the development of self-esteem?

2. How do the authors explain the finding that heredity effects appeared to be larger at Time 2 than at Time 1?

ADOLESCENCE

"Attitudes toward Family Obligations among American Adolescents with Asian, Latin American, and European Backgrounds"

OVERVIEW

This article reports research examining attitudes toward family obligations among U.S. high school students from different cultural backgrounds. The authors contend that the cultures of origin of teens' parents influence the degree to which they exhibit the typical American pattern of emphasizing individual needs and rights more than family obligations. They also went a step further and attempted to determine whether such differences influenced adolescents' overall cognitive and social development.

METHODOLOGY

The authors developed a set of instruments designed to assess the specific variables in which they were interested: current assistance to family members, respect for family, and future assistance to family members. To measure future assistance, for example, the researchers devised a set of statements such as *live or go to a college near your parents*. Participants responded to such statements using a 5-point scale ranging from 1 = *not important at all* to 5 = *very important*. After presenting the instruments to participants, the researchers used a technique called *factor analysis* to determine whether their instruments measured separate variables. After establishing that the three domains of family concepts were statistically separate, the researchers were able to use the instruments to derive domain scores for each participant. The researchers also employed checklists and scales commonly used in research and in therapeutic practice to measure various aspects of parent-teen relationships. Additional measures were used to assess participants' peer relationships and academic achievement. After scoring all the instruments, researchers used *analysis of variance (ANOVA)* to identify relationships among the variables measured by them.

GLOSSARY TERM

■ **Familism** viewpoint and philosophy regarding the obligations of the family members to each other and stressing the need for family members to provide mutual support and to have common goals and common property and living arrangements; also known as *collectivism, sociocentrism,* or *interdependency*

Andrew J. Fuligni, Vivian Tseng, and May Lam

Attitudes toward Family Obligations among American Adolescents with Asian, Latin American, and European Backgrounds

This study was designed to examine the attitudes toward family obligations among over 800 American tenth (M age = 15.7 years) and twelfth (M age = 17.7 years) grade students from Filipino, Chinese, Mexican, Central and South American, and European backgrounds. Asian and Latin American adolescents possessed stronger values and greater expectations regarding their duty to assist, respect, and support their families than their peers with European backgrounds. These differences tended to be large and were consistent across the youths' generation, gender, family composition, and socioeconomic background. Whereas an emphasis on family obligations tended to be associated with more positive family and peer relationships and academic motivation, adolescents who indicated the strongest endorsement of their obligations tended to receive school grades just as low as or even lower than those with the weakest endorsement. There was no evidence, however, that the ethnic variations in attitudes produced meaningful group differences in the adolescents' development. These findings suggest that even within a society that emphasizes adolescent autonomy and independence, youths from families with collectivistic traditions retain their parents' familistic values and that these values do not have a negative impact upon their development.

INTRODUCTION

American families with Asian and Latin American backgrounds often have been described as possessing a collectivistic orientation that emphasizes family members' responsibilities and obligations to one another. This tradition of familism should play a significant role in the lives of children in these families, especially as they enter an adolescent period that is defined by American society as a time for increased individual autonomy and involvement with peers. Yet there have been few studies of whether youths from Asian and Latin American families actually share their cultures' emphasis on filial duty or how this sense of obligation may vary according to factors such as gender or the nativity of adolescents and their parents. Moreover, little is known about how an emphasis on family responsibilities and obligations may be associated with other aspects of the

youths' development such as their family interactions, peer relationships, and academic achievement.

Cultures with a collectivistic orientation emphasize the goals and interests of the group over those of individual members (Triandis, 1995). The decisions, behavior, and self-definition of individuals within such a tradition are expected to reflect the needs, values, and expectations of the larger group (Markus & Kitayama, 1991; Triandis, Bontempo, Villareal, Asai, & Lucca, 1988). Perhaps the most salient domain for the expression of these values is the family. A critical aspect of a collectivistic ideology is a strong concern for the fate and well-being of one's kin, and family members within collectivistic cultures often are expected to support each other and to assist in the maintenance of the household (Kagitcibasi, 1990; Lee, 1983; Triandis, 1990). The needs of the family usually have priority, and individual members often are asked to downplay their own needs and desires if they conflict with those of the larger family (Huang, 1994).

Asian and Latin American families in the United States often have been characterized as placing a greater importance upon familial duty and obligation than their counterparts with European backgrounds. Many traditions within Asian cultures, such as Confucianism, emphasize family solidarity, respect, and commitment (e.g., Ho, 1981; Shon & Ja, 1982; Uba, 1994). Likewise, a devotion and loyalty to family is often an imperative for individuals within Latin American cultures (e.g., Chilman, 1993; Vázquez García, García Coll, Erkut, Alarcón, & Tropp, in press).

Numerous observers have discussed how Asian and Latin American families attempt to socialize their children into these traditions by expecting the children to assist and respect the authority of the family. For example, it is not uncommon for children to be asked to perform chores such as shopping for food, cooking meals, and assisting with the care of other family members (Caplan, Choy, & Whitmore, 1991). As family togetherness is highly valued, children should be present for daily meals, holidays and special occasions (Mordkowitz & Ginsburg, 1987). Children are obligated to make sure that they see and spend time with extended family members such as grandparents, aunts, and uncles. Similar chores and duties exist for children of most cultural backgrounds, but these obligations are usually cited as being especially great among Asian and Latin American families.

Children also are taught to respect the authority and wishes of the family. As in families from other collectivistic traditions, authority within Asian and Latin American households is often hierarchical (Falicov, 1983; Lee, 1983). Children are expected to respect the authority of grandparents, parents, and even older brothers and sisters by seeking the opinions of their elders and following their advice on important matters (Huang, 1994; Shon & Ja, 1982; Uba, 1994). Respect for the family also can be exhibited in a more indirect manner. For example, children often are expected to do well in school and other endeavors in order to provide honor to the family (Chao, 1995). Children also may be asked to make personal sacrifices by sublimating their wishes and desires for the greater good of the larger family.

The obligations of children from Asian and Latin American families extend into their lives as adults. Children ideally should remain at home until marriage and, even then, they should not move far away from their parents (Triandis, 1990; Uba, 1994). Spending time with the family remains an imperative and adult children are still expected to join the family for meals and holidays. Young adult members of Asian and Latin American families are sometimes obligated to continue to assist their families by contributing portions of their earnings to family members or by even taking in their parents when the parents be-

come unable to care for themselves (Feldman, Mont-Reynaud, & Rosenthal, 1992; Zinn, 1994).

Whereas the descriptions of the socialization practices within Asian and Latin American families are numerous, there have been few studies of whether children within these families actually share their cultures' traditional emphasis on family support and respect. Most research has concentrated on more general collectivistic values among young adults and college students, rather than the specific family responsibilities that are salient in the lives of broader samples of children and adolescents. On the one hand, Asian and Latin American adolescents may embrace their duties because they believe in the importance of helping their families deal with the challenges of American society (see Cooper, Baker, Polichar, & Welsh, 1993; see Freeburg & Stein, 1996, for examples among college students). To the extent that such family assistance contributes to the self-images of those from collectivistic cultures, Asian and Latin American children may endorse familistic values as part of the development of their ethnic and cultural identities (Gaines et al., 1997; Markus and Kitayama, 1991; Vázquez García et al., in press).

On the other hand, American society places such a strong emphasis on adolescent autonomy that teen-agers rarely spend time with their families. Instead, adolescents spend the majority of their hours socializing with peers, working in part-time jobs for personal spending money, and participating in extracurricular activities (Fuligni & Stevenson, 1995; Larson, 1983). As a result, adolescents from Asian and Latin American families may appear more like their European American peers than their own parents and place relatively low importance upon their obligations to assist and respect their family. Indeed, numerous observers have posited that familial duties will be one of the most significant sources of conflict between parents and children within Asian and Latin American families (e.g., Zhou, 1997).

The lack of empirical work on the views of children and adolescents also limits our understanding of the extent to which beliefs regarding family obligations differ among Asian and Latin American youths themselves. Foreign-born parents, having been raised in Asian and Latin American societies, may be more likely to emphasize traditional familistic principles in their childrearing than American-born Asian and Latin American parents (Gibson & Bhachu, 1991; Suárez-Orozco & Suárez-Orozco, 1995). In addition, adolescents from immigrant families often are asked to assist the parents with dealing with the outside world because of the youths' greater familiarity with the English language and American customs (Sung, 1987; Zhou, 1997). As a result, youths with immigrant parents may place more importance upon assisting and respecting their families than those with native-born parents. In fact, the importance of family obligations may weaken through the generations so that the views of Asian and Latin American adolescents eventually become indistinguishable from those of their peers from the European majority.

Adolescents' attitudes toward family obligations also may vary according to their gender, family structure, and socioeconomic status. Given the prevalent sex-typing of household duties, girls may place more importance upon assisting their families than do boys (Goodnow, 1988). Adolescents from single-parent families may play a greater role in assisting the family, because their families often lack the assistance of additional adults (Barber & Eccles, 1992). In addition, poorer families may require their adolescents to play a greater role in assisting the family than in wealthier families. Yet it is unclear whether there will be variations in attitudes toward family obligations according to these two latter factors, as the existing evidence for the impact of marital and socioeconomic status upon household responsibilities is inconsistent (Goodnow, 1988).

In addition to examining variations in adolescents' views regarding their family obligations, it is critical to explore how these attitudes are associated with other aspects of their development such as their family interactions, peer relations, and academic achievement. Experience with supporting and assisting the family may have salutatory effects on development, as it provides adolescents the opportunity to develop responsibility and may reflect a close family that cares for and assists one another (Goodnow, 1988). The family cohesion that is reflected by a sense of obligation and respect also may translate into more positive relationships with peers and better educational adjustment. Many Asian and Latin American students, particularly those from immigrant families, attain success in school partly because of an obligation they feel toward their families (Gibson & Bhachu, 1991; Suárez-Orozco & Suárez-Orozco, 1995). Immigration often is undertaken with the explicit intention of creating better lives for the children, and youths within these families often feel that they owe it to their parents to put great effort into their studies (Chao, 1996; Mordkowitz & Ginsburg, 1987).

At the same time, very high levels of family obligations may have less positive effects on adolescents' development than more moderate levels. Youths who believe very strongly in their filial duty may have more difficulty in school, because the effort they spend fulfilling their obligations takes away from the time needed for homework and studying for tests (Henderson, 1997). In addition,

spending a great deal of time on household chores or being with family members may prevent adolescents from becoming active members of their peer groups. It is not unreasonable to suspect that adolescents who place an extremely high importance on their family obligations may be less involved in social relationships outside of the home.

Finally, associations between an emphasis on family obligations and other aspects of adolescents' development may produce group differences in family interactions, peer relations, and academic achievement. For example, some observers have suggested that the poorer academic performance of some Latin American students may be partially due to a competing demand to support and assist the family (see Vázquez García et al., in press, for a description of this argument). It also is possible that a strong emphasis on the family may result in Asian and Latin American youths having extremely close relationships with their parents and siblings at the expense of becoming less involved in peer relationships outside of the home. There have been few studies that have directly tested whether ethnic differences in adolescent development can be attributed to cultural variations in family assistance, support, and respect.

This study was designed to examine expectations and values regarding family obligations among American adolescents from Filipino, Chinese, Mexican, Central and South American, and European backgrounds. The extent to which adolescents believed their views differed from those of their parents was explored, as were variations in the youths' attitudes according to their nativity, gender, family structure, and socioeconomic background. The implications of an emphasis on family obligations for other aspects of adolescents' development were also examined in this study. In particular, the possibility that extremely high levels of expectations and values would have less positive associations with development than more moderate levels was explored. Finally, the extent to which ethnic variations in attitudes produced group differences in adolescents' development was assessed.

METHOD

Sample

Over 1,000 tenth (M age = 15.7 years) and twelfth (M age = 17.7 years) grade students, representing more than 80% of those enrolled in participating schools, completed questionnaires as part of an ongoing study of the development of adolescents in an ethnically diverse community in northern California. Over 90% of the participants completed self-report questionnaires during their social studies classes, whereas the remainder completed surveys that were mailed to their homes. Adolescents' reports of their ethnic backgrounds revealed that over 80% ($N = 820$) of the participating students were from five ethnic backgrounds: Chinese ($N = 103$), Filipino ($N = 312$), Mexican ($N = 120$), Central and South American ($N = 95$), and European ($N = 190$). The sample was evenly balanced across gender and grade level (boys: 46%, girls: 54%; tenth graders: 52%, twelfth graders: 48%).

Adolescents' reports on their own nativity and that of their parents were used to derive the youths' generational status. As shown in Table 1, 29% of the adolescents were of the first generation, having themselves immigrated to the United States. An additional 44% of the students were of the second generation, having been born in the United States, with at least one of their parents having been born elsewhere. The remaining 27% of students were of the third generation or greater, with the student and both parents having been born in the United States. The distribution of generational status varied across ethnic groups. Adolescents from Filipino and Central and South American backgrounds were most likely to be of the first two generations, those from European backgrounds tended to be of the third generation and greater, and students from Mexican and Chinese families were more evenly distributed across generational statuses. (Although the sample size was sufficient to examine generational differences for the overall sample, the ethnic variation in the number of youths within each generation made it possible to detect only large-sized interactions between generation and ethnicity.)

The students' socioeconomic background varied according to ethnicity such that adolescents from Chinese and Filipino families were the most likely to have parents employed in semiprofessional and professional occupations (fathers: 51% and 42%; mothers: 44% and 50%, respectively), followed by adolescents from European, Central and South American, and Mexican families (fathers: 37%, 26%, and 17%; mothers: 36%, 28%, and 20%, respectively). Parental education levels also varied, such that adolescents of Chinese, Filipino, European, and Central and South American backgrounds were more likely to have parents with some college education than those of Mexican backgrounds (fathers: 72%, 88%, 60%, 69%, and 28%; mothers: 65%, 91%, 59%, 57%, and 32%, respectively).

The adolescents of different ethnic backgrounds also varied in the terms of their family structure and composition. Almost one third (29%) of the students of Mexican background lived in single-parent homes as compared to lower proportions of adolescents from the other ethnic backgrounds (European: 25%; Central/South American: 23%; Filipino: 19%; Chinese: 16%). Filipino adolescents tended to have the most siblings living at home ($M = 1.32$), followed by youths with Mexican, Chinese, Central and South American, and European backgrounds ($M = 1.22$, 1.16, 1.15, and 0.97, respectively). Living with grandparents tended to be an infrequent occurrence for most youths (Mexican: 6%; Chinese: 8%; European: 10%; Central/South American: 11%), except for those from Filipino families (18%).

MEASURES

Family Obligations

New measures were created for this study in order to tap youths' attitudes toward specific family obligations that are particularly salient in the lives of adolescents. After conducting a series of focus groups with adolescents and surveying existing literature on filial piety and family obligations, three scales were created to assess the youths' views regarding: (1) current assistance to the family, (2) respect for the family, and (3) future support to the family as adults. Some of the items used in these scales are similar to those in other measures that assess attitudes toward kin collectivism, such as the scales created by Triandis (1991) and Hui (1988), and used in a recent study by Rhee, Uleman, and Lee (1996). Separate factor analyses of the three scales indicated that each set of items loaded onto a single factor; the exact items are listed along with their factor loadings in Table 2. Youths completed each measure twice: The first version asked about the adolescents' perceptions of their parents' views and the second asked about the adolescents' own attitudes.

Current assistance. A measure was created to assess adolescents' expectations for how often they

| TABLE 1 | Sample According to Ethnic Background and Generation |

		GENERATION		
ETHNIC BACKGROUND	N	FIRST	SECOND	THIRD OR LATER
Filipino	312	135	169	8
Chinese	103	18	51	34
Mexican	120	26	63	31
Central/South American	95	43	47	5
European	190	12	31	147
Total	820	234	361	225

TABLE 2	Factor Loadings of Adolescents' Values and Expectations Regarding Family Obligations

	LOADING

Current Assistance

1.	Spend time with your grandparents, cousins, aunts, and uncles	.57
2.	Spend time at home with your family	.76
3.	Run errands that the family needs done	.65
4.	Help your brothers or sisters with their homework	.58
5.	Spend holidays with your family	.48
6.	Help out around the house	.61
7.	Spend time with your family on weekends	.74
8.	Help take care of your brothers and sisters	.61
9.	Eat meals with your family	.66
10.	Help take care of your grandparents	.54
11.	Do things together with your brothers and sisters	.65

Respect for Family

1.	Treat your parents with great respect	.64
2.	Follow your parents' advice about choosing friends	.58
3.	Do well for the sake of your family	.76
4.	Follow your parents' advice about choosing a job or major in college	.59
5.	Treat your grandparents with great respect	.54
6.	Respect your older brothers and sisters	.58
7.	Make sacrifices for your family	.69

Future Support

1.	Help your parents financially in the future	.65
2.	Live at home with your parents until you are married	.59
3.	Help take care of your brothers and sisters in the future	.57
4.	Spend time with your parents even after you no longer live with them	.66
5.	Live or go to college near your parents	.63
6.	Have your parents live with you when you get older	.72

should assist with household tasks and spend time with their family. Using a scale ranging from 1 ("almost never") to 5 ("almost always"), adolescents indicated how often they and their parents expected the youths to engage in 11 activities such as "help take care of your brothers and sisters," "spend time with your family on the weekends," "run errands that the family needs done," and "eat meals with your family." The measure possessed good internal consistencies for both perceived parents' and students' expectations (αs: parents = .83, students = .87) and was similarly reliable across the different ethnic groups, with αs ranging from .79 to .87.

Respect for family. A second scale was created to measure adolescents' beliefs about the importance of respecting and following the wishes of other family members. Using a scale ranging from 1 ("not important at all") to 5 ("very important"), adolescents responded to seven items such as "show great respect for your parents," "follow your parents' advice about what to do after high school," and "respect your older brothers and sisters." The measure possessed good internal consistencies for both perceived parents' and students' values (αs: parents = .79, students = .82) and was reliable across the different ethnic groups (*range* αs = .69–.85).

Future support. A third scale assessed adolescents' beliefs about their obligations to support and be near their families in the future. Using a scale ranging from 1 ("not important at all") to 5 ("very important"), adolescents indicated how important it was that they engage in six behaviors such as "help your parents financially in the future," "spend time with your parents even when you no longer live with them," "help take care of your brothers and sisters in the future," and "live or go to a college near your parents." The scale was internally consistent for both perceived parents' and adolescents' values (αs: parents = .80, students = .81) and possessed good reliabilities within each ethnic group (*range* αs = .72–.82).

Family Relationships

Parent-adolescent conflict. Adolescents' perceptions of conflict with their parents was measured using the Issues Checklist (IC), developed by Prinz, Foster, Kent, and O'Leary (1979) and Robin and Foster (1984). This measure has been used in numerous studies of parent-child relationships during adolescence (e.g., Steinberg, 1987, 1988). Students indicated whether any of 12 specific topics (e.g., spending money, chores, and cursing) were discussed with their mother and father in the last 2 weeks. For each topic that was discussed, the intensity of the discussion was rated from 1 ("very calm") to 5 ("very angry"). To be consistent with previous research (i.e., Steinberg, 1987), a measure of the incidence of parent-adolescent conflict was computed by summing the number of discussions rated as containing anger (2 or greater). Students completed two versions of the checklist, one in reference to each parent. This scale possessed good internal consistencies (αs: father = .80, mother = .79) and similar reliability for the adolescents from all five ethnic groups (*range* αs = .70–.83).

Parent-adolescent cohesion. Students completed the cohesion subscale of the Family Adaptation and

Cohesion Evaluation Scales (FACES) II inventory separately for each parent (Olson, Sprenkle, & Russell, 1979). Using a scale ranging from 1 ("almost never") to 5 ("almost always"), students responded to 10 questions such as "My mother [father] and I feel very close to each other," "My mother and I are supportive of each other during difficult times," and "My mother and I avoid each other at home" (reversed). This scale also has been used in previous research on the changes in parent-child relationships during adolescence (Steinberg, 1987, 1988). This scale possessed good overall internal consistencies (αs: father = .88, mother = .86) and was equally reliable for the adolescents from all four ethnic backgrounds (*range* αs = .83–.90).

Family discussions. Adolescents' responded to five items asking whether or not they discussed a number of different topics (future job plans, current classes, personal problems, future educational plans, future family plans) with each of their parents and with their siblings. The adolescents rated the frequency of these discussions from 1 ("almost never") to 5 ("almost always"). This measure had good internal consistencies overall (αs: mother = .83, father = .84, siblings = .86) and possessed similar reliabilities across ethnic groups, with αs ranging from .79 to .89.

Peer Relationships

Peer discussions. Adolescents responded using a scale that ranged from "almost never" (1) to "almost always" (5) to five items regarding the extent to which they discussed different issues with their friends. These items were identical to the ones they responded to for discussions with family members. The scale possessed a good internal consistency (α = .81) and similar reliabilities across ethnic groups (*range* αs = .73–.86).

Peer time. Adolescents indicated the amount of time they spent socializing with peers on a typical weekday, Saturday, and Sunday. A weekly estimate of the amount of time spent with peers was computed by adding the Saturday and Sunday estimates to five times the weekday estimate.

Friendship value. Adolescents responded to three items that assessed their value of friendships: "How much do you like doing things with your friends?", "For me, making friends is…", and "How useful is the ability to make friends?" The items were rated on three different 5-point scales ranging from "a little" to "a lot", "not at all important" to "very important," and "not at all useful" to "very useful,"

respectively. The scale possessed a modest internal consistency (α = .69) and demonstrated fairly similar reliabilities across ethnic groups (*range* αs = .58–.76).

Academic Adjustment

Study time. A weekly estimate of the amount of time adolescents spent doing homework and studying for tests was computed based upon the students' reports for a typical weekday, Saturday, and Sunday.

Educational aspiration and expectation. Students' aspiration and expectation for educational attainment were measured using two items in which the students were asked (1) how far they would like to go in school and (2) how far they thought they actually would go in school. Students answered using a 5-point scale where 1 = finish some high school, 2 = graduate from high school, 3 = graduate from a 2-year college, 4 = graduate from a 4-year college, and 5 = graduate from law, medical, or graduate school.

Grade point average. The year-end grade point average (GPA) for 91% of the adolescents was computed using the students' course grades that were gathered from their official report cards. Self-reported grades were used for the remainder of the adolescents for whom report cards could not be obtained. GPA was measured on a traditional letter scale, including pluses and minuses, where F = 1, D = 3, C = 6, B = 9, and A = 12. There were no grades of A+.

RESULTS

Variations in Adolescents' Expectations and Values

Ethnicity, Grade, and Gender. Three-way analyses of variance (ANOVAs) were conducted to determine the extent to which adolescents' beliefs about family obligations varied according to their ethnic background, grade, and gender. As shown in Table 3, youths from every Asian and Latin American group held significantly stronger values regarding respect and future obligations to their families than did those from European backgrounds. Adolescents from Asian and Latin American families placed greater importance upon treating their elders with respect, following their parents' advice, and helping and being near their families in the future than did youths from European families. Filipino youths placed the greatest importance upon familial respect, endorsing those items significantly more strongly than the Chinese and Latin American adolescents. Filipino youths also indicated a greater emphasis on their future obligations than those with Mexican backgrounds. These

TABLE 3   Adolescents' Expectations and Values Regarding Family Obligations

| | ETHNIC BACKGROUND | | | | | | |
ATTITUDE	FILIPINO M (SD)	CHINESE M (SD)	MEXICAN M (SD)	CENTRAL AND SOUTH AMERICAN M (SD)	EUROPEAN M (SD)	F	BONFERRONI CONTRASTS
Current assistance	3.23 (.76)	3.07 (.72)	2.89 (.72)	2.80 (.83)	2.68 (.73)	17.43***	F, C > E; F > M, C/S***
Respect	3.92 (.67)	3.51 (.68)	3.55 (.78)	3.61 (.82)	3.00 (.90)	42.27***	F, C, M, C/S > E; F > C, M***; F > C/S**
Future obligations	3.27 (.84)	3.04 (.73)	2.92 (.95)	3.07 (.93)	2.44 (.92)	27.11***	F, C, M, C/S > E***; F > M**

Note: Ns = 791–802. All were 5-point scales; *F* values are based upon three-way ANOVAs that also included grade and gender.

*p <.05; **p < .01; ***p < .001.

ethnic differences in adolescents' values tended to be moderate to very large in size, ranging from .37 to 1.10 standard deviations.

Only Chinese and Filipino adolescents believed that they should spend significantly more time currently helping and spending time with their families than their European American peers. The expectations for current assistance reported by adolescents from the two Latin American groups fell between those with Asian and European backgrounds, and were significantly lower than the expectations reported by Filipino youths. Again, these differences were sizable in magnitude and ranged from .44 to .71 standard deviations.

Tenth- and twelfth-grade adolescents indicated similar expectations and values regarding their obligations to their families, $F(1, 783) = .89$ to $F(1, 772) = 2.86$, $ps > .05$. There also were no gender differences in adolescents' attitudes and none of the grade or gender variations differed according to adolescents' ethnic background, $F(1, 781) = .25$ to $F(1, 783) = 3.06$, $ps > .05$.

Generation

In order to estimate the independent effects of adolescents' generational and ethnic backgrounds, adolescents' generational statuses were dummy-coded and treated as covariates in analyses of covariance (ANCOVAs) along with the youths' ethnic background. Adolescents' generation was not associated with their beliefs regarding their family obligations above and beyond the effect of their ethnic background, $F(2, 786) = .24$ to $F(2, 795) = 2.23$, $ps > .05$. Even after controlling for generational status, all of the previously reported ethnic variations remained significant, $F(4, 795) = 11.64$ to $F(4, 797) = 22.63$, $ps < .001$; Bonferroni contrasts of adjusted means, $ps < .05$.

Additional analyses were conducted in order to examine whether generational differences in adolescents' beliefs varied according to their ethnic background. In only one case did the interaction between adolescents' generational status and their ethnicity emerge as significant, $F(4, 787) = 3.29$, $p < .05$. Separate regressions conducted within each group indicated that first generation Mexican, Chinese, Filipino, and European adolescents reported a higher value of their future obligations than did their third-generation peers, $bs = .20–.62$. In contrast, Central and South American youths from the first generation placed less importance on their future assistance to their family than did those from the third generation, $b = –1.07$.

Socioeconomic Background and Family Composition

ANCOVAs that included adolescents' ethnicity indicated that adolescents' beliefs about their family obligations were unassociated with their socioeconomic background and parents' marital status, the number of siblings in residence, and whether their grandparents lived with them, $F(4, 750) = .44$ to $F(4, 742) = 1.49$, $ps > .05$. Yet the difference between Filipino and Mexican youths in their expectations for current assistance, as well as the difference between Filipino and Central/South American adolescents in their value of respect, were reduced just enough to become no longer significant after controlling for these background variables, Bonferroni contrasts of adjusted means, $ps > .05$. The remainder of the ethnic variations, including the differences between Asian and Latino American youths and their peers from European backgrounds, remained significant even after accounting for the ethnic differences in these family background factors, $F(4, 751) = 11.18$ to $F(4, 737) =$

34.90, $ps < .001$; Bonferroni contrasts of adjusted means, $ps < .05$.

Only 1 out of a possible 12 interactions between aspects of adolescents' family background and their ethnicity emerged as statistically significant. Mexican and Central/South American youths from single-parent families reported slightly higher self-expectations for current assistance ($Ms = 3.09, 2.94$) than those from dual-parent homes ($Ms = 2.82, 2.79$), whereas the reverse was the case for adolescents from Chinese, Filipino, and European backgrounds (single: $Ms = 2.80, 3.12, 2.45$; dual: $Ms = 3.09, 3.25, 2.75$), $F(4, 726) = 2.52, p < .05$.

Perceived Disagreement with Parental Expectations and Values

Within-subject ANOVAs were used to estimate whether adolescents believed that their attitudes differed from those of their parents, and the extent to which this parent-adolescent difference varied by ethnicity, grade, and gender. Overall, youths believed that they had lower expectations for their current assistance to their family and placed less importance upon familial respect than did their parents, $F(1, 780) = 7.86$ and $F(1, 763) = 154.39$, $ps > .01–.001$. As shown in Table 4, adolescents from all five ethnic groups reported only a slight difference with their parents about how often they should currently help out around the house and spend time with family members. Youths perceived a much greater disagreement with their parents over the importance of respecting and following the wishes of other family members; this disagreement was significantly greater among adolescents with European backgrounds than among those from Filipino families.

There was no overall difference in adolescents' reports of how much they and their parents valued their future obligations to their family, $F(1, 758) = 2.31$,

$p > .05$. Slight ethnic variations in this difference were observed such that those from European and Central and South American families actually believed that supporting and living near their families in the future were marginally more important to themselves than to their parents. Youths from the other three ethnic groups believed themselves to be in close agreement with their parents about their future obligations. These ethnic variations, however, were too slight to attain significance in the group contrasts.

The extent to which adolescents believed that their values and expectations differed from those of their parents did not vary according to adolescents' gender or grade level, $F(1, 763) = .02$ to $F(1, 763) = 3.49$, $ps > .05$.

RELATIONS BETWEEN EXPECTATIONS, VALUES, AND OTHER ASPECTS OF DEVELOPMENT

Bivariate Correlations

Partial correlations, after controlling for ethnic background, between adolescents' beliefs and aspects of their family interactions, peer relationships, academic adjustment are presented in Table 5.[1] Adolescents who possessed high expectations and values regarding their obligations to the family generally reported more positive relationships with other family members. These youths felt more emotionally close to their mothers and fathers and were more

---

[1]Due to the ethnic variations in adolescents' beliefs about their family obligations, partial correlations were estimated to avoid the occurrence of significant associations with the other outcomes that were due to simultaneous ethnic differences in both the beliefs and the outcomes. As it was, the partial and unpartialed correlations were virtually identical.

TABLE 4   Adolescents' Perceptions of the Differences between Their Expectations and Values and Those of Their Parents

| | ETHNIC BACKGROUND | | | | | | |
BELIEF	FILIPINO M (SD)	CHINESE M (SD)	MEXICAN M (SD)	CENTRAL AND SOUTH AMERICAN M (SD)	EUROPEAN M (SD)	F	BONFERRONI CONTRASTS
Current assistance	−.02 (.55)	−.02 (.65)	−.14 (.62)	−.06 (.70)	−.12 (.54)	1.46	—
Respect	−.22 (.52)	−.42 (.69)	−.27 (.75)	−.29 (.65)	−.41 (.71)	3.35**	E > F*
Future obligations	−.02 (.68)	−.06 (.91)	0 (.94)	.19 (.89)	.15 (.69)	2.62*	ns

Note: $Ns = 765–787$. Differences are absolute differences, with negative values indicating greater parental endorsement; F values are for ethnic variations in the perceived differences and are based upon within-subject ANOVAs that also included grade and gender.

*$p < .05$; **$p < .01$; ***$p < .001$.

TABLE 5 Partial Correlations between Adolescents' Expectations, Values, and Developmental Outcomes

	CURRENT ASSISTANCE	RESPECT	FUTURE OBLIGATIONS
Family interactions			
Mother conflict	.03	−.03	−.03
Father conflict	.07*	.03	−.01
Mother cohesion	.35***	.38***	.33***
Father cohesion	.36***	.31***	.26***
Mother discussions	.35***	.37***	.29***
Father discussions	.35***	.33***	.23***
Sibling discussions	.28***	.21***	.14***
Peer relationships			
Peer discussions	.13***	.04	.01
Peer time	.04	.04	.07
Friendships value	.12**	.08	.04
Academic adjustment			
Study time	.16***	.15***	.12**
Educational aspiration	.14***	.08*	.02
Educational expectation	.15***	.12***	.03
GPA	.04	.02	−.07

Note: Ns = 591–798. Partial correlations were estimated after controlling for adolescents' ethnic background.

*$p < .05$; **$p < .01$; ***$p < .001$.

likely to seek advice about their current lives and future plans from their parents and siblings. There was only one small association with conflict, as those adolescents who thought that they should spend more of their present time assisting their family also reported more frequent angry discussions with their fathers. Interestingly, youths who emphasized respecting and following the advice of their parents were no less likely to report arguing with their parents than other adolescents.

There was no evidence that adolescents who placed great importance upon their family obligations were less involved in social relationships with other youths. Those who valued assisting, respecting, and following the advice of their family members spent just as much time with their peers as did other adolescents. Youths who believed that they should frequently help out and spend time with their family were actually more likely to value and seek advice from their friends, though these associations tended to be small in magnitude.

Adolescents with attitudes supportive of family obligations tended to be more academically motivated. Youths who believed that they should currently assist and respect their family members tended to have higher aspirations and expectations for pursuing their education beyond high school. Endorsing family obligations also was associated with spending more time studying each week. Even adolescents who believed that they should frequently help out with chores and take care of other family members reported spending more time doing homework and studying for tests. There was no linear association, however, between youths' beliefs about family obligations and the grades that they received at school.

The relations between adolescents' values, expectations, and other aspects of their development tended to be similar for all adolescents, regardless of their ethnicity. Only 4 out of a possible 42 interactions between youths' attitudes and ethnic background emerged, and these differential associations did not follow a consistent pattern, $F(4, 736) = 2.44$ to $F(4, 664) = 4.78$, $ps < .05–.001$. High expectations for current assistance to the family was associated with higher cohesion and discussions with mothers for adolescents from all groups, $bs = .10–.64$, except those from Chinese families, for whom there were negative or virtually no associations, $bs = −.13, .05$. Familial respect was positively associated with discussions with siblings among Filipino, Central and South American, and European adolescents, $bs = .16–.41$, but negatively associated among Mexican and Chinese youths, $bs = −.19, −.34$. Finally, a high value on future obligations was associated with more frequent discussions with siblings among Mexican, Chinese, and European adolescents, $bs = .09–.42$, and fewer discussions among Filipino and Central and South American youths, $bs = −.21, −.33$.

Curvilinear Associations

In order to test the hypothesis that extremely high expectations and values regarding family obligations may have more negative implications than moderate beliefs, regressions were conducted to determine whether curvilinear functions accounted for variations in adolescents' outcomes above and beyond the simple linear relation, after controlling for adolescents' ethnic background. Negative implications for high expectations and values were evident for the students' performance in school, though the curvilinear relations tended to be modest in magnitude. As shown in Figure 1, those who fell into the highest third in terms of their expectations for current assistance and their value of familial respect tended to receive grades nearly as low as or even lower than those who fell into the lowest third, βs = .09, .14, ps < .05, .001. Adolescents possessing moderate levels of these beliefs attained the highest grades. A similar curvilinear pattern was evident for the relation between adolescents' value of their future obligations and their grades, although it was only marginally significant, β = .07, p < .06. These associations remained virtually the same even after controlling for adolescents' socioeconomic background, βs = .09, .13, .06.

Significant curvilinear associations that suggested negative implications of very strong attitudes regarding family obligations did not emerge for any other outcomes, including adolescents' study time and educational aspirations and expectations.

Perceived Disagreement

Analyses also were conducted to determine whether the extent to which adolescents believed that they disagreed with their parents' attitudes was associated with other aspects of their development above and beyond the level of their own values, after con-

trolling for adolescents' ethnic background. In only two cases was perceived disagreement independently associated with adolescents' outcomes. Those who believed that they placed a lower value on familial respect than did their parents tended to feel less close to their mothers (Ms = parent > adolescent, 2.88; parent = adolescent, 3.29; adolescent > parent, 3.38) and spent less time with their peers (Ms = parent > adolescent, 19.32; parent = adolescent, 22.77; adolescent > parent, 23.31) than did other adolescents, $F(2, 754)$ = 5.15 and $F(2, 587)$ = 4.11, ps < .05–.01. Interactions also emerged such that the variations in cohesion with mother and time with peers according to perceived disagreement with parents were greatest among adolescents who placed low importance on familial respect, $F(2, 754)$ = 3.47 and $F(2, 587)$ = 3.41, ps < .05.

Ethnic Variations in Family Interactions, Peer Relationships, and Academic Adjustment

Given the relations between adolescents' beliefs about family obligations and other aspects of their development, analyses were conducted to determine whether the ethnic differences in their attitudes were associated with parallel ethnic variations in family interactions, peer relationships, and academic adjustment. As shown in Table 6, no ethnic differences emerged that followed the pattern of Asian and Latin American youths together being significantly greater or lower than those with European backgrounds. Adolescents from all ethnic backgrounds reported fairly similar relationships with their families and friends. A few differences in family interactions emerged, with a tendency for Filipino youths to be among those who most frequently discussed personal problems and plans with parents and siblings. The most prominent ethnic differences emerged in aspects of adolescents' academic adjustment. Chinese and Filipino adolescents tended to study most often and held higher aspirations and expectations than their peers, and those from Chinese backgrounds possessed the highest grade point averages. Latin American students were as motivated as their counterparts from European families, but the Mexican and Central and South American students tended to receive the lowest grades in their courses.

The strong attitudes of the Filipino youths toward their family obligations appeared to account for their tendency to seek more advice from their parents and siblings than adolescents from other groups, as well the differences in academic motivation between themselves and those from Central/South American families (see Table 6). But the majority of the ethnic differences in educational adjustment

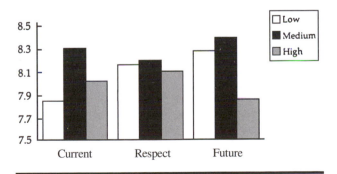

FIGURE 1 Adolescents' grade point average according to their beliefs about family obligations.

TABLE 6   Adolescents' Family Interactions, Peer Relationships, and Academic Adjustment

| | ETHNIC BACKGROUND | | | | | | |
DOMAIN	FILIPINO M (SD)	CHINESE M (SD)	MEXICAN M (SD)	CENTRAL AND SOUTH AMERICAN M (SD)	EUROPEAN M (SD)	F	BONFERRONI CONTRASTS
Family interactions							
Mother conflict	2.83 (2.30)	2.16 (1.91)	2.73 (2.34)	2.92 (2.22)	2.66 (2.43)	1.72	—
Father conflict	1.73 (2.12)	1.55 (2.01)	1.18 (1.63)	1.69 (2.12)	1.57 (1.89)	1.46	—
Mother cohesion	3.09 (.83)	2.98 (.76)	3.11 (.85)	3.18 (.75)	3.16 (.87)	.95	—
Father cohesion	2.80 (.86)	2.75 (.74)	2.45 (.93)	2.79 (.90)	2.92 (.99)	4.39**	F > M**; E > M***
Mother discussions	2.93 (.95)	2.58 (.85)	2.91 (1.08)	3.02 (1.06)	2.91 (.98)	2.77*	F, C/S > C*
Father discussions	2.59 (.95)	2.36 (.89)	2.23 (1.12)	2.67 (.96)	2.59 (.98)	3.63**	F, C/S, E > M*
Sibling discussions	2.62 (1.17)	2.32 (.98)	2.65 (1.18)	2.56 (1.28)	2.22 (1.03)	4.21**	M > E*; F > E**
Peer relationships							
Peer discussions	3.46 (.89)	3.36 (.78)	3.24 (1.10)	3.24 (1.00)	3.32 (.94)	1.64	—
Peer time	22.59 (14.80)	18.99 (12.06)	22.41 (15.43)	20.17 (15.54)	20.10 (12.85)	1.49	—
Friendship value	4.33 (.67)	4.31 (.56)	4.11 (.68)	4.02 (.68)	4.21 (.68)	4.07**	F > C/S**
Academic adjustment							
Study time	16.19 (10.42)	16.82 (9.06)	10.53 (6.61)	11.90 (7.53)	10.26 (7.77)	16.82***	F, C > **C/S****; F, C > M,E***
Educ. aspiration	4.49 (.62)	4.54 (.56)	3.99 (1.01)	4.21 (.73)	4.08 (.80)	16.77***	F, C > **C/S***; F, C > **M,E*****
Educ. expectation	4.25 (.72)	4.39 (.66)	3.60 (1.16)	3.91 (.96)	3.82 (.89)	18.98***	F > **C/S***; C > C/S**;F, C > M,E***
GPA	8.05 (2.23)	9.91 (1.64)	7.05 (2.62)	7.35 (2.36)	8.40 (2.44)	20.31***	F > M; E > C/S**; E > M;C > F, M, C/S,E***

Note: Ns = 594–764. Bold contrasts indicate those ethnic differences that became nonsignificant, *p* > .05, after controlling for youths' attitudes toward family obligations.

*p < .05; **p < .01; ***p < .001.

could not be accounted for by variations in youths' attitudes toward family obligations. Most of the differences in study time, grades, and educational aspirations and expectations remained significant even after controlling for adolescents' values and expectations; Bonferroni contrasts of adjusted means, *ps* < .05. Little evidence was found for even partial mediation, as the percent of variance accounted for by adolescents' ethnic background was reduced by only one third for study time (36%), one quarter for educational aspirations and expectations (26% and 23%), and virtually no reduction was observed for grade point average (3%). Most of these small reductions were likely due to the differences between Filipino and Central/South American youths becoming nonsignificant.

DISCUSSION

Asian and Latin American adolescents possessed stronger values and greater expectations regarding their duty to assist, respect, and support their families than their peers with European backgrounds.

These differences tended to be large and were consistent across the youths' generation, gender, family composition, and socioeconomic background. Although an emphasis on family obligations tended to be associated with more positive outcomes at the individual level, there was no evidence that the ethnic variations in these beliefs produced meaningful group differences in the adolescents' development. These findings suggest that even within a society that emphasizes adolescent autonomy and independence, youths from families with collectivistic traditions retain their parents' familistic values and these values do not have a negative impact upon their development.

The dramatic ethnic differences in the youths' attitudes, sometimes reaching more than a full standard deviation in magnitude, testify to the great importance of family support and respect to those from Asian and Latin American families. The ethnic differences could not be accounted for by variations in socioeconomic background and family composition, and these beliefs generally remained strong regardless of whether the youths and their parents were born in their home countries or in the United States.

The only attitude to decline across generations was the importance of assisting and supporting family members in the future when the adolescents become adults; this value dropped for all groups except for those from Central and South American families. It is likely that the parents of latter-generation youths have greater familiarity and comfort with U.S. society and do not need as much assistance from their adult children. Yet the cultural imperative of family support remains strong even as the actual need for it declines, because third-generation adolescents from Asian and Latin American families still endorsed their future obligations more strongly than their European American peers.

The generational stability in adolescents' attitudes toward family obligations contrasts with previously observed generational differences in other beliefs and values, such as a decline in the importance of education and earlier expectations for behavioral autonomy (Feldman & Rosenthal, 1990; Fuligni, 1997, 1998). Together, these findings suggest that the meaning of being "Chinese" or "Mexican" (or Filipino, Nicaraguan, and so forth) may change across successive generations of adolescents. Among adolescents from immigrant families, being Asian or Latin American appears to include valuing education, postponing dating and other social activities, and believing in the importance of assisting and respecting one's family. In comparison, the identity among youths from latter generations may focus mostly upon duty and obligation to one's family and less upon academics and delayed autonomy. Just as individuals may possess both individualistic and collectivistic attitudes (Sinha & Tripathi, 1994), latter-generation Asian and Latin American youths seem to simultaneously desire greater autonomy and recognize the importance of maintaining a close bond with their families. The retention of the emphasis on family responsibility may be due to the significance of such collectivistic values for the self-images of those from Asian and Latin American families (Markus & Kitayama, 1991). Recent evidence suggests that familistic attitudes are indeed integral to the identities of individuals from these cultural backgrounds (Gaines et al., 1997).

Adolescents believed it was more important to their parents than to themselves that the youths respect their elders, follow their parents' advice, and make sacrifices for the family. Issues of decision making are likely to be points of contention within Asian and Latin American families, leading the adolescents to become frustrated with the assertion of parental authority. As an Asian college student noted to Zhou and Bankston (1998), recalling her parents' rules about dating and socializing: "I had always hoped that my parents would someday open up just a little

to realize that we are living in America and not in Vietnam" (p. 169). Yet it is important to note that issues of authority and decision making are common among other families as well, and that the youths from European backgrounds in this study perceived a similar discrepancy with their parents regarding the importance of respect. In addition, adolescents from all cultural backgrounds believed themselves to be in close agreement with their parents in regards to the importance of helping out at home, spending time with family members, and assisting the family in the future. The perceived discrepancy in views about respect, therefore, may be more a case of common parent-adolescent disagreement over the specific issue of decision making rather than a general clash of cultures within Asian and Latin American families.

At the individual level, youths' desire to assist and respect their family was associated with having close and communicative relationships with their parents and siblings. Adolescents' assumption of their family responsibilities also was associated with a desire to achieve at school. As has been reported in numerous ethnographies, adolescents from Asian and Latin American families are acutely aware of the great sacrifices their parents made to come to this country (Gibson & Bhachu, 1991; Suárez-Orozco & Suárez-Orozco, 1995). The students often are reminded of this sacrifice on a daily basis as their parents work long hours in jobs that are sometimes below their level of training (Caplan et al., 1991). These youths likely feel that achieving in school is an important part of their family obligations and that their academic success will in some way assist the family's fortunes. Yet the associations between a sense of family obligation and academic motivation existed even among those from European American families, suggesting that believing in the importance of assisting and respecting the family tends to be associated with better developmental outcomes even among groups for whom these traditions are relatively less important.

Emphasizing obligation and duty to the family did not compromise adolescents' peer relationships. Youths with high values and expectations regarding their obligations spent just as much time socializing with their friends and were actually slightly more likely to value and seek advice from their peers. These adolescents probably make friends with other youths who hold similar values regarding the family. Observers have noted the existence of distinct peer groups within Asian and Latin American communities in which the adolescents closely align themselves with their families' traditions. For example, the "Mexicanos" noted by Matute-Bianchi (1991) in a community on the central coast of California intentionally differentiated themselves from the more "American-ized" adolescents of Mexican descent through their visible expression of their Mexican heritage, their active use of both Spanish and English, and their involvement in cultural clubs and activities. The existence of peer groups such as the Mexicanos enable adolescents to develop rich and fulfilling social relationships while they pursue their cultural identities within the context of a strong connection to their families. Rather than compromising peer relationships, the sense of family obligation held by these adolescents likely provides a shared value system upon which they can base their friendships.

In one area, however, an extremely high value of family duty and obligation was associated with less positive adolescent development. Whereas a moderate emphasis on family obligations was associated with greater academic success, adolescents who indicated the strongest endorsement of their obligations tended to receive grades just as low as or even lower than those with the weakest endorsement. This modest relation existed after controlling for the students' ethnic and socioeconomic backgrounds, and the associations between adolescents' attitudes and their study time and motivation did not show parallel curvilinear patterns. Yet even at the same level of parental occupation and adolescent motivation, there may be individual variations in family need and responsibility that were not assessed in this study. For example, Suárez-Orozco and Suárez-Orozco (1995) have reported how some adolescents from poor Latin American families feel the need to cut back on their studies during periods of acute economic crisis. One Mexican youth in their study, when asked to describe the thoughts of a girl in a picture who is holding school books while watching her parents labor in the fields, said: "…she is watching her parents working so hard…she feels like they have a big problem. She tries to help her parents, but she also has to study. In the end, she tries to help them" (p. 129). Education remains important to these youths, but the families may face more pressing needs that demand the students' attention. These periodic compromises, in turn, may cumulatively erode the students' progress at school over time.

The link between a very strong sense of obligation and lower school performance also may be due to other individual and family-level phenomena that are independent of ethnic and socioeconomic background. For example, adolescents with the strongest endorsement of their obligations may have parents incapable of effectively managing the household or caring for themselves because of chronic illness or other liabilities. These adolescents may have siblings or grandparents with special needs that demand the

youths' time and attention. Alternatively, the students may strongly emphasize their obligations as a way to affirm their self-worth and place in the family in the face of a lack of success at school (Steele, 1988). More research is needed to better understand this intriguing finding, but the fact that the curvilinear association existed even after controlling for students' ethnic background suggests that the explanations are not likely to be cultural in origin.

Despite the individual-level associations, there was no evidence that the strong emphasis upon family obligations among Asian and Latin American youths produced any major group differences in their development. These results help to clarify the collectivistic nature of relationships within Asian and Latin American families. Although children from these families feel obligated to respect and remain connected to their families, they do not necessarily progress through the adolescent years with closer relationships with their parents and siblings than those with European backgrounds. Rather, the emphasis seems to be more on the importance of instrumentally supporting one another. Cooper et al. (1993) similarly observed that, whereas Chinese and Vietnamese college students placed a strong value on assisting their families, they felt the least comfortable talking about sexuality and dating with their parents. Like most American adolescents, Asian and Latin American youths likely turn to their friends for advice on these and other personal concerns.

Emphasizing duty and obligation to family also does not seem to explain the large ethnic differences in adolescents' achievement at school. There was no evidence that the lower academic performance of the students from Latin American backgrounds, or even the high achievement of Chinese students, were due to the youths' sense of obligation to assist and support their family. It should be noted that the extent to which adolescents believed that they succeeded or had difficulties in school because of their family obligations was not specifically measured in this study. Future research would need to directly measure adolescents' views of how their obligations affected their educational efforts in order to determine the degree to which a sense of obligation actually assisted or prevented certain groups of students from achieving in school. Nevertheless, this study clearly indicates that the individual-level associations between family obligations and academic outcomes cannot be used to explain the ethnic variations in achievement. Factors that contribute group-level variations in academic achievement, although not always clear, can be quite different than those that produce individual differences (Kao, Tienda, & Schneider, 1996). For example, it has been noted that immigrant students from Latin America sometimes get channeled as a group into lower-level academic classes, even though they have already taken similar or even more advanced coursework in their home countries (Suárez-Orozco, 1991).

Although adolescents from Asian and Latin American families clearly place great importance on their family obligations, the extent to which they actually act in accordance with their beliefs remains unclear. The links between beliefs and behavior are not always strong and the demands of adolescent life in American society may make it difficult for youths to fulfill their perceived obligations. For example, in contrast to youths in Asian societies, adolescents in the United States tend to spend a large portion of their time away from the family and socializing with peers in autonomous activities such as dating and attending parties (Fuligni & Stevenson, 1995; Larson, 1983). Even when American adolescents work in part-time jobs, the income they receive tends to be for their own discretionary spending rather than for supporting their families (Greenberger & Steinberg, 1986). The contrast between American behavioral norms and their families' traditions are quite salient to youths from Asian and Latin American families: "To be an American, you may be able to do whatever you want. But to be a Vietnamese, you must think of your family first" (Zhou & Bankston, 1998, p. 166). Additional studies should employ techniques such as naturalistic observation and daily diaries in order to obtain detailed analyses of how Asian and Latin American adolescents negotiate the sometimes competing demands of their family and American society. Such assessments also would provide insight into whether the actual obligatory behaviors of youths have a more direct impact on other aspects of their lives than do their attitudes toward those behaviors.

Additional research also should be conducted on the socialization and implications of family obligations before and after the adolescent years. Studying the acquisition of familistic values at earlier ages would shed light onto how these attitudes are first internalized by children, as well as the role the values play in other aspects of children's development such as their ethnic identity (Gaines et al., 1997). Investigating family obligations during the years of young adulthood would provide insight into how the strength and manifestation of these attitudes change as adolescents move out of the teenage years and into postsecondary education or employment (e.g., Cooper et al., 1993).

Despite the possible concerns of many Asian and Latin American parents who are raising a family in American society, their children appear to retain the traditional cultural values of assisting and respecting their family The extent to which the adolescents act in accordance with their views remains to be seen, but the stability of the attitudes across the different generations suggest that these beliefs serve an important function in the development of these youths. Rather than compromising adjustment in a society that emphasizes individualism, remembering one's obligation to the family may serve as a critical component in the developing identities of Asian and Latin American youths.

REFERENCES

Barber, B. L., & Eccles, J. S. (1992). Long-term influence of divorce and single parenting on adolescent family- and work-related values, behaviors, and aspirations. *Psychological Bulletin, 111,* 108–126.

Caplan, N., Choy, M. H., & Whitmore, J. K. (1991). *Children of the boat people: A study of educational success.* Ann Arbor: University of Michigan Press.

Chao, R. K. (1995). Chinese and European American cultural models of the self reflected in mothers' childrearing beliefs. *Ethos, 23,* 328–354.

Chao, R. K. (1996). Chinese and European American mothers' views about the role of parenting in children's school success. *Journal of Cross-Cultural Psychology, 27,* 403–423.

Chilman, C. S. (1993). Hispanic families in the United States: Research perspectives. In H. P. McAdoo (Ed.), *Family ethnicity: Strength in diversity* (pp. 141–163). Newbury Park, CA: Sage.

Cooper, C. R., Baker, H., Polichar, D., & Welsh, M. (1993). Values and communication of Chinese, Filipino, European, Mexican, and Vietnamese American adolescents with their families and friends. In S. Shulman & W. A. Collins (Eds.), *Father-adolescent relationships* (pp. 73–89). San Francisco: Jossey-Bass.

Falicov, C. J. (1983). Mexican families. In M. McGoldrick, J. K. Pearce, & J. Giodano (Eds.), *Ethnicity and family therapy* (pp. 208–228). New York: Guilford Press.

Feldman, S. S., Mont-Reynaud, R., & Rosenthal, D. A. (1992). When East moves West: The acculturation of values of Chinese adolescents in the U.S. and Australia. *Journal of Research on Adolescence, 2,* 147–173.

Feldman, S. S., & Rosenthal, D. A. (1990). The acculturation of autonomy expectations in Chinese high-schoolers residing in two Western nations. *International Journal of Psychology, 25,* 259–281.

Freeburg, A. L., & Stein, C. H. (1996). Felt obligation towards parents in Mexican-American and Anglo-American young adults. *Journal of Social and Personal Relationship, 13*(3), 457–471.

Fuligni, A. J. (1997). The academic achievement of adolescents from immigrant families: The roles of family background, attitudes, and behavior. *Child Development, 68,* 261–273.

Fuligni, A. J. (1998). Parental authority, adolescent autonomy, and parent-adolescent relationships: A study of adolescents from Mexican, Chinese, Filipino, and European backgrounds [Special issue: Culture and socioemotional development]. *Developmental Psychology, 34,* 782–792.

Fuligni, A. J., & Stevenson, H. W. (1995). Time-use and mathematics achievement among Chinese, Japanese, and American High School Students. *Child Development, 66,* 830–842.

Gaines, S. O., Marelich, W. D., Bledsoe, K. L., Steers, W. N., Henderson, M. C., Granrose, C. S., Barajas, L., Hicks, D., Lyde, M., Takahashi, Y., Yum, N., Rios, D. I., Garcia, B. F., Farris, K. R., & Page, M. S. (1997). Links between race/ethnicity and cultural values as mediated by racial/ethnic identity and moderated by gender. *Journal of Personality and Social Psychology, 72,* 1460–1476.

Gibson, M. A., & Bhachu, P. K. (1991). The dynamics of educational decision making: A comparative study of Sikhs in Britain and the United States. In M. A. Gibson & J. U. Ogbu (Eds.), *Minority status and schooling: A comparative study of immigrant and involuntary minorities* (pp. 63–96). New York: Garland.

Goodnow, J. J. (1988). Children's household work: Its nature and functions. *Psychological Bulletin, 103,* 5–26.

Greenberger, E., & Steinberg, L. (1986). *When teenagers work: The psychological and social costs of adolescent employment.* New York: Basic Books.

Henderson, R. W. (1997). Educational and occupational aspirations and expectations among parents of middle school students of Mexican descent: Family resources for academic development and mathematics learning. In R. W. Taylor & M. C. Wang (Eds.), *Social and emotional adjustment and family relations in ethnic minority families.* Mahwah, NJ: Erlbaum.

Ho, D. Y. F. (1981). Traditional patterns of socialization in Chinese society. *Acta Psychologica Taiwanica, 23,* 81–95.

Huang, L. N. (1994). An integrative approach to clinical assessment and intervention with Asian-American adolescents. *Journal of Clinical Child Psychology, 23*(1), 21–31.

Hui, C. H. (1988). Measurement of Individualism-collectivism. *Journal of Research on Personality, 22,* 17–36.

Kagitcibasi, C. (1990). Family and socialization in cross-cultural perspective: A model of change. In J. Berman (Ed.), *Nebraska Symposium on Motivation, 1989* (pp. 135–200). Lincoln: University of Nebraska Press.

Kao, G., Tienda, M., & Schneider, B. (1996). Racial and ethnic variation in academic performance. *Research in sociology and education, 11,* 263–297.

Larson, R. W. (1983). Adolescents' daily experience with family and friends: Contrasting opportunity systems. *Journal of Marriage and the Family, 45,* 739–750.

Lee, E. (1983). A social systems approach to assessment and treatment for Chinese American families. In M. McGoldrick, J. K. Pearce, & J. Giodano (Eds.), *Ethnicity and family therapy* (pp. 208–228). New York: The Guilford Press.

Markus, H. R., & Kitayama, S. (1991). Culture and the self: Implications for cognition, emotion, and motivation. *Psychological Review, 98,* 224–253.

Matute-Bianchi, M. E. (1991). Situational ethnicity and patterns of school performance among immigrant and non-immigrant Mexican-descent students. In M. A. Gibson & J. U. Ogbu (Eds.), *Minority status and schooling: A comparative study of immigrant and involuntary minorities* (pp. 205–248). New York: Garland.

Mordkowitz, E. R., & Ginsburg, H. P. (1987). Early academic socialization of successful Asian-American college students. *The Quarterly Newsletter of the Laboratory of Comparative Human Cognition, 9*(2), 85–91.

Olson, D. H., Sprenkle, D. H., & Russell, C. S. (1979). Circumplex model of marital and family systems: I. Cohesion and adaptability dimensions, family types, and clinical applications. *Family Process, 18,* 3–28.

Prinz, R. J., Foster, S. L., Kent, R. N., & O'Leary, K. D. (1979). Multivariate assessment of conflict in distressed and nondistressed mother-adolescent dyads. *Journal of Applied Behavioral Analysis, 12,* 691–700.

Rhee, E., Uleman, J. S., & Lee, H. K. (1996). Variations in collectivism and individualism by in-group and culture: Confirmatory factor analyses. *Journal of Personality and Social Psychology, 71,* 1037–1054.

Robin, A. L., & Foster, S. C. (1984). Problem-solving communication training: A behavioral-family systems approach to parent-adolescent conflict. *Advances in child behavior analysis and therapy, 3,* 195–240.

Shon, S. P., & Ja, D. Y. (1982). Asian families. In M. McGoldrick, J. K. Pearce, & J. Giodano (Eds.), *Ethnicity and family therapy* (pp. 208–228). New York: Guilford.

Sinha, D., & Tripathi, R. C. (1994). Individualism in a collectivist culture: A case of coexistence of opposites. In U. Kim, H. C. Triandis, C. Kagitcibasi, S-C Choi, & G. Yoon (Eds.), *Individualism and collectivism: Theory, method, and applications* (pp. 123–137). Thousand Oaks, CA: Sage.

Steele, C. M. (1988). The psychology of self-affirmation: Sustaining the integrity of the self. In L. Berkowitz (Ed.), *Advances in experimental psychology* (Vol. 21, pp. 261–302). New York: Academic Press.

Steinberg, L. (1987). The impact of puberty on family relations: Effects of pubertal status and pubertal timing. *Developmental Psychology, 23,* 451–460.

Steinberg, L. (1988). Reciprocal relation between parent-child distance and pubertal maturation. *Developmental Psychology, 24,* 122–128.

Suárez-Orozco, C., & Suárez-Orozco, M. M. (1995). *Transformations: Immigration, family life, and achievement motivation among Latino adolescents.* Stanford, CA: Stanford University Press.

Suárez-Orozco, M. M. (1991). Immigrant adaptation to schooling: A Hispanic case. In M. A. Gibson & J. U. Ogbu (Eds.), *Minority status and schooling: A comparative study of immigrant and involuntary minorities* (pp. 37–62). New York: Garland.

Sung, B. L. (1987). *The adjustment experience of Chinese immigrant children in New York City.* New York: Center for Migration Studies.

Triandis, H. C. (1990). Cross-cultural studies of individualism and collectivism. In J. Berman (Ed.), *Nebraska Symposium on Motivation* (pp. 41–133). Lincoln: University of Nebraska Press.

Triandis, H. C. (1991). *Manual of instruments for the study of allocentism or collectivism and idiocentrism or individuality.* Unpublished manuscript, University of Illinois, Urbana.

Triandis, H. C. (1995). *Individualism and collectivism.* New York: Simon & Schuster.

Triandis, H. C., Bontempo, R., Villareal, M. J., Asai, M., & Lucca, N. (1988). Individualism and collectivism: Cross-cultural perspectives on self-ingroup relationships. *Journal of Personality and Social Psychology, 54,* 323–338.

Uba, L. (1994). *Asian Americans: Personality patterns, identity, and mental health.* New York: Guilford Press.

Vázquez García, H., García Coll, C. T., Erkut, S., Alarcón, O., & Tropp, L. (in press). Family values of Latino adolescents. In F. A. Villarruel (Ed.), *Latino adolescents: Building on Latino diversity.* New York: Garland Press.

Zhou, M. (1997). Growing up American: The challenge confronting immigrant children and children of immigrants. *Annual Review of Sociology, 23,* 63–95.

Zhou, M., & Bankston, C. L. (1998). *Growing up American: How Vietnamese children adapt to life in the United States.* New York: Russell Sage Foundation.

Zinn, M. C. (1994). Adaptation and continuity in Mexican-origin families. In R. L. Taylor (Ed.), *Minority families in the United States.* Englewood Cliffs, NJ: Prentice Hall.

SELF-STUDY QUESTIONS

Multiple Choice

1. According to the authors, prior research on family obligations
   a. has focused mostly on adults
   b. suggests that Asian and Latin American families emphasize family obligations in bringing up their children
   c. suggests that European American parents value independence more than family obligations
   d. all of the above

2. Which of the following best characterizes the findings of this study?
   a. Ethnic background was unrelated to teens' ideas about family obligations.
   b. Teens with a strong sense of family obligation had higher grades than peers who felt less strongly about their families.
   c. Asian and Latin American teens were more likely to feel obligated to provide their parents with assistance in the future.
   d. European American participants had better peer relationships than their Asian and Latin American peers.

Essay

1. Discuss how findings such as these might lead to both positive and negative stereotypes of Asian, Latin American, and European American culture.

2. The authors of this article imply that a weak sense of family obligations is one cost of socializing children into an individualistic culture. What, in your view, are some of the benefits? What are some of the costs of socializing children into a familistic society?

EARLY ADULTHOOD

"Developmental Aspects in Students' Course Selection"

OVERVIEW

When you enrolled in college for the first time and examined the course offerings in the course catalog, how did you feel? Overwhelmed? Confused? For many college students, the process of deciding which courses to take is a complex and intimidating process. The authors of this article suggest that there is a developmental process in making course selections from the freshman through the senior year. Further, the authors indicate that as students progress through the college years, they move from basing course selections on factors such as "instructor's humor" to variables like "instructor's knowledge and expertise." As you read this article, try to evaluate where you are in your college process and how you select your courses.

METHODOLOGY

Researchers used *correlations* to determine the degree to which an array of variables predicted participants' course selections. Two variables are correlated when they vary together. For example, as a car's mileage increases, it becomes less reliable. This kind of correlation is *negative* because, as mileage goes up, reliability goes down. The price of a new car and the social status it carries also vary together. Unlike mileage and reliability, though, there is a *positive* correlation between price and status because they move in the same direction. As price increases, so does status; as price declines, status does as well.

These researchers also used a measure known as R^2, an indicator of how well a group of variables pre- dicts a particular outcome. For example, most people would agree that, when considered together, intelligence and motivation to succeed predict academic achievement more than either variable alone. If we used tests to measure intelligence and motivation in a group of research participants and used the scores to predict participants' grades, one way of describing the result would be to use R^2. To use researchers' typical way of expressing such findings, we would say that the R^2 indicates that the two predictors *explain* a percentage of variance in grades that is equal to the value of the R^2. Thus, if R^2 is equal to .32, psychologists often say that the predictors explain 32 percent of the variance in the outcome.

GLOSSARY TERMS

- **Conceptual kin** as addressed in this article, course selection, academic major selection, and career selection processes that involve similar types of efforts, procedures, and investigation strategies
- **Jungian types** Carl Jung, a neo-Freudian theorist, believed that people had personality components or "types" that guided the way in which they related to others, and to their preferences for certain types of environments and activities

- **Autonomous thinking** the ability to conceptualize, reason, analyze, and problem-solve on one's own
- **Didactic** the practice of teaching
- **Salient** features or ideas that are noticeable and prominent from all others

Elisha Babad, John M. Darley, and Henry Kaplowitz

Developmental Aspects in Students' Course Selection

Types of information provided in a Student Course Guide to assist in course selection (CS) were content-analyzed. College courses (N = 215) were coded on 9 variables—instructor and course characteristics, subject matter descriptors, and a "criticism" dimension—and were correlated with postcourse student ratings of teaching (SRT). Analyses for course levels revealed a developmental trend, shifting from instructor humor and expressive style to learning value variables as predictors of SRT: (a) In 100-level courses, SRTs were predicted from course guide descriptions of instructor's humor. (b) In 200-level courses, SRTs were predicted by instructor's personality and expressive style. (c) In 300-level courses, lack of criticism was the major predictor, followed by "interesting course" and instructor's humor. (d) At 400-level courses, only academic types of CS information predicted SRTs—interesting readings, interesting course, and instructor's knowledge and expertise.

The time spent in college is an important developmental period, formative in intellectual and social growth. The transition to adulthood involves a choice of occupation and a budding development of a professional identity. Each semester, students are required to make a series of course selection decisions that will determine their subsequent experience by potentially widening or limiting further studies and future occupational opportunities. The selection of one's major field of study and the choice of one's occupation are perhaps more critical as single decisions, but course selection (CS) decisions have much more import on the lives of students making the choices than they realize, because early decisions determine later choices, including career choices, and influence the range of potential possibilities. How do students select courses?

Although CS is an ecologically valid domain for studying commonly occurring decision making processes, the field has been rather neglected, especially compared to the abundance of research in the closest conceptual domains, namely, student ratings of teaching (SRT) and career decision making. Given the scarcity of writings on CS, this introduction is intended to lay a conceptual foundation of CS as a decision making process for this and other studies to follow. Because of the exploratory nature of this study, no

"theory" in the formal sense is presented, although we believe that the developmental findings have both a theoretical base and applied implications.

CS AS A DECISION MAKING PROCESS

In a decision making process, a course of action must be chosen among alternatives, each associated with particular expected outcomes. Criteria, considerations, "aspects" (in Gati's, 1996, terminology), and expected outcome probabilities are available to the decision maker to compare and evaluate the various alternatives, and each action–outcome combination is assigned a value, a level of importance or utility. Few alternatives are perfect in all respects, and decision makers usually trade off certain values or utilities for others to reach the most satisfying decision.

In the case of CS as a decision making process, the information is quite complicated, with disparate utilities (enjoyment, learning, ease, occupational gain, etc.) and multiple considerations pertaining to different aspects. In CS, not one, but multiple, sequential and interdependent decisions must be made concurrently. The projected utilities are sometimes contradictory (e.g., convenience, entertainment, learning), and different courses are selected with different objectives in mind.

Numerous sources of information are available for CS. They include institutional sources (academic advisers, registration and departmental personnel, printed course descriptions, the college bulletin, and sometimes even a computerized system; see Irving,

1990; Shreve & Wildie, 1992); past data of SRT; student course guides, which are usually published by the student union; and informal word of mouth from peers and other sources (Kevin, Harvey, & Crandall, 1975). The types of information about each course typically include information about the instructor's style, course content and materials, various course characteristics, workload and grading leniency, and so on.

All of these aspects must be weighed by their expected contribution in making course decisions. However, one suspects that many CS decisions are not made that way, because it is effortful to consider systematically all factors, and students seek satisfying shortcuts to reduce effort and simplify the complexity of the task. Sometimes one salient characteristic of a course overshadows all other aspects: Choosing a course because of its expected learning value or a particular topic of interest, wishing to hear a charismatic and/or witty instructor, taking an easy course expected to yield a high grade, enrolling in a particular course to make friends, or filling a hole in one's schedule are all likely candidates for quick decision making principles. The present study is focused on the types of information picked up by students in CS as a reflection of their academic and developmental needs. In CS research, the emphasis should be on tracing processes reflecting differential needs, mediated by the importance of each decision, the available and desirable sources of information, students' developmental levels, and other factors.

CS is a "conceptual kin" of career decision making, an area that has been researched very extensively. The choice of a career is obviously a most meaningful and important single decision, whereas CS involves multiple, sequential decisions of lesser importance to the individual. Nevertheless, the similarities in the underlying decision making processes are very strong. Authors in the decision making perspective of career choices (Gati, 1996; Katz, 1993; Philips, 1994; Walsh & Osipow, 1988) are concerned about the complexity of the process in ways that are also relevant to CS. Gati (1986) identified the major problems in career decision making as the lack of information, the lack of resources to collect all information, the cognitive limitations of the decision maker, and the lack of a framework for identifying and processing relevant information. Computer-assisted CS, if constructed, will explicate all aspects and alternatives for each course at the same level of detail as computer-assisted career decision making (Gati, 1990, 1996), but students may not be eager to participate in such a process, favoring informal word of mouth (Borgida, 1978). Moreover, when students choose several courses in a sequence, the process is not uniform in each selection, and each choice can modify the weighting of attributes in the next. As a preliminary investigation, the present study is focused only on the content of the information used in CS.

CS AND SRT

One source of information available to students when they choose courses is the output of the student ratings of instruction forms used in most universities. One of the major declared objectives of SRT (Marsh, 1984; Marsh & Roche, 1997; McKeachie, 1983, 1997; Theall & Franklin, 1990) is to use ratings for improving students' CS, and indeed, SRT data are made available to students in numerous institutions. However, research on the effectiveness of these data in assisting CS is very scarce, and the few published studies show that students do not make much use of empirical student evaluation data and prefer other sources of information (Borgida, 1978; Borgida & Nisbett, 1977; Coleman & McKeachie, 1981; Hendel, 1982).

This is surprising. SRT data should contribute to CS because they provide the most comprehensive informational base for making decisions, and they are made by peers who went through the experience. In theory, CS and SRT should have a circular relationship, CS factors contributing to the evaluations of students who actually selected given courses, and student postcourse ratings contributing to the decision making processes of prospective students. But as mentioned, empirical data show that student ratings contribute relatively little to CS. Perhaps the prospective weighting of utilities in precourse selection is not similar to the retrospective weighting of postcourse evaluation factors. SRT is probably more strongly influenced by salient features of the course, like instructor's personality, wit, and expressive style and can often reflect overall satisfaction rather than actual learning gains (Ambady & Rosenthal, 1993; Feldman, 1986; Murray, Rushton, & Panuonen, 1990). On the other hand, CS can probably give higher weights to other factors that are important to the individual—realization of values, attainment of occupational goals and personal growth on one side and convenience, workload ease, and grading leniency on the other side. Moreover, SRT data are usually presented to students in statistical tables, a format that is often disliked and left unused by its intended audience.

The present study is focused on one particular form of course evaluation information that is often presented to students, and seems to have been designed to overcome the otherwise dry and statistical presentation of student course ratings. We refer to some version of the "student course guide"—an attempt to provide students with informal, juicy, and palatable information based on the experience of their peers. Aware of the deficiencies of statistical tables of SRTs, of college catalogues, of advisers (who may have institutional ulterior motives such as filling empty courses in addition to their concern about each student's learning needs), and of student gossip as sources of information for optimal CS, many student governments have organized alternate sources of information. Student-initiated information books are published and widely read in many institutions to assist students in selecting courses. They are usually written by veteran students from a student-oriented perspective in an attractive, informal, and palatable style, and they provide a rare anchor point for investigating CS decision making. Some of these books (such as the notorious Harvard University "Q-Tips") are widely and eagerly read by students and faculty alike.

In this study we investigated the popular Princeton University "Student Course Guide" which is published in paper form, and now on the internet as well, prior to each semester. For each course, the guide provides a description of the instructor's expertise, personality, and behavioral style; the major contents and readings in the course; various course characteristics, including workload and reading load, types of assignments, and exams; grading leniency; patterns of class participation and instructor-student interaction; contribution of the course to learning and thinking; information about the teaching assistants; and additional informal bits, relevant gossip, and criticism.

There has been some previous research on CS and on SRT–CS connections. (A very large number of studies investigated various factors contributing to and influencing SRT, but we decided to limit this brief review only to research including clear CS elements.) Lorenz (1982) introduced the Student Course Information Program (SCIP) for course selection, which combined student ratings and course descriptions written by the instructors. Hendel (1982) evaluated that program and reported that usage of the SCIP materials had relatively little impact on improving the quality of CS. Borgida (1978) argued that people ignore consensus base-rate information in cognitive processing, and Borgida and Nisbett (1977) found that the provision of mean SRT ratings had little effect on subsequent CS, whereas brief and vivid face-to-face comments from another person had a greater impact despite their informational deficiencies.

Studies on section selection in multisection courses (where many CS elements are missing because all sections are parallel) show some effects of SRT feedback on section selection. Coleman and McKeachie (1981) found that the section rated highest was selected more frequently by those students who had received former students' ratings even though it was rated as requiring more work. Perry, Leventhal, and their associates reported similar findings in a series of studies on instructor's reputation. Leventhal, Abrami, and Perry (1976) reported that students using teacher's reputation or ability to select sections congregated in certain sections and rated instructors more favorably than classmates using other selection criteria. Leventhal, Abrami, Perry, and Breen (1975) reported that published student ratings and reports from other students were the most frequent sources of instructor reputation. They also reported a developmental trend of growing importance of instructor's teaching ability and reputation from freshmen to advanced courses. Hendel (1982) reported that instructor's reputation was more important in CS than course content.

Martin (1989) measured the impact of various sources and kinds of information and investigated the importance assigned to dimensions of course choice information as a function of ego development and three Jungian types. "Sensing" types with high aspirations gave higher weights to career relatedness in CS, whereas "intuitive" types with low aspirations chose according to instructor characteristics. Kevin, Harvey, and Crandall (1975) found that friends were mentioned by 62% of the respondents as their major source of information, with college catalogue and publications lagging far behind (19%). As to the main reasons for CS, personal interest (38%), course content (26%), and the demands in the student's major (22%) were mentioned most frequently. Dellar (1994) reported that the advice offered to students by teachers, parents, and peers was often inappropriate and even detrimental to the students.

In several of these studies, SRT ratings served as independent variables in attempts to predict their effects on subsequent CS. In this research we used postcourse student evaluations as dependent variables and attempted to predict these ratings from CS information provided to students previously in a student course guide.

Most studies mentioned above (with the exception of the Leventhal et al., 1975, study) used samples consisting of college freshmen or high school students, with no regard to developmentally changing needs or to the shifts in the nature of the curriculum along the college years. Respondents were usually asked about courses in general, with no distinction among particular courses along various dimensions. If samples of freshmen are used to draw conclusions about courses and students in general, it would seem to imply that findings are assumed to be generalizable to students at all levels regardless of their developmental stage. But in the college years, students go through an important developmental period of intellectual growth and emotional maturation, and they incrementally develop their occupational identity. The college curriculum is also structured to advance from elementary courses to tasks that demand more autonomy and individual intellectual work. It is therefore reasonable to assume that the decision making process of CS would also undergo changes throughout the college years, reflecting students' growing maturation and changing needs. Another developmental element involves students' accumulated experience and retrospective outlook on the outcomes of previous CS decisions, which can change future decisions. Therefore, this study was planned to examine developmental trends, and we demonstrate later how an overall analysis of all students and courses combined can be misleading.

OVERVIEW OF THE PRESENT RESEARCH

This study was designed to investigate the relationships between precourse CS information provided to college students in a student course guide (with the explicit intent of assisting them in CS), and subsequent postcourse SRTs that these courses received from the students who actually enrolled in them. We believe that students' needs change as a function of both developmental level and situational factors, and they pick up different types of information in course selection depending on their needs at given times. This design (in which N = courses) can identify specific pieces of information that are presumably "picked up" by students and play a role in forming their impressions of each course.

The developmental analysis was carried out through separate computations of correlation and regression coefficients for each course level. At most universities, some signal is given to indicate the assumptions about the level of the class and its intended audience. Often, courses assuming no particular background, and thus thought suitable for freshmen, have identification numbers in the 100 range; courses with a level of preparation characteristic for sophomores receive a 200 number; junior courses in the various domains and subdomains receive 300 numbers; and advanced seminars for seniors are assigned 400 numbers.

We content analyzed the verbal descriptions in the Princeton University "Student Course Guide" and coded each course on nine variables. After establishing the agreement between raters, these coded bits of information from the course guide served as the predictor variables, and the end-of-semester mean ratings of the students who actually took each course (assessed by the standard Princeton "Student Evaluation of Undergraduate Instruction" form and collected routinely each semester) served as the criterion variables. We reasoned that a high correlation between a given aspect from the course guide (e.g., instructor's wit) and a subsequent SRT (e.g., overall lecturer rating) could be interpreted to indicate that this aspect was picked up as important information in CS, whereas inconsequential precourse information would be unrelated to postcourse SRT.

The advantage of this design is that CS information was not derived from students' retrospective self-reports on how they had selected each course, but consisted of the actual information provided in the course guide. Self-reports can be quite informative and useful in a variety of studies, but they are likely to be biased and unreliable to some degree in determining how each bit of information was weighted in the decision making process. The few studies in which CS information was experimentally controlled were focused on section selection in multiple-section courses, and therefore most types of information used in making selections among different courses were irrelevant in those studies.

The initial question was whether the patterns of CS–SRT correlations would be sufficiently distinguished from each other to allow us to draw inferences about the value of specific, differential pieces of information picked up by students from the course guide. Given that the answer to this initial question across all courses would be affirmative, we planned to conduct separate analyses on 100, 200, 300, and 400 level courses to trace developmental changes in students' needs by means of the changing patterns of correlations between course guide variables and postcourse SRTs.

Our development hypothesis came from the design of the college curriculum. The structure of the college curriculum is such that early introductory and basic skill courses are replaced later on by advanced courses requiring autonomous thinking and specialized individual work. Therefore, the hypothesized developmental pattern predicted that advanced students would pick courses not so much on the basis of instructor characteristics and enjoyment value (as we presumed that beginning students might be more likely to do), but on the basis of their expected learning, intellectual investment, and relation to career needs. Cynics might be more pessimistic in their attributions about students, possibly holding an opposing hypothesis predicting a developmental pattern of increasing weight given to expected convenience, entertainment value, low workload, and higher grades.

METHOD

Sample of Courses

All CS information was derived from the Princeton University "Student Course Guide" issued prior to the registration period for a spring semester in the mid-1990s. The guide is issued each semester by a student body with the university's support, and it has a very wide readership in the entire university community. For each course in the guide, the mean SRT ratings received most recently (on four to five major variables) are presented first, followed by a rather long testimonial in the form of a narrative, written by a student who participated in the course recently. The writers seem to be provided with an extensive list of questions to be referred to in their description. The narratives include various anecdotes and numerous details, and they are usually quite engaging to read.

The guide investigated here included undergraduate courses in all departments. First we screened all courses and determined the courses to be included in the analysis. An acceptable course was taught recently in the same format by the same instructor. We rejected new courses, courses taught by new instructors, courses not taught for several years, courses taught by several instructors, changed courses, and cases where the narrative was based mostly on the instructor's description rather than the testimonial of a former class participant. (Comparison of the potential effects of instructor narratives and student narratives could be an interesting research question in subsequent research. In this case, the number of courses with instructor narratives was too small for such comparison, and these narratives differed greatly in style from student narratives and could not be included together in the overall analysis.) The final sample included 215 courses out of the 482 courses in that guide (45%).

The Coding System

Quantitative coding of qualitative material always presents a dilemma between the wish to reduce the material to a manageable number of generalized categories and the wish to preserve the uniqueness of the material and to not lose important information. After several pilot explorations in which over 20 categories had been examined, we designed a coding system consisting of nine variables, each coded on a 3-point scale. The system included four instructor-related variables, four course-related variables, and an overall "criticism" variable. The coding system is presented in Table 1 and explained in detail next.

Variable 1: Instructor's personality. This variable was designed to include all references to the instructor's personality in the narratives. Almost all references were focused on the instructor's expressive style, enthusiasm, and charisma or lack thereof. This variable was coded "1" if instructor's personality was not mentioned at all, or mentioned as normal, reasonable, or average. A very positive reference to instructor's personality was coded "2," and "phenomenal" was coded "3." The reader may wonder about the "phenomenal" category and how rarely it might have been mentioned in the narratives. In fact, such verbal descriptions appeared quite frequently and were not rare at all.

An anonymous reviewer of this article was concerned that the publication of student ratings, and particularly the narrative form, may cause violation of professors' civil rights and defamation of character

---

TABLE 1   Coding Scheme for the Princeton University "Student Course Guide"

VARIABLES	SCORING CATEGORY		
	1	2	3
Instructor variables			
Personality (general, enthusiasm, expressive, etc.)	Reasonable or not mentioned	Very positive	Phenomenal
Knowledge, expertise	Fair or not mentioned	Emphasized	Phenomenal
Approachable, friendly, interpersonal style	Moderate or not mentioned	Very positive	Phenomenal
Humor, wit	No humor	Not mentioned	Witty, funny, dry humor
Course characteristics			
Workload difficulty	Easy	Moderate or not mentioned	High, a lot
Interesting readings, papers, assignments	Not interesting, not relevant	Not mentioned, normal	Emphasized
Grading leniency	Easy	Fair or not mentioned	Difficult
Interesting course	Positive or not mentioned	Special	Phenomenal
Criticism			
Any criticism?	Yes, major criticisms, several criticisms	Minor criticisms (one or two)	None

if students' narrative reports are inaccurate or invalid. The issue of public dissemination of student ratings is the subject of lively debate in many institutions, but in Princeton, all ratings (not only those in the course guide) are open to the public. With regard to the narratives in the course guide, we can testify that much care seems to have been taken to maintain a positive tone of presentation and to avoid malice. Hence, the frequent use of the "phenomenal" category.

Variable 2: Instructor's knowledge and expertise. This category referred to an explicit mention of the instructor's personal knowledge and professional expertise, and was distinguished from the level of interest and knowledge provided by the course itself (Variable 8).

Variable 3: Approachable, friendly. This variable referred to the instructor's interpersonal style and students' ease in interacting with the instructor.

Variable 4: Instructor's humor. It seems that the writers of the narratives were either explicitly asked about instructor's humor, and/or that this aspect is very salient for students, because this particular characteristic was mentioned frequently.

Variable 5: Workload difficulty. This variable referred to the work required in the course, assessing the level of difficulty and demand.

Variable 6: Interesting readings, papers, and assignments. This variable measured the statements about the level of interest and relevance of the readings and the assignments, regardless of the effort or work required and the grading policy.

Variable 7: Grading leniency. This variable separated the grading leniency aspect from the workload and interest aspects of papers, assignments, and exams in the course.

Variable 8: Interesting course. This variable was limited to comments about the course, not the instructor. Because most narratives were quite positive and emphasized the positive aspects of the various courses, we distinguished between three levels of enthusiasm.

Variable 9: Criticism. This variable referred to various criticisms that appeared quite frequently in the narratives. The criticism could focus on the instructor, on aspects of the course itself, on class management (e.g., teaching assistants' work) or any other aspect. In pilot explorations, we found out that it was not feasible to code the contents of the criticisms, and therefore

we decided to focus on rater judgments assessing the severity of criticism. As can be seen in Table 1, this variable was coded in a reversed order, from 1 (*severe criticism*) to 3 (*no criticism*), to facilitate positive rather than negative correlations in the results.

Procedure

In the first stage, the course guide was scrutinized to determine which courses should be included in the analysis. Consequently, the 215 narratives were coded by a graduate level research assistant experienced in college advising and educational research. To ensure that the coding would be based on the narratives only, the numerical ratings for each course (which appeared above the narratives) were erased before the material was given to the coder.

To establish the reliability of the ratings, a second coder, an experienced educational researcher, coded a random sample of 25 narratives from the guide (about 12% of the sample). The overall correlation between the two coders was .83, and joint discussions of coding problems indicated that the coding could proceed in a straightforward and smooth way.

SRT Variables

A few months after the end of the semester, the averaged student ratings for each of the 215 courses were available to us. In the Princeton forms, students rate every item on a 5-point scale (1 = *unacceptable* to 5 = *excellent*). The following variables were used in data analysis.

Lectures. This variable included (a) stimulation of independent thinking, (b) clear presentation of subject matter, and (c) overall quality of lectures (the closest to an "overall instructor" rating in most evaluation questionnaires; see Marsh, 1984).

Readings. This variable included (a) stimulation of independent thinking, (b) clear presentation of subject matter, and (c) overall quality of readings.

Papers, reports, problem sets, and exams. This variable included (a) guidance in preparation of written work, (b) comments in response to written work, (c) overall value of papers, reports, and exams.

General. This variable included (a) contribution to knowledge of subject, (b) contribution to critical evaluation, (c) contribution to interest in subject, and (d) overall quality of the course (similar to the "overall course" variable in most student evaluation questionnaires; see Marsh, 1984).

We realize that a recurrent weakness of field-based studies such as this is the reliance on the institution's existing student ratings questionnaire. Like many "homemade" instruments, the psychometric properties of the Princeton questionnaire are unknown, and that may weaken the power and generalizability of the findings. Of course it would not have been possible to conduct the study if we had to administer another questionnaire in all undergraduate courses. To correct for that weakness as much as possible, we analyzed the interrelationships between the items in the Princeton questionnaire (see Table 3), and used in the final analyses (Tables 4 and 5) only the more robust "overall" summary scores.

RESULTS

All results are reported in correlation and regression coefficients. Preliminary analyses report the correlations within the course guide variables and within the SRT variables. We then report the correlations between course guide and SRT variables, first for the entire sample of 215 courses, and subsequently for each course level separately for the developmental analysis. In these analyses, N = courses. The use of classroom means tends to decrease correlations, and the conventional level of significance underestimates the power of such results.

Preliminary Analyses: Correlations within Course Guide Variables and Within SRT Variables

To examine the psychometric properties of the instruments used in this study in a minimally acceptable manner, we present the correlations within the course guide variables and within the SRT variables in Table 2 and Table 3, respectively. The contrast be-tween the two tables is quite salient: Correlations among SRT variables (see Table 3) were extremely high, whereas correlations among the course guide variables (see Table 2) were quite moderate, often even low. Thus, SRTs on the Princeton questionnaire reflected a rather strong halo effect, whereas the coded CS variables from the "Student Course Guide" seem to have measured separate and distinct aspects and course and instructor characteristics.

In Table 3, the overall course variable was correlated in an order of magnitude of $r = .90+$ with overall lecturer and with the different contribution variables, indicating a virtual identity in students' minds. Other correlations in the table did not lag far behind, and the major implication is that it would be sufficient to present in subsequent tables correlations for the overall variables in each category without losing much information.

In Table 2, the correlations indicate that instructors' personality and other characteristics seemed to contribute to learning. When the instructor was judged more positively, less criticism was expressed and the course contributed more to the students. It should be noted that workload difficulty and leniency of grading were unrelated to instructor characteristics, to criticism, and to the degree to which the course and the readings were interesting. Thus, opinions about workload difficulty and grading leniency were separated from instructor characteristics and level of interest of the course.

Correlations between Course Guide and SRT Variables for the Entire Sample (215 Courses)

Correlations between the course guide variables and the postcourse SRT variables are presented in Table 4 for the entire sample of 215 courses. Had we not

---

TABLE 2   Correlations between Precourse Princeton Student Course Guide-Coded Variables (N = 215 Courses)

VARIABLES	INSTRUCTOR VARIABLES				COURSE CHARACTERISTICS				
	1	2	3	4	5	6	7	8	9
Instructor variables									
1. Personality	—	.17	.35	.36	−.06	.25	−.11	.46	.34
2. Knowledge, expertise		—	.16	.09	.04	.15	.20	.28	.16
3. Approachable			—	.18	−.01	.12	−.05	.22	.21
4. Humor				—	−.11	.07	−.03	.24	.20
Course characteristics									
5. Workload difficulty					—	−.12	.22	−.03	.02
6. Interesting readings, papers						—	.14	.41	.20
7. Grading leniency							—	−.05	−.06
8. Interesting course								—	.25
9. Criticism									—

Note. Correlations above .14 are significant at the $p < .05$ level.

TABLE 3   Matrix of Correlations between Students' Postcourse Evaluations of Instruction on the Standard Princeton University Form (N = 215 Courses)

STUDENTS' RATINGS OF TEACHING	LECTURES			READINGS			PAPERS, EXAMS			CONTRIBUTIONS		
	1	2	3	1	2	3	1	2	3	1	2	3
Lectures												
1. Stimulation of independent thinking	—											
2. Clear presentation of subject matter	.73	—										
3. Overall quality of lectures	.90	.90	—									
Readings												
1. Stimulation of independent thinking	.65	.53	.59	—								
2. Clear presentation of subject matter	.48	.58	.54	.83	—							
3. Overall quality of readings	.54	.56	.56	.93	.94	—						
Papers, exams												
1. Guidance in preparation	.66	.68	.71	.59	.61	.59	—					
2. Comments in response to work	.61	.62	.64	.66	.62	.65	.82	—				
3. Overall value of papers, exams	.69	.65	.72	.67	.65	.65	.87	.84	—			
Contributions												
1. To knowledge of subject	.81	.75	.83	.63	.51	.56	.70	.63	.74	—		
2. To critical evaluation	.84	.73	.83	.69	.56	.61	.71	.68	.76	.90	—	
3. To interest in subject	.83	.73	.84	.69	.57	.62	.68	.69	.74	.87	.88	—
Overall course quality	.88	.82	.91	.68	.59	.62	.74	.70	.79	.92	.91	.93

Note. All correlations in this table are statistically significant at $p < .05$.

taken a developmental approach, this would have been the central table of results in this article. Readers are forewarned that the subsequent developmental analyses reduced the importance of Table 4, and that it is presented for didactic purposes to demonstrate that presenting conventional global findings without consideration of an important developmental dimension can be misleading.

Two patterns are discernible in Table 4, one demonstrating statistically significant moderate-magnitude correlations between certain CS and SRT variables, the other demonstrating no relationships between other CS and SRT variables. Course guide information about instructor's expressivity and hu-

mor, about the level of interest of the course and of the readings, and lack of criticism was positively related to postcourse evaluations. On the other hand, course guide information about workload difficulty, grading leniency, and instructor's approachability was unrelated to SRT ratings.

Developmental Analysis: Correlations between Course Guide and SRT Variables for Course Levels 100, 200, 300, and 400

Course Levels 100, 200, 300, and 400 roughly correspond to freshman, sophomore, junior, and senior class levels. Even if the chronological overlap is not

TABLE 4   Correlations between Precourse Princeton University "Student Course Guide" Variables and Postcourse Student Evaluations of Instruction for All Courses Combined (N = 215 Courses)

POSTCOURSE EVALUATIONS	PRECOURSE VARIABLES								
	PERSONALITY	KNOWLEDGE, EXPERTISE	APPROACHABLE	HUMOR	WORKLOAD DIFFICULTY	INTERESTING READINGS	GRADING LENIENCY	INTERESTING COURSE	CRITICISM
Overall lectures	.34*	.17*	.13	.30*	.03	.14*	−.07	.30*	.26*
Overall readings	.17*	.26*	−.09	.20*	.08	.33*	−.01	.23*	.20*
Overall papers, exams	.15*	.08	.05	.14*	.08	.18*	−.04	.18*	.11
Overall course evaluation	.29*	.17*	.07	.25*	.04	.21*	.00	.29*	.22*

*$p < .05$.

perfect, these course levels represent a developmental scale in the academic sense. We computed a matrix of correlations (9 CS Variables × 4 SRT Overall Variables) and two regression analyses for each course level. The two criteria in the regression analyses were overall course evaluation and overall lectures (i.e., overall instructor), with the nine CS variables serving as predictors.

Table 5 presents the correlations between course guide and SRT variables separately for each course level. Substantial developmental changes are evident, with different CS variables serving as the salient predictors of SRT at the different course levels. In fact, course guide information that predicted SRT at 100-level courses did not predict SRT at the 400 level, and the more powerful predictors at the 400 level did not predict SRT at all at the 100 level. The only common thread to all course levels is the weak predictive power of CS information about workload difficulty and grading leniency.

Next, we examine the patterns of relationships for each course level in Table 5.

100-level courses. For these introductory and entry level courses, the only precourse variable predicting post-course evaluations was instructor's humor, with humorous instructors receiving higher SRTs. In the regression analyses, humor was the only significant predictor of the overall course evaluation ($R^2 = .387$) and of the overall quality of lectures ($R^2 = .351$).

200-level courses. The pattern for the 200 level was more complex, and several CS variables were significantly related to postcourse evaluations. The main emphasis shifted from instructor's humor to instructor's personality and expressive style. Instructor's humor and approachability were also significantly related to SRT, as were lack of criticism and interesting course and readings. Thus, students seem to have picked up "good courses" in terms of the quality of the instructor and more substantive aspects of the course. In the regressions, only instructor's personality emerged as a significant predictor of the overall course ratings ($R^2 = .296$) and overall lecture ratings ($R^2 = .323$), and none of the other CS variables added significantly to those predictions.

300-level courses. Changes from 200- to 300-level courses were more subtle than the shift from 100- to 200-level courses. (Correlations for the 300-level courses were generally lower than the correlations for the other course levels in Table 5 because of the greater number of 300-level courses—98 courses compared to 25–38 courses in the other levels.) The shift seems to be toward greater appreciation of the intel-

lectual quality of the course and the absence of criticism. In the regression analyses for 300-level courses, criticism was the first significant predictor for both overall course rating ($R^2 = .083$) and overall lecture rating ($R^2 = .107$). Compared to the 200-level matrix, correlations for instructor's knowledge and expertise were now statistically significant (together with the significant correlations for interesting course), whereas correlations for instructor's approachability were nonsignificant, and the correlations for instructor's personality style were relatively less salient although statistically significant. In the regressions, interesting course was a significant second predictor of overall course rating (bringing R^2 to .122), and instructor's humor was a significant second predictor of overall lecture ratings (bringing R^2 to .149).

400-level courses. The developmental process seems to have completed its full course in the transition from the 300-to the 400-level courses. At this advanced course level, close to the completion of students' college education, CS predictors of SRT were all academic, focused on potential learning benefits with no regard to instructor's personality or other course characteristics. Very high CS–SRT correlations ($r = .41–.57$) were found for interesting readings, interesting course, and instructor's knowledge and expertise, and none of the other precourse CS variables were significantly related to postcourse SRTs. In the regression analyses, interesting readings emerged as the only significant predictor of overall course ratings ($R^2 = .32$), and interesting course emerged as the only significant predictor of overall lecture ratings ($R^2 = .265$).

DISCUSSION

We found a good many correlations between prior students' evaluations of various courses, summarized and transformed into the text of the course guide, and current students' evaluations of the course. Several principles guided our interpretation of those correlations, and it is worth making them explicit. If a specific course guide datum correlates with a specific similar SRT rating (e.g., on the readings, on workload difficulty, etc.), then this may only indicate reliability of an instructor's behavior over several iterations of the course, but it does not necessarily show that this information plays a role in decisions about course selection. But if some specific course guide aspects correlate with overall course evaluations (or in the present case, several overall evaluations; see Table 5) while other aspects don't, that suggests to us that students chose the course because of the importance to them of the aspects of the course made salient by the

TABLE 5 Correlations between Precourse Princeton University "Student Course Guide" Variables and Postcourse Student Evaluations of Instruction for Course Levels 100, 200, 300, and 400

POSTCOURSE EVALUATIONS	PERSONALITY	KNOWLEDGE, EXPERTISE	APPROACHABLE	HUMOR	WORKLOAD DIFFICULTY	INTERESTING READINGS	GRADING LENIENCY	INTERESTING COURSE	CRITICISM
					PRECOURSE VARIABLES				
100-level courses[a]									
Overall lectures	.31	.22	-.02	.59*	-.01	.17	.14	.07	.19
Overall readings	.30	.27	-.11	.63*	.01	.26	.10	.09	.07
Overall papers, exams	.03	.01	-.16	.39*	-.04	.06	.05	-.06	-.05
Overall course evaluation	.20	.07	-.15	.48*	-.11	.20	.07	-.10	.02
200-level courses[b]									
Overall lectures	.57*	.04	.26*	.37*	-.02	.05	-.27*	.34*	.36*
Overall readings	.36*	.10	.18	.19	-.13	.43*	-.24	.37*	.15
Overall papers, exams	.27*	-.10	.22	.19	.03	.24	-.24	.10	.28*
Overall course evaluation	.54*	.07	.27*	.40*	-.03	.20	-.24	.37*	.42*
300-level courses[c]									
Overall lectures	.29*	.17*	.05	.25*	.09	.09	.04	.28*	.33*
Overall readings	.18*	.21*	-.23	.10	.23*	.25*	.08	.24*	.24*
Overall papers, exams	.09	.06	-.05	.03	.12	.09	.02	.17*	.11
Overall course evaluation	.21*	.18*	.01	.17*	.13	.14	.11	.27*	.29*
400-level courses[d]									
Overall lectures	.24	.41*	.32*	.09	-.01	.46*	-.01	.51*	-.07
Overall readings	-.03	.49*	.02	.27	-.13	.53*	-.05	.18	.25
Overall papers, exams	.28	.45*	.27	.25	.16	.51*	.08	.50*	.00
Overall course evaluation	.30	.44*	.25	.00	.06	.57*	.15	.53*	-.06

[a]N = 24 courses. [b]N = 38 courses. [c]N = 98 courses. [d]N = 25 courses.

*$p < .05$ (one-tailed); $r = .34$ for 100-level courses, $r = .26$ for 200-level courses, $r = .16$ for 300-level courses, $r = .31$ for 400-level courses).

course guide, which influenced their choice of course, and in turn influenced their evaluation of the course. We argue, commonsensically, that students look for information about those salient aspects of future courses they might take in making their selections and that they find this information in the course guide. Of course, that kind of causal chain could not be proven in this research. It is also possible that some or many students obtained the same types of information from other informal sources rather than the course guide (despite the consensus about the extremely wide readership of the guide in hard copy and on the Internet, and the eagerness by which it is awaited in the college community). At the most general level, we argue conceptually that certain stage-relevant types of information are picked up by students and influence their course selection decisions whereas other types of information are discarded as relatively unimportant.

In this research we quantified the narrative information provided for purposes of course selection in the Princeton Course Guide, and attempted to predict actual postcourse SRT ratings. The design made it possible to examine CS–SRT associations empirically, circumventing the need to use students' retrospective self-reports about their decision making process. The nine CS variables we defined covered most (if not all) major considerations that play a role in course selection: entertainment value, instructor personality and expressive style, intellectual challenge and enjoyment, instructor–student rapport, expected effort and grading policy, learning outcomes, occupational outcomes, and so on. The ninth variable—criticism—added information about the smooth running of the course.

The correlational and regression analyses illuminated possible aspects of the decision making process, showing the salience of certain CS aspects over other aspects. The developmental pattern we uncovered suggested that students' considerations and needs change throughout their college years, and at each point they seem to make choices on the basis of stage-relevant information. We could sketch a possible developmental sequence, viewing the early college experience as entailing a tremendous choice open to students searching for but not yet committed to a particular direction or subject matter, somewhat in the nature of "tasting the delights" the college can offer. Subsequent stages are probably characterized by increased commitment to a particular area with a concomitant narrowing of subjective choice and a growing demand for high-quality and useful products. In our results, early courses seemed indeed to be chosen by these criteria. Later this was widened to include other characteristics of the instructor's per-

sonality, with growing importance of the academic substance of the course and the lack of criticism about it (i.e., how well the course is conducted).

These findings are well in line with the current literature on factors contributing to positive SRTs (e.g., d'Apollonia & Abrami, 1997; Marsh & Roche, 1997; McKeachie, 1997), and particularly with experimental studies on the impact of instructor reputation (e.g., Perry, Abrami, Leventhal, & Check, 1979; Perry, Niemi, & Jones, 1974), although these authors did not present a developmental conception and discussed student evaluations in general.

The highest developmental level was reached at the 400 level, where only intellectual considerations and the learning needs of the students predicted subsequent SRT. These empirical findings uncovered an optimistic pattern of growing maturity, highly consonant with the educational objectives of college teaching. Students' needs change throughout their college years, and this was evident in the types of information important for CS at every stage. Therefore, it is important to guarantee that varied and detailed types of information will be made available to students so they may be used according to their changing needs.

Although it was not our purpose to examine the validity of the course guide, the results gave indirect evidence of its usefulness in providing various (and relatively independent; see Table 2) types of helpful information about courses. Previous research showed that statistical feedback data of former SRT ratings is not as efficient in assisting CS. The guide provides personal narratives and anecdotes, gives numerous examples of specific assignments, vividly describes instructors' style and personality, and spells out specific criticisms in a way that cannot fit in empirical feedback data formats. It makes the absorption of full CS information palatable, even enjoyable.

In this study, courses were partitioned according to levels (100 to 400), and the results indeed demonstrated the importance of the developmental analysis, with clear implications for CS and SRT research. Other possible partitions among courses that could not be examined in this study may also be important. One such partition distinguishes among different departments and subject matter domains. Perhaps student needs and considerations differ between the humanities and the natural sciences or among other domains. The sample of courses in this research was too small to allow for such analysis, but in any event such divisions are often quite misleading because there is no perfect overlap between a departmental division and a subject matter division: Humanities and social sciences departments offer some courses heavy in mathematics, biology, or other natural sciences; the science departments offer some historical and philosophical courses; and computer courses that are offered in almost every department are very hard to define within categorizations of disciplines.

A second potential partition of presumed importance for CS research involves the degree of possible choice available for each course. At first glance, a required course is a forced choice, whereas elective courses are completely freely chosen. But electives and required courses are not as dichotomous as it may seem: No course is really compulsory, because the choice of field (which may later lead to required courses) is free, and each track and direction has some choice points built into it. Even required courses are selected by some students who choose to participate without compulsion. On the other hand, elective courses do not always involve totally free choice, because of time constraints and many other extraneous factors. There are often distribution requirements that create categories of courses from which at least one must be taken. Thus, the terms *required course* and *elective course* are somewhat illusory. Still, in future research on bigger samples of courses, this issue will have to be attended to.

A third partition, currently under exploratory investigation, involves students' subjective distinction between primary and secondary courses. In the natural course of events, students presumably choose first the courses that are important to them, in which they expect to invest great effort and commitment. Subsequently, they complete their list by choosing courses that are not as important to them (perhaps chosen because of entertainment value, workload ease, expected high grades, comfortable scheduling, some interest in the topic, or numerous other reasons). We believe that systematic differences may be found between the types of considerations used in selecting primary and secondary courses.

The next issue concerns the potential generalizability of our results beyond the unique environment of a private, highly selective university classified as an R-1 university within the influential Carnegie system. Perhaps some results are due to particular characteristics of Princeton University and cannot be generalized. For instance, the fact that Princeton seniors are required to write a thesis could have influenced the pattern of correlations observed for the 400-level courses. To hazard a guess, we would suggest that the results would generalize to undergraduate students at selective colleges and universities that hold a liberal arts philosophy. We presume that generalizability must be limited somehow, and only the accumulation of future research on varied institutions and varied formats of CS information will reveal those limits.

Another issue concerns our findings on the absence of predictive power of grading leniency information on subsequent student evaluations. In the SRT literature, the trend of published findings shows that higher grades are usually associated with more positive student evaluations, between courses and within courses. Many prominent researchers (e.g., Feldman, 1978, 1979; Howard, Conway, & Maxwell, 1985; Marsh, 1984, 1987; McKeachie, 1979) have acknowledged a modest association between grades and student ratings, but have not held grading leniency as invalidating SRT. Others, most notably Greenwald (1997; Greenwald & Gillmore, 1997), have argued that inflated grades produce inflated ratings and that grading policy does invalidate SRT. Contrary to these various reports, in this study, CS information about grading leniency was unrelated to postcourse SRTs, except for a slight hint of a relationship between grading leniency and SRT at the 200-level courses. This reinforces the optimistic picture of the mature student that emerges out of our results, suggesting that perhaps course selection might be influenced by more substantive considerations than grading leniency. However, we ought to consider another possibility, which is that the students may have won the grading leniency battle in another way. There has been a tendency, perhaps not generalizable to all institutions, over the past decades, toward grade inflation and a resultant shrinkage in grade distribution. As reported in the *Princeton Alumni Weekly* ("Are students getting smarter?" 1996, March 6) and in the *New York Times* (Archibold, 1998, February 18), grades at Princeton and other private highly selective institutions (e.g., Columbia, Dartmouth, Stanford) are very high and rising. In 1994–1995, 41% of all grades awarded at Princeton were As and 42% were Bs. Given this reality, it may be reasonable that grading leniency information no longer plays a role in Princeton CS. It would be useful to examine the question of grading leniency and course selection in a set of courses in which grades have a possibility of significant variation.

This study calls attention to the neglected area of student CS. CS decisions are too important to be made haphazardly, and college educators know that optimal CS contributes to better education, that relevant information must be provided to students in a style that will be acceptable and helpful to them. However, CS decision making processes have not been studied intensively, and solid scientifically based information that will guide modes of practice are still lacking.

On the basis of our research, and on talks with students about the bases for their CS decisions, we can mark the following issues for future research. Students report that their decisions about different courses are based on different considerations, with most serious thought being devoted to selecting among courses within their major field of study for upperclassmen, and to deciding on courses that might help them test out a possible major for under-classmen. It is on decisions about those (primary) courses that the students expend most thought, and come closest to the optimum of rational decision making. Once that subset of courses is fitted into the schedule, decisions about other (secondary) courses can be made in terms of a more complex set of considerations, involving such considerations as workload, time of day the course is given, intrinsic interest in the material that the course presents, and so on. In other words, not all courses are alike in terms of selection criteria. The task of the student is to give himself or herself a semester's set of courses that enables him or her to work hard at the important aspects of education, fulfill whatever distribution requirements that the college has imposed that year, and have a reasonable amount of time for life activities.

If not all courses are alike, neither are all students alike. Students participating in college athletics or carrying a heavy job load to pay for their tuition have more acute scheduling and load considerations in their decision making. A student who arrives at a college sure of his or her choice of major has a sharply different task with course choices than does a person who has not formed career plans as yet. Beyond that, personality differences among students probably have profound effects on CS. Except for very rare beginnings (e.g., Martin, 1989), this area has not been researched as yet. Thus, how the student body should be segmented for purposes of CS guidance needs a good deal of future research.

At a phenomenological level, we were often struck by the thoughtfulness of the students' systems for thinking through these considerations, but also struck by the ways in which the decision criteria made salient by the context of their choices did not mirror well the criteria that we would hope would guide these decisions and link them with considerations of career choice, self-development, and intellectual excitement. How this could be improved is a question that involves course choice, but goes far beyond it.

REFERENCES

Ambady, N., & Rosenthal, R. (1993). Half a minute: Predicting teacher evaluations from thin slices of nonverbal behavior and physical attractiveness. *Journal of Personality and Social Psychology, 64,* 431–441.

d'Apollonia, S., & Abrami, P. (1997). Navigating student ratings of instruction. *American Psychologist, 52,* 1198–1208.

Archibold, R. (1998, February 18). Just because the grades are up, are Princeton students smarter? *The New York Times.*

Are students getting smarter? (1996, March 6). *The Princeton Alumni Weekly.*

Borgida, E. (1978). Scientific education—evidence is not necessarily informative: A reply to Wells and Harvey. *Journal of Personality and Social Psychology, 36,* 477–482.

Borgida, E., & Nisbett, R. (1977). The differential impact of abstract vs. concrete information on decisions. *Journal of Applied Social Psychology, 7,* 258–271.

Coleman, J., & McKeachie, W. (1981). Effects of instructor/course evaluations on student course selection. *Journal of Educational Psychology, 73,* 224–226.

Dellar, G. (1994). The school subject selection process: A case study. *Journal of Career Development, 20,* 185–204.

Feldman, K. (1978). Course characteristics and college students' ratings of their teachers: What we know and what we don't. *Research in Higher Education, 9,* 199–242.

Feldman, K. (1979). The significance of circumstances for college students' ratings of their teachers and courses. *Research in Higher Education, 10,* 149–179.

Feldman, K. (1986). The perceived instructional effectiveness of college teachers as related to their personality and attitudinal characteristics. *Research in Higher Education, 24,* 139–213.

Gati, I. (1986). Making career decisions—a sequential elimination approach. *Journal of Counseling Psychology, 33,* 408–417.

Gati, I. (1990). *Making Better Career Decisions (MBCD): A computer-assisted career decision making system.* Jerusalem, Israel: Hebrew University of Jerusalem, Department of Psychology.

Gati, I. (1996). Computer-assisted career counseling: Challenges and prospects. In M. Savickas & B. Walsh (Eds.), *Handbook of career counseling theory and practice* (pp. 169–190). Palo Alto, CA: Davies-Black.

Greenwald, A. (1997). Validity concerns and usefulness of student ratings of instruction. *American Psychologist, 52,* 1182–1186.

Greenwald, A., & Gillmore, G. (1997). Grading leniency is a removable contaminant of student ratings. *American Psychologist, 52,* 1209–1217.

Hendel, P. (1982, April). *Evaluating the effects of a course evaluation system designed to assist students in electing courses.* Paper presented at the Annual Meeting of the American Educational Research Association, New York.

Howard, G., Conway, C., & Maxwell, S. (1985). Construct validity of measures of college teaching effectiveness. *Journal of Educational Psychology, 77,* 187–196.

Irving, E. (1990). Helping students choose courses. *National Academic Advising Association Journal, 10,* 51.

Katz, M. (1993). *Computer-assisted career decision making.* Hillsdale, NJ: Erlbaum.

Kevin, R., Harvey, M., & Crandall, N. (1975). Student course selection in a non-requirement program: An exploratory study. *Journal of Educational Research, 68,* 175–177.

Leventhal, L., Abrami, P., & Perry, R. (1976). Do teacher rating forms reveal as much about students as about teachers? *Journal of Educational Psychology, 68,* 441–445.

Leventhal, L., Abrami, P., Perry, R., & Breen, L. (1975). Section selection in multi-section courses: Implications for the validation and use of teacher rating forms. *Educational and Psychological Measurement, 35,* 885–895.

Lorenz, G. (1982, April). *Faculty and student views of information systems to improve course selection.* Paper presented at the Annual Meeting of the American Educational Research Association, New York.

Marsh, H. (1984). Student evaluation of university teaching: Dimensionality, reliability, validity, potential biases, and utility. *Journal of Educational Psychology, 76,* 707–754.

Marsh, H. (1987). *Students' evaluation of university teaching: Research findings, methodological issues and directions for future research.* Elmford, NY: Pergamon.

Marsh, H., & Roche, L. (1997). Making students' evaluations of teaching effectiveness effective: The critical issues of validity, bias, and utility. *American Psychologist, 52,* 1187–1197.

Martin, E. (1989). The relationship among college student characteristics and their assigned importance to dimensions of course choices information. *Journal of College Student Development, 30,* 69–76.

McKeachie, W. (1979). Student ratings of faculty: A reprise. *Academe, 65,* 384–397.

McKeachie, W. (1983). The role of faculty evaluation in enhancing college teaching. *National Forum: Phi Kappa Phi Journal, 63,* 37–39.

McKeachie, W. (1997). Student ratings: The validity of use. *American Psychologist, 52,* 1218–1225.

Murray, H., Rushton, L., & Panuonen, S. (1990). Teacher personality traits and student instructional ratings in six types of university courses. *Journal of Educational Psychology, 82,* 250–261.

Perry, R., Abrami, P., Leventhal, L., & Check, J. (1979). Instructor reputation: An expectancy relationship involving student ratings and achievement. *Journal of Educational Psychology, 71,* 776–787.

Perry, R., Niemi, R., & Jones, K. (1974). Effect of prior teaching evaluation and lecture presentation on ratings of teaching performance. *Journal of Educational Psychology, 66,* 851–856.

Philips, S. (1994). Choice and change: Convergence from the decision-making perspective. In M. Savickas & R. Lent (Eds.), *Convergence in career development theories: Implications for science and practice* (pp. 155–163). Palo Alto, CA: Davies-Black.

Shreve, C., & Wildie, A. (1992, January). *PASS—Placement/Advisement for Student Success.* Paper presented at the Annual Winter Institute on Institutional Effectiveness and Student Success, Jacksonville, FL.

Theall, M., & Franklin, J. (Eds.). (1990). *Student ratings of instruction: Issues for improving practice.* (New Directions for Teaching and Learning Series, No. 43). San Francisco: Jossey-Bass.

Walsh, W., & Osipow, S. (Eds.). (1988). *Career decision making.* Hillsdale, NJ: Erlbaum.

SELF-STUDY QUESTIONS

Multiple Choice

1. Course selection variables described in this study include all but the following:
   a. intellectual challenge
   b. criticism and entertainment value
   c. political and religious affiliation
   d. instructor-student rapport

2. Identify some of the major problems in career-decision making as it relates to developmental aspects in students' course selection.
   a. lack of information
   b. inability to identify and process information
   c. lack of resources to collect information
   d. ability of the decision-maker
   e. all of the above

Essay

1. Based on the information presented concerning how a student's developmental process influences course selection, describe what decision-making strategies you utilize to select your courses. What developmental level do you think you are at in your college career?

2. Evaluate the sources you use to make course selection decisions. Consider sources such as yourself, family, mentors, employers, library information, academic counselors, etc. How might your course and/or academic major selection efforts be applied to your career selection research efforts?

EARLY ADULTHOOD

"Envisioning Fatherhood: A Social Psychological Perspective on Young Men without Kids"

OVERVIEW

Historically, the responsibilities associated with pregnancy and child-rearing have been placed largely on women. In recent years, however, fatherhood has gained more attention in the media and in research. This article explores how young men who are not fathers think about themselves with respect to fatherhood, particularly with regard to the "readiness" of these men to become fathers as well as the ideas and values they have regarding fatherhood and motherhood. Programs designed to educate men regarding fatherhood's responsibilities are also discussed. If you are a man, consider your own ideas about fatherhood. Have you ever thought about fatherhood using some of the ideas set forth in this article? If you are a woman, what do you think about the trend to examine the importance of fatherhood more closely, as well as the growth of programs on fatherhood education?

METHODOLOGY

The goal of the authors of this study was to develop a comprehensive theoretical model describing young men's ideas about fatherhood. They conducted interviews with participants and coded their responses according to a set of theoretical themes. Their coding strategy was based on a technique called *grounded theory analysis*. This approach allowed them to adjust the criteria they used to code participants' responses to interview questions while still collecting data. Such studies often result in the development of a rich source of information for theory-building.

GLOSSARY TERMS

- **Fecundity**   ability to produce children
- **Paternity**   fatherhood; the state of being a father
- **Social psychology**   a branch of psychology that examines behavior, beliefs, attitudes, and emotions within the context of groups
- **Generativity**   a term used in theories of adult development that describes the desire to contribute to and care for a younger generation

- **Doubling of self**   a method of thinking from which a person gains a sense of who she or he is in the present by examining who she or he was in the past

William Marsiglio, Sally Hutchinson, and Mark Cohan

Envisioning Fatherhood: A Social Psychological Perspective on Young Men without Kids

Using in-depth interviews and a purposive sample of 32 men ages 16–30 who have not yet fathered a child, our grounded theory study examined how men envision aspects of fatherhood. Informed by symbolic interactionist and life course perspectives, our interpretive data analyses yielded two interrelated substantive dimensions: fatherhood readiness *and* fathering visions. *We introduce five interrelated theoretical themes to sharpen our understanding of these dimensions, and discuss how these dimensions and themes inform interventions aimed at heightening young men's procreative responsibility.*

Interest in the social psychology of fatherhood has grown significantly in recent years (Marsiglio, 1998). Much of the scholarship in this area focuses on how individuals construct meaning in relation to paternity, fathering, and the negotiation of family roles. Research on men's evolving identities as fathers, and their commitments to their children, is critical for understanding these social processes and the micro-level dimensions to the fatherhood terrain. This work is particularly vital when considering the diverse paths men take on their way to acknowledging and embracing their fecundity, paternity, and father roles, respectively.

While much of the research germane to this area focuses on men who have already become fathers, we extend this literature by studying young, single men's subjective experiences who have not yet, to their knowledge, sired a child or, in the case of most of our participants, impregnated a woman. Our analyses build upon earlier work with these data that focused on how males become aware of their perceived fecundity, experience themselves as procreative beings once they become aware, and view responsibility issues while orienting themselves toward their sexual and potential paternal roles (Marsiglio, Hutchinson, & Cohan, in press). We now focus on several issues that relate more directly to the social psychology of fatherhood. In particular, we highlight two main interrelated dimensions associated with men's efforts to envision aspects of fatherhood: sense of readiness for

becoming fathers (*fatherhood readiness*); and views about the ideal fathering experience, images of the good or ideal father, and visions of future fathering experiences (*fathering visions*). In a more limited fashion, we discuss men's fantasies about what their children might be like and the comparative appraisals they use to organize their thinking about fatherhood.

Throughout our discussion, we also emphasize how gender and relationship commitments can influence the way some men perceive specific issues. Because paternity, and in many instances social fatherhood, can be viewed as joint accomplishments involving a man and woman, we explore how men's orientation to prospective fatherhood is sometimes influenced by their involvement with particular romantic partners. We examine young men's thoughts about the prospects of fatherhood independent of specific romantic relationships as well.

Consistent with our grounded theory perspective, we have read our data with an eye toward capturing distinctive features of the way men express their thoughts about procreation, social fathering, and children. Our analyses revealed, for example, several preliminary themes that appear to cut across the dimensions listed above that characterize men's efforts to envision fatherhood. We introduce and define these themes when we analyze men's sense of being "ready" for fatherhood. These themes provide an explicit organizational structure for this section. Further, because we suspect that men's sense of readiness is linked to their image of what represents a good or ideal father, we then selectively use three of these themes to illuminate men's views about fathering in general, and more specifically, their visions about how they themselves plan to act as fathers. In this context, we consider the significance and symbolic meaning underlying men's desire to father their own biological child someday, and discuss men's perceptions of their own fathers. Finally, we comment briefly on the nature of men's visions of their hypothetical children.

Our research with men who are not yet fathers is warranted because many men who eventually do become fathers begin to develop their paternal identities prior to their child's birth, and for some, even before their child is conceived. This study is also consistent with recent initiatives to incorporate males into important policy debates and program interventions that address sex, pregnancy, paternity, and social fatherhood issues (Federal Interagency Forum on Child and Family Statistics, 1998; Levine & Pitt, 1995; Marsiglio, 1998; Moore, Driscoll, & Ooms, 1997; Sonenstein, Stewart, Lindberg, Pernas, & Williams, 1997). These efforts embrace broader schemes for conceptualizing and promoting responsible fatherhood, especially among teens and young adults. Thus, our study generates insights relevant to both theory and program development.

BACKGROUND

Though our study used grounded theory methodology (Glaser, 1978, 1992; Strauss, 1987), our analysis of young men's subjective lives as persons capable of procreating and assuming father roles is informed by the symbolic interactionist (Mead, 1934) and life course perspectives (Marsiglio, 1995). The former directs our attention to how men construct and interpret their perceptions about their potential experiences as fathers, and the latter reminds us that men's views about the timing of fatherhood are shaped by their ideas about how they would like to sequence and time other critical life course events, including education, work, and relationships (marriage in particular). From an interactionist perspective, we are interested in the meanings men assign to situations, events, acts, others, and themselves as they relate to aspects of fatherhood and the social psychological processes by which this occurs. These processes include both the identity work men do by themselves as they attempt to define what they value for themselves and others, and the interactions they share with partners (and others) as they co-construct their views about fathering and children.

Using samples of men, most of whom are not fathers, researchers have studied different facets of young men's perceptions regarding sexual and contraceptive responsibility, as well as pregnancy resolution (see Marsiglio, 1998 for review). Additionally, some research has attempted to unravel how men of varying ages think and feel during their partner's

pregnancy and the transitional period to first time fatherhood (Herzog, 1982; LaRossa & LaRossa, 1989; May, 1980; Sherwen, 1987; Soule, Stanley, & Copans, 1979; Zayas, 1988). These types of analyses are grounded on men's lived experiences with the pregnancy and childbirth processes. Much less is known about how young men who have not yet become fathers envision fatherhood and children (Gohel, Diamond, & Chambers, 1997). Thus, the bulk of what we know about young men's sense of the meanings and responsibilities of fatherhood comes from studies of acknowledged fathers and their partners (Allen & Doherty, 1996; Furstenberg, 1995).

Because of the stigma associated with teen pregnancy and unplanned paternity, many young men are hesitant to establish legal paternity or even report informally that they have fathered a child; others may not be aware that they have sired a child. Consequently, information regarding young fathers comes only from those who acknowledge their paternity, a subset of the larger population that may have special characteristics. This potential bias in the data gathered from fathers further emphasizes the need to explore young men's perceptions about fatherhood and children before they experience paternity.

Insights gleaned from surveys of social service providers who have developed male involvement and pregnancy prevention programs throughout the U.S. are also relevant to our study (Levine & Pitt, 1995; Sonenstein et al., 1997). While it is beyond our purposes here to present Sonenstein et al.'s full summary of the practical advice and program philosophies of these programs, it is useful to repeat their observation that:

> …these programs try to change males' attitudes toward themselves, their relationships with women, and their futures. Most focus on comprehensive life issues—improving self-esteem, relationship skills, and employment skills— to give young men the tools they will need to take control in multiple areas of their lives, to exercise responsibility, and to give them hope for positive futures (p. 143).

Most of the program insights have emerged out of interventions in low-income, inner-city areas, but some can and should be adapted to teenage and young adult men in more advantaged neighborhoods as well as other groups (e.g., military and prison populations).

METHODS
Sample

The purposive sample we used for this analysis is part of a larger ongoing project in which we secured interviews with single men ages 16–30 who had dated at least one woman in the past three years (or had been married). These men fit one of five primary procreative experience profiles: (1) "procreative novices," no pregnancy or fertility experience; (2) "abortion veterans," responsible for a pregnancy that was aborted within the previous 12 month period; (3) "fathers-in-waiting," partners are currently pregnant with their first child; (4) "new fathers," those whose child is between 6–12 weeks old; and, (5) fathers. For this paper, we restricted our focus to those 32 men who had not yet fathered a child (we included the 6 participants who were involved with their pregnant partner at the time of our initial interview with them).

We conducted 17 interviews with procreative novices, 11 with abortion veterans, 6 with fathers-in-waiting, and 2 miscarriage veterans (a few men are categorized in more than one category). We used these experience profiles to broaden the range of data available to us as we examined men's views on fathering, rather than as a basis for examining differences and commonalities among the different categories of participants. We use pseudonyms throughout the text to refer to all participants, and we abbreviate quoted excerpts to eliminate redundancies (e.g., "then, then I knew") and extraneous utterances (e.g., "you know," "uhm").

Our recruitment strategy sought to enhance diversity by taking into account men's procreative life experiences mentioned above as well as their age, race/ethnicity, education, financial status, and relationship status. Of the 32 participating men, 19 were White, 10 were African American (one bi-racial), 2 were Hispanic, and 1 was Native American Indian. The mean age of the sample was 21.6 years, with 7 being younger than 19 and 7 others being 26 or older. Three of our participants were still in high school, another 7 had no college experience (one of these men had not completed high school), 21 had some college experience (one of these men had not completed high school), and 1 was a college graduate. Three participants were either separated or divorced.

We recruited participants in a number of ways. Screening interviewers arranged 16 interviews with men who were visiting a local Department of Motor Vehicles' office, and we identified the remaining participants through abortion clinics, a prenatal clinic, a prepared child birth class, a local employment agency, homeless shelter, personal contacts, and word of mouth.

Interviews

Our semi-structured, audio-taped face-to-face interviews lasted between 60 and 90 minutes and took place in on-campus offices, public libraries, and other locations convenient to the participants. Four interviewers—2 White males, an African-American male, and a White female, aged 30, 40, 45 and 55 respectively—conducted the interviews. With an eye toward the past, present, and future, we encouraged our participants to talk about their perceptions and experiences involving paternity, social fatherhood, children, and relationships. We focused extensively on their current relationship, if they had one. Men had the opportunity to discuss moments and events that shaped the level and type of awareness they currently had of themselves as procreative beings and potential fathers. Our analyses for this article were informed by interview questions that dealt primarily with the following: (1) instances where they thought they might have impregnated someone; (2) instances where they talked to someone about impregnating a girl/woman or becoming a father; (3) talk about situations or events that happened to them that changed how they thought about impregnating someone; (4) the importance for them to father their own biological child; (5) relationships in which they thought about what it would be like to have a child with a particular partner; (6) whether or not they saw kids in their future; and (7) imagery they had about their possible children and of themselves as fathers.

While interviewing, we were aware that interviewees could respond to our sensitive and sometimes personal questions with idealized responses, telling us what they thought we wanted to hear. To minimize "correct answers" we attempted to portray a non-judgmental attitude while emphasizing the importance and value of their feelings, beliefs, and experiences for our understanding.

Sensitivity to temporal issues implicit in our interview questions was also important. Our questions about procreative events often prompted men to reference different time frames as they discussed their views and experiences. Thus, they sometimes described their experiences by moving back and forth in the narrative between their past, present, and future selves.

Data Analysis

Data were subjected to the methods of grounded theory analysis (Glaser, 1978, 1992; Strauss, 1987), including substantive and theoretical coding, memoing (the writing of theoretical notes), and theoretical sampling. The constant comparative method facilitated the comparisons of incident with incident and incidents with the developing codes. Data collection and analysis occurred simultaneously, permitting the data analysis to inform data collection by suggesting the importance of a particular code and/or the need to obtain more data on a particular code. Memoing helped in the identification of relationships among codes. As a technique to enhance dependability, the first two authors of this paper coded each interview separately and then together (Lincoln & Guba, 1985). As we analyzed our data, we attempted to differentiate between the narratives men used to depict their orientation to procreative issues independent of the interview context and questions per se, and those responses that were more clearly constructed for the first time in direct response to an interviewer's questioning. Our analyses were designed to expand and enrich theoretical concepts rather than identify factors that reliably predict or shape whether individuals think about fatherhood or think about it in particular ways.

ENVISIONING FATHERHOOD

Because our sample included participants ranging in age from 16–30, it is not surprising that most had given at least passing thought to their ability to impregnate a sex partner. All of our participants recognized the connection between sexual intercourse and conception. While we interviewed a few notable exceptions, those participants who were older and more experienced in having relationships, negotiating sex, contraception, and in some instances resolving a pregnancy, typically had given more thought to being a father. However, some men, despite being sexually active, had not thought about the prospects of fatherhood or imagined what it would be like to some day be a father. While it is noteworthy that these latter participants did not think about fatherhood, our analyses focused primarily on those men who had reflected on this topic.

As we listened to participants discuss their images and concerns about fatherhood and children, several interrelated themes emerged from the data. The present analyses examine these themes, among a sample of nonfathers, in order to better understand what being "ready" for fatherhood means, how men perceive ideal fathering, and how they envision fathering for themselves. We have labeled the more prominent themes: degree and form of collaboration, focus of attention (relational and substantive), temporal orientation, experience (source and intensity), and degree of clarity. Again, we use each of these themes to organize our analysis of fatherhood readiness while incorporating three themes (focus of attention, temporal orientation, and degree of clarity) into our subsequent analysis of fathering visions. In both analysis sections, we highlight, where possible, how the relevant themes intersect with one another.

Fatherhood Readiness

Many participants commented on the nature of their preparedness to become fathers and assumed the responsibilities associated with social fathering. Their remarks underscored the connection, as well as the subtle distinction, between men's desires to become fathers now or in the future, and their sense of being ready to do so at this point in their lives. Some men were receptive to the idea of paternity or fathering a child in an abstract sense, but they realized that they were currently not inclined or prepared to embrace all aspects of being a father. Desmond, a 30-year-old African American, remarked:

> …I do not mind being [becoming] a father…if I had a child, I could be ready to be a father. What I do not want to give up is the time. I'd like my son, well let's just say son, may not be a son, might be a daughter, but I'd like my child to be very well educated, to have good advantages, to do well in life, to be all it can be, and I would support it as best I could. But, I wish there was a way to do that without, right now, without giving up the time.

In this excerpt, Desmond talks about his fatherhood readiness in terms of a contradiction: He has high aspirations for this hypothetical (male) child, and is willing to commit to supporting these aspirations, but he is not currently willing to make the time commitment he associates with fatherhood. Considered at the present time, fatherhood holds seemingly irreconcilable positives and negatives: helping a child "be all it can be" versus time demands.

Degree and form of collaboration. We found that men were attentive to their sense of readiness by reflecting on it alone and/or when they discussed it with others. Patterns of private reflection and more collaborative experiences had distinctive features, yet were likely to reinforce one another over time. Both may also be relevant intermittently to men's sense of readiness as it varied over time within and between relationships. While a few men recalled instances where they had acknowledged their sense of readiness without discussing it with someone, most men reported having at least fleeting conversations with others about their own sense of readiness. Most of these conversations did not include truly collaborative exchanges where men were constructing and negotiating their sense of readiness with others, rather they tended to serve as reinforcement for the orientations men had developed previously.

Seeing pregnant teenagers and young parents out in public triggered some men to reflect privately about how ill-prepared they were to become a father at the time. Thus, some men, like Arthur, a 21-year-old man raised in a rural area, attended to their sense of readiness privately when they reflected on how others (e.g., family, friends, individuals in school or in public, persons on TV. talk shows) were affected by off-time parental responsibilities. In Arthur's case, he based his sense of readiness and explicit preference to delay fatherhood until he was about 28 on his desire to improve upon the meager material life his father provided for him when he was a child:

> ...when I grew up my dad, he didn't have nothin'. They [parents] had me when they were like eighteen, and they pretty much didn't have anything. We drove ol' beat up cars, lived in an old mobile home, and I just don't want to be like that for the rest of my life.

Arthur was also quick to add his personal conviction: "I want to be sure it's [having child] with the person I'm going to be with for the rest of my life. Not just go and make a buncha kids." Although it does not appear that Arthur spent much time thinking about these issues in private, our reading of Arthur's interview suggests that he had given some thought to these issues, away from his family and partner. In other portions of his interview, he did make it clear that he had also talked explicitly to his partner, mother, and grandmother about wanting to wait to have children until he was in his late twenties.

Marcus, a 19-year-old bi-racial participant, provided a specific example of a collaborative process when he recalled his conversation with one of his girl-friends: "And then we just talked about, she was like, I can't have no kids right now. I'm like, you? I can't have none neither. Too damn young." While this excerpt illustrates a rather superficial type of exchange, talk of this variety can be important if it activates the men's sense of procreative responsibility and provides them with an opportunity to establish, or reassert their own views about their fatherhood readiness.

Desmond offered another colorful example of a form of collaboration men can experience as they fashion their sense of readiness. During his interview, he reenacted for the interviewer a conversation he had in which a friend shared with him some folk wisdom about girlfriends and father readiness. Desmond had said to his friend, "You know, I could have a baby from this girl. I'd like to give this girl a baby." His friend responded "Well, you don't know that yet, until [you], look in her eyes." To which Desmond asked, "Why?" The friend replied: "If you can look in her eyes and, when you look at her, see your children in her eyes, then that's when you know." Desmond went on to tell the interviewer how he attempted to put his friend's advice into practice: "I tried to do that, and it kind of, I kind of saw what they [the friend and other friends] were talking about."

Focus of attention.   When men talked about their degree of readiness they varied in their focus of attention. Our data showed that this focus involved both a relational object (self, partner, child) as well as substantive features (e.g., financial and occupational stability, educational attainment, emotional well-being, time). Most men focused primarily or exclusively on their own well-being or personal development. Typically they reported fears about not being able to complete their education or career plans, and/or having their mobility or leisure activities unduly restricted. For example, Alex, 18 years old and White, asserted that: "There's a lot I want to do, a lot of things I want to see. A lot of things I want to accomplish before I want to settle down and have a family."

A more dramatic and unique example was provided by Kyle, a White, 21-year-old devout Christian. Following on the heels of his comments about how little he has thought about girls and pregnancy, Kyle remarked:

> ...I need to know what a husband and father needs to be and start working towards that. As I started realizing the character qualities that need to be there, and I realize I'm not anywhere near that and how much work is gonna need to be done on myself to prepare myself for that, the list keep[s] on getting longer, and I'm tackling them one at a time or whatever ones I can handle at each moment, but I think by just having them in my thoughts, maybe it's just like a physical maturing now...I want to be a good husband, I want to be a good father—I don't have any concept of what a husband or a good father is but, the Bible does.... I have notes of character qualities and then verse after verse that talks about it.

While Kyle hadn't thought about impregnating a girl, this passage clearly reveals that he had thought extensively about his degree of fatherhood readiness. Kyle was unique in our sample, and uncharacteristic of the more general population, because of the commitment and effort he has made to prepare himself for fatherhood, even before becoming sexually active. Another way Kyle was unique was that his preparation for becoming a good father focused primarily on his personal and moral development. Instead of being worried about how fatherhood would thwart his personal life or development, as we saw with Alex above, Kyle drew attention to how his current stage of personal and moral development would restrict his ability to be a good Christian father. He clearly felt he was ill-prepared to be a good father at this point in his life.

Kyle's orientation to self was also instructive because it illustrated how some men in our sample portrayed aspects of their personal character and then linked them to their degree of readiness for fatherhood. These types of portrayals required men to have a degree of self-awareness, the ability to articulate it, and an understanding of how it may influence their preparedness for being a father.

A smaller number of men voiced their concern about how an unplanned pregnancy and birth would affect their child's well-being. These comments tended to emphasize the financial aspects of providing for children. Reflecting on the financial struggles his single mother grappled with as she tried to raise three kids, Jerry, a White 19-year-old, said:

> …she always did what she had to do to get us what we wanted and what we needed, even if it was sacrificing stuff she needed at the time, but she couldn't get. She just wanted to make sure we had everything. Like come Christmas time she'd do whatever she could to give us presents and stuff, but then you see some people where their parents don't have enough money to even buy them things, and so lot of things like that makes you want to, like makes you think that you need to have the money, and definitely want to be able to take care of your kids as well as you can.

Though it was not common, a few participants explicitly mentioned or hinted at how their sense of readiness was, or would be, tied to their partners' circumstances. Not surprisingly, men voiced their concerns for their partners in conjunction with their concerns about their own well-being, sometimes mentioning, for example, that they were both still in school. After stating that he wanted kids someday, and then being asked the ideal age at which this might occur, Jerry said: "…when I'm through with college, and when I have a job, and my life's steady, and if I'm with someone that her life's steady, and just when we know the time's right, when you have the money that you're going to be able to take care of it and stuff."

In addition to associating their degree of readiness to their concerns about either their partner, child, themselves, or some combination, our participants' views often implicated specific substantive concerns. In light of prevailing gendered beliefs about fathering and breadwinning in the U.S., it was not surprising to find that financial considerations were by far the most consistently mentioned concern. As Desmond's earlier remarks indicate, some men identified the loss of time as a nonfinancial worry affecting their sense of fatherhood readiness. Furthermore, Tom, a Native American 22-year-old, responded to a question about what being ready to have a child means to him:

> Steadiness, 'cause right now I've got a lifestyle that's like, I'll go work in a place for a while, and get set up. And get as much money saved up and then try to go off and move somewhere else a little better. I just haven't really found a place yet that I'm comfortable with staying.

Our data consistently shows, either implicitly or explicitly, that most men's focus of attention was multifaceted and not limited to just relational or substantive concerns. Kyle's earlier comments implicitly suggested, for instance, that while his focus of attention is self-oriented, he believes his child and partner would suffer because he has not yet developed the traits that would allow him to express himself as a Christian father. Moreover, his comments reveal that he combines his explicit relational focus on self with his substantive interests regarding Christian fatherhood.

Temporal orientation. When men were asked to reflect upon their perceptions about being ready to become a father, they organized their replies by introducing a temporal orientation to the way they both conceptualized their readiness and depicted it in their narratives. In various ways, men's description of their sense of readiness was framed by their tendency to contrast perceptions, experiences, and desires they associated with different time periods. We saw this, for example, with Arthur, who linked fatherhood readiness with improving upon the financial circumstances he experienced as a child. Thus, men sometimes drew upon their previous familial or personal experiences to mold a message for themselves about their readiness to be a father. In other words, men assessed what they had witnessed in the past (e.g., living in poverty) and then speculated on how assuming or postponing father roles would influence them now and/or in the future.

Men sometimes characterized transformations over time that they had personally experienced in terms of their readiness to have children. Miller, a White 28-year-old, recalled that he: "Never even really gave much thought to it [having children]. You know, I like to travel. I like to work and take my time off and go and see and do. I never really made a place in that life for a, for a kid." He then added that "I'm getting to almost to the point where I should start settling down a little bit and actually, possibly looking for a house to live in and a job that I work at for more than a year or so." Here, Miller juxtaposes his previous and perhaps fading lifestyle with his emerging thoughts about a "nesting" strategy that would foster a more stable life-style, one that apparently would be more conducive to fathering a child. The narrative device he uses reveals his slowly evolving shift in identity while highlighting the more continuous features of his procreative consciousness and sense of readiness to be a father.

In other instances, men privileged their current experience and did their best to avoid other time references. Marcus, for example, noted that he and his partner "…wouldn't really talk about what if we have a kid because we were scared to talk about like, I didn't even want to look…at that. I just wanted to talk about things right now, didn't want to talk about the future."

Men commonly compared, either implicitly or explicitly, their current situation with what they projected for themselves in the future. One 17-year-old Hispanic participant, Reynaldo, provided a useful example:

> I'm hoping to at least be out of college, have a steady job, be financially stable and be mature about things, and hopefully be married. And then I can think about being a father. But, right now I don't really think about myself being a father, it's just in the distant future. Like when I'm 26, 27 around there. But, I'm picturing myself being a good father.

Reynaldo, like some of our other participants, was able to visualize relatively long term goals that he wanted to accomplish prior to becoming a father.

Experience (source and intensity).

We earmarked men's first-hand experiences with aspects of the reproductive realm and child care because some men viewed these experiences as salient to their father readiness. They also warranted attention, given men's limited exposure to certain types of experiences that result from the gendered nature of the reproductive realm and child care. Several men's sense of readiness was affected by their fertility-related experiences. Indeed, some men found that being confronted with the prospect of becoming a father to an unplanned child acted as a wake-up call for them to think about fatherhood issues more seriously. When asked if his abortion experience affected the way he thought about kids, Austin, 21 years of age and White explained "…it's definitely reminded me that I'm definitely not ready for that kind of responsibility. I knew that I wasn't before this happened, but if anything it reminded me that I wasn't ready for that at all." In Tom's case, on the other hand, his miscarriage experience deflated his desire and sense of readiness to have another child.

> Before the miscarriage I was more 'amped' to have a child, I guess you could say and more willing. And nowadays I'm going to be very selective, it's going to be a while till I have another, try to have another kid.

Tom's description not only identifies miscarriage as the source of his experiential connection to his sense of readiness, but his use of the word 'amped' reveals that the miscarriage must have been an intense experience to transform his earlier readiness to have a child.

Nonfertility experiences can also act as turning points in men's lives by affecting the way they think about fatherhood. In his response to a question about whether he sees kids in his future, Marcus conveyed how his sense of fatherhood readiness had been shaped by his frequent interaction with his niece. After describing his niece as "the cutest thing on earth to me right now," he provided a detailed account of a day of babysitting her as a way of explaining why he is not ready to be a father:

> I picked her up at twelve thirty, and I was with her from…twelve thirty to like seven…. And just being around her from twelve thirty to seven thirty and just constantly having to like give her bottles…and changing the diaper, and when I put her down, she cries, she wants to hold me, she wants me to walk around the house with her. She doesn't want to be put down. I can't watch TV, I mean I can watch TV but I have to keep an eye on her. It's just things like that, that right there's being responsible…. I have a lot of other things in my life right now to take care of before I have children. So that's why I say that she makes me want to have one [a child]…and, then again, she doesn't.

As Marcus observed, his exposure to the moral labor of child care offered him a dose of reality that convinced him that he's not quite ready to be a hands-on father, despite the possible appeal of having his own child. However, similar types of moral labor experiences may encourage other men to decide that they are actually ready for fatherhood. Likewise, opportunities to be involved in the more playful aspects of spending time with children may encourage men to embrace the idea of fatherhood and increase their sense of readiness. The following three excerpts capture a sentiment that was shared by a number of the men:

> I've always liked kids, like my cousin had a little kid a couple of years ago and I just like messing, playing with them and stuff. (Cal, 16, White)

> Eventually I'd love to be a father. I mean I love kids. I love playing with them. (Alex, 18, White)

> I've always liked kids. You know, I have like nieces and nephews I love, I want to have me a kid, you know…(Harper, 29, African American)

While the attraction to the playful aspects of spending time with kids may have enhanced Cal's and Alex's fatherhood readiness, this does not necessarily mean that they will challenge prevailing gendered patterns of parental involvement once they become fathers. In other words, their sense of readiness may actually hinge on their willingness to express more traditional forms of father involvement that center on play, rather than attending to their children's everyday needs (Lamb, 1997).

Degree of clarity. Many of the excerpts we have presented thus far illustrate men's level of clarity about their perceived fatherhood readiness. Given the age range of our sample, it is not surprising that most participants were relatively clear about not being ready to have a child. However, as we just saw with Marcus, some men expressed a degree of ambivalence about the prospects of fatherhood and others, like Desmond, indicated a considerable amount of clarity that they have been ready at various times in their lives to have a child. Desmond shared his thoughts about the possibility of having children with two recent partners:

> *It was all positive, just thinking about raising a child. Because, really, the last two, I probably could have married them in the wink of an eye. So I thought about how we would look in a house, raising a family, with a child, being accepted, being loved, nurtured, cared for, and all of those things.*

Desmond reveals his clarity about being ready for fatherhood in these relationships by contrasting his recent orientation with the way he responded during his early twenties to a pregnancy scare. His narrative construction about his evolving fatherhood readiness over time is consistent with the "doubling of self" technique involving identity work (Denzin, 1987). Those who use this technique explicitly construct and present their current identity by contrasting it to an identity they had previously expressed. Commenting on his reaction to his partner's possible pregnancy, Desmond said: "…I immediately tried to distance myself from it or, it was just, I wasn't ready to deal with that. When I look back at it, that was not fair to her because I probably hurt her feelings at the time. When you're young and immature, sometimes you're not in control of your feelings." In addition to highlighting how some men used a "doubling of self" technique to make sense of changes in their procreative identity, Desmond's narrative is instructive because it illustrates how an understanding of men's subjective experiences is fostered by attending to the intersection of multiple themes, such as, the focus of attention, temporal orientation, and degree of clarity.

Fathering Visions

Since our earlier analysis implied that men's sense of readiness is related to their expectations of how fa-

thers should ideally express themselves as fathers, we now address men's views of the ideal fathering experience, the good or ideal father, and their visions of how they expect to act as fathers toward their future children. While some had given considerable thought to these matters, others had not. In this section, we selectively emphasize several of the themes we introduced previously while broadening our analysis to highlight men's penchant for biological fatherhood, their thoughts about their own fathers, and their ideas about what their children might be like.

When asked about the importance of fathering their own biological children, most men were quick to point out that being genetically related to children they might "father" in the future was an important feature of what they would consider to be their ideal fathering experience. Marcus, for example, indicated that biological paternity was important to him, "Cuz it's gonna be my seed. It's gonna be me. I made that being, that human being, that person. And I'm going to father it jis like my father fathered me." Meanwhile, Justin stressed his affinity for the intergenerational connection by first commenting on how proud his parents were when he graduated high school, and then noted:

> *…I see children as, it's like you're passing on your genes, you're passing on your hereditary information. …it's like you get to a certain point in your life where you're not going to achieve much more. You're just at a stand still and you can bring up a child who can achieve great things and continue on the family.*

In Justin's everyday words, he associates his desire for biological paternity and social fathering with what theorists of adult development refer to as generativity—the need to nurture and guide younger generations (Hawkins & Dollahite, 1997). While most participants focused, as Justin did, on the relationship between themselves as a father and their potential children when evaluating the importance of biological paternity, Jerry accentuated the shared experience among prospective parents that can accompany a pregnancy.

> *Just the whole thing that you and your wife will go through. Just her becoming pregnant, going to the doctors with her, and when she has her checkups, and just the whole experience pretty much. Going to the hospital with her and, being there in the delivery…*

Jerry's comments reflect his appreciation for a type of collaborative approach to the prebirth process that he associates with the ideal fatherhood experience; fathering is made special by sharing the gestation process with the prospective mother.

Consistent with research that has sampled fathers (Allen & Doherty, 1996; Daly, 1993), our sample of men reported several key features of good fathering and indicated that men's own fathers can serve as positive or negative role models. While economic provisioning was mentioned by a number of men, participants were quick to stress the importance of fathers spending time with their kids and their desire to be actively involved in their own children's lives. Responding to what being a father meant to him, Antoine, a 19-year-old African American offered a reply that reflects the sentiments of a number of participants.

> ...Always there, no matter what you do, right or wrong, thick and thin, whatever. Somebody that's not just a provider, not just put a roof over you head, but taking care of you, gives you advice. Just your mentor and everything, friend, best friend.

Using glowing language, Reynaldo reinforced Antoine's comment by noting how his father can be a good father even while he is unemployed:

> ...my dad is a real man right now 'cause, he can support us even though he's unemployed right now, but you know, whenever he had a job, he was doing good. And he supported us and right now he is showing how he can get us through tough times right now.

Thus, for many in our sample, the essence of being a good father involved being present, approachable, a friend, and a dispenser of measured discipline.

During the course of the interviews, this general conception of the "good father" appeared to be closely related to how participants assessed their own fathers. Whether they described their fathers as positive or negative role models, the benchmark against which they articulated their assessments amounted to a fairly consistent ideal. Typically, their fathers' contributions as disciplinarians and providers were appreciated, but the men wanted these necessary roles balanced with direct involvement and emotional concern. Not surprisingly, those facets in which particular men found their own fathers lacking were the ones which they seemed most eager to improve on when they become fathers, and those qualities that the men most appreciated were the ones they hoped to emulate. At one extreme, men who felt their fathers were absent physically vowed not to leave their children fatherless. The comments of Warren, a 23-year-old African American, were representative of this small, but important group:

> I was just thinking that I didn't want to have children in X number of cities and also have a wife who wasn't the mother of those children [pause] cause that's pretty much how, what it was with my father.... I never felt cheated out of a father, 'cause I think my life turned out a little better, but at the same time I would have liked to [have] known him.

At the other end of the spectrum, some men praised their fathers for developing a strong emotional connection with them or knowing how to provide just the right amount of discipline and supervision:

> I'd be a very loving father like my father was. And I would try to model myself as he raised me...I'd be firm but I'd never hit the child. I'd be very loving and supportive no matter what. Just be his best friend. [Mitchel, White, 22 years old]

> Like my father is good, so I'm gonna pretty much be the same way that he is to me. You know, not strict but having a level head and keeping me down and not letting me get out of control really. Giving me a little bit of line but not too much. [Reynaldo, Hispanic, 17 years old]

Men whose experiences fell somewhere in between these two poles presented a similar dynamic. For instance, David, who is 28 years old and White, praised his father's achievement of the provider ideal, but sees himself being emotionally closer to his children:

> Well he was a good provider. You know, he worked full time and he brought home the money, paid the bills but he wasn't like real affectionate. It didn't seem like he made an effort to like go out of his way to do things with his kids.... I think I would be a lot closer to my kids than he was.

Talking about their fathers, then, became an opportunity for these men to refine their visions of themselves as future fathers by reflecting on what they valued or missed in their experience of being fathered.

Focus of attention, degree of clarity, and temporal orientation.

Of the five themes we discussed in connection with fatherhood readiness, the focus of attention, degree of clarity, and temporal orientation themes were the most relevant to how participants attempted to bridge the conceptual divide between the father ideal and how they expected to be with their children. As they contemplated their future fathering behavior, men's focus of attention typically involved their child(ren) as well as the dynamic relationship between them and their child(ren). For a few men, their focus of attention evolved around some type of child development and/or family process philosophy. Miller, for instance, forcefully concluded that:

> ...kids are spastic. What are you going to do?...I hate that, when you constantly see parents who are like, 'Don't do that. No, don't touch that. No don't do that. No don't do this.' I mean, for Christ's sake: Just buy a leash, put the kid on the leash, and deal with it that way, if you're going to be that neurotic about it.

With this philosophy as a backdrop, Miller asserted that: "My kids are going to experience and go out and do and see the stuff. Because that's how life should be." These excerpts demonstrate Miller's degree of clarity about children's personalities in general, and his future role as a laid-back father. He has a definite belief about children's temperament and how a parent (father) should treat them.

Warren's comments provide us with another angle for thinking about the degree of clarity theme. This 23-year-old African American presented his vision of himself as a father someday in the context of a story that emphasizes the pitfalls of parenting. He recalled that his mother once "beat" both him and his sister because his sister did something wrong but would not "fess up." While Warren clearly disliked that experience as a child, he now anticipates that as a father he cannot guarantee that such situations will never arise, any more than his mother could. Consequently, he resigns himself to the idea that fathering will be a "learning experience," noting that: "I can have a blueprint set up right now and then when you have children, who's to say that that blueprint is going to work." Ironically, then, Warren asserted his clarity about fathering by emphasizing what he perceived to be the uncertainty associated with parenting. Notice, too, that he did so by first assuming a temporal orientation directed toward the past as he drew a lesson from his mother's actions when he was a child.

In most cases, men's visions of themselves as fathers carried with them implicit or explicit visions of the children they would father. As earlier analyses with these data revealed, men emphasized gender, personality, and physical features in addition to imagining doing specific activities with their children (Marsiglio, Hutchinson, & Cohan, in press). Moreover, some men tended to focus on these hypothetical children as small children, whereas others referenced their children's development through the years. Justin, a White 18-year-old acknowledged trying to imagine his and his partner's children "but at most they're just like infants, really young children." In contrast, Tom admitted to thinking about the differences in raising a girl or a boy. From his perspective, gender differences do not become relevant to parenting until the children reach puberty. At that point, he anticipates that if he had a daughter he would be uncomfortable with her emerging sexuality:

> …like girls would start getting interested in boys and start looking at them. Uhm, I'd don't think I'd be as comfortable taking them to like baseball games and stuff. [Interviewer: why not?] Uhm. I don't know. I've seen a lot of like young girls out there…hollering at the guys. I don't know. I wouldn't even want to think that my daughter's got that part where the rear-ends get her excited.

These men differ not only in how far into the future they "forecast" the lives of their hypothetical children, but they also focus their attention differently in this regard. While Justin's child visions were linked with a specific partner, Tom's thoughts at least gave the impression of being independent of a particular relationship.

PROGRAM IMPLICATIONS

We have organized our analysis of how men envision fatherhood around two key interrelated substantive dimensions: fatherhood readiness and fathering visions. Both of these dimensions is relevant to the expanding number of male involvement and pregnancy prevention programs in the U.S. and, taken together, provide a substantive foundation for these types of interventions. Likewise, the five theoretical themes (degree and form of collaboration, focus of attention, temporal orientation, experience, and degree of clarity) that emerged from our data are instructive because they provide insights for strengthening these types of programs. These themes supplement the practical advice Sonenstein and her colleagues (1997) offered based on their review of model programs, and are also relevant to programs suitable for high schools, colleges, the military, and prisons. Our purpose in this section, then, is to show briefly how the two substantive dimensions and five interrelated theoretical themes can inform efforts designed to heighten young men's procreative responsibility and encourage them to consider their long-term visions for fathering prior to impregnating a partner. More specifically, we recommend that programs develop opportunities for men to address at least the following five areas: (a) self knowledge, appraisals, and aspirations; (b) relationship issues with partners; (c) past experiences with fathers (painful and valued); (d) current paternal role models; and (e) philosophies of fathering and child visions.

Consistent with Sonenstein et al.'s (1997) stated goal of encouraging men to respect themselves, we add that it is critical for young men to "know" themselves. Efforts to enhance men's self-awareness should not only encourage men to identify their self-perceptions about a range of personal attributes (character portrayals) and long-term aspirations, but men should also be prompted to identify the sources that have affected their perceptions about these matters. Men should be prompted to ask themselves what they value and how they came to feel that way. What are their long-term aspirations in terms of education, employment, finances, and family? How important do they feel it is to travel, be independent, spend time with friends, and nurture others? Much of this self-knowledge may have little, if anything, to do directly with their views of fathering, children, and family. However, men's values and perceptions about human capital issues are likely to be related indirectly to their future approach to family-related matters, and opportunities should be created for men to discover these connections.

Part of men's self-knowledge involves understanding how their identities as men are affected by their perceptions of their romantic partner(s) and/or women in general. What are the qualities they would like in a partner? What are the qualities they desire in the mother of their child? What does a "good" relationship look like? Encouraging men to think about these issues should, in many instances, lead men to become introspective and evaluate themselves, partners, family, and friends. In addition, these questions may assist men in considering alternative definitions of masculinity. Thus, programs should help men expand their self-knowledge by enlightening them about the competing images of masculinity, and how these images implicate different ways to relate to one's female partner. Depending on the nature of the program, a range of ideological perspectives on gender relations from pro-feminism to religious conservatism could be presented and debated.

Our data showed that men's interactions with their female partners contributed to the diverse criteria men use to evaluate their sense of being ready for fatherhood. Efforts to raise young men's level of procreative consciousness should therefore encourage men to recognize how their sense of readiness may be related to their partner's perceptions and experiences. By alerting men explicitly to the three primary foci of attention (self, partner, and child), programs could help young men recognize that their procreative abilities can have diverse consequences, not only for them, but others as well. Developing men's gender/partner sensitivity and child sensitivity is important. For example, assisting men to forecast the short- and long-term outcomes of a birth for their partner and for the unintended child may promote a revisioning of that scenario. Such discussions could also sensitize men to a range of possible situations they or others might encounter. For example, they might be appraised that those men who perceive themselves to be in love with their partner may be more likely than those in casual dating relationships to recognize the possible negative consequences an unplanned pregnancy and birth may have for their partner. Or, men could be reminded that their affection for their partner may in some instances obscure their ability to see beyond the idealized image of creating a child (and family) with their beloved. Messages such as these can sharpen men's understanding of the tacit and explicit collaboration that can take place among partners as men develop their sense of readiness for fatherhood.

As is commonly shown in fatherhood research, men's relationships with their fathers played a significant role in shaping our participants' views about the ideal father and the visions they had for fathering their own children. Our data showed that, when given a chance, men often linked their visions about their future experiences as fathers with their positive and negative experiences with their own fathers. Programs therefore should be designed to provide young men focused opportunities to think systematically about the connections they make between their childhood experiences and their fathering visions.

In addition to having men identify their personal visions of fathering, programs can encourage men to consider how they perceive children in general and whether they have given thought to what their own children might be like. A number of men in our study remarked that they "loved" or "really liked" children and enjoyed "playing" with them. While a few mentioned how their first-hand experiences with the everyday care of children made them question whether they were ready for fatherhood, many men had a limited understanding of the demands of full-time parenting. Thus, whenever possible, programs should provide men supervised chances to develop first-hand experience with childcare responsibilities so that they are better informed about what active father involvement entails.

Two main assumptions guiding our previous suggestions are that it is worthwhile to target young men, and it is possible to reach them prior to their involvement in an unplanned pregnancy that they may be ill-prepared to handle. While designing programs that are sensitive to the various developmental stages for teenage and young adult males is a challenging task, we found that males of varying ages are eager to talk about fatherhood and related issues. Getting men to not only understand the full significance of paternity and social fatherhood, but also make sexual and contraceptive decisions that reflect that understanding should be a critical goal for those who work with young men in schools, social service agencies, the military, prisons, and the health care arena. Based on this research we advocate programs that promote introspection, evaluation, and a temporal orientation that assists men in a "doubling of self" to examine their past and present in order to project their future. Programs may be most effective in this regard when they provide an organizational context, a structured format, and an appropriate set of concepts (e.g., fatherhood readiness, father visions, child visions) that allow men to construct and share narratives about their procreative selves in the presence of their peers.

CONCLUSION

By using the grounded theory method and in-depth interviews with a sample of young men who have not yet fathered a child, we have been able to offer fresh theoretical insights about the way men envision aspects of fatherhood. Although our sample may not be suitable for generalizing to specific groups, it permitted us to conceptualize and explore sensitizing concepts, including the two substantive dimensions to the process of envisioning fatherhood (fatherhood readiness, father visions) and the five theoretical themes (degree of collaboration, focus of attention, temporal orientation, experience, and degree of clarity). These concepts advance the social psychology of fatherhood by emphasizing aspects of prospective fatherhood and can be incorporated into other studies of fatherhood with different samples of men.

Our study serves the dual purpose of informing both theory and program development. With additional work, researchers can tease out the dimensions, phases, contexts, degrees, contingencies, types, and other theoretical codes that permit further expansion, integration, and grounding of the concepts, thus moving towards theory generation. This theoretical work can promote effective program development by attending to young men's voices, i.e., their subjective perspectives about envisioning fatherhood.

While we studied a diverse sample of young men with varied educational, economic, and ethnic backgrounds, our sample was small, and the number of men who represented any category was even smaller. In the future, we will expand and diversify our sample and examine both within and between group data, concentrating on the similarities and differences of, for example, the father visions of specific groups such as young inner city Black males, rural males, males with varying degrees of experience with sex and pregnancy, and the like. We will also augment our theoretical sampling by obtaining more data on the interrelationships of the substantive dimensions and the theoretical themes. These additional data will provide the foundation for developing and enhancing more client specific programs. In addition, the generated concepts can be useful in evaluating existing programs and, with further refinement, the conceptualization of outcome variables for intervention studies.

REFERENCES

Allen, D. A., & Doherty, W. J. (1996). The responsibilities of fatherhood as perceived by African American teenage fathers. *Families in society: The Journal of Contemporary Human Services, March*, 142–155.

Daly, K. (1993). Reshaping fatherhood: Finding the models. *Journal of Family Issues, 14*, 510–530.

Denzin, N. K. (1987). *The recovering alcoholic.* Thousand Oaks, CA: Sage.

Federal Interagency Forum on Child and Family Statistics (1998). *Nurturing fatherhood: Improving data and research on male fertility, family formation, and fatherhood.* Washington, DC.

Furstenberg, F. F., Jr. (1995). Fathering in the inner city: Paternal participation and public policy. In W. Marsiglio (Ed.), *Fatherhood: Contemporary theory, research, and social policy* (pp. 119–147). Thousand Oaks. CA: Sage.

Glaser, B. (1978). *Theoretical sensitivity.* Mill Valley, CA: Sociology Press.

Glaser, B. (1992). *Basics of grounded theory analysis.* Mill Valley, CA: Sociology Press.

Gohel, M., Diamond J. J., Chambers C. V. (1997). Attitudes toward sexual responsibility and parenting: An exploratory study of young urban males. *Family Planning Perspectives, 29*, 280–283.

Hawkins, A. J., & Dollahite, D. (1997). *Generative fathering: Beyond deficit perspectives.* Thousand Oaks, CA: Sage.

Herzog, J. M. (1982). Patterns of expectant fatherhood: A study of fathers of premature infants. In S. H. Cath, A. R. Gurwitt, & J. M. Ross (Eds.), *Father and child: Development and clinical perspectives* (pp. 301–314). Boston: Little, Brown.

Lamb, M. E. (1997). *The role of the father in child development* (3rd edition). New York: John Wiley & Sons, Inc.

LaRossa, R., & LaRossa, M. M. (1989). Babe care: Fathers vs. mothers. In B. J. Risman & P. Schwartz (Eds.). *Gender in intimate relationships: A micro-structural approach.* Belmont, CA: Wadsworth.

Levine, J. A., & Pitt, E. W (1995). *New expectations: Community strategies for responsible fatherhood.* New York: Families and Work Institute.

Lincoln, Y., & Guba, E. (1985). *Naturalistic inquiry.* Beverly Hills, CA: Sage.

Marsiglio, W. (1998). *Procreative Man.* NY: New York University Press.

Marsiglio, W. (1995). Fathers' diverse life course patterns and roles: Theory and social interventions. In W. Marsiglio (Ed.), *Fatherhood: Contemporary theory, research, and social policy* (pp. 78–101). Thousand Oaks, CA: Sage.

Marsiglio, W., Hutchinson, S., & Cohan, M. (in press). Young men's procreative identity: Becoming aware, being aware, and being responsible. *Journal of Marriage and the Family.*

May, K. A. (1980). A typology of detachment/involvement styles adopted during pregnancy by first-time fathers. *Western Journal of Nursing Research, 2,* 445–453.

Mead, G. H. (1934). *Mind, self, and society: From the standpoint of a social behaviorist.* Chicago: University of Chicago Press.

Moore, K. A., Driscoll, A. K., & Ooms, T (1997). *Not just for girls: The roles of boys and men in teen pregnancy prevention.* Washington, DC: National Campaign to Prevent Teen Pregnancy.

Sherwen, L. N. (1987). The pregnant man. In L. N. Sherwen (Ed.), *Psychosocial dimensions of the pregnant family* (pp. 157–176). New York: Springer.

Sonenstein, F. L., Stewart, K., Lindberg, D. L., Pernas, M., & Williams, S. (1997). *Involving males in preventing teen pregnancy: A guide for program planners.* The California Wellness Foundation: The Urban Institute.

Soule, B., Stanley, K., & Copans, S. (1979). Father identity. *Psychiatry, 42,* 255–263.

Strauss, A. (1987). *Qualitative analysis for social scientists.* New York: Cambridge University Press.

Zayas, L. H. (1988). Thematic features in the manifest dreams of expectant fathers. *Clinical Social Work Journal, 16,* 282–296.

SELF-STUDY QUESTIONS

Multiple Choice

1. In this study, what factor tended to cause some men to realize they were not yet ready to become fathers?
   a. parental disapproval
   b. knowing that they had not yet seen the world
   c. observing friends who had become fathers
   d. seeing teenagers who were pregnant or parenting

2. What were necessary, missing ingredients for being a "good father" for some men in the study?
   a. providing adequate shelter and food on the table
   b. religious and social skills training
   c. emotional concern and direct involvement
   d. sports participation and attendance

Essay

1. Traditionally speaking, the father has been thought of as the playful, "rough and tumble" parent with his child, while the responsibility of everyday care has been assumed by the mother. How does fatherhood readiness influence a man's ability to take on a more comprehensive fatherhood role?

2. In your opinion, what should a man know about himself and his partner before becoming a father?

EARLY/MIDDLE ADULTHOOD

"Children of Lesbian and Gay Parents: A Review of the Literature"

OVERVIEW

Sexual orientation is a topic that has "come out of the closet" in the past thirty or so years, and a growing number of children are being raised by parents who are openly homosexual. Consequently, questions have arisen about the possible impact of parental sexual orientation on children's development. These questions have been posed by opponents of homosexual rights, psychologists interested in the influence of a variety of parent variables on children's development, and gay and lesbian parents who, like other parents, are committed to providing the best environment for their children. In response, psychol-

ogists and other behavioral scientists are carrying out a growing number of studies of the development of children raised by gay and lesbian parents. In this article, the author discusses the findings of several such studies. As you read it, think about your own ideas about gay and lesbian families. Do you believe that this family structure has the same types of hopes, dreams, and goals for its children as those of a heterosexual family? How do you think our society and institutions have helped or hindered the overall well-being of the members of gay and lesbian families?

METHODOLOGY

This article reports a *literature review*. When a researcher carries out a literature review, he or she typically looks for studies that address a particular topic or set of research questions in books, scientific journals, and among papers presented at professional meetings. Literature reviews are important in lifespan

development because they summarize the implications of a large number of similar studies. Typically, literature reviews focus on the major findings and implications of a large number of studies rather than on particular methodologies.

GLOSSARY TERMS

- **Homophobia** an irrational fear of people who are homosexual
- **"Coming out"** an expression used to describe an individual's process of revealing his or her sexual orientation to others
- **Sexual orientation** while this term usually refers to a person's attraction to sexual partners, it also refers to the emotional attraction a person feels for a partner
- **Sex-role stereotyping** the assignment of what is considered by a society, culture, institution, or

individual to be appropriate behavior and/or activities for a person based on her or his gender
- **Sex-role socialization** the incorporation of culturally defined norms or appropriate behavior, goals, beliefs, and values into one's personality
- **Gender-identity** a person's sense of identity as being either male or female
- **Gender-role** an individual's roles and functions, attitudes and behaviors that are regarded by a society and its culture as being appropriately female or male

Bridget Fitzgerald

Children of Lesbian and Gay Parents: A Review of the Literature

The purpose of this paper is to review the research literature concerning the development of children with gay and lesbian parents. It begins by discussing some of the social, theoretical, and legal implications of studying this population, and critiques a number of the assumptions guiding this research. The review then proceeds to include studies on children of divorced lesbian and gay parents, as well as studies conducted on children of gay and lesbian families that are planned. The body of literature generally concludes that children with lesbian and gay parents are developing psychologically, intellectually, behaviorally, and emotionally in positive directions, and that the sexual orientation of parents is not an effective or important predictor of successful child development. The paper also includes a discussion of the limitations of these studies, provides suggestions for future research, and discusses the challenge these families pose for the meaning and definition of family. [Article copies available for a fee from The Haworth Document Delivery Service: 1-800-342-9678. E-mail address: getinfo@haworthpressinc.com <Website: http://www.haworthpressinc.com>]

Studies on children of lesbian and gay parents first started to appear in the 1970s, mostly out of a need for evidence in custody cases showing that these children were just as "normal" as kids with heterosexual parents. These studies were few in number and they began with case studies such as those by Osman (1972), Mager (1975), and Weeks, Derdeyn and Langman (1975). In the late '70s and early '80s, as more gay and lesbian parents ended their marriages and sought custody of their children, larger empirical studies began to be conducted, also in an effort to dispel myths and stereotypes concerning gays and lesbians. As these studies clearly indicated, the number of gay and lesbian parents was large and the characteristics of these families were widely diverse. It is estimated, for example, that there are between 2–6 million gay/lesbian parents who have 6–14 million children (Bozett, 1987, Editors of the Harvard Law Review, 1990, Gottman, 1989, Patterson, 1992, Pennington, 1987). The fact that such estimates range so widely results from the difficulty of establishing exact numbers for a population that is largely invisible due to homophobia and the threat of losing custody. The diversity of their families and their desire to have children is not unlike their heterosexual counterparts. Some gay/lesbian families are formed after the dissolution of a heterosexual marriage, which can result in single-parent homes or stepfamilies. Others are planned families that are formed after the individual has already "come out." This latter form is established in a variety of ways, such as through artificial insemination by a known or unknown donor, adoption, surrogacy, or foster parenting.

When discussing the results of previous studies, therefore, the above distinction is maintained, with the children of divorced lesbian/gay parents being discussed first, followed by a review of studies dealing with planned lesbian/gay families. This distinction between "divorced" and "planned" families is made because the studies themselves have generally been identified as one or the other. The importance of these categories is due mainly to the possible significance of very early family experiences on later gender and social development of children. Consequently, a common argument proceeds as follows: Children who were originally raised in heterosexual households who not only had male and female parents, but who also experienced divorce and single parenting, may then develop differently from children raised by lesbian and gay parents since birth (Golombok & Tasker, 1994). The remaining sections of the paper will address the limitations of these studies, provide suggestions for future research, and discuss the challenge these families pose for the meaning and definition of the concept family. But first, I would like to address some of the social, theoretical, and legal implications of studying children with lesbian and gay parents.

Why is it important to study this population? First of all, as mentioned above, this is a fairly large population that helps to represent the wide diversity of current family forms. The large numbers and diversity of these families alone should warrant further study so that we may better understand families in general. These families are also intricately connected to our society as a whole, both resisting the dominant culture that takes a negative view of lesbians and gays. Such adverse views are directed especially at the desire of gays and lesbians to become parents and contribute to the ongoing transformation of these families. As Laura Benkov writes:

> The process of invention interweaves social and personal change. As lesbians and gay men create new family forms, they work within the set of limits and possibilities of the cultural context. In this process, they also feed back into the culture, transforming the set of constraints and possibilities therein. (1994:13)

Another important issue raised by research on gay and lesbian parenting relates to the theoretical implications of these studies in the sense of potentially posing a challenge to psychological theories of child development. Questions are raised about the importance of having parents of each sex in order for normal development to occur. As Patterson (1997) indicates, theories of psychological development, such as psychoanalytic and social learning, emphasize the importance of having both a mother and a father for healthy social development. Consequently, these theories predict a negative outcome for children who are not raised in such an environment. "An important theoretical question thus concerns the extent to which such predictions are sustained by results of research on children of gay and/or lesbian parents" (p. 238).

These families also contest the role of the state and legal institutions in regulating our personal relationships. How much influence should the state and the judiciary have in defining what a family is or should be? Should we follow former President George Bush's declaration that "homosexuals raising children is not normal" (quoted in Benkov, 1994)? These studies, then, which for the most part are assessing the "normality" of these children, have important ramifications in custody cases and in pub-

lic policy debates around adoption and foster parenting. For example, there are still five states that have *per se* precedents that guide all lesbian and gay custody rulings (Benkov, 1994). This precedent establishes an irrebuttable presumption that homosexuality in and of itself constitutes unfitness. A 1988 Tennessee appellate court case expressed its opinion that a parent's homosexuality will adversely affect the morality of the child. "Homosexuality has been considered contrary to the morality of man for well over two thousand years. It has been and is considered to be an unnatural, immoral act" (quoted in Dooley 1990:414). Under this approach, the courts' presumptions preempt the need for serious and accurate appraisal of the parents' capabilities and of the needs of the child. As Theodore Stein (1996:445) writes, "The moral arguments offered to justify a per se rule are little more than an effort to cloak prejudice and to legitimize discrimination. Such decision making substitutes abstract references to morality for sound legal reasoning."

Increasingly most jurisdictions, in turn, do follow the "best interests of the child" standard, utilizing a nexus approach. The nexus approach is a step forward in that it does away with presumptions of the gay parents' unfitness, but continues to state that custody can be denied if a parent's homosexuality can be proven to adversely affect the child. Thus it retains the dubious assumption that homosexuality may be harmful to children (Dooley, 1990; Patterson & Redding, 1996).

During most custody cases, the courts often are concerned with several issues surrounding the social and psychological development of children being raised by gay or lesbian parents. A few of these issues include a concern that the parent's homosexuality will adversely affect the child's gender and emotional development; a likelihood of social stigma or peer rejection due to parental homosexuality; and a fear that there is an increased likelihood for the child to become homosexual. The validity of these concerns will be addressed in the following two sections which first look at studies of children with divorced lesbian or gay parents and examine those families in which gays or lesbians planned and conceived children after having come out.

An important caveat is necessary that is concerned with my feelings about the importance of critically addressing the assumptions that guide the research and language used by most of the following studies. These comments pertain to the notion that certain gender identity traits exist that are deemed 'appropriate' or 'normal' for both males and females. This notion is problematic through its normalizing tone that reinforces hegemonic gender roles, fails to allow for differences, and refrains from challenging the existing oppressive gender order. Although I do believe that these studies are contributing in a positive way to debunking myths and stereotypes about gay parents and their children, they are acquiescing to hegemonic ideas of masculinity and femininity. The promotion of gender hegemony is accomplished by judging 'appropriate' child development in terms of such outcomes as girls wearing dresses and being emotionally supportive, and boys playing with trucks and displaying independent, aggressive behavior. Sandra Pollack (1987:321) writes,

> A number of the comparison studies focus on the sex roles of children. Again, my reservation is the underlying assumption that there are appropriate sex roles for boys and girls. What these studies really examine is whether the children conform to acceptable societal norms. Yet this very assumption of appropriate roles is what feminists are committed to eliminating...While we might use these studies as a courtroom tactic because the children 'do just fine,' we must remain aware of the acceptance of sex-role stereotyping on which such an argument is based.

This reinforcement of oppressive, hierarchical, socially constructed gender identities is highly constraining and detrimental to both men and women. Assumptions of this kind denigrate those who do not conform to the dominant gender order, which contributes to limited self-expression and to ongoing prejudice and discrimination. A more constructive approach is to discuss children's development in terms of how successful they are in areas of self-management, adjustment, self-esteem, and how well they are equipped to maneuver through life, rather than if they exhibit traditional, 'normal' gender-role behavior.

The related question as to whether or not the children of homosexuals are more likely to be gay themselves is immensely problematic for obvious reasons in the sense that to be gay or lesbian is assumed to be a negative, unwelcome outcome. This position tends to reinforce homophobia, even if unintentionally. Nancy Polikoff (1987:326) emphasizes this when discussing lesbian mothers:

> When we constantly assert in the public arena that we will raise our children to be heterosexual, and that we will protect them from the manifestations of our sexuality...we essentially concede it is preferable to be heterosexual, thereby foreclosing an assertion of pride and of the positive value in homosexuality.

Thus I urge the reader to keep these comments in mind as they read through the following studies.

CHILDREN OF DIVORCED LESBIAN AND GAY PARENTS

Gender Development

When discussing issues of traditional gender development, a distinction is usually made between gender identity, gender-role behavior, and sexual orientation. Gender identity concerns a person's self-identification as male or female. Gender-role includes behaviors and attitudes that are regarded by a particular culture as appropriately male or female. Sexual orientation refers to a person's attraction to sexual partners as homosexual, heterosexual, or bisexual (Golombok & Tasker, 1994).

Of the investigators who have examined the gender identity of children with lesbian mothers, none have found any evidence of gender identity confusion. For example, Green (1978), using protective measures such as toy, game, clothing and peer group preferences, found that 36 out of 37 children were developing along typical lines for their sex. Similarly, Kirkpatrick, Smith, and Roy (1981) found no indication of differences in gender identity between a group of children being raised by lesbian mothers and a group being brought up by single heterosexual mothers. These researchers evaluated the sex of first-drawn figure, the history of play preferences, and behavior exhibited in the playroom, all of which resulted in the conclusion that there were no identifiable differences between the two groups. Green, Mandel, Hotvedt, Gray, and Smith (1986) also conducted a study comparing the two different types of single-parent households, reporting that their data did not support the fear that lesbian mothers would produce gender identity conflict in their children. Golombok, Spencer and Rutter (1983), using systematic standardized interviews with 37 children and their lesbian mothers, and 38 children and their heterosexual mothers, along with parent and teacher questionnaires, found no significant differences between the psychosexual and gender identity development of the two groups. Other studies also have come to the same conclusion that a parent's sexual orientation does not detrimentally affect or confuse their children's formation of what is deemed by dominant Western medical-scientific discourses to be an appropriate gender identity (Gottman, 1989; Hotvedt & Mandel, 1982; Schwartz, 1986).

The above studies also conducted research on gender-role behaviors that resulted in similar findings. Specifically, the general result was that no significant difficulties existed for children of homosexual parents to display what is considered suitable gender behaviors and attitudes (Golombok et al.,

1983; Gottman, 1989; Green, 1978; Green et al., 1986; Hotvedt & Mandel, 1982; Kirkpatrick et al., 1981; Schwartz, 1986). Moreover, both Kweskin and Cook (1982) and Hoeffer (1981) compared the sex-role behaviors of children of lesbians and children of heterosexual single mothers, with the conclusion being that the two groups exhibited no significant differences. Hoeffer stated that the most notable thing about her findings was not the differences, but the similarities between the two groups in their acquisition of sex-role behavior. Moreover, regardless what the mother's sexual orientation was, both boys and girls preferred toys that were traditionally associated with their gender.

The third dimension of gender development, sexual orientation, has also received empirical investigation to examine if a greater instance of homosexuality exists among children being raised by homosexual parents. All of the studies conducted thus far, with one exception (Cameron & Cameron, 1996), indicate that gay and lesbian parents are no more likely to produce gay and lesbian children than their heterosexual counterparts. A study conducted by Bailey, Bobrow, Wolfe, and Mikach (1995) examined 55 gay or bisexual fathers' reports of their 82 sons' sexual orientations. Results indicated that 90% of these sons were heterosexual, suggesting that having a gay father does not substantially increase the likelihood of sons becoming gay adults. Furthermore, sexual orientation was not a positive correlate of the amount of time that sons lived with their fathers, again suggesting that environmental transmission of homosexuality cannot be corroborated in this sample.

Huggins (1989) studied 36 children who ranged in age from 13 to 19 years of age. Half of the children had lesbian mothers and half had heterosexual mothers. The major finding was that only one of these adolescents self-identified as homosexual and this particular youth was the child of one of the heterosexual mothers.

Golombok and Tasker (1996) conducted one of the few longitudinal studies to investigate the impact on children raised by lesbian mothers. The data were collected in 1977 from 25 children of lesbian mothers and a control group of 21 children of heterosexual single mothers with follow-up data collected in 1992. The average age of the children at the two times of data collection were 9.5 and 23.5 years of age, respectively. The researchers used standardized interviews to obtain data on sexual orientation, which resulted in the finding that a substantial majority of children who grew up in lesbian families self-identified as being heterosexual. However, some interesting additional findings were evident:

Although no significant difference was found between the proportions of young adults from lesbian and heterosexual families who reported feelings of attraction toward someone of the same gender, those who had grown up in a lesbian family were more likely to consider the possibility of having lesbian or gay relationships...However, the commonly held assumption that children brought up by lesbian mothers will themselves grow up to be lesbian or gay is not supported by the findings of the study; the majority identified as heterosexual in adulthood. (p. 8)

Saffron (1996) also indicates that the children of lesbian and gay parents whom she interviewed had a more open and accepting attitude toward diverse sexual identities.

Parents who are comfortable with their homosexual identity are likely to impart a liberal understanding of sexuality to their children...Some [of the children] expressed uneasiness with labels and the limits they impose on people's understanding of each other...Many spoke of their willingness to question their own sexuality. (p. 195)

Several other studies have arrived at the same conclusion as the above studies. *Specifically, the incidence of homosexuality is no higher if one is raised by a gay or lesbian parent, than if one is raised by a heterosexual parent* (Golombok et al., 1983; Gottman, 1989; Green, 1978; Green et al., 1986; Miller, 1979; Schwartz, 1986).

The fact that a vast majority of homosexuals had heterosexual parents is an additional indication that sexual orientation is not learned from the parent, nor a result of having only one male or one female as primary caregivers. As Marciano (1985:300) writes:

The absence of consistent same-sex and opposite-sex models does not produce gay children. Those in widow-headed households, homes of divorce or desertion, do not have consistent models and there is little talk of their gay vulnerabilities.

Moreover, concern over the issue of whether or not children of gays or lesbians are more likely to become gay or lesbian and tendencies to deny custody based solely on this issue, carry with them implicit moral judgements that gay children are less desirable than heterosexual ones.

In conclusion, all of the studies cited above, with one exception, indicate that these children of lesbian and gay parents do not exhibit more frequent nonconventional gender-role behaviors than do their counterparts being raised by heterosexual parents. Moreover, these children usually develop what is considered to be, by the dominant and often repressive, Western medical/social-scientific community, an appropriate psychosexual identity and a typical heterosexual orientation.

Emotional Well-Being and the Development of Self-Esteem

The extant research on children's emotional and personal development also reveals that concerns over their development being in some way abnormal is not substantiated. No significant differences were found between children of lesbian and gay parents and children of heterosexual parents in reference to the development of self-concept, behavioral problems, intelligence, and psychiatric evaluations.

Huggins (1989) conducted a study of 36 adolescent children who were equally divided into two groups according to their mothers' sexual orientation and then were further divided by sex within each group. She administered the SEI (Coopersmith Self-Esteem Inventory) to assess each group's self-esteem. Her findings indicated that there were no significant statistical differences between the SEI scores of the two main groups, with daughters of heterosexual mothers having the highest mean score, and sons of heterosexual mothers having the lowest. In addition, she found that children of both lesbian and heterosexual mothers had higher scores if their mother was living with a lover or was remarried. "These data, therefore, seem to bring into question the validity of denying child custody to a lesbian mother" simply because she is living with her female partner.

Tasker and Golombok (1995), in their longitudinal study concerning the sexual orientation of children in lesbian families, found that young adults from these families were generally positive about their relationships with their mother, father, and mother's partner. Moreover, children with lesbian mothers had been able to establish closer relationships with their mother's partner than children from heterosexual households had with their mother's male partner. This study also reported that young adults from lesbian versus heterosexual households did not differ in their likelihood of experiencing anxiety or depression. Other investigators of children with lesbian and gay parents also have concluded that the healthy emotional and self-concept development of children occurs normally and does not differ significantly from that which occurs with heterosexual parents (Golombok et al., 1983; Gottman, 1989; Green et al., 1986; Puryear, 1983; Smith, 1982).

Social Development

The last issue of this section addresses concerns frequently expressed over children's social development, relationships with peers, and the potential for exposure to feelings of being stigmatized. In several studies the majority of children of gay and lesbian parents demonstrated evidence of positive peer relationships and social development, and reported feeling popular both in their neighborhoods and in schools (Golombok et al., 1983; Green et al., 1986; Hotvedt & Mandel, 1982; Schwartz, 1986). Tasker and Golombok (1995) also assessed their sample for recollections of being teased or bullied by their peers, with results indicating that children from lesbian families were no more likely to experience these consequences than were their heterosexual counterparts. In contrast, children from lesbian families were more likely to remember peer group teasing about their own sexuality, but not differ from heterosexual counterparts on the proportion who had experienced peer stigma due to their family backgrounds or mothers' lifestyles. Four studies have reported, in turn, that the children from lesbian homes often were affected by the perceived need for secrecy where custody was a concern. Moreover, these children also reported being affected by feelings that their parents' homosexuality must be kept secret due to being afraid of teasing and name-calling by peers (Afzal Javaid, 1993; Bozett, 1987; Lewis, 1992; Paul, 1987). These findings suggest, of course, that the real problem is not with the parent's sexual orientation, but instead with the legal system's and society's prejudices.

Schulenberg (1985), in a questionnaire distributed to several children under age 12, asked about whether or not they had experienced any peer stigma due to their parent's homosexuality. She noted that, of those children who indicated that other people knew their parent was gay, only one child reported being harassed. As these studies indicate, compared to other kids, children of lesbian and gay parents are not necessarily being stigmatized disproportionately simply because of their particular family form. Moreover, as Dooley (1990) indicates, courts will deny custody by relying on the presumption that these children will, at some point, experience prejudice and stigmatization. As such, these decisions are based not on actual incidences of harassment, but only on presumptions, that the above studies indicate do not happen on a regular basis. "Using potential stigmatization of the child as a reason for denying custody to the gay parent, courts are giving allegiance to societal prejudices, which is disallowed under equal protection" (1990:418). Thus, courts are actually reinforcing the stigmas that they find so damaging in the first place.

In summary, the studies to date provide no empirical evidence that the children of lesbian and gay parents are 'different' from other kids. Children reared in homosexual households do not have problems with their conventional gender development, emotional and social development, nor in their relationships with peers as a result of their parent's homosexuality. These studies suggest that the sexual orientation of parents is not a meaningful predictor of successful child development.

PLANNED LESBIAN AND GAY FAMILIES

A growing trend for both lesbians and gays is to choose to become parents after coming out. Fostered by donor insemination and adoption, the larger number of lesbians who have chosen motherhood since the 1980s has been referred to as a "lesbian baby boom" (Clunis & Green, 1995; McCandlish, 1987; Ratkin, 1990; Weston, 1991). Because this is a fairly recent phenomenon, much less research has been conducted on planned families than on families headed by divorced lesbian and gay parents. The few studies that have been conducted all conclude that children in these families are developing in a positive manner.

Steckel (1985) compared the process of separation-individuation among preschool children, of which 11 were born to lesbian couples and 11 were born to heterosexual couples. She utilized structured parent interviews, parent and teacher Q sorts, as well as a Structured Doll Technique in order to assess independence, ego functions, and object relations of these children. She found much similarity in the children's development within both groups, with neither family experience revealing greater psychopathology or difficulties in separation-individuation. She also reported, however, that differences existed in the experiences of separation, with children of heterosexuals having a more aggressively tinged separation. Specifically, these children viewed themselves as more aggressive and were correspondingly characterized by both parents and teachers as more assertive, bossy, domineering, and negativistic. In contrast, she describes the children of lesbian mothers as possessing a more lovable self-image, with parents and teachers describing these children as more affectionate, responsive, and protective of younger children. She concluded that the presence of a female co-parent, rather than a father, does not negatively affect a child's process of intrapsychic separation, but that it does contribute to a qualitatively different separation experience.

Another study by McCandlish (1987) provided a qualitative research project consisting of comprehensive family interviews with five lesbian couples who were raising seven children born to them through donor insemination. These preschool children formed secure attachments to both mothers, showed no psychological or behavioral difficulties,

and displayed what is considered to be conventional gender identities.

More recently Patterson (1994) conducted a study on children between the ages of 4 and 9 years old, who were born to or adopted by lesbian mothers, in order to assess their psychosocial development. Comparing their social competence, behavior adjustment, and sexual identity with available standardized norms, she found that these children scored within normal ranges. These children did differ from youngsters of heterosexual parents, however, by reporting more negative reactions to stress (such as anger and fear), while at the same time reporting a greater sense of well-being (such as joy and contentment) about themselves. Patterson offers two possible interpretations of these results. The first is that children of lesbian mothers actually experience more stress in their daily lives than do other children. Patterson (1994: 169–170) notes:

> As a result of heterosexist, homophobic, and/or other aspects of their environment, children with lesbian mothers may actually encounter more stressful events and conditions than do children with heterosexual mothers…their more frequent reports of emotional responses to such stress might simply reflect the more stressful nature of their experience.

A second interpretation, in turn, is that these children, regardless of actual stress levels, may be more willing to acknowledge and report a variety of strong emotional experiences, both negative and positive. This finding does not replicate Steckel's (1985) results which indicated that children of lesbian mothers see themselves as less aggressive and more sociable than children of heterosexual parents. Despite these differences, Patterson's main conclusion is that the children of the lesbian baby boom in this sample had experienced an ordinary process of psychosocial development.

An additional study found many similarities between children raised by lesbian couples who had conceived through donor insemination and a matched sample of children from two-parent heterosexual families (Flaks, Ficher, Masterpasqua, & Joseph, 1995). Children's cognitive functioning and behavioral adjustment were assessed for 30 children, divided equally between the two groups. Results for all the hypotheses tested failed to reveal statistically significant main effects for parental sexual orientation, with 17 of the 24 comparisons between the two groups actually suggesting tendencies that favored the children of lesbian parents.

Although few in number, these studies nevertheless demonstrate consistent results which indicate that children of lesbian mothers are developing psychologically, intellectually, behaviorally, and emotionally in positive directions. As Flacks et al. (1995) indicate, the implications of this research suggest that, for healthy child development to occur, neither father presence nor parental heterosexuality are critical. Moreover, as Pollack (1987) emphasizes, an important thing to keep in mind is the intention of these studies to demonstrate that few differences exist between homosexual and straight families. This demonstrates, in turn, that

> neither lesbians nor their children have pathological problems that are very different from heterosexual single mothers and their young. My concern centers on the underlying assumption that the lesbian mother should be judged on how well she compares to the heterosexual. (p. 320)

Dolores Maggiore (1992:xxv) continues this criticism by stating that comparison studies tend to

> [hold] up the model of heterosexual mothers, their mothering, and their families and, in so doing, casts the lesbian and her family in second-class status, accepting the 'sanctity' of the heterosexual model and the patriarchal family. Thus, one does nothing to change the system, validate the lesbian family, or affirm the right of a lesbian to raise her family as she wishes.

LIMITATIONS OF STUDIES AND SUGGESTIONS FOR FUTURE RESEARCH

Many of these studies suffer from similar limitations and weaknesses, with the main obstacle being the difficulty in acquiring representative, random samples on a virtually invisible population. Many lesbian and gay parents are not open about their sexual orientation due to real fears of discrimination, homophobia, and threats of losing custody of their children. Those who do participate in this type of research are usually relatively open about their homosexuality and, therefore, may bias the research towards a particular group of gay and lesbian parents (Bozett, 1987; Victor & Fish, 1995).

Because of the inevitable use of convenience samples, sample sizes are usually very small and the majority of research participants end up looking quite homogeneous—e.g., white, middle-class, urban, and well-educated. Another pattern is the wide discrepancy between the number of studies conducted with children of gay fathers and those with lesbian mothers. The few studies of children with gay fathers are most likely due to maternal custody patterns, which reflect the fact that fathers, gay or nongay, are less likely to be custodial parents (Bozett, 1987).

Another potential factor of importance is the possibility of social desirability bias when research subjects respond in ways that present themselves and their families in the most desirable light possible. Such a phenomenon does seem possible due to the desire of this population to offset and reverse negative images and discrimination. Consequently, the findings of these studies may be patterned by self-presentation bias (Gartrell, Hamilton, Banks, Mosbacher, Reed, Sparks, & Bishop, 1996; Lott-Whitehead, & Tully, 1992; Tasker & Golombok, 1995; Turner, Scadden, & Harris, 1990).

In summary, faced with these frequent methodological difficulties, the generalizability of these studies is limited and overall, they can best be described as descriptive and suggestive, rather than conclusive. As Patterson and Redding (1996) indicate, since the problem of obtaining representative, random samples on this population will likely remain an issue, "it is not the results obtained from any one specific sample but the accumulation of findings from many different samples that will be most meaningful" (p. 44).

Keeping this in mind, research is needed in which larger sample sizes are acquired whenever feasible and where multiple methodologies are utilized. Longitudinal studies are needed "which seek to assess not only child adjustment over time, but also the family processes, relationships, and interactions to which child adjustment may be linked. Family processes, in turn, should be viewed in the context of surrounding ecological conditions of family life" (Patterson, 1992, 1039). Pollack makes a similar suggestion stating that "studies that look at the actual lives of [these] children may be more useful than those focusing on sex-role identities" (1987:322). There is additional need for intergenerational research involving reports and interviews with children of various ages and adults. Greater diversity is needed in future studies, both in terms of demographic characteristics and in various family forms such as adoptive and foster parenting, stepfamilies, planned lesbian families, and gay families with co-parents.

Another important area of research is needed to examine how homophobia affects children in lesbian and gay families, or, more specifically, how the young and their families cope with our heterosexist, homophobic society. As Allen and Demo (1995) write, "detailed investigations of lesbian and gay families will help family researchers shed new light on such little-understood phenomena as the…ability of families to cope with stigma while forging permanent, enduring bonds without societal support" (p. 124). Finally, sociology's minimal contribution to the study of families of gays and lesbians, as pointed out by Allen and Demo's review article, needs to be remedied not only in terms of quantity, but quality as well.

> *We concur with other commentators that heterosexism underlies the limited information accumulated to date about lesbian and gay families and the impact of sexual orientation on family life…extant sociological work treats homosexuality as deviant, focuses on sexual behavior and attitudes, and ignores the family context and family relations of lesbians and gay men…This distortion… is not harmless or value-free. Our silence as family researchers on this issue contributes to a general climate of intolerance and to maintenance of the status quo. (1995:121–124)*

CONCLUSION

At the beginning of this paper, I discussed some of the possible theoretical implications of research on children of lesbian and gay parents and specifically on the effect it may have on psychoanalytic and social learning theories of child development. As Patterson (1997) wrote, "An important theoretical question thus concerns the extent to which such [negative] predictions are sustained by results of research on children of lesbian and/or gay parents" (p. 238).

If, as I have stated throughout this review, the presence of a heterosexual parent of each gender is not crucial to healthy child development, then the traditional psychoanalytic and social learning theories necessarily come into question. I do not mean to suggest that these theories are now somehow irrelevant, but it does seem important that they adapt to the findings of these studies on nontraditional families. As Flaks et al. (1995) state, "it would appear that theories of child development will have to take into account the preeminence of process variables over structural ones in predicting the most desirable family environment for raising children" (p. 113). However, it is important to determine which types of structural variables would be considered less relevant than process variables to examine (e.g., number, gender, or sexual orientation of parent(s) and the legal and/or biological relationships between parent and child), and which structural variables may still be quite pertinent (such as race, ethnicity, and class). Process and form should not necessarily be considered as opposites, but as variables that often influence each other. In short, a more holistic approach that takes both issues into account may be the most constructive.

These results also have important legal implications for gays and lesbians and their families. Because these studies consistently indicate that parental homosexuality is not detrimental to children's

healthy growth and development, the legal community must not support policies of outright denial of rights to such things as adoption, foster parenting, reproductive technology, or retention of custody, simply on the basis of sexual orientation. Furthermore, planned lesbian and gay families should also be afforded the same legal protections and benefits as heterosexual families. For example, the non-biological parent or the second same-sex parent in an adoption, should be granted full parental status, with all the rights and responsibilities therein (Editors of the *Harvard Law Review,* 1990; Flacks et al., 1995; Patterson, 1994).

More recently, significant progress was made regarding second parent adoptions when a gay couple both became the legal parents of a boy they had been foster parenting. This groundbreaking legal case occurred in New Jersey, which became the first state to allow homosexual couples the right to adopt children on an equal basis with heterosexual married couples. Hopefully, in the future a parent's sexual orientation or preference will no longer be considered an important factor bearing on adoption and parents' sexual orientation will not be addressed in discussions of custody. But until that time, it is important that more research be conducted which addresses the limitations noted in the studies reviewed in order to provide more accurate information and to dispel existing myths and stereotypes regarding parenting in gay and lesbian families.

The theoretical and legal implications generated by studying nontraditional families raises an important question and challenges to family researchers and to the society as a whole—What is a "family" and how should it be defined? How do the current dominant definitions affect children in these nontraditional families?

The formation of openly gay- and lesbian-headed families demonstrates that there are many unique family forms which challenge the traditional portrait of who parents are and what families look like (Clunis & Green, 1995). Gay and lesbian families challenge the traditional model by "raising fundamental questions about the relation between gender and parenting, the significance of biological versus social connections, and the role of the state in family life" (Benkov, 1994:6). These families point us toward concentrating on the quality of relationships within a family, rather than on how the household is structured. Lesbian and gay families dispute one of the central notions of family, namely the obligatory and strict linking of biological kinship with who constitutes being included in a definition of family. In many cases membership in lesbian and gay families is not primarily based on blood relationships or necessarily on legal ties, but on a collective commitment to sharing, loving and taking care of one another (Clunis & Green, 1995; Saffron, 1996). As Laura Benkov (1994:6–7) writes:

> I have serious trouble with rhetoric that idealizes traditional "family values." When people frame the nuclear family as morally superior, they focus on the shape of families (how many parents? Of what gender composition?) rather than on the quality of the relationships both within and beyond the family. At the same time, idealizing the traditional family obscures the violence and gender inequity often hidden behind closed doors. Perhaps most important, the emphasis on "family values" diverts attention from societal problems such as poverty and racism by locating all difficulties in "the breakdown of the family." (pp. 6–7)

In conclusion, I feel it is important to note that several of these studies have also indicated that significant positive outcomes may result from growing up with a gay or lesbian parent. For example, a more open climate usually exists in these families for discussing issues relating to sexuality and for exposure to new and diverse points of view that allow for varied role models for children. Greater potential also exists for more egalitarian family relationships to develop that are not based on strict, often repressive definitions of gender roles (Clunis & Green, 1995; Lewis, 1992; Lott-Whitehead & Tully, 1992; Rafkin, 1990).

Dorothy Riddle (1978) writes,

> Rather than posing a menace to children, gays may actually facilitate important developmental learning…children have the possibility of learning that it is possible to resist traditional sex-role socialization…children become exposed to the concept of cultural and individual diversity as positive rather than threatening. (as quoted in Pollack. 1987: 322)

Many of these children can take advantage of being a part of a nontraditional family that teaches increased empathy, tolerance for others, and a healthy respect for all kinds of difference. Miller (1992) suggests that children from these families are more socially responsible because they become aware of and are concerned with inequality and prejudice not only with respect to sexual orientation, but also in terms of gender, race, and class. Saffron (1990) also makes an important point:

> Children are growing up in a changing society, where there are few certainties and no blue-prints for living. In this society, at this time in history, there is a wealth of sexual identities, cultures, lifestyles, types of families and values. The most important lesson for our children is to teach them to value diversity, to be empathic with people who are oppressed and not to be afraid of difference… (p. 192)…parents teach these values by the way they live their lives. If they are comfortable with their sexuality, they model pride and self-acceptance. If they know a variety of people and types of families, they teach children to value diversity and to understand that there are many routes to happiness and self-fulfillment. (p. 179)

Finally, what the research suggests is that gay and lesbian parents are completely capable of providing a positive home environment in which to raise children. A parent's sexual preferences do not matter nearly as much as helping and encouraging children to become self-reliant and self-respecting adults, and providing surroundings in which love, respect, and emotional support predominate.

REFERENCES

Afzal Javaid, G. (1993). The children of homosexual and heterosexual single mothers. *Child Psychiatry and Human Development, 23,* 4, 235–248.

Allen, K. & Demo, D. (1995). The families of lesbians and gay men: A new frontier in family research. *Journal of Marriage and the Family, 57,* 111–127.

Bailey, J. M., Bobrow, D., Wolfe, M., & Mikach, S. (1995). Sexual orientation of adult sons of gay fathers. *Developmental Psychology, 31,* 1, 124–129.

Benkov, L. (1994). *Reinventing the family.* New York: Crown Publishers.

Bozett, Frank W. (1987). *Gay and lesbian parents.* New York: Praeger Publishers.

Cameron, P. & Cameron, K. (1996). Homosexual parents. *Adolescence, 31,* 757–776.

Clunis, D. M. & Green, G. D. (1995). *The lesbian parenting book: A guide to creating families and raising children.* Seattle: Seal Press.

Dooley, D. (1990). Immoral because they're bad, bad because they're wrong: Sexual orientation and presumptions of parental unfitness in custody disputes. *Case Western Law Review, 26,* 395–424.

Editors of the *Harvard Law Review.* (1990). *Sexual orientation and the law.* Cambridge: Harvard University Press.

Flaks, D., Ficher, I., Masterpasqua, F., & Joseph, G. (1995). Lesbians choosing motherhood: A comparative study of lesbian and heterosexual parents and their children. *Developmental Psychology, 31,* 1, 105–114.

Gartrell, N., Hamilton, J., Banks, A., Mosbacher, D., Reed, N., Sparks, C., & Bishop, H. (1996). The national lesbian family study: 1. Interviews with prospective mothers. *American Journal of Orthopsychiatry, 66,* 2, 272–281.

Golombok, S., Spencer, A., & Rutter, M. (1983). Children in lesbian and single-parent households: Psychosexual and psychiatric appraisal. *Journal of Child Psychology and Psychiatry, 24,* 4, 551–572.

Golombok, S. & Tasker, F. (1994). Children in lesbian and gay families: Theories and evidence. In J. Bancroft (Ed.), *Annual Review of Sex Research, Volume 5.* Mount Vernon, Iowa: The Society for the Scientific Study of Sexuality.

Golombok, S. & Tasker, F. (1996). Do parents influence the sexual orientation of their children? Findings from a longitudinal study of lesbian families. *Developmental Psychology, 32* (1), 3–11.

Gottman, J. (1989). Children of gay and lesbian parents. *Marriage & Family Review,* 14 (3–4), 177–196.

Green, R. (1978). Sexual identity of 37 children raised by homosexual or transsexual parents. *American Journal of Psychiatry,* 135(6), 692–697.

Green, R., Mandel, J., Hotvedt, M., Gray, J., & Smith, L. (1986). Lesbian mothers and their children: A comparison with solo parent heterosexual mothers and their children. *Archives of Sexual Behavior, 15, 2,* 167–184.

Hoeffer, B. (1981). Children's acquisition of sex-role behavior in lesbian-mother families. *American Journal of Orthopsychiatry, 51, 3,* 536–544.

Hotvedt, M. & Mandel, J. (1982). Children of Lesbian Mothers. In W. Paul, J. Weinrich, J. Gonsiorek, & M. Hotvedt (Eds.), *Homosexuality: Social, psychological, and biological issues* (pp. 275–285). Beverly Hills: Sage Publications.

Huggins, S. (1989). A comparative study of self-esteem of adolescent children of divorced lesbian mothers and divorced heterosexual mothers. *Marriage & Family Review, 18,* 1–2, 123–135.

Kirkpatrick, M., Smith, C. & Roy, R. (1981). Lesbian mothers and their children: A comparative survey. *American Journal of Orthopsychiatry, 51, 3, 545–551.*

Kweskin, S. & Cook, A. (1982). Heterosexual and homosexual mothers' self-described sex-role behavior and ideal sex-role behavior in children. *Sex Roles, 8,* 967–975.

Lewis, K. (1992). Children of lesbians: Their point of view. In D. Maggiore (Ed.), *Lesbians and child custody: A casebook.* New York: Garland Publishing, Inc.

Lott-Whitehead, L. & Tully, C. (1993). The family lives of lesbian mothers. *Smith College Studies in Social Work, 63,* 265–280.

Mager, D. (1975). Faggot father. In K. Jay & A. Young (Eds.), *After you're out.* New York: Links Books.

Maggiore, D. (1992). Introduction. In D. Maggiore (Ed.), *Lesbians and child custody: A casebook.* New York: Garland Publishing, Inc.

Marciano, T. D. (1985). Homosexual marriage and parenthood should not be allowed. In H. Feldman & M. Feldman (Eds.), *Current controversies in marriage and family.* Beverly Hills: Sage Publications.

McCandlish, B. (1987). Against all odds: Lesbian mother family dynamics. In F. Bozett (Ed.), *Gay and lesbian parents* (pp. 23–38), New York: Praeger Publishers.

Miller, B. (1979). Gay fathers and their children. *Family Coordinator, 28,* 544–552.

Miller, N. (1992). *Single parents by choice: A growing trend in family life.* New York: Insight Books.

Osman, S. (1972). My stepfather is a she. *Family Process, 11,* 209–218.

Patterson, C. (1992). Children of lesbian and gay parents. *Child Development, 63,* 1025–1042.

Patterson, C. (1994). Children of the lesbian baby boom: Behavioral adjustment, self-concepts, and sex role identity. In B. Greene, & G. Herek (Eds.), *Lesbian and gay psychology: Theory, research, and clinical applications* (pp. 156–175), Thousand Oaks, CA: Sage Publications.

Patterson, C. (1997). Children of lesbian and gay parents. In T. Ollendick & R. Prinz (Eds.), *Advances in clinical child psychology, Volume 19.* New York: Plenum Press.

Patterson, C. & Redding, R. (1996). Lesbian and gay families with children: Implications of social science research for policy. *Journal of Social Issues, 52,* 3, 29–50.

Paul, J. (1987). Growing up with a gay, lesbian, or bisexual parent: An exploratory study of experiences and perceptions (unpublished doctoral dissertation, University of California, Berkeley). *Dissertation Abstracts International-A, 47/07,* 2756.

Pennington, S. (1987). Children of lesbian mothers. In F. W. Bozett (Ed.), *Gay and lesbian parents.* New York: Praeger Publishers.

Polikoff, N. (1987). Lesbian mothers, lesbian families: Legal obstacles, legal challenges. In S. Pollack & J. Vaughn (Eds.), *Politics of the heart: A lesbian parenting anthology.* Ithaca, NY: Firebrand Books.

Pollack, S. (1987). Lesbian mothers: A lesbian-feminist perspective on research. In S. Pollack & J. Vaughn (Eds.), *Politics of the heart: A lesbian parenting anthology.* Ithaca, NY: Firebrand Books.

Puryear, D. (1983). Familial experiences: A comparison between the children of lesbian mothers and the children of heterosexual mothers (unpublished doctoral dissertation, California School of Professional Psychology, Berkeley). *Dissertation Abstracts International-B, 44/12,* 3941.

Rafkin, L. (1990). *Different mothers: Sons and daughters of lesbians talk about their lives.* Pittsburgh: Cleis Press.

Saffron, L. (1990). *What about the children?: Sons and daughters of lesbian and gay parents talk about their lives.* New York: Cassell.

Schulenberg, J. (1985). *Gay Parenting.* New York: Doubleday.

Schwartz, J. (1986). An exploration of personality traits in daughters of lesbian mothers. (unpublished doctoral dissertation, California School of Professional Psychology, San Diego). *Dissertation Abstracts International-B, 47/02,* 805.

Smith, K. V. R. (1982). Children raised by lesbian mothers (unpublished doctoral dissertation, University of California, Los Angeles). *Dissertation Abstracts International-B, 42/08,* 3444.

Steckel, A. (1985). Separation-individuation in children of lesbian and heterosexual couples (unpublished doctoral dissertation, The Wright Institute). *Dissertation Abstracts International-B, 46/03,* 982.

Stein, T. (1996). Child custody and visitation: The rights of lesbian and gay parents. *Social Service Review, 70,* 3, 435–450.

Tasker, F. & Golombok, S. (1995). Adults raised as children in lesbian families. *American Journal of Orthopsychiatry, 65,* 2, 203–215.

Turner, P., Scadden, L., & Harris, M. (1990). Parenting in gay and lesbian families. *Journal of Gay and Lesbian Psychotherapy, 1,* 3, 55–66.

Victor, S. & Fish, M. (1995). Lesbian mothers and their children: A review for school psychologists. *School Psychology Review, 24,* 3, 456–479.

Weeks, R. B., Derdeyn, A.P., & Langman, M. (1975). Two cases of children of homosexuals. *Child Psychiatry and Human Development, 6,* 26–32.

Weston, K. (1991). *Families we choose: Lesbians, gays, kinship.* New York: Columbia University Press.

SELF-STUDY QUESTIONS

Multiple Choice

1. Fitzgerald states that studies on the adjustment of children who have gay or lesbian parents show that their adjustment is similar to that of children of heterosexual parents. What is her overriding concern about these studies?
   a. use of the scientific method
   b. failure to clarify gay and lesbian family structures
   c. the promotion of the idea that there must be something wrong with being homosexual
   d. differences in heterosexual versus homosexual parenting styles

2. One study in the article reported that young adults who were raised in lesbian families are often
   a. close to their mother's female partner
   b. more depressed and anxious
   c. resentful and bitter over their lives being different from others
   d. morally unfit

Essay

1. The author suggests that philosophies of child development have focused on the child's ability to behave in roles that are gender appropriate, which may promote prejudice and discrimination. She also suggests that it might be more productive if we focused on helping children achieve a sense of positive self-worth, confidence, and the ability to face and master the challenges of life. What are your views on raising a child?

2. If your sexual orientation is heterosexual, what would your thoughts be if your friend's parent(s) were gay or lesbian?

EARLY/MIDDLE ADULTHOOD

"The Family in Jewish Tradition"

OVERVIEW

We often hear the term *traditional family* used to describe two-parent families, often in contrast to terms such as *single-parent family*. However, in its full meaning, the term *traditional family* refers to much more than just a particular configuration of individuals who live in the same household. Specifically, as this article suggests, ideas about what is or is not a traditional family are grounded in particular cultural frameworks that provide individuals with a more or less rigid set of role-based prescriptions for behavior. Moreover, as the author's analysis of the Jewish traditional family suggests, the meanings and functions of these roles can change substantially as a result of forces outside the particular culture in question. However, the author also contends that, even taking into consideration such changes, there can be considerable continuity in the assumptions and values that govern a culture's ideas about families and family roles across many generations. As you read this article, explore your own ideals and values regarding family life. Compare what you think are the structures and standards of current family life with those of the ancient Jewish family.

METHODOLOGY

This article reports no formal research or statistical techniques. The author uses a variety of documentary and historical evidence to support his assertions about change and continuity in the Jewish traditional family.

GLOSSARY TERMS

- **Genealogies** the tracing of a family's descent; lineage or ancestry
- **Consanguineous** related by birth; descended from the same ancestor; of the same blood
- **Patriarchal** a society that has a male ruler or a father who is head of the family or tribe; descent, kinship, and property ownership are traced through the eldest male
- **Nuclear family** parents and children who live in the same household
- **Kinship** family relationship
- **Monogamy** the practice of marrying only one person at a time
- **Polygamy** the practice of having two or more wives, husbands, or mates at the same time
- **Talmud** a book of rabbinic interpretations of the Jewish scriptures

The Family in Jewish Tradition

INTRODUCTION

The family is a feature of human society that predates modern thinking about it. Although the precise origin of the family is unknown, there is evidence of family life in every record of early mankind. It is found in every known society, both civilized and preliterate. An accurate sociological description of the family and its legal status in Biblical times is not readily available, as the relevant evidence is not of a strictly socio-descriptive nature.

The lack of suitable documents dealing with everyday life makes it necessary to utilize literary allusions in developing a picture of the family and its functions in Biblical times. The use of these literary images as a basis for framing a discussion of family in many eras and historical transitions suggests that a shared knowledge of what was noted could help unwind some of the assumptions that define family in terms of sociological discourse. The Book of Genesis, which contains stories of the patriarchs and their families, is the original source for forming images and deriving values of Jewish family life in the classical tradition. One focal point for tales of family life is the period of occupation and settlement in the land of Canaan. A second source of information is genealogies, found particularly in Genesis and in Chronicles, which depict the family trees of the main tribal leaders and groups.

Strictly legal passages in the Bible on the subject of family law are few in number, scattered throughout, and of limited scope. Social legislation pertaining specifically to the family is found primarily in Deuteronomy, including the laws relating to Levirate marriage (Deut. 25:5–10) and a brief outline of the process of divorce (Deut. 24:1–4). Although discoveries from ancient Israel have not yielded any legal documents pertaining to marriage, it is believed that such documents were used by the Israelites in matters of marriage and divorce. Written marriage contracts are not mentioned until a later period. As a result of such limited sources, therefore, no early

Jewish writing was devoted specifically to the family, and no straightforward definition of the family can be found in the Bible or other early sacred writings. The Talmud, encompassing the written laws governing all aspects of life, devoted a whole book to marriage and to divorce, but none to the functions of the family. Most of what we know about the family was established during the period of the Bible, and very little has been added until modern times.

MARRIAGE, PROCREATION, AND DIVORCE

Leviticus gives the "forbidden degrees," that is, a list of those relationships that were considered consanguineous (blood relations or 'near kin') and, therefore, made marriage forbidden. The Bible strictly prohibited marriage among consanguineous relatives, and the ties of blood relationship that forbade sexual relations were spelled out in order to prevent any violations (Lev. 18:6–18; 20:11–14; 17:19–21). These taboos included 26 relationships considered as "secondary incest," such as daughter-in-law or sister-in-law. No restrictions were placed, however, on marrying within the extended family; instead these marriages were accepted and even encouraged.

The Israelite family as reflected in all genealogical and narrative sources was patriarchal. There is no word in the Old Testament that corresponds precisely to the modern "nuclear family," consisting of father, mother and children. The closest equivalent to the family in the Bible was aptly termed "bet av" or "father's house" (Gen. 24:38), with the establishment of a new family being termed "house building" (Deut. 25:10). This household, composed of several generations, was formed by parents, children, sons- and daughters-in-law, as well as dependents. The father was the head of the Biblical family unit, the owner of family property, and the person through whom genealogy was traced.

The family (father's house) was tied through various relationships to a much broader circle of family relatives that included the parents' brothers, particularly from the father's side, their in-laws and their children. The term "bayit" or "house" usually described a subdivision of the "mishpahah" (which re-

Reprinted from *Marriage & Family Review*, 1999, *28*, 43–54. Copyright 1999 by The Haworth Press, Inc., Binghamton, NY. Reprinted with permission.

fers to the "clan" or "family" in the larger sense) (Josh. 7:14) and the "shevet" (or "tribe") (Ex. 12:21). Even the nation ("am") or the "house of Israel" was considered to be an extension of the family (Num. 25:15). In fact, the root of the word "mishpahah" means to incorporate or to bind together, and, as such, the concept of family was rather loosely defined.

The concept of the family, therefore, included numerous "father-houses" and the resulting kinship of all the persons constituting such a political division. This division held from generation to generation and was usually named after an ancient father who was a common ancestor. Thus, family was viewed not only as a smaller, nuclear unit, but also as an extended framework for a larger unit of society. The criteria for membership in a family (in the broader sense) were blood relationship and descent from a common ancestor; legal ties, such as common habitation and marriage; and geographical proximity.

The genealogies of I Chronicles sometimes refer to the clan leader as the "father" of a town or towns in his district (I Chron. 2:51–52). A common livelihood or profession was probably a major factor in family and clan solidarity. Besides those families who engaged primarily in farming their own lands, there were others who practiced a specific trade. From an economic standpoint, the larger family was the strongest and most stable institution, while the smaller "father-houses" were split and eventually disappeared.

Roles and Functions in the Family

As a social institution, the family provided a framework for regulating sexual relations, conserving lines of descent, securing property ownership, dictating inheritance rights, and executing justice. It also assigned roles for the division of labor and the responsibility for socializing children, as well as defining the roles of its members in relation to the external world. In the Bible, the division between the roles of women and men in daily family life was sharply drawn. The men were dominant in the public sphere, as leaders in the political arena, while the women dominated the private sphere, confining themselves to domestic duties such as cooking.

The head of the Biblical family was the patriarch who exercised authority over his wife and children (Num. 26:54–55). Marriage was based primarily on the patriarchal model with the woman joining and enlarging her husband's family, and virtually becoming his possession (Ex. 20:14). A woman was required to go along with her husband into servitude if he could not repay his debts (Ex. 21:2–3); however, she was not a slave that he might sell as he could his daughter.

Despite subordination to their husbands, women retained some rights, such as possessing and trading property even while married, and inheriting property from their fathers in the absence of sons (Num. 26:28–34; 27:1–11). At the death of a husband, a woman could become the actual, and probably the legal, head of the household if there were no sons of responsible age (II Kings 8:1–6).

Women were not simply portrayed as docile characters who were subservient to their husbands' authority. They argued (Gen. 30:1) and gave orders (Gen. 16:2); some had very strong characters, even if their power was not always displayed openly. The influence of famous mothers in epic tradition, such as Sarah (Gen. 21:12), is illustrative of the significance attached to their role. While the status of the woman in the family was not nearly as high as her husband's, she was considered to be the undisputed mistress of the household. In bearing sons, she gave to the tribe its most valuable possession, and as such, her position did afford her some compensations.

The modern definitions of monogamy and polygamy were not strictly applicable to the ancient world. Polygamy was commonly practiced by men who held two or more wives at a time. However, a woman had an advantage if she were the senior wife of a harem or the sole wife of a monogamous marriage. Wives had their own private rooms that no strange man was allowed to enter; yet, they were by no means forbidden to associate with men and even took part at banquets.

Despite the practice of polygamy, the taboo against adultery was enforced as one of the Ten Commandments, and violations were severely punished. The law operated on a double standard and was much stricter for women, whose infidelity was punishable with death by stoning. The adulterer was not punished unless he committed the crime with a married woman. In that case, his sin was considered to be a violation of the husband's rights, while the adulteress was viewed as a wicked woman responsible for wounding the honor of her husband and destroying the basis of the family (Num. 5:11–31).

The most important function of the wife was the bearing of children. In accordance with the command to "be fruitful and multiply" (Gen. 1:28), procreation was regarded as the supreme duty. Motherhood was considered a blessing, and childlessness the greatest misfortune, even a punishment from God (Gen. 30:23). The number of children a woman had influenced her status, whereas her honor deteriorated within the family if she proved unable to bear children. As a mother, particularly of a son, a woman occupied a position of distinction within the family. Sons were especially desired because they alone assured the continuity of the family name, and the absence of sons threatened a man's house with extinction (Num. 27:4,8). Without sons, a man perceived himself as a "dried up wood" because after his death, his name would be forgotten (Gen. 29:30–31). The father's first-born son held a special position above his brothers and was entitled to double inheritance over them (Deut. 21:15–17).

If a woman was barren, her husband was entitled to take either another wife or a concubine. According to Jewish law, servants were considered to be part of the family (Gen. 12:16). In fact, the word "servant" shares the same root with the word "family." Thus, the wife might voluntarily offer her handmaiden for childbearing purposes in order to protect her status as well as to ensure the inheritance of her home (Gen. 16:1–2). The legal status of the concubine was lower than that of the wife, and her children were not necessarily entitled to inherit equally. Biblical law insisted, however, that they should not be completely deprived of their rights (Gen. 21:10; 25:6).

The distinction between legitimacy and illegitimacy in their present significance did not exist. Insofar as the father was known, all children were considered to be legitimate, whether borne by concubines or lawful wives (Gen. 21:10). The subject of adoption, as used today in its legal meaning, is not mentioned directly in the Bible; nevertheless, some clues can be found that it was practiced. Adoption was not addressed as such probably due to the great importance attached to family boundaries and the significance of blood relations within the social organization.

Divorce

Childlessness was the most common motive for a man to divorce his wife. So essential was procreation as a purpose of marriage that a man was not only permitted, but even encouraged, to divorce his wife after ten years of barrenness (Yev. 6:6). According to Biblical law, it was only the husband who was allowed to take the initiative in a divorce proceeding and could do so with or without the consent of his wife (Deut. 24:1–4). This did not change until the turn of the 11th century, when Gershom ben Judah ruled that a divorce could be implemented only with the consent of both parties.

Although divorce was permitted in the Bible and the Talmud, overall it was frowned upon by the sages. Despite this reluctance, however, the sages did lay down the grounds for divorce by both the husband and the wife (Git. 90a). In practice, divorce was a rarity in Jewish communities and was considered a stigma. The powerful bond which united parents and children with mutual responsibilities was expected to strengthen the family unit enough to enable it to withstand all stresses, both internal and external.

THE ESSENCE OF FAMILY LIFE

Domestic harmony was an ideal toward which Jewish families strove. The guidelines for achieving this harmony were clearly outlined: "A man should spend less than his means on food, up to his means on clothes, and beyond his means in honoring wife and children because they are dependent on him" (Hul. 84b). Yet, harmony was achieved not only through the give and take of interpersonal relationships, but also through the experience of ritual and holy events. The customs and strong values inherent in the Jewish way of life served to unify the family and sustain family bonds even in the hardest of times.

There was great emphasis placed on the value of the family as the social unit responsible for nurturing domestic and religious virtues. This resulted in the Jewish home becoming the most vital factor in the survival of Judaism and the preservation of the Jewish way of life, more so even than the synagogue or school in later times. The traditional Jewish home was the center of religious practice and ceremony, with a religious spirit of observance dictating dietary habits and other aspects of daily life.

The family unit was regarded somewhat as a closed one (Num. 24:5). Usually a woman and her children would reside in her own tent or house, thereby forming sub-groups of mothers' children (Gen. 30:14–16). Within these units, the first-born male would instruct and protect his brothers. By subdividing the family into small units centered around the mother, women were able to enjoy rights and roles that the written law did not allow. Thus, a woman could function as a ruler in her own domicile, even if not on a legal basis.

The mother was primarily responsible for the early training and education of her children (Prov. 1:8) until they grew older (6 years old) and the father assumed his duties of teaching his children religion, Jewish values, and moral behavior (Gen. 18:19, Ex. 12:26–27). It was the father's duty to teach his sons a craft or trade, while mothers taught their daughters at home about the domestic responsibilities of a Jewish woman. Special weight was laid upon early religious training, as the family functions were religious as well as social.

The wealthier class also used special tutors to teach reading and writing. There is, however, no mention of school in the Old Testament. Schools were established at a much later period, and then only in the larger cities. Education was always considered to be important, and all knowledge was based on fear of God and obedience to parents (Prov. 1:7).

Children were expected to "honor" and "revere" both parents and to demonstrate their respect through obedience (Ex. 20:12, Deut. 21:18–21). This commandment required that children refrain from sitting in their parents' seats (a practice that is followed even in modern times), interrupting them, or taking sides in a dispute. Strict discipline was maintained, and children who assaulted or even cursed their parents could be punished by the death penalty (Ex. 21:15–17); a rebellious son was to be stoned to death (Deut. 21:18–21). According to the Talmud, this practice was never enacted, though the threat served as a deterrent to rebellious behavior.

As the head of the family, the father's authority over his children was almost absolute. Children were regarded as the father's property and could be seized for payment of debt (II Kings 4:1). His control included the right to sell a daughter into marriage, although there were limitations on selling her into slavery (he could not sell her to foreigners). Moreover, an absolute ban existed on selling daughters into prostitution (Ex. 21: 7–11, Lev. 19:29).

Historically, children were viewed as extensions of their parents and were pressured to conform to their expectations. A son was expected to grow up into a scholar, and likewise to bring honor to the family by marrying the daughter of a scholar. Genealogical lists were drawn up and carefully preserved to monitor the purity of the family. The status of certain families as "pure" and "impure" was well known, and references were made to "families of scribes which produced scribes, of scholars who produced scholars, and of plutocrats who produced plutocrats" (Eccl. R. 4:9).

Both purity of descent and health considerations were regarded as important, and there were warnings against marrying into a family with a history of such diseases as epilepsy or leprosy (Yev. 64b). By custom, marriages outside the clan were discouraged, while marriages with relations within the extended family were preferred. Because marriage was a question of admitting a woman into the family, it became a family affair. Consequently, it was greatly frowned upon for the son to marry a woman against the will of his parents.

The responsibility of the individual member of a family towards the good name of the family as a whole is constantly stressed. This is evident from the many Biblical passages delivering the message:

A family is like a heap of stones. Remove one, and the whole structure can collapse. (Gen. R. 100:7)

Whosoever brings disrepute upon himself brings disrepute upon his whole family. (Num. R. 21:3)

Here too, the family is perceived as a "system" to which modern system concepts apply. This strong regard for the family honor gave rise to the ceremony of "kezazah" in which all the members of the family participated when one of them married a woman who was not considered to be worthy of them (Ket. 28b). Such heavy emphasis on the worthiness of the family as a prime consideration in choosing a marriage partner has persisted throughout the history of Jewish social life. This is symbolically reflected in the notion that still exists today that one should be able to "sit down at the table" with the respective families of the potential bride and groom.

Family honor was also used as the basis for justifying the system of retribution. Family solidarity was demonstrated through customs such as blood revenge that was exacted upon members of another clan who had killed a kinsman. A whole family could be held responsible for one member's wrongdoing on the premise that

there is not a family containing a publican of which all the members are not publicans or containing a thief in which they are not all thieves. (Shev. 39a)

Members of the same family were perceived as "brothers," and the relationship between brothers was highly significant in the Israelite family. Blood revenge was the primary responsibility of the immediate family relatives of the victim (Num. 35:9–34; Deut. 19:1–13). However, in the absence of a brother or another close relative, the circle of people who were responsible for the revenge was enlarged. The extended family then had to select the avenger (go'el) who would be considered as a "brother."

Thus, each member of the group was entitled to protection by that group, and the avenger had obligations extending to many matters of family honor. When brothers departed from each other in order to establish a new "father-house" of their own, they were still tied to each other with a reciprocal responsibility to protect and support each other. A near kinsman was required to redeem a relative who had been forced by poverty to sell his land or other family property or to sell himself into slavery to pay a debt (Lev. 25:25, 47–49).

It was even the responsibility of a man to marry his brother's widow if he died without sons to take over the household. This was the practice of the Levirate marriage that was instituted to carry on the name of the deceased brother and to ensure the continuance of his estate. Thus, the son born of such a marriage was considered as the child of the deceased

(Deut. 25: 5–10). Later, daughters were given the right to inherit in the absence of sons, thereby enabling the preservation of the family estate. At that point, the Levirate requirements became limited to cases in which the deceased had left no children at all (Num. 27:4).

DISCUSSION

As evident from this discussion of the family in Jewish tradition, most of what the term "family" describes was established during the Biblical period and remained largely unchanged until the last century. Very little was added during the subsequent periods of the Settlement, the Kingdom, and the Second Temple until modern times.

Most major family concepts, such as family structure, mate selection, engagement, marriage, inheritance and divorce, including adultery and incest, were all established during the Biblical period. No recorded changes are known during the Settlement and Kingdom periods. The controversy between monogamy and polygamy continues as a result of influence by other nations. Very few changes took place during the Babylonian period (after the destruction of the Second Temple). The dowry was replaced by the marriage contract ("Ktuba"), and the engagement and marriage ceremonies were combined into one. Whereas the age of marriage during Biblical times was "when the children grow up," namely, 12 for girls and 13 for boys, it rose to 18 during the Mishna and Talmud period (4th Century). At that time, the marriage certificate became an official contract, thus protecting the woman against a forced divorce. No major changes or additions were found during the Middle Ages, with the exception of Rabbi Gershon's improvement in the 11th Century. This principle stipulated that a man could not marry two women, nor divorce his wife against her will. An exception occurred only if the wife was mentally ill, a circumstance meaning that a second wife could be taken. Capital punishment and killing for blood revenge, of course, have long since been abolished.

The subject of the family during Biblical times must be regarded, therefore, under two aspects: one, the family in its wider sense of individuals related by marriage or common ancestry; and two, the smaller family unit consisting of parents and children. In Jewish tradition, the family constitutes a very closely knit unit in which all members are bound by mutual ties of responsibility. These ties provided the primary focus of Biblical life, and considerable attention was given to the interactions of various family members within the context of the patriarchal community. Biblical heroes did not attain identity and glory away from their families, and their problems and preoccupations were deeply domestic. Because family was the point around which life revolved, it was simultaneously the source of intimate connection and the scene of spiritual struggle.

In the post-Biblical period, as the land was settled and interaction with institutions outside the structure of the family developed, the ties of the larger clan tended to weaken and the smaller monogamous family unit took on increasing importance. Although polygamy was permitted by both the Bible and the Talmud, the ideal set forth was always of husband, wife, and children forming one unit. The passage from Psalms, "thy wife shall be a fruitful vine in the innermost part of thy house; thy children like olive plants round about thy table" (Ps. 128:2–3), formed the basis of innumerable homilies in the Talmud extolling the virtues of domestic bliss. Finally in the year 1000, monogamy was formally decreed as the normal state of marriage by Gershom ben Judah.

The pattern of Jewish family life set down in the Talmud was the model and practice until modern times. The age of marriage was set at 18 (Avot. 5:24), although some sages encouraged earlier marriage (Kid. 29b). Marriages were usually arranged by the parents of both families, with the betrothal being considered a formal marriage that could be dissolved only through divorce or death. Sexual life was strictly regulated and great importance was attached to ritual aspects; celibacy was discouraged and rare. The Talmud pointed to the Biblical verse, "he created it (the world) not a waste; he formed it to be inhabited" (Is. 45:18), as a justification for the religious duty not only to marry but also to establish a family.

CONCLUSION

The family was regarded as the smallest social unit through which the cultural and religious heritage of Judaism could be transmitted. The sanctity of the home was especially apparent in Jewish life during the Middle Ages. Throughout those centuries of persecution and migration, the home became the pillar of moral and social strength and the key to maintaining a Jewish consciousness. The observances of the faith were so entwined with the daily customs of the home that Jewish religion and its family life became bonded as one.

The Jewish tradition did not distinguish between religious rules, moral behavior, and law, but demanded that all be equally followed by the people. Those persons who did not perform accordingly would be bound by social sanctions. Such orders were based on God's commandments rather than on logical constructs. Throughout the coming centuries, even while the law evolved into a different form of government executed by court houses, this set of orders remained in force only on the basis of social sanctions.

Thus, in the beginning, Biblical law took the form of religious charisma that was maintained as God's law, and only much later was the legal process assumed by the "dayanim" (religious judges). Since Jewish tradition is based on the Halacha (Jewish law), it does not recognize a Jewish nation that is not a Biblical nation.

Traditional practices were maintained and reinforced within the context of the Jewish family, whose concepts and laws were as old as Biblical times. Consequently, the family served as a source of values and philosophy of life. Jewish values and Jewish traditions were transmitted from generation to generation within the family context. It is only in the last 200 years that this solid structure has begun to waver.

Jewish law has never lost its original character; but exists side by side with the State and even binds the State. In fact, the 1953 law of the Rabbinical Court (Marriage and Divorce) states clearly that all Jews residing in Israel as Israeli citizens will be under the jurisdiction of the Rabbinical law.

Despite the influence of tradition, the reality of the Jewish people since the 19th century has changed, and many Jews no longer live "by the Bible." Major changes in the status of women and the family have had a radical impact on modern society. Social and demographic trends in Western society have brought changes in marriage and family life that have altered the family structure. The State of Israel has developed new laws in recent years to keep up with the changes created by the new era; these may not be sufficient and many more should follow.

Nevertheless, it is interesting to note that so many basic structures and functions of the family have never been changed or challenged. New laws can continue to be established without losing the ancient meanings and values. The old concepts can still be used; it is necessary only to adopt new laws and new sanctions rather than to replace the concepts themselves. For example, the stigma attached to adultery still exists even though it is no longer punished by public stoning. Another concept that is still alive is the familial responsibility to educate children, even though the specific parental roles spelled out in the Bible are no longer applicable to modern times.

All of the meanings that we attach to the structure and functions of the Jewish family were established very early in the history of Jewish social life. In this tradition, most of what the term "family" describes has been stable until the last century. Not only within the Jewish communities, but also in the general western secular society the concepts associated with the Biblical views of marriage, children, and family responsibilities are often retained in evaluating and interpreting social practice. However, it is useful to remember that these ideas are seen through the lens of contemporary problems and practice. This brief review of the major ideas in Jewish tradition of Biblical interpretation can be used to enlighten current debates on the family in today's policy work.

Despite the fact that there is not a current definition of the family that is universally accepted, the loosely defined family unit that is bound and incorporated together fits family systems theories and can be used for research in the social sciences. Even in the absence of a clear definition, however, we can continue to adapt the concept of family in our struggle to understand it. This process might help us account for the survival of the oldest institution on earth.

REFERENCES

Biblical encyclopedia. (1968). (pp. 582–588). Jerusalem: Bialik.

Childress, J. F., & Macquarrie, J. (Eds.). (1986). *The Westminster dictionary of Christian ethics* (pp. 224–226). Philadelphia: The Westminster Press.

Cornfeld, G., & Luria, B. Z. (Eds). (1967). *Encyclopedia of the Bible and second temple* (Vol. 1, pp. 782–790; Vol. 2, pp. 408–418). Tel Aviv: Achiasaf.

Douglas, J. D. (Ed.). (1972). *The new Bible dictionary* (pp. 415–418). London: Inter-Varsity Press.

Encyclopedia Judaica. (1971). (Vol. 6, pp. 1164–1172). Jerusalem: Keter House, Ltd.

Ferm, V. (Ed.). (1964). *An encyclopedia of religion* (pp. 271–272). Paterson, New Jersey: Littlefield, Adams & Co.

Harley, D. (1982). *The world's religion.* Tel Aviv: Devir Publishing.

Hoffman, Y. (Ed.). (1988). *The Israeli encyclopedia of the Bible* (pp. 562–564). Massada.

Jackson, S. M. (Ed.). (1967). *The new Schaff-Herzog encyclopedia of religious Knowledge* (pp. 273–277). Grand Rapids, Michigan: Baker Book House.

Lor, G. (1982). *The relationship between God and nation as man-woman relationship.* Unpublished dissertation (Chapter 1). The University of Haifa.

MacGregor, G. (1990). *The everyman dictionary of religion and philosophy* (pp. 191–192, 400). London: J. M. Dent & Sons, Ltd.

McGraw-Hill encyclopedia of world biography. (1973). (pp. 371–372).

Radi, Z. (1989). *The new Biblical dictionary.* (pp. 339–340).

Singer, I. (Ed) (1903). *The Jewish encyclopedia* (Vol. 5, pp. 337–338). New York and London: Funk and Wagnalls Company.

Solialy, M. (Ed). (1965). *Biblical lexicon* (pp. 576–581). Tel Aviv: Devir Publishing.

Wigoder, G. (Ed). (1989). *The encyclopedia of Judaism* (pp. 255–258, 284). NY: Macmillan Publishing Company.

APPENDIX

Abbreviations for Biblical and Talmudic Sources

Abbreviation	Source	Abbreviation	Source
Avot	Avot	Kid.	Kidushin
Chron. I, II	Chronicles	Kings I, II	Kings
Deut.	Deuteronomy	Hul.	Hulin
Eccl.	Ecclesiastes	Lev.	Leviticus
Ex.	Exodus	Num.	Numbers
Gen.	Genesis	Prov.	Proverbs
Gen. R.	Genesis Raba	Ps.	Psalms
Git.	Gittin	Shev.	Shevuot
Is.	Isaiah	Yev.	Yevanot
Josh.	Joshua		

SELF-STUDY QUESTIONS

Multiple Choice

1. In ancient Jewish law and tradition, divorce was permitted under what circumstances?
   a. adultery
   b. childlessness
   c. lack of religious training
   d. a and b only

2. In ancient times, what was the most threatening disciplinary action that Jewish parents could take against rebellious children?
   a. selling a child into slavery
   b. permitting a child to be seized to pay debts
   c. not allowing a child to sit in the parent's chair
   d. stoning to death an abusive, cursing child

Essay

1. How have the roles and functions of women evolved in modern times in the areas of marriage, career, child-bearing, and parenting? Compare this evolution with the same roles and functions for women stated in the article.

2. In Jewish tradition, the family is viewed as being the responsible "social unit" for conveying domestic and religious as well as other values. What do you think are the most important responsibilities of the family unit today?

MIDDLE ADULTHOOD

"Women's Personality in Middle Age: Gender, History, and Midcourse Corrections"

OVERVIEW

The authors of this article examined several groups of middle-aged women who came of age and were influenced dramatically by the social protests and reform movements of the 1960s. Their focus was on how Baby Boomer women, as compared to women in earlier cohorts, explore their identities, develop a sense of purpose and freedom, and achieve generativity in midlife. As you read this article, stop to think about what you know about the social and historical events of this past century. In what ways have your family members, supervisors, co-workers, and others been influenced by these past events? What about you? What historical events of your childhood and adolescence have or will impact your sense of who you are and how you relate to others, and the goals and values your have formed for life?

METHODOLOGY

This article is a summary of the authors' and other researchers' studies that help support the authors' assertions about the characteristics of middle-aged female members of the Baby Boom generation. As such, it reports no specific methods or statistical analyses.

GLOSSARY TERMS

- **Midlife crisis** feelings of anxiety, depression, and loss over one's life being "half over"
- **Generativity** the desire to make a valuable, even permanent, contribution to the betterment of society and the next generation
- **Empty nest** a time when children have left home and are beginning their own lives
- **Menopause** the time in a woman's life when she ceases to menstruate and is no longer capable of reproduction
- **Identity** one's sense of who one is; one's perception of his or her roles and functions, beliefs, attitudes, and values
- **Age cohort** a group of individuals born during the same historical period

- **Feminism** a term usually associated with the Women's Movement and the Equal Rights Amendment of the early 1970s, stressing equal access and opportunities for women and other disadvantaged groups in education, career, salary, and family life
- **Executive personality** in midlife, behavior and belief that one can institute plans and direct others in order to accomplish goals
- **Personal authority** a person's feeling and knowledge that she or he has the ability to take charge and to make certain requirements of a given situation

Abigail J. Stewart and Joan M. Ostrove

Women's Personality in Middle Age: Gender, History, and Midcourse Corrections

This article examines several key features of the course of adult development in the cohort of women born during the baby boom. By focusing on the women in this group and comparing their experience with that of older cohorts and research on men, the authors demonstrate the need for models of aging that take account of the intersections of history, gender, and individual development. Concepts proposed as universal features of middle age (midlife crisis, generativity, aging), as well as those proposed as specific to women (empty nest, menopause) are examined. Perhaps most important, certain features not commonly viewed as particularly important in women's middle aging (midlife review, identity, confident power) are shown to be central. The need for further research examining these same processes among men and different groups of women is underscored.

Psychologists aim for universal accounts of human development. Our accounts of middle age are no different. Concepts like the midlife crisis, generativity, and the empty nest are intended to have broad applicability, even as we know they do not characterize everyone. At the same time, depictions of the middle age of famous baby boomers in the United States—most recently Hillary Rodham Clinton's 50th birthday—have allowed us to ask new questions about middle age. When does it start and end? How is it affected by the lengthening average life expectancy? Are the roles and tasks in middle age different for the people in this generation than for their parents? Have changes in gender roles changed the way middle age is experienced by men and women? In short, the presence of the baby boom's middle aging in popular consciousness has raised doubts about the universality of earlier accounts of middle age.

It makes sense that generations raised with different expectations and in different historical circumstances may age differently. In fact, some psychologists have pointed to the often profound implications of historical experience for individuals' development (e.g., Elder, 1974; Erikson, 1975), such that small differences in people's ages may make big differences in their lives. For example, Elder (1986)

showed that military experience in World War II provided opportunities for upward mobility for disadvantaged men who were late adolescents or young adults at the time; it did not play that role for disadvantaged men who were older. Although previous research and theory have not focused on the difference history might make to middle age, they provide a framework for recognizing that developmental processes may differ in different generations. Stewart and Healy (1989) provided a model of how history might differentially affect different stages of individual development, and thereby create psychologically distinct cohorts. According to their account, the social historical events that occur in a person's childhood shape the individual's background assumptions about life and the world, while those that occur in late adolescence shape the individual's conscious identity. Events that take place during the busy years of adulthood inevitably affect the opportunities that individuals have open to them, but maybe not their values or their identities. A concrete example of how this might work is that there is considerable evidence that women entered the labor force in unusual numbers during World War II. For middle-class White women who were adults at the time, with gender identities shaped in the 1930s, that was an interesting and novel opportunity. For some younger women, however, it may have contributed to the development of a vocational identity that was at odds with the postwar pressures for domesticity. For young girls, whose sisters were

Reprinted from *American Psychologist*, 1998, *53*, 1185–1194. Copyright © 1998 by the American Psychological Association. Reprinted with permission.

celebrated as contributing to the war effort, it may have offered a model of women's potential social role and contribution that shaped a background assumption about women's possibilities. According to this model, then, social events play an important role in individuals' lives regardless of their stage of development, but the nature of that role depends on their life stage. Further, there is a special importance to events that coincide with the identity-forming adolescent years, because once identities are formed they are posited to have persistent effects.

Given the importance of events coinciding with late adolescence according to this theory, we would expect it to matter that baby boomers' formative years coincided with several social movements (including, e.g., civil rights and Vietnam War protest). The women's movement may have had particular relevance to the lives of women in this cohort, because it ushered in dramatic changes in women's access to education and occupational opportunities, women's workforce participation, norms for egalitarian household arrangements, and support for girls' more equal participation in math, science, and athletics. It is no accident that in the wake of those changes psychologists—probably also often baby boomers!—have also increasingly recognized the ways in which gender might matter over the course of development (e.g., Franks & Fodor, 1990; Grambs, 1989; Levinson, 1996).

In this article, we bring together these notions of the importance of gender and generation with insights about middle age derived from theories that posit a universal pattern of adult development.

ACCOUNTS OF MIDDLE AGE IN THEORIES OF ADULT DEVELOPMENT

Psychological theories and research have described several features of middle-aged personality that distinguish it from personality in other life stages. These developmental approaches do not focus on traits that are assumed to persist across the lifespan but instead on aspects of personality (structures, preoccupations, etc.) that are hypothesized to change. For example, Jung (1954), Jacques (1965), and Levinson, Darrow, Klein, Levinson, and McKee (1978) suggested that middle age is characterized by a midlife crisis, involving radical changes, disrupted family lives, and desperate efforts to retrieve youth (see Chiriboga, 1989, for a useful discussion). Neugarten (1968) proposed, in contrast, that middle age is characterized by the confident "executive personality," while Erikson (1982) described middle-aged people as generative "maintainers of the world" (Erikson, Erikson, &

Kivnick, 1986). These images suggest that middle-aged people are the responsible pillars of society, confidently in command and filled with concern about the next generation. Karp (1988) focused instead on inner experience—a shift from a focus on time since birth to time until death, from the external world of events to the internal world of spirituality, reflection, and introspection. These theories offer valuable constructs for describing many people's experience of internal changes that coincide with midlife. While ideas about gender and history are implicit in m any of them, our goal is to illuminate the ways in which personality development in middle-age must be examined in the context of attention to gender and generation.

GENDER AND MIDDLE AGE

Building on Jung (1954), Gutmann (1987) suggested that there is "gender crossover"—that middle age is when the gendered young adult personality is developed in new directions. Whereas Gutmann (and others; see, e.g., James & Lewkowicz, 1997) explicitly addressed gender, much of the literature on people's middle age invokes a gender dimension indirectly. *Women's* middle age is often discussed in terms of menopause (Dan & Bernhard, 1989), the empty nest (Bart, 1971), and new opportunities for activity and self-expression (Levinson, 1996), and *men's* middle age is discussed more often in terms of crisis and acting out (Levinson et al., 1978), executive personality (Howard & Bray, 1988), and, more recently, withdrawal from the youthful male world of competition and achievement (Franz, 1997). Generally the imagery in popular culture mirrors these, though the middle-aged woman is most commonly depicted in popular culture in even more negative terms—as over the hill, unattractive, and sexually irrelevant (Greer, 1992; Heilbrun, 1988). This image is stressed by the substantial literature on middle-aged women focusing on menopause as the key issue, though there is considerable evidence that most women do not experience it that way (see Datan, 1986; Gergen, 1990; Mitchell & Helson, 1990; Neugarten & Kraines, 1965, for critiques of this emphasis).

Neither popular culture nor psychological theory has systematically considered the possibility that middle age is gendered differently for different generations. One exception is discussion of the empty nest. In that discussion, researchers first noticed that the psychological meaning of the empty nest depended on women's other activities (Barnett & Baruch, 1978). Scholars have debated whether women who were not employed outside the home found the empty nest liberating or depressing (Adelmann, Antonucci, Crohan, & Coleman, 1989). They agreed, though, that an empty nest would be much more salient in those women's daily lives than in the lives of women who were employed outside the home.

It is interesting that Antonucci and Akiyama (1997) concluded that

> women who experienced their early adulthood during the time of the feminine mystique were much more likely to report lower levels of psychological well-being when their children left the home than women who were young adults during World War II, when women were encouraged to enter the labor force. (p. 159)

Theorizing about middle age that is gendered from the beginning—like the empty nest debate—has tended to incorporate awareness of generation or cohort. Many other concepts that were initially considered "universal" have not yet been fully analyzed in terms of either gender or generation.

GENERATIONS AND MIDDLE AGE

The timing of middle age itself may well have changed across generations. Though 40 is frequently selected as a marker of early middle age both in older and more recent theorizing (Jung, Jacques, Levinson, Gergen), the upper limit continues to be raised. Changes in life expectancy and improvements in the quality of life for older adults have resulted in not only a deferral of "old age" but also changes in people's retirement expectations (Grambs, 1989). Earlier cohorts expected to remain healthy and active for only a short time after retiring. Today many middle-aged adults plan second careers or serious volunteer or leisure commitments (Osherson, 1980). Changes in the relative centrality of work and family in adult life (Antonucci & Akiyama, 1997) or in valuing community or individual achievement (Veroff, Douvan, & Kulka, 1981), like changes in life expectancy, may well change the psychological meaning of middle age for different cohorts. Helson pointed out that "middle age will have different meanings in different times and places for different individuals" (1997, p. 23); it may, more narrowly, have different meanings for those in different cohorts.

GENDER AND GENERATION IN MIDDLE AGE: WOMEN IN THE BABY BOOM

We can examine gender and generation in middle age by focusing on the increasingly documented experience of middle aging in one cohort of women and comparing it with accounts based on the experience of other cohorts or men. In an ideal world we would have full comparative data on multiple cohorts and for both women and men at several times. In this world we often must rely on indirect comparisons with theoretical and empirical accounts when direct comparative data are unavailable.

In the remainder of this article, we bring notions of gender and generation to bear on explorations of college-educated women's middle aging. Our goal is both to provide evidence of how middle age is experienced by contemporary women and to illustrate a strategy for using gender and cohort as analytic tools for understanding both middle age in other groups and other psychological phenomenon.

We summarize findings based on five samples of college-educated women who are currently middle-aged. These include (a) Ravenna Helson's longitudinal study of Mills College graduates of 1958 and 1960 (Helson, 1993); (b) the Radcliffe Longitudinal Study of the class of 1964 (Stewart & Vandewater, 1993); (c) a sample of women who graduated from Smith College in 1964 (Stewart, Ostrove, & Helson, 1908); (d) Sandra Tangri's study of University of Michigan graduates of the Class of 1967 (Tangri & Jenkins, 1993); (e) and a sample of African American alumnae of about the same period at the University of Michigan (see Cole & Stewart, 1996). Clearly these samples are not representative of all American women of this cohort. First, by virtue of their college education, women in all of these samples are at least middle class in adulthood. There is variance among them, though. Some of the colleges they attended were private and selective, while the two University of Michigan samples, perhaps because they are drawn from a public institution, reflect substantial social class diversity in their families of origin (see also Ostrove & Stewart, 1994, 1998; Stewart & Ostrove, 1993). Four of the samples are nearly entirely White. We have also drawn on the Berkeley Guidance sample's data archived at the Institute of Human Development to compare these women to women almost 20 years older (Clausen, 1993).

The world in which the five samples of college-educated women were raised was the postwar U.S. baby boom—the Truman and Eisenhower years of increasing prosperity and traditional gender roles. The identity-formative college years were the Kennedy years and coincided with the civil rights movement, establishment of the Peace Corps, and—harbinger of the years ahead—the Kennedy assassination. Betty Friedan's *The Feminine Mystique* appeared at the same time (1963), and in the next years (after graduation) the Vietnam war and the various movements of the late 1960s gathered steam. For many of these women, the demands for more inclusive graduate and professional education came too late—more than half of them were married within one year of graduation; two years later, more than one fourth were full-time mothers at home. For them, the late 1960s felt a little remote, something they watched from the sidelines with little ability to participate. One of the women in the Radcliffe sample described those years for herself. She said,

> I remember when I was recovering from the birth of my daughter, a friend of mine who was a little bit more feminist than I was, bringing me a copy of this article about "The Myth of the Vaginal Orgasm." And I remember looking at this thing and thinking, "You just don't get it. I just had a baby; it really hurts; I don't want to think about this. Take it away."

There were, of course, others—those who went on to graduate school or quickly divorced and reentered the world of education and job seeking. So this cohort of mostly White, mostly middle- or upper-class young women was divided—they were all affected by the same events but not in the same ways (see also Stewart, 1994). Moreover, as the women's movement left a lasting legacy of opened doors in education and the workplace (at least for middle-class White women) members of this cohort were able to take advantage of new opportunities as their lives permitted or demanded. The woman just quoted, who could not relate to the women's movement in the late 1960s, eventually went to graduate school and is now a feminist scholar.

One way to evaluate the historical location of this generation of women is to compare them to other generations. We are able to do that for women from the Radcliffe sample (the Class of 1964), with two comparison samples of women from other graduating classes. Stewart and Ostrove (1993) reported some comparative data for the Radcliffe Class of 1947. They found that by middle age the two groups were quite similar in their rates of marriage (94% for the Class of 1947 and 92% for the Class of 1964) and child bearing (96% and 88%, respectively). Moreover, the two cohorts married and had their first children at virtually identical ages (ages 24 and 23 for marriage; age 27 for both classes for first child). However, by middle age they were also very different. The younger women had fewer children overall (2.45 vs. 3.22 on average), were more likely to get divorced (41% vs. 25%), and were over time more likely to gain graduate educations (44% vs. 17%) and professional careers (48% vs. 30%). In comparing these two cohorts 17 years apart, then, there is *little* evidence of social change in young adulthood but quite a bit by middle age.

A comparison of the Radcliffe sample (Class of 1964) with a sample from the Radcliffe Class of 1975

in early adulthood is also instructive (see Stewart & Salt, 1983, for details about the sample). These data come from 1978, when the women in the Class of 1975 were 24 years old. At a comparable age nearly two thirds of the women in the Class of 1964 were married, and 16% were mothers; only 13% of the Class of 1975 were married, and none were mothers—this points to a dramatic social change! By this early point after graduation nearly 80% of the Class of 1975 women were pursuing careers of some kind, with 58% in graduate school—the contrast with the Class of 1964 women on these indicators is equally as striking as those involving marriage and motherhood. The 11 years that separated these two cohorts produced dramatic differences in their experience of early adulthood. For the women who are currently middle-aged, then, the period of early adulthood provides a critical context for their midlife tasks, hopes, and experiences.

Midlife Crisis or Midcourse Corrections?

Both theorists and researchers have proposed that a midlife crisis is a common experience (see, e.g., Gould, 1978; Levinson et al., 1978; Vaillant, 1977). However, doubt has been expressed both about the concept in general (Haan, 1981; McCrae & Costa, 1984; Pearlin, 1975) and about its applicability to women (Baruch & Brooks-Gunn, 1984; Hunter & Sundel, 1989). We suspect that it may be useful to rethink the concept a bit, recognizing that midlife may often be a period of change or transition but one that is neither universal nor necessarily as dramatic as "crisis" suggests. Instead, perhaps many individuals make modest (and some not so modest) "corrections" in their life trajectories—literally, "midcourse corrections." Some of those corrections may actually resemble crises; for example, one woman in the Radcliffe sample commented in an interview at age 50:

> I know a lot of women…who started out with one set of expectations and…[later] fell into a crack, got divorced, …became professor of something or other, or they went to business school. It's like their lives have this cleft right down the middle.

In fact, about *two thirds* of the women in this sample made major changes in their educational or work lives between ages 37 and 43 (Stewart & Vandewater, in press; see also Stewart & Vandewater, 1993). What is even more important, though, is the underlying motivation for those changes. Stewart and Vandewater asked the Radcliffe women in the Class of 1964 when they were 37 years old whether they would make the same life pattern decisions if they had it to do over again; a sizable number (34%) said they would not. Most of those said they would have pursued educational or work opportunities more extensively before making family commitments; those were called, then, "traditional role regrets." As one woman said, "When I was in college I considered a career in medicine. Due to lack of support from family members and future husband, I didn't pursue it. I would have at least tried it if I were 20 today." Another woman expressed regret this way: "I would not have let my husband take sole responsibility for determining the course of our lives. His career has always been the only deciding factor in our lives, which has not been fair to me or the children."

What were the consequences of this acknowledgment of regret? One possibility was that it would spark a process of goal setting and change making during the subsequent period. As one woman told us in an interview when she was 50, "For me, 35 was the big waking up—looking around and saying, 'Is this it? Is this all there is? Is this what life has dealt me?' If so, I'm getting up and doing something about it." Some women went to graduate school, others looked for jobs consistent with their talents and training.

In the Radcliffe sample, Stewart and Vandewater (1993) coded women's future goals for the expression of goals in the area of education and work and found that women with traditional role regrets were much more likely to express a *desire* to make major changes in this area. However, they also found that women with these regrets were *not* more likely than other women to actually *make* changes in this area over the next several years (perhaps partly because so many women without regrets also made major changes in this period). Some of the women who made changes were, presumably, motivated by something other than regret (e.g., new aspirations or opportunities, the impact of other family members' changes, etc.).

In any case, in the Radcliffe sample, the women who had expressed regrets and made life changes by age 43 in the area of their age 37 regrets were as well off, in terms of psychological adjustment in their mid-40s, as the women who had no regrets at all. In contrast, the one group with relatively low well-being was the group of women who had expressed regret and *not* made changes. Stewart and Vandewater (in press) assessed external constraints (like caregiving responsibilities, or demands from husbands' careers) that might be inhibiting them; these constraints were unrelated to having regrets and making changes. However, they did find that the women who had regrets but did not make life changes by age 43 were significantly higher on a Q-sort measure of rumination (including items such as "tends to ruminate," "is subtly negativistic," and "tends to interpret clear-cut situations in complicated ways").

Stewart and Vandewater (in press) replicated these findings with the University of Michigan sample. A larger proportion of Michigan women had traditional role regrets (61%), but all of the other findings were identical: Regrets resulted in goal setting but not necessarily in changes. Those who expressed regrets and made changes were as well off in later middle age as those without regrets. Those who expressed regrets but did not make changes were higher not only in depression but also in rumination and lower in effective instrumentality by age 47.

Overall, then, in both of these longitudinal studies (Radcliffe Class of 1964, Michigan Class of 1967) there is evidence for a long period of midcourse correction initiated at least by the late 30s. This process was most consequential among women with traditional role regrets, and for some of them it set off a process involving pursuit of educational or career opportunities in middle age that had been abandoned much earlier. For others, there was instead a long period of relative immobilization, and those women by their late 40s were lower in well-being than the other women.

It is important to underscore that the vast majority of the women we studied were, by age 47 or 48, reporting high levels of psychological adjustment and low levels of depression. Similarly, most women in both the Radcliffe and Michigan samples were not characterized by a ruminative style but rather by an effective, instrumental personality. The cohort of women who were middle-aged in the 1990s may have been more prone to midlife review focused on traditional role regrets than later cohorts will be, because they were more likely to have left dreams behind in early adulthood. It may be that for their male peers, and later cohorts of women, the early adult trajectory is less constrained, so the midlife corrections are less drastic. This seems likely because the process of midcourse correction was psychologically critical only among the women with traditional role regrets. Even if the early adult constraints affect only a minority of women in future generations, we should not ignore the risks they pose for later personality development and well-being.

Middle Age: Is It the Prime of Life?

The evidence that some women engaged in a life-review process in early middle age suggests that internal developments in this period are important. One possibility is that middle age is actually a period of relative happiness and psychological well-being. Though early adulthood is often romanticized and middle age maligned, Veroff and Feld (1970) found that a national sample described early adulthood (not middle age) as the time of greatest emotional difficulty for them. One literary critic called her book *Safe at Last in the Middle Years,* because fictional representations of middle age imply that it is a haven from the more turbulent years of early adulthood (Gullette, 1988). Similarly, Mitchell and Helson (1990) were so struck with their findings in a large sample of Mills alumnae of diverse ages that they labeled the 50s "women's prime of life." Women in the Smith College sample were asked directly "How do you feel about turning 50?" Nearly half (48%) said only positive things about it ("Great!" and "I'm a better 50 year old than I was at other ages; I've been waiting for it"). Another 21% were neutral ("no big deal" was a typical response). Less than a third (31%) were negative at all, with only 18% strongly so ("Lousy" or "I hate it"). Clearly something positive was happening for these college-educated women as they reached middle age; we sought a clearer understanding of just what was happening by looking directly at women's subjective experience of aging.

Stewart, Ostrove, and Helson (1998) developed scales based on items first used by Helson and Moane (1987) for the Mills sample and expanded for use with the Michigan and Smith samples. The four scales assessed *identity certainty,* or the subjective sense of having a strong and clear identity (often discussed as an adolescent issue but widely recognized as a later adult development issue for many women); a sense of *generativity,* which we defined, as Erik Erikson (1982) had, as including an enlarged vision of one's role in the social world and a sense of responsibility and commitment; and feelings of *confident power* or efficacy. Finally, we assessed conscious and direct *awareness of aging* itself. These feelings were assessed by three samples of women in their 40s and 50s, both for that age and retrospectively for earlier ages (i.e., 30s in all cases, 40s in some).

Identity certainty, generativity, confident power, and awareness of aging were all experienced as more prominent in middle age (the 40s) than in early adulthood (the 30s). In addition, wherever data on the 50s were available, identity certainty, confident power, and awareness of aging were all rated even higher than they were in the 40s. Generativity was also higher for the women in the Smith sample (there was no age 50 data for the Michigan or Mills sample). We take these findings as confirming that there is indeed something common to all of these women about middle age, and that something includes a realistic sense of aging, but it also includes an enhanced sense of personal identity, an enlarged vision of the self in the social world, and a capacity to be effective and have an impact. Because these findings are at least partly cross-sectional, it is diffi-

cult to articulate the connections among these different developments. Perhaps the early formation of a strong personal identity enhances the likelihood of development of "executive personality" in middle age. This, in turn, may foster efforts to express generative impulses in the larger social world outside the family. This developmental model is consistent with some features of Erikson's theory (1982; e.g., the basis for generativity in resolution of an earlier identity struggle). Moreover, Erikson's ontogenetic account included fairly cryptic assertions that each stage continued to reverberate in later states (thus, that identity would continue to play a role even after resolution). However, once we incorporate attention to gender and generation, it is clear why identity and generativity are *both* live, powerful issues in middle age for women of this generation.

IDENTITY AND MIDDLE AGE IN WOMEN

Helson, Stewart, and Ostrove (1995) specifically explored the impact of social change on identity development by comparing women's midlife identities in three samples, one of which was considerably older than the baby boom cohorts. In that study the Radcliffe women were the youngest cohort, the Mills women the next oldest, and the Berkeley Guidance Study women the oldest (women who were born in 1928 and 1929). The three cohorts came of age, then, in the 1950s, the early 1960s, and the late 1960s. Data were available to assess the identities of all three groups when they were in their 40s, using a Q-sort-based measure of identity originally designed to assess Marcia's (1966) four identity statuses. The measure produced two dimensions: identity integration and identity search. Consistent with the hypothesis of decreasing gender-based constraint on identity formation, Helson, Stewart, and Ostrove found that the youngest sample was highest on both identity integration and the searching style.

They were particularly interested in the implications of identity formation for midlife well-being. They found that well-defined identities were associated with well-being for women in the two younger cohorts but not in the older Berkeley Guidance sample. Because that group of women became adults in the 1950s, an integrated personal identity—whether struggled for or accepted—carried few rewards in middle age because there were few opportunities for women to pursue independent careers and interests during the "feminine mystique." Similarly, for this group, failure to establish an integrated identity carried few costs, as they were rewarded instead for accommodation to the demands and needs of their husbands and children's lives and activities. In this sense, then, the changing social context affected not only the personality developments in women's lives but also the implications of those developments for well-being.

Predicting Midlife Well-Being

Women's identity development was encouraged by the women's movement, and having a well-developed identity in fact supported the well-being of women in the cohort most directly shaped by that movement. Moreover, in the longitudinal sample of Michigan alumnae, Ostrove, Deitch, and Stewart (1998) found that adoption of certain feminist identities was associated with midlife well-being. It makes sense, then, to consider the well-being implications of domains other than identity affected by the women's movement. For example, the women's movement encouraged women to pursue work and family lives that are personally fulfilling rather than accepting gender-based constraints on them. Moreover, educational and occupational opportunities substantially improved for women during baby boom women's early adulthood. It is important to consider whether pursuit of those opportunities actually resulted in improved well-being for women. Vandewater, Ostrove, and Stewart (1997) assessed a model linking roles, personality development, and psychological adjustment in two samples: the Radcliffe and Michigan longitudinal studies. As they predicted, combining work and family roles in early adulthood was related to identity achievement, which in turn supported high levels of midlife work and family role quality and the development of generativity. Midlife role quality and generativity were in turn the only direct predictors of later midlife well-being. For all of these samples of women who came of age in the 1960s, then, in contrast to the Berkeley Guidance sample, identity achievement did facilitate both generativity and well-being.

Is Generativity a Midlife Phenomenon?

In characterizing the development of generativity among women, Erikson suggested that they (like men) did experience a midlife generativity crisis, focused on the desire to make a lasting contribution to the next generation. This crisis results in a capacity and commitment to care—for ideas, cultural products, institutions, values, and people (see especially Erikson, Erikson, & Kivnick, 1986). While some research has suggested that generativity (at least some measures of it) is indeed higher in middle age than in early adulthood (see, e.g., McAdams, de St. Aubin, & Logan, 1993; McAdams, Hart, & Maruna, 1998; Ochse

& Plug, 1986; Peterson & Stewart, 1990; Ryff & Heincke, 1983; Ryff & Migdal, 1984; Vaillant, 1993), other studies have been equivocal (see, e.g., Gruen, 1964; MacDermid, Franz, & De Reus, 1998; McAdams, de St. Albin, & Logan, 1993; Ryff & Migdal, 1984; Whitbourne, Zuschlag, Elliot, & Waterman, 1992).

Recently, Stewart and Vandewater (1998) argued that these conflicting results can be reconciled by positing three separate forms of generativity with different developmental courses: *generative desires*, which peak in early adulthood and decline in middle and later age; *felt capacity for generativity*, which may rise from early to middle adulthood and then decline somewhat; and a sense of *generative accomplishment*, which may rise across adulthood to a peak in old age. Middle age, then, should be distinguished by relatively high levels of all three forms of generativity, but it is the felt capacity for generativity that should distinguish it from other periods of adulthood. One of the women in the Radcliffe sample captured both the early desire for generativity and the midlife felt capacity in an interview. She said,

> In my 20s, when we were trying to end the war in Vietnam, we simultaneously thought we had all the power in the world and that we had no power at all. Neither was true.... I now have a much more limited, more accurate, and in some important ways more energizing and empowering sense of my own powers and limitations.... It's "inch by inch" and it's "row by row," and you have some "elbow room," but that's all you've got.

What is different about midlife generativity, then, is partly that these women feel like "what they've got" is enough—that they are now capable of enacting the generative contributions they imagined and desired much earlier.

Different forms of generativity may, then, have different optimal "seasons" in women's adult lives; young motherhood, like the early years of career building, may indeed be a period in which women long to be effective and responsible contributors to society and the next generation (see supporting evidence in Espin, Stewart, & Gomez, 1990; Peterson & Stewart, 1993). But it is in middle age that they are much more likely to feel that they are actually able to do that and only in even later middle age that they feel they have actually done it.

Enacting Early Adult Ideology, Identity, and Midlife Generativity

Erikson's (1982; Erikson, Erikson, & Kivnick, 1986) theory and the model of midlife well-being tested by Vandewater, Ostrove, and Stewart (1997) suggest an intimate link between identity development and the capacity for generativity. Moreover, both also suggest that early adult activities—in this case, role combination—play an important role in shaping identity. Stewart, Settles, and Winter (1998) found that for women in this cohort, any level of involvement (even being an interested observer rather than a participant) in the social movements of the late 1960s was consequential for midlife personality and ideology. It is clear, then, that midlife personality, including generativity, is importantly shaped by early adult activities. Similarly, Erikson posited and subsequent research has shown that generative desires are expressed in midlife behavioral commitments and pursuits (see McAdams & de St. Aubin, 1992; Stewart & Healy, 1986). Is there a connection, then, between the identities, including political ideologies, shaped in a particular generation or cohort, and the generative activities of the women in that cohort, including their efforts to contribute in the political sphere?

Cole and Stewart (1996) examined this possibility in Tangri's longitudinal samples (Tangri & Jenkins, 1993) of women who graduated from the University of Michigan in 1967 and Cole and Stewart's (1996) sample of African American women who graduated between 1967 and 1973. Both groups were studied when they were 47 years old but were asked to report on their political ideology (presumably shaped in their college and early adult years), their college political activism, their midlife personalities, and their midlife political participation.

Cole and Stewart (1996) were interested in two questions: Was student political activism related to the development of a politicized middle-aged identity and a felt capacity for generativity? and were having a politicized identity and generativity important predictors of midlife political-participation? They found that for the White women both of these propositions were true. For them, student activism was associated with development of a politicized personal identity and a felt capacity for generativity. For the African American women, student activism was associated with midlife generativity but not with politicized identity. In terms of predictors of *midlife political participation*, the same pattern held. Politicized identity and generativity were both associated with mid-life political activism for White women, while again only generativity predicted it for the African American women. Since the African American women scored significantly higher on political identity than the White women, and showed less variance on it, we suspect that having a politicized identity is simply more normative for Black than White women and is therefore less likely to relate to any particular political activity. These analyses suggested, though, that the politicized identities

and capacity for generativity that resulted from many of these women's activism in the 1960s and 1970s were associated not only with personality development (in terms of identity and generativity) but also with political participation in middle age.

SUMMARY: MIDDLE AGING IN WOMEN

What have we learned from reviewing the picture of middle age that emerges from these different analyses? First, what seems to be common to middle age for "women in general," at least college-educated women? It seems that common to most of the women are an increased sense of personal identity and confidence in personal efficacy, paralleled by a somewhat increased preoccupation with aging itself. These feelings were reported to increase by women in all of the samples, regardless of cohort. This pattern of feelings is *not* consistent with the popular images of middle-aged women but is confirmed by their interview statements. In fact, there is an exuberance in these women that is hard to miss, along with a sense of personal authority and agency. One woman said,

I've now accumulated a certain amount of experience professionally that will be useful! I can teach somebody else some of that—not just the mechanics, but how to get along in certain situations…Five years ago I don't think I would have looked at it the same way.

Another woman said, "I never thought of myself as having that kind of authority, where I could—in just a calm manner—just say, 'this is it, these are your choices.' I think I always wanted to make sure everything was okay, and nobody was mad."

Many women described more freedom from inhibitions. One woman commented that in meetings, in the past,

My usual censor mechanisms came in of "well, maybe you'd better wait," and "is this the time," and "do you know the group?" And the other part said, "Oh, the hell with it. If you've got something that you think is important they should listen to—throw it out there!"

Perhaps this is what Neugarten and Berkowitz (1964) meant by the "executive personality," and perhaps it is part of middle age when all goes well for both men and women of all cohorts. It is possible, though, that some part of the "high" for this group comes from the lifting of the burden of inhibition and constraint specific to the historical period of their young adulthood. It will be important to study whether still younger generations of women will feel *better* as young adults and therefore not quite so elated in middle age.

It was common for the women in these samples to make changes in early middle age, and to engage in a process of life review and midcourse correction. Most of the women weathered this process very well indeed, whereas a few seemed unable to transform their lives and experienced a kind of paralyzed depression in middle age. It remains to be seen what later middle age will look like for these women—we are still hoping they will find their way. We may also hope that younger cohorts of women will find more opportunities earlier and that fewer will therefore feel they must drastically transform their lives in middle age.

What about things that are common only to some cohorts of women—things affected by the particularities of the social context? Even within the span of these studies, more recent cohorts are more likely to report that as they grow older they have an increased capacity for generativity, while the oldest cohort reported high levels of generativity at all ages. In addition, secure identity formation did not play an important role in the development of personality or well-being in cohorts that came of age in the 1950s. We suspect that for women personality development in terms of individualized identity was both unlikely and unrewarding in that era. For younger women, though, identity achievement is strongly associated with continued personality development, establishment of a satisfying life structure, and later midlife well-being. Will the formation of a strong personal identity continue to play such an important role for future generations of women faced perhaps with less contradictory but also perhaps with less flexible and varied pressures for adult role performance? Does the formation of a strong personal identity play such an important role in cultures where individualism is less highly valued than in the United States?

Finally, the baby boom cohort—the Radcliffe, Smith, and Michigan samples—was powerfully influenced by the social movements that occurred in their late adolescence and young adulthood (see also Agronick & Duncan, 1998; Duncan & Agronick, 1995). Participation in these movements, and adoption of politicized identities, have been consequential both for their midlife activities, like political participation, and their midlife personalities. For this cohort, the civil rights and women's movements left traces not only in the world of opportunities but also in personality, and those traces matter as they confront new demands in later stages of life. Stewart, Settles, and Winter (1998) showed that these traces may be found both in women's private and public lives. They quoted one woman who said that the women's movement led her to feel "freer to leave my husband for a more fulfilling sex life" and an-

other who said that the movements generally "made the whole free-thinking, autonomous style of my life possible, both then and now," and a third who said "I totally identified with them…. I felt comfortable joining the antinuclear movement in the '80s as if I was returturng home."

There is a great deal the studies discussed here in detail cannot tell us about middle age. What is it like to reach middle age in poverty, having had few life chances and having accumulated many burdens? Is the growth in personal authority and generativity something that only relatively educated, economically privileged women experience? The studies of Kansas City adults conducted in the 1950s and published by Bernice Neugarten and her colleagues (Gruen, 1964; Neugarten & Berkowitz, 1964) *did* include a representative cross-section of adults, and they did not find differences in midlife generativity as a function of social class. More recently, McAdams, de St. Aubin, and Logan, 1993 (see also McAdams, Hart, & Maruna, 1998) measured various facets of generativity in a racially and economically diverse sample and found that education was slightly correlated with some measures but not with others and that income was uncorrelated with any of them. There is reason to believe, then, that individuals who face more externally imposed challenges than rewards in the course of adulthood *do* experience similar kinds of personality development in middle age. Indeed the cumulation of life experiences that build a sense of confidence, a knowledge of personal capacities, and a felt capacity to make a contribution to the community and the next generation does *not* depend on a lifetime of economic and racial privilege—that cumulation may even be more likely without such privilege. For example, Schulz (1998) described some of the strength and confidence a sample of Navajo women draw from their experiences coping with adversity. She quoted one woman as saying that to be Navajo is "to be able to handle any problem—even if we get to a place where we can't go forward, we always find a way." This sense of competence derives not from privilege, then, but from successfully handling difficulties. We need more research that explores the bases of midlife confidence among those whose earlier lives include deprivation and discrimination, as well as those with many advantages.

There is, too, the question of men—if gender and changes in gender expectations for women have affected the experience of middle age for women, they may also have done so for men. It is important for future research to assess whether men in the same cohort as these women experience the same increase in confidence and authority as the women. Perhaps the early adoption of a confident and authoritative stance. associated with cultural expectations of men, means that middle age for men involves more acknowledgement of doubt and vulnerability. Perhaps, too, the social changes of recent years will mean that young men who make major investments in domestic life will experience middle age differently than their fathers did. We also know little about the meanings of these same social events in the lives of men from the same cohort, though it is likely that the social events and movements of the 1960s did make a difference in their lives and personalities too.

Finally, the centrality of the women's movement and the civil rights and Vietnam protest movements to women's lives in the cohort we've been discussing in the United States is incontrovertible. Researchers have demonstrated that the psychology of some earlier generations in the United States was equally powerfully shaped by the Great Depression and World War II (see, e.g., Clausen, 1993; Elder, 1974, 1986; Elder & Clipp, 1989). But what are the critical social influences on the generations that have been shaped by the years since the 1960s, not to mention those in other cultures and nations? Within the U.S. context, recent generations may have been shaped, among other things, by a Republican-dominated Presidency and now by a Republican Congress, the rise of environmentalism, the gay rights and gay pride movements, the end of apartheid in South Africa, the end of communism in Eastern Europe, the discovery and spread of AIDS, the backlash against affirmative action and feminism in the United States, the Persian Gulf War, the war in Bosnia, and unnerving new forms of terrorism. Will these and other social events and movements shape the psychological experience of cohorts that have followed those who came of age in the 1960s? Will some of them affect background assumptions and values, while others shape identities or opportunities? We do not yet know whether the same kinds of events play all of these roles equally. Perhaps it is most common, for example, for social movements to affect identities (unless they result in large social changes, as perhaps the women's movement did that in turn may shape background assumptions of a younger generation). It is important to try to sort out how history does and does not change both women's—and men's—experience of middle age.

REFERENCES

Adelmann, P. K., Antonucci, T. C., Crohan, S. E., & Coleman, L. M. (1989). Empty-nest, cohort, and employment in the well-being of midlife women. *Sex Roles, 20*, 173–189.

Agronick, G. S., & Duncan, L. E. (1998). Personality and social change: Individual differences, life path, and importance attributed to the women's movement: A longitudinal analysis. *Journal of Personality and Social Psychology, 74*, 1545–1555.

Antonucci, T., & Akiyama, H. (1997). Concern with others at midlife: Care, comfort, or compromise? In M. E. Lachman & J. B. James (Eds.), *Multiple paths of midlife development* (pp. 147–169). Chicago: University of Chicago Press.

Barnett, R. C., & Baruch, G. K. (1978). Women in the middle years: A critique of research and theory. *Psychology of Women Quarterly, 3*, 187–197.

Bart, P. B. (1971). Depression in middle-aged women. In V. Gornick & B. K. Moran (Eds.), *Women in sexist society* (pp. 163–186). New York: New American Library.

Baruch, G., & Brooks-Gunn, J. (Eds.). (1984). *Women in midlife.* New York: Plenum.

Chiriboga, D. A. (1989). Mental health at the midpoint: Crisis, challenge, or relief? In S. Hunter & M. Sundel (Eds.), *Midlife myths: Issues, findings, and practice implications* (pp. 116–144). Newbury Park, CA: Sage.

Clausen, J. A. (1993). *American lives: Looking back at the children of the Great Depression.* Berkeley, CA: University of California Press.

Cole, E. R., & Stewart, A. J. (1996). Meanings of political participation among Black and White women: Political identity and social responsibility. *Journal of Personality and Social Psychology, 71*, 130–140.

Dan, A. J., & Bernhard, L. A. (1989). Menopause and other health issues for midlife women. In S. Hunter & M. Sundel (Eds.), *Midlife myths: Issues, findings, and practice implications* (pp. 51–66). Newbury Park, CA: Sage.

Datan, N. (1986). Corpses, lepers, and menstruating women: Tradition, transition, and the sociology of knowledge. *Sex Roles, 14*, 693–703.

Duncan, L. E., & Agronick, G. S. (1995). The intersection of life stage and social events: Personality and life outcomes. *Journal of Personality and Social Psychology, 69*, 558–568.

Elder, G. H., Jr. (1974). *Children of the Great Depression.* Chicago: University of Chicago Press.

Elder, G. H., Jr. (1986). Military times and turning points in men's lives. *Developmental Psychology, 22*, 233–245.

Elder, G. H., Jr., & Clipp, E. C. (1989). Combat experience and emotional health: Impairment and resilience in later life. *Journal of Personality, 57*, 311–341.

Erikson, E. H. (1975). *Life history and the historical moment.* New York: Norton.

Erikson, E. H. (1982). *The life cycle completed: A review.* New York: Norton.

Erikson, E. H., Erikson, J. M., & Kivnick, H. Q. (1986). *Vital involvement in old age.* New York: Norton.

Espin, O., Stewart, A. J., & Gomez, C. A. (1990). Letters from V: Adolescent personality development in socio-historical context. *Journal of Personality, 58,* 347–364.

Franks, V., & Fodor, I. (Eds.). (1990). Women at midlife and beyond [Special issue]. *Psychology of Women Quarterly, 14.*

Franz, C. E. (1997). Stability and change in the transition to midlife: A longitudinal study of midlife adults. In M. E. Lachman & J. B. James (Eds.), *Multiple paths of midlife development* (pp. 45–66). Chicago: University of Chicago Press.

Friedan, B. (1963). *The feminine mystique.* New York: Norton.

Gergen, M. M. (1990). Finished at 40: Women's development within the patriarchy. *Psychology of Women Quarterly, 14,* 471–494.

Gould, R. L. (1978). *Transformation: Growth and change in adult life.* New York: Simon & Schuster.

Grambs, J. D. (1989). *Women over 40: Visions and realities.* New York: Springer.

Greer, G. (1992). *The change: Women, aging, and the menopause.* New York: Knopf.

Gruen, W. (1964). Adult personality: An empirical study of Erikson's theory of ego development. In B. L. Neugarten (Ed.), *Personality in middle and late life: Empirical studies* (pp. 1–14). New York: Atherton.

Gullette, M. M. (1988). *Safe at last in the middle years: The invention of the midlife progress novel: Saul Bellow, Margaret Drabble, Anne Tyler, and John Updike.* Berkeley, CA: University of California Press.

Gutmann, D. L. (1987). *Reclaimed powers: Toward a new psychology of men and women in later life.* New York: Basic Books.

Haan, N. (1981). Common dimensions of personality development: Early adolescence to middle life. In D. H. Eichorn, J. A. Claussen, N. Haan, M. P. Honzik, & P. H. Mussen (Eds.), *Present and past in middle life* (pp. 17–151). New York: Academic Press.

Heilbrun, C. G. (1988). *Writing a woman's life.* New York: Norton.

Helson, R. (1993). In K. D. Hulbert & D. T. Schuster (Eds.), *Women's lives through time* (pp. 190–210). San Francisco: Jossey-Bass.

Helson, R. (1997). The self in middle age. In M. E. Lachman & J. B. James (Eds.), *Multiple paths of midlife development* (pp. 21–43). Chicago: University of Chicago Press.

Helson, R., & Moane, G. (1987). Personality change in women from college to midlife. *Journal of Personality and Social Psychology, 53,* 176–186.

Helson, R., Stewart, A. J., & Ostrove, J. (1995). Identity in three cohorts of midlife women. *Journal of Personality and Social Psychology, 69,* 544–557.

Howard, A., & Bray, D. (1988). *Managerial lives in transition: Advancing age and changing times.* New York: Guilford.

Hunter, S., & Sundel, M. (1989). Introduction: An examination of key issues concerning midlife. In S. Hunter & M. Sundel (Eds.), *Midlife myths: Issues, findings, and practice implications* (pp. 8–28). Newbury Park, CA: Sage.

Jacques, E. (1965). Death and the midlife crisis. *International Journal of Psychoanalysis, 46,* 502–514.

James, J. B., & Lewkowicz, C. J. (1997). Themes of power and affiliation across time. In M. E. Lachman & J. B. James (Eds.), *Multiple paths of midlife development* (pp. 109–143). Chicago: University of Chicago Press.

Jung, C. G. (1954). The development of personality. In W. McGuire (Ed.), *The collected works of C. G. Jung* (Vol. 17, pp. 167–186). Princeton, NJ: Princeton University Press.

Karp, D. A. (1988). A decade of reminders: Changing age consciousness between fifty and sixty years old. *The Gerontologist, 28,* 727–738.

Levinson, D. J. (1996). *The seasons of a woman's life.* New York: Knopf.

Levinson, D. J., Darrow, C. M., Klein, E. B., Levinson, M. H., & McKee, B. (1978). *The seasons of a man's life.* New York: Ballantine Books.

MacDermid, S. M., Franz, C. E., & De Reus, L. A. (1998). Generativity: At the crossroads of social roles and personality. In D. P. McAdams & E. de St. Aubin (Eds.), *Generativity and adult development: How and why we care about the next generation* (pp. 181–226). Washington, DC: American Psychological Association Press.

Marcia, J. (1966). Development and validation of ego-identity status. *Journal of Personality and Social Psychology, 3,* 551–558.

McAdams, D. P., & de St. Aubin, E. (1992). A theory of generativity and its assessment through self-report, behavioral acts, and narrative themes in autobiography. *Journal of Personality and Social Psychology, 62,* 1003–1015.

McAdams, D. P., de St. Aubin, E., & Logan, R. L. (1993). Generativity among young, midlife, and older adults. *Psychology and Aging, 8,* 221–230.

McAdams, D. P., Hart, H. M., & Maruna, S. (1998). The anatomy of generativity. In D. P. McAdams & E. de St. Aubin (Eds.), *Generativity and adult development: How and why we care about the next generation* (pp. 7–44). Washington, DC: American Psychological Association Press.

McCrae, R. R., & Costa, P. T., Jr. (1984). *Emerging lives, enduring dispositions: Personality in adulthood.* Boston: Little, Brown.

Mitchell, V., & Helson, R. (1990). Women's prime of life: Is it the fifties? *Psychology of Women Quarterly, 14,* 451–470.

Neugarten, B. L. (1968). The awareness of middle age. In B. L. Neugarten (Ed.), *Middle age and aging.* Chicago: University of Chicago Press.

Neugarten, B. L., & Berkowitz, H. (1964). *Personality in middle and late life: Empirical studies.* New York: Atherton.

Neugarten, B. L., & Kraines, R. J. (1965). "Menopausal symptoms" in women of various ages. *Psychosomatic Medicine, 27,* 266–273.

Ochse, R., & Plug, C. (1986). Cross-cultural investigations of the validity of Erikson's theory of personality development. *Journal of Personality and Social Psychology, 50,* 1240–1252.

Osherson, S. D. (1980). *Holding on or letting go: Men and career change at mid-life.* New York: Free Press.

Ostrove, J. M., Deitch, S. J., & Stewart, A. J. (1998). *Feminist consciousness and well-being among women at midlife.* Manuscript submitted for publication.

Ostrove, J. M., & Stewart, A. J. (1994). Meanings and uses of marginal identities: Social class at Radcliffe in the 1960s. In C. E. Franz & A. J. Stewart (Eds.), *Women creating lives: Identities, resilience and resistance* (pp. 289–307). Boulder, CO: Westview.

Ostrove, J. M., & Stewart, A. J. (1998). Representing Radcliffe: Perceptions and consequences of social class. *Journal of Adult Development, 5*(3), 183–193.

Pearlin, L. (1975). Sex roles and depression. In N. Datan & L. H. Ginsberg (Eds.), *Life-span developmental psychology: Normative life crises* (pp. 191–207). New York: Academic Press.

Peterson, B. E., & Stewart, A. J. (1990). Using personal and fictional documents to assess psychosocial development: A case study of Vera Brittain's generativity. *Psychology and Aging, 5,* 400–411.

Peterson, B. E., & Stewart, A. J. (1993). Generativity and social motives in young adults. *Journal of Personality and Social Psychology, 65,* 186–198.

Ryff, C. D., & Heincke, S. G. (1983). Subjective organization of personality in adulthood and aging. *Journal of Personality and Social Psychology, 44,* 807–816.

Ryff, C. D., & Migdal, S. (1984). Intimacy and generativity: Self-perceived transitions. *Signs, 9,* 470–481.

Schulz, A. J. (1998). Navajo women and the politics of identities. *Social Problems, 45*(3), 336–355.

Stewart, A. J. (1994). The women's movement and women's lives: Linking individual development and social events. In A. Lieblich & R. Josselson (Eds.), *The narrative study of lives: Exploring identity and gender* (Vol. 2, pp. 230–250). Thousand Oaks, CA: Sage.

Stewart, A. J., & Healy, J. M., Jr. (1986). The role of personality development and experience in shaping political commitment: An illustrative case. *Journal of Social Issues, 42,* 11–31.

Stewart, A. J., & Healy, J. M., Jr. (1989). Linking individual development and social changes. *American Psychologist, 44,* 30–42.

Stewart, A. J., & Ostrove, J. M. (1993). Social class, social change, and gender: Working-class women at Radcliffe and after. *Psychology of Women Quarterly, 17,* 475–497.

Stewart, A. J., Ostrove, J. M., & Helson, R. (1998). *Middle aging in women: Patterns of personality change from the 30s to the 50s.* Manuscript submitted for publication.

Stewart, A. J., & Salt, P. (1983). Changing sex roles: College graduates of the sixties and seventies. In M. D. Hor-

ner, C. Nadelson, & M. Notman (Eds.), *The challenge of change* (pp. 275–296). New York: Plenum.

Stewart, A. J., Settles, I. H., & Winter, N. J. G. (1998). Women and the social movements of the 1960s: Activists, engaged observers, and nonparticipants. *Political Psychology, 19,* 63–94.

Stewart, A. J., & Vandewater, E. A. (1993). The Radcliffe Class of 1964: Career and family social clock projects in a transitional cohort. In K. D. Hulbert & D. T. Schuster (Eds.), *Women's lives through time* (pp. 235–258). San Francisco: Jossey-Bass.

Stewart, A. J., & Vandewater, E. A. (1998). The course of generativity. In D. P. McAdams & E. de St. Aubin (Eds.), *Generativity and adult development: Psychosocial perspectives on caring for and contributing to the next generation* (pp. 75–100). Washington, DC: American Psychological Association Press.

Stewart, A. J., & Vandewater, E. A. (in press). "If I had it to do over": Women's midlife review and midcourse corrections. *Journal of Personality and Social Psychology.*

Tangri, S., & Jenkins, S. (1993). The University of Michigan Class of 1967: The women's life paths study. In K. D. Hulbert & D. T. Schuster (Eds.), *Women's lives through time* (pp. 259–281). San Francisco: Jossey-Bass.

Vaillant, G. E. (1977). *Adaptation to life.* Boston: Little, Brown.

Vaillant, G. E. (1993). *The wisdom of the ego.* Cambridge, MA: Harvard University Press.

Vandewater, E. A., Ostrove, J. M., & Stewart, A. J. (1997). Predicting women's well-being in midlife: The importance of personality development and social role involvements. *Journal of Personality and Social Psychology, 72,* 1147–1160.

Veroff, J. E., Douvan, E., & Kulka, R. (1981). *The inner American: A self-portrait from 1957 to 1976.* New York: Basic Books.

Veroff, J. E., & Feld, S. (1970). *Marriage and work in America: A study of motives and roles.* New York: Van Nostrand Reinhold.

Whitbourne, S. K., Zuschlag, M. K., Elliot, L. B., & Waterman, A. S. (1992). Psychosocial development in adulthood: A 22-year sequential study. *Journal of Personality and Social Psychology, 63,* 260–271.

SELF-STUDY QUESTIONS

Multiple Choice

1. Navajo women debunk the idea that personal authority and generativity
   a. are experienced only by educated, upper class women
   b. are experienced because to be a Navajo woman implies the ability to tackle any problem in life
   c. are experienced because of their facing adversity and resolving conflicts that they face
   d. all of the above

2. In comparing the Radcliffe class of 1947 with the Radcliffe class of 1964, the authors found that by middle age, the 1964 class was experiencing all of these trends except
   a. having fewer children
   b. getting divorced more frequently
   c. entering politics on a state level
   d. gaining graduate educations and professional careers

Essay

1. The authors suggest that young adulthood may be a more difficult and challenging time of life, and middle age a more rewarding and positive time of life. Do you agree? Explain why or why not.
2. Explain how a woman's having a well-developed identity might contribute to her feelings of well-being in midlife.

MIDDLE ADULTHOOD

"Creativity: Cognitive, Personal, Developmental, and Social Aspects"

OVERVIEW

Do you remember all those standardized tests you took in school to measure your intelligence? The author of this article suggests that the testing approach to intelligence focuses on a very narrow set of abilities and entirely ignores analyzing creativity. In addition, the emphasis on declining abilities in adulthood, he argues, causes lay people and psychologists alike to fail to recognize that some intellectual abilities, including creativity, may actually increase in middle and late adulthood. The author reviews historical and current theories of intelligence and creativity. He argues that both our genetic inheritance and characteristics of our environments contribute to the development of creativity.

METHODOLOGY

The author of this article reviews his own and others' research on creativity to illustrate the various approaches psychologists take to studying it. Thus, there are no references to specific research methods or statistical analyses.

GLOSSARY TERMS

- **Creativity** the ability used in the production of original ideas and/or solutions to various problems
- **Cognitive processes** aspects of mental activity such as thinking, reasoning, perception, ability to learn, memory, language acquisition, insight, and problem-solving
- **Primary-process thinking** Freud's description of the kind of thinking characteristic of the personality component he called the *id*, where our basic instincts, wishes, and desires reside; the id tries to satisfy a need or longing either by direct action on an object that would supply satisfaction or on an image of that object that would satisfy basic cravings

- **Cognitive unconscious** the process whereby one idea or concept stimulates the formation of another idea or concept
- **Brainstorming** a popular technique that encourages the production of creative ideas and problem-solving in groups, especially in industrial or organizational settings
- **Sternberg's triarchic theory of intelligence** a theory that proposes three types of intelligence
- **Gardner's theory of multiple intelligences** a theory that hypothesizes seven different types of intelligence
- **Guilford's structure-of-intellect model** a theory proposing 360 separate types of intelligence

Creativity: Cognitive, Personal, Developmental, and Social Aspects

Although many psychologists have expressed an interest in the phenomenon of creativity, psychological research on this topic did not rapidly expand until after J. P. Guilford claimed, in his 1950 APA presidential address, that this topic deserved far more attention than it was then receiving. This article reviews the progress psychologists have made in understanding creativity since Guilford's call to arms. Research progress has taken place on 4 fronts: the cognitive processes involved in the creative act, the distinctive characteristics of the creative person, the development and manifestation of creativity across the individual life span, and the social environments most strongly associated with creative activity. Although some important questions remain unanswered, psychologists now know more than ever before about how individuals achieve this special and significant form of optimal human functioning.

Creativity is certainly among the most important and pervasive of all human activities. Homes and offices are filled with furniture, appliances, and other conveniences that are the products of human inventiveness. People amuse themselves with the comics in the daily paper, take novels with them to while away the hours on a plane or at the beach, go to movie theaters to see the latest blockbusters, watch television shows and commercials, play games on the computer, attend concerts from classical and jazz to rock and soul, visit museums that display the artistic artifacts of cultures and civilizations—again all implicitly bearing ample testimony to the consequences of the creative mind. The buildings people enter, the cars they drive, the clothes they wear—even the music they hear in elevators—are all exemplars of some form of creativity. The only way to escape this phenomenon is to walk stark naked deep within some primeval forest, and even then a person must take care not to hum a single tune, not to recall even one line of poetry, or not to even to look up in the sky for fear of seeing some jet or its contrail.

Not surprisingly, creativity is seen as a good attribute for people to possess. Teachers expect their students to display some creativity in their science projects and term papers. Executives at high-tech firms expect their research and development units to devise new products and their marketing units to conceive novel strategies to promote those products. At a more personal level, creativity is often seen as a sign of mental health and emotional well-being. In fact, various art and music therapies have emerged that promote psychological adjustment and growth through creative expression. In a nutshell, creativity can be counted among those very special ways that human beings can display optimal functioning

Despite the significant and omnipresent nature of creativity, psychologists have seldom if ever viewed it as a central research topic (Sternberg & Lubart, 1996). For example, of all the numerous recipients of APA's Award for Distinguished Scientific Contributions since 1956, only one, J. P. Guilford, can be credited with devoting a substantial part of his career to the psychological study of creativity. To be sure, other recipients of this high honor have addressed this topic as a side excursion of their primary investigations. Examples include figures as diverse as Wolfgang Köhler, Carl Rogers, B. F. Skinner, Jerome Bruner, James E. Birren, Herbert A. Simon, Donald T. Campbell, and David C. McClelland. Nevertheless, probably only Guilford can be said to enjoy simultaneous prominence in psychological science in general and in the more specialized domain of creativity research. Indeed, in his classic 1950 presidential address before the American Psychological Association, Guilford made a plea on behalf of making creativity a more focal point of psychological inquiry (Guilford, 1950). Fortunately, many psychologists responded to the call, and creativity research really boomed in the 1960s and early 1970s. Moreover, after a slight lull of a decade or so, psychologists have shown a renewed interest in the phenomenon. Although not yet a mainstream research topic, psychologists now know far more about creativity than ever before. That knowledge reveals a great deal about antecedents, correlates, and consequences of this particular form of optimal human functioning. In fact, this literature has now become so vast and rich that this article can accomplish no more than a review of the mere highlights.

OVERVIEW

The literature on creativity spans several of the core sub-disciplines of psychology. This breadth is immediately apparent in the four main topics discussed below: cognitive processes, personal characteristics, life span development, and social context.

Cognitive Processes

The creative act is often portrayed as a mysterious and even mystical process, more akin to divine inspiration than to mundane thought. This view dates back to the ancient Greeks, who believed that creativity required the intervention of the muses. One of the principal goals of psychological studies has been to try to remove this mystery, replacing it with a deeper scientific understanding. For example, Sigmund Freud and other psychoanalytic thinkers attempted to accomplish this end by explicating creativity in terms of primary-process thinking (Gedo, 1997). However, with the advent of contemporary cognitive science, psychology has come much closer to appreciating the mental processes that must participate in the creative act. Recent developments in four areas of research—insightful problem solving, creative cognition, expertise acquisition, and computer simulation—deserve special mention.

Insightful problem solving.   The Gestalt psychologists were the first psychologists to study creativity through the process of insight. Cognitive psychologists have built upon this early tradition by developing new experimental methodologies and theoretical models (Sternberg & Davidson, 1995). By manipulating priming stimuli, assessing feeling-of-

knowing states, using protocol analysis, and applying other techniques, psychologists better understand how creative insights emerge during the incubation period. Especially striking is the empirical demonstration of intuitive information processing as a regular manifestation of the *cognitive unconscious* (e.g., Bowers, Farvolden, & Mermigis, 1995; Schooler & Melcher, 1995). The magic behind the sudden, unexpected, and seemingly unprepared inspiration has now been replaced by the lawful operation of subliminal stimulation and spreading activation.

Creative cognition.   One of the more significant events in recent cognitive psychology is the emergence of *the creative cognition approach* (Smith, Ward, & Finke, 1995). According to this research program, creativity is a mental phenomenon that results from the application of ordinary cognitive processes (see also Ward, Smith, & Vaid, 1997). In addition, just as laboratory experiments have provided tremendous insights into human cognition, the same methodology can be applied to the study of creative thought. Particularly provocative are the experimental studies showing how visual imagery can function in the origination of creative ideas (Finke, Ward, & Smith, 1992). Another exciting feature of these experiments is the use of open-ended problems that demand genuine creativity, in contrast to much laboratory research that relies on problems that have fixed solutions. Nevertheless, these investigations concur with those on insightful problem solving in one fundamental message: The optimal functioning embodied by creativity entails ordinary cognitive processes, and hence creative thought is accessible to almost anyone.

Expertise acquisition.   Recent research has amply demonstrated that exceptional talents are less born than made (Ericsson, 1996). Whether the domain is competitive sports, chess, or music performance, it usually requires about a decade of extensive deliberate practice before a person can attain world-class proficiency. Furthermore, evidence increasingly shows that to a certain extent, creativity demands a comparable level of systematic training and practice. Even the creative genius cannot escape this inherently laborious period of apprenticeship (Hayes, 1989; Simonton, 1991b). Creative individuals do not produce new ideas de novo, but rather those ideas must arise from a large set of well-developed skills and a rich body of domain-relevant knowledge. Like the work on creative cognition, this conception of creative expertise has rather egalitarian implications regarding the ability of anyone to acquire this form of optimal functioning (see Howe, Davidson, & Sloboda, 1998).

Computer simulation. A final development that has great promise is the increased use of computers to test explicit cognitive models of the creative process (Boden, 1991; Johnson-Laird, 1993). For instance, Newell and Simon's (1972) classic theory of human problem solving has inspired the emergence of several "discovery programs" that purport to uncover laws and principles from empirical data—often using the same raw data to make the same discoveries made by eminent scientists (Langley, Simon, Bradshaw, & Zythow, 1987; Shrager & Langley, 1990). Other computer programs have endeavored to reproduce creative behavior in art, literature, and music, sometimes with remarkable success (Boden, 1991). Additional strategies that have promising futures are genetic algorithms and genetic programming (Martindale, 1995). Although originally designed by computer scientists to solve practical problems, it is becoming increasingly apparent that these programs may eventually provide valuable theoretical models of how the creative process operates in the human mind (Simonton, 1999b).

In the long term, as the simulations of these computer models become ever more convincing, psychologists may eventually understand how best to increase the creative potential of all human beings.

Personal Characteristics

Psychologists have long been interested in the individual attributes that enable some persons to display more creativity than others do. The empirical literature, both classic and current, falls naturally under two headings: intelligence and personality.

Intelligence. Many investigators have been interested in the extent to which creativity requires superior intelligence, a tradition that dates back to the pioneer work of Galton (1869) and Terman (1925). Using performance on standard IQ tests as the gauge of intellectual capacity, the early research indicated that a certain threshold level of intelligence was required for the manifestation of creativity but that beyond that threshold, intelligence bore a minimal relation with creative behavior (Barron & Harrington, 1981). More critical was the realization that the simplistic, exclusive, and unidimensional concept of intelligence had to be replaced by a more complex, inclusive, and multidimensional conception. Examples include Guilford's (1967) structure-of-intellect model, Stern-

berg's (1985) triarchic theory of intelligence, and Gardner's (1983) theory of multiple intelligences. The last theory is especially provocative insofar as it includes abilities that are not a standard part of psychometric tests (e.g., musical, bodily-kinesthetic, interpersonal, and intrapersonal intelligences). Moreover, each intelligence is associated with a specific manifestation of creativity, such as painting, choreography, or psychology (Gardner, 1993).

Personality. It has been long recognized that creativity is as much a dispositional as an intellectual phenomenon (e.g., Dellas & Gaier, 1970). This was made quite apparent, for example, in the early research on the creative personality conducted at the Institute for Personality Assessment and Research at the University of California, Berkeley (e.g., Barron, 1969; MacKinnon, 1978). Although interest in the dispositional correlates of creativity waned somewhat with the arrival of the cognitive revolution, personality research has seen a revival in recent years. As a result, researchers have now compiled a fairly secure profile of the creative personality (e.g., Martindale, 1989; Simonton, 1999a). In particular, such persons are disposed to be independent, nonconformist, unconventional, even bohemian, and they are likely to have wide interests, greater openness to new experiences, a more conspicuous behavioral and cognitive flexibility, and more risk-taking boldness.

Particularly fascinating is what the research has contributed to the long-standing mad-genius controversy. There is now sufficient evidence showing that creativity often tends to be associated with a certain amount of psychopathology (e.g., Eysenck, 1995; Jamison, 1993; Ludwig, 1995). At the same time, this association is not equivalent to the claim that creative individuals must necessarily suffer from mental disorders. On the contrary, research has shown that (a) numerous creators, even of the highest order, have no apparent tendencies toward psychopathology; (b) the incidence rates vary according to the domain of creative activity, with some domains showing rather low rates; (c) those creators who seemingly exhibit symptoms usually possess compensatory characteristics that enable them to control and even channel their proclivities into productive activities; and (d) many characteristics that appear abnormal may actually prove quite adaptive to the individual's lifelong adjustment (see, e.g., Barron 1969; Csikszentmihalyi, 1997; Ludwig, 1995; Rothenberg 1990). In fact, the creative personality often provides a fine illustration of how supposed psychological weaknesses can sometimes be converted into a form of optimal functioning.

Life Span Development

Creativity is more than a cognitive and dispositional attribution in which individuals may vary. It is also an activity that develops over the course of the human life span. Researchers into the developmental psychology of creativity have focused on two aspects of this longitudinal transformation. First, investigators have examined what childhood and adolescent experiences appear to be associated with the development of creative potential. Second, researchers have scrutinized how that potential is actualized during the course of the creator's adulthood and final years. Many of the studies in either category have concentrated on the development of individuals who have attained some acclaim for their creative achievements, albeit there is no shortage of inquiries into the emergence of more everyday forms of creative behavior.

The acquisition of creative potential. A very large inventory of developmental antecedents has been documented over the past several decades of research (Simonton, 1987). A great number of these influences concern the family environments and circumstances that seem to most favor the emergence of creative personalities. These factors include birth order, early parental loss, marginality, and the availability of mentors and role models. Other developmental variables refer to an individual's experience and performance in primary, secondary, and higher education. Perhaps the most remarkable generalization to be drawn from both sets of developmental influences is that exceptional creativity does not always emerge from the most nurturant environments (e.g., Eisenstadt 1978; Goertzel, Goertzel, & Goertzel, 1978; Simonton 1984). On the contrary, creative potential seems to require a certain exposure to (a) diversifying experiences that help weaken the constraints imposed by conventional socialization and (b) challenging experiences that help strengthen a person's capacity to persevere in the face of obstacles (Simonton, 1994). These developmental inputs may be especially important for artistic forms of creative behavior. In any case, it is startling testimony to the adaptive power of the human being that some of the most adverse childhoods can give birth to the most creative adulthoods.

One other major movement in the recent literature deserves mention. Back in 1869, Galton first introduced the notion that exceptional creativity might have a genetic foundation. With the advent of modern behavioral genetics, this possibility has received increased attention (Lykken, 1998; Simonton, 1999c; Waller, Bouchard, Lykken, Tellegen, & Blacker, 1993).

Although it is still too early to tell exactly how much individual variation in creativity owes its existence to genetic endowment, there is no doubt that certain intellectual and dispositional traits required for creativity display respectable heritability coefficients (Bouchard, 1994; Eysenck, 1995). It is becoming increasingly clear that the acquisition of creative potential requires the simultaneous contribution of both nature and nurture.

The actualization of creative potential. Many investigators have been fascinated with how creativity is manifested during the course of a person's career (e.g., Gardner, 1993; Root-Bernstein, Bernstein, & Gardier, 1993). Especially notable is the *evolving systems approach* of Howard Gruber (1989) and his colleagues. Taking advantage of laboratory notebooks, sketchbooks, diaries, and other archival sources, these researchers have examined how creative ideas emerge and develop in a complex and dynamic interaction between the creator's personal vision and the sociocultural milieu in which that creativity must take place (see Wallace & Gruber, 1989). A distinctive feature of these inquiries is their emphasis on the qualitative and idiographic case-study method, an approach that permits an in-depth understanding of how creativity works in individual lives.

However, large-sample quantitative and nomothetic investigations on this topic are also abundant. The question that has received the most attention has been the relation between creativity and age (Simonton, 1988). Sometimes this issue is addressed by gauging how performance on psychometric measures of creativity changes across the adult life span (e.g., McCrae, Arenberg, & Costa, 1987), but the more common approach is to assess how the output of creative products chances as a function of age (e.g., Lehman, 1953; Lindauer, 1993b). Because this research has consistently found that creativity is a curvilinear (inverted backward J) function of age, one might conclude that older individuals would not be creative. However, the empirical and theoretical literature shows that such a pessimistic conclusion is unjustified (Csikszentmihalyi, 1997; Dennis, 1966; Simonton, 1991a, 1997a). Numerous factors operate that help maintain creative output throughout the life span. Indeed, it is actually possible for creators to display a qualitative and quantitative resurgence of creativity in their final years (Lindauer, 1993a; Simonton, 1989). Considering these findings, the picture for creativity in the later years of life is optimistic rather than pessimistic. Given that the 21st century will see a huge generation of "baby boomers" entering their golden years, this particular generalization about optimal functioning will acquire even more importance.

Social Context

The original research on creativity tended to adopt an excessively individualistic perspective. Creativity was viewed as a process that took place in the mind of a single individual who possessed the appropriate personal characteristics and developmental experiences. Beginning in the late 1970s, however, more psychologists began to recognize that creativity takes place in a social context (e.g., Harrington, 1990). Indeed, in the 1980s, an explicit social psychology of creativity emerged to supplement the cognitive, differential, and developmental perspectives (e.g., Amabile, 1983). The methods adopted in this burgeoning field range from laboratory experiments and field observations to content analytical and historiometric studies. These investigations have also looked at a diversity of external conditions, with perhaps the greatest emphasis on the interpersonal, disciplinary, and sociocultural environments.

Interpersonal environment. Although there has long existed the popular image of the lone genius, it is clear that much creativity takes place in interpersonal settings. The student may be expected to display creativity on a term paper or essay exam, or the worker may be expected to exhibit some creativity on the job. The particular nature of the interpersonal expectations may then serve to either enhance or inhibit the amount of creativity shown by the individual. A good illustration of the possibilities may be found in the research of Amabile and her associates (e.g., Amabile, 1996) on the repercussions of rewards, evaluation, surveillance, and other circumstances. Particularly valuable are their inquiries into the impact of intrinsic and extrinsic incentives for performing a task. Creativity usually appears more favored when individuals perform a task for inherent enjoyment rather than for some external reason that has little to do with the task itself. However, circumstances also occur in which the extrinsic motivation can contribute to the amplification of individual creativity (Amabile, 1996; Eisenberger & Cameron, 1996). This research has obvious implications for how to best nurture creativity in both schools and the workplace.

Before advancing to the next variety of social context, I should at least mention the current status of research on brainstorming. This technique was first introduced as a way of stimulating the production of creative ideas in problem-solving groups (Osborn, 1963). In a sense, brainstorming purports to

generate creativity from an interpersonal rather than an intrapersonal process. Brainstorming has become a very popular approach in industrial and organizational settings (Farr, 1990). Unfortunately, although the research literature is not uniform in its assessment of the method's validity, it is clear that brainstorming has utility only with rather specific types of instructions and guidance (e.g., Diehl & Stroebe, 1987). At present, it is impossible to say whether this method will be rendered more effective by the current research on electronic brainstorming in which the interactions occur through computer mediation (e.g., Roy, Gauvin, & Limayem, 1996).

Disciplinary environment. Most creators do not function in isolation from other creators, but rather their creativity takes place within a particular artistic, scientific, or intellectual discipline. For example, in the systems view put forward by Csikszentmihalyi (1990), creativity requires the dynamic interaction between three subsystems, only one of which entails the individual creator. The second subsystem is the domain, which consists of the set of rules, the repertoire of techniques, and any other abstract attributes that define a particular mode of creativity (e.g., the paradigm that guides normal science, according to Kuhn, 1970). The third subsystem is the field, which consists of those persons who work within the same domain, and thus have their creativity governed by the same domain-specific guidelines. These colleagues are essential to the realization of individual creativity, according to the systems view, because creativity does not exist until those making up the field decide to recognize that a given creative product represents an original contribution to the domain.

Once psychologists recognize that creativity emerges out of an interaction of individual, field, and domain, then the phenomenon becomes far more complex. One illustration of this complexity may be found in Martindale's (1990) research on stylistic change in the arts, especially in poetic literature. Although the poet wants to reach as wide a public as possible, Martindale argued that the most important audience for poetry is fellow writers (as well as a few select critics), who play the major part in evaluating whether an author's poetry qualifies as creative. That evaluation is based on two considerations. First, the poetry must conform to the stylistic rules of the time, rules that define the acceptable form and content for that particular domain of creativity. Second, the poetry must be original, rather than merely rehashing what has already been said. In the early history of a particular style, poets can attain this second end by ever more extensive use of what Martindale called "primordial thought" (i.e., primary-process thinking in psychoanalytic terms), but as time goes on, originality can only be obtained by stretching, even outright violating, the various rules of the game. After a few generations, the stylistic conventions begin to break down, and the domain loses its coherence—which means it becomes increasingly difficult for anyone to judge what is good and bad among contemporary poems. Fortunately, a new style usually emerges, with distinctive sets of form and content prescriptions, and the whole cyclical process begins once again. Martindale has empirically documented this progression not just in poetry, but in most other forms of creativity as well, including music and painting.

Needless to say, once psychologists acknowledge that creativity is a systemic rather than a totally individualistic phenomenon, it becomes far more difficult to study using the more commonplace methods of psychology. Experimental studies of human problem solving become far less enlightening to the extent that the laboratory cubical isolates the person from a disciplinary domain and field. Psychometric inquiries into the creative personality are likewise rendered less insightful to the degree that the creator has been unrooted from his or her disciplinary matrix. To circumvent these limitations, psychologists have adopted a number of strategies. Some, like Martindale (1990), have taken advantage of archival data to study the interplay between creators and their disciplines (see also Simonton, 1992b). Others have engaged in some form of participant observation, such as Dunbar's (1995) provocative in situ examination of scientific discovery in biomedical research laboratories. Although these alternative methods are much more arduous than the more commonplace experimental and psychometric investigations, they have contributed findings that could not be acquired in any other way. In particular, such investigations have amply proven that creativity cannot be divorced from its disciplinary context.

Sociocultural environment. Beyond the realm of interpersonal and disciplinary interactions, there exists the larger external milieu. Sociologists and anthropologists have long argued that creativity is mostly if not entirely a sociocultural phenomenon (e.g., Kroeber, 1944), but only in the past couple of decades have psychologists begun to scrutinize the extent to which creative achievements depend on the impersonal and pervasive zeitgeist (Simonton, 1984). Two findings warrant special mention here:

1. It has become increasingly clear that certain political environments affect the degree of creativity manifested by the corresponding population. Some of these political influences operate directly on the adult creator, such as when warfare depresses the output of creative ideas (Simonton, 1984). Other political effects function during the developmental stages of an individual's life, either encouraging or discouraging the acquisition of creative potential. Thus, on the one hand, growing up in times of anarchy, when the political world is plagued by assassinations, coups d'état, and military mutinies, tends to be antithetical to creative development (e.g., Simonton, 1976). On the other hand, growing up when a civilization is fragmented into a large number of peacefully coexisting independent states tends to be conducive to the development of creative potential (e.g., Simonton, 1975). In fact, nationalistic revolts against the oppressive rule of empire states tends to have a positive consequence for the amount of creativity in the following generations (Kroeber, 1944; Simonton, 1975; Sorokin, 1947/1969). Many nations have experienced golden ages after winning independence from foreign domination, with ancient Greece providing a classic example.

2. The rationale for the last mentioned consequence may be that nationalistic rebellion encourages cultural heterogeneity rather than homogeneity (Simonton, 1994). Rather than everyone having to speak the same language, read the same books, follow the same laws, and so on, individuals are left with more options. This suggests that cultural diversity may facilitate creativity, and there is evidence that this is the case. Creative activity in a civilization tends to increase after it has opened itself to extensive alien influences, whether through immigration, travel abroad, or studying under foreign teachers (Simonton. 1997b). By enriching the cultural environment, the ground may be laid for new creative syntheses. This finding is consistent with a host of other empirical results, such as the creativity-augmenting effects of ethnic marginality, bilingualism, and even exposure to ideological or behavioral dissent (e.g., Campbell, 1960; Lambert, Tucker, & d'Anglejan, 1973; Nemeth & Kwan, 1987; Simonton, 1994).

These and other sociocultural forces are potent enough that they can completely extinguish creativity in a given nation, sometimes producing a dark age that may last for generations (Simonton, 1984). However, it requires emphasis that zeitgeist factors serve to raise or lower the general level of creative activity at a given time and place, but cannot easily account for individual differences in the development and manifestation of creativity. For example, the general milieu may largely explain why the Renaissance began in Italy but not why Michelangelo towered over his Italian contemporaries.

CONCLUSION

Although psychologists have made tremendous progress in the understanding of creativity, much work remains to be done. Certainly, many substantive questions demand considerably more empirical scrutiny. Consider, for example, the following three desiderata:

1. Psychologists still have a long way to co before they come anywhere close to understanding creativity in women and minorities (see, e.g., Helson, 1990). So far, creativity in such groups seems to display a complex pattern of divergence and convergence relative to what has been observed in majority-culture male study participants (e.g., Simonton, 1992a, 1998). The details of these differences and similarities must be empirically documented before psychologists can be said to understand how this form of optimal functioning operates in the entire human race.

2. Psychologists must carry out more ambitious longitudinal studies that examine how creativity develops during the course of childhood, adolescence, and adulthood. Terman's (1925) classic investigation followed a cohort of intellectually gifted children throughout their life courses, but most current work has been obliged to scrutinize a narrower slice of the life span (e.g., Csikszentmihalyi, Rathunde, & Whalen, 1993; Getzels & Csikszentmihalyi, 1976; Subotnik & Arnold, 1994). Although such investigations have told psychologists much about creative development, only more extensive studies can complete the picture of the origins of creative potential.

3. Psychologists also need to carry out more research on the attributes of the creative product. Ironically, although psychologists have made considerable advances in their understanding of what contributes to the success of an aesthetic composition (e.g., Martindale, 1990; Simonton, 1980), they still know very little about what determines the creativity of a scientific contribution (e.g., Shadish, 1989; Sternberg & Gordeeva, 1996).

Beyond expanding the scope of empirical inquiries, more attention must be devoted to the development of more comprehensive and precise theories of creativity. At present, two theoretical movements look the most promising: (a) economic models that examine the individual's willingness to invest in "human capital" and to engage in risk-taking behaviors (see, e.g., Rubenson & Runco, 1992; Sternberg & Lubart, 1995); and (b) evolutionary models that have elaborated Campbell's (1960) variation-selection model of creativity into more complete explanations of the creative process, person, and product (see, e.g., Eysenck, 1995; Simonton, 1999b). Both the economic and evolutionary theories have supported the emergence of mathematical models that make predictions susceptible to empirical tests (e.g., Simonton, 1997a).

Finally, and perhaps most important, the scientific understanding of creativity should be extended to lead to ever more useful applications. To the world at large, creativity is not just an interesting psychological phenomenon but a socially and personally valued behavior besides. It is partly for this reason that there are so many workshops and self-help books that purport to enhance personal creativity; yet the gap between scientific knowledge and practical interventions is often so wide that doubts are cast on both science and practice. However, if creativity research continues to expand and diversify, a time will come when scientific theories prove their utility by successfully stimulating creativity in the everyday world. Ultimately, ever more human beings may be able to display optimal functioning through creativity.

REFERENCES

Amabile, T. M. (1983). *The social psychology of creativity.* New York: Springer-Verlag.

Amabile, T. M. (1996). *Creativity in context.* Boulder, CO: Westview.

Barron, F. X. (1969). *Creative person and creative process.* New York: Holt, Rinehart, & Winston.

Barron, F. X., & Harrington, D. M. (1981). Creativity, intelligence, and personality. *Annual Review of Psychology, 32,* 439–476.

Boden, M. A. (1991). *The creative mind: Myths & mechanisms.* New York: Basic Books.

Bouchard, T. J., Jr. (1994). Genes, environment, and personality. *Science, 264,* 1700–1701.

Bowers, K. S., Farvolden, P., & Mermigis, L. (1995). Intuitive antecedents of insight. In S. M. Smith, T. B. Ward, & R. A. Finke (Eds.), *The creative cognition approach* (pp. 27–51). Cambridge, MA: MIT Press.

Campbell, D. T. (1960). Blind variation and selective retention in creative thought as in other knowledge processes. *Psychological Review, 67,* 380–400.

Csikszentmihalyi, M. (1990). The domain of creativity. In M. A. Runco & R. S. Albert (Eds.), *Theories of creativity* (pp. 190–212). Newbury Park. CA: Sage.

Csikszentmihalyi, M. (1997). *Creativity: Flow and the psychology of discovery and invention.* New York: Harper Collins.

Csikszentmihalyi, M., Rathunde, K., & Whalen, S. (1993). *Talented teenagers: The roots of success and failure.* Cambridge, England: Cambridge University Press.

Dellas, M., & Gaier, E. L. (1970). Identification of creativity: The individual. *Psychological Bulletin, 73,* 55–73.

Dennis, W. (1966). Creative productivity between the ages of 20 and 80 years. *Journal of Gerontology, 21,* 1–8.

Diehl, M., & Stroebe, W. (1987). Productivity loss in brainstorming groups: Toward the solution of a riddle. *Journal of Personality and Social Psychology, 53,* 497–509.

Dunbar, K. (1995). How scientists really reason: Scientific reasoning in real-world laboratories. In R. J. Sternberg & J. E. Davidson (Eds.), *The nature of insight* (pp. 365–396). Cambridge, MA: MIT Press.

Eisenberger, R., & Cameron, J. (1996). Detrimental effects of reward: Reality or myth? *American Psychologist, 51,* 1153–1166.

Eisenstadt, J. M. (1978). Parental loss and genius. *American Psychologist, 33,* 211–223.

Ericsson, K. A. (Ed.). (1996). *The road to expert performance: Empirical evidence from the arts and sciences, sports, and games.* Mahwah, NJ: Erlbaum.

Eysenck, H. J. (1995). *Genius: The natural history of creativity.* Cambridge, England: Cambridge University Press.

Farr, J. L. (1990). Facilitating individual role innovation. In M. A. West & J. L. Farr (Eds.), *Innovation and creativity at work: Psychological and organizational strategies* (pp. 207–230). New York: Wiley.

Finke, R. A., Ward, T. B., & Smith, S. M. (1992). *Creative cognition: Theory, research, and applications.* Cambridge, MA: MIT Press.

Galton, F. (1869). *Hereditary genius: An inquiry into its laws and consequences.* London: Macmillan.

Gardner, H. (1983). *Frames of mind: A theory of multiple intelligences.* New York: Basic Books.

Gardner, H. (1993). *Creating minds: An anatomy of creativity seen through the lives of Freud, Einstein, Picasso, Stravinsky, Eliot, Graham, and Gandhi.* New York: Basic Books.

Gedo, J. E. (1997). Psychoanalytic theories of creativity. In M. A. Runco (Ed.), *The creativity research handbook* (Vol. 1, pp. 29–39). Cresskill, NJ: Hampton Press.

Getzels, J., & Csikszentmihalyi, M. (1976). *The creative vision: A longitudinal study of problem finding in art.* New York: Wiley.

Goertzel, M. G., Goertzel, V., & Goertzel, T. G. (1978). *300 eminent personalities: A psychosocial analysis of the famous.* San Francisco: Jossey-Bass.

Gruber, H. E. (1989). The evolving systems approach to creative work. In D. B. Wallace & H. E. Gruber (Eds.), *Creative people at work: Twelve cognitive case studies* (pp. 3–24). New York: Oxford University Press.

Guilford, J. P. (1950). Creativity. *American Psychologist, 5,* 444–454.

Guilford, J. P. (1967). *The nature of human intelligence.* New York: McGraw-Hill.

Harrington, D. M. (1990). The ecology of human creativity: A psychological perspective. In M. A. Runco & R. S. Albert (Eds.). *Theories of creativity* (pp. 143–169). Newbury Park, CA: Sage.

Hayes, J. R. (1989). *The complete problem solver* (2nd ed.). Hillsdale, NJ: Erlbaum.

Helson, R. (1990). Creativity in women: Outer and inner views over time. In M. A. Runco & R. S. Albert (Eds.), *Theories of creativity* (pp. 46–58). Newbury Park, CA: Sage.

Howe, M. J. A., Davidson, J. W., & Sloboda, J. A. (1998). Innate talents: Reality or myth? *Behavioral and Brain Sciences, 21,* 399–442.

Jamison, K. R. (1993). *Touched with fire: Manic-depressive illness and the artistic temperament.* New York: Free Press.

Johnson-Laird, P. N. (1993). *Human and machine thinking.* Hillsdale, NJ: Erlbaum.

Kroeber, A. L. (1944). *Configurations of culture growth.* Berkeley: University of California Press.

Kuhn, T. S. (1970). *The structure of scientific revolutions* (2nd ed.). Chicago: University of Chicago Press.

Lambert, W. E., Tucker, G. R., & d'Anglejan, A. (1973). Cognitive and attitudinal consequences of bilingual schooling: The St. Lambert project through grade five. *Journal of Educational Psychology, 65,* 141–159.

Langley, P., Simon, H. A., Bradshaw, G. L., & Zythow, J. M. (1987). *Scientific discovery.* Cambridge, MA: MIT Press.

Lehman, H. C. (1953). *Age and achievement.* Princeton, NJ: Princeton University Press.

Lindauer, M. S. (1993a). The old-age style and its artists. *Empirical Studies and the Arts, 11,* 135–146.

Lindauer, M. S. (1993b). The span of creativity among long-lived historical artists. *Creativity Research Journal, 6,* 231–239.

Ludwig, A. M. (1995). *The price of greatness: Resolving the creativity and madness controversy.* New York: Guilford Press.

Lykken, D. T. (1998). The genetics of genius. In A. Steptoe (Ed.), *Genius and the mind: Studies of creativity and temperament in the historical record* (pp. 15–37). New York: Oxford University Press.

MacKinnon, D. W. (1978). In *search of human effectiveness.* Buffalo, NY: Creative Education Foundation.

Martindale, C. (1989). Personality, situation, and creativity. In J. A. Glover, R. R. Ronning, & C. R. Reynolds (Eds.), *Handbook of creativity* (pp. 211–232). New York: Plenum Press.

Martindale, C. (1990). *The clockwork muse: The predictability of artistic styles.* New York: Basic Books.

Martindale, C. (1995). Creativity and connectionism. In S. M. Smith, T. B. Ward, & R. A. Finke (Eds.), *The creative cognition approach* (pp. 249–268). Cambridge, MA: MIT Press.

McCrae, R. R., Arenberg, D., & Costa, P. T. (1987). Declines in divergent thinking with age: Cross-sectional. longitudinal. and cross-sequential analyses. *Psychology and Aging, 2,* 130–136.

Nemeth, C. J., & Kwan, J. (1987). Minority influence, divergent thinking and detection of correct solutions. *Journal of Applied Social Psychology, 17,* 788–799.

Newell, A., & Simon, H. A. (1972). *Human problem solving.* Englewood Cliffs, NJ: Prentice-Hall.

Osborn, A. F. (1963). *Applied imagination: Principles and procedures of creative problem-solving* (3rd ed.). New York: Scribner.

Root-Bernstein, R. S., Bernstein, M., & Garnier, H. (1993). Identification of scientists making long-term, high-impact contributions, with notes on their methods of working. *Creativity Research Journal, 6,* 329–343.

Rothenberg, A. (1990). *Creativity and madness: New findings and old stereotypes.* Baltimore: Johns Hopkins University Press.

Roy, M. C., Gauvin, S., & Limayem, M. (1996). Electronic group brainstorming: The role of feedback on productivity. *Small Group Research, 27,* 215–247.

Rubenson, D. L., & Runco, M. A. (1992). The psychoeconomic approach to creativity. *New Ideas in Psychology, 10,* 131–147.

Schooler, J. W., & Melcher, J. (1995). The ineffability of insight. In S. M. Smith, T. B. Ward, & R. A. Finke (Eds.), *The creative cognition approach* (pp. 97–133). Cambridge, MA: MIT Press.

Shadish, W. R., Jr. (1989). The perception and evaluation of quality in science. In B. Gholson, W. R. Shadish, Jr., R. A. Neimeyer, & A. C. Houts (Eds.), *The psychology of science: Contributions to metascience* (pp. 383–426). Cambridge, England: Cambridge University Press.

Shrager, J., & Langley, P. (Eds.). (1990). *Computational models of scientific discovery and theory formation.* San Mateo, CA: Kaufmann.

Simonton, D. K. (1975). Sociocultural context of individual creativity: A transhistorical time-series analysis. *Journal of Personality and Social Psychology, 32,* 1119–1133.

Simonton, D. K. (1976). Philosophical eminence, beliefs, and zeitgeist: An individual-generational analysis. *Journal of Personality and Social Psychology, 34,* 630–640.

Simonton, D. K. (1980). Thematic fame, melodic originality, and musical zeitgeist: A biographical and transhistorical content analysis. *Journal of Personality and Social Psychology, 38,* 972–983.

Simonton, D. K. (1984). *Genius, creativity, and leadership: Historiometric inquiries.* Cambridge, MA: Harvard University Press.

Simonton, D. K. (1987). Developmental antecedents of achieved eminence. *Annals of Child Development, 5,* 131–169.

Simonton, D. K. (1988). Age and outstanding achievement: What do we know after a century of research? *Psychological Bulletin, 104,* 251–267.

Simonton, D. K. (1989). The swan-song phenomenon: Last-works effects for 172 classical composers. *Psychology and Aging, 4,* 42–47.

Simonton, D. K. (1991a). Career landmarks in science: Individual differences and interdisciplinary contrasts. *Developmental Psychology, 27,* 119–130.

Simonton, D. K. (1991b). Emergence and realization of genius: The lives and works of 120 classical composers. *Journal of Personality and Social Psychology, 61,* 829–840.

Simonton, D. K. (1992a). Gender and genius in Japan: Feminine eminence in masculine culture. *Sex Roles, 27,* 101–119.

Simonton, D. K. (1992b). Leaders of American psychology, 1879–1967: Career development, creative output, and professional achievement. *Journal of Personality and Social Psychology, 62,* 5–17.

Simonton, D. K. (1994). *Greatness: Who makes history and why.* New York: Guilford Press.

Simonton, D. K. (1997a). Creative productivity: A predictive and explanatory model of career trajectories and landmarks. *Psychological Review, 104,* 66–89.

Simonton, D. K. (1997b). Foreign influence and national achievement: The impact of open milieus on Japanese civilization. *Journal of Personality and Social Psychology, 72,* 86–94.

Simonton, D. K. (1998). Achieved eminence in minority and majority cultures: Convergence versus divergence in the assessments of 294 African Americans. *Journal of Personality and Social Psychology, 74,* 804–817.

Simonton, D. K. (1999a). Creativity and genius. In L. Pervin & O. John (Eds.), *Handbook of personality theory and research* (2nd ed., pp. 629–652). New York: Guilford Press.

Simonton, D. K. (1999b). *Origins of genius: Darwinian perspectives on creativity.* New York: Oxford University Press.

Simonton, D. K. (1999c). Talent and its development: An emergenic and epigenetic model. *Psychological Review, 106,* 435–457.

Smith, S. M., Ward, T. B., & Finke, R. A. (Eds.). (1995). *The creative cognition approach.* Cambridge, MA: MIT Press.

Sorokin, P. A. (1969). *Society, culture, and personality.* New York: Cooper Square. (Original work published 1947)

Sternberg, R. J. (1985). *Beyond IQ: A triarchic theory of human intelligence.* New York: Cambridge University Press.

Sternberg, R. J., & Davidson, J. E. (Eds.). (1995). *The nature of insight.* Cambridge, MA: MIT Press.

Sternberg, R. J., & Gordeeva, T. (1996). The anatomy of impact: What makes an article influential? *Psychological Science, 7,* 69–75.

Sternberg, R. J., & Lubart, T. I. *(1995). Defying the crowd: Cultivating creativity in a culture of conformity.* New York: Free Press.

Sternberg, R. J., & Lubart, T. I. (1996). Investing in creativity. *American Psychologist, 51,* 677–688.

Subotnik, R. F., & Arnold, K. D. (Eds.). (1994). *Beyond Terman: Contemporary longitudinal studies of giftedness and talent.* Norwood, NJ: Ablex.

Terman, L. M. (1925). *Mental and physical traits of a thousand gifted children.* Stanford, CA: Stanford University Press.

Wallace, D. B., & Gruber, H. E. (Eds.). (1989). *Creative people at work: Twelve cognitive case studies.* New York: Oxford University Press.

Waller, N. G., Bouchard, T. J., Jr., Lykken, D. T., Tellegen, A., & Blacker, D. M. (1993). Creativity, heritability, familiality: Which word does not belong? *Psychological Inquiry, 4,* 235–237.

Ward, T. B., Smith, S. M., & Vaid, J. (Eds.). (1997). *Creative thought: An investigation of conceptual structures and processes.* Washington, DC: American Psychological Association.

SELF-STUDY QUESTIONS

Multiple Choice

1. With respect to the "mad genius" controversy, creative individuals tend to
   a. channel their creativity into activities that are productive
   b. justify aspects of their own psychopathology with the demands of being creative
   c. seek genetic counseling to check for genius levels of intelligence
   d. join others who are creative so that any feelings of isolation can be understood by other creative individuals

2. Factors that influence the creative process include all but the following:
   a. interpersonal environment
   b. intrapersonal environment
   c. sociocultural environment
   d. genetic inheritance only

Essay

1. Discuss how the cognitive processes, such as insightful problem-solving, creative cognition, expertise acquisition, and computer simulation, might influence the process of creativity in a person.

2. Discuss how personal characteristics such as intelligence and personality might contribute to or detract from a person's own creativity.

MIDDLE/LATE ADULTHOOD

"Differences in Familism Values and Caregiving Outcomes among Korean, Korean American, and White American Dementia Caregivers"

OVERVIEW

Anthropologists and others who study culture often distinguish between *individualism* and *familism* or *collectivism*. They suggest that Western culture values the independence and self-sufficiency of a person more highly than his or her social relationships. In contrast, they say, non-Western cultures value a collective ideal of the family as a group or unit as being more important than any one individual within that family. But what are the values of families and individuals who migrate from a familistic culture to a society that is more individualistic? Do they maintain the values of the cultures of origin, or do they abandon them in favor of the views of their adopted nation? This article addresses precisely these questions. The authors report research examining differences among Korean, Korean American, and Western European American ("White") caregivers in the levels of stress they experience while taking care of elderly family members who have dementia as well as their beliefs about family responsibility to care for such members. As you read this article, think about your own ideas about how the elderly should be cared for and by whom.

METHODOLOGY

The researchers used structured interviews with elder caregivers from the three cultural groups. In a structured interview, each participant is asked the same questions. Many of the interview questions employed a *Likert-type* scale. A Likert scale requires a participant to describe his or her response in terms of a continuum such as *strongly agree, agree, disagree,* or *strongly disagree*. After compiling all of the interview data, the researchers used a statistical technique called *multiple analysis of variance (MANOVA)* to identify relationships among the variables examined in the study.

GLOSSARY TERMS

- **Familism**   viewpoint and philosophy regarding the role of the family members toward each other stressing the need for family members to provide mutual support and to have common goals and common property and living arrangements
- **Filial piety**   a family value where children, no matter what their age, must respect, honor, and obey the wishes of their parents, the ultimate authorities in their lives
- **Elder care**   various types of care for an elderly person whether in the person's home, an adult day care setting, an assisted living facility, or a skilled-care facility (nursing home)
- **Acculturation**   the process that a person who is an immigrant or who is from another culture goes through in order to adapt to the standards, norms, and values of a dominant or host culture
- **Dementia**   an impairment or decline in cognitive functioning as well as in personality functioning

Gahyun Youn, Hyun-Suk Jeong, Bob G. Knight,
and Donna Benton

Differences in Familism Values and Caregiving Outcomes among Korean, Korean American, and White American Dementia Caregivers

Recent theories have suggested that burden and distress among dementia caregivers may be higher in American culture, which emphasizes individualism, and lower in cultures with higher levels of familism. However, immigrants may experience higher levels of burden because of acculturation with attendant values, conflicts and stresses. Forty-four Korean caregivers and 32 Korean American caregivers were compared with 54 White American caregivers on sociodemographic variables, familism, burden, anxiety, and depression. Familism was highest in Korean caregivers and lowest in Whites, with Korean Americans in the middle. Koreans and Korean Americans reported higher levels of burden. Koreans showed higher levels of depression and of anxiety than White American caregivers, with Koreans and Korean Americans higher than Whites on anxiety. These results suggest a need for greater specificity in theories about familism values, with attention to the specific meaning of familism in different cultures.

Caring for an older relative with dementia has been recognized for some time as a source of burden and distress for the caregiver (Zarit, Reever, & Bach-Peterson, 1980). A large literature has accumulated that documents the effects of caregiving on self-reported distress, mostly in White caregiver samples (Schulz, O'Brien, Bookwala, & Fleissner, 1995). Although there has been a rapid increase in articles about family caregivers for frail elderly persons in the past 2 decades, attention to cultural differences in the caregiving context has been limited. Research has tended to focus on White caregivers of European origins. Attention to care-givers from other nations and to recent immigrants from those nations can shed light on the role of culture and of acculturation in the caregiving process. Aranda and Knight (1997) proposed a sociocultural stress and coping model, which integrates ethnicity into the stress and coping model for caregiving distress.

The understanding of caregiver distress has come from the stress and coping theory developed by Laz-

arus and Folkman and their colleagues (e.g., Lazarus & Folkman, 1984). In general, stress and coping models include the following categories of variables: (a) context variables such as gender, age, socioeconomic status, care-giving history, relationship of the caregiver to the patient, and so forth; (b) demands on the caregiver (objective stressors or objective burden); (c) the caregiver's appraisal of demands as stressful or satisfying (subjective caregiver burden, which is likely to be influenced by cultural values); (d) the potential mediators between appraisal and outcomes (coping styles and social support); and (e) the consequences of caregiving demands (emotional distress and health outcomes). In the sociocultural adaptation of this model, burden as appraisal of caregiving stress is hypothesized to be directly influenced by cultural values such as familism (Aranda & Knight, 1997). The nature of caregiving, and the emotional distress outcomes of caregiving, can be affected by between-group differences in status variables among ethnic groups, such as typical gender and familial relationship of caregivers, mean caregiver age, mean educational levels, health of caregivers, and so forth. Culture is also posited to affect potential mediating variables such as social support. In their review, Aranda and Knight noted that African American caregivers have often appraised caregiving as less burdensome than did White caregivers (Haley et al., 1995; Lawton, Rajagopal, Brody, & Kleban, 1992; Morycz, Malloy, Bozich, & Martz, 1987), and the lowered stress appraisal has been related to lower depression outcomes (Haley et al., 1996). However, Latino caregivers appear to have similar levels of burden and depression as do White caregivers (Cox & Monk, 1990; Mintzer et al., 1992; see Aranda & Knight for review).

Korean American older adults have been one of the fastest growing subgroups in the United States during the past 2 decades, increasing from 3,270 persons in 1970 to 14,616 in 1980 (Koh & Bell, 1987) to about 34,248 in 1990 (Moon, 1996). Because Korea is a rapidly developing country, with large changes in urbanization, industrialization, and Westernization in the last 3 decades, both Koreans and Korean Americans have been found to show lower levels of a variety of sociodemographic status variables (e.g., income, education, health) than Whites in the United States, with Korean Americans typically somewhat better off than Koreans with regard to these variables (Koh & Bell, 1987; Moon, 1996). These demographic differences can be interpreted as representing differences in social resources that groups with differing backgrounds bring to caregiving (using the ethnicity as a disadvantaged, minority-group framework). Alternately, these ethnic differences in sociodemographic variables could be seen as potential confounds in caregiving stress and coping models in the sense that they would produce distress in all group members, not only in caregivers. Therefore, in this study we examined ethnic differences between the groups as a whole and then reanalyzed the differences with continuous status variables such as age and education controlled statistically as covariates and by limiting the samples to homogeneous subgroups of gender and family relationship to care recipient.

A key area of the operation of cultural values appears to be in the selection of the primary caregiver. For Koreans, the adult son (especially the eldest son) is responsible for his elderly parents physically as well as financially (Choi, 1993; Youn & Song, 1992). This choice is grounded in Korean cultural traditions of filial piety and in Confucian teachings (Sung, 1992). Even though he does not live in the same household with the parent who has dementia or his other parent is available to take care of the demented parent, it is traditionally assumed that the son's family has the most responsibility for a parent with dementia. The responsibility for daily care would typically be that of the oldest son's wife. In summary, in Korea if an elderly woman or a widower becomes frail, the primary caregiver is almost always the oldest son's wife. For a married older man, the wife may provide care in some instances.

This rule for who becomes the primary caregiver is different from the American majority population in which the spouse is the typical first-choice provider (Gatz, Bengtson, & Blum, 1991; Horowitz, 1985). When a spouse is unavailable, elder care in America has traditionally been provided by daughters (Gatz et al., 1991). Daughters tend to live closer to parents than sons, and women are more likely to live with daughters than sons when care is needed (Horowitz, 1985). In the U.S. hierarchy of caregiving responsibility, the next step is daughters-in-law (Gatz et al., 1991). Given these rules, the majority of primary caregivers for Americans is spouses and daughters whereas that for Koreans is daughters-in-law (Choi, 1993; Youn & Song, 1992).

After immigration to the United States, many Korean Americans will not adhere to the Korean tradition. Korean Americans are much more likely to be Christian than are Koreans and adopt a variety of Western values fairly quickly, including separate households for healthy elders (Koh & Bell, 1987; Moon, 1996). Thus, a Korean American daughter-in-law is more likely to feel it is unfair to restrict her outside activities when she cares for the parent-in-law than is a daughter-in-law living in Korea. Nevertheless, the Korean American son and his wife may feel guilty when they do not take care of the parent but also may experience severe distress when they do care for the parent at home. We hypothesize that among Korean Americans, many spouses or daughters take responsibility for their frail elders, following U.S. selection norms rather than Korean ones. Because of the departure from traditional selection norms and because of the internal conflict between Korean and American values, we hypothesized Korean American caregivers to appraise caregiving as more burdensome than either Korean or U.S. caregivers. In a similar way, Aranda and Knight (1997) noted with regard to Latino immigrant groups that immigrants caught between two cultures often report the highest levels of emotional distress, a finding that is attributed to the difficulty of resolving conflicting cultural values.

A key cultural value that is hypothesized to explain differences between the U.S. mainstream culture and other cultural groups is that of familism. Landrine (1992) argued that the concept of an independent and individualized self is congruent with Western European-American dominant culture but is not held by persons from other cultural backgrounds, including many U.S. minority populations. In other cultures, the self is defined in relationship to the family and other social groupings. With regard to caregiving, this conceptualization would support the hypothesis that the appraisal of caregiving as a burden is most likely within the context of White, U.S. culture. Other cultures would be more likely to appraise caregiving as a natural extension of family life, rather than as an interruption of the individual life of the caregiver. For example, Lawton et al. (1992) reported that Black caregivers reported higher levels of traditional caregiving ideology and less intrusiveness of caregiving responsibilities in their lives. More recently, Haley et al. (1996) reported the results of a structural equation model that showed that race affected stressfulness appraisals, which in turn affected depression outcome. They speculated that White caregivers perceived caregiving as unexpected and disruptive, whereas Black caregivers perceived it as expected and natural.

Of course, the test of the accuracy of this theoretical perspective rests on being able to measure individual versus familial values orientations across cultures and testing whether groups higher in familism are lower in burden and emotional distress. It should be possible, for example, to measure the values orientation of familism (e.g., Bardis, 1959c) versus the individualism characteristic of American majority culture. We expected that Korean culture would provide an exception to this developing model in that familism values are high, but the daughter-in-law and dependent elder relationship is traditionally expected to be high in conflict (Choe, 1991). In this case, familism values could be expected to increase burden. We also anticipated that acculturation processes could result in Korean Americans having lower familism than Koreans but possibly higher levels of burden and distress that are due to experiencing the conflict between Korean and U.S. values.

In discussions of African American and Latino caregivers, researchers assume that familism values are linked to larger and more tightly integrated extended family support systems that provide additional resources for the caregiver facing caregiving distress. Johnson and Barer (1990) described African American family structures that included extended family and fictive kin and that appeared more active than the networks of White caregivers, although not necessarily larger. Aranda and Knight (1997) speculated that the caregiving unit for Latinos may be the family, rather than a single primary caregiver.

Although there is very little research on caregivers as such, recent studies suggest that the situation may be different for modern Korean and Korean American families. Family-based support is small by U.S. standards, probably because of modernization and urbanization, and Korean families have not yet developed support networks outside the family (Sung, 1991). Korean American elderly persons report more support from church and community organizations and more flexible support from kin than do Koreans, but the amount of quantitative social support is still low (Koh & Bell, 1987; Moon, 1996). We tentatively hypothesized that Korean culture may provide an example in which familism values do not translate into large and flexible family support systems, in part because the culture narrowly defines who is responsible for parent care.

In summary, we hypothesized that familism values would be highest in the Korean caregivers and lowest in the White caregivers, with Korean Americans in the middle. Given the value conflicts of acculturation and the likelihood that caregiving would often be performed by relatives other than the daughter-in-law (who would feel that she was performing a task not culturally defined as her own), we hypothesized that Korean American caregivers would show the highest levels of burden, with Koreans having the lowest, and Whites in the middle. Because emotional distress outcomes are seen in stress and coping models as being influenced by burden (as the appraisal of caregiving as stressful) and by social support, we hypothesized that Korean Americans would have the highest levels of emotional distress (depression and anxiety) because they would have higher burden and lower social support.

METHOD

Participants

White caregivers were recruited under the auspices of the Research Training and Information Transfer Core of the Alzheimer's Disease Research Center (ADRC), Southern California Consortium. Sources included the caregivers of ADRC dementia sample enrollees, the Los Angeles Caregiver Resource Center, and other community sources. The White caregivers were collected as part of a study comparing African American and White caregivers on health and mental health variables for which a selection requirement was that caregivers be more than 50 years of age. Korean American caregivers were recruited from the Korean Health, Education, Information and Research Center, the Los Angeles Koreatown Multi-Purpose Senior Center, and from Divine Home Care. Others were volunteers responding to a newspaper article about the study in *The Korea Times*, a Los Angeles–area Korean language newspaper. All Korean American caregivers were Korean-born immigrants to the United States. Korean caregivers were recruited from the Korea Gerontological Research Society, the Korea Hotline for the Elderly, the Institute of Social Science, and from many small-sized community senior centers.

In all cases, caregivers were caring for a relative who had a physician-confirmed diagnosis of dementia. We relied on the caregivers' reports of this physician diagnosis. Cross-national and cross-cultural diagnostic practices might differ, of course. Although we discussed ways of measuring these differences, available methods (e.g., translating a cognitive-impairment screening tool into Korean) would not have resolved questions fully and, in our judgment, would have discouraged participation by Korean and Korean American caregivers. We do note that the caregivers' reports of problems with the care receivers (Revised Memory and Behavior Problem Checklist [R-MBPC] scores, Teri et al., 1992; see below for details) did not differ significantly across the three groups (see Table 1), $F(2, 127) = 2.91$, $p = .06$, $MSE = 218.41$ (power was moderately strong at .56).

The White and Korean American caregivers were residents of Los Angeles or Orange Counties, California. The average duration of stay in America for the Korean American caregivers was 17.8 years. The Korean caregivers resided in the metropolitan Kwangju area (population = approximately 1.4 million) located in southwestern Korea. In all three groups, most caregivers were seeking help, and thus information and referral to support groups and other services were provided.

All caregivers were interviewed at their own home or at another convenient place for the caregiver. Caregivers were encouraged to pick a time when the relative with dementia was in respite care or likely to be quiet in the home setting. Interviewers were G. Youn and H.-S. Jeong for the Korean and Korean American caregivers and graduate students in psychology and gerontology for the White caregivers. Interview sessions typically lasted about 2 hr. The order of tests was invariant across caregivers.

The sample included 54 White, 44 Korean, and 32 Korean American caregivers caring for the older relatives with dementia who were not currently institutionalized. The caregivers must have identified themselves as the primary caregiver.

Across the three groups, the majority of the primary caregivers in the sample were women, married, and currently living in the same household with the elderly patient.

There was a major difference in the relationship between the caregiver and the care receiver: 70% of the White caregivers were the spouses for the elderly patients, whereas almost 80% of the Korean caregivers were daughters-in-law. Among Korean American caregivers, about 40% were spouses, 37% were daughters, and only 19% were daughters-in-law. This represents a considerable cultural shift in the definition of the primary caregiver role between Ko-

rea and Koreatown. Because the White caregivers were screened for being over 50 years of age, the average age for the White caregivers was higher than those for the other two groups, which did not differ from each other. This selection by age also accounts for the somewhat higher proportion of spouses in this sample compared with other samples of U.S. caregivers because spouses tend to be older than adult child caregivers. Demographic data characterizing the three different caregiver groups are presented in Table 1.

Procedure

The inventories written in English were translated into Korean and back-translated into English using techniques by Brislin (1986) to ensure that they were understandable and culturally sensitive. The instruments were translated into Korean by two bilingual adults and then translated into English by two different bilingual adults. The translators were all native speakers of Korean who had lived in the United States for at least 10 years and were doctoral students at the University of Southern California or the University of California, Los Angeles. During this back-translation process, there were no significant discrepancies in content, as verified by native speakers of English comparing the back-translated English version to the original English version.

Measures

Caregivers provided information concerning their gender, age, years of education, marital status, health, and annual household income. Economic status for the American, Korean, and Korean American caregivers was measured by the annual household income. The following ranges of annual income for each caregiver household were used: (a) less than $9,500; (b) $9,501–13,500; (c) $13,501–19,500; (d) $19,501–28,500; (e) $28,501–38,500; (f) $38,501–53,500; and (g) $53,500 and above. The caregivers' health and functional abilities were assessed by two questions that rated physical condition ("How would you describe your health?") and functional ability ("How would you describe your ability to do your day to day tasks such as dress, shop, etc.") on a 4-point Likert-type scale that ranged from *excellent* to *poor*, with higher numbers reflecting poorer health or functional ability.

The number of persons providing instrumental social support was elicited by the question, "How many people help you with the tasks of caregiving at any time (i.e., keeping an eye on the person, helping with bathing, feeding, etc.)?" The number of persons providing emotional support was the answer to the

TABLE 1   Demographic Characteristics of the Caregivers

VARIABLE	WHITE (n = 54)		KOREAN (n = 44)		KOREAN AMERICAN (n = 32)	
	M	SD	M	SD	M	SD
Female (%)	64.8		93.2		87.5	
Marital status						
Single	13.0		0.0		9.4	
Married	83.3		90.9		87.5	
Widowed	3.7		9.1		3.1	
Relationship (%)						
Husband	25.9		0.0		9.4	
Wife	44.4		6.8		31.3	
Son	9.3		6.8		0.0	
Daughter	20.4		6.8		37.5	
Son-in-law	0.0		0.0		3.1	
Daughter-in-law	0.0		79.5		18.8	
Living with patient (%)	94.4		97.7		81.3	
Age (years)	67.7_a	10.5	52.8_b	8.0	56.4_b	15.4
Years of education	15.1_a	2.9	9.6_c	3.0	12.0_b	4.2
Caregiving duration (years)	4.5	3.5	2.9	2.1	3.8	4.4
No. of emotional helpers	3.9_a	3.4	1.3_b	1.5	2.2_b	2.0
No. of instrumental helpers	1.4_a	1.6	0.6_b	1.0	1.6_a	1.7
Health (1–4)	2.1_b	0.8	2.8_a	0.8	1.8_b	1.0
Functional abilities (1–4)	1.7_b	0.8	2.0_a	0.4	1.3_c	0.5
Economic status (1–7)	5.0_a	1.8	4.3_b	1.0	4.2_b	1.7
R-MBPC (0–96)	41.6	16.0	42.0	15.1	34.5	12.1

Note. Discrete variable entries are percentages of the subsample (White, Korean, Korean American) falling in that category. For continuous variables, entries are means and standard deviations. For physical health and functional ability, higher numbers refer to worse health and ability. Means with different subscripts differ ($p < .05$) on the basis of Tukey's post-hoc comparison tests. R-MBPC = Revised Memory and Behavior Problems Checklist (Teri et al., 1992).

question, "How many people can you talk to about things related to caregiving that are difficult for you?"

R-MBPC. The R-MBPC (Teri et al., 1992) consists of 24 items that ask caregivers to measure observable behavioral problems (i.e., memory-related, depression, and disruptive behavior) in dementia patients. In this study, only the frequency of behaviors was asked in the Korean speaking samples, and these frequency scores are the basis for all R-MBPC scores reported in this article (including the English-speaking caregivers). Items include questions about "trouble losing or misplacing things" (memory), "waking you or family members up at night" (behavior), and "appears sad or depressed" (recipient depression).

Each item is rated for frequency of occurrence of the behavior or problem from 0 (*never occurs*) to 4 (*occurs daily or more often*). We recoded "don't know or not applicable" to "never occurs" to use the scale to assess present behavior. Higher scores of the R-MBPC reflect more frequent present problems in the patient. Convergent and discriminant validities were established for the memory problems and de-

pression sub-scales, similar scales were not available for disruptive behavior (Teri et al., 1992). In our samples, Cronbach's alphas were .90 for the English-Language Scale and .87 for the Korean Scale.

Burden. Subjective burden was measured by the Burden Interview (Zarit et al., 1980). The Burden Interview is a 22-item scale that can either be self-administered or included in an interview. Items are scored from 0 to 4, with higher scores indicative of greater caregiver burden. Knight et al. (1998) have selected 14 items from the total of 22, which tap three factors of Embarrassment–Anger, Reaction to Patient Dependency, and Self-Criticism. For the subscales, alphas were .89, .64, and .70, respectively, for the English version and .83, .60, and .64 for the Korean version. Items included "feel embarrassed over relative's behavior" (Embarrassment–Anger), "feel you do not have enough time for yourself" (Reaction to Patient Dependency), and "feel you should be doing more for your relative" (Self-Criticism). Cronbach's alphas for the 14-item Burden Scale were .88 in English and .82 in Korean.

Familism. This is a 16-item scale measuring ideal-typical familism, which refers to strong in-group feelings, emphasis on family goals, common property, mutual support, and the desire to pursue the perpetuation of the family (Bardis, 1959c). Response formats are from *strongly disagree* (1) *to strongly agree* (5), with higher scores representing stronger attitudes toward ideal-typical familism. In the scale's development samples (Michigan college students), Spearman-Brown split-half reliability coefficients ranged from .77 to .84, with 30-day retest reliability of .90 (Bardis, 1959a, 1959b, 1959c). Validity was established by report of expected mean differences between reference groups (the Michigan college students with Greek students "in a familistic community"; Bardis, 1959b). Cronbach's alphas for our sample were .83 in English and .83 in Korean. Items included, "A person should always support his or her uncles or aunts if they are in need"; "A person should always be completely loyal to his or her family"; and "A person should avoid every action of which his or her family disapproves."

Depression. Depression was measured by the Center for Epidemiologic Studies Depression Scale (CES–D; Radloff, 1977). The CES–D Scale is a 20-item self-report scale developed to screen for depressive symptomology in the general population. Each response is scored from 0 to 3. Total scores range from 0 to 60, with higher scores indicating more depressive symptomology. Validity of the scale was tested through correlation with other self-report measures and with clinical ratings of depression. In a review of studies using the CES–D with older adults, Radloff and Teri (1986) concluded that the sensitivity and specificity of the scale is as good or better with older adults as it is with younger adults. In our caregiving sample, Cronbach's αs = .74 for the English scale and .92 for the Korean scale. The CES–D has been shown to have four factors in both younger and in older adults (Hertzog, Van Alstine, Usala, & Hultsch, 1990; Radloff, 1977): Depressive Mood, Psychomotor Retardation, Lack of Well-Being, and Interpersonal Isolation. The alphas for the subscales were .80, .73, .60, and .11, respectively, for the English version and .90, .73, .83, and .69 for the Korean version.

Anxiety. Anxiety was measured by the State Anxiety Scale from the Spielberger State–Trait Anxiety Inventory (STAI—Form Y; Spielberger, Gorsuch, Lushene, Vagg, & Jacobs, 1985). The STAI is a 40-item self-administered scale for measuring two related, yet different, constructs. Responses to each item in the anxiety questionnaire were scored from 1 to 4. The scores for state anxiety range from 20 to 80, with higher scores indicating more anxiety. The STAI has been shown to have excellent psychometric properties for the assessment of anxiety in elderly persons (Patterson, O'Sullivan, & Spielberger, 1980). Cronbach's alphas for our samples were .96 in English and .94 in Korean.

RESULTS

Demographic Characteristics for the Sample

We conducted comparisons of the three groups on status and resource variables using a one-way multivariate analysis of variance (MANOVA). The variables included in this comparison were age, years of education, economic status, duration of caregiving, perceived physical condition, functional abilities for the caregivers, reported problems with the care recipient (R-MBPC), and numbers of both emotional and instrumental helpers. For 3 White caregivers, missing data in economic status were replaced with the mean value of 5.

The combined status variables varied significantly as a function of ethnic group, $F(18, 240) = 12.72$, $p < .001$. Follow-up univariate results indicated significant differences for seven variables (see Table 1). The results from post-hoc comparisons among means using Tukey's honestly significant differences are also shown in Table 1. As noted above, age was significantly different between the White caregivers and the two Korean samples, which did not differ from one another. Years of education distinguished the three groups, with Koreans having the lowest, Whites the highest, and Korean Americans in the middle.

The Korean caregivers assessed both their physical condition and their functional ability as worse than the other two groups. Korean Americans were not different from Whites on perceived physical health, but they rated their functional ability as better than Whites.

As for the number of emotional helpers, slightly less than one fifth of the White and Korean American caregivers answered that they have no helper, but more than two fifths of the Korean caregivers did so, Kruskal-Wallis Test, $\chi^2(2, N = 130) = 20.92$, $p < .001$. The White group reported a higher mean number of emotional helpers for the caregiving situation than the other two groups, who did not differ significantly. In addition, more than 40% of the White caregivers, more than one third of the Korean American caregivers, and about two thirds of the Korean caregivers said that they have no instrumental helpers at all, $\chi^2(2, N = 130) = 8.85$, p < .05. The Korean group reported lower mean number of instrumental helpers for the caregiving situation than did the White or Korean American groups. With regard to quantitative social support, it appears that Korean caregivers were more likely to be isolated. Economic status differed significantly among the group, with White caregivers reporting a slightly higher economic status than the other two groups, who did not differ.

In the remaining analyses, first, MANOVA results are reported for the entire sample, as collected without covariates, to present the observed differences between the groups as they were selected in this study. This analysis compared the three groups on the dependent variables of familism, burden, depression, and state anxiety. Second, the MANOVAs are repeated, with the covariates of age, education, and perceived physical health included in the analysis. This step adjusted the sample means of outcome variables for the differences in observed status variables and in health. This step corrected for differences between the groups that may have been due to selection factors or to differences in the groups from which the caregivers were drawn. For example, it is likely that the differences in education and in health were characteristic of Korean-American national differences and not specific to caregivers from those nations.[1] When significant differences were obtained in total burden or in total depression scores, MANOVAs were reported on

---

[1]We treat health as a background variable rather than as an outcome variable, which is the common practice in many caregiving articles. Health (especially perceived health) works better as an outcome variable when one is comparing caregivers with presumably similar noncaregivers, in which case health differences can be attributed to caregiving. In our study, we compared groups of caregivers that we felt were likely to be different on a variety of characteristics, including health. In this study, we think differences in health are more likely to be a function of nationality than to be outcomes of ethnic differences in caregiving.

the subscales of these measures to further explore the between-group differences.

In later sections, the same analyses were repeated in subsamples selected from the total study sample to adjust for two categorical variables that may have been confounded with cultural differences as an explanation. Results are reported for groups of female caregivers only and for groups composed only of children (and children-in-law) caring for parents. Given the large number of MANOVAS, differences were considered significant at the $p = .01$ level.

Analyses for the Total Sample

The between-subjects MANOVA without covariates was significant: multivariate $F(8, 250) = 18.18$, $p < .001$. Follow-up univariate results indicated significant differences for familism, $F(2, 127) = 80.46$, $p < .001$, $MSE = 53.60$; anxiety, $F(2, 127) = 43.59$, $p < .001$, $MSE = 138.72$; CES–D, $F(2, 127) = 10.43$, $p < .001$, $MSE = 99.28$; and burden, $F(2, 127) = 6.33$, $p < .01$, MSE = 80.33. Means and standard deviations are shown in Table 2. Familism differed among the groups as predicted: Koreans were highest, Korean Americans were in the middle, and Whites were lowest. Anxiety was highest among Koreans, followed by Korean Americans, with Whites having the lowest anxiety scores. For depression scores, Korean caregivers showed higher levels of depression than the other two groups, who did not differ from each other. Burden was lowest among Whites, with Koreans and Korean Americans both significantly higher and not different from one another. Because reported problems with the care recipient (R-MBPC scores) were close to being significantly different, this analysis was repeated using R-MBPC scores as a covariate.

TABLE 2   Means and Standard Deviations for the Total Sample

FACTOR	WHITE (n = 54)		KOREAN (n= 44)		KOREAN AMERICAN (n = 32)	
	M	SD	M	SD	M	SD
Familism (16–80)	42.6$_c$	9.0	61.2$_a$	5.5	53.8$_b$	6.2
Anxiety (20–80)	37.1$_c$	11.5	58.7$_a$	13.5	52.8$_b$	9.4
CES-D (0–60)	16.2$_b$	9.1	25.4$_a$	11.9	19.7$_b$	8.3
Depressed Mood (0–21)	5.0$_b$	3.9	8.5$_a$	5.6	5.6$_b$	3.1
Psychomotor Retardation (0–21)	6.1	4.0	7.4	4.4	6.1	3.2
Lack of Well-Being (0–12)	4.7$_c$	2.7	8.7$_a$	2.8	7.2$_b$	2.6
Interpersonal Isolation (0–6)	0.3	0.7	0.8	1.3	0.9	1.1
Burden Interview (0–56)	26.9$_b$	10.5	31.5$_a$	7.2	33.4$_a$	8.2
Embarrassment-Anger (0–36)	14.7$_b$	18.0	20.5$_a$	6.0	22.8$_a$	5.9
Patient's Dependency (0–12)	8.9	2.5	8.1	2.1	7.6	2.4
Self-Criticism (0–8)	3.1	2.0	3.0	1.4	3.1	1.4

Note. Means with different subscripts differ ($p < .05$) on the basis of Tukey's post-hoc comparison tests. CES–D = Center for Epidemiologic Studies Depression Scale.

All results remained significant: multivariate $F(4, 123)$ = 9.81, $p < .001$. In the univariate contrasts, all variables remained significantly different with $p < .001$; familism, $F(2, 126) = 80.28$, $MSE = 53.56$; anxiety, $F(2, 126) = 49.99$, $MSE = 125.47$; CES–D, $F(2, 126) = 10.7\ 1$, $MSE = 95.06$; and burden, $F(2, 126) = 11.76$, $MSE = 63.40$. Because R-MBPC made no difference in this analysis, it was not used as a covariate in tests with the subsamples.

With the three covariates of age, education, and physical health, the MANOVA was also significant: multivariate $F(8, 244) = 8.09$, $p < .001$. Follow-up univariate results indicated significant differences for familism, $F(2, 124) = 29.53$, $p < .001$, $MSE = 54.03$, and for anxiety, $F(2, 124) = 4.75$, $p < .01$, $MSE = 118.12$. The differences for depression and burden were apparently due to the covariates of age, health, and educational level.

For the CES–D subscales, a between-subjects MANOVA without the covariates was significant (as expected because the total score was different): multivariate $F(8, 250) = 7.75$, $p < .001$. Univariate analyses indicated significant differences in Depressed Mood, $F(2, 127) = 7.91$, $p < .001$, $MSE = 19.36$, and for Lack of Well-Being, $F(2, 127) = 26.37$, $p < .001$, $MSE = 7.48$. Tukey's post-hoc tests indicated that the Korean caregivers showed higher levels of Depressed Mood than the other two groups, who were not different from each other. For Lack of Well-Being, the Korean caregivers showed the highest levels, Korean Americans were in the middle, and White caregivers were the lowest. With the three covariates, the differences between groups were not significant at the $p = .01$ level, $F(8, 244) = 2.36$.

The MANOVA for the Burden Interview subscales was significant, multivariate $F(6, 252) = 11.83$, $p < .001$. The univariate tests showed that Embarrassment-Anger, $F(2, 127) = 26.79$, $p < .001$, $MSE = 10.83$, was different, with Korean and Korean American caregivers reporting higher levels and not significantly different from one another. With the three covariates, the subscale differences were significant, $F(6, 246) = 5.78$, $p < .001$. The univariate contrasts indicated that the difference was due to Embarrassment–Anger, $F(2, 124) = 5.82$, $p = .004$. The White caregivers were lower than the Koreans and Korean Americans, who did not differ significantly.

Analyses for Women Only

As shown in Table 1, the percentage of female caregivers in the White group was much lower compared with those of the other two groups. To avoid confounding ethnic differences with gender differences, analyses were recalculated using only the female caregivers (35 Whites, 41 Koreans, and 28 Korean Americans).

The between-subjects MANOVA without covariates on the female-only sample was significant, multivariate $F(8, 198) = 15.26$, $p < .001$. Follow-up univariate results indicated significant differences for familism, $F(2, 101) = 90.29$, $p < .001$, $MSE = 48.14$; anxiety, $F(2, 101) = 27.42$, $p < .001$, $MSE = 143.21$; and CES–D, $F(2, 101) = 6.93$, $p < .01$, $MSE = 105.97$. Means and standard deviations are shown in Table 3. The familism results were the same as those for the analysis that included the men. For anxiety, the pattern of means was the same as in the larger sample, but the

TABLE 3   Means and Standard Deviations for Female Caregivers

FACTOR	WHITE ($n = 35$)		KOREAN ($n = 41$)		KOREAN AMERICAN ($n = 28$)	
	M	SD	M	SD	M	SD
Familism (16–80)	40.0_c	9.1	61.2_a	5.4	54.5_b	5.9
Anxiety (20–80)	38.7_b	11.6	58.6_a	13.8	53.9_a	9.2
CES–D (0–60)	16.1_b	9.6	24.9_a	11.9	$20.5_{a,b}$	8.5
Depressed Mood (0–21)	5.2_b	4.3	8.4_a	5.6	$6.0_{a,b}$	3.0
Psychomotor Retardation (0–21)	5.7	4.0	7.1	4.3	6.2	3.3
Lack of Well-Being (0–12)	4.8_b	2.6	8.6_a	2.8	7.3_a	2.7
Interpersonal Isolation (0–6)	0.4	0.8	0.9	1.4	1.0	1.1
Burden Interview (0–56)	29.2	10.3	32.6	6.3	33.7	8.1
Embarrassment-Anger (0–36)	16.9_b	7.6	21.3_b	5.4	23.3_a	5.5
Patient's Dependency (0–12)	9.3_a	2.5	$8.4_{a,b}$	1.7	7.5_b	2.5
Self-Criticism (0–8)	3.0	1.9	2.9	1.2	3.0	1.4

Note. Means with different subscripts differ ($p < .05$) on the basis of Tukey's post-hoc comparison tests. Double subscripts are used when a middle score falls between two significantly different means and does not differ from either. CES–D = Center for Epidemiologic Studies Depression Scale.

difference between Koreans and Korean Americans no longer reached significance, most likely because of lower power in the subsample. Depression for the women differed, with Korean caregivers being most depressed, Whites the least, and Korean Americans in the middle and not different from the other two. Burden was not significantly different between groups with the men excluded from the sample (power in this smaller sample was moderately strong at .51), suggesting that the difference obtained above was due to White men reporting lower levels of burden, a well-known finding (e.g., Lutzky & Knight, 1994) that was replicated in this sample among Whites (men had a mean burden score of 22.5 compared with 29.2 for women, $t(52) = 2.34$, $p = .02$. The MANOVA with the three covariates for female caregivers was significant, $F(8, 192) = 7.37$, $p < .001$. Follow-up univariate results indicated a significant difference for familism, $F(2, 98) = 34.59$, $p < .001$, $MSE = 24.08$. Tukey's post-hoc comparisons for familism scores indicated the same results as in the total sample.

The CES-D subscales analysis was significant, multivariate $F(8, 198) = 5.39$, $p < .001$. The univariate analyses indicated significant differences in Depressed Mood, $F(2, 101) = 4.86$, $p < .01$, $MSE = 21.14$, and Lack of Well-Being, $F(2, 94) = 18.51$, $p < .001$, $MSE = 7.44$. Tukey's post-hoc tests for the latter MANOVA results indicated that the White caregivers showed the lowest level of Depressed Mood and the Korean caregivers the highest. Scores of the Korean American group were in the middle and not different from those of the other two groups. For Lack of Well-Being, the White caregivers showed the lowest level whereas the other two groups did not differ from each other.

In passing, it can be noted that the approximate equality in total Burden Scale scores may conceal a difference. The univariate tests of subscales show compensating differences in Embarrassment–Anger, $F(2, 101) = 19.34$, $p < .001$, $MSE = 8.67$, and in Patient's Dependency, $F(2, 101) = 5.46$, $p < .01$, $MSE = 4.91$. Post-hoc comparisons show that Korean and Korean American women scored highest on Embarrassment–Anger, with Whites being significantly lower; on the other hand, Whites scored highest on Patient's Dependency, Korean Americans scored the lowest, and Koreans were in the middle and not different from either group.

Analyses for Children Only

Looking at the caregivers' relationships to the patients in Table 1, the proportion of spouses in the White group was over 70%, but those for the Korean and Korean American groups were approximately 7% and 41%, respectively. When spouse caregivers were excluded, most of the adult-children caregivers for the White and Korean American group were daughters, but those for the Korean group were daughters-in-law. Because the relationship between spouses is different in nature than that between child and parent (Horowitz, 1985), a comparison that is limited to children and children-in-law is also of interest. This comparison is based on 16 Whites, 41 Koreans, and 19 Korean Americans.

First, the MANOVA without covariates was significant, multivariate, $F(8, 142) = 10.97$, $p < .001$. The follow-up univariate results indicated significant differences for familism, $F(2, 73) = 44.26$, $p < .001$, $MSE = 44.36$; for anxiety, $F(2, 73) = 10.85$, $p < .001$, $MSE = 162.40$; but not for burden at $p = .01$, $F(2, 73) = 4.16$, $p = .02$, $MSE = 62.00$. Although depression was not significantly different across groups in this reduced sample, power was low at .29. Means and standard deviations are shown in Table 4. Tukey's post-hoc comparisons indicated that the results with children replicated those of the total sample for familism. For anxiety, the pattern of means is the same as in the total sample, but as with the female subsample, the difference between Koreans and Korean Americans is no longer significant, likely because of lower power in the subsamples.

Second, a between-subjects MANOVA with the three covariates for the four major measures was conducted. The combined, dependent variables varied significantly as a function of ethnic group, $F(8, 136) = 6.79$, $p < .001$. Follow-up univariate results indicated significant differences for familism, $F(2, 70) = 24.06$, $p < .001$, $MSE = 45.04$. Tukey's post-hoc comparisons for familism scores indicated the same results as in the total sample. With covariates, the Burden subscales were different, $F(6, 138) = 5.99$, $p < .01$, $MSE = 59.90$. Korean Americans were highest, Whites were lowest, and Koreans had a mean between the other two that was not different from the White sample mean. The difference in burden was mainly due to the Embarrassment-Anger subscale, $F(2, 70) = 10.76$, $p < .001$, $MSE = 33.57$.

DISCUSSION

As hypothesized, the Korean caregivers showed much higher levels of familism than did White American caregivers, with Korean Americans between the two, suggesting that they are acculturating to American values. This difference in familism was robust when differences in status variables and in health were controlled in the analysis. In the total sample, burden was higher in Korean Americans and in Koreans, a finding

TABLE 4	Means and Standard Deviations for Children and Children-in-Law						
	WHITE (n = 16)		KOREAN (n = 41)		KOREAN AMERICAN (n = 19)		
FACTOR	M	SD	M	SD	M	SD
Familism (16–80)	43.4$_c$	9.5	61.6$_a$	5.4	54.4$_b$	6.3
Anxiety (20–80)	40.3$_b$	13.9	57.7$_a$	13.5	53.9$_a$	9.6
CES–D (0–40)	20.5	7.1	24.6	11.9	20.7	8.7
Depressed Mood (0–21)	6.6	2.8	8.0	5.5	6.1	3.0
Psychomotor Retardation (0–21)	8.3	3.4	7.2	4.5	6.6	3.4
Lack of Well-Being (0–12)	4.8	2.6	8.5	2.8	6.9	2.9
Interpersonal Isolation (0–6)	0.8	1.1	0.9	1.4	1.2	1.2
Burden Interview (0–56)	27.5	9.2	31.1	7.2	35.2	8.1
Embarrassment-Anger (0–36)	14.8	6.3	20.2	6.1	24.4	5.4
Patient's Dependency (0–12)	8.9	2.0	8.1	2.0	7.6	2.5
Self-Criticism (0–8)	3.8	1.8	2.8	1.3	3.2	1.6

Note. Means with different subscripts differ ($p < .05$) on the basis of Tukey's post hoc comparison tests. CES–D = Center for Epidemiologic Studies Depression Scale.

that disconfirms the hypothesis that Korean Americans have higher burden because of acculturative stress. When demographic variables and health were controlled, burden was roughly equal across groups, suggesting that differences were due to group differences in gender, education, age, and health. The U.S. sample contained most of the men, and men are known to report lower levels of burden (e.g., Lutzky & Knight, 1994). Among female caregivers, the differences in total burden were not significant, although there was some suggestion of compensating subscale differences, which would be of interest if replicated. When the sample was limited to children and children-in-law who were caring for parents, burden was significant again, with covariates controlled. Thus, it appears that the greater adherence to familism values does not protect Korean caregivers from burden. When burden was found to be higher among Korean and Korean American caregivers, these groups reported higher levels on the Embarrassment–Anger subscale than the other two groups. This may suggest that these caregivers were more sensitive to shame that was related to the demented relative's behaviors.

As found in studies of older Koreans and older Korean Americans, in this study the Korean caregivers reported that they had the smallest levels of emotional support and of instrumental support while they had taken the caregiving roles, with Korean Americans having more social support than Koreans but less than that reported by Whites. Choi (1993), in a study of Korean caregivers, noted that the caregivers expressed a lack of socioemotional support and of social acknowledgment, which increased feelings of entrapment and abandonment. He argued that emo-

tional support for caregivers is a key element in maintaining familial support under changing social structures, as South Korea urbanizes and Westernizes. Another point of interest in understanding the role of familism in Korean culture is that familism does not seem to reflect a strong tradition of mutual support, as is hypothesized to be true of African American and of Latino caregivers in the United States.

Zarit, Orr, and Zarit (1985) argued that the caregiving distress for the primary caregivers could be lessened by social support such as other family members visiting them. Their finding may not generalize to Koreans. Youn and Kim (1995) found that many Korean daughters-in-law who were the primary caregivers reported that they felt much more burden whenever their sisters-in-law (i.e., sisters of their husbands or wives of their brothers-in-law) visited their caregiving situations.

American White caregivers were less depressed and less anxious. Because the contrast was not significant when age, education, health, and gender were statistically controlled, we speculate that this effect was a general cultural difference rather than one specific to caregiving. Future research should include a noncaregiver sample to test this conjecture.

Limitations

Limitations to this study should be noted before generalizing the results. Although the samples were similar to those of other caregiver studies and although they provided an important first comparison among Korean, White, and acculturating Korean Americans, a larger sample size would increase the power of the analysis and may result in the identification of statistically significant differences that were not apparent in this study. The small sample size and low power are particularly important to keep in mind in interpreting failures to find significant differences between ethnic groups in the women-only and child-only subsample analyses.

As noted previously, the absence of a noncaregiver comparison group leaves open the possibility that results were due to general ethnic or cross-national differences rather than to Ethnicity × Caregiving interactions. Haley et al. (1995), for example, found that some differences between African American and White caregivers were due to general group differences between African Americans and Whites, independent of caregiving status.

The probable lack of comparability of diagnostic procedures for dementia across groups and the very limited information on the care recipients mean that the degree of impairment and the type of care are largely unknown and could be unequal across groups. The available information suggests that the great majority of caregivers in all three groups resided with the person who had dementia, had been caregiving for similar periods of time, and reported similar numbers of problems in the care recipient. However, these groups could well differ in important ways not assessed in this study.

In a similar manner, the question of scale equivalence across cultures, although strengthened by the use of back-translation procedures and by the finding of similar reliabilities, is not conclusive. It has been suggested that the CES–D may have a different factor structure in elderly, Mexican American persons compared with older White, non-Latino research participants (Miller, Markides, & Black, 1997). This sample is too small for confirmatory factor analysis, on equivalence of factor structure across ethnic groups. We also note that Miller et al. reported that the two-factor model found in older Mexican Americans has been reported in White, non-Latino populations as well, leaving the case for ethnic differences in factor structure unclear.

Summary and Implications

Nonetheless, the results provide strong support for the difference in familism values among the three groups and point to changes in the selection of the family caregiver and in familism values among Korean Americans. The results also call attention to the (at least) equivalent levels of caregiver burden and the higher levels of anxiety and depression in Korean and Korean American caregivers. These high levels of emotional distress may, in fact, be general among Koreans and Korean Americans and not limited to caregivers. These findings suggest a need for greater attention in research and practice to the needs of this rapidly growing population in the United States as well as for greater attention to mental health and family caregiving services in South Korea. The finding that high levels of familism do not correspond to lower levels of appraisal of caregiving as burdensome or to lower levels of emotional distress is consistent with the Korean culture's perception of the daughter-in-law caregiving role as a duty, with expected high levels of conflict. The clear specification of the daughter-in-law as the expected caregiver appears to function to isolate the primary caregiver among Koreans, with more instrumental help available to Korean Americans. It does, however, suggest a need for greater precision in cross-cultural theories that suggest that high familism reflects more positive appraisals of familial relationships and lower emotional distress outcomes than does the American emphasis on individualism. Familism that emphasizes obligation over reciprocal affective ties (e.g., Roberts & Bengtson, 1990) does not protect against distress and may increase it.

REFERENCES

Aranda, M. P., & Knight, B. G. (1997). The influence of ethnicity and culture on the caregiver stress and coping process: A sociocultural review and analysis. *The Gerontologist, 37,* 342–354.

Bardis, P. D. (1959a). Attitudes toward the family among college students and their parents. *Sociology and Social Research, 43,* 352–358.

Bardis, P. D. (1959b). A comparative study of familism. *Rural Sociology, 24,* 362-371.

Bardis, P. D. (1959c). A familism scale. *Marriage & Family Living, 21,* 340–341.

Brislin, R. W. (1986). The wording and translation of research instruments. In W. J. Looner & J. W. Berry (Eds.), *Field methods in cross-cultural research* (pp. 137–164). Beverly Hills, CA: Sage.

Choe, H. (1991). *Research on the relations between mothers- and daughters-in-law from social psychological perspectives.* Unpublished doctoral dissertation, Chung Ang University, Seoul, Korea.

Choi, H. (1993). Cultural and noncultural factors as determinants of caregiver burden for the impaired elderly in South Korea. *The Gerontologist, 33,* 8–15.

Cox, C., & Monk, A. (1990). Minority caregivers of dementia victims: A comparison of Black and Hispanic families. *Journal of Applied Gerontology, 9,* 340–354.

Gatz, M., Bengtson, V. L., & Blum, M. J. (1991). Caregiving families. In J. E. Birren & K. W. Schaie (Eds.), *Handbook of the psychology of aging* (3rd ed., pp. 405–426). San Diego, CA: Academic Press.

Haley, W. E., Roth, D. L., Coleton, M. I., Ford, G. R., West, C. A. C., Collins, R. P., & Isobe, T. L. (1996). Appraisal, coping, and social support as mediators of well-being in Black and White family caregivers of patients with Alzheimer's disease. *Journal of Consulting and Clinical Psychology, 64,* 121–129.

Haley, W. E., West, C. A. C., Wadley, V. G., Ford, G. R., White, F. A., Barrett, J. S., Harrell, L. E., & Roth, D. L. (1995). Psychological, social, and health impact of caregiving: A comparison of Black and White dementia family caregivers and noncaregivers. *Psychology and Aging, 10,* 540–552.

Hertzog, C., Van Alstine, J., Usala, P. D., & Hultsch, D. F. (1990). Measurement properties of the Center for Epidemiological Studies Depression Scale (CES–D) in older populations. *Psychological Assessment, 2,* 64–72.

Horowitz, A. (1985). Sons and daughters as caregivers to older parents: Differences in role performance and consequences. *The Gerontologist, 25,* 612–617.

Johnson, C., & Barer, B. (1990). Families and networks among older inner-city Blacks. *The Gerontologist, 30,* 726–733.

Knight, B. G., Fox, L. S., & Chou, C. (1998). *Factor structure of the burden interview.* Manuscript submitted for publication.

Koh, J. Y., & Bell, W. G. (1987). Korean elders in the United States: Intergenerational relations and living arrangements. *The Gerontologist, 27,* 66–71.

Landrine, H. (1992). Clinical implications of cultural differences: The referential versus the indexical self. *Clinical Psychology Review, 12,* 401–415.

Lawton, M. P., Rajagopal, D., Brody, E., & Kleban, M. (1992). The dynamics of caregiving for a demented elder among Black and White families. *Journal of Gerontology: Social Sciences, 47,* S156–SI64.

Lazarus, R. S., & Folkman, S. (1984). *Stress, appraisal, and coping.* New York: Springer.

Lutzky, S. M., & Knight, B. G. (1994). Explaining gender differences in caregiver distress: The roles of emotional attentiveness and coping styles. *Psychology and Aging, 4,* 513–519.

Miller, T. Q., Markides, K. S., & Black, S. A. (1997). The factor structure of the CES–D in two surveys of elderly Mexican-Americans. *Journal of Gerontology: Social Sciences, 52B,* S259–S269.

Mintzer, J. E., Rubert, M. P., Loewenstein, D., Gamez, E., Millor, A., Quinteros, R., Flores, L., Miller, M., Rainerman, A., & Eisdorfer, C. (1992). Daughters caregiving for Hispanic and Non-Hispanic Alzheimer's patients: Does ethnicity make a difference? *Community Mental Health Journal, 28,* 293–303.

Moon, A. (1996). Predictors of morale among Korean immigrant elderly in the USA. *Journal of Cross-Cultural Gerontology, 11,* 351–367.

Morycz, R. K., Malloy, J., Bozich, M., & Martz, P. (1987). Racial differences in family burden: Clinical implications for social work. *Gerontological Social Work, 10,* 133–154.

Patterson, R. L., O'Sullivan, M., & Spielberger, C. D. (1980). Measurement of state and trait anxiety in elderly mental health clients. *Journal of Behavioral Assessment, 2,* 89–97.

Radloff, L. S. (1977). The CES–D Scale: A self-report depression scale for research in the general population. *Applied Psychological Measurement, 1,* 385–401.

Radloff, L. S., & Teri, L. (1986). Use of the Center for Epidemiological Studies—Depression Scale with older adults. *Clinical Gerontologist, 5,* 119–136.

Roberts, R. E., & Bengtson, V. L. (1990). Is intergenerational solidarity a unidimensional construct? A second test of a formal model. *Journals of Gerontology, 45,* S12–S20.

Schulz, R., O'Brien, A. T., Bookwala, J., & Fleissner, K. (1995). Psychiatric and physical morbidity effects of dementia caregiving: Prevalence, correlates, and causes. *The Gerontologist, 35,* 771–791.

Spielberger, C. D., Gorsuch, R., Lushene, R., Vagg, P., & Jacobs, G. *(1985). Manual for the State–Trait Anxiety Inventory (Form Y).* Palo Alto, CA: Consulting Psychology Press.

Sung, K. (1991). Family-centered informal support networks of Korean elderly: The resistance of cultural traditions. *Journal of Cross-Cultural Gerontology, 6,* 431–447.

Sung, K. (1992). Motivations for parent care: The case of filial children in Korea. *International Journal of Aging and Human Development, 34,* 109–124.

Teri, L., Truax, P., Logsdon, R., Uomoto, J., Zarit, S., & Vitaliano, P. (1992). Assessment of behavioral problems in dementia: The Revised Memory and Behavior Problems Checklist. *Psychology and Aging, 7,* 622–631.

Youn, G., & Kim, H. (1995, November). *Family caregiving strain and depression of the daughters-in-law who care for the demented and the healthy elderly parents.* Paper presented at the Fifth Asia/Oceania Regional Congress of Gerontology, Hong Kong.

Youn, G., & Song, D. (1992). Aging Koreans' perceived conflicts in relationships with their offspring as a function of age, gender, cohabitation status, and marital status. *Journal of Social Psychology, 132,* 299–305.

Zarit, S. H., Orr, N. K., & Zarit, J. M. (1985). *The hidden victims of Alzheimer's disease: Families under stress.* New York: New York University Press.

Zarit, S. H., Reever, K., & Bach-Peterson, J. (1980). Relatives of impaired elderly: Correlates of feelings of burden. *The Gerontologist, 20,* 373–377.

SELF-STUDY QUESTIONS

Multiple Choice

1. According to the authors of this article, which group is less likely to value the independence of an individual?
   a. British Americans
   b. Irish Americans
   c. German Americans
   d. African Americans

2. Korean caregivers reported that they experienced _____ level(s) of _____ than did Korean Americans or Americans of Western European family backgrounds.
   a. higher; emotional support
   b. same; instrumental support
   c. same; social acknowledgment
   d. lower; emotional and instrumental support

Essay

1. Based on the points discussed regarding the differences in attitudes toward providing care for elderly family members, how would you evaluate your own cultures's attitudes toward this type of caregiving?

2. Why might a family from another culture experience various levels of distress and burden regarding the caretaking of an elderly family member that is different from that of mainstream American culture?

LATE ADULTHOOD

"The Meaning of Aging and the Future of Social Security"

OVERVIEW

Modern society, and especially Western culture, has moved away from demonstrating respect and reverence for people as they age. In fact, it is not uncommon for older people to report that they feel society or their loved ones no longer value them for their wisdom, skills, knowledge, and the contributions they have to offer. At the same time, improvements in health and increases in longevity have changed the way many people think about the physical and mental capabilities of older adults. Thus, more frequently than in the past, older Americans are volunteering, taking care of younger family members, and working full- or part-time to supplement their retirement income. For the vast majority of Americans, this extra income supplements their monthly Social Security check, and, as this article suggests, changing ideas about old age may be influencing opinions about the Social Security system itself.

METHODOLOGY

This article is an essay describing the authors' view of the link between a society's beliefs about aging and the elderly and the institutions it creates to care for them. Thus, it reports no specific research techniques or statistical analyses.

GLOSSARY TERMS

- **Social Security Act** sweeping legislation passed in 1935 that provided workers with a guaranteed, taxpayer-funded retirement income
- **Post-modern culture** a term used to describe how our present-day society views people as being able to reinvent themselves and create new realities
- **Existentialism** a school of thought in philosophy and psychology that examines humanity's search for purpose, fulfillment, and meaning in our lives and deaths
- **Demographics** characteristics such as age, gender, race, nationality, religion, education, marital status, sexual orientation, and socioeconomic status
- **Age-wave** the ongoing increase in the numbers of aging individuals in America, particularly with respect to members of the Baby Boom generation (those born from 1946 to 1964)
- **Modernized view of aging** a current movement in thought and theory that seeks to remove limitations of aging but appears to lack sufficient explanation or emphasis on meaning and significance of older age

Thomas R. Cole and David G. Stevenson

The Meaning of Aging and the Future of Social Security

What vision of a secure old age should be embedded in this cornerstone of the American welfare state?

Later life in the West today is a season in search of its purposes. For the first time in human history, most people can expect to live into their seventies in reasonably good health; those over eighty-five are the fastest-growing age group in the population. Yet the words of *Ecclesiastes*—"To every thing there is a season, and a time to every purpose under heaven"—carry little conviction when applied to the second half of life.

Between the sixteenth century and the third quarter of the twentieth century, Western ideas about aging underwent a fundamental transformation, spurred by the development of modern society. Ancient and medieval understandings of aging as a mysterious part of the eternal order of things gradually gave way to the secular, scientific, and individualist tendencies of modernity. Old age was removed from its place as a way station along life's spiritual journey and redefined as a problem to be solved by science and medicine. By the mid-twentieth century, older people were moved to society's margins and defined primarily as patients or pensioners.

Because long lives have become the rule rather than the exception, and because collective meaning systems have lost their power to infuse aging with widely shared significance, we have become deeply uncertain about what it means to grow old. Ancient myths and modern stereotypes alike fail to articulate the challenges or capture the uncertainty of generations moving into the still-lengthening later years. The modernization of aging has generated a host of unanswered questions: Does aging have an intrinsic purpose? Is there anything really important to be done after children are raised, jobs left, careers completed? Is old age the culmination of life? Does it contain potential for self-completion? What are the avenues of spiritual growth in later life? What are the roles, rights, and responsibilities of older people? What are the particular strengths and virtues of old age? Is there such a thing as a good old age?

In 1979, the English writer Ronald Blythe wrote in *The View in Winter* that "the ordinariness of living to be old" was too new to appreciate. "The old have …been sentenced to life and turned into a matter for public concern," he wrote. "They are the first generations of full-timers and thus the first generations of old people for whom the state, experimentally, grudgingly, and uncertainly, is having to make special supportive conditions." Blythe suggested that it would soon be necessary for people to learn to grow old as they had once learned to grow up.

These perceptive remarks already have the feel of a bygone era. At the turn of the twenty-first century, the long-rising tide of modernity is turning; beneath the much heralded "age wave," uncharted postmodern cultural currents are breaking up conventional images, norms, and expectations about aging and old age. The large percentage of public economic and medical resources devoted to older people has spawned a fierce debate over intergenerational equity in shrinking welfare states. Meanwhile, writers, filmmakers, advocates, and elders are defying negative stereotypes and images of old age. Within the last decade, we have also seen renewed interest in the search for meaning in later life—variously called "conscious aging," "spiritual eldering," or "spirituality and aging." And in 1999, the United Nations' International Year of the Older Person program is making a concerted effort to emphasize that older people are active agents as well as dependent beneficiaries, sources of wisdom and guidance as well as recipients of healthcare and income transfers.

The meaning of later life is not only a matter of cultural values and personal experience; it is also linked to values and assumptions built into social policy. In our view, the current debate over the future of Social Security needs to be examined not

Reprinted with permission from *Generations*, 1999–2000, *23*, 72–76. Copyright © The American Society on Aging, San Francisco, California.

only in the usual fiscal terms but also in moral and existential terms: What vision of a secure old age should be embedded in this cornerstone of the American welfare state? We begin with a historical review of the value tensions that have shaped Social Security since its inception and offer a brief analysis of the social meanings at stake in the current debate over the future of the program.

HISTORICAL ORIGINS OF SOCIAL SECURITY

Social security has always been defined by competing values. From the program's beginnings in 1935, proponents have struck a balance between the rhetoric of offering assistance and the rhetoric of administering insurance. Although the Social Security act included public assistance for low-income elders, Old Age Assistance (Title I) was meant to provide temporary relief until the contributory system (Title II) could take effect. In particular, President Roosevelt and his advisors thought that it was important to distinguish Social Security from welfare to ensure support for the program. Even in the midst of the Depression, "welfare" had a stigma that could have prevented the program's success.

Rather than representing major shift in opinion about individual or governmental responsibility, income support for retirees was promoted as a logical response to the Depression. In part, the Social Security Act arose from the realization that poverty could result from factors beyond human control (Achenbaum, 1986). Individual and family misfortune did not necessarily indicate lax morals or an inadequate work ethic and, hence, was worthy of public intervention.

Yet, Social Security was also created within the context of a culture that valued independence and self-sufficiency. Economic assistance was acceptable as long as it did not compromise these principles. The underlying conflict between Social Security as insurance and Social Security as assistance reflected a deeper ambivalence between self-reliance and mutual responsibility. Americans cherished the former while recognizing the need for the latter, and Social Security had to marry both of these concepts to be successful.

In rhetoric and in practice, workers have always "earned" their right to Social Security. Benefits are based on contributions and have a direct relationship to earnings. Under this model, the government's primary role is viewed as administrative rather that redistributive. This system is equitable in the sense that individuals are treated in accordance with their individual contributions. Yet, Social Security also adheres to a broader notion of fairness by proving a minimum benefit to all who are eligible. This broader concept of public assistance is not based on individual merit but instead on membership within a larger community. The equity promoted within such a system is based on the conviction that each individual is deserving of the benefit regardless of individual circumstance. Throughout the history of Social Security, policy makers have tried to balance these two conflicting concepts of equity within the program.

SOCIAL MEANING OF SECURITY

How we structure our Social Security program is inextricably linked to how we define a secure old age. Security for American elders is often promoted through the ideal of choice. Choice ensures security because it supports individual control, autonomy, and independence—cherished traits in America throughout adulthood. Successful aging in this context means the combination of increased freedom in retirement with undiminished physical and cognitive functioning. It should not be surprising that many of us fail to meet this standard. Indeed, this myth of independence is perpetuated by the misguided belief that individuals should be able to fend for themselves, a belief reinforced by the popular misconception that Social Security is a contract in which the beneficiary and the contributor are perceived to be one.

Independence throughout old age and a fully funded Social Security system are in fact both myths. Most older individuals need to rely on external support at some point before they die, and Social Security is a pay-as-you-go system (current payments from younger generations go directly to older generations). Consequently, both independence in old age and the Social Security system rely on a transfer between generations. Rather than deny the existence of these transfers, we should embrace them and contemplate the relationships that are necessary to support them.

Burdenless living, independence, and self-sufficiency imply nothing about human solidarity. In fact, these ideals imply an absence of human relationships, at least in the interdependent sense. Instead of relationships, freedom is exalted as the primary good. This freedom no doubt includes the ability to conduct relationships on one's own terms—free of any necessity of exchange. Yet, as Michael Ignatieff (1984) has argued, if the welfare state serves the needs of freedom alone, it neglects the needs of solidarity and renders us "a society of strangers." As we move forward in the Social Security debate, we need to realign the values that will guide future reform and emphasize community over isolated self-reliance.

MEANING OF SOCIAL SECURITY

Over the years, Social Security has kept many of our nations's elderly out of poverty (poverty rates for both older men and women are about one-fifth what they would be without Social Security) and has managed to do so without high administrative cost or major scandal. However, demographic and economic projections do not bode well for the program's future solvency. Although the program is not in imminent financial crisis, policy makers point to the coming "age wave" in their push to save Social Security for future generations.

As we engage in this debate, it is important to ponder exactly what we are trying to save. What kind of program do we want Social Security to be? What ends should it serve? How will potential reforms alter the nature of the program? The inevitable cycle of dire predictions and fiscal rescue plans obscures the fact that larger questions about Social Security's meaning and purpose are often not addressed. If we want to ensure the sustainability—rather than just the affordability—of Social Security into the next millennium, we must address these more difficult questions before we proceed.

We must first decide what vision of social insurance we want to guide our Social Security program. Should we regard Social Security as a contract between and for individuals, or should it be an expression of community? Each option entails a different sense of fairness. If we envision Social Security as a contract that provides individual benefits in accordance with contributions, individual retirement accounts are perhaps a reasonable way to proceed. For many, individual accounts foster a sense of ownership and control that in turn promotes feelings of security. Regardless of the overall fiscal health of the Social Security program, each individual would have his or her own personal account. At a time when many assume that Social Security will not exist when they retire, it is easy to see the appeal of such an approach.

However, the individualized approach is deeply flawed. Individual accounts undermine the vision of social insurance as an expression of solidarity. Reliance on individual accounts subordinates the notion of mutual protection to the principle of individual choice. While this approach is consistent with the manner in which many older Americans find security, sacrificing the commitment to a basic retirement benefit for all is too high of a price to pay. If we bolster our social commitment to—and our collective confidence in—a decent minimum benefit, we would find security more easily in provisions of community than in arrangements for individual choice. Ultimately, we must reestablish the priority of sheltering individuals from risk over the ideal of personal gain.

Somewhat along these lines, some have advocated that Social Security benefits be targeted by income. Although the underlying logic of this position is appealing, the extreme of this approach—means-testing benefits—could result in the transformation of Social Security from social insurance to a welfare program. If what has happened to support for the means-tested benefit Medicaid is any indication, the widespread support that Social Security currently enjoys would dissipate considerably. A more reasonable approach is to reduce benefit payments to those with higher incomes, while maintaining a strong commitment to a decent minimum standard of living. Such an approach would be unfair from the perspective of individual equity (i.e., that individuals should receive benefits based on their own contributions), but would be beneficial for those who arguably need support the most.

Any discussion of targeting benefits naturally leads to consideration of the larger role of Social Security in retirement and, more specifically, the level of benefits Social Security should seek to provide. When Social Security began, retirement was a different entity than it is today. Average life expectancy and cultural norms about work and leisure meant that retirement was a short and unfortunate necessity. Social Security was created in part to encourage older people to retire from the workforce and to make way for younger workers. As individuals live longer and healthier lives, the possibility for an extended period of time after retirement becomes more likely. Indeed, our society has come to expect a long period of leisure when obligations of work and family life are complete.

In this context, Social Security influences retirement trends in important ways. First, the magnitude of individual Social Security benefits has a profound impact on retirement savings. The initial, modest aim of keeping older people out of the poorhouse has expanded dramatically to provide the majority of post-retirement income. Two-thirds of today's older people rely on Social Security for at least half of their total income, and even the richest quintile relies on Social Security for more than 20 percent of income. In times of scarce resources, some critics ask whether it is efficient or desirable to offer a retirement benefit that makes individual savings less necessary.

In addition, the eligibility age for Social Security benefits influences when people retire. Although the eligibility age for full benefits will increase from 65 to 67 by the year 2027, some believe that this change should be accelerated and even increased—perhaps to age 70—to reflect the improved health (and productive potential) of today's elders. Clearly, such a shift will have to grapple with cultural beliefs about when we are entitled to retire and receive pension benefits and also with such issues as job availability and age discrimination in employment.

SECURITY OF SOCIAL MEANING

Although Daniel Callahan's *Setting Limits* (1987) received less attention for its discussion of meaning and old age than for its resource allocation proposals, Callahan makes a persuasive case for the place of meaning in discussions of public policy. He argues that our modernized view of aging is hamstrung by its drive to remove the limitations of age and that it "lacks that most important of all ingredients for old age: a sense of collective meaning and purpose." Our orientation, Callahan posits, is toward an individualistic old age that gives us more of what we want (e.g., more years and less limitation) but illuminates little about the meaning and significance of those years.

The American vision of security in old age illustrates Callahan's point. As described above, we tend to feel secure when we are self-sufficient and in control. However, there are two main limitations to such an approach. First, such a standard of security is almost impossible to maintain. Second, and more important, even if we were able to maintain control until the day we die, a tenuous notion of independence does nothing to anchor our connection to a higher spiritual or ethical purpose.

If we cling to our needs and aspirations as individuals alone, we will fail to realize a deeper sense of meaning that can only be achieved through connection to the larger social and spiritual community. To achieve this kind of security—rather than just financial security—we need to develop a fundamental trust that we understand the order of the world in which we live (see Hashimoto, 1996). This cannot be done through reliance on a transitory notion of individual control. It must develop through a grounding in social relationships and spiritual beliefs.

The discussion of security almost inevitably turns to a contemplation of human need. Social Security (as well as Medicare) is premised on the idea that older Americans have a need for—and a corresponding right to—security. A narrow view of these needs can be found in the typical realm of the welfare state—food, shelter, and medical care. In this context, the provision of Social Security is important for the delivery of the monthly benefits check alone. However, as Ignatieff (1984) has argued, our needs as individuals extend beyond mere survival and include the need to achieve our potential as human beings. This realm of need includes things that the state cannot compel—love, respect, and community. It is in this gap between our claims on the collectivity and our needs *for* the collectivity where meaning can be lost.

And yet this gap between rights and needs is also where meaning is to be found. Ideals of later life are carved out of three basic dimensions of meaning: individual, social, and cosmic (Cole, 1992). We have reached the limits of what can be gained through the realm of the individual alone. It is high time that we accept the inevitable emptiness of such an approach and begin to foster our connection to the larger social and spiritual community. Our cult of independence is inevitably—and ironically—plagued by a lack of true security and, ultimately, by a lack of meaning. A truly sustainable Social Security program must be grounded in the security of shared social meanings.

Public policy has a role to play in our search for lasting security and meaning. As Social Security reform inches more and more toward a vision of individual equity, we must pause to consider the aspects of security that we are sacrificing in the process. Fiscal soundness matters, but it is not *all* that matters. Social Security reform and aging policy in the United States need to be socially and spiritually sound as well. Unless we look beyond the balance sheets of the future, our hopes and aspirations for growing older will be reduced to actuarial projections. We cannot afford to be so shortsighted.

REFERENCES

Achenbaum, W. A. 1986. *Social Security: Visions and Revisions.* New York: Cambridge University Press.

Blythe, R. 1979. *The View in Winter: Reflection on Aging.* London: Harcourt Brace.

Callahan, D. 1987. *Setting Limits: Medical Goals in an Aging Society.* New York: Simon and Schuster.

Cole, T. R. 1992. *The Journey of Life: The Cultural Aging History of Aging in America.* New York: Cambridge University Press.

Hashimoto, A. 1996. *The Gift of Generations: Japanese and American Perspectives on Aging and the Social Contract.* New York: Cambridge University Press.

Ignatieff, M. 1984. *The Needs of Strangers.* London: The Hogarth Press.

SELF-STUDY QUESTIONS

Multiple Choice

1. Benefit payments that recognize the importance of a worker's contribution to Social Security and its contribution to self-reliance and responsibility reflect a view that the government role is
   a. redistributive
   b. welfare-based
   c. administrative
   d. imperative

2. This article suggests that we utilize the Social Security system to guarantee economic freedom for aging Americans, yet we fail to create meaningful relationships with them. Instead, we create
   a. a society of independent elders
   b. a society of generational boundaries
   c. a society of visionaries
   d. a society of strangers

Essay

1. Discuss the idea set forth in this article that poverty and need can be due at times to situations that are beyond a person's control.

2. Programs such as Social Security and Medicare were designed to provide a certain level of financial security to older Americans. The article suggests that an older person may have additional needs in life that need to be met in order to reach his or her life's potential. Discuss these factors that the article proposes.

EARLY, MIDDLE, AND LATE ADULTHOOD

"Unasked-For Support and Unsolicited Advice: Age and the Quality of Social Experience"

OVERVIEW

In this article, the question of how older and younger adults respond to advice or an offering of support when they have not asked for it is explored. The basic notion is that receiving such support may undermine an adult's sense of competence. Strategies that each group of participants used for coping with these events, such as evaluating who the person was who was offering the advice or support, the method in which the advice or support was delivered, and whether the advice or support was offered in a way that was pleasant or unpleasant are also examined. Interestingly, regardless of age, the authors found that living alone was the best buffer against getting unsolicited advice or unasked-for support for adults of all ages. As you read this article, pay close attention to the ways in which younger people and older people welcome or are threatened by unasked-for support or unsolicited advice.

METHODOLOGY

These authors used a variety of techniques to compile data about participants' experiences and beliefs about unasked-for support. They employed a technique called *regression analysis* as well as *analysis of variance (ANOVA)* to explore relationships among variables. These techniques allow researchers to find such relationships and to determine how they work together to influence a particular outcome variable. From these analyses, the researchers are able to build theoretical models, called *path models* (see Figure 4) that predict occurrences of unasked-for support and individuals' evaluations of such experiences. Variables to which greater weights are applied in the model contribute more to these outcomes. In addition, the models suggest that some variables contribute to these outcomes indirectly by contributing to factors that do directly influence them.

GLOSSARY TERMS

- **Taxonomy**   the science of classification
- **Cognition**   mental processes such as thinking, reasoning, perception, learning, memory, and language development
- **Affect**   feelings or emotions
- **Autonomy-eroding**   taking away a person's sense of self, independence, and authority

Jacqui Smith and Jacqueline J. Goodnow

Unasked-For Support and Unsolicited Advice: Age and the Quality of Social Experience

The present study (N = 122) examined whether older adults (M = 79 years) differed from younger age groups (Ms = 25 and 45 years) in their experience of 35 situations of unsolicited support selected from 7 content areas (e.g., health, cognition, finances, life management). Examined were reported occurrence, affective quality, interpretation, and strategies used when support was unwelcome. At all ages, unasked-for support was regarded as more unpleasant than pleasant, primarily because it implied incompetence. Unexpectedly, compared with the younger adults, older adults reported less occurrence overall (with some variations by content area) but the same level of unpleasant affect. Cognitive and social–relational factors that are age related (e.g., the use of active discounting strategies) played a role in reported occurrence and affective appraisal and may determine whether unsolicited support has positive or negative outcomes.

Interactions involving support and advice are widely regarded as markers of the quality of social experience, especially in late adulthood (e.g., Antonucci, 1990; M. M. Baltes, 1996; Rook, 1995). Specifying the positive and negative dimensions of supportive interactions and the ways in which they arise has come to be seen as steps toward refining the concept of social support and toward clarifying how social experience may chance with age (Carstensen, 1993). In the present study we focused on occasions in everyday life when offers of support or advice are unsolicited. These occasions may range from offers to carry a heavy bag to reminders about an appointment or suggestions about how to improve one's state of health. The context in which unsolicited support is offered conveys messages about the images that the giver holds about the intended recipient. The ways in which recipients interpret and react to unsolicited offers of support or advice likely reflect their own beliefs about relationships and self as well as their past experiences of similar transactions (e.g., Burleson, Albrecht, & Sarason, 1994).

Two sets of questions were central to our study. The first set concerned the possibility of relationships between age and content area in the reported occurrence and affective appraisal of occasions of unsolicited support. Do older adults report receiving more offers of unsolicited support or advice than younger adults, especially in areas in which older individuals are generally perceived to be in need of assistance (e.g., physical activity, cognitive tasks)? The second set had to do with the extent to which differences in reported occurrence and affective appraisal depend on the norms people bring to occasions when assistance is offered and the strategies they use in the face of unwanted support or advice. These foci allowed us to explore the argument that the analysis of interactions involving support requires attention not only to characteristics such as age but also to the cognitive and social-relational dimensions of interactions (e.g., M. M. Baltes, 1996; Burleson et al., 1994; Carstensen, 1993; Dunkel-Schetter, Folkman, & Lazarus, 1987; Rook, 1995).

UNASKED-FOR SUPPORT OR ADVICE: AGE LINKS TO OCCURRENCE AND AFFECT

Analyses of social support take several forms. Some focus on occasions of crisis (e.g., times of illness or of loss). Others focus on everyday events (e.g., assistance with shopping and emotional comfort). Everyday events—the focus of the present study—seem more likely to bring out the quality of social experience (Barnes & Duck, 1994; Dunkel-Schetter et al., 1987; Zautra, Affleck, & Tennen, 1994).

Analyses of support also concentrate on the processes and consequences of giving, receiving, or seeking support. The focus on receiving unasked-for support in the present study was based on its particular advantages for exploring links to age. To begin with, this category of support has attracted contrasting hypotheses about its occurrence. Late adulthood has been seen as both a time when others feel increasingly free to offer advice and a time when older adults increasingly exercise selective control over their social contacts, potentially reducing the extent to which they are exposed to unwanted interactions (Carstensen, 1992, 1993; Rook, 1989).

Occasions of unasked-for support or advice have also attracted contrasting hypotheses with regard to the affect they provoke. At any age, assistance given without its being asked for may be experienced as pleasant (Eckenrode & Wethington, 1990). Also at any age, the same support may be perceived as an attempt at control or interference and for that reason be unwelcome (e.g., Cutrona & Suhr, 1994; Hughes & Gove, 1981; La Gaipa, 1990). In late adulthood, a time when adults may be increasingly sensitive to attempts at influence, this unwelcome quality may be particularly pronounced (Rook, 1989, 1995).

Social control in the context of personal relationships can be direct (e.g., regulatory actions or interventions) or indirect (e.g., felt obligation) and, although successful in preventing or moderating risk-related behavior, usually provokes frustration, anger, or distress (Hughes & Gove, 1981; Rook, 1995). To date, as Rook, Thuras, and Lewis (1990) noted, there is no strong empirical support for the argument that influence attempts in late adulthood give rise to the distress that social control theory suggests. That lack of evidence, however, may reflect the use of measures of general levels of distress (e.g., depression, life satisfaction) rather than reports of specific feelings in particular circumstances (Rook, 1989). One first research step in the analysis of affective impact, then, needs to consist of asking people to comment on both positive and negative feelings relative to specific occasions.

For the analysis of both occurrence and affect relative to age, two other steps are required. First, direct comparative data are needed. Late adulthood may be associated with an increase in the occurrence and the affective quality of unasked-for support and advice. Without direct comparisons with younger ages, however, researchers cannot tell what is specific to late adulthood. It is possible, for example, that both early adulthood and late adulthood are life phases attracting unwelcome support and advice. It is also possible that at all ages unasked-for support tends to be experienced more often as unpleasant than pleasant.

Second, researchers need to sample a variety of situations involving unasked-for support or advice. It is unlikely that all offers will be equally frequent or equally pleasant or unpleasant. Furthermore, some situations might be age specific. A variety of situations may also allow researchers to ask whether the two variables of social experience—the likelihood of occurrence and affective quality—are interrelated. It may be, for example, that the more unpleasant a particular offer of support, the more it may be avoided in most social interactions and so becomes infrequent.

The literature suggests two approaches to obtaining information about situations of unsolicited support (e.g., Zautra et al., 1994). The first involves collecting personal experiences from different age groups, increasing the likelihood that the occasions covered will be part of everyday social experience. This was part of Scheidt and Schaie's (1978) approach to building a taxonomy of everyday situations that call for competence in late adulthood. In the present study, we began with pilot interviews with individuals aged 70–80 years.

The second approach consists of a theory-guided selection of situations considered to be areas of potential vulnerability or sensitivity. This approach is linked to the argument that the experience of stress varies by life domain (e.g., Lazarus & Folkman, 1984). It is also consistent with the argument that late adulthood may bring a decline in several areas of competence, forcing choices with regard to the areas one will try to maintain or to have others perceive one as maintaining (e.g., P. B. Baltes & Baltes, 1990; Carstensen, 1993).

This second approach was adopted in the present study. We presented participants with 35 situations reflecting seven areas of potential sensitivity. The content ranged from tangible aid (e.g., someone warns of a potential danger) to areas involving health (e.g., advice to have a checkup), finances (e.g., advice on the management of money), cognition (e.g., a reminder to turn out the lights), physical competence (e.g., advice to get more exercise), age identity (e.g., being told that something is inappropriate for one's age), and life management (e.g., the rearrangement of a desk so that things can be more easily found). In some of these areas, it seems especially likely that age differences will appear. The occurrence and the unpleasantness of someone speaking more deliberately or more slowly than is needed, for example (cognitive area), seems likely to attract age differences. In contrast, advice with regard to money may involve such strong cultural norms with regard to privacy that few age differences will be found.

COGNITIVE AND SOCIAL–RELATIONAL MEDIATORS OF THE OCCURRENCE AND AFFECTIVE IMPACT OF UNSOLICITED SUPPORT

At any age, what factors might underlie the frequency with which unasked-for support is received and the sense that the experience is pleasant or unpleasant? To what extent do these factors in themselves vary with age or account for age effects?

Without regard to age, general studies of the receipt of social support emphasize two underlying factors: how the other's action is interpreted (e.g., Nadler & Fisher, 1986; Sarason, Sarason, & Pierce, 1994) and the way offers of support are embedded within social relationships (e.g., Barnes & Duck, 1994; Dunkel-Schetter et al., 1987).

Issues of interpretation, within analyses of late adulthood, are highlighted by Rook's (1995) suggestion that the kind of affect provoked by any attempt at influence will depend on the extent to which these attempts are seen as well intended or as "condescending, patronizing, autonomy-eroding" (p. 451). Needed, then, are data indicating the ways in which specific offers of support or advice are interpreted. In the present study, asking why an offer of support or advice was experienced as pleasant or unpleasant provided that kind of information. On the basis of the literature, we surmised that unsolicited offers of support would be viewed as pleasant because they indicate communal concern and friendliness or because the support was actually needed. The interpretation of such offers as unpleasant, on the other hand, would be because the support was perceived as interference (unwanted social control) or because it indicated that the recipient was judged to be incompetent.

An emphasis on social–relational factors is to be found within several analyses of late adulthood (e.g., Acitelli & Antonucci, 1994; Antonucci, 1994; Antonucci & Jackson, 1990; Rook, 1989). Much research has shown the different effects on well-being of social support received from spouse, same-aged friends, or family members and the varying expectations about the reciprocal exchange of support linked with these various social partners. The question is how to ground this general emphasis in specific measures that might bring out particular links to age.

One way to examine the influence of social–relational factors is to ask who makes offers of support. On the basis of the literature, we expected that unasked-for offers of support would come mainly from people whom the receiver knew well (e.g., a partner or family member). We wondered, however, whether this would be true for all age groups. Op-

portunities for exposure to unsolicited support may also depend on the circumstances of the individual's life (e.g., whether he or she lives alone or with others; Hughes & Gove, 1981). Given that many adults over the age of 70 years are widowed and live alone, they may have less exposure on a day-to-day basis to unsolicited offers of support from close partners.

A second way to examine the influence of social–relational factors is to ask about the strategies that people use in the face of unwanted offers of support. At least at younger ages, the extent to which people receive offers of assistance varies with the extent to which these offers are invited or discouraged by the approaches people take toward everyday social interactions (Dunkel-Schetter et al., 1987). Old age might bring with it a change in the strategies that people use to deal with unwelcome offers of support. In turn, these strategies might alter not only the frequency with which unasked-for offers are made but also the perceived unpleasantness of the offers that do break through an individual's protective screen. In the present study, we examined whether there would be age differences in strategies for dealing with unwanted support (i.e., assertively ignore, actively discount, accommodate) and whether these strategies would be associated with reported occurrence of unsolicited support.

A third and last way forward combines attention to cognitive and social–relational factors. This consists of considering the norms or expectations that people bring to occasions of support or advice. All relationships, it has been argued, are regulated by norms that specify what people should contribute and what they should receive (e.g., Clark, Patarki, & Carver, 1996; Fiske, 1992). The sense that these norms have been violated is a strong contributor to feelings of disappointment or pleasure in one's interactions with others (e.g., Clark & Reis, 1988).

Reciprocity is undoubtedly an important norm in most social interactions. It is also a feature of social relationships that appears to be subject to change in old age. Late adulthood has been proposed as a time when people may feel less able to make a return for the support they receive (e.g., Antonucci, 1994; Beckman, 1981; Ingersoll-Dayton & Antonucci, 1988). Reciprocity, however, is only one of the norms that people bring to occasions of support or advice. People may find unpleasant, for example, "actions that violate implicit norms of trust, respect, reciprocity, and status equality" (Rook, 1989, p. 171).

There are few analyses of the norms expected to apply specifically to occasions of support or advice, with or without regard to age. In the present study, we developed an exploratory set of items describing possible norms. The items were derived from several sources: general analyses of advice (e.g., Rook, 1989; Wiseman, 1986), answers in our pilot interviews to questions about why an offer of support might be pleasant or unpleasant, and empirical findings about what young adults regard as reasonable and unreasonable ways to offer a particular kind of support (reminding an individual that a task has not yet been completed; Goodnow & Warton, 1992). Goodnow and Warton, for example, reported that young adults believe reasonable reminders avoid any implication that the other is incompetent, unreliable, or of distinctly inferior status.

The items used in the present study covered expectations ranging from the view that people should offer advice only when they are sure it is needed to the view that people should actively protect "the face" of the other. The set of items, as noted earlier, was exploratory. It does, however, provide a base for asking about the extent to which the endorsement of the norms described varies with age and is correlated with the experience of unasked-for support as pleasant or unpleasant.

CENTRAL QUESTIONS

A number of possible interconnections between age and several factors of experience with unasked-for offers of support have been introduced above. In the present study we examined two sets of specific questions. The opening questions had to do with the extent to which variations in age (being a young, middle-aged, or older adult) and in content area were associated with differences in (a) the occurrence of encounters with unasked-for support, (b) the extent to which these experiences are found to be pleasant or unpleasant, and (c) the reasons offered for the sense of pleasantness or unpleasantness. A second set of questions asked, without reference to specific content areas, about variations with age in the extent to which people endorse a variety of normative statements related to the giving of support or advice and in the strategies people typically use in responding to unwanted offers. We also asked about the possible connections among these variables and used regression analyses to examine predictors of occurrence and affect.

METHOD

Participants

The volunteer sample ($N = 122$) included 41 young (21 women and 20 men; $M = 25.2$ years, range = 20–30), 39 middle-aged (21 women and 18 men; $M = 45.1$ years,

range = 39–53), and 42 older (21 women and 21 men; $M = 78.9$ years, range = 70–91) adults. All participants were German nationals living in Berlin. They were recruited through newspaper advertisements and from an existing address list of older adults (initially established through media announcements) who had participated in previous studies of psychological functioning in old age (e.g., Freund & Smith, in press). Participants were paid DM 30 (approximately $20).

Table 1 shows the sample characteristics in terms of educational level, present life conditions, and performance on two psychometric tests. We attempted to recruit participants so that there would be a wide range of educational levels within each age group. The final sample, however, was positively biased in terms of education (35% of the younger adults were university students). Because the experimental method involved verbal knowledge, we assessed whether age group differences might be confounded by differences in intellectual functioning. Two subtests of intellectual abilities were included for this purpose: one assessed fluid intelligence (the Digit Symbol Substitution test; Wechsler, 1955), and the other assessed verbal ability (Spot-a-Word; Lehrl, 1977). As can be seen in Table 1, raw scores on the Digit Symbol Substitution test showed the typical age-related differences reported in the literature. As expected, however, given the high educational levels of the participants, the measure of verbal ability showed no significant age differences.

Materials

All measures dealt with situations of unsolicited offers of support or advice and were developed for this study.

Situations: Measure of occurrence. In pilot work, short descriptions were devised for 35 situations of unsolicited support and advice (SUSA Interview) likely to be encountered in everyday interpersonal interactions (the complete list is provided in the Appendix). The situations were devised so that they (a) might be experienced by men and women in different age groups, (b) arise in a variety of interpersonal contexts (e.g., between partners, friends, or strangers), and (c) characterize different areas of potential vulnerability and sensitivity. The average number of situations reported as having been experienced in the present sample was 15.8 ($SD = 6.1$, range = 1–30).

Each description began with the refrain, "Have you ever experienced that without your asking, someone…" The situations described advice or actions in seven content areas: (a) age identity (four vignettes:

TABLE 1   Characteristics of the Sample: Age Group Differences and Similarities

CHARACTERISTIC	YOUNG (n = 41)	MIDDLE AGED (n = 39)	OLDER (n = 42)	TOTAL (N = 122)
Sex (% women)	51	54	50	52
Age (in years)				
M	25.2	45.0	78.9	49.8***
SD	2.4	3.8	5.4	22.8
Education (%)**				
Primary	—	20	21	14
Lower secondary	17	36	29	27
Higher secondary	83	44	50	59
Vocational training (%)	59	72	68	66
Employed (%)	49	97	—	49***
Marital status (%)***				
Married	20	42	38	34
Widowed	—	—	36	12
Divorced	2	23	12	12
Single	78	33	14	42
Children (% yes)	5	59	76	47***
No. of children (n = 56)				
M	1	1.6	2.2	1.9
SD	0.00	0.95	1.2	1.1
Live alone (%)	32	36	57	42*
Hearing difficulty (%)[a]	2	5	24	11**
Walking distance[b]				
M	6.5	6.4	6.2	6.4
SD	0.97	0.96	0.87	0.94
Life satisfaction[c]				
M	3.5	3.5	3.7	3.5
SD	0.71	0.72	0.67	0.89
Subjective health[d]				
M	3.5	3.3	3.3	3.4
SD	0.74	0.71	0.90	0.79
Digit Symbol[e]				
M	64.5	53.1	42.3	53.2***
SD	9.3	8.4	11.8	13.6
Verbal ability[f]				
M	22.9	22.0	22.6	22.5
SD	4.4	4.5	4.7	4.5

Note. Dashes indicate empty cells. [a]Question was "Is it a problem for you to hear well what people say?" % = Yes. [b]Single item: "What distance can you walk without a rest?" Response scale: 1 = *can no longer walk*, 7 = > *5 km.* [c]Single item: "How satisfied are you with your life at the present?" Response scale: 1 = *very dissatisfied*, 5 = *very satisfied.* [d]Single item: "How would you rate your health at the present?" Response scale: 1 = *very poor*, 5 = *very good.* [e]Digit Symbol Substitution test (Wechsler, 1955). [f]Spot-a-Word Test (Lehrl, 1977).

*p < .05. **p < .01. ***p < .001.

e.g., suggested that you should organize your life in a more age-appropriate way, suggested that someone your age would not understand); (b) tangible aid (seven vignettes; e.g., offered to carry a suitcase or shopping bags for you, bought clothes for you); (c) health (four vignettes; e.g., suggested that you should eat more vitamins or vegetables, suggested that you should take better care of yourself); (d) finances (three vignettes; e.g., suggested how you should orga-nize your finances, suggested what you could afford); (e) cognition (seven vignettes; e.g., checked that you had turned off the lights, told you that you had already said something [were repeating things]); (f) compe-tence (five vignettes; e.g., warned you not to overex-ert yourself, underestimated your capabilities); and (g) life management (five vignettes; e.g., told you how to spend your time, rearranged your room or desk so that you could find things more easily).

Participants responded yes or no to each situation. The proportion of situations experienced within each content area was calculated to provide a general measure of likelihood of occurrence.

Measure of affect. After participants indicated that they had experienced a situation, they rated on a 4-point scale the affect associated with this experience (ranging from *very pleasant* to *very unpleasant*). In a later part of the interview (after the rating of reasons for the affective quality of situations experienced), we also obtained affect ratings for situations that had not been personally encountered. In this later section, the informants were asked how they would feel if such an interaction happened to them in the future. This procedure enabled us to obtain affective appraisals from all participants for the 35 situations.

Source of the unsolicited support. For those situations that participants indicated they had experienced, there were two follow-up questions regarding the source of the offer of support. The first question asked who gave the offer and provided a forced choice between three response alternatives: a significant other (e.g., partner, parent, adult children, sibling, or other family members), a friend or acquaintance (e.g., neighbor), or a stranger. The second question asked about the relevance of the source for the evaluation of the situation as pleasant or unpleasant. Specifically, participants were asked, "Was this person relevant to your experience of the situation as pleasant or unpleasant?" Three forced-choice response categories were listed: "Yes, relevant because I knew the person," "Yes, relevant because I did not know the person," and "No, the person was not relevant."

Reasons for appraisal as pleasant or unpleasant. After the evaluations of affect and the questions about the source of the offer, participants were asked to rate a set of four potential reasons for either the perceived pleasantness or the perceived unpleasantness. Each reason was rated on a 5-point scale (ranging from *applies very well* to *does not apply at all*).

The reasons presented for a situation viewed as pleasant were (a) because I thought the support was given out of friendliness (coded as *friendliness*); (b) because I believe that people should help each other *(communion)*; (c) because I really needed the support *(needed support)*; and (d) it was pleasant because it indicated that the other person thinks about my needs and wishes *(others think of me)*. The four reasons presented if a situation was seen as unpleasant were (a) because I felt offended (coded as *belittled*); (b) because it indicated that the other person saw me as incompetent or incapable *(incompetent)*; (c) because it felt like the other person was interfer-

ing in my affairs *(interference)*; and (d) because it seemed like the other person had the wrong image of me *(wrong image)*. As with the ratings for affect, we also obtained ratings of reasons for situations not personally encountered.

General strategies for dealing with situations of unsolicited support. In the final section of the questionnaire, participants responded to 12 items outlining general strategies for dealing with situations of unsolicited and unwanted support or advice. These items were framed generally (i.e., they were not specific to the 35 situations). Responses were given on a 5-point scale (5 = *applies very well to me*, 1 = *does not apply to me at all*). Exploratory principal-components factor analysis indicated that the items could be summarized in terms of three factors (eigenvalues of 2.6, 2.1, and 1.8 together explaining 54% of the variance) that were relatively independent (correlations ranged from −.03 to .02). Cronbach alphas for the subscales (each with four items) were acceptable given the small number of items and the sample size (.59–.71). The factors were labeled as follows: (a) Assertively Ignore or reject (e.g., "When something like that happens I make a point of telling the other person why I don't like what they did"; "I just continue doing things my way, regardless what others say to me"); (b) Active Discounting (e.g., "I just tell myself that the other person has a problem, not me"; "I try to see the funny side of such situations"); and (c) Accommodate (e.g., "I try to avoid such situations"; "I generally try to fit in with the other person").

Beliefs about relationship norms. A 12-item scale was developed to capture individuals' beliefs about the interpersonal relationship norms that were violated in situations of unsolicited support that were unpleasant. This scale was completed by participants as a separate questionnaire in the final section of the interview. Task instructions outlined the notion that situations involving unsolicited support might be perceived as being unpleasant because they violated unwritten norms. Participants were asked to indicate the extent to which they believed that unpleasant situations involving unsolicited support reflected a violation of the particular norm described in 12 items using a 5-point response scale (5 = *applies very well*, 1 = *does not apply at all*). Exploratory principal-components factor analysis indicated that the items could be summarized in terms of four factors (eigenvalues of 3, 1.6, 1.3, and 1.1) together accounting for 58% of the variance. Interfactor correlations ranged from .01 to .24. Cronbach alphas for the subscales were acceptable (.56–.73). The factors were labeled as follows: (a) Preserve

Equal Status (four items; e.g., "One should not behave as if one knows everything better than others"); (b) Actively Protect the Other's Face (three items; e.g., "One should not highlight the other's weaknesses"); (c) Avoid Interference (two items; e.g., "One should not meddle in the private affairs of others"); and (d) Respect the Other's Position (three items; e.g., "One should not make decisions for others when they can make them themselves").

Procedure

Data were collected in group settings of 4–6 persons for the young and middle-aged participants. In these groups, after the psychometric tests were completed and general instructions were given about the question and response format, individuals completed a printed SUSA Interview booklet at their own pace. A research assistant was available for the duration of the session to respond to any questions that arose. Older participants were individually interviewed because pilot work had indicated that this procedure was not only more acceptable to the individual but also helped to minimize missing data. Individual interviews required 90 min on average. For practical reasons, it was not possible to conduct individual interviews with the 80 younger participants.

The data collection sessions consisted of four parts. Sample-descriptive information about subjective health, life satisfaction. and two short measures of intellectual functioning (Digit Symbol Substitution test [Wechsler, 1955], and Spot-a-Word [Lehrl, 1977]) as well as biographical information was completed first. The second part of the session focused on participants' experiences of the 35 situations. Situations were presented one at a time (the order was randomized). Participants indicated for each one whether they had encountered the situation and then rated the associated affect, source, and reasons for their appraisal.

In the third section of the procedure, participants were asked about the situations that they had not encountered. Specifically, we asked about the affect and reasons that they thought they would associate with the situation should it occur to them in the future. In the final part of the session, participants completed the general scales about their own strategies for dealing with unwanted help and their beliefs about relationship norms that are violated by situations of unwanted support.

RESULTS

The results presented below focus on two central sets of questions. To begin, we report analyses of age- and content-related differences in reported occurrence, sources of unsolicited support, affective appraisal of such situations, and the reasons underlying, appraisal. We then examine age differences in normative beliefs and preferred strategies for dealing with unwanted support and use regression analyses to explore the relationships between (a) age, strategies, and reported occurrence and (b) age, beliefs, strategies, and affect. A variable coding whether participants lived alone or with others was included in the regression analyses.

Age and Content Effects

Reported occurrence of unsolicited support.   We had expected that, overall, older adults would report more incidents of unsolicited support. The results, however, showed the opposite. Younger adults reported encountering proportionally more of the 35 situations presented than did the middle-aged or the older adults, $F(2, 119) = 14.8$, $MSE = 0.03$, $p < .001$. On average, young adults said that 55% ($SD = 0.17$) of the situations had happened to them personally, middle-aged adults reported 48% ($SD = 0.18$), and older adults only 34% ($SD = 0.35$). Figure 1 displays differences by age group and content area (the Appendix provides item-specific information).

To examine the significance of age- and content-related differences, we calculated for each participant the percentage of situations experienced in each domain and entered these scores into a repeated measures analysis of variance (ANOVA), with age group (3) and gender (2) as between-subjects variables and content area (7) as the within-subjects variable.[1] This analysis confirmed the overall significant main effect for age, $F(2, 116) = 16.3$, $MSE = 0.20$, $p < .001$, $\eta^2 = .22$, and also revealed a main effect for content area, $F(6, 696) = 36.7$, $MSE = 0.06$, $p < .001$, $\eta^2 = .24$, together with a significant Age × Content Area interaction, $F(12, 696) = 1.8$, $MSE = 0.06$, $p < .05$, $\eta^2 = .03$.

With regard to content area, participants reported encountering proportionately more situations associated with everyday cognition ($M = 0.56$, $SD = 0.29$), competence ($M = 0.54$, $SD = 0.31$), and

---

[1]Throughout, we report the results of repeated measures analyses of variance that included gender as a between-subjects variable. Because we did not have specific expectations about differences between men and women, these analyses were not our first concern but are nevertheless important. Women and men did not differ in the reported occurrence of unsolicited support or affective appraisal. There were, however, several interactions involving gender. These interactions were not predicted or readily interpretable, and for that reason are not discussed in this article. A summary of gender-related findings can be obtained from us.

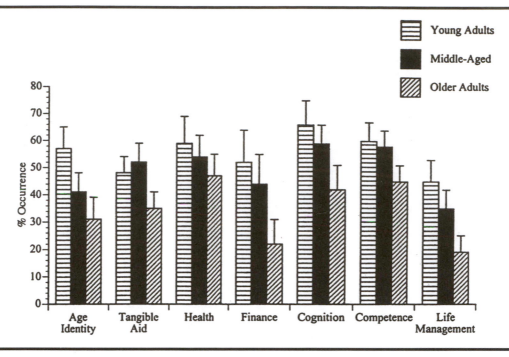

FIGURE 1 Age differences in the reported occurrence of unsolicited support among the seven content areas examined in the study.

health ($M = 0.52$, $SD = 0.29$) than with situations having to do with finances ($M = 0.38$, $SD = 0.40$) or life management ($M = 0.32$, $SD = 0.27$). Situations categorized as reflecting age identity ($M = 0.42$, $SD = 0.29$) and tangible aid ($M = 0.44$, $SD = 0.23$) ranked in the middle. These variations may reflect the particular items included in our study. For example, in the cognitive area, five of the seven items had been encountered by more than 50% of the sample. In the life management area, only one of the three had this status (see the Appendix).

Follow-up analyses for the Age × Content Area interaction confirmed that, compared with middle-age and older adults, young adults reported proportionately more encounters in the areas of age identity, $F(2, 119) = 9.8$, $MSE = 0.07$, $p < .001$, and cognition, $F(2, 119) = 6.1$, $MSE = 0.06$, $p < .01$. Older adults reported significantly less experience than young and middle-aged adults with finance, $F(2, 119) = 6.6$, $MSE = 0.15$, $p < .01$, competence, $F(2, 119) = 9.4$, $MSE = 0.09$, $p < .001$, and life management, $F(2, 119) = 10.6$, $MSE = 0.06$, $p < .001$. Age differences in the areas of health ($p = .15$) and tangible aid ($p = .09$) did not reach significance.

In further analyses, we examined the extent to which age group variations in personal living arrangements might have contributed to the finding that older adults reported the least experience of un-

asked-for help or advice. We expected that offers of unasked-for support or advice usually come from significant others and that living alone might entail less opportunity for such encounters on a day-to-day basis. More older adults lived alone (57%) than did the other age groups (middle aged = 36%; young = 32%). Overall, those who lived alone reported a relatively lower occurrence of unsolicited support than people who lived with others, $F(1, 120) = 6.7$, $MSE = 0.21$, $p < .01$, $\eta^2 = .24$. Further analyses (reported below) of the sources of unsolicited support confirmed that the proportion of occurrence with significant others and strangers differed as a function of living arrangements. When age was included as a covariate, the effects associated with living alone or together with others on reported occurrence were no longer significant. Hierarchical regressions predicting reported occurrence in which age was entered either before or after living arrangements indicated that 15% of the variance in reported occurrence was uniquely accounted for by age, whereas living arrangements accounted for only 2.5%. The variance shared by age and living arrangements was 3.5% (the total variance explained was 21%). It appears that factors associated with age, in addition to living arrangements, play a role in determining the experience of situations of unsolicited support.

Affect. Reported occurrence of the situation produced a significant difference in the affect rating given to 15 items (indicated in the Appendix) but did not alter whether the situation was viewed primarily as pleasant or unpleasant: Three pleasant situations were rated more positively and 12 unpleasant items were rated less negatively by individuals who reported that the situations had happened to them. For all analyses reported below, the affect rating was collapsed across reported occurrence because our aim was to obtain general information about the affect appraisals of the situations. The majority (80%) of the situations presented were perceived as being more unpleasant than pleasant with variations by content area (see Figure 2 and the Appendix). Participants varied in their judgments (range = 0%–94% seen as unpleasant) but, on average, considered that 65% of the items described relatively unpleasant situations. The overall mean affect rating on the 4-point scale (1 = *pleasant*, 4 = *unpleasant*) was 2.81 (*SD* = 0.27).

Mean affect ratings for each content domain were entered into a repeated measures ANOVA, with age group (3) and gender (2) as between-subjects variables and content area (7) as the within-subjects variable. The appraisal of affect was significantly associated with the content area (main effect): $F(6, 696)$ = 67.2, MSE = 0.15, $p < .001$, η^2 = .37). Situations concerned with tangible assistance were seen as the least unpleasant (*M* = 2.3, *SD* = 0.37), followed by unsolicited advice about health (*M* = 2.6, *SD* = 0.46). Unsolicited comments about finances (*M* = 3.2, *SD* = 0.37) and life management (*M* = 3.1, *SD* = 0.43) were rated as the most unpleasant. Although the main effect for age was not significant (p = .08), there was a significant interaction between age and content area, $F(12, 696)$ 12.2, MSE = 0.15, $p < .01$, η^2 = .04. Follow-up analyses revealed that this interaction (illustrated in Figure 2) was located in the health and life management domains. Alpha-adjusted Tukey group contrasts ($p < .05$) indicated that younger adults considered the situations related to health (*M* = 2.7, *SD* = 0.46) and life management (*M* = 3.2, *SD* = 0.39) more unpleasant than did the middle-aged (health, *M* = 2.5, *SD* = 0.40; life management *M* = 3.0, *SD* = 0.46) and older adults (health, *M* = 2.5, *SD* = 0.48; life management, *M* = 3.0, *SD* = 0.43).

Reasons for appraisal as pleasant or unpleasant. Two approaches were adopted to investigate the reasons underlying affective evaluations. In the first approach, participants who reported that they had encountered a situation were asked (a) who gave the offer of support in each situation and (b) whether the

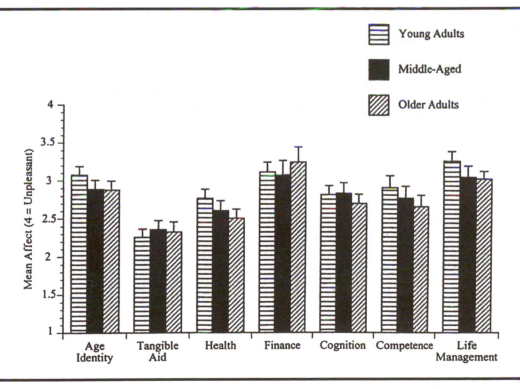

FIGURE 2 Mean ratings of affect (unpleasantness) associated with offers of unsolicited support: interactions between age and content area. The affect ratings shown here were independent of reported occurrence of the situations.

source mattered for their evaluation of the situation. Answers to the first question about the source brought out an effect common to all age groups (no main effect for age in a repeated measures ANOVA). The large majority of occurrences were part of close relationships: Fifty-eight percent were with significant others, 28% were with friends, leaving only 14% with strangers.

People who lived alone were, as one might expect, less likely to receive offers from significant others: Fifty percent of occurrences for this group were with significant others compared with 64% for those who lived with others, $F(1, 120) = 9.82$, $MSE = 0.50$, $p < .01$, $\eta^2 = .28$. Living arrangements did not make a difference in the proportion of occurrences with friends (living alone = 31%, living with others = 26%), but those who lived alone did report more occurrences with strangers (respectively, 18% vs. 10%), $F(1, 120) = 7.38$, $MSE = 0.16$, $p < .01$, $\eta^2 = .25$. The second question about source ("Was the person relevant to the experienced affect?") divided the sample: Forty-four percent said it made no difference who the person was, and 56% said it did matter (with the majority commenting, that their knowing the person made the difference).

The second approach to the bases for appraisal involved asking all participants (regardless of reported occurrence) to rate a set of four reasons for

finding each situation pleasant or unpleasant.[2] The profile of mean ratings across the seven content areas is illustrated separately for unpleasant (see Figure 3a) and pleasant evaluations (see Figure 3b). Because different percentages of situations were judged to be pleasant versus unpleasant within each domain, we conducted separate repeated measures ANOVAs for the pleasant and the unpleasant reasons within the seven domains. Each analysis involved two between-subjects variables, age (3) and gender (2), and one within-subjects variable, reason (4).

As can be seen in Figure 3a, there was variation in the mean ratings given to the four reasons for appraised unpleasantness. Overall, the highest rated reason was the statement coded as incompetence ("because it indicated that the other person saw me as incompetent or incapable"; $M = 3.4$, $SD = 0.53$). The statement coded as belittling ("because I felt offended") received the lowest endorsement ($M = 3.0$, $SD = 0.60$). The order of mean ratings differed by content area. For age identity and tangible aid, the rea-

---

[2]The analyses related to reasons are independent of reported occurrence. These analyses describe the participants' perceptions of each situation. Analyses broken down by reported occurrence versus nonoccurrence did not indicate that the profile of reasons differed.

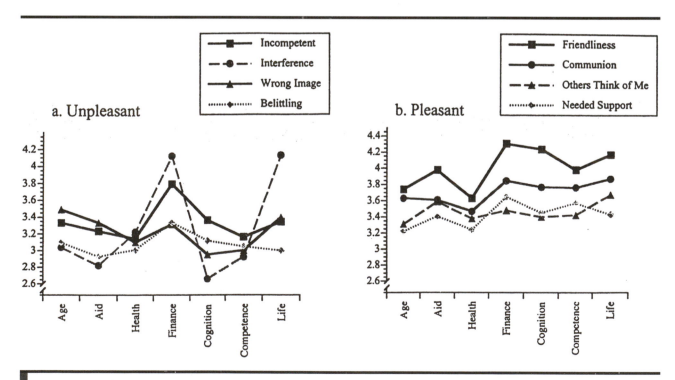

FIGURE 3 Profile of reasons why offers of unsolicited support are viewed as unpleasant (a) or pleasant (b). For situations viewed as unpleasant, the profile of ratings differed by content area.

sons coded as wrong image and incompetent were rated higher than those coded as interference and belittling (respective main effects for reasons), $F(3, 342) = 11.36$, $MSE = 0.45$, $p < .001$, $\eta^2 = .09$; $F(3, 342) = 16.3$, $MSE = 0.41$, $p < .001$, $\eta^2 = .13$. In the area of health, all reasons were rated equally. In relation to competence and cognition, the reason incompetent was rated highest (respective main effects for reasons), $F(3, 324) = 3.0$, $MSE = .37$, $p < .03$, $\eta^2 = .03$; $F(3, 333) = 19.9$, $MSE = 0.53$, $p < .001$, $\eta^2 = .15$, whereas for the domains of finance and life management, the reason interference was seen as most relevant (respective main effects for reasons), $F(3, 327) = 26.1$, $MSE = 0.66$, $p < .001$, $\eta^2 = .19$; $F(3, 339) = 65.8$, $MSE = 0.41$, $p < .001$, $\eta^2 = .37$.

Overall, for the set of unpleasant reasons, older adults gave higher ratings to the statement coded as wrong image ($M = 3.4$, $SD = 0.56$) than did younger adults ($M = 3.1$, $SD = 0.55$). Specific to content areas, Age × Reason interactions were found for age identity, $F(6, 342) = 3.23$, $MSE = 0.45$, $p < .004$, $\eta^2 = .05$, cognition, $F(6, 333) = 2.7$, $MSE = 0.53$, $p < .01$, $\eta^2 = .05$, finances, $F(6, 327) = 3.1$, $MSE = 0.66$, $p < .006$, $\eta^2 = .05$, and life management, $F(6, 339) = 5.2$, $MSE = 0.41$, $p < .001$, $\eta^2 = .08$. Alpha-adjusted Tukey group contrasts revealed that older adults were more concerned than younger adults that the unsolicited advice implied that others saw them as incompetent in the areas of age identity (older, $M = 3.6$, $SD = 0.60$; younger, $M = 3.2$, $SD = .079$), finances (older, $M = 4.1$, $SD = 0.66$; younger, $M = 3.6$, $SD = 0.86$), and life management (older, $M = 3.6$, $SD = 0.85$; younger, $M = 3.2$, $SD = 0.94$). Young adults ($M = 4.4$, $SD = 0.59$) more than older adults ($M = 3.9$, $SD = 0.67$) were concerned about interference in relation to life management. In the area of cognition, middle-aged adults ($M = 3.3$, $SD = 1.03$) gave higher ratings to the reason belittling than did older adults ($M = 2.8$, $SD = 0.86$).

The reasons for pleasant evaluations did not vary significantly by content area (see Figure 3b). Unsolicited advice or actions, when experienced as pleasant, were most commonly viewed as having been primarily given out of friendliness ($M = 3.9$, $SD = 0.47$). The statement "because I really needed the support" received the lowest ratings ($M = 3.4$, $SD = 0.61$). An Age × Reason interaction occurred only in relation to age identity, $F(6, 156) = 4.07$, $MSE = 0.48$, $p < .004$, $\eta^2 = .04$. Older adults gave higher ratings than young adults to the items suggesting that givers offered their advice for reasons of communion (i.e., that others showed concern for their welfare), $F(2, 58) = 6.2$, $MSE = 0.75$, $p < .003$ (older, $M = 4.1$, $SD = 0.50$; younger, $M = 3.1$, $SD = 1.1$), and to the item stating that others think of my needs and wishes, $F(2, 58) = 7.7$, $MSE = 0.68$, $p < .001$ (older, $M = 3.5$, $SD = 0.60$; younger, $M = 2.6$, $SD = 1.2$).

Normative Beliefs

The analysis of reasons suggested that appraisals might depend on whether situations of unsolicited support violated normative beliefs about interpersonal relationships (e.g., situations are viewed as unpleasant if one feels that others are interfering in one's private affairs). For a more direct analysis of normative beliefs, we had included a 12-item scale covering possible view-points that were reducible to four factors (labeled as Preserve Equal Status, Actively Protect the Other's Face. Avoid Interference, and Respect the Other's Position). A repeated measures ANOVA on the four factor scores revealed a significant main effect for age, $F(2, 116) = 8.74$, $MSE = 0.70$, $p < .001$, $\eta^2 = .13$, together with an Age × Belief interaction, $F(6, 348) = 4.58$, $MSE = 1.1$, $p < .000$, $\eta^2 = .07$. Follow-up analyses of each factor revealed significant age differences only for two beliefs, Actively Protect the Other's Face, $F(2, 119) = 7.2$, $MSE = 3.2$, $p < .001$, $\eta^2 = .33$, and Avoid Interference, $F(2, 119) = 16.94$, $MSE = 9.1$, $p < .001$, $\eta^2 = .42$. Alpha-adjusted Tukey group contrasts indicated that compared with the young and with middle-aged adults, older adults gave higher ratings to items stressing the importance of actively protecting the other's face or self-esteem and of avoiding interference. Middle-aged adults gave higher ratings than young adults on items regarding avoiding interference. Age group means and standard deviations on the four belief factors are provided in Table 2.

Preferred Strategies for Dealing with Unwelcome Support

Table 2 also shows the means and standard deviations for the age groups on the three strategies for dealing with unwelcome offers of support derived from a 12-item scale (assertively ignore, active discounting, and accommodate). A repeated measures ANOVA of unit-weighted factor scores revealed a significant main effect for age, $F(2, 115) = 4.79$, $MSE = 0.96$, $p < .01$, $\eta^2 = .08$, together with an Age × Strategy interaction, $F(4, 236) = 9.31$, $MSE = 0.87$, $p < .001$, $\eta^2 = .14$. Follow-up analyses were undertaken for each strategy. In contrast to young and middle-aged adults, the older adults reported greater preferences for ways of coping that involved active discounting strategies (e.g., rationalizing denigrating offers as signs of the giver's immaturity), $F(2, 120) = 20.9$, $MSE = 15.8$, $p < .001$, $\eta^2 = .51$; Tukey-adjusted group contrasts, $p < .05$. Middle-aged adults also gave higher ratings to this strategy than did younger adults. Both young and older adults reported using assertive strategies (e.g., telling the donor why they did not

TABLE 2   Means for the Three Age Groups on the Four Normative Beliefs and Three Strategy Subscales

| | AGE GROUP | | | | | |
| | YOUNG ADULTS | | MIDDLE AGED | | OLDER ADULTS | |
SCALE AND DIMENSION	M	SD	M	SD	M	SD
Normative beliefs						
Preserve equal status	4.4	0.93	4.3	0.95	4.2	1.17
Actively protect the other's face	3.2	1.07	3.5	0.90	3.8	0.84
Avoid interference	2.9	0.82	3.4	1.01	3.8	0.94
Respect the other's position	4.3	1.12	4.7	1.07	4.3	0.93
Strategies						
Assertively ignore	3.1	0.97	2.8	0.83	3.2	1.09
Active discounting	2.8	0.93	3.3	1.01	3.6	0.62
Accommodate	3.5	0.96	3.6	1.10	3.3	0.92

want their support or ignoring the offer) more than did middle-aged participants, $F(2, 120) = 3.6$, $MSE = 3.5$, $p < .05$, $\eta^2 = .24$; Tukey-adjusted group contrasts, $p < .05$. The young and older adults did not differ on this strategy. There were no age differences for items describing accommodation strategies.

Correlational Analyses

As exploratory steps toward understanding the interrelationships among the various measures collected in the present study, we calculated the zero-order correlations between selected variables (see Table 3) and conducted two sets of hierarchical regression analyses (path models), one predicting reported occurrence and the other predicting affect.

As can be seen from Table 3, the intercorrelations were moderate to small. Highest relationships (as expected from the analyses reported above) were those between age and occurrence ($r = -.46$), active discounting ($r = .51$), protect the other's face ($r = .37$), and avoid interference ($r = .41$). The overall correlation between occurrence and mean affect (higher

scores indicate more unpleasantness) was not significant ($r = -.11$, $p = .21$). Content-specific correlations (not given in Table 3) between occurrence and affect were significant for tangible aid ($r = -.24$, $p < .01$), cognition ($r = -.18$, $p < .05$), competence ($r = 18$, $p < .05$), and finances ($r = -.23$, $p < .01$): For these areas, higher perceptions of unpleasantness were associated with lower reported occurrence. Although relatively small, the relationships are consistent with the suggestion that actions might be taken to avoid situations viewed as potentially unpleasant.

The two hierarchical regression analyses (path models) provided some initial insight into the links between age and reported occurrence and age and affect (see Figures 4a and 4b). The figures include the standardized regression coefficients for the significant paths.

In the first set of analyses, age and unit-weighted factor scores on the three general strategies for dealing with unwanted help (active discounting, accommodate, and assertively ignore) were entered as predictors of reported occurrence. These variables were selected to follow up the proposal of Dunkel-

TABLE 3   Zero-Order Correlations Among the Variables Entered Into the Regression Analyses

VARIABLE	1	2	3	4	5	6	7	8	9
1. Age	—								
2. Live alone[a]	.26**	—							
3. Occurrence	−.46**	−.25**	—						
4. Affect	−.14	.21*	−.11	—					
5. Active discounting	.51**	.03	−.16	−.23*	—				
6. Assertively ignore	.10	.26**	−.20*	.16	−.02	—			
7. Accommodate	−.11	.01	−.08	.15	.01	.03	—		
8. Protect the other's face	.37**	.07	−.20*	−.22*	.23*	−.14	−.13	—	
9. Avoid interference	.41**	.25**	−.21*	−.06	.20*	.15	.03	−.01	—

[a]1 = *live alone,* 2 = *live with others.*

*$p < .05$. **$p < .01$.

a.

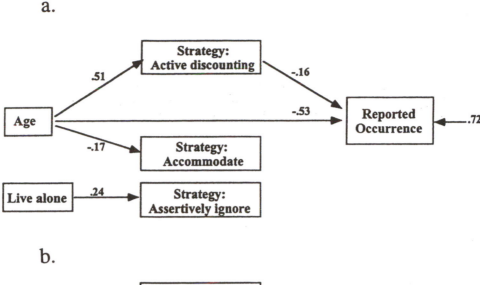

b.

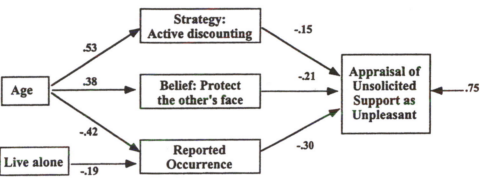

FIGURE 4 Results of regression analyses (path models) predicting reported occurrence of unsolicited support (a) and affective appraisal of situations of unsolicited support (b).

Schetter et al. (1987) that, at least in young adults, strategies might determine whether offers were invited or discouraged. Living alone (1 = *alone*, 0 = *living with others*) was added to the analyses as a covariate because we had found that this also was linked to reported occurrence. Twenty-eight percent of the variance in occurrence was explained. As expected, age was the strongest predictor, with a direct path to reported occurrence ($\beta = -.53$) and an indirect path through the strategy of active discounting. Older adults reported proportionately fewer occurrences and also more use of active discounting strategies ($\beta = .51$). This strategy was the only one to have a direct relationship with reported occurrence ($\beta = -.16$). Greater use of this strategy was related to fewer reported occurrences of unwanted support. Living alone was associated with the strategy assertively ignore ($\beta = .24$), but after age and the other strategies were partialed, the path to reported occurrence was not significant.

In the second set of analyses we examined proposals in the literature that beliefs about relationships

as well as personal strategies and past experiences of similar transactions contribute to feelings of disappointment or pleasure in one's interactions with others (e.g., Burleson et al., 1994; Clark & Reis, 1988). We wondered whether the low relationship between age and affective appraisal at the zero-order level might reflect age differences in strategies and beliefs. Again, the variable of living alone was added to these analyses. The regression analysis, which accounted for 25% of the variance in appraised unpleasantness, indeed revealed an interesting set of mediators that counteracted the effect of age on appraisal. As can be seen in the right-hand side of Figure 4b, affective appraisal was predicted directly from the active discounting strategy ($\beta = -.15$), the belief that unwanted support violated the norm that interpersonal interactions should protect the other's face ($\beta = -.21$), and reported occurrence of the 35 examples of unsolicited support ($\beta = -.30$). In each case, the path beta values reflect relationships after the effects of the other four predictor variables (including age and living alone) were partialed. The more active discounting was a preferred strategy, the less unpleasant the situations of nonsolicited support were perceived to be. The more personal encounters with the 35 situations, the less participants also viewed the situations as unpleasant. Furthermore, the more individuals believed that unwanted support violated the norm that interpersonal interactions should protect the other's face, the less unpleasant they rated situations of unsolicited support.

At first glance, this latter finding with regard to beliefs about protecting the other's face may seem surprising. However, it likely reflects the double-sided reference of normative beliefs about protecting face. There is, on the one side, an expectation that others respect the norm in interactions with oneself. On the other side, individuals who believe that it is important to protect the other's face in interpersonal interactions are also likely to react to violations of this norm in ways that do not accentuate the other's indiscretion. Hence, in situations of unwanted unsolicited support, the recipient recognizes that the other person has violated the relationship norm (and so finds the situation unpleasant) but reacts in such a way to repair the broken norm (i.e., by protecting the perpetrator's face). The end effect is that the recipient downgrades the appraised unpleasantness of the situation, perhaps by using active discounting strategies (the correlation between active discounting and the normative belief was .23). This downgrading process may also possibly serve to protect the recipient's self-esteem.

The effects of age on appraisal were indirectly mediated through strategies, beliefs, and occurrence. On the one hand, with increasing age, individuals reported a greater preference for active discounting strategies ($\beta = .53$) and the protective norms ($\beta = .38$). These beliefs, in turn, predicted that unsolicited support was viewed as being less unpleasant. On the other hand, as a counteracting effect, older adults reported proportionately fewer personal encounters of unsolicited support, and this predicted higher appraisals of unpleasantness. Living alone was associated only with less reported occurrence.

GENERAL DISCUSSION

This study began with two interrelated questions. The first had to do with whether age would cause an increase in the likelihood of encountering unasked-for offers of support or advice and in the extent to which such offers were felt to be unpleasant. The second had to do with the role of cognitive and social–relational factors: factors that might themselves be associated with age and partially account for age effects.

On the first score, the results were not in the expected direction (namely greater occurrence and

higher rating of unpleasant affect in late adulthood). When age differences occurred, they were in the direction of the oldest group reporting the least likelihood of occurrence and less unpleasant affect. What could underlie this intriguing finding? To begin, one problem in interpreting, it is that the questions used in this study did not clearly specify a temporal window. It is not known how far back in time each participant searched his or her memory for experience of each of the 35 situations. This would need to be specifically addressed in future work. The finding that younger rather than older adults reported a higher occurrence of unsolicited support needs replication but suggests that further age-comparative studies on this topic would be worthwhile.

Possible explanations for the present findings in relation to age highlight the significance of social–cognitive and social–relational factors, such as life circumstances (e.g., living alone or with others), the reasons for finding offers pleasant or unpleasant, the norms people expect to regulate offers of support, and the strategies they bring to bear on unwanted offers. These variables were themselves related to age and, in some cases, accounted in part for age effects. For example, more of the older than the younger adults lived alone and so may actually have received fewer offers of nonsolicited support on an everyday basis. Young adults may not only have more opportunities for exposure (e.g., in interactions with parents and family as well as intimate partners) but may also be less selective than older adults in their social interactions (cf. Carstensen, 1993). It could also be that in long-term relationships (e.g., with adult children or siblings), strategies of active support seeking replace the more passive strategy of waiting for it to be offered. Alternatively, older adults may indeed experience more or a similar amount of unsolicited support than younger adults, but to protect and maintain self-esteem, belief systems have been changed. With age, individuals may positively interpret or learn to ignore encounters that earlier in life might have been sources of irritation and anger. In part, this explanation fits with our findings regarding the mediating effects (and associated age differences) of active cognitive coping strategies and relationship beliefs.

In more general terms, the results support and expand several proposals related to age and interactions involving the receipt of support. They also point to several useful ways of extending the present study. Supported first of all are suggestions that interactions involving support or advice need to be considered as having both positive and negative aspects, as being experienced in both positive and negative fashion (e.g., Allan, 1986; M. M. Baltes, 1996; La Gaipa, 1990; Rook, 1989, 1995). In fact, occasions of unasked-for support seem especially well suited to the exploration of negative aspects, correcting what Rook (1995) described as an uncritical tendency to think of social interactions in late adulthood only in terms of them increasing the likelihood of welcome or beneficial support. Together with the investigation of age differences in the occurrence and appraisal of situations involving support seeking, occasions of unasked-for support may extend the understanding of conditions underlying the costs and benefits of support in late adulthood.

The present study also supported proposals that everyday situations of various kinds provide useful indexes of the quality of interactions for individuals (e.g., Barnes & Duck, 1994; Dunkel-Schetter et al., 1987; Zautra et al., 1994). We have now generated a collection of situations that might be built on in several ways. One way to do so is to add other items to the collection. These additions might be chosen especially to boost the number of situations experienced as pleasant or, a potentially overlapping direction, the number of situations that involve expressive support (e.g., comforting, sympathizing; Burleson, 1990) rather than the instrumental support bias that marks the current collection. In any expansion, however, it would be advisable to keep in mind the need to sample a variety of content areas. The links between age and particular content areas are likely to display some variation with the particular items used but covering a range remains an essential step toward asking why particular items or particular content areas vary from one another. It is noteworthy, for example, that the areas in which the oldest group showed particular concern with the implications of incompetence had to do with age identity (e.g., someone suggested that someone your age would not understand) and finances (e.g., someone suggested what you could afford).

A second way to build on the present set is to add procedures similar to those used by Scheidt and Schaie (1978). They asked people aged 70 years to Q-sort 80 situations three times: for pleasantness or unpleasantness, ease or difficulty in coping, and frequency of occurrence. These Q-sorts yielded results similar to some in the present study: Situations that were rated as difficult to deal with tended to be rated as unpleasant, and unpleasant situations tended to be rated as infrequent. The methodological steps described by Scheidt and Schaie (1978) could be used to assess other "context-specific competencies" (p. 855) and to isolate situations that are difficult to deal with but also frequent (i.e., not easy to avoid). Intervention might then be directed at ways of coping with precisely those situations.

The third proposal supported by the present study consists of arguments that the analysis of situations involving support should turn to considering the interpretative and social–relational dimensions of interactions (e.g., Antonucci, 1990; M. M. Baltes, 1996; Burleson et al., 1994; Carstensen, 1992, 1993; Dunkel-Schetter et al., 1987; Rook, 1995). These factors have been translated in the present study into several specific measures, covering the reasons for pleasantness and unpleasantness, the norms that people think should apply to situations of support or advice, life circumstances (e.g., whether one lives alone), and strategies for dealing with unwelcome offers of support. These several measures were found to be related to the occurrence of unasked-for offers, their affective quality, and their links to age. They also point to a possible general picture of how age differences may come to occur or to be minimized.

Across age groups, for example, there is not only variation but also considerable consensus about the types of situations that have been encountered and that are experienced as unpleasant. The same result applies when it comes to the norms that people think should be respected and to the reasons for various types of unasked-for support.

The similarities that occur might well be attributed to the three age groups being part of a common culture and by their all encountering most offers of support in a broadly similar context: the context of a close relationship (e.g., parent or partner). What, then, contributes to differences across age groups and variations within an age group? We suggest that these reflect the balance of two sets of conditions. One set influences the extent to which the individual is sensitive to the particular implications of lesser competence or lesser value. To the extent that increasing age brings with it the perception of a drop in a competence or a quality that is valued and part of one's identity, age is one such condition (e.g., P. B. Baltes & Baltes, 1990).

The other set of conditions has to do with the extent to which individuals are protected from imputations of lesser competence or lesser value. That protection may come from life circumstances that reduce the number of occasions on which an offer of support might occur. In all age groups, for example, living alone is associated with the lesser occurrence of unasked-for offers. One way in which age then exerts an influence is through its increasing the likelihood that people will live alone rather than with others. The opportunities for comment on what one has done or might do are then reduced.

Protection or insulation may also come from individuals taking more specific steps. They may avoid situations in which unwelcome offers may arise or head them off by signaling that an offer will be unwelcome. When these situations nonetheless occur, people may actively challenge an offer (asking, e.g., why it has been made or pointing out that it is inappropriate). They may also actively discount the source of the unwelcome implication (e.g., regarding the person from whom it comes as uninformed, as lacking in social skills, or as grossly unaware of how people should behave in such situations). The source of the difficulty then shifts from themselves to others. Again, age emerges as exerting an influence by virtue of the extent to which it alters the availability and the effectiveness of these several forms of protection, these several ways of reducing the occurrence or the sting of unwelcome offers. Age also emerges as influencing effects by way of a path from occurrence to affective quality. Situations that are infrequent tend to be experienced as especially unpleasant. They have apparently either broken through the protective screen or the individual is out of practice in ways of coping.

Across groups and within groups, the particular combinations of these conditions may vary. We would certainly expect, for example, a different pattern to occur—and for different results to emerge—in an 80-year-old group living under the nursing home circumstances described by M. M. Baltes (1996). These are circumstances that alter the likelihood that people can avoid interactions that call their competence or their value into question. These are also situations in which the offers of support or advice come from people with whom the individual is not in a close relationship but instead is in a position of some dependency. One might expect, then, that the

need becomes all the stronger to rely, if possible, on cognitive strategies such as discounting the knowledge or the social nous of the other.

Can a similar pattern of conditions be seen as applying to the experience of an offer of support or advice as pleasant? The results point to offers as being experienced as pleasant when they are interpretable as being based on a positive concern for the receiver, as being consistent with what the receiver is likely to appreciate, and as being in keeping with the norms that are expected to regulate offers of support. Such offers may not affirm the competence of the recipient, but they seem likely to respect the recipient's feelings and his or her value in the eyes of others. These circumstances appear to underlie, for example, the widespread approval of the surprise birthday party in all age groups.

Overall, we suggest that the general principle is that the occurrence and the affective quality of offers of support stem not simply from age per se but from the combination of interpretative and social-relational factors. Normative beliefs and expectations about interpersonal interactions promote vulnerability or sensitivity on the one hand and either provide reminders of one's strengths and worth or call into play a variety of ways to protect oneself from uncomfortable implications of lesser competence or lesser value on the other hand. The presence and the interplay of these several conditions in relation to age and to particular life circumstances then become the issues to be addressed.

REFERENCES

Acitelli, L. K., & Antonucci, T. C. (1994). Gender differences in the link between marital support and satisfaction in older couples. *Journal of Personality and Social Psychology, 67,* 688–698.

Allan, G. (1986). Friendship and care for elderly people. *Ageing and Society, 6,* 1–12.

Antonucci, T. C. (1990). Social supports and social relationships. In R. H. Binstock & L. K. George (Eds.), *Handbook of aging and the social sciences* (3rd ed., pp. 205–226). San Diego, CA: Academic Press.

Antonucci, T. C. (1994). A life-span view of women's social relations. In B. F. Turner & L. E. Troll (Eds.), *Women growing older: Psychological perspectives* (pp. 239–269). Thousand Oaks, CA: Sage.

Antonucci, T. C., & Jackson, J. (1990). The role of reciprocity in social support. In B. R. Sarason, I. G. Sarason, & G. R. Pierce (Eds.), *Social support: An interactional view* (pp. 173–198). New York: Wiley.

Baltes, M. M. (1996). *The many faces of dependency in old age.* Cambridge, England: Cambridge University Press.

Baltes, P. B., & Baltes, M. M. (1990). Psychological perspectives on successful aging: The model of selective optimization with compensation. In P. B. Baltes & M. M.

Baltes (Eds.), *Successful aging: Perspectives from the behavioral sciences* (pp. 1–34). New York: Cambridge University Press.

Barnes, M. K., & Duck, S. (1994). Everyday communicative contexts for social support. In B. R. Burleson, T. L. Albrecht, & I. G. Sarason (Eds.), *Communication of social support: Messages, interactions, relationships, and community* (pp. 175–194). Thousand Oaks, CA: Sage.

Beckman, L. J. (1981). Effects of social interaction and children's relative inputs on older women's psychological well-being. *Journal of Personality and Social Psychology, 41,* 1075–1086.

Burleson, B. R. (1990). Comforting as social support: Relational consequences of supportive behaviors. In S. Duck, with R. C. Silver (Eds.), *Personal relationships and social support* (pp. 66–82), London: Sage.

Burleson, B. R., Albrecht, T. L., & Sarason, I. G. (Eds.). (1994). *Communication of social support: Messages, interactions, relationships, and community.* Thousand Oaks, CA: Sage.

Carstensen, L. L. (1992). Social and emotional patterns in adulthood: Support for socioemotional selectivity theory. *Psychology and Aging, 7,* 331–338.

Carstensen, L. L. (1993). Motivation for social contact across the life span: A theory of socioemotional selectivity. *Nebraska Symposium on Motivation, 40,* 209–254.

Clark, M. S., Patarki, S. P., & Carver, V. H. (1996). Some thoughts and findings on self-presentation of emotions in relationships. In G. J. O. Fletcher & J. Fitness (Eds.), *Knowledge structures in close relationships: A social psychological approach* (pp. 247–274). Mahwah, NJ: Erlbaum.

Clark, M. S., & Reis, H. T. (1988). Interpersonal processes in close relationships. *Annual Review of Psychology, 39,* 609–672.

Cutrona, C. E., & Suhr, J. A. (1994). Social support communication in the context of marriage: An analysis of couples' supportive interactions. In B. R. Burleson, T. L. Albrecht, & I. G. Sarason (Eds.), *Communication of social support: Messages, interactions, relationships, and community* (pp. 113–135). Thousand Oaks, CA: Sage.

Dunkel-Schetter, C., Folkman, S., & Lazarus, R. C. (1987). Correlates of social support receipt. *Journal of Personality and Social Psychology, 53,* 71–80.

Eckenrode, J., & Wethington, E. (1990). The process and outcome of mobilizing social support. In S. Duck, with R. C. Silver (Eds.), *Personal relationships and social support* (pp. 83–103). London: Sage.

Fiske, A. P. (1992). The four elementary forms of sociality: Framework for a unified theory of social relations. *Psychological Review, 99,* 689–723.

Freund, A. M., & Smith, J. (in press). Temporal stability of older person's spontaneous self definition. *Experimental Aging Research.*

Goodnow, J. J., & Warton, P. (1992). Understanding responsibility: Adolescents' views of delegation and follow-through within the family. *Social Development, 1,* 89–106.

Hughes, M., & Gove, W. R. (1981). Living alone, social integration, and mental health. *American Journal of Sociology, 87,* 48–74.

Ingersoll-Dayton, B., & Antonucci, T. C. (1988). Reciprocal and nonreciprocal social support: Contrasting sides of intimate relationships. *Journal of Gerontology: Social Sciences, 43,* S65–S73.

La Gaipa, J. J. (1990). The negative effects of informal support systems. In S. Duck, with R. C. Silver (Eds.), *Personal relationships and social support* (pp. 122–139). London: Sage.

Lazarus, R. S., & Folkman, S. (1984). *Stress, appraisal, and coping.* New York: Springer.

Lehrl, S. (1977). *Mehrfachwahl-Wortschatz-Test (MWT-B)* [Multiple choice verbal ability test]. Erlangen, Germany: Straube.

Nadler, A., & Fisher, J. D. (1986). The role of threat to self-esteem and perceived control in recipient reaction to help: Theory development and empirical validation. *Advances in Experimental Social Psychology, 19,* 81–122.

Rook, K. S. (1989). Strains in older adults' friendships. In R. G. Adams & R. Blieszner (Eds.), *Older adult friendship: Structure and process* (pp. 166–194). Newbury Park, CA: Sage.

Rook, K. S. (1995). Support, companionship, and control in older adults' social networks: Implications for well-being. In J. F. Nussbaum & J. Coupland (Eds.), *Handbook of communication and aging research* (pp. 437–463). Mahwah, NJ: Erlbaum.

Rook, K. S., Thuras, P. D., & Lewis, M. A. (1990). Social control, health risk taking, and psychological distress among the elderly. *Psychology and Aging, 5,* 327–334.

Sarason, I. G., Sarason, B. R., & Pierce, G. R. (1994). Relationship-specific social support: Toward a model for the analysis of supportive interactions. In B. R. Burleson, T. L. Albrecht, & I. G. Sarason (Eds.), *Communication of social support: Messages, interactions, relationships, and community* (pp. 91–112). Thousand Oaks, CA: Sage.

Scheidt, R. J., & Schaie, K. W. (1978). A taxonomy of situations for an elderly population: Generating situational criteria. *Journal of Gerontology, 33,* 848–857.

Wechsler, D. (1955). *Wechsler Adult Intelligence Scale manual* New York: Psychological Corporation.

Wiseman, J. P. (1986). Friendship: Bonds and binds in a voluntary relationship. *Journal of Social and Personal Relationships, 3,* 191–211.

Zautra, A. J., Affleck, G., & Tennen, H. (1994). Assessing life events among older adults. *Annual Review of Gerontology and Geriatrics, 14,* 324–352.

APPENDIX

The 35 Situations of Unsolicited Support and Advice (SUSA Interview):
Percentage of Reported Occurrence and Ratings of Affect as a Function of Age

CONTENT AREA AND ITEM[a]	% OCCURRENCE[b]			AFFECT[c]		
	Y	M	O	Y	M	O
Age identity						
Suggested that your generation would not be interested	51	37	24	3.07	3.0	3.08
Suggested that something was too young or too old for you	68	46	41	3.05	2.92	2.88
Suggested that someone your age would not understand because you have no experience	81	68	36	2.93	2.82	2.76
Suggested that you organize your life in a more age-appropriate way	27	11	21	3.27	2.84	2.81

(continued)

(Continued)

CONTENT AREA AND ITEM[a]	% OCCURRENCE[b]			AFFECT[c]		
	Y	M	O	Y	M	O
Tangible aid						
Offered to help carry a suitcase or shopping bags for you	51	61	74	1.8[d]	2.16	1.9
Planned an outing for you	34	55	19	2.29	2.45	2.45
Gave you an inappropriate present	17	27	14	2.71	2.53	2.63
Organized for you to meet with someone	49	55	26	2.98[e]	2.87	2.67
Warned you of a danger	63	55	43	2.22	2.34	2.34
Planned a birthday surprise	49	47	48	1.56[d]	1.82	2.0
Bought clothes for you	71	65	21	2.83[e]	2.74	3.1
Health						
Suggested that you should eat more vitamins, vegetables, less sugar etc.	85	82	79	2.88	2.58	2.21
Told you that you needed a checkup	32	32	24	2.59[e]	2.66	2.54
Told you how much exercise or rest you should have	59	55	50	2.8	2.55	2.24
Suggested that you should take better care of yourself	61	47	33	2.8[e]	2.66	3.0
Finances						
Suggested how you should organize your finances	53	47	14	3.13[e]	3.03	3.36
Suggested what you could afford	51	41	29	3.12	3.11	3.15
Cognition						
Explained something you already knew about	98	90	83	3.07	2.97	2.71
Told you that you had already said something (repeating yourself)	61	55	57	2.95	2.97	2.93
Corrected your grammar	85	74	45	2.93	3.0	2.83
Deliberately spoke louder or slower than needed to you	27	36	22	3.27[e]	3.03	2.71
Checked that you turned out the lights, switched off the gas, etc.	61	63	33	2.76	2.61	2.6
Suggested that you should use a memory aid (e.g., make notes or lists)	37	26	14	2.83[e]	2.82	2.74
Checked that you had paid a bill or answered a letter	93	73	43	2.73[e]	2.71	2.88
Competence						
Warned you not to overexert yourself	73	58	43	2.95	2.81	2.6
Underestimated your capabilities	37	37	15	3.24	3.13	2.9
Was surprised at what you could accomplish (e.g., sport, gymnastics)	37	37	15	1.83[d]	1.84	1.74
Took over a task because they thought that you were not physically capable	34	32	10	2.72[e]	2.58	2.6
Suggested what clothes would better suit you	90	87	71	2.34[e]	2.39	2.36
Life management						
Told you how you should spend your time	71	55	33	3.39	3.0	3.02
Rearranged your desk, room, or cupboards so that you might find things better	39	32	7	3.44[e]	3.29	3.52
Told you where you should live	20	19	17	3.22[e]	2.95	2.98
Told you how to plan your future	54	37	19	3.22	2.89	2.95
Told you how to manage your relationships	39	34	19	3.07	3.16	2.74

Note. Y = younger; M = middle aged; 0 = older.

[a]Each item begins "Have you ever experienced that without your asking, someone…" [b]The response to the items was yes or no. [c]Affect was rated on a 4-point scale (1 = very pleasant, 2 = somewhat pleasant, 3 = somewhat unpleasant, and 4 = very unpleasant). [d]Rated more pleasant ($p < .01$) by individuals who reported it had happened to them. [e]Rated less unpleasant ($p < .01$) by individuals who reported it had happened to them.

SELF-STUDY QUESTIONS

Multiple Choice

1. What are coping strategies that are used to deal with unwanted support or advice?
   a. assertively ignore
   b. accommodate and actively discount
   c. emotional or rational responding
   d. a and b only

2. Which of the following is not suggested in the article to explain why unsolicited advice and support might be pleasant?
   a. patronization
   b. communal concern
   c. actual need for support
   d. friendliness of offer

Essay

1. Examine how the experience of unasked-for support or unsolicited advice might vary depending on the relationship between the giver and the receiver and on the norms associated with that relationship.

2. In older adults, how might an inability to reciprocate (return the favor) be a threat to the competence and independence of the receiver? How would this inability to reciprocate impact the pleasantness or unpleasantness of the offer?

DEATH

"Holocaust Survivors' Perspectives on the Euthanasia Debate"

OVERVIEW

Genocide is the intentional killing of a particular group of people. One of the most graphic examples of genocide, the *Holocaust,* occurred during the rise and fall of the Nazi regime in Germany in the 1930s and 1940s. Approximately six million Jews, as well as numerous others, perished in Nazi concentration camps and labor camps, and in their attempts to hide or escape from the pursuing Nazis. As a result, the Holocaust is often used as a standard by which to measure practices and events that may suggest genocidal intent. Just such a parallel has been drawn by critics of the current right-to-die movement who suggest that legalized euthanasia may enable authorities to choose who is or is not worthy of continued life in the same way that the Nazis deemed Jews, protectors and friends of Jews, homosexuals, the disabled, and their political opponents to be suitable only for medical experimentation, forced labor, and, ultimately, extermination. This study utilizes a qualitative method of investigation to explore the views of Holocaust survivors regarding the appropriateness of this analogy.

METHODOLOGY

The author of this article employed a *qualitative* or *phenomenological approach.* Such techniques examine how human beings construct and give meaning to their own life experiences. In contrast to techniques in which the researcher's goal is to avoid subjectivity, the purpose of such research is to examine, in as much depth as possible, individual human beings' ideas about their own experiences. Consequently, the researcher conducted in-depth interviews with Holocaust survivors and solicited their views about possible parallels between Nazi concentration camp practices and euthanasia. From these interviews, the researcher derived common themes. Such research helps psychologists and other behavioral scientists gain insight into the ways in which individuals cognitively and emotionally experience life in the real world.

GLOSSARY TERMS

- **Holocaust** the Nazi persecution, incarceration, and systematic killing of Jews and others in Europe between 1939 and 1945
- **Bioethics** the study of the ethical considerations and dilemmas associated most frequently with advances in modern medicine
- **Metacommunication** a message about a message, typically a nonverbal one given

Ronit D. Leichtentritt, Kathryn D. Rettig, Steven H. Miles

Holocaust Survivors' Perspectives on the Euthanasia Debate

The paper reports on a qualitative analysis of 15 personal interviews with holocaust survivors in Israel concerning their perceptions of similarities and differences between socially-assisted dying and the holocaust policies. The design of the study was exploratory/descriptive and asked the following questions: "Some discussions have expressed similarities between Nazi Germany and euthanasia. Do you believe the comparison is justified? In what ways are euthanasia and the holocaust similar? In what ways are they different?" Participants concluded that profound differences existed between Nazi Germany and socially assisted dying. These differences were established from four different perspectives in 10 different themes, and demonstrated by 24 different examples of the themes. Informants further cautioned philosophers about comparisons between the holocaust and other human behaviors. The survivors perceived that such a comparison has negative consequences for their own well-being, the dignity of their family members, the next generation and the Israeli society.

1. INTRODUCTION

"I will use my power to help the sick to the best of my ability and judgment; I will abstain from harming or wronging any man by it" (Hippocratic oath).

An intensive public debate is currently focused on whether a person who is incurably ill and suffering has the right to ask for and receive help in dying. The public discourse about right-to-die issues in the United States has included the arguments of bioethicists who are debating similarities and differences between the Nazi's euthanasia and different levels of socially assisted dying.[1] The first approach to these controversial issues denies either factual similarities or definitional equivalence between the Nazis' euthanasia program and today's examples of socially assisted dying. First, "[t]he *decision* to terminate the life of a patient under the Nazi program was taken, not by the individual or by his or her relatives, but by an official body...Second, [t]he *criterion* was not the welfare of the individual patient, but whether or not the patient's life was judged to be of 'value' or 'worth to the community'" (Macklin, 1992, p. 199). A third reason for the lack of similarities between the Nazi era and the current controversy regarding socially assisted death focuses on different uses of the term 'euthanasia', and concludes that the term used in Nazi Germany does not have our meaning (Dawidowicz, 1985). This argument assumes the existance of a single universal meaning for the term 'euthanasia' (Macklin, 1992).

The second approach to the controversy finds similarities between Nazi policies and euthanasia and concludes that today we are faced with the prospect that society will accept and legalize the crime of crimes against humanity for which Nazi doctors were hanged at Nuremberg (Kronberg, 1988; Neuhaus, 1988). "It has been noted [that] euthanasia [is] precisely the way the Nazis justified mercy killing" (Emanuel, 1994, p. 1895). This perspective finds the practices involving termination of life-sustaining

---

[1]Three main subcategories of definitions exist within the euthanasia construct: active vs. passive, voluntary vs. involuntary and physician-assisted vs. nonphysician assisted (Brigham and Pfeifer, 1996). Active euthanasia is considered an intentional act that causes death, whereas passive euthanasia is an intentional act to avoid the prolongation of life (Hunter, 1980). Involuntary euthanasia refers to the termination of life of an impaired person who has not requested an early death, whereas voluntary euthanasia refers to termination of life of a competent person who has specifically asked for such assistance (Hunter, 1980). Physician assisted death occurs when a physician intentionally and willfully takes actions that help a patient to end his or her life.

Reprinted from *Social Science & Medicine*, 1998, *48*, 185–196, with permission from Elsevier Science Ltd. All rights reserved.

treatment and withholding food and water to be unacceptable, since physicians in Nazi Germany often chose the policy of starvation rather then wasting medication on those who were selected for death (Lifton, 1986). For example, a testimony given by one of the physicians in the concentration camps concluded: "We do not kill with poison, injection, etc. No, our method is much simpler and more natural" (Lifton, 1986, p. 62).

The connections made between euthanasia and the holocaust are partly based on the 'slippery slope' argument. The slippery slope refers to "an argument that claims a proposal is not really morally objectionable in itself, but should be rejected nonetheless, because it will inevitably, or almost inevitably, lead to morally objectionable actions" (Devettere, 1995, p. 473). The slippery slope argument can never prove that unwanted abuses *will* occur if we legally accept euthanasia, only that they *might* occur.

The slippery slope argument implies that the mass murders of human beings in concentration camps did not start overnight. Leo Alexander (1949) concluded:

> Started from small beginnings. The beginnings at first were merely a subtle shift in emphasis in the basic attitude of the physicians…that were in such a thing as a life not worthy to be lived. This attitude in its early stages concerned itself merely with the severely and chronically sick. Gradually the sphere of those to be included in this category was enlarged to encompass the socially unproductive, the ideologically unwanted, and finally all non-Germans. But it is important to realize that the infinitely small wedged-in lever from which this entire trend of mind received its impetus was the attitude towards the nonrehabilitable sick (p. 93).

The relevancy of the slippery slope argument is partly based on the pervasive role of medical doctors in the Nazi euthanasia programs, and the full extent to which Nazism permeated German medicine (Lifton, 1986; Muller-Hill, 1988; Proctor, 1988; Karter, 1989). Forty-five percent of German physicians belonged to the Nazi party, a percentage higher than that for any other profession (Lerner and Rothman, 1995). The goal of producing a pure Aryan race took preference in physician's perspectives over fundamental ethical principles, such as the integrity of the body and commitment to the well-being of the individual patient (Lerner and Rothman, 1995).

Based on these arguments some have gone one step further pointing out how history repeats itself through the experiences in The Netherlands. A 1991 Dutch report acknowledged that there have been hundreds of cases of nonvoluntary euthanasia, although they violated the established euthanasia guidelines. The report analyzed the 129,000 deaths in Holland during 1990 and found that 2300 of them were reported as euthanasia. In more than a third of these cases (about 1000), a crucial guideline, accepted by the Dutch Medical Association, was violated because the patients had made no clear request for euthanasia. A few of those patients were children (Devettere, 1995).

2. THE ISRAELI CONTEXT

The holocaust survivors who were interviewed in the current study lived in Israel, a culture that is distinctive in several ways. First, the patient's rights of withholding and withdrawing treatment (passive euthanasia) were accepted in the Israeli parliament very recently (May, 1996). Second, the Hebrew language has only one phrase that can be applied to euthanasia in all of its meanings: *Mavet Mitoch Rachamim*, literally means 'death out of mercy'. The lack of appropriate terminology makes it difficult to discuss issues surrounding end-of-life decisions. The third distinctive aspect of Israeli culture is the orthodox Jewish influence on the cultural norms and the resulting conservative attitudes towards euthanasia (see for example Sonnennblick et al., 1993).

Active euthanasia is forbidden within orthodox Jewish perspectives, although several rabbis have concluded that passive euthanasia is religiously acceptable. These liberal perspectives are not widely accepted by the traditional outlook of orthodox Judaism. The orthodox Jewish codes state that physicians must use medical skills to heal the sick, as the preservation of human life takes precedence over all biblical injunctions. Life value is absolute and supreme. Questions regarding the *quality* of life, which is to be preserved, are not relevant in determining whether therapeutic procedures should or should not be instituted or whether life support systems should or should not be withheld or withdrawn (Bleich, 1986). The orthodox Jewish literature that addresses the subject of euthanasia uses powerful language to emphasize the importance of non acceptance especially an active form of the process:

> We could as a nation, have preferred the euthanasia of a pleasant death to our election as a people with a special purpose. We could have given up our uniqueness and joined the majority, and have disappeared as so many other bigger nations disappeared. If we were, nevertheless determined to stay alive, despite a great deal of suffering, it was because we were convinced that where there is life there is hope (Jakobovits, 1986, p. 95).

The current research is part of a larger study that attempts to interpret the meanings and attitudes held by elderly persons in Israel toward life-sustaining therapies. Previous phases of the study found that participants made *no* distinctions between the different forms of euthanasia: active vs. passive, voluntary vs. involuntary and that *previous life experiences* were important contributors to individual meanings and attitudes toward euthanasia (Leichtentritt and Rettig, 1998). The purpose of the current phase of the study was to explore the similarities and differences between the holocaust and euthanasia as they were perceived by fifteen Israeli holocaust survivors. The study contributes to the existing literature by (a) moving from philosophically-based arguments towards a more empirical understanding, (b) reaching an interpretive understanding based on the holocaust survivors subjective meanings, (c) highlighting the survivors voices, as they are rarely heard or taken into consideration and (d) examining the euthanasia debate in a country where discussions about 'right-to-die' issues are difficult and rare.

3. METHOD

The current research is a qualitative investigation that used a phenomenological data analysis method. Qualitative research is a method of choice when the underlying theories are not formulated, the existing theories are questioned, or when the phenomenon has received minimal empirical examination and requires an exploratory descriptive approach. Qualitative research is especially suited for studying "meanings, interpretations and subjective experiences" (Daly, 1992, p. 3–4). The phenomenological approach belongs to a family of qualitative methods concerned with interpretive practices. These approaches, examine how human beings construct and give meaning in concrete social situations (Holstein and Gubrium, 1995). Phenomenology is concerned with understanding human behavior from the actor's own frame of reference.

3.1. Participants

Fifteen holocaust survivors living in the northern part of Israel participated in this study. A summary of the participants' characteristics is presented in Table 1. A holocaust survivor is a Jew who lived through Nazi persecution in Europe between 1939 and 1945, in the ghettos, concentration camps, labor camps, in hiding or as a partisan in the woods (Kamien, 1991). Ten participants (coded 01 to 10) were healthy and living in the community, and five (coded 11 to 15) were at a geriatric-rehabilitation

TABLE 1	Participants' Characteristics	
SUBJECT	GENDER	EXPERIENCE DURING WORLD WAR II
01	M	concentration camp—1 year
02	F	concentration camp—2 years
03	M	concentration camp—5 years
04	F	concentration camp—7 months
05	F	concentration camp—3 years
06	M	concentration camp—2 years
07	F	concentration camp—3 years
08	F	concentration camp—2.5 years
09	F	hide
10	F	concentration camp—1 year
11	M	hide
12	M	concentration camp—2 years
13	F	concentration camp—3 years
14	M	concentration camp—4 years
15	F	concentration camp—1.5 years

hospital at time of the interviews. The snowball sampling method (Patton, 1990) was used to locate participants with the help of the 'Institute for Holocaust Education'. Social workers helped in recruiting participants from different units at the hospital.

3.2. Data Collection

An active interviewing method was used to collect data. "Active interviewing involves the researcher and the participant in constructing meanings and perspectives" (Holstein and Gubrium, 1995, p. 16). Active interviewing views the research participant as a narrator possessing a fund of knowledge that is simultaneously substantive, reflexive and emergent. The research participant's responses are viewed as knowledge-in-the-making, with the researcher helping to activate different stocks of knowledge. "The interviewer intentionally, concertedly provokes responses by indicating narrative positions, resources, orientations and precedents" (Holstein and Gubrium, 1995, p. 39). The interviews were conducted mostly in Hebrew, but participants sometimes used German words and phrases. The interviewer spoke Hebrew, German and English languages and was therefore able to follow the ideas of the survivors, regardless of the language used. The interviews lasted about 2 h and were translated to English by the researchers. The research questions were presented to participants as follows: "Some discussions have expressed similarities between Nazi Germany and mercy killing. Do you believe the comparison is justified? In what ways are mercy killing and the holocaust similar? In what ways are they different"?

3.3. Ethical Considerations

Several ethical issues were potentially problematic in the described research. First, the interviews brought forward painful memories and information. Some participants had not previously spoken about these experiences: "I do not think I ever talked about that with anyone, I do not think anyone ever heard these things from me before…" (02). Second, introducing new connections made some of the participants think about these meaningful issues in ways that might prevent them from returning to their original way of thinking. Third, the interviews were individual, but the researcher raised questions about how family members might be affected by these issues. Efforts were made to minimize the risks[2].

3.4. Data Analysis

Participants' responses were recorded and transcribed. The phenomenological method was used in the data analysis process and contains five steps (Speigelberg, 1960; Gioigi, 1985).

1. Gaining a sense of the whole. The first step involves reading the interview over and over again in order to gain an overall sense of the ideas provided by the participants.
2. Identifying meaning units. A meaning unit is "a part of the description whose phrases require each other to stand as a distinguishable moment" (Wertz, 1985, p. 165). This step in the analysis process also involved identifying units of the text that describe similarities and differences between euthanasia and the holocaust.
3. Transforming the participant's language into a more abstract language. Similar meaning units (often based on nonverbal communication) were clustered together and were identified as themes.
4. Watching modes of appearing. The fourth step of phenomenological analysis gives attention to the way in which participants presented their perspectives, paying attention not only to *what* appears, but also to the *way* ideas appear, with the goal of distinguishing between different types and layers of information presentation (Speigelberg, 1960). A metacommunication analysis was performed at this stage.

5. Synthesizing meaning units into a consistent statement of the phenomenon being studied. The phenomenological analysis ended in a higher level of syntax which aimed to identify the "fundamental structure of the phenomenon" (Colaizzi, 1978, p. 61).

3.5. Evaluating the Research Process

Validity in qualitative research has to do with description and explanation and whether or not a given explanation fits a given description (Janesick, 1994). Several methods were used to establish validity in this study. First, the results were checked with other colleagues. Second, the length of interviews allowed the researchers to check consistencies in meanings expressed by the informant over time. Third, follow-up sessions were performed with some of the participants who read the current manuscript regarding the accuracy in which the writing represents their perspectives. Fourth, the detailed description of the analysis process and quotes are given to the reader for evaluation (Rosenblatt and Fischer, 1993).

4. RESULTS

The following paragraphs present a part of one interview in order to provide the reader with a 'sense of a whole,' which is the first step in a qualitative-phenomenological method. The interview was translated by the researcher and condensed in order to focus on the one similarity and 10 major differences that were identified between euthanasia and holocaust policies.

5. INTERVIEW TEXT

When I was younger I had no opinion on the subject of mercy killing. Who thought about those things? The only thing we needed to believe was life and to act as if we are going to survive. Life was the focus, not death. Only in the last few years I have started to think about this issue. I believe most people here, in Israel, did not think about mercy killing before…the last 5 or 7 years. Maybe it existed in hospitals, maybe they did it quietly without anyone knowing what is going on, which is actually more frightening and dangerous than legitimizing [euthanasia]…

Today I think that if there is no other option, and there is no way out, then it is better than letting the person suffer or letting his family suffer when they watch him and care for him. But this is only when there is no hope and there is no way the person can

---

[2]The research was approved by the Institutional Review Board: Human subject committee (code number 9605S11203). Participants were given an explanation about the research intentions, potential risks and benefits of involvement in the project, and were clearly told they could withdraw from the project at any time.

become better, *only then* I am in favor…It has to be the person's choice. No one else can decide for him, not even a close family member, and by no means a physician can receive that amount of power. No one else can take that authority in making life and death decisions. This is how you set the boundaries…

Mercy killing has *no* connection with my childhood or what happened during World War II. I saw a lot during that time, I saw a lot of dead bodies, sometimes not even full bodies but parts all over the place. I saw deaths and murders which had no mercy in them…And those were things that happened on a daily basis, part of the routine in the camp, someone being hung, another is lying on the floor after being shot, all of these on a daily routine …I can tell you that life in the camps, the way death occurred, all of that horror, has nothing in common with the situation when a person is lying sick, terminally ill, and *wishing* to die. You see, not I nor anyone else *deserved* the humiliation that happened in the camps…

How can one compare between Nazi Germany and the understanding that one should have more control over his own life and death? One is for my own self benefit and the other comes from a pathological ideology. I wish mercy killing was accepted here. Allowing people to die in dignity, this is something no one had the *luxury* to enjoy while being in a concentration camp. You can find everything in a concentration camp: hunger, diseases, but dignity—this notion was simply *not* there…Nazi Germany and mercy killing are not alike, the differences between the two are like between day and night, and after experiencing the 'night', I wish to experience some of the 'day', the light instead of the dark, if you wish to call it that way [laugh]…

It is not fair to us to say that Nazi Germany and mercy killing are the same…mercy killing, as I understand it, is something you ask for, it is something that comes out of passion and choice…it implies a dignified death—nothing like the holocaust. Maybe people who make the comparison do not know what happened during the war, maybe they only think about the similar outcome…

I want to die with no pain! What does it mean? It means that when the situation arrives, I wish to receive an injection and to get it over with! I know this is what I want for myself, if there is no hope for cure, then it is better to get it over with [long silence]. This way you avoid the suffering, not only for yourself, but also for the people who are around you. I do not think I ever talked about that with anyone. I do not think anyone knows what I want. But if you ask me—an injection and get it over with…Death itself

does not frighten me. The problem is what is connected and surrounding death. I believe I have endured my assigned portion of suffering in this world …I cannot take any more (02).

6. SENSE OF THE WHOLE

The first step of the analysis involved gaining an overall sense of the major ideas that were provided by the participants. It was evident that the idea and the vocabulary for choosing one's own death was new for most of the people. Therefore, the interviews were meaning-making and reality-constructing processes. The evidence in the interviews did not support the western debate about the Nazi euthanasia program. *All* of the participants concluded that *profound* differences existed between Nazi Germany and socially assisted dying, regardless of their overall attitudes toward euthanasia, 'pro' (nine participants) or 'con' (six participants). Both verbal and nonverbal channels of communication were used to highlight the distinctive differences between the two phenomena.

7. IDENTIFYING, LABELING AND DEFINING THEMES

The second and third stages of the qualitative analysis involved the selection of meaning units that led to the identification of themes that were stated in a more abstract language than the words used by participants. Eleven themes were identified, one theme that focused on the similarity, and ten themes describing differences between euthanasia and the holocaust.

7.1. Themes of Similarities

When similarities between the holocaust and euthanasia were discussed, the emphasis was on the end result—death. This similarity was addressed by the participants only in the last minutes of the interview. "One may say that these two are similar or alike because, in both cases, the individual dies in the end. Maybe we should not completely ignore that…but based only on this—to say that similarities exist between Nazi policy and euthanasia? It does not sound very logical to me" (12).

7.2. Themes of Differences

Table 2 reports four different perspectives, in 10 different themes, and 24 different examples of the

TABLE 2 Perspectives, Themes and Examples Distinguishing the Nazi Era from Euthanasia

PERSPECTIVES	DEFINITIONS OF THEMES	EXAMPLES FROM THE INTERVIEWS
Physicians as actors	*Authority taken vs. authority requested;* participants' perceptions of the physician's right to act or to make final decisions, and the source of that authority	I did not appoint them to become my physicians, I did not even appoint myself as being the 'patient'.... They just took over, or maybe they received their power from…I do not know from whom, mostly I think from themselves, and from the Nazi party (12); I would *ask* the physician for assistance in the case of a mercy killing; In the case of mercy-killing, it is not him who decides for me, it is my decision, but he has the knowledge to assist me (04)
	Intention to kill vs. intention to assist; participants' perceptions concerning the motivation of physicians in regard to the participants' wishes	In one case, the physician's intentions are to kill, or to use one's body for some crazy experimental procedures, while the other, the intention is completely different, it is to help *you* die; You became the center of the process (02); My family physician came over to the hospital to visit me, she talked with the physician here, so she will be able to provide me with the right treatment when I will be released back home (11)…on the other hand he [Mengele] killed thousands, thousands of people are no longer alive because of him…he did not kill, he just 'played' with his stick moving it from one side to another, one side to another; One side was for life and the other death…and he *enjoyed* it! (01); To say that physician in the camp wanted to assist you to die—that will be *very* sarcastic (06)
Participants as actors	*Wish to live vs. the wish to die;* the motivation of the participant concerning the wish to prolong life or to hasten death	During the war, I was willing to do anything in order to survive; My basic instinct was life; You will not believe from where and how I managed to stay alive…now I have different goals; I no longer have that urge to survive; I do not feel the same today; Today, what is important for me is to avoid suffering. I no longer wish to live at all costs; There, are prices which I am no longer willing to pay in order to stay alive (08); *There,* life was our focus, not death (02)
	Motivation to survive: the continuity of the Jewish people vs. the survival of one person; the motivation of the participant to survive for the benefit of the group or the self	While being in the camps I had the urge to survive, not *only* for myself, but for others as well, surviving was my answer to the fact that they killed my mother, my father, my whole family…surviving was my response to the Nazi idea of killing the Jewish people; My wish to live was influenced by the idea that surviving was important for more than me; When we are referring to the acts of mercy killing, the question of whether I am alive is less important [pause]; People today can decide these issues as their lives do not bare the burden of being one of few survivors, of being the only survivor from the whole family.… It puts a whole different perspective on the same result—death (10); My life was much more important there; Surviving the camps was a personal goal, as well as a family and social goal; I was there for four years; That makes a statement! Four years and they did not get me! I was there for four years and still you can find descendants of may parents [gives the full names of his parents], here today alive, and well; There is still a Jewish state…Life and death had different meanings then; One does not have the privilege to choose death over life then, you just could not afford that…(14)
	Decision of self vs. decision of others; the amount of control the participant has over the timing of death, power taken in making decisions about the circumstances of one's death	Give people the right to choose; That is what democracy is all about…I should have the final decision about my and my own body, my own life and death; In the concentration camps someone else was in charge of all these domains; In some cases, someone else was also in charge of other people's souls…If a person chooses euthanasia as the way he wishes to die, why call it Nazi Germany? Why not call it democracy? (12) Summarize my life in the camps, summarize the main idea of the Nazi torturing process: Take control away from people, 'leave them in the dark'…I did not know if I am going to be dead or alive tomorrow morning, I did not know if I am going to be alive in the next seven minutes; This is exactly the opposite from mercy killing, where the person gains control over one of the processes in human life that tends to be the least in our control—that is exactly the opposite; Regardless of one's moral attitudes towards gaining control over death and dying, how can you say they are the same? (06)

(continued)

TABLE 2 *(Continued)*		
PERSPECTIVES	DEFINITIONS OF THEMES	EXAMPLES FROM THE INTERVIEWS
Physician– participant relationships	*Power differentiation vs. power equality;* the participants' perceptions concerning differences in authority to control and capacity to act	Power differentiation between Jews and German…between Jews and German's physicians; The power differences…that was like, like God on one side and dirt, which you crash over on the other (cry)…Here the physician and I are luckily holding equal rights; I have ways in which I can defend myself here (08)
	Abusive vs. respecting relationships; the participants' perceptions regarding attitudes and behaviors of physicians toward patients, ranging from abusive mistreatment to consideration and respect	What are people talking about? My body was used by Mengele; I was humiliated…I never answered any question that he asked me, as I was not able to tell if that was a question I was supposed to answer, or if it was better to shut up; I was terrified by that man, by his voice, by the sound of his walk…I was terrified by the man; I was terrified. I do not think I can even give words to how scared I was; Do you know a more strong word than 'terrified'? Because that does not seems to say strongly enough how afraid I was (01); If I will not be treated today in ways I think I should by a physician, I will just go to a different physician…I will not tolerate disrespectful attitudes (08)
Social context	*Social ideology vs. individual needs and preferences;* the participants' perceptions concerning the origin of justifications for end-of-life decisions, ranging from pathological ideologies to patient wishes	Their goal was to reach a pure Aryan race…the whole idea has its root in an ideology…Nazi Germany justifications for end-of-life decisions, were society based on superior and inferior races (09); One is for my own self benefits and the other comes from a pathological ideology…If there is no option, and there is no way out…only if there is suffering and there is no hope, and there is no way the person can become better…and it has to be the person's choice (02); In the case of mercy killing, the physician wishes to release the patient from his misery (12)
	Decisions by dictator vs. democratic procedures; the participants' perceptions concerning the presence or absence of appropriate social structures for life and death decisions, with safeguards against unethical practices and abuse of power	There is a need to look at the process of how things occurred; What were the social rules which allowed such a horror to happen? (10) He [physician] was a dictator and everyone was terrified by him…He was *the one* who decided to send people to the crematorium, or to save human life…(01); As far as I know, the whole idea of euthanasia, as it is being practiced in The Netherlands, requires a committee; It involves the decision of several people, including oneself or his/her family members; It is not something which can be concluded and practiced by one physician…it is not something which is being decided in the flash of the moment (03)
	Injustice vs. justice and fairness; the participants' perceptions concerning the outcomes of end-of-life decisions and the extent to which the values of fairness and justice were or were not upheld	There was not even one drop of justice in that place; It was a corrupted environment even before Hitler gained power (09); People over there did not even receive a decent funeral; There was no burial, no funeral, no mourning, nothing, like the person never existed…*No one* should be treated like that…it was an undignified, unjust, inhuman, humiliating and frightening environment…and even those words do not capture what it was like! I do not think you can ever understand, as it is so much different from what you know today…(04); I want to die when my time comes…(laugh) but I can see no harm with giving people the option and I think it is fair…(01)

themes that distinguish the Nazi era from euthanasia. The perspectives include the viewpoints of physicians, individuals, the physician-participant relationship and the social context. The 10 themes are each defined and quotation-examples from the interviews are provided. The themes that address the participants' perspectives of the physicians as the main actor include (a) authority taken vs. authority requested, and (b) intention to kill vs. intention to assist. Themes addressing informants' perceptions of

themselves as the main actor include: (c) the wish to live vs. the wish to die, (d) the motivation to survive for the continuity of the Jewish people vs. survival for one person and (e) decision of self vs. decision of others. The relationships between physicians and individuals are included in the themes of (f) power differentiation vs. power equality and (g) abusive vs. respectful relationships. The last set of themes addressed societal differences between Nazi Germany and Israel and were captured through the notions of

(h) social ideology vs. individual needs and preferences, (i) decisions by dictators vs. democratic procedures and (j) injustice vs. justice and fairness.

8. MODES OF APPEARING

The fourth step of the phenomenological method required paying attention to the way in which the perspectives were presented and involved a meta-communication analysis. The participants' different modes of expression while discussing euthanasia and experiences during World War II were closely examined. The theme analysis examined the surface or content level, a metacommunication level qualifies what is said in the first level (Watzlawick et al., 1967). Metacommunication is "a message about a message, typically nonverbal, offered simultaneously with the verbal message, structuring, qualifying or adding meaning to that message" (Goldenberg and Goldenberg, 1996, p. 426).

Participants used various forms of metacommunication to emphasize the distinct separation between euthanasia and Nazi Germany: (a) changing between Hebrew and German languages, (b) choosing different terminology, (c) using metaphors, (d) changing the tone of voice, (e) using personal vs. group-oriented grammar, (f) changing the described and visible emotions and (g) using a sarcastic or ironic tone of voice. The sarcastic tone was especially noticed in the discussion of similarities between the two phenomena "You see, I can find some similarities, is not that scary?! (laugh)" (02). Don't you just 'love' strong conclusions that are based on no, or very few justifications? It takes a second to create them and several years to get rid of these misleading conclusions" (10).

8.1. Changing between Languages

The changes between Hebrew and German languages occurred while describing highly emotional events, or when the participant had the need to distance emotionally from the described experience.

No one explained to us what was going on. It happened two days after we were brought to the camp, [German] they went like one marks wild animals for property identifications, they marked each one of us. *We were standing one after another my father, I, my brother and my uncle, so we have sequential numbers (02).*

We arrived on May 20th 1944 to Auschwitz and Mengele said: [German] you are twins! Just like that, we were afraid to say that this is wrong, or this is true. He took us from the line to his [German] experiments [pause] he conducted experiments on my sister and I *(01).*

8.2. Choosing Different Terminology

Several words and phrases were used by informants only in regard to their experiences during the war, such a 'crematorium', while other words, such as 'death', were avoided while informants described their holocaust experiences. Instead, the phrase 'did not survive' was frequently used. When talking about death that occurred after the war, different phrases were introduced in the interview: "I came to Israel, my parents, on the other hand, *stayed in the camps*…I buried two people by now, two very close people, my wife and my son, *died*" (02).

8.3. Using Metaphors

Metaphor is "a figure of speech in which a word or phrase that ordinarily applies to one kind of object or idea is applied to another, thus suggesting a likeness or analogy between them" (Rosenblatt, 1994, p. 12). The following quotations are some examples of the metaphors presented in the interviews:

It is like we speak a different language…It is like if you are not familiar with a language, then you will not be able to tell the differences between that language and a new language people present to you. You cannot see the nuances. Seeing the holocaust and assisting a person to die as the same is a mistake. I have been there, and I can tell you there is nothing like that (01).

I was nothing in Nazi Germany, much less than a human being, much less than a dog on the street (11).

Saying that the two are alike, is like saying that two books on the same topic are the same. This kind of understanding ignores the fact that the authors are different, the plots are different, the context, as well as the size of the books, are completely different (03).

8.4. Changing the Tone of Voice

The participants used a softer, quieter tone of voice, even a whisper, while describing experiences during the war. A more confident tone of voice was present while addressing euthanasia. This nonverbal communication was explicitly expressed by one of the participants: "How can someone see the two processes alike …one is so *quiet*, like the *silence* you experience while visiting holy places. It comes from respect, while the other one is all *screaming* and *shouting*…" (04).

8.5. Using Personal vs. Group-Oriented Grammar

The participants' overall orientation changed from personal to group-oriented language while talking about euthanasia compared to the holocaust experience. "Now I am talking not only for myself, or my own experiences, I am talking on behalf of all those who did not survive. This is why I use the term we" (02). Physicians, as well as Jews in the camps, were often grouped in the descriptions of the holocaust experience. While addressing the issue of euthanasia, a personal/individual orientation was introduced, highlighting the individual's own wants, wishes and attitudes: "I know what I want, if you ask me, I am capable of picturing the 'ideal' death for you…I wish I could introduce this picture to my own dying process…" (09).

8.6. Changing the Described and Visible Emotions

Different feelings were visible and verbally introduced by the participants while addressing the notion of euthanasia in comparison to the holocaust. The use of words such as betrayal, shame, humiliation, hate and horror were associated with discussion of the physician's role during World War II and the Nazi policies: "Can you think of more disrespectful and fraudulent ways of dying…? People thought they were going to take a shower, at least in the beginning we were thinking about showers, until we smelled that smell [pause] horror" (04).

The participants who perceived euthanasia as an acceptable option (*n* = 9), described the underlying feelings surrounding end-of-life decision making with the feelings of dignity, honor, and respect. "We should allow people to reach a dignified death…to die in the way they wish to—this is respect. This is the complete opposite of what was the ideology of Nazi Germany" (09). The participants who disagreed with end-of-life decision making expressed feelings of confusion, anger, sadness and frustration: "People ask to die [pause] people no longer value life. That is sad. Life is much less important, less holy today… that is sad" (02).

9. 'UNIVERSAL WISDOM': AN OVERALL DIMENSION

The last step of a phenomenological method of analysis requires the researcher to move from working with parts of individual interviews to address all interviews as a whole. The goals in the last step of the analysis are to reach a synthesis of the identified meaning units, as well as to identify the fundamental structure of the phenomenon (Colaizzi, 1978).

The emphasis on the differences between socially assisted dying and Nazi policy did not allow for a synthesis of this level to occur. Since, "what is

unique cannot be universal. What's universal threatens, and is threatened by, what's unique" (Cleveland, 1992, p. 18). The holocaust experience was perceived as a unique part of history. The participants did not generalize or try to find universal understandings across the two situations of euthanasia and the holocaust. The distinct differences between the two situations did provide a global-universal understanding, as participants shared their experiences and wisdom. The survivors emphasized the need to incorporate past experiences, in a constructive way, into current life. The move from the particularistic understanding of similarities and differences, towards a more universal wisdom was accomplished by a change in emphasis from past and current towards a past–current–future time orientation.

A holistic perspective, in the eyes of the survivors, moves beyond the ethical debates of similarities and differences. The universal wisdom was perceived to include three main ideas. First, the need to 'remember and not to forget'. Second, the issue of 'never again' which was raised by most of the informants. Third, the need of individuals, as well as the Israeli society, to 'incorporate the past into current life experiences and future social rules in constructive and beneficial ways'.

> We cannot take every action, or human behavior and compare it to the extreme. Nazi Germany was the extreme …this way of thinking will lead us nowhere (09). We cannot let that piece of history control our life… our shadows should not become our children's fears…and this by no means implies that we have forgotten what happened…or are ignoring the fact that it could happen again (05).

Finally, participants identified the political implications for such a comparison. "Combining the two implies that neither I, nor my children or my grandchildren, will reach the point when we will have more control over our life and death…[long silence]. Don't you think it is sad? It is like the Biblical statement—the fathers have eaten sour grapes and the children's teeth are set on edge" (12).

10. DISCUSSION

This research asked 15 holocaust survivors in Israel about their perspectives concerning the connections often made between socially assisted dying and Nazi Germany, and analyzed the text of their interviews by using the phenomenological method. The research is unique in its presentation of data as a means of understanding the similarities and differences between Nazi Germany and euthanasia, rather than relying on theoretical or philosophical arguments.

There are also several limitations of the current work. First, the study included a small number of the holocaust survivors and only survivors in Israel. It is likely that Israeli survivors may have different perspectives from survivors who live in other countries throughout the world. Moreover, meanings and attributions are concepts that develop and change within cultures and also over time. The one-time interviews had limited potential for capturing these developments. Readers may also question the decision to inquire into this issue more than 50 years after the Second World War in a culture where euthanasia is not yet legally accepted. Further research on euthanasia is certainly needed, since attitudes and meanings towards euthanasia have seldom been researched within the Israeli society. The current research results need to be followed by collecting data from other survivors, the children of holocaust survivors and other Israeli citizens.

Social phenomena, especially in regard to life and death issues, involve, not merely questions of social laws, but also morality, philosophy, sociology and medical ethics debates. Societies have different priorities, values, historical and traditional backgrounds, and therefore tend to treat end-of-life decision making in diverse ways. Researchers who focus on euthanasia in terms of isolated events at a specific time and place may misrepresent the social understanding of the phenomenon and the implications of historical and traditional forces on social norms and laws. Euthanasia needs to be understood in terms of *process*, based on *historical* and *traditional* influences (Heissing et al., 1996).

One of the main historical events influencing the Israeli society is the holocaust. Seeing theoretical similarities between the holocaust and euthanasia may partly explain the conservative end-of-life policies in Israel, as well as the relative absence of public discourse on the right-to-die issues. Moreover, concluding similarities between the holocaust and socially assisted dying have serious consequences. Informants cautioned philosophers to be careful in the comparisons they use. Euthanasia, by most of the participants' perspectives, can be morally and ethically justified. The holocaust, on the other hand, had *no* moral justification. The comparison, therefore, is inappropriate and was perceived as unjust and unfair. Participants strongly urged ethicists to recognize the consequences of such connections. Bioethics tends to use the similarities arguments as a means of describing socially assisted dying as an immoral act. Participants pointed to a different conclusion which is equally likely to be reached by perceiving euthanasia and the holocaust as equal— "it might give justification for the holocaust ...this debate puts the holocaust on an inappropriate level, a level that you can debate over, think whether it was or it was not justified..."(15).

The perspectives of holocaust survivors as they were expressed in the current research, demonstrate, on one hand, the strong disagreements with such a comparison, and on the other hand, the range of diverse attitudes towards euthanasia. These findings call for (a) bioethicists to avoid, or to be careful when discussing similarities and (b) the Israeli policy makers to acknowledge and to accommodate the different perspectives towards end-of-life decision making into the laws of the state.

One of the goals of the current research was to empower the survivors by giving voice to their perspectives and by giving them a stage for raising their voices. The theoretical debate is based on arguments about the similarities of the Nazi euthanasia and present risks of legitimizing socially assisted dying. Yet no one has asked the survivors for their viewpoints, or made an effort to listen to their wisdom concerning these important end-of-life issues. Participants shared their life-long wisdom, which called generations to involve themselves in the healing process which will allow the Israeli society to learn and incorporate the past into the future, instead of being limited by it. Informants of the current study shared the conclusion that "it is hoped that an optimism for our future may flow from the lesson learned from our tragic past" (Frankl, 1984, p. 13). It may be surprising to some opponents of socially assisted dying that holocaust survivors could find so few similarities and that they made such extensive efforts to demonstrate the differences between Nazi euthanasia and the current rights of individuals to make choices about their own death. The survivors were strongly insistent in demanding that comparisons could not be ethically justified and would have negative consequences for their own well-being, the dignity of their family members, the next generation and the Israeli society.

REFERENCES

Alexander, L., 1949. Medical science under dictatorship. New England Journal of Medicine 24, 39–47.

Bleich, J. D., 1986. Risks versus benefits in treating the gravely ill patient: ethical and religious considerations. In: Jewish Values in Bioethics. Human Science Press, New York, pp. 57–74.

Brigham, J. C., Pfeifer, J. E., 1996. Euthanasia: an introduction. Journal of Social Issues 52 (2), 1–12.

Cleveland, H., 1992. The age of people power. The Futurist 26 (1), 18.

Colaizzi, P. F., 1978. Psychological research as the phenomenologist views it. In: Runald, V. S., Mark, K. (Eds.), Existential Phenomenological Alternatives for Psychology. Oxford University Press, New York, pp. 59–66.

Daly, K., 1992. The fit between qualitative research and characteristics of families. In: Gilgun, J., Daly, K., Handel, G. (Eds.), Qualitative Methods in Family Research. Sage, Newbury Park, CA, pp. 3–11.

Dawidowicz, L., 1985. The Holocaust and the Historians. Harvard University Press, Cambridge, MA.

Devettere, R. J., 1995. Practical Decision-making in Health Care Ethics: Cases and Concepts. Georgetown University Press, Washington, DC.

Emanuel, E. J., 1994. Euthanasia: historical, ethical, and empiric perspectives. Archives of International Medical Journal 154, 1890–1901.

Frankl, V., 1984. Men's Search for Meaning: an Introduction to Logotherapy. Simon and Schuster, New York.

Gioigi, A., 1985. Phenomenology and Psychological Research. Duquesne University Press, Pittsburgh.

Goldenberg, I., Goldenberg, H., 1996. Family Therapy: an Overview. Brooks/Cole Pub, New York.

Heissing, D. J., Blad, J. R., Pieterman, R., 1996 Practical reasons and reasonable practice: the case of euthanasia in The Netherlands. Journal of Social Issues 52 (2), 149–168.

Holstein, J. A., Gubrium, J. F., 1995. The Active Interview. Sage, Thousand Oaks, CA.

Hunter, R.C.A., 1980. Euthanasia: a paper for discussion psychiatrists. Canadian Journal of Psychiatry 25, 439–445.

Jakobovits, I., 1986. Ethical Problems Regarding the Termination of Life: Jewish Values in Bioethics. Human Science Press, New York, pp. 84–102.

Janesick, V. J., 1994. The dance of qualitative research design: metaphor, methodolatry and meanings. In: Denzin, N. K., Lincoln, Y. S. (Eds.), Handbook of Qualitative Research. Sage, Thousand Oaks, CA, pp. 199–208.

Kamien, F., 1991. Inheriting the holocaust. Unpublished master's thesis. University of New York, New York.

Karter, M. H., 1989. Doctors under Hitler. University of North Carolina Press, NC.

Kronberg, M. H., 1988. How to stop the resurgence of Nazi euthanasia today. EIR special report, No. 129.

Leichtentritt, R. D., Rettig, K. D., 1998. Meanings and attitudes towards end-of-life preferences in Israel. Death Studies (in press).

Lerner, B. H., Rothman, D. J., 1995. Medicine and the holocaust: learning more of the lessons. Journal of International Medicine 122 (10), 793–794.

Lifton, R. J., 1986. The Nazi Doctors: Medical Killing and the Psychology of Genocide. Basic Books, New York.

Macklin, R., 1992. Which way down the slippery slope: Nazi medical killing and euthanasia today. In: Caplan, A. L. (Ed.), When Medicine Went Mad: Bioethics and the Holocaust. Humana Press, NJ, pp. 173–200.

Muller-Hill, B., 1988. Murderous Science: Eliminating by Scientific Selection of Jews, Gypsies and Others, Germany 1933–1945. Oxford University Press, Oxford.

Neuhaus, R. J., 1988. The turn of eugenics. Commentary 85, 15–26.

Patton P., 1990. Qualitative Evaluation and Research Methods. Sage, Nebury Park.

Proctor, R. N., 1988. Racial Hygiene: Medicine under the Nazis. Harvard University Press, Cambridge MA.

Rosenblatt, P. C., 1994. Metaphors of Family Systems Theory: Towards a new Constructions. Guilford Press, New York.

Rosenblatt, P. C., Fischer, L. R., 1993. Qualitative family research. In: Boss, P. B., Doherty, W. J., LaRossa, R., Schumm, W. R., Steinmetz, S. K. (Eds.), Sourcebook of Family Theories and Methods: A Contextual Approach. Plenum Press, New York, pp. 167–180.

Sonnennblick, M., Friedlandar, Y., Steinberg, A., 1993. Disassociation between the wishes of terminally ill patients and decisions by their offspring. Journal of American Geriatrics Society 41, 599–604.

Speigelberg, H., 1960. The Phenomenological Movement: a Historical Introduction. Martinus Niijhoff, The Hague.

Watzlawick, P., Beavin, J. H., Jackson, D. D., 1967. Pragmatics of Human Communication. W. W. Norton, New York.

Wertz, F. J., 1985. Methods and findings in a phenomenological psychological study of a complex life-event: being criminally victimized. In: Amedeo, G. (Ed.), Phenomenology and Psychological Research. Duquesne University Press Pittsburgh, PA, pp. 153–174.

SELF-STUDY QUESTIONS

Multiple Choice

1. One of the central attitudes of the Holocaust survivors that attempts to distinguish the Nazi era from our current understanding of euthanasia includes all but which of the following?
   a. survival of the concentration camp inmate
   b. survivors' feelings of disrespect, shame, and humiliation
   c. survivors' feelings about individual control over physician-assisted death in specific situations
   d. a lack of fairness regarding timing and type of death?

2. From the article, euthanasia is most likely to receive individual and public acceptance when it is
   a. involuntary
   b. voluntary

c. active
d. passive

Essay

1. Under what circumstances, if any, do you believe euthanasia to be morally acceptable?

2. Describe the importance of interviewing Holocaust survivors about their recollections of their lives during the time of the Nazi reign in Europe. Include a discussion of "Universal Wisdom".